Rover 214 & 414
Service and Repair Manual

Mark Coombs and Christopher Rogers

(1689-288-5AC5)

Models covered

Rover 214 and 414 models fitted with eight or sixteen-valve 1397 cc 'K-series' engine

Covers major mechanical features of Cabriolet

Does not cover Diesel engine models

© Haynes Publishing 1999

A book in the **Haynes Service and Repair Manual Series**

ABCDE
FGHIJ
KLMNO

2

Printed by **J H Haynes & Co Ltd, Sparkford, Nr Yeovil, Somerset BA22 7JJ, England**

Haynes Publishing
Sparkford, Nr Yeovil, Somerset BA22 7JJ, England

Haynes North America, Inc
861 Lawrence Drive, Newbury Park, California 91320, USA

Editions Haynes S.A.
Tour Aurore - La Défense 2, 18 Place des Reflets,
92975 PARIS LA DEFENSE Cedex, France

Haynes Publishing Nordiska AB
Box 1504, 751 45 UPPSALA, Sweden

ISBN **1 85960 458 7**

British Library Cataloguing in Publication Data
A catalogue record for this book is available from the British Library.

Contents

LIVING WITH YOUR ROVER 214 & 414

Roadside Repairs

Weekly Checks

Lubricants, Fluids, Capacities and Tyre Pressures

MAINTENANCE

Contents

REPAIRS AND OVERHAUL

Introduction

The Rover 214 Hatchback and 414 Saloon models covered in this Manual are a much-developed version of the original 213 and 216 models first launched in 1984. The 214 five-door model was the first to be introduced in October 1989 and was closely followed by the 414 model introduced in March 1990. The 214 model range was further updated in September 1990 when a three-door variant was introduced.

All models are fitted with the new 1.4 litre 'K' series engine. The 214 S model (first introduced in September 1990) has an eight-valve single overhead camshaft version of the engine which is fed by an SU KIF carburettor.

All other 214 and 414 models are equipped with a sixteen-valve double overhead camshaft version of the engine which is controlled by a Rover/Motorola Modular Engine Management System (MEMS) with either single-point fuel injection (SPi) or multi-point fuel injection (MPi). All versions of the engine are able to accept a full range of emission control systems, up to and including a three-way regulated catalytic converter.

The five-speed transmission, which is a joint development by Rover and Peugeot engineers, is of Peugeot design and produced by Rover. The transmission is fitted to the left-hand end of the engine. The complete engine/transmission unit is mounted transversely across the front of the car and drives the front wheels through unequal-length driveshafts.

The front suspension incorporates MacPherson struts and the rear is of the double wishbone type.

Braking is by discs at the front and drums at the rear, with a dual-circuit hydraulic system. On all models in the range, an Anti-lock Braking System (ABS) was offered as an optional extra. If ABS is fitted, then braking is by discs both at the front and rear.

Rover 214 SEi

Rover 414 SLi

Your Rover 214 & 414 Manual

The aim of this manual is to help you get the best value from your vehicle. It can do so in several ways. It can help you decide what work must be done (even should you choose to get it done by a garage), provide information on routine maintenance and servicing, and give a logical course of action and diagnosis when random faults occur.

However, it is hoped that you will use the manual by tackling the work yourself. On simpler jobs it may even be quicker than booking the car into a garage and going there twice, to leave and collect it. Perhaps most important, a lot of money can be saved by avoiding the costs a garage must charge to cover its labour and overheads.

The manual has drawings and descriptions to show the function of the various components so that their layout can be understood. Then the tasks are described and photographed in a clear step-by-step sequence.

References to the "left" or "right" of the vehicle are in the sense of a person in the driving seat, facing forwards.

Acknowledgements

Thanks are due to Champion Spark Plug who supplied the illustrations showing spark plug conditions, and to Duckhams Oils who provided lubrication data. Thanks are also due to Draper Tools Limited, who supplied some of the workshop tools, and to all those people at Sparkford who helped in the production of this Manual.

We take great pride in the accuracy of information given in this manual, but vehicle manufacturers make alterations and design changes during the production run of a particular vehicle of which they do not inform us. No liability can be accepted by the authors or publishers for loss, damage or injury caused by any errors in, or omissions from the information given.

Working on your car can be dangerous. This page shows just some of the potential risks and hazards, with the aim of creating a safety-conscious attitude.

General hazards

Scalding

• Don't remove the radiator or expansion tank cap while the engine is hot.
• Engine oil, automatic transmission fluid or power steering fluid may also be dangerously hot if the engine has recently been running.

Burning

• Beware of burns from the exhaust system and from any part of the engine. Brake discs and drums can also be extremely hot immediately after use.

Crushing

• When working under or near a raised vehicle, always supplement the jack with axle stands, or use drive-on ramps. *Never venture under a car which is only supported by a jack.*
• Take care if loosening or tightening high-torque nuts when the vehicle is on stands. Initial loosening and final tightening should be done with the wheels on the ground.

Fire

• Fuel is highly flammable; fuel vapour is explosive.
• Don't let fuel spill onto a hot engine.
• Do not smoke or allow naked lights (including pilot lights) anywhere near a vehicle being worked on. Also beware of creating sparks (electrically or by use of tools).
• Fuel vapour is heavier than air, so don't work on the fuel system with the vehicle over an inspection pit.
• Another cause of fire is an electrical overload or short-circuit. Take care when repairing or modifying the vehicle wiring.
• Keep a fire extinguisher handy, of a type suitable for use on fuel and electrical fires.

Electric shock

• Ignition HT voltage can be dangerous, especially to people with heart problems or a pacemaker. Don't work on or near the ignition system with the engine running or the ignition switched on.

• Mains voltage is also dangerous. Make sure that any mains-operated equipment is correctly earthed. Mains power points should be protected by a residual current device (RCD) circuit breaker.

Fume or gas intoxication

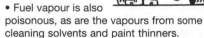

• Exhaust fumes are poisonous; they often contain carbon monoxide, which is rapidly fatal if inhaled. Never run the engine in a confined space such as a garage with the doors shut.
• Fuel vapour is also poisonous, as are the vapours from some cleaning solvents and paint thinners.

Poisonous or irritant substances

• Avoid skin contact with battery acid and with any fuel, fluid or lubricant, especially antifreeze, brake hydraulic fluid and Diesel fuel. Don't syphon them by mouth. If such a substance is swallowed or gets into the eyes, seek medical advice.
• Prolonged contact with used engine oil can cause skin cancer. Wear gloves or use a barrier cream if necessary. Change out of oil-soaked clothes and do not keep oily rags in your pocket.
• Air conditioning refrigerant forms a poisonous gas if exposed to a naked flame (including a cigarette). It can also cause skin burns on contact.

Asbestos

• Asbestos dust can cause cancer if inhaled or swallowed. Asbestos may be found in gaskets and in brake and clutch linings. When dealing with such components it is safest to assume that they contain asbestos.

Special hazards

Hydrofluoric acid

• This extremely corrosive acid is formed when certain types of synthetic rubber, found in some O-rings, oil seals, fuel hoses etc, are exposed to temperatures above 400°C. The rubber changes into a charred or sticky substance containing the acid. *Once formed, the acid remains dangerous for years. If it gets onto the skin, it may be necessary to amputate the limb concerned.*
• When dealing with a vehicle which has suffered a fire, or with components salvaged from such a vehicle, wear protective gloves and discard them after use.

The battery

• Batteries contain sulphuric acid, which attacks clothing, eyes and skin. Take care when topping-up or carrying the battery.
• The hydrogen gas given off by the battery is highly explosive. Never cause a spark or allow a naked light nearby. Be careful when connecting and disconnecting battery chargers or jump leads.

Air bags

• Air bags can cause injury if they go off accidentally. Take care when removing the steering wheel and/or facia. Special storage instructions may apply.

Diesel injection equipment

• Diesel injection pumps supply fuel at very high pressure. Take care when working on the fuel injectors and fuel pipes.

⚠️ *Warning: Never expose the hands, face or any other part of the body to injector spray; the fuel can penetrate the skin with potentially fatal results.*

Remember...

DO

• Do use eye protection when using power tools, and when working under the vehicle.

• Do wear gloves or use barrier cream to protect your hands when necessary.

• Do get someone to check periodically that all is well when working alone on the vehicle.

• Do keep loose clothing and long hair well out of the way of moving mechanical parts.

• Do remove rings, wristwatch etc, before working on the vehicle – especially the electrical system.

• Do ensure that any lifting or jacking equipment has a safe working load rating adequate for the job.

DON'T

• Don't attempt to lift a heavy component which may be beyond your capability – get assistance.

• Don't rush to finish a job, or take unverified short cuts.

• Don't use ill-fitting tools which may slip and cause injury.

• Don't leave tools or parts lying around where someone can trip over them. Mop up oil and fuel spills at once.

• Don't allow children or pets to play in or near a vehicle being worked on.

The following pages are intended to help in dealing with common roadside emergencies and breakdowns. You will find more detailed fault finding information at the back of the manual, and repair information in the main chapters.

If your car won't start and the starter motor doesn't turn

☐ If it's a model with automatic transmission, make sure the selector is in 'P' or 'N'.
☐ Open the bonnet and make sure that the battery terminals are clean and tight.
☐ Switch on the headlights and try to start the engine. If the headlights go very dim when you're trying to start, the battery is probably flat. Get out of trouble by jump starting (see next page) using a friend's car.

If your car won't start even though the starter motor turns as normal

☐ Is there fuel in the tank?
☐ Is there moisture on electrical components under the bonnet? Switch off the ignition, then wipe off any obvious dampness with a dry cloth. Spray a water-repellent aerosol product (WD-40 or equivalent) on ignition and fuel system electrical connectors like those shown in the photos. Pay special attention to the ignition coil wiring connector and HT leads. (Note that Diesel engines don't normally suffer from damp.)

A Check that the distributor HT lead connections are clean and secure

B Check that the spark plug HT lead connections are clean and secure - cover removed

C Check that the ignition coil HT and LT lead connections are clean and secure

Check that electrical connections are secure (with the ignition off) and spray them with a water-dispersing spray like WD40 if you suspect a problem due to damp

D Check the security and condition of the battery connections

E The ECU wiring plugs may cause problems if dirty or not properly connected

Jump starting

HAYNES HINT *Jump starting will get you out of trouble, but you must correct whatever made the battery go flat in the first place. There are three possibilities:*

1 *The battery has been drained by repeated attempts to start, or by leaving the lights on.*

2 *The charging system is not working properly (alternator drivebelt slack or broken, alternator wiring fault or alternator itself faulty).*

3 *The battery itself is at fault (electrolyte low, or battery worn out).*

When jump-starting a car using a booster battery, observe the following precautions:

✔ Before connecting the booster battery, make sure that the ignition is switched off.

✔ Ensure that all electrical equipment (lights, heater, wipers, etc) is switched off.

✔ Take note of any special precautions printed on the battery case.

✔ Make sure that the booster battery is the same voltage as the discharged one in the vehicle.

✔ If the battery is being jump-started from the battery in another vehicle, the two vehicles MUST NOT TOUCH each other.

✔ Make sure that the transmission is in neutral (or PARK, in the case of automatic transmission).

1 Connect one end of the red jump lead to the positive (+) terminal of the flat battery

2 Connect the other end of the red lead to the positive (+) terminal of the booster battery.

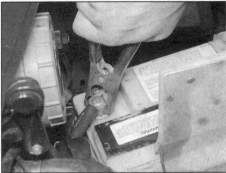

3 Connect one end of the black jump lead to the negative (-) terminal of the booster battery

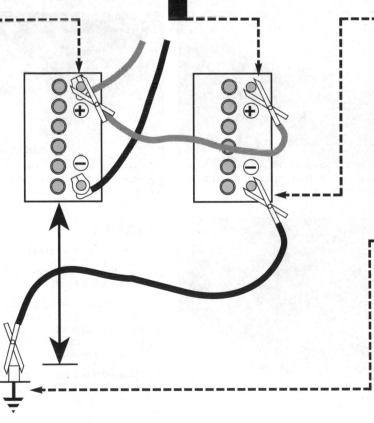

4 Connect the other end of the black jump lead to a bolt or bracket on the engine block, well away from the battery, on the vehicle to be started.

5 Make sure that the jump leads will not come into contact with the fan, drive-belts or other moving parts of the engine.

6 Start the engine using the booster battery and run it at idle speed. Switch on the lights, rear window demister and heater blower motor, then disconnect the jump leads in the reverse order of connection. Turn off the lights etc.

Wheel changing

Some of the details shown here will vary according to model. For instance, the location of the spare wheel and jack is not the same on all cars. However, the basic principles apply to all vehicles.

 Warning: Do not change a wheel in a situation where you risk being hit by other traffic. On busy roads, try to stop in a lay-by or a gateway. Be wary of passing traffic while changing the wheel – it is easy to become distracted by the job in hand.

Preparation

☐ When a puncture occurs, stop as soon as it is safe to do so.
☐ Park on firm level ground, if possible, and well out of the way of other traffic.
☐ Use hazard warning lights if necessary.

☐ If you have one, use a warning triangle to alert other drivers of your presence.
☐ Apply the handbrake and engage first or reverse gear (or Park on models with automatic transmission).

☐ Chock the wheel diagonally opposite the one being removed – a couple of large stones will do for this.
☐ If the ground is soft, use a flat piece of wood to spread the load under the jack.

Changing the wheel

1 Location of spare wheel and tools in boot

2 Unscrew the spare wheel retaining cap

3 Remove the trim to expose the wheelnuts

4 Use the wheel brace to slightly loosen the wheelnuts

5 Locate the jack head in the correct jacking point

6 Raise the jack until the wheel is clear of the ground

7 Remove the wheelnuts and lift off the wheel

8 Fit the replacement wheel and tighten the nuts

Finally...

☐ Remove the wheel chocks.

☐ Stow the jack and tools in the correct locations in the car.

☐ Check the tyre pressure on the wheel just fitted. If it is low, or if you don't have a pressure gauge with you, drive slowly to the nearest garage and inflate the tyre to the right pressure.

☐ Have the damaged tyre or wheel repaired as soon as possible.

Identifying leaks

Puddles on the garage floor or drive, or obvious wetness under the bonnet or underneath the car, suggest a leak that needs investigating. It can sometimes be difficult to decide where the leak is coming from, especially if the engine bay is very dirty already. Leaking oil or fluid can also be blown rearwards by the passage of air under the car, giving a false impression of where the problem lies.

 Warning: Most automotive oils and fluids are poisonous. Wash them off skin, and change out of contaminated clothing, without delay.

 The smell of a fluid leaking from the car may provide a clue to what's leaking. Some fluids are distinctively coloured. It may help to clean the car carefully and to park it over some clean paper overnight as an aid to locating the source of the leak.
Remember that some leaks may only occur while the engine is running.

Sump oil

Engine oil may leak from the drain plug...

Oil from filter

...or from the base of the oil filter.

Gearbox oil

Gearbox oil can leak from the seals at the inboard ends of the driveshafts.

Antifreeze

Leaking antifreeze often leaves a crystalline deposit like this.

Brake fluid

A leak occurring at a wheel is almost certainly brake fluid.

Power steering fluid

Power steering fluid may leak from the pipe connectors on the steering rack.

Towing

When all else fails, you may find yourself having to get a tow home – or of course you may be helping somebody else. Long-distance recovery should only be done by a garage or breakdown service. For shorter distances, DIY towing using another car is easy enough, but observe the following points:
☐ Use a proper tow-rope – they are not expensive. The vehicle being towed must display an 'ON TOW' sign in its rear window.
☐ Always turn the ignition key to the 'on' position when the vehicle is being towed, so that the steering lock is released, and that the direction indicator and brake lights will work.
☐ Only attach the tow-rope to the towing eyes provided.
☐ Before being towed, release the handbrake and select neutral on the transmission.
☐ Note that greater-than-usual pedal pressure will be required to operate the brakes, since the vacuum servo unit is only operational with the engine running.
☐ On models with power steering, greater-than-usual steering effort will also be required.
☐ The driver of the car being towed must keep the tow-rope taut at all times to avoid snatching.
☐ Make sure that both drivers know the route before setting off.
☐ Only drive at moderate speeds and keep the distance towed to a minimum. Drive smoothly and allow plenty of time for slowing down at junctions.
☐ On models with automatic transmission, special precautions apply. If in doubt, do not tow, or transmission damage may result.

Introduction

There are some very simple checks which need only take a few minutes to carry out, but which could save you a lot on inconvenience and expense.

These *"Weekly Checks"* require no great skill or special tools, and the small amount of time they take to perform could well prove to be very well spent, for example:

☐ Keeping an eye on tyre condition and pressures, will not only help to stop them wearing out prematurely but could also save your life.

☐ Many breakdowns are caused by electrical problems. Battery-related faults are particularly common and a quick check on a regular basis will often prevent the majority of these.

☐ If your car develops a brake fluid leak, the first time you might know about it is when your brakes don't work properly. Checking the level regularly will give advance warning of this kind of problem.

☐ If the oil or coolant levels run low, the cost of repairing any engine damage will be far greater than fixing the leak.

Underbonnet Check Points

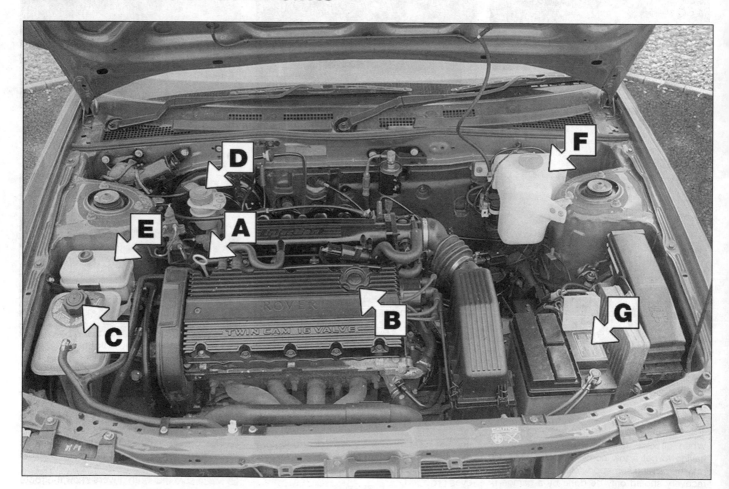

K16 MPi engine with plastic inlet manifold

A *Engine oil level dipstick*
B *Engine oil filler cap*
C *Coolant expansion tank*

D *Brake fluid reservoir*
E *Power steering fluid reservoir*

F *Screen washer fluid reservoir*
G *Battery*

Engine oil level

Before you start

✔ Make sure that your car is on level ground.
✔ Check the oil level before the car is driven, or at least 5 minutes after the engine has been switched off.

HAYNES HINT *If the oil is checked immediately after driving the vehicle, some of the oil will remain in the upper engine components, resulting in an inaccurate reading on the dipstick.*

The correct oil

Modern engines place great demands on their oil. It is very important that the correct oil for your car is used (see "Lubricants and Fluids" on page 0•16).

Car Care

● If you have to add oil frequently, you should check whether you have any oil leaks. Place some clean paper under the car overnight, and check for stains in the morning. If there are no leaks, then engine may be burning oil (see "Fault Finding").

● Always maintain the level between the upper and lower dipstick marks. If the level is too low, severe engine damage may occur. Oil seal failure may result if the engine is overfilled by adding too much oil.

1 The dipstick is located at the rear right-hand end of the engine (see "Underbonnet Check Points" on page 0•10 for exact location). Withdraw the dipstick.

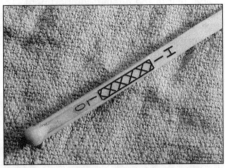
3 Note the oil level on the end of the dipstick, which should be between the upper HI mark and the lower LO mark. Approximately 1.0 litre of oil will raise the level from the lower mark to the upper mark.

2 Using a clean rag or paper towel, wipe all the oil from the dipstick. Insert the clean dipstick into the tube as far as it will go, then withdraw it again.

4 Oil is added through the filler cap. Rotate the cap through a quarter-turn anti-clockwise and withdraw it. Top-up the level. A funnel may help to reduce spillage. Add the oil slowly, checking the level on the dipstick often. Do not overfill.

Coolant level

Warning: Do not attempt to remove the expansion tank pressure cap when the engine is hot, as there is a very great risk of scalding. Do not leave open containers of coolant about, as it is poisonous.

Car Care

● With a sealed-type cooling system, adding coolant should not be necessary on a regular basis. If frequent topping-up is required, it is likely there is a leak. Check the radiator, all hoses and joint faces for signs of staining or wetness, and rectify as necessary.

● It is important that antifreeze is used in the cooling system all year round, not just during the winter months. Don't top up with water alone, as the antifreeze will become diluted.

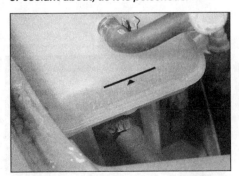
1 When the engine is cold, the coolant level should be between the expansion tank ridge/seam and the level indicated above COOLANT LEVEL on the side of the expansion tank, which is located in the front right-hand corner of the engine compartment.

2 If topping-up, wait until the engine is cold, then cover the filler cap with a layer of rag and start unscrewing the cap. Wait until any hissing ceases, indicating that all pressure is released, then slowly unscrew the cap until it can be removed. At all times keep well away from the filler opening.

3 Add a mixture of water and antifreeze through the expansion tank filler neck, until the coolant is up to the upper level. Refit the cap, turning it clockwise as far as it will go until it is secure.

Brake fluid level

Warning: Brake fluid can harm your eyes and damage painted surfaces, so use extreme caution when handling and pouring it. Do not use fluid which has been standing open for some time, as it absorbs moisture from the air, which can cause a dangerous loss of braking effectiveness.

Before you start

✔ Make sure that the car is on level ground.
✔ Cleanliness is of great importance when dealing with the braking system, so take care to clean around the reservoir cap before topping-up. Use only clean brake fluid from a container which has stood for at least 24 hours (to allow air bubbles to separate out).

Safety first

● If the reservoir requires repeated topping-up, this is an indication of a fluid leak somewhere in the system, which should be investigated immediately.
● If a leak is suspected, the car should not be driven until the braking system has been checked. Never take any risks where brakes are concerned.

1 The brake master cylinder and fluid reservoir is mounted on the vacuum servo unit in the engine compartment. The MAX and MIN level marks are indicated on the side of the reservoir and the fluid level should be maintained between these marks at all times.

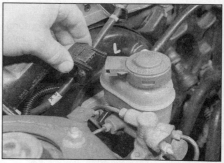

2 If topping-up is necessary, unplug the electrical connector and wipe the area around the filler cap with a clean rag before removing the cap. When adding fluid, pour it carefully into the reservoir to avoid spilling it on surrounding painted surfaces. Be sure to use only the specified brake hydraulic fluid since mixing different types of fluid can cause damage to the system.

3 Before adding fluid, it's a good idea to inspect the reservoir. The system should be drained and refilled if dirt is seen in the fluid (see Chapter 9 for details).

4 Carefully add fluid avoiding spilling it on surrounding paintwork. Use only the specified fluid; mixing different types can cause damage to the system. After filling to the correct level, refit the cap securely, to prevent leaks and the entry of foreign matter. Ensure that the fluid level switch plunger is free to move. Wipe off any spilt fluid.

Screen washer fluid level

Car care

● Screenwash additives not only keep the windscreen clean during bad weather, they also prevent the washer system freezing in cold weather - which is when you are likely to need it most. Don't top up using plain water, as the screenwash will become diluted and will freeze in cold weather.
● Check the operation of the windscreen and rear window washers. Adjust the nozzles using a pin if necessary, aiming the spray to a point slightly above the centre of the swept area.

Warning: On no account use engine coolant antifreeze in the screen washer system - this will damage the paintwork.

1 The reservoir for the windscreen and rear window (where fitted) washer systems is located on the left-hand side of the engine compartment.

2 When topping-up the reservoir(s) a screenwash additive should be added in the quantities recommended on the bottle.

Power steering fluid level

Before you start
✔ Make sure that the car is on level ground.
✔ Set the front roadwheels in the straight-ahead position.
✔ The engine should be stopped.
✔ Do not operate the steering once the engine is stopped.

Safety first
● If the reservoir requires repeated topping-up, there is a fluid leak somewhere in the system which should be investigated immediately.
● If a leak is suspected, the car should not be driven until the power steering system has been checked.

1 The power steering fluid reservoir is located on the right-hand side of the engine compartment, just behind the cooling system expansion tank. MAX and MIN level marks are indicated on the side of the reservoir and the fluid level should be maintained between these marks at all times.

2 If topping-up is necessary, first wipe the area around the filler cap with a clean rag before removing the cap. When adding fluid, pour it carefully into the reservoir to avoid spillage. Be sure to use only the specified fluid.

3 After filling the reservoir to the proper level, make sure that the cap is refitted securely to avoid leaks and the entry of foreign matter into the reservoir.

Wiper blades

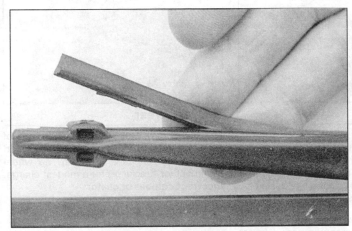

1 Check the condition of the wiper blades. If they are cracked or show any signs of deterioration, or if the glass swept area is smeared, renew them. For maximum clarity of vision, wiper blades should be renewed annually, as a matter of course.

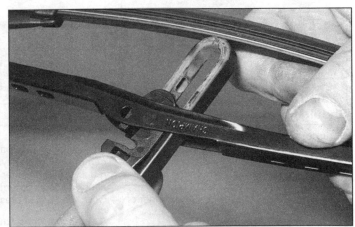

2 To remove a wiper blade, pull the arm fully away from the glass until it locks. Swivel the blade through 90º, press the locking tab with a finger nail and slide the blade out of the arm's hooked end. On refitting, ensure that the blade locks securely into the arm.

Tyre condition and pressure

It is very important that tyres are in good condition, and at the correct pressure - having a tyre failure at any speed is highly dangerous. Tyre wear is influenced by driving style - harsh braking and acceleration, or fast cornering, will all produce more rapid tyre wear. As a general rule, the front tyres wear out faster than the rears. Interchanging the tyres from front to rear ("rotating" the tyres) may result in more even wear. However, if this is completely effective, you may have the expense of replacing all four tyres at once! Remove any nails or stones embedded in the tread before they penetrate the tyre to cause deflation. If removal of a nail does reveal that

the tyre has been punctured, refit the nail so that its point of penetration is marked. Then immediately change the wheel, and have the tyre repaired by a tyre dealer.

Regularly check the tyres for damage in the form of cuts or bulges, especially in the sidewalls. Periodically remove the wheels, and clean any dirt or mud from the inside and outside surfaces. Examine the wheel rims for signs of rusting, corrosion or other damage. Light alloy wheels are easily damaged by "kerbing" whilst parking; steel wheels may also become dented or buckled. A new wheel is very often the only way to overcome severe damage.

New tyres should be balanced when they are fitted, but it may become necessary to re-balance them as they wear, or if the balance weights fitted to the wheel rim should fall off. Unbalanced tyres will wear more quickly, as will the steering and suspension components. Wheel imbalance is normally signified by vibration, particularly at a certain speed (typically around 50 mph). If this vibration is felt only through the steering, then it is likely that just the front wheels need balancing. If, however, the vibration is felt through the whole car, the rear wheels could be out of balance. Wheel balancing should be carried out by a tyre dealer or garage.

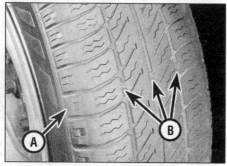

Tread Depth - visual check

1 The original tyres have tread wear safety bands (B), which will appear when the tread depth reaches approximately 1.6 mm. The band positions are indicated by a triangular mark on the tyre sidewall (A).

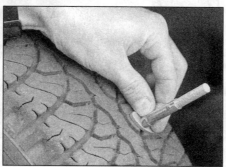

Tread Depth - manual check

2 Alternatively tread wear can be monitored with a simple, inexpensive device known as a tread depth indicator gauge.

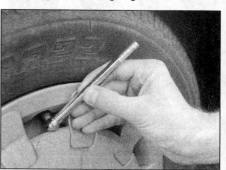

Tyre Pressure Check

3 Check the tyre pressures regularly with the tyres cold. Do not adjust the tyre pressures immediately after the vehicle has been used, or an inaccurate setting will result. Tyre pressures are shown on page 0•16

4 *Tyre tread wear patterns*

Shoulder Wear

Underinflation (wear on both sides)
Under-inflation will cause overheating of the tyre, because the tyre will flex too much, and the tread will not sit correctly on the road surface. This will cause a loss of grip and excessive wear, not to mention the danger of sudden tyre failure due to heat build-up.
Check and adjust pressures
Incorrect wheel camber (wear on one side)
Repair or renew suspension parts
Hard cornering
Reduce speed!

Centre Wear

Overinflation
Over-inflation will cause rapid wear of the centre part of the tyre tread, coupled with reduced grip, harsher ride, and the danger of shock damage occurring in the tyre casing.
Check and adjust pressures

If you sometimes have to inflate your car's tyres to the higher pressures specified for maximum load or sustained high speed, don't forget to reduce the pressures to normal afterwards.

Uneven Wear

Front tyres may wear unevenly as a result of wheel misalignment. Most tyre dealers and garages can check and adjust the wheel alignment (or "tracking") for a modest charge.
Incorrect camber or castor
Repair or renew suspension parts
Malfunctioning suspension
Repair or renew suspension parts
Unbalanced wheel
Balance tyres
Incorrect toe setting
Adjust front wheel alignment
Note: *The feathered edge of the tread which typifies toe wear is best checked by feel.*

Electrical system

✔ Check all external lights and the horn. Refer to the appropriate Sections of Chapter 12 for details if any of the circuits are found to be inoperative, and replace the fuse if necessary. Most fuses are located behind the cover in the right-hand lower facia panel. Other fuses are located in the fusebox on the left-hand side of the engine compartment. To replace a blown fuse, pull it from position, using the plastic tool provided. Fit a new fuse of the same rating. If a second fuse blows, it is important that you find the reason - do not use a fuse with a higher rating.

✔ Visually check all accessible wiring connectors, harnesses and retaining clips for security, and for signs of chafing or damage.

> **HAYNES HINT** *If you need to check your brake lights and indicators unaided, back up to a wall or garage door and operate the lights. The reflected light should show if they are working properly.*

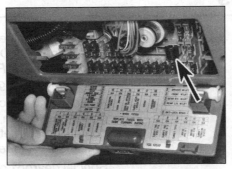

1 If a single indicator light, brake light or headlight has failed, it is likely that a bulb has blown and will need to be replaced. Refer to Chapter 12 for details. If both brake lights have failed, it is possible that the brake light switch operated by the brake pedal is faulty. Refer to Chapter 9 for details.

2 If more than one indicator light or headlight has failed, it is likely that either a fuse has blown or that there is a fault in the circuit (see Chapter 12).

Battery

Caution: Before carrying out any work on the vehicle battery, read the precautions given in "Safety first" at the start of this manual.

✔ Make sure that the battery tray is in good condition, and that the clamp is tight. Corrosion on the tray, retaining clamp and the battery itself can be removed with a solution of water and baking soda. Thoroughly rinse all cleaned areas with water. Any metal parts damaged by corrosion should be covered with a zinc-based primer, then painted.

✔ Periodically (approximately every three months), check the charge condition of the battery as described in Chapter 5A.

✔ If the battery is flat, and you need to jump start your vehicle, see *"Jump starting"*.

> **HAYNES HINT**
>
>
>
> *Battery corrosion can be kept to a minimum by applying a layer of petroleum jelly to the clamps and terminals after they are reconnected.*

1 The battery is located on the left-hand side of the engine compartment. The exterior of the battery should be inspected periodically for damage such as a cracked case or cover.

2 Check the tightness of battery clamps to ensure good electrical connections. You should not be able to move them. Also check each cable for cracks and frayed conductors.

3 If corrosion (white, fluffy deposits) is evident, remove the cables from the battery terminals, clean them with a small wire brush, then refit them. Accessory stores sell a useful tool for cleaning the battery post ...

4 ... as well as the battery cable clamps

Lubricants and fluids

Engine	Multigrade engine oil, viscosity SAE 10W/40 to spec. API-SG or SG/CD, CCMC G4, or RES.22.OL.G4 (*Duckhams QXR Premium Petrol Engine Oil, or Duckhams Hypergrade Petrol Engine Oil*)
Cooling system	Antifreeze to spec. BS 6580 and BS 5117. Ethylene-glycol based with non-phosphate corrosion inhibitors, containing no methanol. Mixture 50% by volume (*Duckhams Antifreeze and Summer Coolant*)
Gearbox	Special gearbox oil. Refer to your Rover dealer (*Duckhams Hypoid Gear Oil 75W-80W GL-5 may be used for topping-up only*)
Braking system	Hydraulic fluid to spec. SAE J 1703 or DOT 4 (*Duckhams Universal Brake and Clutch Fluid*)
Power steering system	Automatic transmission fluid (ATF) to Dexron II D specification (*Duckhams ATF Autotrans III*)
General greasing	Multi-purpose lithium-based grease to NLGI consistency No. 2 (*Duckhams LB 10*)

Capacities

Engine oil	4.5 litres - including filter
Cooling system	5.8 litres
Gearbox	2.0 litres
Power steering reservoir	1.2 litres
Fuel tank	55 litres
Washer system reservoir	3.1 litres

Tyre Pressures (tyres cold)

	Front	Rear
155 SR 13 tyres		
Normal driving conditions	2.1 bar (30 psi)	2.1 bar (30 psi)
Loads in excess of four persons	2.1 bar (30 psi)	2.3 bar (34 psi)
Speeds in excess of 100 mph - all loads	2.2 bar (32 psi)	2.2 bar (32 psi)
175/65 TR 14 tyres		
All loads - up to 100 mph	2.1 bar (30 psi)	2.1 bar (30 psi)
All loads - over 100 mph	2.2 bar (32 psi)	2.2 bar (32 psi)
185/60 HR 14 tyres		
All loads - up to 100 mph	2.1 bar (30 psi)	2.1 bar (30 psi)
All loads - over 100 mph	2.5 bar (36 psi)	2.5 bar (36 psi)

Note: *Pressures apply only to original equipment tyres and may vary if any other make or type is fitted. Check with the tyre manufacturer or supplier for correct pressures if necessary*

Chapter 1
Routine maintenance and servicing

Contents

1

Degrees of difficulty

Easy, suitable for novice with little experience	**Fairly easy,** suitable for beginner with some experience	**Fairly difficult,** suitable for competent DIY mechanic	**Difficult,** suitable for experienced DIY mechanic	**Very difficult,** suitable for expert DIY or professional

Specifications

Lubricants, fluids and capacities
Refer to the end of "Weekly Checks"

Engine
Oil filter type . . . . Champion B104

Cooling system
Antifreeze properties - 50 % antifreeze (by volume):
    Commences freezing . . . . −36°C
    Frozen solid . . . . −48°C

Ignition system
Firing order . . . . 1-3-4-2 (No 1 cylinder at timing belt end)
Crankshaft rotation . . . . Clockwise (viewed from right-hand side of vehicle)
Distributor rotor arm rotation . . . . Anti-clockwise (viewed from left-hand side of vehicle)
Ignition timing:
    Carburettor engines - @ 1500 rpm (vacuum pipe disconnected) . . . . 9° ± 1° BTDC
    Fuel-injected engines . . . . See text
Spark plugs:
    Type . . . . Champion RC9YCC
    Electrode gap . . . . 0.8 mm
Spark plug (HT) leads:
    Resistance . . . . 25 k ohms per lead, maximum

Fuel system

Air cleaner filter element:
Carburettor engines . . . .   Champion W218
SPi fuel-injected engines . . . .   Champion W221
MPi fuel-injected engines . . . .   Champion U631
Fuel filter (fuel-injected engines) . . . .   Champion L219
Idle speed . . . .   850 ± 50 rpm
CO level at idle speed - engine at normal operating temperature:
Carburettor engines:
Without catalytic converter (at exhaust tailpipe) . . . .   2.0 to 3.0 %
With catalytic converter (at gas-sampling pipe) . . . .   1.0 to 3.0 %
Fuel-injected engines:
Without catalytic converter (at exhaust tailpipe) . . . .   0.5 to 2.0 %
With catalytic converter (at gas-sampling pipe) . . . .   0.5 to 2.0 %
Recommended fuel:
Without catalytic converter . . . .   95 RON unleaded (unleaded Premium) or 97 RON leaded (4-star)
With catalytic converter . . . .   95 RON unleaded (unleaded Premium)

Braking system

Front and rear brake pad friction material minimum thickness . . . .   3.0 mm
Rear brake shoe friction material minimum thickness . . . .   2.0 mm

Suspension and steering

Power steering pump drivebelt deflection . . . .   7.5 to 8.5 mm @ 10 kg pressure

Tyre pressures

Refer to the end of "Weekly checks"

Electrical system

Alternator drivebelt deflection:
With air conditioning . . . .   9 to 10 mm @ 10 kg pressure
Without air conditioning . . . .   6 to 8 mm @ 10 kg pressure
Wiper blades - front and rear . . . .   Champion X-45

Torque wrench settings

	Nm	lbf ft
Engine		
Oil drain plug	42	31
Timing belt cover fasteners		
Upper right-hand/outer cover	4	3
Lower and upper left-hand inner covers	9	6
Fuel system		
Air cleaner intake duct-to-cylinder head support bracket bolt - K16 engine	8	6
System pressure release bolt - at fuel filter	12	9
Fuel filter inlet union	40	30
Fuel filter outlet union	35	26
Ignition system		
Spark plug cover screws - K16 engine	2	1.5
Spark plugs	25	18
Distributor cap screws	2	1.5
Distributor rotor arm grub screw - fuel-injected engines	10	7
Distributor mounting bolts - carburettor engines	25	18
Starting and charging systems		
Alternator mounting/pivot/adjusting arm bolts	25	18
Gearbox		
Oil filler/level and drain plugs	25	18
Brake system		
Front brake caliper guide pin bolts	32	24
Rear brake drum retaining screws	10	7
Suspension and steering		
Power steering/alternator drivebelt adjuster pulley nut and bolt	25	18
Roadwheel nuts	100	74

The maintenance intervals in this manual are provided with the assumption that you will be carrying out the work yourself. These are based on the minimum maintenance intervals recommended by the manufacturer for vehicles driven daily. If you wish to keep your vehicle in peak condition at all times, you may wish to perform some of these procedures more often. We encourage frequent maintenance because it enhances the efficiency, performance and resale value of your vehicle.

If the vehicle is driven in dusty areas, used to tow a trailer, or driven frequently at slow speeds (idling in traffic) or on short journeys, more frequent maintenance intervals are recommended.

When the vehicle is new, it should be serviced by a factory-authorised dealer service department, in order to preserve the factory warranty.

Every 250 miles (400 km) or weekly

- ☐ Refer to "Weekly Checks"

Every 1000 miles (1500 km) or monthly - whichever comes first

- ☐ Check operation of all locks, hinges and latch mechanisms (Section 3)
- ☐ Check operation of seat belts (Section 4)
- ☐ Check operation of brakes (Section 5)
- ☐ Check for signs of fluid leakage (Section 6)
- ☐ Check battery electrolyte level (Section 7)
- ☐ Check headlamp alignment (Section 8)

Every 6000 miles (10 000 km) or 6 months - whichever comes first

Note: Frequent oil and filter changes are good for the engine. We recommend changing the oil at the mileage specified here, or at least twice a year if the mileage covered is less

- ☐ Renew engine oil and filter (Section 9)

Every 12 000 miles (20 000 km) or 12 months - whichever comes first

- ☐ Drain, flush and refill cooling system with new antifreeze (Section 10)*
- ☐ Check operation of radiator cooling fan (Chapter 3)
- ☐ Replenish carburettor piston damper oil (Section 11)
- ☐ Check idle speed and mixture, where possible (Section 12)
- ☐ Check operation of lambda sensor, where fitted (Chapter 4 and Section 13)
- ☐ Check exhaust system (Section 14)
- ☐ Check distributor cap, ignition HT coil and spark plug (HT) leads (Section 15)
- ☐ Check clutch operation (Section 16)
- ☐ Check gearbox oil level (Section 17)
- ☐ Check driveshaft gaiters and CV joints (Section 18)
- ☐ Check brake pedal operation (Section 19)
- ☐ Check front brake pads, calipers and discs (Section 20)
- ☐ Check rear brake shoes, wheel cylinders and drums - non-ABS models (Section 21)
- ☐ Check rear brake pads, calipers and discs - ABS models (Section 22)
- ☐ Check handbrake adjustment (Section 23)
- ☐ Check suspension and steering (Section 24)

- ☐ Check roadwheels (Section 25)
- ☐ Check and adjust power steering pump drivebelt (Section 26)
- ☐ Check exterior paintwork, body panels and underbody sealer (Section 27)
- ☐ Lubricate all locks, hinges, latch and sunroof mechanisms (Section 28)
- ☐ Check alternator drivebelt (Section 29)

* If Rover-recommended antifreeze is used exclusively, this task need only be carried out after the first three years of the vehicle's life and every two years thereafter.

Every 24 000 miles (40 000 km) or 2 years - whichever comes first

- ☐ Check air conditioning refrigerant (Section 30)
- ☐ Renew air cleaner filter element (Section 31)
- ☐ Renew fuel filter - fuel injected models only (Section 32)
- ☐ Check crankcase breather hoses (Chapter 4)
- ☐ Check and adjust ignition timing, where possible (Section 33)
- ☐ Renew spark plugs (Section 34)
- ☐ Renew brake system hydraulic fluid (Section 35)

Every 48 000 miles (80 000 km) or 4 years - whichever comes first

- ☐ Check timing belt (Section 36)

Every 60 000 miles (100 000 km) or 3 years - whichever comes first

- ☐ Overhaul brake system master cylinder, brake calipers and (where applicable) rear wheel cylinders (Chapter 9).

Every 60 000 miles (100 000 km) or 5 years - whichever comes first

- ☐ Renew timing belt (Chapter 2)
- ☐ Check evaporative emission control system components (Chapter 4)

1

Underbonnet view of a Rover 214 with K16 SPi engine

1 Engine oil level dipstick
2 Engine oil filler cap
3 Coolant expansion tank filler cap
4 Braking system fluid reservoir cap
5 Power steering fluid reservoir cap
6 Battery
7 Air cleaner housing
8 Distributor
9 Cooling system filler neck
10 Fuel filter - non catalyst model
   shown
11 Clutch cable
12 Speedometer cable
13 Washer fluid reservoir
14 Front suspension strut mounting
   nuts
15 Reverse gear interlock cable
16 Left-hand engine/gearbox
   mounting
17 Engine management ECU
18 Intake air temperature control
   valve
19 Alternator
20 Windscreen wiper motor
21 Braking system pressure
   regulating valve
22 Engine compartment fusebox
23 Bonnet lock

Front underbody view (typical) - undercover panel removed

1 Engine oil drain plug
2 Oil filter
3 Gearbox oil drain plug
4 Gearbox oil level plug
5 Rear engine/gearbox mounting
6 Left-hand driveshaft inner constant
   velocity joint
7 Right-hand driveshaft inner constant
   velocity joint
8 Starter motor
9 Front towing eye
10 Front suspension tie bar
11 Front suspension lower arm
12 Anti-roll bar connecting link
13 Steering gear track rod balljoint
14 Anti-roll bar
15 Fuel lines
16 Gearchange lever mounting plate
17 Front exhaust pipe
18 Intermediate exhaust pipe

Underbonnet view of a Rover 214 with K16 MPi engine - plastic inlet manifold

1 Engine oil level dipstick
2 Engine oil filler cap
3 Coolant expansion tank filler cap
4 Braking system fluid reservoir cap
5 Power steering fluid reservoir cap
6 Battery
7 Air cleaner housing
8 Distributor
9 Spark plug cover
10 Fuel filter
11 Washer fluid reservoir
12 Front suspension strut mounting nuts
13 Engine management ECU
14 Throttle housing
15 Inlet manifold chamber
16 Windscreen wiper motor
17 Braking system pressure regulating valve
18 Engine compartment fusebox
19 Bonnet lock
20 Exhaust manifold

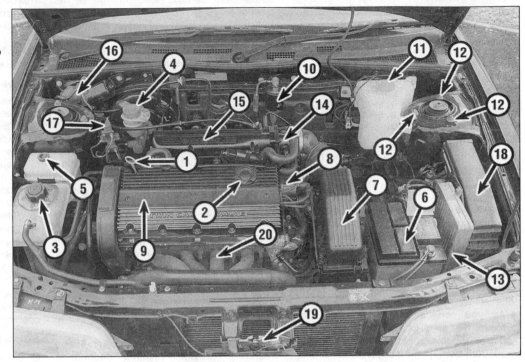

Rear underbody view (typical)

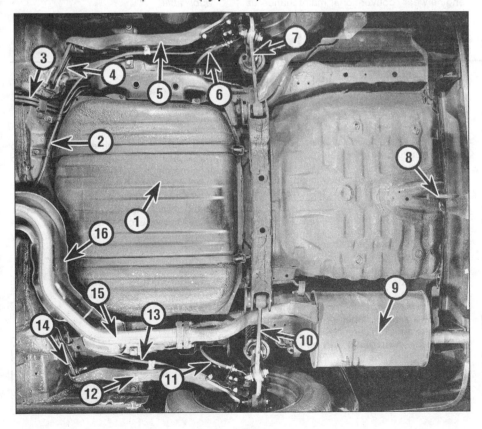

1 Fuel tank
2 Left-hand handbrake cable
3 Fuel lines
4 Rear suspension left-hand front lateral link
5 Rear suspension left-hand trailing arm
6 Flexible brake hose
7 Rear suspension left-hand lower lateral link
8 Rear towing eye
9 Exhaust tailpipe
10 Rear suspension right-hand lower lateral link
11 Flexible brake hose
12 Rear suspension right-hand trailing arm
13 Right-hand handbrake cable
14 Rear suspension right-hand front lateral link
15 Intermediate exhaust pipe
16 Exhaust heatshield

1

1 Introduction

1 This Chapter is designed to help the home mechanic maintain his/her vehicle for safety, economy, long life and peak performance.

2 The Chapter contains a master maintenance schedule, referring to Sections dealing specifically with each task in the schedule, or other Chapters. Visual checks, adjustments, component renewal and other helpful items are included. Refer to the accompanying illustrations of the engine compartment and the underside of the vehicle for the locations of the various components.

3 Servicing your vehicle in accordance with the mileage/time maintenance schedule and the following Sections will provide a planned maintenance programme, which should result in a long and reliable service life. This is a comprehensive plan, so maintaining some items but not others at the specified service intervals will not produce the same results.

4 As you service your vehicle, you will discover that many of the procedures can be grouped together, because of the particular procedure being performed, or because of the close proximity of two otherwise-unrelated components to one another. For example, if the vehicle is raised for any reason, the exhaust can be inspected at the same time as the suspension and steering components.

5 The first step in this maintenance programme is to prepare yourself before the actual work begins. Read through all the Sections relevant to the work to be carried out, then make a list and gather together all the parts and tools required. If a problem is encountered, seek advice from a parts specialist, or a dealer service department.

2 Irregular maintenance?

1 If, from the time the vehicle is new, the routine maintenance schedule is followed closely and frequent checks are made of fluid levels and high-wear items, as suggested throughout this Manual, the engine will be kept in relatively good running condition and the need for additional work will be minimised.

2 It is possible that there will be times when the engine is running poorly due to the lack of regular maintenance. This is even more likely if a used vehicle, which has not received regular and frequent maintenance checks, is purchased. In such cases, additional work may need to be carried out, outside of the regular maintenance intervals.

3 If engine wear is suspected, a compression test will provide valuable information regarding the overall performance of the main internal components. Such a test can be used as a basis to decide on the extent of the work to be carried out. If, for example, a compression test indicates serious internal engine wear, conventional maintenance as described in this Chapter will not greatly improve the performance of the engine, and may prove a waste of time and money, unless extensive overhaul work is carried out first.

4 The following series of operations are those most often required to improve the performance of a generally poor-running engine:

Primary operations

a) Clean, inspect and test the battery
b) Check all the engine-related fluids
c) Check the condition and tension of the auxiliary drivebelt(s)
d) Renew the spark plugs
e) Inspect the distributor cap and HT leads - as applicable
f) Check the condition of the air cleaner filter element, and renew if necessary
g) Renew the fuel filter (if fitted)
h) Check the condition of all hoses, and check for fluid leaks
i) Check the idle speed and mixture settings - as applicable

5 If the above operations do not prove fully effective, carry out the following secondary operations:

Secondary operations

a) Check the charging system
b) Check the ignition system
c) Check the fuel system
d) Renew the distributor cap and rotor arm - as applicable
f) Renew the ignition HT leads - as applicable

Every 1000 miles or monthly - whichever comes first

3 Lock, hinge and latch mechanism check

1 Check the security and operation of all hinges, latches and locks, adjusting them where required. For lubrication, refer to Section 28.

2 On 214 models, check the condition and operation of the tailgate strut. Renew the strut if it is leaking or no longer able to support the tailgate when raised.

4 Seat belt check

HAYNES HiNT *If seat belts become dirty, clean them with a damp cloth using a small amount of detergent only.*

1 Check the webbing of each belt for signs of fraying, cuts or other damage, pulling the belt out to its full extent to check its entire length.

2 Check the operation of the belt buckles by fitting the belt tongue plate and pulling hard to ensure that it remains locked in position.

3 Check the retractor mechanism (inertia reel only) by pulling out the belt to the halfway point and jerking hard. The mechanism must lock immediately to prevent any further unreeling but must allow free movement during normal driving.

4 Ensure that all belt mounting bolts are securely tightened. Note that the bolts are shouldered so that the belt anchor points are free to rotate.

5 If there is any sign of damage, or any doubt about a belt's condition, then it must be renewed. If the vehicle has been involved in a collision, then any belt in use at the time must be renewed as a matter of course and all other belts checked carefully.

6 Use only warm water and non-detergent soap to clean the belts. Never use any chemical cleaners, strong detergents, dyes or bleaches. Keep the belts fully extended until they have dried naturally and do not apply heat to dry them.

5 Brake check

1 Make sure that the vehicle does not pull to one side when braking and that the wheels do not lock prematurely when braking hard.

2 Check that there is no vibration through the steering when braking.

3 Check that the handbrake operates correctly without excessive movement of the lever and that it holds the vehicle stationary on a slope.

6 Fluid leakage check

HAYNES HiNT *Leaks in the cooling system will usually show up as white or rust-coloured deposits around the area adjoining the leak.*

1 Visually inspect the engine joint faces, gaskets and seals for any signs of coolant or oil leaks. Pay particular attention to the areas around the rocker cover, cylinder head, oil filter and sump joint faces. Bear in mind that over a period of time some very slight seepage from these areas is to be expected but what you are really looking for is any indication of a serious leak. Should a leak be found, renew the offending gasket or oil seal by referring to the appropriate Chapter of this Manual.

2 Similarly, check the transmission for oil leaks and investigate and rectify any problems found.

3 Check the security and condition of all engine related pipes and hoses. Ensure that all cable ties or securing clips are in place and in good condition. Clips which are broken or missing can lead to chafing of the hoses, pipes or wiring which could cause more serious problems in the future.

4 Carefully check the condition of all coolant, fuel, power steering and brake hoses. Renew any hose which is cracked, swollen or deteriorated. Cracks will show up better if the hose is squeezed. Pay close attention to the hose clips that secure the hoses to the system components. Hose clips can pinch and puncture hoses, resulting in leaks. If wire type hose clips are used, it may be a good idea to replace them with screw-type clips.

5 With the vehicle raised, inspect the fuel tank and filler neck for punctures, cracks and other damage. The connection between the filler neck and tank is especially critical. Sometimes a rubber filler neck or connecting hose will leak due to loose retaining clamps or deteriorated rubber.

6 Similarly, inspect all brake hoses and metal pipes. If any damage or deterioration is discovered, do not drive the vehicle until the necessary repair work has been carried out. Renew any damaged sections of hose or pipe.

7 Carefully check all rubber hoses and metal fuel lines leading away from the petrol tank. Check for loose connections, deteriorated

hoses, crimped lines and other damage. Pay particular attention to the vent pipes and hoses which often loop up around the filler neck and can become blocked or crimped. Follow the lines to the front of the vehicle carefully inspecting them all the way. Renew damaged sections as necessary.

8 From within the engine compartment, check the security of all fuel hose attachments and pipe unions, and inspect the fuel hoses and vacuum hoses for kinks, chafing and deterioration.

9 Check the condition of all exposed wiring harnesses.

7 Battery electrolyte level check

HAYNES HiNT *Persistent need for topping-up the battery electrolyte suggests that alternator output is excessive or the battery is approaching the end of its life.*

1 A "maintenance-free" (sealed for life) battery is standard equipment on all vehicles covered by this Manual. Although this type of battery has many advantages over the older refillable type and should never require the addition of distilled water, it should still be routinely checked. The electrolyte level can be seen through the battery's translucent case. Although it should not alter in normal use, if the level has lowered (for example, due to electrolyte having boiled away as a result of overcharging) it is permissible to gently prise up the cell cover(s) and to top up the level.

2 If a conventional battery has been fitted as a replacement, the electrolyte level of each cell should be checked and, if necessary, topped up until the separators are just covered. On some batteries the case is

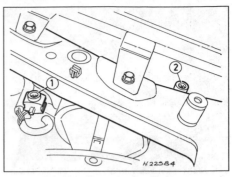

8.2 Headlamp unit adjusters

1 Vertical adjuster   2 Horizontal adjuster

translucent and incorporates MINIMUM and MAXIMUM level marks. The check should be made more often if the vehicle is operated in high ambient temperature conditions.

3 Top up the electrolyte level using distilled or de-ionized water. This should not be necessary often under normal operating conditions. If regular topping-up becomes necessary and the battery case is not fractured, the battery is being over-charged and the voltage regulator will have to be checked.

8 Headlamp beam alignment check

1 If the headlamps are thought to be out of alignment, then accurate adjustment of their beams is only possible using optical beam setting equipment, and this work should therefore be carried out by a Rover dealer or workshop with the necessary facilities.

2 For reference, the headlamps can be adjusted by using a suitably sized crosshead screwdriver to rotate the two adjuster assemblies fitted to the rear of each lamp **(see illustration)**. Access to the lower adjuster can be gained through the hole in the bonnet lock platform.

Every 6000 miles or 6 months - whichever comes first

9 Engine oil and filter renewal

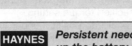

HAYNES HiNT *Frequent oil changes are the most important preventative maintenance procedure that can be undertaken by the DIY owner. As engine oil ages, it becomes diluted and contaminated, which leads to premature engine wear.*

1 Before starting this procedure, gather together all the necessary tools and materials.

Ensure that you have plenty of clean rags and newspapers handy to mop up any spills.

2 The engine oil should be warm as it will drain better and more built-up sludge will be removed with it. Take care not to touch the exhaust or any other hot parts of the engine when working under the vehicle. To avoid any possibility of scalding and to protect yourself from possible skin irritants and other harmful contaminants in used engine oils, it is advisable to wear gloves when carrying out this work.

3 The engine oil drain plug is located on the front of the sump and can be reached easily, without having to raise the vehicle. Remove the oil filler cap and use a spanner, or preferably a suitable socket and bar, to slacken the drain plug about half a turn **(see**

illustration). Position the draining container under the drain plug, then remove the plug

9.3 Unscrewing engine oil drain plug

9.7 Using an oil filter removal tool

9.9 Applying a light coat of clean engine oil to oil filter sealing ring

completely. If possible, try to keep the plug pressed into the sump while unscrewing it by hand the last couple of turns. As the plug releases from the threads, move it away sharply so the stream of oil issuing from the sump runs into the container, not up your sleeve.

4 Allow some time for the old oil to drain. It may be necessary to reposition the container as the flow of oil slows to a trickle. Work can be speeded-up by removing the oil filter, as described below, while the oil is draining.

5 After all the oil has drained, wipe off the drain plug with a clean rag and renew its sealing washer. Clean the area around the drain plug opening and refit the plug. Tighten the plug to the specified torque setting.

6 Move the container into position under the oil filter, which is located next to the drain plug on the front of the engine.

7 Using an oil filter removal tool, slacken the filter initially then unscrew it by hand the rest of the way **(see illustration)**. Empty the oil in the filter into the container and allow any residual oil to drain out of the engine.

8 Use a clean rag to remove all oil, dirt and sludge from the filter sealing area on the engine. Check the old filter to make sure that the rubber sealing ring has not stuck to the engine. If it has, carefully remove it.

9 Apply a light coating of clean engine oil to the new filter's sealing ring **(see illustration)**. Screw the filter into position on the engine until it seats, then tighten it through a further half-turn. Tighten the filter by hand only.

10 Remove the old oil and all tools from under the vehicle.

11 Refill the engine with fresh oil, using the correct grade and type of oil. Pour in half the specified quantity of oil first, then wait a few minutes for the oil to fall to the sump. Continue adding oil a small quantity at a time until the level is up to the lower mark on the dipstick. Adding a further 1 litre will bring the level up to the upper mark on the dipstick.

12 Start the engine and run it for a few minutes while checking for leaks around the oil filter seal and the sump drain plug.

13 Switch off the engine and wait a few minutes for the oil to settle in the sump once more. With the new oil circulated and the filter now completely full, recheck the level on the dipstick and add more oil as necessary.

14 Dispose of the used engine oil safely.

Every 12 000 miles or 12 months - whichever comes first

10 Coolant renewal

 Warning: Wait until the engine is cold before renewing the coolant. Do not allow antifreeze to come into contact with your skin or painted surfaces of the vehicle. Rinse off spills immediately with plenty of water. Never leave antifreeze lying around in an open container or in a puddle in the driveway or on the garage floor. Children and pets are attracted by its sweet smell; antifreeze is fatal if ingested.

Antifreeze mixture

1 Antifreeze should always be renewed at the specified intervals. This is necessary not only to maintain the antifreeze properties but also to prevent corrosion which would otherwise occur as the corrosion inhibitors become progressively less effective.

Note: *If Rover-recommended antifreeze is used exclusively, this task need only be carried out after the first three years of the vehicle's life and every two years thereafter.*

2 Always use an ethylene glycol-based antifreeze which is suitable for use in mixed-metal cooling systems.

3 The type of antifreeze and levels of protection afforded are indicated in "Weekly Checks" and Specifications. To give the recommended 50% concentration, 2.9 litres of antifreeze must be mixed with 2.9 litres of clean, soft water. This should provide enough to refill the complete system but it is best to make up a larger amount so that a supply is available for subsequent topping-up.

Draining

4 To drain the cooling system, remove the expansion tank filler cap then move the heater air temperature control to the maximum heat position.

5 Place a large drain tray beneath the coolant drain tap fitted to the bottom right-hand corner of the radiator then open up the tap and allow the coolant to drain into the container. Once the system had drained completely, securely close the tap.

Flushing

6 With time, the cooling system may gradually lose its efficiency due to the radiator core having become choked with rust, scale deposits and other sediment. To minimise this, as well as using only good quality antifreeze and clean soft water, the system should be flushed as follows whenever the coolant is renewed.

7 With the coolant drained, ensure the drain tap is closed then refill the system with fresh water. Refit the expansion tank filler cap, start the engine and warm it up to normal operating temperature, then stop it and (after allowing it to cool down completely) drain the system again. Repeat as necessary until only clean water can be seen to emerge, then refill finally with the specified coolant mixture.

8 If the specified coolant mixture has been used and has been renewed at the specified intervals, the above procedure will be sufficient to keep clean the system for a considerable length of time. If, however, the system has been neglected, a more thorough operation will be required, as follows.

9 First drain the coolant, then disconnect the radiator top and bottom hoses from the radiator. Insert a garden hose into the radiator top hose outlet and allow water to circulate through the radiator until it runs clean from the bottom outlet.

10 To flush the engine, insert the garden hose into the top hose and allow water to circulate until it runs clear from the bottom hose. If, after a reasonable period, the water still does not run clear, the cooling system should be flushed with a good proprietary cleaning agent.

11 In severe cases of contamination, reverse-flushing of the radiator may be necessary. To do this, remove the radiator, invert it and insert a garden hose into the bottom outlet. Continue flushing until clear water runs from the top hose outlet. If necessary, a similar procedure can be used to flush the heater matrix.

12 The use of chemical cleaners should be necessary only as a last resort as regular renewal of the coolant will prevent excessive contamination of the system.

10.15a Unscrew cooling system bleed screw to allow trapped air to escape

10.15b Unscrewing filler cap bolt whilst retaining filler stem with an open-ended spanner

10.16 Filling cooling system slowly via filler stem

Filling

13 With the cooling system drained and flushed, ensure that the drain tap is securely closed. Check all hose unions for security and all hoses for condition. Fresh antifreeze has a searching action which will rapidly find any weaknesses in the system.

14 Prepare a sufficient quantity of the specified coolant mixture, allowing for a surplus so as to have a reserve supply for topping-up.

15 Slacken the bleed screw from the coolant rail situated underneath the distributor to allow the escape of air trapped during refilling, then remove the cooling system filler cap bolt (where fitted). Use a suitable open-ended spanner to retain the filler stem neck whilst the cap bolt is removed to prevent any strain being placed on the hose **(see illustrations)**.

16 Fill the system slowly through the filler stem **(see illustration)**. When coolant can be seen emerging from the bleed screw in a steady stream, tighten the bleed screw securely. Continue filling until the coolant reaches the neck of the filler stem. Refit the filler stem cap bolt and tighten it securely whilst retaining the neck with an open-ended spanner. Top up the expansion tank to the correct level, then refit the filler cap.

17 Start the engine and run it at no more than idle speed until it has warmed up to normal operating temperature and the radiator electric cooling fan has cut in. Watch the

temperature gauge to check for signs of overheating.

18 Stop the engine and allow it to cool down completely, then remove the expansion tank filler cap and top up the tank to the correct level. Refit the filler cap and wash off any spilt coolant from the engine compartment and bodywork.

19 After refilling, check carefully all system components for signs of coolant leaks. A label should now be attached to the radiator or expansion tank stating the type and concentration of antifreeze used and the date installed. Any subsequent topping-up should be made with the same type and concentration of antifreeze.

20 If, after draining and refilling the system, symptoms of overheating are found which did not occur previously, then the fault is almost certainly due to trapped air at some point in the system causing an air-lock and restricting the flow of coolant. Usually, air is trapped because the system was refilled too quickly. In some cases air-locks can be released by tapping or squeezing the various hoses. If the problem persists, stop the engine and allow it to cool down completely before unscrewing the bleed screw to allow the trapped air to escape.

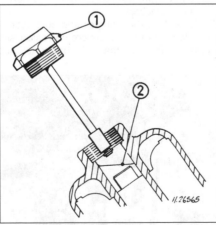

11.2b Topping up carburettor piston damper

1 Piston damper   2 Oil level

11 Carburettor piston damper oil replenishment

1 Remove the air cleaner housing.

2 Unscrew the piston damper from the top of the carburettor suction chamber and top up the chamber to the top of the damper cylinder with engine oil **(see illustrations)**. Note that since the advent of modern low-viscosity multigrade engine oils, there is no need to use a special carburettor oil in SU carburettors.

3 Raise and lower the carburettor piston, ensuring that it moves smoothly without sticking, then refit and tighten (carefully but securely) the piston damper.

4 Refit the air cleaner assembly, ensuring that all vacuum pipes are correctly reconnected.

12 Idle speed and mixture check

Carburettor engines

1 Before beginning any form of carburettor adjustment, check the following:

a) *Check that the ignition timing is accurate.*

b) *Check that all spark plugs are in good condition and correctly gapped.*

c) *Check that the accelerator and choke cables are correctly adjusted.*

d) *Check that the carburettor idle bypass system is functioning correctly.*

e) *Check that the piston damper is topped-up.*

f) *Check that the crankcase breather hose(s), the float chamber vent hose and the full load air bleed hose are clear.*

g) *Check that the air cleaner filter element is clean and that the exhaust system is in good condition.*

h) *If the engine is running very roughly, check its compression pressures whilst bearing in mind the possibility that one of the hydraulic tappets might be faulty, producing an incorrect valve clearance.*

1

11.2a Removing piston damper from carburettor suction chamber

2 Take the vehicle on a journey of sufficient length to warm the engine up to normal operating temperature. Any adjustment should be completed within two minutes of return, without stopping the engine. If this cannot be achieved, or if the radiator electric cooling fan operates, wait for the cooling fan to stop and clear any excess fuel from the inlet manifold by racing the engine two or three times to between 2000 and 3000 rpm, then allow it to idle again.

3 Ensure all electrical loads are switched off. If the vehicle is not equipped with a tachometer, connect one following the manufacturer's instructions. Note the idle speed, comparing it with that specified.

4 The idle speed adjusting knob is located under the air cleaner assembly, on the rear right-hand corner of the carburettor. Screw the knob in or out as necessary to obtain the specified speed **(see illustration)**.

5 Idle mixture is set at the factory and should require no further adjustment. If, due to a change in engine characteristics caused by carbon build-up, bore wear, etc., or after a major carburettor overhaul, the mixture becomes incorrect, then it can be reset. Note, however, that an exhaust gas analyser (CO meter) will be required to check the mixture and to set it with the necessary standard of accuracy. If a meter is not available, then the vehicle must be taken to a Rover dealer for the work to be carried out.

6 If an exhaust gas analyser is available, follow the manufacturer's instructions to check the CO level. If adjustment is required, it is made by turning the idle air bypass screw, which is set in a deep recess on the carburettor left-hand side, beneath the breather hose **(see illustration)**. Using a Torx-type screwdriver (size TX10) turn the screw in very small increments until the level is correct. Screwing the screw in (clockwise) richens the idle mixture and increases the CO level.

7 When adjustment is complete, disconnect any test equipment and refit any components removed for access.

Fuel-injected engines

8 Experienced home mechanics who have a considerable amount of skill and equipment (including a good-quality tachometer and a good-quality, carefully-calibrated exhaust gas analyser) may be able to check the exhaust CO level and the idle speed but, if these are found to be in need of adjustment, the vehicle must be taken to a suitably-equipped Rover dealer

9 Adjustments can be made only by re-programming the fuel-injection/ignition system ECU using Rover diagnostic equipment connected to the system by the diagnostic connector. For most owners, the best solution will be to carry out those maintenance operations that they feel able to undertake, with the vehicle then being taken to a Rover dealer for expert attention to the remaining items.

13 Lambda sensor operation check

1 This task can only be carried out using Rover diagnostic equipment. Do not neglect to have this check made at the specified intervals, especially as the vehicle's mileage increases, as it is the only means of checking (in conjunction with a CO level check) whether the catalytic converter's closed-loop control system is working properly. Lambda sensors are delicate components working under arduous conditions and do not last for ever. If the sensor is no longer effective, it must be renewed.

14 Exhaust system check

1 With the engine cold, check the complete exhaust system from the engine to the end of the tailpipe. Ideally, the inspection should be carried out with the vehicle raised to permit unrestricted access.

2 Check the exhaust pipes and connections for evidence of leaks, severe corrosion and damage. Ensure that all brackets and mountings are in good condition and secure. Leakage at any of the joints or in other parts of the system will usually show up as a black sooty stain in the vicinity of the leak.

3 Rattles and other noises can often be traced to the exhaust system, especially the brackets and mountings. Try to move the pipes and silencers. If any component can come into contact with the body or suspension parts, then secure the system with new mountings or, if possible, separate the joints and twist the pipes as necessary to provide additional clearance.

15 Distributor cap, rotor arm and HT lead check

HAYNES HINT *Ensure that all HT leads are numbered before removal, to avoid confusion when refitting.*

Spark plug (HT) leads

1 The spark plug leads should be checked whenever new spark plugs are fitted.

2 Pull each lead from its plug by gripping the end fitting. Do not grip the lead, otherwise the lead connection may be fractured **(see illustration)**.

3 Check inside the lead end fitting for signs of corrosion, which will look like a white crusty powder. Push the end fitting back onto the spark plug ensuring that it is a tight fit. If not, remove the lead again and use pliers to carefully crimp the metal connector inside the end fitting until it fits securely on the end of the plug.

4 Using a clean rag, wipe the entire length of each lead to remove any built-up dirt and grease. Once the lead is clean, check for burns, cracks and other damage. Do not bend the lead excessively or pull the lead lengthwise, otherwise the conductor inside might break.

5 Disconnect the other end of each lead from

12.4 Turning idle speed adjusting knob to alter engine idle speed

12.6 Adjusting idle mixture (air cleaner removed for clarity)

15.2 Pull each spark plug lead by gripping its end fitting

15.5 Disconnecting an HT lead from the distributor cap

15.7 Distributor cap is retained by two offset screws

15.9 Removing distributor rotor arm grub screw - fuel-injected engines

the distributor cap **(see illustration)**. Again, pull only on the end fitting. Check for corrosion and a tight fit in the same manner as the spark plug end.

6 If an ohmmeter is available, check the resistance of each lead by connecting the meter between the spark plug end of the lead and the segment inside the distributor cap. Refit each lead securely on completion.

Distributor cap and rotor arm

7 Unscrew the two screws and remove the distributor cap **(see illustration)**.

8 Wipe the cap clean and carefully inspect it inside and out for signs of cracks, carbon tracks (tracking) and worn, burned or loose contacts. Check that the cap's centre carbon brush is unworn, free to move against spring pressure and making good contact with the rotor arm.

9 Inspect the rotor arm. On fuel-injected engines, it is retained by a small grub screw **(see illustration)**. If checking components with a meter, note that the rotor arm has an in-built resistor.

10 Renew any components which are found to be faulty. It is common practice to renew the cap and rotor arm whenever new spark plug leads are fitted.

11 When fitting a new cap, remove the leads from the old cap one at a time and fit them to the new cap in exactly the same location. Do not simultaneously remove all the leads from the old cap or firing order confusion may occur. Note that the screw locations are offset so that the cap may be refitted only one way. Tighten the cap retaining screws and, where necessary the rotor arm grub screw, to the specified torque wrench settings.

16 Clutch check

1 Check that the clutch pedal moves smoothly and easily through its full travel and that the clutch itself functions correctly, with no trace of slip or drag.

2 If excessive effort is required to operate the clutch, check first that the cable is correctly routed and undamaged, then remove the pedal to ensure that its pivot is properly greased before suspecting a fault in the cable itself. If the cable is worn or damaged, or if its self-adjusting mechanism is no longer effective, then renew it.

3 No adjustment is possible. If any fault develops in the clutch, the gearbox must be removed so that the clutch can be overhauled.

17 Gearbox oil level check

Note: *The manufacturer states that, provided only the recommended oils are used, the gearbox is filled for life and the oil does not require regular changes. If, however, the gearbox oil has to be drained and refilled for any reason, the operation is described in Chapter 7.*

1 The gearbox oil level must be checked with the vehicle standing on its wheels on level ground. Also, the level must be checked before the vehicle is driven, or at least 5 minutes after the engine has been switched off. If the oil is checked immediately after driving the vehicle, some of the oil will remain distributed around the gearbox components, resulting in an inaccurate level reading.

2 Wipe clean the area around the filler/level plug, which is located at the rear of the gearbox, next to the left-hand driveshaft inner constant velocity joint. Unscrew the plug and clean it, discarding the sealing washer. To avoid rounding-off the corners of the plug hexagon, use only good quality, close-fitting, single-hexagon or surface drive spanners or sockets.

3 The oil level should reach the lower edge of the filler/level hole. A certain amount of oil will have gathered behind the filler/level plug and will trickle out when it is removed; this does not necessarily indicate that the level is correct **(see illustration)**.

4 To ensure that a true level is established, wait until the initial trickle has stopped, then add oil as necessary until a trickle of new oil can be seen emerging. The level will be correct when the flow ceases. Use only good quality oil of the specified type. Adding oil is an extremely awkward operation. Above all, allow plenty of time for the oil level to settle properly before checking it.

5 If the gearbox has been overfilled so that oil flows out as soon as the filler/level plug is removed, check that the vehicle is completely level (front to rear and side to side) and allow the surplus to drain off into a suitable container.

6 When the level is correct, fit a new sealing washer and refit the filler/level plug, tightening it to the specified torque wrench setting. Wash off any spilt oil.

18 Driveshaft rubber gaiter and CV joint check

1 With the vehicle raised and securely supported on axle stands, turn the steering onto full lock then slowly rotate the roadwheel. Inspect the condition of the outer constant velocity (CV) joint rubber gaiters while squeezing the gaiters to open out the

17.3 Gearbox oil level is correct when oil has just stopped trickling from filler/level plug hole

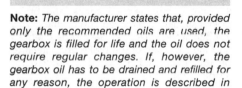

18.1 Checking driveshaft outer CV joint rubber gaiter

20.2 Front brake pad friction material (arrowed) can be checked through slot in caliper body

folds **(see illustration)**. Check for signs of cracking, splits or deterioration of the rubber which may allow the grease to escape and lead to the entry of water and grit into the joint. Also check the security and condition of the gaiter retaining clips. Repeat these checks on the inner CV joints. If any damage or deterioration is found, then renew the gaiters.
2 Check the general condition of the CV joints by first holding the driveshaft and attempting to rotate the roadwheel. Repeat this check by holding the inner joint and attempting to rotate the driveshaft. Any appreciable movement indicates wear in the joints or driveshaft splines, or a loose driveshaft nut.

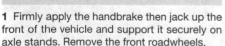

19 Brake pedal check

1 Check that the brake pedal pivot is properly greased and that the pedal moves smoothly and easily through its full travel.
2 With the engine switched off, the pedal should have a small amount of free play, then firm resistance. If the pedal feels spongy or has a long travel, then the brake system should be checked further.

20 Front brake pad, caliper and disc check

1 Firmly apply the handbrake then jack up the front of the vehicle and support it securely on axle stands. Remove the front roadwheels.
2 For a quick check, the thickness of friction material remaining on each brake pad can be measured through the slot in the caliper body **(see illustration)**. If any pad's friction material is worn to the specified thickness or less, all four pads must be renewed as a set.
3 For a comprehensive check, the brake pads should be removed and cleaned. This will permit the operation of the caliper to be checked and the condition of the brake disc itself to be fully examined on both sides. Refer to Chapter 9 for further information.

21 Rear brake shoe, wheel cylinder and drum check

1 Chock the front wheels then jack up the rear of the vehicle and support it on axle stands.
2 For a quick check, the thickness of friction material remaining on one of the brake shoes can be measured through the slot in the brake backplate that is exposed by prising out its sealing grommet **(see illustration)**. If a rod of the same diameter as the specified minimum thickness is placed against the shoe friction material, the amount of wear can quickly be assessed. If any shoe's friction material is worn to the specified thickness or less, all four shoes must be renewed.
3 For a comprehensive check, the brake drums should be removed and cleaned. This will permit the wheel cylinders to be checked and the condition of the brake drum itself to be fully examined. Refer to Chapter 9 for further information.

22 Rear brake pad, caliper and disc check

1 Chock the front wheels then jack up the rear of the vehicle and support it on axle stands.

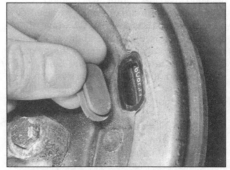

21.2 Remove grommet to check rear brake shoe friction material thickness

2 For a quick check, the thickness of friction material remaining on each brake pad can be measured through the slot in the caliper body **(see illustration 20.2)**. If any pad's friction material is worn to the specified thickness or less, all four pads must be renewed as a set.
3 For a comprehensive check, the brake pads should be removed and cleaned. This will permit the operation of the caliper to be checked and the condition of the brake disc itself to be fully examined on both sides. Refer to Chapter 9 for further information.

23 Handbrake check

Checking

1 The handbrake should be capable of holding the parked vehicle stationary, even on steep slopes, when applied with moderate force. The mechanism should be firm and positive in feel with no trace of stiffness or sponginess from the cables and should release immediately the handbrake lever is released. If the mechanism is faulty in any of these respects then it must be checked immediately.
2 To check the handbrake setting, first apply the footbrake firmly several times to establish correct shoe-to-drum clearance. Applying normal, moderate pressure, pull the handbrake lever to the fully-applied position whilst counting the number of clicks emitted from the handbrake ratchet mechanism. If adjustment is correct, there should be 8 to 10 clicks before the handbrake is fully applied. If this is not the case, then adjustment is required.

Adjustment

3 To adjust the handbrake, chock the front wheels then jack up the rear of the vehicle and support it on axle stands.
4 Lift out the ashtray from the rear of the centre console to gain access to the handbrake adjusting nut **(see illustrations)**.
5 Apply the handbrake and check that the equalizer and cables move freely and

23.4a Remove ashtray from centre console . . .

23.4b . . . to gain access to handbrake cable adjuster nut and equalizer mechanism

24.2 Checking a steering gear rubber gaiter

24.4 Rocking a roadwheel to check steering/suspension wear

smoothly, then set the lever on the first notch of the ratchet mechanism. With the lever in this position, rotate the handbrake lever adjusting nut until only a slight drag can be felt when the rear wheels are turned. Once this is so, fully release the handbrake lever and check that the wheels rotate freely. Check adjustment by applying the handbrake fully whilst counting the clicks emitted from the handbrake ratchet and, if necessary, re-adjust.

6 Once adjustment is correct, refit the ashtray and lower the vehicle to the ground.

24 Suspension and steering check

Front suspension and steering

1 Raise the front of the vehicle and securely support it on axle stands.
2 Inspect the balljoint dust covers and the steering gear rubber gaiters for splits, chafing or deterioration **(see illustration)**. Any wear of these components will cause loss of lubricant, together with dirt and water entry, resulting in rapid deterioration of the balljoints or steering gear.
3 On vehicles equipped with power steering, check the fluid hoses for chafing or deterioration and the pipe and hose unions for fluid leakage. Also check for signs of fluid leakage under pressure from the steering gear rubber gaiters which would indicate failed fluid seals within the steering gear.
4 Grasp the roadwheel at the 12 o'clock and 6 o'clock positions and try to rock it **(see illustration)**. Very slight free play may be felt but if the movement is appreciable then further investigation is necessary to determine the source. Continue rocking the wheel while an assistant depresses the brake pedal. If the movement is now eliminated or significantly reduced, it is likely that the hub bearings are at fault. If the free play is still evident with the brake pedal depressed, then there is wear in the suspension joints or mountings.

5 Now grasp the roadwheel at the 9 o'clock and 3 o'clock positions and try to rock it as before. Any movement felt now may again be caused by wear in the hub bearings, or in the track rod balljoints. If a balljoint is worn the visual movement will be obvious. If the inner joint is suspect it can be felt by placing a hand over the steering gear rubber gaiter and gripping the track rod. If the wheel is now rocked, movement will be felt at the inner joint if wear has taken place.
6 Using a large screwdriver or flat bar check for wear in the suspension mounting bushes by levering between the relevant suspension component and its attachment point. Some movement is to be expected as the mountings are made of rubber, but excessive wear should be obvious. Also check the condition of any visible rubber bushes, looking for splits, cracks or contamination of the rubber.
7 With the vehicle standing on its wheels, have an assistant turn the steering wheel back and forth about an eighth of a turn each way. There should be very little, if any, lost movement between the steering wheel and the roadwheels. If this is not the case, closely observe the joints and mountings previously described but in addition, check for wear of the steering column universal joint and the steering gear itself.

Rear suspension

8 Chock the front wheels then jack up the rear of the vehicle and support it on axle stands.
9 Working as described for the front suspension, check the rear hub bearings and the trailing arm and lateral link bushes for wear.

25 Roadwheel check

1 Remove each roadwheel and clean any dirt or mud from its inside and outside surfaces. Examine the wheel rim for signs of rusting, corrosion or other damage. Light alloy wheels

are easily damaged by 'kerbing' whilst parking and, similarly, steel wheels may become dented or buckled. Renewal of the wheel is very often the only course of remedial action possible.
2 If the wheels are not removed for inspection, check that the wheel nuts are securely fastened by first removing the wheel trim then slackening each nut in turn through one-quarter of a turn before tightening it to the specified torque wrench setting. Refit the trim.

26 Power steering pump drivebelt check

1 The power steering pump is situated on the rear right-hand end of the engine and is driven by the crankshaft pulley via a belt.

Check and adjustment

2 Apply the handbrake then jack up the front of the vehicle and support it on axle stands. Remove the right-hand front roadwheel.
3 From underneath the front of the vehicle, slacken and remove the three bolts securing the bumper flange to the body. Remove the seven bolts securing the front undercover panel to the body and remove the panel.
4 Check the power steering pump drivebelt for cracks, splitting, fraying or damage, whilst rotating the crankshaft using a suitable spanner applied to the crankshaft pulley bolt, so that the entire length of the belt is examined. Check also for signs of glazing (shiny patches) and for separation of the belt plies. Renew the belt if worn or damaged.
5 The drivebelt tension is checked by measuring the amount of deflection that takes place when a force of 10 kg is applied (using a spring balance, or similar) midway between the crankshaft and power steering pump pulleys on the belt's upper run. If the deflection measured is any more or less than that specified, the drivebelt must be adjusted as follows.

1

26.6a Slacken adjuster pulley spindle nut . . .

26.6b . . . and rotate adjuster bolt until power steering pump drivebelt tension is correct

26.10 Power steering pump drivebelt removal

6 Slacken the drivebelt adjuster (idler) pulley spindle nut and bolt, then rotate the adjuster bolt, situated on the underside of the pulley assembly, clockwise or anti-clockwise as required to obtain the correct belt tension **(see illustrations)**.
7 When the correct tension is achieved, tighten the adjuster pulley spindle bolt and nut to the specified torque setting and rotate the crankshaft several times to settle the drivebelt. Recheck the belt tension, repeating the adjustment procedure if necessary.
8 Refit the undercover panel and roadwheel then lower the vehicle to the ground.

Renewal

9 Carry out the operations described in paragraphs 2 and 3.
10 Slacken the drivebelt adjuster (idler) pulley spindle nut and bolt and slacken the adjuster bolt until the drivebelt can be slipped off the pulleys and removed from the vehicle **(see illustration)**.
11 Clean the belt pulleys carefully, removing all traces of oil or grease and checking that the grooves are clear. Fit the new belt to the pulleys and tighten the adjuster bolt until the tension is approximately correct, then check and adjust the tension as described above.
12 Start the engine and allow it to idle for approximately 10 minutes to settle the drivebelt in position. Stop the engine then recheck the drivebelt tension and, if necessary, repeat the adjustment procedure.
13 Refit the undercover panel and roadwheel then lower the vehicle to the ground.

27 Vehicle exterior check

Paintwork and body panels

1 Wash the vehicle thoroughly, removing all tar spots and other surface blemishes.
2 Carefully check all paintwork, looking closely for chips or scratches. Check with particular care vulnerable areas such as the front (bonnet and spoiler) and around the

wheelarches. Any damage to the paintwork must be rectified as soon as possible to comply with the terms of the manufacturer's cosmetic and anti-corrosion warranties. Check with a Rover dealer for details.
3 If a chip or (light) scratch is found that is recent and still free from rust, then it can be touched-up using the appropriate touch-up pencil which can be obtained from Rover dealers. Any more serious damage, or rusted stone chips, can be repaired as described in Chapter 11. If damage or corrosion is so severe that a panel must be renewed, then seek professional advice.
4 Check that the door and ventilator opening drain holes and pipes are completely clear so that water can drain out.

Underbody sealer check

5 The wax-based underbody protective coating should be inspected annually, preferably just prior to winter, when the underbody should be washed down as thoroughly but gently as possible and any damage to the coating repaired.
6 If any body panels are repaired or renewed, do not forget to replace the coating and to inject wax into door panels, sills, box sections etc, to maintain the level of protection provided by the vehicle's manufacturer.
7 Check carefully that the wheel arch liners and undercover panel are in place and securely fastened and that there is no sign of underbody damage or of developing corrosion. If any corrosion is found, seek immediate professional advice.

28 Lock, hinge, latch and sunroof lubrication

1 Lubricate the hinges of the bonnet, doors and tailgate with a light oil.
2 Lightly grease the bonnet release mechanism and cable.
3 The door and tailgate latches, strikers and locks must be lubricated using only the special Rover Door Lock and Latch Lubricant supplied in 25 gram sachets under Part Number VWN 10075. Inject 1 gram into each

lock and wipe off any surplus, then apply a thin film to the latches and strikers.
4 Do not lubricate the steering lock mechanism with oil or any other lubricant which might foul the ignition switch contacts. If the lock is stiff, try to introduce a graphite-based powder into the mechanism.
5 If a sunroof is fitted, lubricate very sparingly the seal lip with Rover's Non-Staining Grease (Corning No. 7) available under Part Number BAU 5812.

29 Alternator drivebelt check

1 The alternator is located on the front right-hand side of the engine unit, just above the engine oil filter, and is driven by the crankshaft pulley via a belt. On models equipped with air conditioning, an extended alternator drivebelt is fitted which also drives the air conditioning compressor which is situated just below the alternator.

Checking

2 Apply the handbrake then jack up the front of the vehicle and support it on axle stands. Remove the right-hand front roadwheel.
3 From underneath the front of the vehicle, slacken and remove the three bolts securing the bumper flange to the body. Remove the seven bolts securing the front undercover panel to the body and remove the panel.
4 Check the drivebelt for cracks, splitting, fraying or damage, whilst rotating the crankshaft clockwise using a suitable spanner applied to the crankshaft pulley bolt, so that the entire length of the belt is examined. Check also for signs of glazing (shiny patches) and for separation of the belt plies. Renew the belt if worn or damaged.

Adjustment - models with air conditioning

5 Carry out the operations described in paragraphs 2 and 3.
6 The drivebelt tension is checked by measuring the amount of deflection that takes place when a force of 10 kg is applied (using a

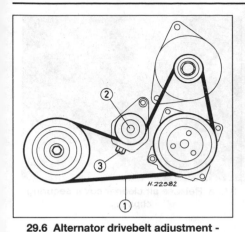

29.6 Alternator drivebelt adjustment - models with air conditioning

1 Drivebelt tension checking point
2 Adjuster pulley spindle bolt
3 Adjuster bolt

spring balance, or similar) midway between the crankshaft and air conditioning pulleys on the belt's lower run. If the deflection measured is more or less than that specified, the drivebelt must be adjusted as follows **(see illustration)**.

7 Slacken the drivebelt adjuster (idler) pulley spindle nut and bolt, then rotate the adjuster bolt (situated on the underside of the pulley assembly) clockwise or anti-clockwise as required to obtain the correct belt tension.

8 When the correct tension is achieved, tighten the adjuster pulley spindle bolt and nut, and rotate the crankshaft several times to settle the drivebelt. Recheck the belt tension, repeating the adjustment procedure if necessary.

9 Refit the undercover panel and roadwheel, then lower the vehicle to the ground.

Adjustment - models without air conditioning

10 Carry out the operations described in paragraphs 2 and 3.

29.12a Slacken alternator upper pivot mounting bolts (arrowed) . . .

11 The drivebelt tension is checked by measuring the amount of deflection that takes place when a force of 10 kg is applied (using a spring balance, or similar) midway between the crankshaft and alternator pulleys on the belt's upper run. If the deflection measured is more or less than that specified, the drivebelt must be adjusted as follows.

12 Slacken both the alternator upper pivot mounting bolts and the lower adjusting arm mounting bolt. Rotate the adjuster bolt clockwise or anti-clockwise as required to obtain the correct belt tension **(see illustrations)**.

13 When the correct tension is achieved, tighten the alternator adjusting arm and pivot bolts to the specified torque and rotate the crankshaft several times to settle the drivebelt. Recheck the belt tension and re-adjust if necessary.

14 Refit the undercover panel and roadwheel, then lower the vehicle to the ground.

Renewal

15 Carry out the operations in paragraphs 2 and 3.

16 If the vehicle is equipped with power

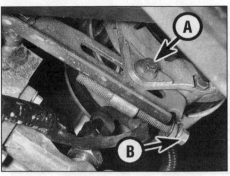

29.12b . . . and lower adjusting arm bolt (A) then rotate adjuster bolt (B) - models without air conditioning

steering, remove the power steering pump drivebelt, as described in Section 26.

17 Slacken the drivebelt adjuster (idler) pulley spindle nut and bolt (models with air conditioning), or the alternator pivot and adjusting arm mounting bolts (models without air conditioning) and slacken the adjuster bolt until the drivebelt can be slipped off the pulleys and removed from the vehicle.

18 Clean the belt pulleys carefully, removing all traces of oil or grease and checking that the grooves are clear. Fit the new belt to the pulleys and tighten the adjuster bolt until the belt tension is approximately correct, then check and adjust the tension as described above.

19 Where necessary, refit the power steering pump drivebelt.

20 Start the engine and allow it to idle at the specified speed for approximately 10 minutes to settle the drivebelt in position. Stop the engine then recheck the drivebelt tension as described above and, if necessary, repeat the adjustment procedure.

21 Refit the undercover panel and roadwheel, then lower the vehicle to the ground.

Every 24 000 miles or 2 years - whichever comes first

30 Air conditioning refrigerant check

1 The refrigerant condition and level is checked via the sightglass on the top of the receiver drier. The receiver drier is situated in the engine compartment where it is located just to the left of the radiator.

2 Start the engine then switch on the air conditioning system and allow the engine to idle for a couple of minutes whilst observing the sightglass. If the air conditioning system is operating normally then occasional bubbles should be visible through the sightglass.

3 If a constant stream of bubbles is visible, the refrigerant level is low and must be topped

up. If the sightglass has become clouded or streaked, there is a fault in the system. If either condition is present, the vehicle must be taken to a Rover dealer or suitable professional refrigeration specialist for the air conditioning system to be checked further and overhauled.

31 Air cleaner filter element renewal

Carburettor and single-point injection engines

1 Release the clips securing the air cleaner assembly cover, then unscrew the retaining

screws and carefully unclip the cover from the assembly **(see illustrations)**. If the assembly

31.1a Release air cleaner assembly cover retaining clips . . .

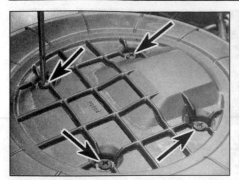

31.1b . . . then remove retaining screws and lift off cover - carburettor engine shown

31.3 Ensure new filter element is correctly seated on refitting

31.4a Release air cleaner cover securing clips . . .

is dislodged, lift it carefully and check that none of the vacuum pipes, hoses or wiring (as applicable) connected to its underside have been damaged or disconnected.

2 Lift out the air cleaner filter element and discard it. Wipe clean the inside of the assembly and the cover, then check that there is no foreign matter visible either in the air cleaner intake duct or in the inlet tract.

3 Place the new element in the air cleaner assembly. Ensure the element is correctly seated and clip the cover back onto the assembly (see illustration). Refit the retaining screws and clips to secure the cover.

Multi-point injection engines

4 Release the clips securing the air cleaner assembly cover and lift the cover off the housing just enough to allow the filter element to be withdrawn (see illustrations). If it is found necessary to remove the cover from the vehicle, then the throttle housing-to-air cleaner hose will have to be unclipped.

5 Remove the filter element and discard it (see illustration). Wipe clean the inside of its housing and cover, then check that there is no foreign matter lodged in the inlet tract.

6 Place the new element in the housing. Ensure the element is correctly seated and clip the cover back into position.

7 Ensure any disturbed hose connections are secure.

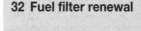

32 Fuel filter renewal

⚠ *Warning: Certain procedures require the removal of fuel lines and connections which may result in some fuel spillage.*
Before carrying out any operation on the fuel system refer to the precautions given in Safety first! at the beginning of this Manual and follow them implicitly. Petrol is a highly dangerous and volatile liquid and the precautions necessary when handling it cannot be overstressed.

1 Depressurise the fuel system as described in Chapter 4. Place wads of rag beneath the fuel filter unions to catch any spilled fuel.

2 Using two spanners to prevent damage to any of the fuel system pipes or components, disconnect the fuel filter inlet and outlet unions then remove the filter mounting clamp bolt and withdraw the filter from its mounting (see illustration).

3 Fit the new filter with its arrows pointing in the direction of the fuel flow, ie. to the right of the vehicle on models not equipped with a catalytic converter and downwards on models equipped with catalytic converters.

4 Tighten the filter mounting clamp bolt, connect the fuel pipes to the filter and tighten their unions securely, to the specified torque

wrench settings if possible. Start the engine and check carefully for any signs of fuel leaks from any of the disturbed components.

5 Dispose safely of the old filter. Note that it will be highly inflammable and may explode if thrown on a fire.

33 Ignition timing check

⚠ *Warning: Voltages produced by an electronic ignition system are considerably higher than those produced by conventional ignition systems. Extreme care must be taken when working on the system with the ignition switched on. Persons with surgically-implanted cardiac pacemaker devices should keep well clear of the ignition circuits, components and test equipment.*

Carburettor engines

1 Firmly apply the handbrake then jack up the front of the vehicle and support it on axle stands. Remove the right-hand roadwheel. From underneath the front of the vehicle, slacken and remove the three bolts securing the bumper flange to the body. Remove the seven bolts securing the front undercover panel to the body and remove the panel.

31.4b . . . lift cover off housing . . .

31.5 . . . and withdraw air filter element - MPi engine

32.2 Use two spanners when slackening fuel filter unions - non catalyst model shown

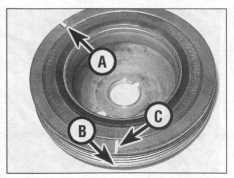

33.3a Crankshaft pulley engine assembly mark (A) factory timing mark (B) and home-made timing mark (C)

33.3b Ignition timing marks on pulley (arrowed) must be clarified before ignition timing can be checked

33.3c Ignition timing reference marks on timing belt lower cover

2 Before the ignition timing can be checked, the crankshaft pulley timing marks must be clarified. When looking at a brand-new pulley, the only obvious timing mark is the straight line (emphasised by the factory with white paint) cut radially in the pulley's outer (right-hand) face. This mark is, however, an engine assembly mark which, when aligned with the single, separate mark (at the 12 o'clock position) on the timing belt lower cover sets the crankshaft to 90° BTDC. The ignition timing mark is a tiny notch cut in the rim of the pulley's inner (left-hand) rim at approximately 100° anti-clockwise from the engine assembly mark; it is virtually invisible and care is required to identify it.

3 Rotate the pulley so that the engine assembly mark points vertically downwards, whereupon the ignition timing mark can be seen clearly enough to scribe a line squarely across the pulley rims. A hacksaw can then be used to enlarge the mark in the pulley outer (right-hand) rim and white paint can be used to highlight it **(see illustrations)**.

4 Start the engine and warm it up to normal operating temperature, then stop the engine and connect a timing light, according to the manufacturer's instructions. Disconnect the vacuum pipe from the distributor and plug it temporarily.

5 Start the engine and have an assistant increase engine speed to the specified amount, then aim the timing light at the timing marks. The highlighted mark should stand out clearly. Check that the crankshaft pulley mark aligns with the correct cover reference mark, or within the specified tolerance.

6 If adjustment is required, slacken the distributor mounting bolts until the distributor body is just able to rotate, then turn the body clockwise (viewed from the vehicle's left-hand side) to advance the ignition timing, or anti-clockwise to retard it. Tighten the bolts to the specified torque setting when the correct position is found, then recheck the ignition timing to ensure that it has not altered.

7 Increase engine speed and check that the pulley mark advances to beyond the beginning of the cover reference marks, returning to close to the TDC mark when the engine is allowed to idle. This shows that the centrifugal advance mechanism is functioning, but a detailed check must be left to a Rover dealer who has the necessary equipment.

8 Unplug and reconnect the vacuum pipe. The ignition timing should advance as the pipe is reconnected, retarding again when it is disconnected. If the ignition timing does not alter, check that the pipe is clear of blockages or kinks and that it is not leaking. Suck on the carburettor end of the pipe. If there is no effect on the ignition timing, then the vacuum diaphragm unit is faulty and must be renewed. On models equipped with a catalytic converter, the thermostatically-operated vacuum switch may be at fault (refer to Chapter 5 for further information). This can be eliminated by connecting a vacuum pipe directly from the carburettor to the distributor. If the vacuum advance is then restored to normal, the switch is faulty and must be renewed. Again, more detailed tests must be left to a Rover dealer.

9 When the ignition timing is correct, stop the engine and disconnect the timing light and tachometer, then reconnect the vacuum pipe. Refit the undercover and the roadwheel.

Fuel-injected engines

10 Home mechanics with a timing light and a good-quality tachometer may be able to check the ignition timing, the procedure being as described in paragraphs 1 to 5 above, except that the check should be made at idle speed and there is no vacuum pipe to disconnect. If, however, the timing is found to be in need of adjustment, then the vehicle must be taken to a suitably-equipped Rover dealer as adjustment can be made only by re-programming the fuel-injection/ignition system ECU using Rover diagnostic equipment connected to the system by the diagnostic connector. Note also that the timing and idle speed are under ECU control and may, therefore, vary significantly from the nominal values given in Chapters 4 and 5. Without the full equipment, any check is therefore nothing more than a rough guide.

34 Spark plug renewal

1 The correct functioning of the spark plugs is vital for the correct running and efficiency of the engine. It is essential that the plugs fitted are as specified for the engine. If the correct type is used and the engine is in good condition, then the spark plugs should not need attention between scheduled replacement intervals. Spark plug cleaning is rarely necessary and should not be attempted unless specialised equipment is available, as damage can easily be caused to the firing ends.

Removal

2 To gain access to the plugs, first remove the air cleaner housing metal intake duct. On K8 (carburettor) engines the plugs are then easily reached along the front of the engine. On K16 (fuel-injected) engines, undo the two retaining screws and remove the spark plug cover from the centre of the cylinder head cover **(see illustration)**.

3 Mark the HT leads one to four to correspond to the cylinder each lead serves (No. 1 cylinder is at the timing belt end of the engine). Pull the leads from the plugs by gripping their end fittings, not the lead,

34.2 Remove spark plug cover . . .

1

34.3 . . . then disconnect HT leads from spark plugs - K16 engine

34.5a Spark plugs are easily accessed on K8 engine

34.5b Removing a spark plug

otherwise the lead connection may be fractured **(see illustration)**.

4 Remove all dirt from the spark plug recesses using a clean brush, vacuum cleaner or compressed air before removing the plugs, so as to prevent dirt from dropping into the cylinders.

5 Unscrew the plugs using a spark plug spanner, suitable box spanner or a deep socket and extension bar **(see illustrations)**. Keep the socket aligned with the spark plug, otherwise if it is forcibly moved to one side, the ceramic insulator may be broken off. As each plug is removed, examine it as follows.

Examination

6 Examination of the spark plugs will give a good indication of the condition of the engine. If the insulator nose of the spark plug is clean and white, with no deposits, this is indicative of a weak mixture or too hot a plug (a hot plug transfers heat away from the electrode slowly, a cold plug transfers heat away quickly).

7 If the tip and insulator nose are covered with hard black-looking deposits, then this is indicative that the mixture is too rich. Should the plug be black and oily, then it is likely that the engine is fairly worn, as well as the mixture being too rich.

8 If the insulator nose is covered with light tan to greyish brown deposits, then the mixture is correct and it is likely that the engine is in good condition.

9 The spark plug electrode gap is of

considerable importance as, if it is too large or too small, the size of the spark and its efficiency will be seriously impaired. The gap should be set to the specified value.

10 To set the electrode gap, measure the gap with a feeler gauge and then bend open, or close, the outer electrode until the correct gap is achieved **(see illustrations)**. The centre electrode should never be bent, as this will crack the insulator and cause plug failure.

11 Special spark plug electrode gap adjusting tools are available from most motor accessory shops.

Refitting

12 Before refitting the spark plugs check that the threaded connector sleeves are tight and that the plug exterior surfaces and threads are clean.

13 Refit the spark plugs, reconnect the HT leads in their correct order and refit all components removed for access.

35 Brake fluid renewal

1 This procedure is similar to that described for the bleeding of the hydraulic system, as described in Chapter 9, except that the brake fluid reservoir should be emptied by syphoning and allowance should be made for all old fluid to be expelled when bleeding a section of the circuit.

HAYNES HiNT

It is very often difficult to insert spark plugs into their holes without cross-threading them. To avoid this possibility, fit a short length of rubber hose over the end of the spark plug. The flexible hose acts as a universal joint to help align the plug with the plug hole. Should the plug begin to cross-thread, the hose will slip on the spark plug, preventing thread damage to the aluminium cylinder head. Remove the rubber hose and tighten the plug to the specified torque using the spark plug socket and a torque wrench.

2 Working as described in Chapter 9, open the first bleed nipple in the sequence and pump the brake pedal gently until nearly all the old fluid has been emptied from the master cylinder reservoir. Top up to the MAX level on the reservoir with new fluid and

34.10a Measuring a spark plug electrode gap with a feeler gauge

34.10b Measuring a spark plug electrode gap using a wire gauge

34.10c Adjusting a spark plug electrode gap with a special tool

continue pumping until only new fluid remains in the reservoir and new fluid can be seen emerging from the bleed nipple.Old hydraulic fluid is much darker In colour than the new, making it easy to distinguish the two.

3 Tighten the nipple and top the reservoir level up to the MAX level line.

4 Work through all the remaining nipples in the sequence until new fluid can be seen emerging from all of them. Be careful to keep the master cylinder reservoir topped up to above the MIN level at all times, or air may enter the system and greatly increase the length of the task.

5 When the operation is complete, check that all nipples are securely tightened and that their dust caps are refitted. Wash off all traces of spilt fluid and recheck the master cylinder reservoir fluid level.

6 Check the operation of the brakes before taking the vehicle on the road.

Every 48 000 miles or 4 years - whichever comes first

36 Timing belt check

1 Working as described in Chapter 2, remove the timing belt upper right-hand (outer) cover.

2 Apply the handbrake and ensure that the transmission is in neutral, then jack up the front of the vehicle and support it on axle stands. Remove the right-hand roadwheel.

3 From underneath the front of the vehicle, slacken and remove the three bolts securing the bumper flange to the body. Remove the seven bolts securing the front undercover panel to the body and remove the panel to gain access to the crankshaft pulley.

4 Using a spanner or socket and extension bar applied to the crankshaft pulley bolt, rotate the crankshaft in a clockwise direction so that the full length of the timing belt can be checked. Examine the belt carefully for any signs of uneven wear, splitting or oil

contamination, and renew it if there is the slightest doubt about its condition.

5 Note that Rover state that there is no need to adjust belt tension once it has been installed. If, however, the belt is thought to be incorrectly tensioned, especially if it has been disturbed for other servicing/repair work, the tensioner can be reset following the procedure outlined in Chapter 2.

6 Refit all removed components and lower the vehicle to the ground once the check is complete.

1

Notes

Chapter 2 Part A
Engine in-car repair procedures

Contents

Degrees of difficulty

Easy, suitable for novice with little experience	**Fairly easy,** suitable for beginner with some experience	**Fairly difficult,** suitable for competent DIY mechanic	**Difficult,** suitable for experienced DIY mechanic	**Very difficult,** suitable for expert DIY or professional

Specifications

General

Type	Four-cylinder in-line, four-stroke, liquid-cooled
Designation:	
1.4 8-valve sohc	K8
1.4 16-valve dohc	K16
Bore	75.00 mm
Stroke	79.00 mm
Capacity	1396 cc
Firing order	1-3-4-2 (No 1 cylinder at timing belt end)
Direction of crankshaft rotation	Clockwise (seen from right-hand side of vehicle)
Compression ratio:	
K8	9.75 : 1
K16 (single-point injection)	9.5 : 1
K16 (multi-point injection)	10.0 : 1
Minimum compression pressure	10.3 bar
Maximum compression pressure difference between cylinders	1.4 bar

Cylinder block/crankcase

Note: *Service liners are Grade B*

Material	Aluminium alloy
Cylinder liner bore diameter - 60 mm from top of bore:	
Standard - grade A (Red)	74.975 to 74.985 mm
Standard - grade B (Blue)	74.986 to 74.995 mm
Service limit	75.045 mm

Crankshaft

Number of main bearings	5
Main bearing journal diameter	47.979 to 48.000 mm
Main bearing journal size grades:	
Grade A	47.993 to 48.000 mm
Grade B	47.986 to 47.993 mm
Grade C	47.979 to 47.986 mm
Crankpin journal diameter	42.986 to 43.007 mm
Crankpin journal size grades:	
Grade A	43.000 to 43.007 mm
Grade B	42.993 to 43.000 mm
Grade C	42.986 to 42.993 mm
Main bearing and crankpin journal maximum ovality	0.010 mm
Main bearing and big-end bearing running clearance	0.021 to 0.049 mm
Crankshaft endfloat:	
Standard	0.10 to 0.30 mm
Service limit	0.50 mm
Thrustwasher thickness	2.61 to 2.65 mm

Gudgeon pins

Diameter	18.0 mm
Fit in connecting rod	Interference

Pistons and piston rings

Note: *Service pistons are Grade B*

	Grade A	Grade B
Piston diameter:		
K8	74.940 to 74.955 mm	74.956 to 74.970 mm
K16	74.945 to 74.960 mm	74.960 to 74.975 mm
Piston-to-bore clearance:		
K8 - standard	0.015 to 0.045 mm	
K16 - standard	0.010 to 0.040 mm	
Service limit - all	0.080 mm	
Piston ring end gaps (fitted 20 mm from top of bore):		
Top compression ring:		
K8	0.25 to 0.45 mm	
K16	0.30 to 0.50 mm	
Second compression ring - all models	0.30 to 0.50 mm	
Oil control ring:		
K8 - standard	0.25 to 1.00 mm	
K16:		
standard	0.25 to 0.50 mm	
service limit	0.60 mm	
Piston ring-to-groove clearance:		
Top compression ring:		
K8	0.04 to 0.09 mm	
K16	0.04 to 0.07 mm	
Second compression ring:		
K8	0.04 to 0.08 mm	
K16	0.04 to 0.07 mm	
Oil control ring - all models	0.02 to 0.06 mm	

Cylinder head

Material	Aluminium alloy
Height	118.95 to 119.05 mm
Reface limit	0.20 mm
Maximum acceptable gasket face distortion	0.05 mm
Valve seat angle	45°
Valve seat width	1.5 mm
Seat cutter correction angle:	
Upper	30°
Lower	60°
Valve stem installed height:	
K8:	
new	38.95 to 40.81 mm
service limit	41.06 mm
K16:	
new	38.93 to 39.84 mm
service limit	40.10 mm

Valves

Seat angle:	
Inlet	45°
Exhaust	44° 30'
Head diameter:	
Inlet:	
K8	34.0 mm
K16	28.0 mm
Exhaust:	
K8	31.0 mm
K16	24.0 mm
Stem outside diameter:	
Inlet:	
K8	6.967 to 6.975 mm
K16	5.952 to 5.967 mm
Exhaust:	
K8	6.952 to 6.967 mm
K16	5.947 to 5.962 mm
Guide inside diameter:	
K8	7.000 to 7.025 mm
K16	6.000 to 6.025 mm
Stem-to-guide clearance:	
Inlet:	
standard	0.03 to 0.04 mm
service limit	0.07 mm
Exhaust:	
standard	0.07 to 0.08 mm
service limit	0.11 mm
Valve timing:	
K8:	
Inlet opens	13° BTDC
Inlet closes	47° ABDC
Exhaust opens	53° BBDC
Exhaust closes	7° ATDC
K16:	
Inlet opens	15° BTDC
Inlet closes	45° ABDC
Exhaust opens	55° BBDC
Exhaust closes	5° ATDC
Valve spring free length:	
K8	46.2 mm
K16	50.0 mm
Valve guide fitted height	6.0 mm

Camshaft

Drive	Toothed belt
Number of bearings	6
Bearing journal running clearance:	
Standard	0.060 to 0.094 mm
Service limit	0.150 mm
Camshaft endfloat:	
Standard	0.060 to 0.190 mm
Service limit	0.500 mm
Valve lift:	
K8	9.0 mm
K16	8.2 mm
Hydraulic tappet outside diameter	32.959 to 32.975 mm

Lubrication system

System pressure	1.0 bar @ idle speed
Oil pump type	Trochoidal, eccentric-rotor
Oil pump clearances:	
Rotor endfloat	0.02 to 0.06 mm
Outer rotor-to-body clearance	0.28 to 0.36 mm
Rotor lobe clearance	0.05 to 0.13 mm
Pressure relief valve operating pressure	4.1 bar
Oil pressure warning lamp lights at	Below 0.3 to 0.5 bar

2A

Torque wrench settings

	Nm	lbf ft
Spark plug (HT) lead clip screws - K8	9	7
Air intake duct support bracket-to-cylinder head screws	4	3
Spark plug cover screws - K16	2	1.5
Cylinder head cover bolts	9	7
Camshaft bearing cap/carrier-to-cylinder head bolts	9	7
Cylinder head bolts:		
1st stage	20	15
2nd stage	Tighten through 180°	
3rd stage	Tighten through (a further) 180°	
Timing belt cover fasteners:		
Upper right-hand (outer) cover	4	3
Lower and upper left-hand (inner) covers	9	7
Timing belt tensioner backplate clamp bolt	25	19
Timing belt tensioner pulley Allen screw	45	33
Camshaft sprocket bolt	33	24
Crankshaft pulley bolt	160	118
Oil pump-to-cylinder block/crankcase bolt and screws	9	7
Alternator mounting bracket-to-cylinder block/crankcase bolts	45	33
Dipstick tube-to-cylinder block/crankcase bolts	9	7
Flywheel bolts	85	63
Transmission-to-engine bolts	85	63
Flywheel cover plate screws	9	7
Flywheel rear cover plate bolt and nut	38	28
Big-end bearing cap bolts:		
1st stage	20	15
2nd stage	Tighten through 45°	
Main bearing ladder-to-cylinder block/crankcase bolts	10	7
Oil rail-to-main bearing ladder nuts	9	7
Oil pump pick-up/strainer pipe bolts	9	7
Sump bolts	10	7
Engine oil drain plug	42	31
Engine/transmission right-hand mounting:		
Bracket-to-cylinder block/crankcase bolts	45	33
Mounting-to-bracket nuts	100	74
Mounting-to-body through-bolt and nut	85	63
Engine/transmission left-hand mounting:		
Mounting-to-body bolts	45	33
Mounting-to-transmission bracket bolts	60	44
Transmission bracket bolts	100	74
Engine/transmission rear mounting:		
Mounting bracket-to-transmission bolt	85	63
Connecting link-to- transmission bracket bolt	60	44
Connecting link-to-body bolt	85	63
Anti-beaming bracket-to-support bracket bolt	45	33

1 General information and precautions

How to use this Chapter

This Part of the Chapter describes those repair procedures that can reasonably be carried out on the engine whilst it remains in the vehicle. If the engine has been removed from the vehicle and is being dismantled as described in Part B of this Chapter, any preliminary dismantling procedures can be ignored.

Note that whilst it may be possible physically to overhaul items such as the piston/connecting rod assemblies with the engine in the vehicle, such tasks are not usually carried out as separate operations and usually require the execution of several additional procedures (not to mention the cleaning of components and of oilways). For this reason, all such tasks are classed as major overhaul procedures and are described in Part B of this Chapter.

Engine information

The engine is of four-cylinder, in-line type, mounted transversely at the front of the vehicle with the clutch and transmission on its left-hand end. The engine is available in two forms - the K8 engine, which is the eight-valve single overhead camshaft engine fitted to the carburettor-equipped 214 S model, and the K16 engine, which is a sixteen-valve double overhead camshaft engine which is fitted to all fuel-injected models. Apart from the different cylinder head designs, both engines are of identical construction.

Apart from the pressed steel sump, the plastic timing belt covers and the aluminium alloy cylinder head cover, the engine consists of three major castings which are the cylinder head, the cylinder block/crankcase and the crankshaft main bearing ladder. There is also an oil rail underneath the main bearing ladder and the camshaft carrier/bearing caps.

All major castings are of aluminium alloy and are clamped together by ten long through-bolts which perform the dual role of cylinder head bolts and crankshaft main bearing fasteners. Since these bolts pass through the cylinder block/crankcase and the main bearing ladder, the oil rail is secured also to the main bearing ladder (by two nuts) and the main bearing ladder is secured also to the cylinder block/crankcase (by ten smaller bolts) so that the cylinder head can be removed without disturbing the rest of the engine. The passages provided for the bolts in the major castings are used as breather passages or as returns for the oil to the sump.

The crankshaft runs in five main bearings. Thrustwashers are fitted to the centre main bearing (upper half) to control crankshaft endfloat.

The connecting rods rotate on horizontally-split bearing shells at their big-ends. The pistons are attached to the connecting rods by gudgeon pins which are an interference fit in the connecting rod small-end eyes. The aluminium alloy pistons are fitted with three piston rings, comprising two compression rings and an oil control ring.

The cylinder bores are formed by replaceable wet liners which are located from their top ends. Two sealing rings are fitted at the base of each liner to prevent the escape of coolant into the sump.

The inlet and exhaust valves are each closed by coil springs and operate in guides pressed into the cylinder head. The valve seat inserts are pressed into the cylinder head and can be renewed separately if worn.

On the K8 engine, the camshaft is driven by a toothed timing belt and operates the eight valves via self-adjusting hydraulic tappets, thus eliminating the need for routine checking and adjustment of the valve clearances. The camshaft rotates in six bearings that are line-bored direct in the cylinder head and the (bolted-on) bearing caps. This means that the bearing caps are not available separately from the cylinder head and must not be interchanged with others from another engine. The distributor is driven from the left-hand end of the camshaft and the mechanical fuel pump is operated by an eccentric on the camshaft.

Apart from the fact that it has two camshafts, one inlet and one exhaust, each controlling eight valves and both retained by a single camshaft carrier, the same applies to the K16 engine. On the K16 engine, the distributor is driven from the left-hand end of the inlet camshaft. The fuel pump is electrically-operated.

On both engine types, the coolant pump is driven by the timing belt.

Lubrication is by means of an eccentric-rotor trochoidal pump mounted on the crankshaft right-hand end. It draws oil through a strainer located in the sump and then forces it through an externally-mounted full-flow cartridge-type filter into galleries in the oil rail and cylinder block/crankcase, from where it is distributed to the crankshaft (main bearings) and camshaft(s). The big-end bearings are supplied with oil via internal drillings in the crankshaft, while the camshaft bearings and the hydraulic tappets receive a pressurised supply. The camshaft lobes and valves are lubricated by splash, as are all other engine components.

Repair operations possible with the engine in the car

The following work can be carried out with the engine in the vehicle:
a) *Compression pressure - testing.*

b) *Cylinder head cover - removal and refitting.*
c) *Crankshaft pulley - removal and refitting.*
d) *Timing belt covers - removal and refitting.*
e) *Timing belt - removal, refitting and adjustment.*
f) *Timing belt tensioner and sprockets - removal and refitting.*
g) *Camshaft oil seal(s) - renewal.*
h) *Camshaft(s) and hydraulic tappets - removal, inspection and refitting.*
i) *Cylinder head - removal and refitting.*
j) *Cylinder head and pistons - decarbonising.*
k) *Sump - removal and refitting.*
l) *Oil pump - removal, overhaul and refitting.*
m) *Crankshaft oil seals - renewal.*
n) *Engine/transmission mountings - inspection and renewal.*
o) *Flywheel - removal, inspection and refitting.*

Precautions

Note that a side-effect of the above described engine design is that the crankshaft cannot be rotated once the cylinder head and block through-bolts have been slackened. During any servicing or overhaul work the crankshaft always must be rotated to the desired position before the bolts are disturbed.

2 Engine oil and filter - renewal

1 Details of checking the engine oil levels and renewing both the oil and filter are contained in *"Weekly Checks"* and Chapter 1.

3 Compression test - description and interpretation

1 When engine performance is down, or if misfiring occurs which cannot be attributed to the ignition or fuel systems, a compression test can provide diagnostic clues as to the engine's condition. If the test is performed regularly it can give warning of trouble before any other symptoms become apparent.
2 The engine must be fully warmed up to normal operating temperature, the battery must be fully charged and the spark plugs must be removed. The aid of an assistant will be required.
3 Disable the ignition system by disconnecting the ignition HT coil lead from the distributor cap and earthing it on the cylinder block. Use a jumper lead or similar wire to make a good connection.
4 Fit a compression tester to the No 1 cylinder spark plug hole. The type of tester which screws into the plug thread is preferred (see illustration).

5 Have the assistant hold the throttle wide open and crank the engine on the starter motor. After one or two revolutions, the compression pressure should build up to a maximum figure and then stabilise. Record the highest reading obtained.
6 Repeat the test on the remaining cylinders, recording the pressure in each.
7 All cylinders should produce very similar pressures. Any difference greater than that specified indicates the existence of a fault. Note that the compression should build up quickly in a healthy engine. Low compression on the first stroke, followed by gradually increasing pressure on successive strokes, indicates worn piston rings. A low compression reading on the first stroke, which does not build up during successive strokes, indicates leaking valves or a blown head gasket (a cracked head could also be the cause). Deposits on the undersides of the valve heads can also cause low compression.
8 If the pressure in any cylinder is reduced to the specified minimum or less, carry out the following test to isolate the cause. Introduce a teaspoonful of clean oil into that cylinder through its spark plug hole and repeat the test.
9 If the addition of oil temporarily improves the compression pressure, this indicates that bore or piston wear is responsible for the pressure loss. No improvement suggests that leaking or burnt valves, or a blown head gasket, may be to blame.
10 A low reading from two adjacent cylinders is almost certainly due to the head gasket having blown between them and the presence of coolant in the engine oil will confirm this.
11 If one cylinder is about 20 percent lower than the others and the engine has a slightly rough idle, a worn camshaft lobe could be the cause.
12 If the compression reading is unusually high, the combustion chambers are probably coated with carbon deposits. If this is the case, the cylinder head should be removed and decarbonised.
13 On completion of the test, refit the spark plugs and reconnect the ignition system.

3.4 Measuring compression pressure

2A

4 Top Dead Centre (TDC) for number one piston - locating

General

1 The crankshaft pulley, crankshaft and camshaft sprockets are provided by the factory with clear marks which align only at 90° BTDC. This positions the pistons half-way up the bores so that there is no risk of damage as the engine is reassembled. These marks do not indicate TDC. Use only the ignition timing marks, as described in this Section, to find TDC.

2 Top dead centre (TDC) is the highest point in its travel up-and-down the cylinder bore that each piston reaches as the crankshaft rotates. While each piston reaches TDC both at the top of the compression stroke and again at the top of the exhaust stroke, for the purpose of timing the engine, TDC refers to the piston position (usually No 1) at the top of its compression stroke.

3 While all engine reassembly procedures use the factory timing marks (90° BTDC), it is useful for several other servicing procedures to be able to position the engine at TDC.

4 No 1 piston and cylinder is at the right-hand (timing belt) end of the engine. Note that the crankshaft rotates clockwise when viewed from the right-hand side of the vehicle.

Locating TDC

5 Disconnect the battery negative lead and remove all the spark plugs.

6 Trace No 1 spark plug (HT) lead from the plug back to the distributor cap and use chalk or similar to mark the distributor body or engine casting nearest to the cap's No 1 terminal. Undo the distributor cap retaining screws and remove the cap.

7 Apply the handbrake and ensure that the transmission is in neutral, then jack up the front of the vehicle and support it on axle stands. Remove the right-hand roadwheel.

8 From underneath the front of the vehicle, slacken and remove the three bolts securing the bumper flange to the body. Remove the seven bolts securing the front undercover panel to the body and remove the panel to gain access to the crankshaft pulley and ignition timing marks.

9 Using a spanner, or socket and extension bar, applied to the crankshaft pulley bolt, rotate the crankshaft clockwise until the notch on the crankshaft pulley's inboard (left-hand) rim is aligned with the TDC mark on the timing belt lower cover (see Chapter 1 for details of ignition timing marks).

10 With the crankshaft in this position, Nos 1 and 4 cylinders are now at TDC, one of them on the compression stroke. If the distributor rotor arm is pointing at (the previously-marked) No 1 terminal, then No 1 cylinder is correctly positioned. If the rotor arm is pointing at No 4 terminal, rotate the crankshaft one full turn (360°) clockwise until the arm points at the

5.3a Disconnecting breather hose from cylinder head cover - K8 engine

marked terminal. No 1 cylinder will then be at TDC on the compression stroke.

11 Once No 1 cylinder has been positioned at TDC on the compression stroke, TDC for any of the other cylinders can then be located by rotating the crankshaft clockwise 180° at a time and following the firing order.

5 Cylinder head cover - removal and refitting

Removal

1 Disconnect the battery negative lead.

2 Remove the air cleaner assembly and metal intake duct.

3 Using a suitable pair of pliers, release the retaining clip(s) and disconnect the breather hose(s) from the cylinder head cover **(see illustrations)**.

K8 engines

4 Undo the bolts securing the HT lead mounting and air intake support brackets to the cylinder head cover, then remove the brackets and position the HT leads clear of the cover.

5 Remove the two uppermost retaining screws securing the timing belt upper right-hand/outer cover to the cylinder head cover, then slacken the remaining screws and bolts, as necessary, until the timing belt cover can be prised clear of the cylinder head cover without damaging it.

6 Working progressively and in the **reverse** of the tightening sequence **(see illustration 5.14),**

5.12a Ensure seal is correctly seated in cylinder head cover groove . . .

5.3b Disconnecting breather hoses from cylinder head cover - K16 engine

slacken and remove the cylinder head cover retaining bolts.

7 Remove the cover, peel off the rubber seal and check it for cuts, other damage or distortion. Renew the seal if necessary.

K16 engines

8 Undo the two spark plug cover retaining screws and lift off the cover. Disconnect the HT leads from the plugs and withdraw them from the cylinder head, along with the clip plate and the grommet which is fitted to the left-hand end of the cylinder head cover.

9 Working progressively and in the **reverse** of the tightening sequence **(see illustration 5.22),** slacken and remove the cylinder head cover retaining bolts, noting the correct fitted position of the air intake duct support bracket.

10 Carefully lift off the cylinder head cover, taking care not to damage the gasket. Check that the gasket sealing path is undamaged and is attached to the gasket all around its periphery. If the sealing path is undamaged, then the gasket is re-usable and should remain in place on the cover until reassembly, unless its removal is necessary for other servicing work.

Refitting

K8 engines

11 On reassembly, carefully clean the cylinder head mating surfaces and the cover seal's groove and remove all traces of oil.

12 Seat the seal in its groove in the cover and refit the bolts, pushing each through the seal, then apply a smear of silicone-RTV sealant to each corner of the seal **(see illustrations)**.

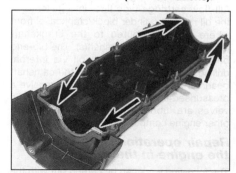

5.12b . . . then refit bolts and apply sealant at locations arrowed - K8 engine

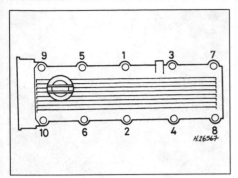

5.14 Cylinder head cover bolt tightening sequence - K8 engine

5.20a Fit gasket to cylinder head cover dowels (arrowed) so that . . .

5.20b . . . stamped markings would appear as shown if gasket were placed on camshaft carrier

13 Refit the cover to the cylinder head, ensuring that the seal remains seated in its groove. Fit all bolts, finger-tight.

14 Tighten the cylinder head cover bolts in the sequence shown to the specified torque wrench setting **(see illustration)**.

15 Refit the timing belt upper right-hand/outer cover to the cylinder head cover and tighten all the disturbed screws and bolts to the specified torque setting.

16 Refit the HT lead mounting clips and air cleaner intake support brackets to the cylinder head, then tighten the retaining bolts to the specified torque. Ensure the HT leads are correctly routed.

17 Connect the breather hose to the cylinder head cover and secure it in position with the retaining clip.

18 Refit the air cleaner housing and reconnect the battery negative lead.

K16 engines

19 On reassembly, carefully clean the mating surfaces, removing all traces of oil. If the gasket has been removed, the oil separator elements can be cleaned by removing them from the cover and washing them in solvent. Use compressed air to blow dry the elements before refitting them to the cover.

20 If a new gasket is to be fitted, press it onto the cover locating dowels so that if it were laid on the camshaft carrier its stamped markings would be legible. The TOP mark should be nearest the inlet manifold and the EXH MAN SIDE mark should have its arrows pointing to the exhaust manifold **(see illustrations)**.

21 Lower the cover onto the cylinder head, ensuring that the gasket is not damaged or displaced. Install the cover retaining bolts, not forgetting to refit the air intake duct support bracket to its original position, and tighten them finger-tight.

22 Working in the sequence shown, tighten the cylinder head cover retaining bolts to the specified torque setting **(see illustration)**.

23 Reconnect the HT leads to the spark plugs, then locate the clip plate and grommet in the left-hand end of the cylinder head cover. Ensure the HT leads are correctly routed then refit the spark plug cover and tighten its retaining screws to the specified

torque. Tighten the air intake support bracket screws.

24 Connect both the breather hoses to the cylinder head cover and secure them in position with the retaining clips.

25 Refit the air cleaner housing and reconnect the battery negative lead.

---

6 Crankshaft pulley - removal and refitting

Removal

1 Apply the handbrake then jack up the front of the vehicle and support it on axle stands. Remove the right-hand roadwheel.

2 From underneath the front of the vehicle, slacken and remove the three bolts securing the bumper flange to the body. Remove the seven bolts securing the front undercover panel to the body and remove the panel.

3 If necessary, rotate the crankshaft until the relevant timing marks align.

4 Remove the power steering pump and/or alternator drivebelt(s) (as applicable).

5 To prevent crankshaft rotation while the pulley bolt is unscrewed, select top gear and have an assistant apply the brakes firmly. If the engine has been removed from the

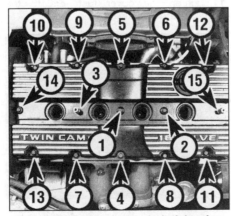

5.22 Cylinder head cover bolt tightening sequence - K16 engine

vehicle, lock the flywheel using the arrangement shown **(see illustration 18.2)**.

6 Unscrew the pulley bolt, noting the special washer behind it, then remove the pulley from the crankshaft.

Refitting

7 Align the crankshaft pulley centre notch with the locating lug on the crankshaft timing belt sprocket then refit the washer, ensuring that its flat surface is facing the pulley. Fit the retaining bolt **(see illustration)**.

8 Lock the crankshaft by the method used on removal and tighten the pulley retaining bolt to the specified torque setting.

9 Refit the power steering pump and/or alternator drivebelt(s) (as applicable) and adjust them as described in Chapter 1.

10 Refit the undercover panel and roadwheel then lower the vehicle to the ground.

2A

---

7 Timing belt covers - removal and refitting

Removal

Upper right-hand (outer) cover

1 Slacken the bolt situated at the cover's bottom corner, immediately behind the engine/gearbox unit right-hand mounting bracket.

6.7 Ensure notch in crankshaft pulley centre fits over crankshaft timing belt sprocket locating lug (arrowed)

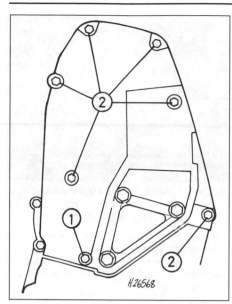

7.2a Timing belt upper right-hand (outer) cover fasteners - K8 engine

1 Slacken screw - cover should be slotted
2 Remove fasteners

2 Unscrew the remaining cover retaining bolts and withdraw the cover, noting the rubber seal fitted to the mounting bracket edge. Note that if the cover is not slotted at the bottom corner screw's location, the screw

7.9a Timing belt upper left-hand (inner) cover fasteners (arrowed) - K8 engine

7.9b Timing belt upper left-hand (inner) cover fasteners (arrowed) - K16 engine

7.2b Timing belt upper right-hand (outer) cover fasteners (arrowed) - K16 engine, raised for clarity

will have to be removed fully. If this is the case, the cover can be slotted to ease future removal and refitting **(see illustrations)**.

Lower cover

3 Remove the crankshaft pulley.
4 Remove the cover retaining screws, including the one which also secures the upper cover's bottom front corner. Remove the cover whilst noting the rubber seal fitted to its mounting bracket edge **(see illustration)**.

Upper left-hand (inner) cover

5 Remove the timing belt.
6 Remove the camshaft sprocket(s) and the timing belt tensioner.
7 Unscrew the bolt securing the cover to the coolant pump.
8 On K16 engines, unbolt the engine/gearbox unit right-hand mounting bracket from the cylinder block/crankcase.
9 Remove the remaining cover retaining bolts and withdraw the cover **(see illustrations)**.

Refitting

Upper right-hand (outer) cover

10 Refitting is the reverse of the removal procedure. Ensure that the seal fits correctly between the cover and the mounting bracket and that the cover edges mate correctly with those of the inner cover and (K8 engines only) cylinder head cover **(see illustration)**.
11 Tighten the cover fasteners to the specified torque setting.

7.9c Removing timing belt upper left-hand (inner) cover - K16 engine

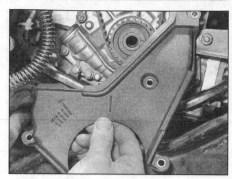

7.4 Removing timing belt lower cover

Lower cover

12 Refitting is the reverse of the removal procedure. Ensure that the seal fits correctly between the cover and the mounting bracket and tighten the cover fasteners to the specified torque setting.

Upper left-hand (inner) cover

13 Refitting is the reverse of the removal procedure. Tighten all disturbed fasteners to their specified torque wrench settings.

8 Timing belt - removal, inspection, refitting and adjustment

HAYNES HINT *If the timing belt is to be re-used, use white paint or similar to mark the direction of rotation on the belt.*

Removal

1 Disconnect the battery negative lead.
2 To improve access to the timing belt, remove the expansion tank mounting bolts then free the coolant hose from any relevant retaining clips and position the tank clear of the engine. On models equipped with power-assisted steering, undo all the power steering hose retaining clip bolts then slide the fluid reservoir out of its retaining clip and position it

7.10 Ensure timing belt upper right-hand (outer) cover engages correctly with cylinder head cover - K8 engine

8.6 Crankshaft pulley mark aligned with timing belt lower cover mark at 90° BTDC

8.7 Camshaft sprocket marks (A) aligned with timing belt upper left-hand (inner) cover mark (B) - K16 engine

8.11 Removing engine/gearbox unit right-hand mounting bracket - K8 engine

clear of the timing belt covers. Take great care not to place any undue strain on hoses and mop up any spilt fluid immediately.

3 Remove the timing belt upper right-hand (outer) cover.

4 Firmly apply the handbrake then jack up the front of the vehicle and support it on axle stands. Remove the right-hand roadwheel

5 From underneath the front of the vehicle, slacken and remove the three bolts securing the bumper flange to the body. Remove the seven bolts securing the front undercover panel to the body and remove the panel to gain access to the crankshaft pulley bolt.

6 Using a suitable spanner or socket on the crankshaft pulley bolt, rotate the crankshaft in a clockwise direction until the long white-painted mark on the crankshaft pulley's outboard (right-hand) face is aligned with the single, separate mark on the timing belt lower cover so that the crankshaft is in the 90° BTDC position (see Chapter 1 for details of the pulley/cover marks) **(see illustration)**.

7 Check that the camshaft sprocket mark(s) align as described in paragraph 15, showing that Nos 1 and 4 cylinders are at 90° BTDC so that there is no risk of the valves contacting the pistons during dismantling and reassembly. If the camshaft sprocket mark(s) are 180° out, rotate the crankshaft through one complete turn (360°) to align the marks as described **(see illustration)**.

8 On K16 engines, use the tool described in Section 9 to lock up the camshaft sprockets

so that they cannot move under valve spring pressure when the timing belt is removed.

9 Remove the crankshaft sprocket and timing belt lower cover.

10 Position a trolley jack with a wooden spacer beneath the sump then gently jack it up to take the weight of the engine.

11 Slacken and remove the engine/gearbox unit right-hand mounting through-bolt and nut and the mounting-to-bracket nuts. Remove the mounting, along with the two rubber washers which are fitted on each side of the mounting. On K8 engines only, unscrew the retaining bolts securing the bracket to cylinder block/crankcase and remove it from the engine unit **(see illustration)**.

12 Slacken both the timing belt tensioner pulley Allen screw and the tensioner backplate clamp bolt through half a turn each, then push the pulley assembly downwards to remove all the tension from the timing belt. Hold the tensioner pulley in this position and re-tighten the backplate clamp bolt securely **(see illustration)**.

13 Slip the belt off the sprockets **(see illustration)**. Do not rotate the crankshaft until the timing belt has been refitted.

Inspection

14 Check the timing belt carefully for any signs of uneven wear, splitting or oil contamination and renew it if there is the slightest doubt about its condition. If the engine is undergoing an overhaul and has

covered more than 48 000 miles (80 000 km) since the original belt was fitted, renew the belt as a matter of course, regardless of its apparent condition. If signs of oil contamination are found, trace the source of the oil leak and rectify it, then wash down the engine timing belt area and all related components to remove all traces of oil.

Refitting

15 On reassembly, thoroughly clean the timing belt sprockets and check that they are aligned as follows. It is most important that these marks are aligned exactly as this sets valve timing. Note that in this position, Nos 1 and 4 cylinders are at 90° BTDC so that there is no risk of the valves contacting the pistons during dismantling and reassembly.

a) *Camshaft sprocket on K8 engine - The EX line and the mark stamped on the sprocket rim must be at the front (looking at the sprocket from the right-hand side of the vehicle) and aligned exactly with the cylinder head top surface* **(see illustration)**.

b) *Camshaft sprockets on K16 engine - Both EXHAUST arrow marks must point to the rear (looking at the sprockets from the right-hand side of the vehicle) with the IN lines and the sprocket rim marks aligned exactly with the line on the timing belt upper left-hand/inner cover (representing the cylinder head top surface).* **See illustration 8.7.**

2A

8.12 Timing belt tensioner pulley bolt (A) and tensioner backplate clamp bolt (B)

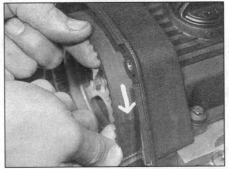

8.13 Mark direction of rotation of timing belt before removal

8.15a Camshaft sprocket marks (A) aligned with cylinder head top surface (B) - K8 engine

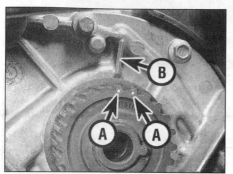

8.15b Crankshaft sprocket dots (A) aligned on each side of oil pump raised rib (B)

8.16 Refitting timing belt - K16 engine

c) *Crankshaft sprocket - The two dots must be positioned on each side of the raised rib on the oil pump body* (see illustration).

16 If a used belt is being refitted, ensure that the arrow mark made on removal points in the normal direction of rotation. Fit the timing belt over the crankshaft and camshaft sprockets, ensuring that the belt front run (and, on K16 engines, the top run) is taut, ie: all slack is on the tensioner pulley side of the belt, then fit the belt over the coolant pump sprocket and tensioner pulley. Do not twist the belt sharply during refitting and ensure that the belt teeth are correctly seated centrally in the sprockets and that the timing marks remain in alignment (see illustration)..

17 Slacken the tensioner backplate clamp bolt and check that the tensioner pulley moves to tension the belt. If the tensioner assembly is not free to move under spring tension, rectify the fault or the timing belt will not be correctly tensioned.

18 On K16 engines, remove the camshaft sprocket locking tool.

19 On K8 engines, refit the engine/gearbox unit right-hand mounting bracket, tightening its bolts to the specified torque wrench setting.

20 On all engines, refit the timing belt lower cover and the crankshaft pulley.

21 Using a suitable spanner or socket, rotate the crankshaft two full turns clockwise to settle and tension the belt. Realign the crankshaft pulley (90° BTDC) mark and check that the sprocket timing mark(s) are still correctly aligned.

22 If all is well, first tighten the tensioner pulley backplate clamp bolt to the specified torque, then tighten the tensioner pulley Allen screw to the specified torque.

23 Reassemble the engine/gearbox unit right-hand mounting, ensuring that the rubber washers are correctly located, then tighten the mounting nuts and bolts to their specified torque settings. Remove the jack from underneath the engine unit.

24 Refit the front undercover panel and roadwheel, then lower the vehicle to the ground.

25 Refit the timing belt upper right-hand (outer) cover.

26 Where necessary, refit the power steering fluid reservoir to the mounting bracket and secure the hydraulic hose clamps in position with the retaining bolts.

27 Refit the coolant expansion tank and tighten the mounting bolts securely. Secure the coolant hose in position with any necessary retaining clips and reconnect the battery negative lead.

Adjustment

28 As the timing belt is a 'fit-and-forget' type, the manufacturer states that tensioning need only be carried out when a belt is (re)fitted. No re-tensioning is recommended once a belt has been fitted and therefore this operation is not included in the manufacturer's maintenance schedule.

29 If the timing belt is thought to be incorrectly tensioned, then adjust the tension as described in paragraphs 1 to 7, 17, 21, 22 and 24 to 27 above.

30 If the timing belt has been disturbed, adjust its tension following the same procedure, omitting as appropriate the irrelevant preliminary dismantling/reassembly steps.

9 Timing belt tensioner and sprockets - removal, inspection and refitting

HAYNES HINT *If both camshaft sprockets on K16 engines are to be removed, it is good practice to mark them (inlet or exhaust) so that they can be returned to their original locations on reassembly.*

Note: *This Section describes as individual operations the removal and refitting of the components concerned. If more than one*

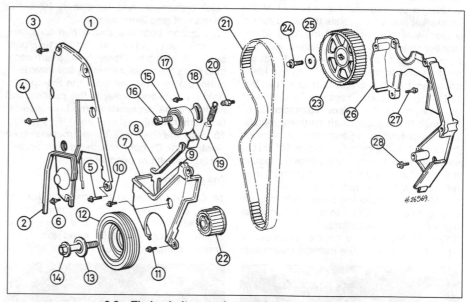

9.2a Timing belt, sprockets and covers - K8 engine

1 Timing belt upper right-hand (outer) cover
2 Seal
3 Bolt
4 Bolt
5 Bolt
6 Shouldered bolt
7 Timing belt lower cover
8 Seal
9 Seal
10 Bolt
11 Bolt
12 Crankshaft pulley
13 Washer
14 Crankshaft pulley bolt
15 Timing belt tensioner pulley assembly
16 Tensioner pulley Allen screw
17 Tensioner backplate clamp bolt
18 Tensioner pulley spring
19 Sleeve
20 Pillar bolt
21 Timing belt
22 Crankshaft sprocket
23 Camshaft sprocket
24 Camshaft sprocket bolt
25 Washer
26 Timing belt upper left-hand (inner) cover
27 Bolt - cover to water pump
28 Bolt

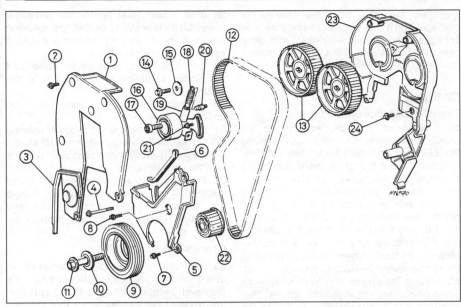

9.2b Timing belt, sprockets and covers - K16 engine

1 Timing belt upper right- hand (outer) cover	10 Washer	18 Tensioner pulley spring
2 Bolt	11 Crankshaft pulley bolt	19 Sleeve
3 Seal	12 Timing belt	20 Pillar bolt
4 Bolt	13 Camshaft sprockets	21 Tensioner backplate
5 Timing belt lower cover	14 Bolt	clamp bolt
6 Seal	15 Washer	22 Crankshaft sprocket
7 Bolt	16 Timing belt tensioner	23 Timing belt upper left-
8 Bolt	pulley assembly	hand (inner) cover
9 Crankshaft pulley	17 Tensioner pulley Allen	24 Bolt
	screw	

component needs to be removed at the same time, start by removing the timing belt, then remove each component as described below whilst ignoring the preliminary dismantling steps.

Removal

1 Disconnect the battery negative lead.

2 To improve access to the timing belt components **(see illustrations)**, remove the expansion tank mounting bolts then free the coolant hose from any relevant retaining clips and position the tank clear of the engine. On models equipped with power-assisted steering, undo all the power steering hose retaining clip bolts then slide the fluid

reservoir out of its retaining clip and position it clear of the timing belt covers. Take great care not to place any undue strain on hoses and mop up any spilt fluid immediately.

3 Remove the timing belt upper right-hand (outer) cover.

4 Apply the handbrake then jack up the front of the vehicle and support it on axle stands. Remove the right-hand roadwheel.

5 From underneath the front of the vehicle, slacken and remove the three bolts securing the bumper flange to the body. Remove the seven bolts securing the front undercover panel to the body and remove the panel.

6 Using a suitable spanner or socket on the crankshaft pulley bolt, rotate the crankshaft in

a clockwise direction until the long white-painted mark on the crankshaft pulley's outboard (right-hand) face is aligned with the single, separate mark on the timing belt lower cover so that the crankshaft is in the 90° BTDC position (see Chapter 1 for details of the pulley/cover marks).

7 Check that the camshaft sprocket mark(s) align as described in Section 8, paragraph 15 then proceed as described under the relevant sub-heading.

Camshaft sprocket(s)

8 Slacken through half a turn each, the timing belt tensioner pulley Allen screw and the tensioner backplate clamp bolt. Push the pulley assembly down to release all tension from the timing belt, then re-tighten the backplate clamp bolt securely.

9 Remove the belt from the camshaft sprocket(s), taking care not to twist it too sharply. Use fingers only to handle the belt. Do not rotate the crankshaft until the timing belt is refitted.

10 On K8 engines, slacken the camshaft sprocket retaining bolt and remove it, along with its washer. To prevent the camshaft from rotating, use Rover service tool 18G 1521 to retain the sprocket. If the tool is not available, then an acceptable substitute can be fabricated from two lengths of steel strip (one long, the other short) and three nuts and bolts. One nut and bolt should form the pivot of a forked tool with the remaining two nuts and bolts at the tips of the forks to engage with the sprocket spokes, as shown in illustration 9.23a.

11 On K16 engines, unscrew the appropriate camshaft sprocket retaining bolt and remove it, along with its washer. To prevent a camshaft from rotating, lock together both sprockets using Rover service tool 18G 1570. This tool is a metal sprag shaped on both sides to fit the sprocket teeth and is inserted between the sprockets. If the tool is not available, then an acceptable substitute can be cut from a length of square-section steel tube or similar to fit as closely as possible around the sprocket spokes **(see illustrations)**.

12 On all engines, remove the sprocket(s) from the camshaft end(s), noting the locating roll pin(s) **(see illustration)**. If a roll pin is a

2A

9.11a Camshaft locking tool cut from steel section . . .

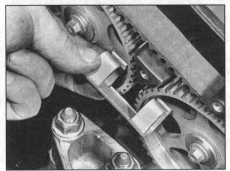

9.11b . . . to fit sprocket spokes as closely as possible - K16 engine

9.12 Removing camshaft sprocket (roll pin arrowed) - K8 engine

loose fit in the camshaft end, remove it and store it with the sprocket for safe-keeping.

Crankshaft sprocket

13 On K16 engines, use the tool described in paragraph 11 to lock together the camshaft sprockets so that they cannot move under valve spring pressure when the timing belt is removed.

14 Remove the crankshaft pulley and timing belt lower cover.

15 Slacken through half a turn each the timing belt tensioner pulley Allen screw and the tensioner backplate clamp bolt, push the pulley assembly down to release all the tension from the timing belt, then re-tighten the backplate clamp bolt securely.

16 Work the belt clear of the crankshaft sprocket, taking care not to twist it too sharply. Use fingers only to handle the belt. Do not rotate the crankshaft until the timing belt is refitted.

17 Remove the sprocket from the crankshaft.

Tensioner assembly

18 On K16 engines, use the tool described in paragraph 11 to lock together the camshaft sprockets so that they cannot move under valve spring pressure when the timing belt is removed.

19 Using a suitable pair of pliers, unhook the tensioner spring from the pillar bolt. Unscrew the tensioner pulley Allen screw and the tensioner backplate clamp bolt then withdraw the tensioner assembly from the engine unit. Do not rotate the crankshaft until the timing belt is re-tensioned.

Inspection

20 Clean thoroughly the camshaft/crankshaft sprockets and renew any that show signs of wear, damage or cracks.

21 Clean the tensioner assembly but do not use any strong solvent which may enter the pulley bearing. Check that the pulley rotates freely on the backplate, with no sign of stiffness or of free play. Renew the assembly if there is any doubt about its condition or if

there are any obvious signs of wear or damage. The same applies to the tensioner spring, which should be checked with great care as its condition is critical for the correct tensioning of the timing belt.

Refitting

Camshaft sprocket(s)

22 If removed, refit the roll pin to the camshaft end, ensuring that its split is facing the centre of the camshaft, then refit the sprocket so that the timing marks are facing outwards (to the right). On K16 engines, ensure that the appropriate sprocket keyway engages with the camshaft locating pin (ie: if refitting the inlet camshaft sprocket, engage its IN keyway with the roll pin and so on) then refit the sprocket retaining bolt and washer **(see illustration)**. Where necessary, repeat the procedure for the second sprocket.

23 Prevent the sprocket(s) from rotating by using the method employed on removal, then tighten the sprocket retaining bolt(s) to the specified torque setting. Check that the sprocket timing marks align as described in Section 8, paragraph 15 **(see illustrations)**.

24 Fit the timing belt over the camshaft sprockets, ensuring that the belt front run (and, on K16 engines, the top run) is taut, that is, all slack is on the tensioner pulley side of the belt. Do not twist the belt sharply while refitting it and ensure that the belt teeth are correctly seated centrally in the sprockets and that the timing marks remain in alignment.

25 Slacken the tensioner backplate clamp bolt and check that the tensioner pulley moves to tension the belt. If the tensioner assembly is not free to move under spring tension, rectify the fault or the timing belt will not be correctly tensioned.

26 On K16 engines, remove the camshaft sprocket locking tool.

27 Using a suitable spanner or socket, rotate the crankshaft two full turns clockwise to settle and tension the belt. Realign the crankshaft pulley (90° BTDC) mark and check that the sprocket timing mark(s) are still correctly aligned.

28 If all is well, first tighten the tensioner pulley backplate clamp bolt to the specified torque, then tighten the tensioner pulley Allen screw to the specified torque.

29 Refit the front undercover panel and roadwheel, then lower the vehicle to the ground.

30 Refit the timing belt upper right-hand (outer) cover.

31 Where necessary, refit the power steering fluid reservoir to the mounting bracket and secure the hydraulic hose clamps in position with the retaining bolts.

32 Refit the coolant expansion tank and tighten the mounting bolts securely. Secure the coolant hose in position with any necessary retaining clips and reconnect the battery negative lead.

Crankshaft sprocket

33 Refit the sprocket to the crankshaft so that it locates correctly on the crankshaft's flattened section, noting that the sprocket flange must be innermost so that the two timing marks are on the outside (right-hand side) of the sprocket. Check that the sprocket timing marks align as described in Section 8, paragraph 15.

34 Fit the timing belt over the crankshaft sprocket, ensuring that the belt front run (and, on K16 engines, the top run) is taut, that is, all slack is on the tensioner pulley side of the belt. Do not twist the belt sharply while refitting it and ensure that the belt teeth are correctly seated centrally in the sprockets and that the timing marks remain in alignment.

35 Slacken the tensioner backplate clamp bolt and check that the tensioner pulley moves to tension the belt. If the tensioner assembly is not free to move under spring tension, rectify the fault or the timing belt will not be correctly tensioned.

36 On K16 engines, remove the camshaft sprocket locking tool.

37 Refit the lower timing belt cover and the crankshaft pulley.

38 Carry out the operations described in paragraphs 27 to 32.

9.22 Camshaft sprockets have two keyways. Engage EX keyway with exhaust camshaft roll pin and IN keyway with inlet camshaft roll pin - K16 engine

9.23a Using fabricated tool to hold camshaft pulley in position - K8 engine

9.23b Locking camshafts in position with fabricated tool - K16 engine

9.39 Ensure timing belt tensioner spring is correctly hooked onto pillar bolt

10.4 Fitting a new camshaft right-hand oil seal - K16 engine

10.8 Remove air intake duct support bracket to reach exhaust camshaft left-hand oil seal - K16 engine

Tensioner pulley

39 Refit the tensioner pulley assembly and tighten the pulley Allen screw and the backplate clamp bolt lightly. Hook the tensioner spring over the pillar bolt and check that the tensioner is free to move under spring tension and that the pulley bears correctly against the timing belt **(see illustration)**.
40 On K16 engines, remove the camshaft sprocket locking tool.
41 Carry out the operations described above in paragraphs 27 to 32.

10 Camshaft oil seals - renewal

Note: If a right-hand oil seal is to be renewed with the timing belt still in place, then check that the belt is free from oil contamination. Renew the belt if signs of oil contamination are found. Cover the belt to protect it from contamination while work is in progress and ensure that all traces of oil are removed from the area before the belt is refitted.

Right-hand seal(s)

1 Remove the camshaft sprocket(s).
2 Punch or drill two small holes opposite each other in the oil seal. Screw a self-tapping screw into each and pull on the screws with pliers to extract the seal.
3 Clean the seal housing and polish off any burrs or raised edges which may have caused the seal to fail in the first place.
4 Lubricate the lips of the new seal with clean engine oil and drive it into position until it seats on its locating shoulder. Use a suitable tubular drift, such as a socket, which bears only on the hard outer edge of the seal **(see illustration)**. Take care not to damage the seal lips during fitting and note that the seal lips should face inwards.
5 Refit the camshaft sprocket(s).

Left-hand seals - K16 engines

6 Disconnect the battery negative lead.
7 To reach the inlet camshaft seal, remove the distributor.
8 To reach the exhaust camshaft seal,

unfasten the rubber strap securing the air intake duct to its support bracket, disconnect the vacuum pipe from the air temperature control valve and unclip the pipe from the support bracket. Undo the bracket's retaining bolts and remove the bracket from the cylinder head **(see illustration)**.
9 Remove the old seal and install the new one as described above in paragraphs 2 to 4.
10 On the inlet camshaft, refit the distributor.
11 On the exhaust camshaft, refit the air intake duct support bracket, tightening its screws to the specified torque wrench setting. Reconnect and secure the air temperature control valve vacuum pipe and refit the rubber strap to secure the air intake duct.
12 Connect the battery negative lead.

11 Camshafts and hydraulic tappets - removal, inspection and refitting

> **HAYNES HINT** *If faulty tappets are diagnosed and the engine's service history is unknown, it is always worth trying the effect of renewing the engine oil and filter (using only good quality engine oil of the recommended viscosity and specification) before going to the expense of renewing any of the tappets.*

Note: Prior to removing the camshaft(s), obtain Rover sealant kit LVV 10002 which also contains a plastic scraper. Read the instructions supplied with the kit and take care not to allow the sealant to contact the fingers, as it will bond the skin. If difficulty is experienced with the removal of hardened sealant from mating surfaces, it will be necessary to use a foam action gasket remover.

Removal

K8 engines

1 Remove the cylinder head cover **(see illustration 11.0a overleaf)**.
2 Remove the distributor.
3 Remove the camshaft sprocket.

4 Carefully prise the oil feed tube away from the camshaft bearing caps and remove it from the head assembly. Remove the O-rings from the oil rail and discard them. The O-rings must be renewed whenever they are disturbed.
5 The camshaft right and left-hand end bearing caps are noticeably different and cannot be confused. The intermediate bearing caps (which are all similar) are marked by the manufacturer with a number (1, 2, 3, or 4) stamped in the boss next to the oil feed hole. Before unbolting any of the caps, make written notes to ensure that each can be easily identified and refitted in its original location.
6 Working in the **reverse** of the tightening sequence **(see illustration 11.29)**, slacken the camshaft bearing cap bolts progressively, by one turn at a time. Work only as described to release the pressure of the valve springs on the bearing caps gradually and evenly.
7 Withdraw the bearing caps, noting the presence of the locating dowels on the end caps, then remove the camshaft and withdraw the oil seal.
8 Obtain eight small, clean plastic containers, number them 1 to 8, and then fill them with clean engine oil. Using a rubber sucker, withdraw each hydraulic tappet in turn **(see illustration)**, and place it in its respective container, to prevent oil loss. Do not interchange the hydraulic tappets or the rate of wear will be much increased and do not allow them to lose oil or they will take a long

11.8 Use a valve-grinding sucker to extract hydraulic tappets

2A

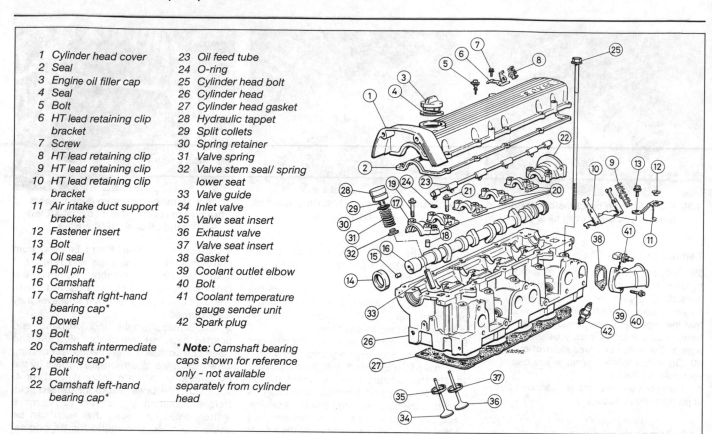

1 Cylinder head cover
2 Seal
3 Engine oil filler cap
4 Seal
5 Bolt
6 HT lead retaining clip bracket
7 Screw
8 HT lead retaining clip
9 HT lead retaining clip
10 HT lead retaining clip bracket
11 Air intake duct support bracket
12 Fastener insert
13 Bolt
14 Oil seal
15 Roll pin
16 Camshaft
17 Camshaft right-hand bearing cap*
18 Dowel
19 Bolt
20 Camshaft intermediate bearing cap*
21 Bolt
22 Camshaft left-hand bearing cap*

23 Oil feed tube
24 O-ring
25 Cylinder head bolt
26 Cylinder head
27 Cylinder head gasket
28 Hydraulic tappet
29 Split collets
30 Spring retainer
31 Valve spring
32 Valve stem seal/ spring lower seat
33 Valve guide
34 Inlet valve
35 Valve seat insert
36 Exhaust valve
37 Valve seat insert
38 Gasket
39 Coolant outlet elbow
40 Bolt
41 Coolant temperature gauge sender unit
42 Spark plug

* **Note:** Camshaft bearing caps shown for reference only - not available separately from cylinder head

11.0a Top end components - K8 engine

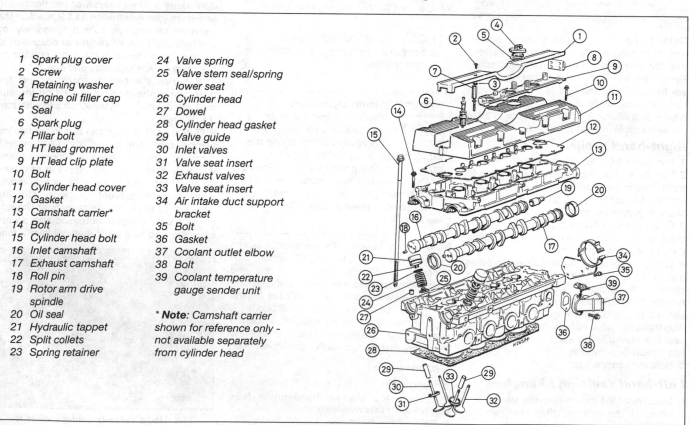

1 Spark plug cover
2 Screw
3 Retaining washer
4 Engine oil filler cap
5 Seal
6 Spark plug
7 Pillar bolt
8 HT lead grommet
9 HT lead clip plate
10 Bolt
11 Cylinder head cover
12 Gasket
13 Camshaft carrier*
14 Bolt
15 Cylinder head bolt
16 Inlet camshaft
17 Exhaust camshaft
18 Roll pin
19 Rotor arm drive spindle
20 Oil seal
21 Hydraulic tappet
22 Split collets
23 Spring retainer

24 Valve spring
25 Valve stem seal/spring lower seat
26 Cylinder head
27 Dowel
28 Cylinder head gasket
29 Valve guide
30 Inlet valves
31 Valve seat insert
32 Exhaust valves
33 Valve seat insert
34 Air intake duct support bracket
35 Bolt
36 Gasket
37 Coolant outlet elbow
38 Bolt
39 Coolant temperature gauge sender unit

* **Note:** Camshaft carrier shown for reference only - not available separately from cylinder head

11.0b Top end components - K16 engine

11.9 Secure partly-removed timing belt upper left-hand (inner) cover clear of cylinder head - K16 engine

time to refill with oil on restarting the engine, resulting in incorrect valve clearances.

K16 engines

9 Remove both camshaft sprockets, then unscrew the inner cover's upper retaining bolts so that the cover can be pulled away from the cylinder head just far enough for adequate working clearance. Take care not to distort or damage the cover or the timing belt **(see illustration)**.
10 Remove the cylinder head cover **(see illustration 11.0b)**.
11 Remove the distributor.
12 Unclip the air temperature control valve vacuum pipe from the air intake duct support bracket, then unbolt the bracket from the cylinder head.
13 Working in the **reverse** of the tightening sequence **(see illustration 11.36)**, evenly and progressively slacken the camshaft carrier bolts by one turn at a time. Once all valve spring pressure has been relieved, remove the bolts.
14 Withdraw the camshaft carrier, noting the presence of the locating dowels, then remove the camshafts and slide off the oil seals. The inlet camshaft can be identified by the distributor rotor arm drive spindle (or its location), therefore there is no need to mark the camshafts.
15 Obtain sixteen small, clean plastic containers, number them 1 to 16, and then fill them with clean engine oil. Using a rubber

sucker, withdraw each hydraulic tappet in turn **(see illustration 11.8)**, and place it in its respective container, to prevent oil loss. Do not interchange the hydraulic tappets or the rate of wear will be much increased and do not allow them to lose oil or they will take a long time to refill with oil on restarting the engine, resulting in incorrect valve clearances.

Inspection

16 Check each hydraulic tappet for signs of obvious wear (scoring, pitting, etc) and for ovality. Renew if necessary.
17 If the engine's valve clearances have sounded noisy, particularly if the noise persists after initial start-up from cold, then there is reason to suspect a faulty hydraulic tappet. Only a good mechanic experienced in these engines can tell whether the noise level is typical, or if renewal is warranted of one or more of the tappets.
18 If any tappet's operation is faulty, then it must be renewed.
19 Carefully remove all traces of old sealant from the mating surfaces of the bearing caps or camshaft carrier and cylinder head by using a plastic scraper. Examine the camshaft bearing journals and the cylinder head bearing surfaces for signs of obvious wear or pitting. If any such signs are evident, renew the component concerned.
20 To check the bearing journal running clearance, remove the hydraulic tappets, carefully clean the bearing surfaces and refit the camshaft(s) and carrier/bearing caps with a strand of Plastigauge across each journal. Tighten the carrier/bearing cap bolts to the specified torque wrench setting whilst taking great care not to rotate the camshaft(s), then remove the carrier/bearing caps and use the scale provided with the Plastigauge kit to measure the width of each compressed strand.
21 If the running clearance of any bearing is found to be worn to the specified service limit or beyond, fit a new camshaft and repeat the check. If the clearance is still excessive, then the cylinder head must be renewed.
22 To check camshaft endfloat, remove the hydraulic tappets, carefully clean the bearing surfaces and refit the camshaft(s) and carrier/bearing caps. Tighten to the specified

torque wrench setting the carrier/bearing cap bolts, then measure the endfloat using a Dial Test Indicator (DTI) or dial gauge mounted on the cylinder head so that its tip bears on the camshaft right-hand end.
23 Tap the camshaft fully towards the gauge, zero the gauge, then tap the camshaft fully away from the gauge and note the gauge reading. If the endfloat measured is found to be worn to the specified service limit or beyond, fit a new camshaft and repeat the check. If the clearance is still excessive, then the cylinder head must be renewed.
24 The camshaft itself should show no signs of marks, pitting or scoring on the lobe surfaces. If such marks are evident, renew the camshaft.
25 If a camshaft is renewed, extract the roll pin from the old one and fit the pin to the new camshaft with its split towards the camshaft's centre.

Refitting
K8 engines
26 Liberally oil the cylinder head hydraulic tappet bores and the tappets **(see illustration)**. Note that if new tappets are being fitted, they must be charged with clean engine oil before installation. Carefully refit the tappets to the cylinder head, ensuring that each tappet is refitted to its original bore and is the correct way up. Some care will be required to enter the tappets squarely into their bores.
27 Liberally oil the camshaft bearings and lobes then refit the camshaft. Position the shaft so that its No 1 cylinder lobes are pointing away from their valves and the roll pin in the camshaft's right-hand end is in the 4 o'clock position when viewed from the right-hand end of the engine **(see illustration)**.
28 Ensure that the locating dowels are pressed firmly into their recesses. Check that the mating surfaces are completely clean, unmarked and free from oil, then apply a thin bead of special Rover sealant to the mating surfaces of the front and rear bearing caps as shown **(see illustration 11.29)**. Carefully follow the instructions supplied with the sealant kit. Refit the bearing caps, using the notes made on removal, to ensure that each is installed correctly and in its original location **(see illustration)**.

11.26 Lubricate hydraulic tappets thoroughly and refit correct way up - K8 engine

11.27 Camshaft roll pin location at TDC position (for refitting camshaft bearing caps) - K8 engine

11.28 Apply sealant (arrowed) and fit camshaft bearing caps - K8 engine

2A

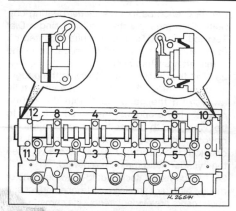

11.29 Camshaft bearing cap bolt tightening sequence - K8 engine

Note: Apply thin bead of sealant to end bearing cap mating surfaces along paths shown by heavy black lines

11.30a Fill oil holes with clean engine oil - K8 engine

11.30b Renew O-rings (arrowed) before refitting oil feed tube - K8 engine

29 Working in the sequence shown **(see illustration)**, progressively tighten the camshaft bearing cap bolts by one turn at a time until the caps touch the cylinder head evenly. Now go round again, working in the same sequence, and tighten all the bolts to the specified torque setting. Work only as described to impose the pressure of the valve springs gradually and evenly on the bearing caps. Wipe off all surplus sealant so

that none is left to find its way into any oilways.
30 Squirt clean engine oil into each camshaft bearing cap oil hole, then fit new O-rings to each of the oil feed tube stubs **(see illustration)**. Refit the oil feed tube to the cylinder head and press it firmly into position in the camshaft bearing caps.
31 Fit a new camshaft oil seal **(see illustration)**, then refit the cylinder head cover and camshaft sprocket.
32 Refit the distributor.

K16 engines

33 Liberally oil the cylinder head hydraulic tappet bores and the tappets. Note that if new tappets are being fitted, they must be charged with clean engine oil before installation. Carefully refit the tappets to the cylinder head, ensuring that each tappet is refitted to its original bore and is the correct way up. Some care will be required to enter the tappets squarely into their bores.
34 Liberally oil the camshaft bearings and lobes and refit them to the cylinder head. Position each shaft so that its No 1 cylinder lobes are pointing away from their valves. With the shafts in this position, the roll pin in the inlet camshaft's right-hand end will be in the 4 o'clock position when viewed from the right-hand end of the engine, while that of the

exhaust camshaft will be in the 8 o'clock position **(see illustration)**.
35 Ensure that the locating dowels are pressed firmly into their recesses, check that the mating surfaces are completely clean, unmarked and free from oil, then apply a thin bead of special Rover sealant to the mating surfaces of the camshaft carrier as shown **(see illustration)**. Carefully follow the instructions supplied with the sealant kit. Refit the carrier.
36 Working in the sequence shown **(see illustration)**, progressively tighten the camshaft carrier bolts by one turn at a time until the carrier touches the cylinder head evenly. Now go round again, working in the same sequence, tightening all bolts to the specified torque setting. Work only as described to impose the pressure of the valve springs gradually and evenly on the carrier. Wipe off all surplus sealant so that none is left to find its way into any oilways.
37 Fit new camshaft oil seals, then refit the cylinder head cover, inner timing cover retaining bolts and camshaft sprockets.
38 Refit the distributor.
39 Refit the air intake duct support bracket, tightening its screws to their specified torque wrench setting, then reconnect and secure the air temperature control valve vacuum pipe and refit the rubber strap to secure the air intake duct.

11.31 Fitting a new camshaft right-hand oil seal - K8 engine

11.34 Camshaft roll pin locations at TDC position for refitting camshaft carrier (arrowed) - K16 engine

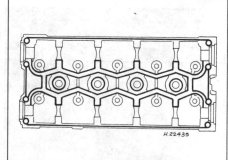

11.35 Apply thin bead of sealant to camshaft carrier mating surfaces along paths shown by heavy black lines - K16 engine

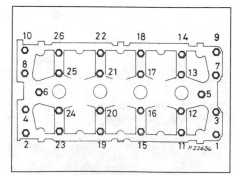

11.36 Camshaft carrier bolt tightening sequence - K16 engine

12 Valve clearances - general information

1 It is necessary for a clearance to exist between the tip of each valve stem and the valve operating mechanism. This allows for expansion of the various engine components as the engine reaches normal operating temperature.

2 On most older engine designs, this meant that the valve clearances (also known as 'tappet' clearances) had to be checked and adjusted regularly. If the clearances were too slack, the engine would be very noisy, its power output would suffer and its fuel consumption would increase. Conversely, if the clearances were too tight, the engine's power output would be reduced and the valves and their seats could be severely damaged.

3 The engines covered in this Manual employ hydraulic tappets which use engine oil pressure to automatically take up the clearance between each camshaft lobe and its respective valve stem. This means that there is no need for regular checking and inspection of the valve clearances, but it is essential that only good quality oil of the recommended viscosity and specification is used in the engine and that this oil is scrupulously changed at the recommended intervals. If this advice is not followed, the oilways and tappets may become clogged with particles of dirt or deposits of burnt engine oil, so that the system cannot work properly. Ultimately, one or more of the tappets may fail and expensive repairs may be required.

4 On starting the engine from cold, there will be a slight delay while full oil pressure builds up in all parts of the engine, especially in the tappets. The valve clearances, therefore, may well rattle for about 10 seconds or so and then quieten. This is a normal state of affairs and is nothing to worry about, provided that all tappets quieten quickly and stay quiet.

5 After the vehicle has been standing for several days, the valve clearances may rattle for longer than usual as nearly all the oil will have drained away from the engine's top end components and bearing surfaces. While this is only to be expected, care must be taken not to damage the engine by running it at high speed until all the tappets are refilled with oil and operating normally. With the vehicle stationary, hold the engine at no more than a fast idle speed (maximum 2000 to 2500 rpm) for 10 to 15 minutes or until the noise ceases. Do not run the engine at more than 3000 rpm until all tappets are fully recharged with oil and all noise has ceased.

6 If the valve clearances are thought to be noisy, or if a light rattle persists from the engine's top end after it has reached normal operating temperature, take the vehicle to a Rover dealer for expert advice. Depending on the mileage covered and the usage to which each vehicle has been put, some vehicles may be noisier than others. Only a good mechanic experienced in these engines can tell if the noise level is typical for the vehicle's mileage or if a genuine fault exists. If any tappet's operation is faulty, then it must be renewed.

13 Cylinder head - removal and refitting

Note: *Due to engine design, it will become very difficult, almost impossible, to turn the crankshaft once the cylinder head bolts have been slackened. The manufacturer states that the crankshaft will be 'tight' and should not be rotated more than absolutely necessary once the head has been removed. If the crankshaft cannot be rotated, then it must be removed for overhaul work to proceed. With this in mind, the crankshaft always must be rotated to the desired position before the bolts are disturbed.*

Removal

1 Disconnect the battery negative lead.
2 Drain the cooling system.
3 Remove the camshaft sprocket(s).
4 Unscrew the bolts securing the timing belt upper left-hand (inner) cover to the cylinder head, so that the cover can be pulled away from the cylinder head just far enough for adequate working clearance. Take care not to distort or damage the cover or the timing belt.
5 Remove the cylinder head cover.
6 Disconnect the exhaust system front pipe from the manifold and, where fitted, disconnect or release the lambda sensor wiring so that it is not strained by the weight of the exhaust.
7 Note that the following text assumes that the cylinder head will be removed with both inlet and exhaust manifolds attached. This is easier but makes it a bulky and heavy assembly to handle. If it is wished first to remove the manifolds, proceed as described in the relevant Sections of Chapter 4.
8 On carburettor engines, disconnect the following from the carburettor and inlet manifold as described in the relevant Sections of Chapter 4A:
a) *Fuel pump feed hose - plug both openings to prevent loss of fuel and entry of dirt into system.*
b) *Carburettor idle bypass solenoid wires.*
c) *Accelerator cable.*
d) *Choke cable.*
e) *Vacuum servo unit vacuum hose.*
f) *Inlet manifold PTC heater wire.*
g) *Inlet manifold heater temperature switch wiring.*
9 On fuel-injected engines, refer to the relevant Sections of Chapter 4B or C, and disconnect or remove all throttle body/fuel rail components appertaining to cylinder head removal, noting the following:

a) *The fuel system must be depressurised before any component is disconnected.*
b) *Plug the open ends of all disconnected pipes to prevent loss of fuel and entry of dirt into system.*
c) *Discard all sealing washers and O-rings, these must be renewed.*
10 Working as described in Chapter 3, disconnect the connector plug from the coolant temperature sensor screwed into the coolant outlet elbow, then disconnect the coolant hoses from the (three) inlet manifold unions and from the coolant outlet elbow.
11 Unclip the engine wiring harness from the inlet manifold or its support stays. Slacken the bolts securing the stays to the manifold, then unbolt the support stays and the carburettor metal overflow pipes from the cylinder block/crankcase.
12 Remove the distributor cap, complete with the spark plug HT leads. Remove the spark plugs.
13 On K16 engines equipped with air conditioning, undo the nuts and bolts securing the heat shields to the rear of the alternator and air conditioning compressor and remove both heat shields. Slacken the two lower alternator mounting bolts then remove the upper mounting bolt and pivot the alternator away from the cylinder head.
14 Working in the reverse of the tightening sequence **(see illustrations 13.29a or 13.29b)**, progressively slacken the ten cylinder head bolts by one turn at a time. A female Torx-type socket (No 12 size) will be required. Remove each bolt in turn and store it in its correct fitted order by pushing it through a clearly-marked cardboard template.
15 The joint between the cylinder head and gasket and the cylinder block/crankcase must now be broken without disturbing the wet liners. Although these liners are better located and sealed than some wet liner engines, there is still a risk of coolant and foreign matter leaking into the sump if the cylinder head is lifted carelessly. If care is not taken and the liners are moved, there is also a possibility of the bottom seals being disturbed, causing leakage after refitting the head.
16 To break the joint, obtain two L-shaped metal bars which fit into the cylinder head bolt holes and gently rock the cylinder head free towards the front of the vehicle **(see illustration)**. Do not try to swivel the head on

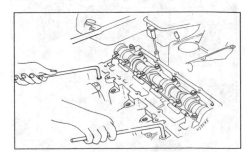

13.16 Using two cranked bars to break cylinder head joint

2A

13.20 Checking condition of cylinder head bolt threads - cylinder head removed

13.26a Fit new cylinder head gasket on two locating dowels (arrowed) . . .

13.26b . . . so that TOP mark is upwards and FRONT arrow points to timing belt end

the cylinder block/crankcase as it is located by dowels as well as by the tops of the liners.
17 With the joint broken, lift the cylinder head away, using assistance if possible as it is a heavy assembly, especially if complete with the manifolds. Remove the gasket, noting the two locating dowels, and discard it.
18 Further to the warnings given in the note at the beginning of this Section, do not attempt to rotate the crankshaft with the cylinder head removed, otherwise the wet liners may be displaced. Operations that would normally require the rotation of the crankshaft (eg: cleaning the piston crowns) must be carried out with great care to ensure that no particles of dirt or foreign matter are left behind. If cylinder liner clamps are to be used, they must be clamped in place using

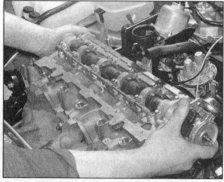

13.27 Refitting the cylinder head

spacers fitted under the heads of the cylinder head bolts.
19 If the cylinder head is to be dismantled, remove the camshaft(s) then refer to the relevant Sections of Part B of this Chapter.

Refitting

20 Check the condition of the cylinder head bolts, particularly their threads. Keeping all bolts in their correct fitted order, wash them and wipe dry. Check each bolt for any sign of visible wear or damage, renewing as necessary. Lightly oil the threads of each bolt, carefully enter it into its original hole and screw it in, by hand only until finger-tight. Measure the distance from the cylinder block/crankcase gasket surface to under the bolt's head **(see illustration)**.
21 If the distance measured is under 97 mm, the bolt may be re-used. If the distance measured is more than 97 mm, the bolt must be renewed. Considering the task these bolts perform and the pressures they must withstand, owners should consider renewing all the bolts as a matched set if more than one of the originals fail inspection or are close to the limit set.
22 The mating faces of the cylinder head and cylinder block/crankcase must be perfectly clean before refitting the head. Use a hard plastic or wood scraper to remove all traces of gasket and carbon.
23 Check the mating surfaces of the cylinder block/crankcase and the cylinder head for

nicks, deep scratches and other damage. If slight, they may be removed carefully with a file, but if excessive, machining may be the only alternative to renewal.
24 If warpage of the cylinder head gasket surface is suspected, use a straight-edge to check it for distortion. Refer to Part B of this Chapter if necessary.
25 Wipe clean the mating surfaces of the cylinder head and cylinder block/crankcase. Check that the two locating dowels are in position at each end of the cylinder block/crankcase surface.
26 Position a new gasket on the cylinder block/crankcase surface so that its TOP mark is uppermost and the FRONT arrow points to the timing belt end **(see illustrations)**.
27 Refit the cylinder head, locating it on the dowels **(see illustration)**.
28 Keeping all the cylinder head bolts in their correct fitted order, wash them and wipe dry. Lightly oil under the head and on the threads of each bolt, carefully enter it into its original hole and screw it in, by hand only, until finger-tight.
29 Working progressively and in the sequence shown **(see illustrations)**, use first a torque wrench, then an ordinary socket extension bar to tighten the cylinder head bolts through the specified stages. To tighten the bolts through the specified angles, simply use a felt-tip pen or similar to mark the position on the cylinder head of each bolt head's radial mark. The second stage then

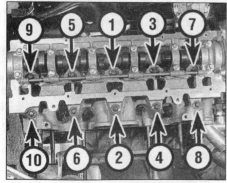

13.29a Cylinder head bolt tightening sequence - K8 engine

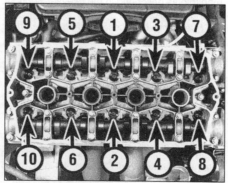

13.29b Cylinder head bolt tightening sequence - K16 engine

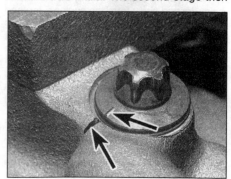

13.29c Alignment of bolt head radial marks with cylinder head to establish tightening angles (arrowed)

tightens each bolt through half a turn so that the marks face away from each other and the third stage tightens them through another half-turn so that all the bolt-head marks will then align again with their cylinder head counterparts. If any bolt is overtightened past its mark, slacken it through 90°, then re-tighten until the marks align (see illustration).
30 Refit and tighten the inlet manifold support stay bolts, then secure the engine wiring harness using the clips provided.
31 On K16 engines equipped with air conditioning, refit the alternator mounting bolts and tighten them to the specified torque setting. Refit the compressor and alternator heatshields, tightening their retaining bolts and nuts securely.
32 Connect all disturbed coolant hoses, securing them in position with their retaining clips. Reconnect the coolant temperature sensor wiring.
33 Working as described in Chapter 4, connect or refit all disturbed wiring, hoses and control cable(s) to the inlet manifold and fuel system components, then adjust the choke and or accelerator cable(s).
34 Reconnect the exhaust system front pipe to the manifold and (if applicable) reconnect the lambda sensor wiring.
35 Refit the cylinder head cover, inner timing cover retaining bolts and camshaft sprocket(s).
36 Refit the spark plugs and distributor cap then reconnect the battery negative lead.
37 Refill the cooling system.

14 Sump - removal and refitting

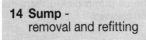 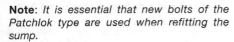

Note: It is essential that new bolts of the Patchlok type are used when refitting the sump.

Removal

1 Disconnect the battery negative lead.
2 Drain the engine oil then clean and refit the engine oil drain plug, tightening it to the specified torque wrench setting. If the engine is nearing its service interval when the oil and filter are due for renewal, it is recommended that the filter is also removed and a new one fitted. After reassembly, the engine can then be replenished with fresh engine oil.
3 Apply the handbrake, then jack up the front of the vehicle and support it on axle stands. Remove the right-hand roadwheel.
4 From underneath the front of the vehicle, slacken and remove the three bolts securing the bumper flange to the body. Remove the seven bolts securing the front undercover panel to the body and remove the panel.
5 Working as described in Chapter 4, disconnect the exhaust system front pipe from the manifold and, where fitted, disconnect or release the lambda sensor

14.6 Remove flywheel lower cover plate to reach sump bolts

wiring so that it is not strained by the weight of the exhaust.
6 Unscrew the three retaining bolts and remove the flywheel lower cover plate (see illustration).
7 Slacken and remove the bolts securing the anti-beaming bracket to the engine and transmission and remove the bracket.
8 Progressively slacken the sump retaining bolts then remove them along with the anti-beaming bracket support. Make a note of the correct fitted position of the support and of the longer bolts at positions 4, 8 and 12 (see illustration 14.14) to ensure correct refitment on reassembly.
9 Break the joint by striking the sump with the palm of the hand, then lower the sump and withdraw it (see illustration).
10 While the sump is removed, take the opportunity to unbolt the oil pump pick-up/strainer pipe and clean it using a suitable solvent. Inspect the strainer mesh for signs of clogging or splitting and renew if necessary.

Refitting

11 Clean all traces of gasket from the mating surfaces of the cylinder block/crankcase and sump, then use a clean rag to wipe out the sump and the engine's interior. If the oil pump pick-up/strainer pipe was removed, fit a new sealing O-ring to its end and refit the pipe, tightening its retaining bolts to the specified torque setting.
12 If the sump gasket is damaged or shows signs of deterioration, then it must be renewed. Fit the gasket to the sump mating

14.12 Sump gasket pegs must engage with sump mating surface holes

14.9 Removing the sump

surface so that its 7 locating pegs fit into the sump holes (see illustration).
13 Offer up the sump to the cylinder block/crankcase then fit the new sump retaining bolts, not forgetting the anti-beaming bracket support. Tighten the bolts finger-tight only.
14 Working in the sequence shown (see illustration), tighten the sump bolts to the specified torque setting.
15 Refit the anti-beaming bracket and tighten the mounting bolts to the specified torque setting.
16 Install the flywheel lower cover plate and tighten the retaining bolts to the specified torque wrench setting.
17 Reconnect the exhaust system front pipe to the manifold and, where necessary, reconnect the lambda sensor wiring.
18 Refit the undercover panel and wheel, then lower the vehicle to the ground and reconnect the battery negative lead.
19 Replenish the engine oil.

15 Oil pump - removal and refitting

Note: The oil pressure relief valve can be dismantled without removing the oil pump from the vehicle. See Section 16 for details.

Removal

1 Remove the crankshaft sprocket and secure the timing belt clear of the working

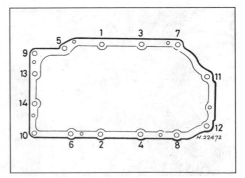
14.14 Sump bolt tightening sequence

2A

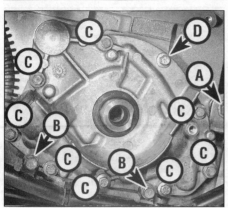

15.4 Alternator adjuster link nut (A) wiring guide screws (B) oil pump bolts (C) and special oil pump bolt (D)

area so that it cannot be contaminated with oil.

2 Drain the engine oil, then clean and refit the engine oil drain plug, tightening it to the specified torque wrench setting. If the engine is nearing its service interval when the oil and filter are due for renewal, it is recommended that the filter is also removed and a new one fitted. After reassembly, the engine can then be replenished with fresh engine oil.

3 Where necessary, unscrew the alternator adjuster link retaining nut and unbolt the engine wiring harness guide retaining screws, then move the link and guide clear of the oil pump.

4 Unscrew the oil pump retaining bolts, noting the fitted position of the special bolt, and withdraw the oil pump **(see illustration)**. Recover the pump gasket and discard it, then carefully lever the crankshaft right-hand oil seal out of the oil pump. The oil seal should be renewed whenever it is disturbed.

Refitting

5 Thoroughly clean the mating faces of the oil pump and cylinder block/crankcase. Use grease to stick a new gasket in place.

6 Prime the pump before installation by injecting clean engine oil into it and turning it by hand.

7 Offer up the pump, ensuring that its inner

16.4 Unscrewing oil pressure relief valve threaded plug

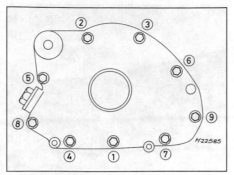

15.8 Oil pump bolt tightening sequence

gear engages fully on the crankshaft flats, then push the pump fully into position.

8 Refit the pump retaining bolts, ensuring that the special bolt is refitted to its original position. Tighten the retaining bolts to the specified torque setting in the order shown **(see illustration)**.

9 If removed, refit the alternator adjuster link and the engine wiring harness guide, then tighten securely the retaining nut and screws.

10 Fit a new crankshaft right-hand oil seal.

11 Remove all traces of surplus oil then refit the crankshaft sprocket.

12 Replenish the engine oil.

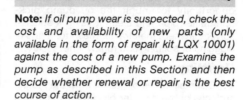

16 Oil pump - dismantling, inspection and reassembly

Note: *If oil pump wear is suspected, check the cost and availability of new parts (only available in the form of repair kit LQX 10001) against the cost of a new pump. Examine the pump as described in this Section and then decide whether renewal or repair is the best course of action.*

Dismantling

1 Remove the oil pump.

2 Unscrew the Torx screws (size T25) and remove the pump cover plate. Discard the sealing ring.

3 Note the identification marks on the outer rotor then remove both the rotors from the body.

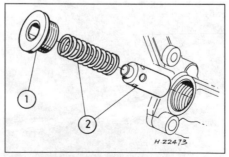

16.5 Oil pressure relief valve assembly

1   Threaded plug
2   Valve spring and plunger

4 The oil pressure relief valve can be dismantled, if required, without disturbing the pump. If this is to be done with the pump in position and the engine still installed in the vehicle, it will first be necessary to jack up the front of the vehicle and remove the right-hand roadwheel to gain access to the valve **(see illustration)**.

5 To dismantle the valve, unscrew the threaded plug and recover the valve spring and plunger **(see illustration)**. Discard the plug sealing washer.

Inspection

6 Inspect the rotors for obvious signs of wear or damage and renew if necessary. If the pump body or cover plate is scored or damaged, then the complete oil pump assembly must be renewed.

7 Using feeler gauge blades of the appropriate thickness, measure the clearance between the outer rotor and the pump body, then between the tips of the inner and outer rotor lobes (a and b respectively) **(see illustration)**.

8 Using feeler gauge blades and a straight-edge placed across the top of the pump body and the rotors, measure the rotor endfloat (c).

9 If any measurement is outside the specified limits, the complete pump assembly must be renewed.

10 If the pressure relief valve plunger is scored, or if it does not slide freely in the pump body bore, then it must be renewed, using all the components from the repair kit.

11 To complete a thorough inspection of the oil pump components, the sump should be removed and the oil pump pick-up/strainer pipe removed and cleaned.

Reassembly

12 Lubricate the pump rotors with clean engine oil and refit them to the pump body,

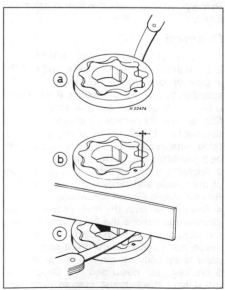

16.7 Checking oil pump rotors for wear - see text for details

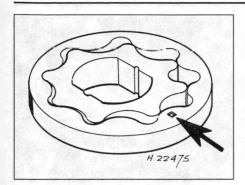

16.12 Oil pump outer rotor outside face identifying mark (arrowed)

18.2 Using fabricated tool to lock flywheel in position

ensuring that the outer rotor's identification mark faces outwards **(see illustration)**.

13 Fit a new sealing ring to the pump body and refit the cover plate. Apply thread-locking compound to the threads of the cover plate Torx screws and tighten them securely.

14 Check that the pump rotates freely, then prime it by injecting oil into its passages and rotating it. If a long time elapses before the pump is refitted to the engine, prime it again before installation.

15 Refit the oil pressure relief valve plunger, ensuring that it is the correct way up, then install the spring. Fit a new sealing washer to the threaded plug and tighten the plug securely.

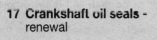

17 Crankshaft oil seals - renewal

Right-hand seal

1 Remove the crankshaft sprocket and secure the timing belt clear of the working area so that it cannot be contaminated with oil.

2 Punch or drill two small holes opposite each other in the seal. Screw a self-tapping screw into each and pull on the screws with pliers to extract the seal.

3 Clean the seal housing and polish off any burrs or raised edges which may have caused the seal to fail in the first place.

4 Lubricate the lips of the new seal with clean engine oil and drive it into position until it seats on its locating shoulder. Use a suitable tubular drift, such as a socket, which bears only on the hard outer edge of the seal. Take care not to damage the seal lips during fitting. Use either grease or a thin layer of insulating tape to protect the seal lips from the edges of the crankshaft flats but be careful to remove all traces of tape and to lubricate the seal lips if the second method is used. Note that the seal lips should face inwards.

5 Wash off any traces of oil, then refit the crankshaft sprocket.

Left-hand seal

6 Remove the flywheel.

7 Taking care not to mark either the crankshaft or any part of the cylinder block/crankcase, lever the seal evenly out of its housing.

8 Clean the seal housing and polish off any burrs or raised edges which may have caused the seal to fail in the first place.

9 Lubricate with grease the lips of the new seal and the crankshaft shoulder, then offer up the seal to the cylinder block/crankcase.

10 Ease the sealing lip of the seal over the crankshaft shoulder by hand only, then press the seal evenly into its housing until its outer flange seats evenly on the housing lip. If necessary, a soft-faced mallet can be used to tap the seal gently into place.

11 Wash off any traces of oil, then refit the flywheel.

18 Flywheel - removal, inspection and refitting

Removal

1 Remove the gearbox and the clutch assembly.

2 Prevent the flywheel from turning by locking the ring gear teeth **(see illustration)** or by bolting a strap between the flywheel and the cylinder block/crankcase.

3 Slacken and remove the flywheel retaining bolts and discard them The bolts must be renewed whenever they are disturbed.

4 Remove the flywheel. Do not drop it, as it is very heavy.

Inspection

5 If the flywheel's clutch mating surface is deeply scored, cracked or otherwise damaged, then the flywheel must be renewed, unless it is possible to have it surface ground. Seek the advice of a Rover dealer or engine reconditioning specialist.

6 If the ring gear is badly worn or has missing teeth, then it must be renewed. This job is best left to a Rover dealer or engine reconditioning specialist. The temperature to which the new ring gear must be heated for installation (350°C - shown by an even light blue colour) is critical and, if not done

accurately, the hardness of the teeth will be destroyed.

7 Examine the reluctor ring (fitted to the rear of the flywheel) for signs of damage and check that it is securely fastened by the two retaining screws. If the reluctor ring is damaged, then it must be renewed.

Refitting

8 Clean the mating surfaces of the flywheel and crankshaft. Clean any remaining adhesive from the threads of the crankshaft threaded holes by making two saw cuts at opposite points along the (carefully-cleaned) threads of one of the original flywheel bolts and screwing it into each hole in turn. **Do not** use a tap to clean the threads in this way.

9 Position the flywheel over the crankshaft's locating dowel, press it into place and fit six **new** bolts.

10 Lock the flywheel using the method employed on dismantling, then tighten the retaining bolts to the specified torque wrench setting.

11 Refit the clutch, then remove the locking tool and refit the gearbox.

19 Engine/gearbox mountings - inspection and renewal

Inspection

1 If improved access is required, raise the front of the vehicle and support it securely on axle stands.

2 Check the mounting rubber to see if it is cracked, hardened or separated from the metal at any point. Renew the mounting if any such damage or deterioration is evident.

3 Check that all mounting fasteners are securely tightened. Use a torque wrench to check, if possible.

4 Using a large screwdriver or a pry bar, check for wear in the mounting by carefully levering against it to check for free play. Where this is not possible, enlist the aid of an assistant to move the engine/gearbox unit back and forth or from side to side while you watch the mounting. While some free play is to be expected even from new components, excessive wear should be obvious. If excessive free play is found, check first that the fasteners are correctly secured, then renew any worn components as described below.

Renewal

Right-hand mounting

5 Disconnect the battery negative lead.

6 To improve access to the mounting, remove the expansion tank mounting bolts then free the coolant hose from any relevant retaining clips and position the tank clear of the engine. On models equipped with power-assisted steering, undo all the power steering hose retaining clamp bolts then slide the fluid

2A

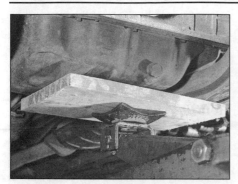

19.7a Use trolley jack with wooden spacer to adjust height of engine/gearbox unit

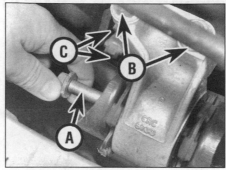

19.7b Right-hand mounting through-bolt (A), mounting-to-bracket nuts (B), bracket-to-cylinder block/crankcase bolts (two arrowed - C)

19.12 Check rubber washers are correctly installed before tightening through-bolt nut

reservoir out of its retaining clip and position it clear of the timing belt covers. Take great care not to place any undue strain on hoses and mop up any spilt fluid immediately.

7 Support the weight of the engine/gearbox unit by using a trolley jack, with a wooden spacer to prevent damage to the sump. Unscrew the mounting through-bolt and nut and the mounting to bracket nuts. Remove the mounting, noting the two rubber washers **(see illustrations)**.

8 Where necessary, unscrew the retaining bolts and remove the bracket from the cylinder block/crankcase.

9 Check carefully for signs of wear or damage on all components and renew them where necessary.

10 On reassembly, refit the bracket to the

19.18 Slacken and remove gearbox bracket-to-mounting bolts . . .

cylinder block/crankcase and tighten the retaining bolts to the specified torque setting.

11 Locate the rubber washers on the mounting, one on each side of its centre boss, then refit the mounting to the bracket and tighten the retaining nuts, finger-tight only.

12 Using the trolley jack to position the engine unit at the correct height, refit from rear to front the mounting-to-body through-bolt, ensuring that the rubber washers are correctly seated, then refit the nut **(see illustration)**.

13 Tighten the mounting to bracket nuts and the through-bolt to the specified torque wrench settings, then lower and remove the jack.

14 Where necessary, refit the power steering fluid reservoir to its mounting bracket and secure the hydraulic hose clamps in position with the retaining bolts.

15 Refit the coolant expansion tank and tighten the mounting bolts securely. Secure the coolant hose in position with any necessary retaining clips and reconnect the battery negative lead.

Left-hand mounting

16 Disconnect the battery negative lead then disconnect the clutch cable.

17 To improve access to the mounting, unclip the engine wiring harness and position it clear of the mounting.

18 Support the weight of the engine/gearbox

unit by using a trolley jack, with a wooden spacer to prevent damage to the gearbox casing. Slacken and remove the two bolts securing the gearbox bracket to the mounting **(see illustration)**.

19 Lower the engine/gearbox unit, then remove the four bolts securing the mounting to the body and manoeuvre the mounting out of position. If required, slacken and remove the two bolts which secure the bracket to the gearbox and remove the bracket **(see illustrations)**.

20 Although the mounting rubber is secured by two nuts to a metal outer section, the two parts can be renewed only as a complete assembly. Check all components carefully for signs of wear or damage and renew where necessary.

21 On reassembly, refit the bracket to the gearbox and tighten the retaining bolts to the specified torque setting.

22 Manoeuvre the mounting into position then refit the retaining bolts and tighten them to the specified torque setting.

23 Use the trolley jack to raise the gearbox to the correct height, then refit the mounting bracket to mounting bolts and tighten them to the specified torque setting. Refit the wiring harness to its retaining clip.

24 Refit the clutch cable and reconnect the battery negative lead.

Rear mounting

25 Apply the handbrake then jack up the

19.19a . . . then lower gearbox and remove four left-hand mounting-to-body bolts (arrowed) . . .

19.19b . . . and remove mounting

19.19c Gearbox bracket is retained by two bolts (one arrowed)

front of the vehicle and support it securely on axle stands.

26 Support the weight of the engine/gearbox unit by using a trolley jack, with a wooden spacer to prevent damage to the transmission casing. Unbolt the mounting bracket from the gearbox and the connecting link from the underbody bracket, then remove the mounting **(see illustrations)**.

27 Unscrew the through-bolt to separate the connecting link from the bracket. Check carefully for signs of wear or damage, paying particular attention to the connecting link rubber bushes. Renew as necessary.

28 Reassembly is the reverse of the removal procedure. Tighten all mounting bolts to the specified torque setting.

19.26a Unbolt rear mounting to gearbox bolts (arrowed) . . .

19.26b . . . then undo connecting link-to-underbody bracket bolt and remove mounting

2A

Notes

Chapter 2 Part B Engine removal and general overhaul procedures

Contents

Degrees of difficulty

Easy, suitable for novice with little experience	Fairly easy, suitable for beginner with some experience	Fairly difficult, suitable for competent DIY mechanic	Difficult, suitable for experienced DIY mechanic	Very difficult, suitable for expert DIY or professional 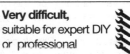

2B

Specifications

Refer to Part A of this Chapter

1 General information

Included in this part of the Chapter are details of removing the engine/gearbox unit from the vehicle and general overhaul procedures for the cylinder head, cylinder block/crankcase and all other engine internal components.

The information given ranges from advice concerning preparation for an overhaul and the purchase of replacement parts to detailed step-by-step procedures covering removal, inspection, renovation and refitting of engine internal components.

After Section 5, all instructions are based on the assumption that the engine has been removed from the vehicle. For information concerning in-car engine repair, as well as the removal and refitting of those external components necessary for full overhaul, refer to Part A of this Chapter and to Section 5. Ignore any preliminary dismantling operations described in Part A that are no longer relevant once the engine has been removed from the vehicle.

2 Engine overhaul - general information

It is not always easy to determine when, or if, an engine should be completely overhauled, as a number of factors must be considered.

High mileage is not necessarily an indication that an overhaul is needed, while low mileage does not preclude the need for an overhaul. Frequency of servicing is probably the most important consideration. An engine which has had regular and frequent oil and filter changes, as well as other required maintenance, should give many thousands of miles of reliable service. Conversely, a neglected engine may require an overhaul very early in its life. If a complete service does not remedy any problems, major mechanical work is the only solution.

Excessive oil consumption is an indication that piston rings, valve seals and/or valve guides are in need of attention. Make sure that oil leaks are not responsible before deciding that the rings and/or guides are worn. Perform a compression test to determine the likely cause of the problem.

Check the oil pressure with a gauge fitted in place of the oil pressure switch and compare it with that specified. If it is extremely low, the main and big-end bearings and/or the oil pump are probably worn out.

Loss of power, rough running, knocking or metallic engine noises, excessive valve gear noise and high fuel consumption may also point to the need for an overhaul, especially if they are all present at the same time.

An engine overhaul involves restoring all internal parts to the specification of a new engine. During an overhaul, the cylinder liners, the pistons and the piston rings are renewed. New main and big-end bearings are generally fitted and, if necessary, the crankshaft may be renewed to restore the journals. The valves are serviced as well, since they are usually in less than perfect condition at this point. While the engine is being overhauled, other components, such as the distributor, starter and alternator, can be overhauled as well. The end result should be an as-new engine that will give many trouble-free miles.

Critical cooling system components such as the hoses, thermostat and coolant pump should be renewed when an engine is overhauled. The radiator should be checked carefully to ensure that it is not clogged or leaking. Also it is a good idea to renew the oil pump whenever the engine is overhauled.

Before beginning the engine overhaul, read through the entire procedure to familiarize yourself with the scope and requirements of the job. Overhauling an engine is not difficult if you follow carefully all of the instructions, have the necessary tools and equipment and pay close attention to all specifications. However, it can be time-consuming. Plan on the vehicle being off the road for a minimum of two weeks, especially if parts must be taken to an engineering works for repair or reconditioning. Check on the availability of parts and make sure that any necessary special tools and equipment are obtained in advance. Most work can be done with typical hand tools, although a number of precision measuring tools are required for inspecting parts to determine if they must be renewed. Often the engineering works will handle the inspection of parts and offer advice concerning reconditioning and renewal.

Always wait until the engine has been completely dismantled and all components, especially the cylinder block/crankcase, the cylinder liners and the crankshaft have been inspected before deciding what service and repair operations must be performed by an engineering works. Since the condition of these components will be the major factor to consider when determining whether to overhaul the original engine or buy a reconditioned unit, do not purchase parts or have overhaul work done on other components until they have been thoroughly inspected. As a general rule, time is the primary cost of an overhaul, so it does not pay to fit worn or substandard parts.

As a final note, to ensure maximum life and minimum trouble from a reconditioned engine, everything must be assembled with care in a spotlessly clean environment.

3 Engine/gearbox removal - methods and precautions

If you have decided that the engine must be removed for overhaul or major repair work, several preliminary steps should be taken.

Locating a suitable place to work is extremely important. Adequate work space, along with storage space for the vehicle, will be needed. If a shop or garage is not available, at the very least a flat, level, clean work surface is required.

Cleaning the engine compartment and engine/gearbox before beginning the removal procedure will help keep things clean and organised.

An engine hoist or A-frame will also be necessary. Make sure the equipment is rated in excess of the combined weight of the engine and gearbox (290 lb/130 kg approximately). Safety is of primary importance, considering the potential hazards involved in lifting the engine/gearbox unit out of the vehicle.

If the engine/gearbox unit is being removed by a novice, a helper should be available. Advice and aid from someone more experienced would also be helpful. There are many instances when one person cannot simultaneously perform all of the operations required when lifting the unit out of the vehicle.

Plan the operation ahead of time. Before starting work, arrange for the hire of or obtain all of the tools and equipment you will need. Some of the equipment necessary to perform engine/gearbox removal and installation safely and with relative ease are (in addition to an engine hoist) a heavy duty trolley jack, complete sets of spanners and sockets as described at the front of this Manual, wooden blocks and plenty of rags and cleaning solvent for mopping up spilled oil, coolant and fuel. If the hoist must be hired, make sure that you arrange for it in advance and perform all of the operations possible without it beforehand. This will save you money and time.

Plan for the vehicle to be out of use for quite a while. An engineering works will be required to perform some of the work which the do-it-yourselfer cannot accomplish without special equipment. These places often have a busy schedule, so it would be a good idea to consult them before removing the engine in order to accurately estimate the amount of time required to rebuild or repair components that may need work.

Always be extremely careful when removing and refitting the engine/gearbox unit. Serious injury can result from careless actions. Plan ahead, take your time and a job of this nature, although major, can be accomplished successfully.

4 Engine/gearbox - removal and refitting

Note: *The engine can be removed from the vehicle only as a complete unit with the gearbox.*

Removal

1 Park the vehicle on firm, level ground then remove the bonnet.
2 If the engine is to be dismantled, drain the oil and remove the oil filter, then clean and refit the drain plug, tightening it to its specified torque setting.
3 Firmly apply the handbrake then jack up the front of the vehicle and support it securely on axle stands. Remove both front roadwheels.
4 From underneath the front of the vehicle, slacken and remove the three bolts securing the bumper flange to the body. Remove the seven bolts securing the front undercover panel to the body and remove the panel.
5 Drain the gearbox oil, then clean and refit the drain plug, tightening it to its specified torque setting.
6 Drain the cooling system.
7 Remove the battery, followed by the battery tray and support bracket.
8 Remove the complete air cleaner assembly, including the intake duct and mounting bracket, intake hose and resonator.
9 Disconnect the ignition coil HT lead from the distributor cap.
10 Undo the nut and disconnect the battery positive lead from the main starter motor solenoid terminal, then carefully disconnect the spade connector from the solenoid.
11 Undo the two bolts securing the engine compartment fusebox to the body, then disconnect the two engine wiring harness block connectors from the underside of the fusebox. Undo the bolt securing the wiring harness earth lead to the bonnet platform, then disconnect the LT wiring connector from the ignition coil. On fuel-injected engines, also disconnect the wiring connector and vacuum pipe from the engine management ECU. Free the engine wiring harness from any relevant clips or ties so that it is free to be removed with the engine/gearbox unit **(see illustrations)**.

4.11a Disconnecting engine harness wiring connectors from underside of fusebox . . .

4.11b ... and ignition coil LT wiring connector

4.11c Disconnecting vacuum pipe from engine management ECU - fuel-injected engines

12 Trace the clutch cable back from the clutch release lever to the bulkhead and remove the C-clip which retains the outer cable spring in position. Unhook the inner cable from the release lever and free the outer cable from its mounting bracket and position it clear of the gearbox.

13 From underneath the vehicle, pull out the rubber retaining pin which secures the lower end of the speedometer cable to the gearbox housing. Withdraw the cable from the speedometer drive and remove the O-rings from the cable lower end. Renew the O-rings, regardless of their condition.

14 In the absence of the special gearchange linkage balljoint separator (Rover service tool number 18G 1592), use a suitable flat-bladed screwdriver to carefully lever the link rod balljoints off the gearbox upper and lower selector levers, taking care not to damage the balljoint gaiters.

15 Unscrew the reverse interlock cable nut from the top of the gearbox housing. In the absence of the special spanner (Rover service tool number 18G 1591), use a close-fitting spanner to unscrew the plastic nut, noting that it is easily damaged. Plug the gearbox orifice to prevent the entry of dirt.

16 Disconnect the coolant hose from the bottom of the expansion tank, the expansion tank hose from the inlet manifold union, both heater hoses from the heater matrix unions and the radiator top hose from the coolant outlet elbow. Either remove the radiator bottom hose or secure it so that it will not hinder engine/gearbox removal.

17 Slacken and remove the union bolt which secures the vacuum servo unit vacuum hose to the inlet manifold. Discard the sealing washers as they must be renewed whenever they are disturbed.

18 On carburettor engines, disconnect the feed hose from the fuel pump, then disconnect the accelerator and choke cables from the carburettor.

19 On fuel-injected engines, depressurise the fuel system and disconnect the fuel feed and return hoses from the throttle body/fuel rail. Disconnect the accelerator cable from the throttle housing.

20 Remove the expansion tank mounting bolts and position the tank clear of the engine unit.

21 Remove the alternator.

22 On models equipped with power-assisted steering, remove the power steering pump.

23 On models equipped with air conditioning, slacken and remove the two compressor heatshield retaining bolts then remove the heatshield and disconnect the compressor wiring connector. Undo the four bolts securing the compressor to the mounting bracket and the single bolt securing the air conditioning pipe to the mounting bracket. Position the compressor clear of the engine unit. Secure it to the body to avoid placing any strain on the air conditioning pipes and hoses

24 Disconnect the exhaust system front pipe from the manifold and, where necessary, disconnect the lambda sensor wiring connector.

25 Slacken and remove the bolt and washer securing the anti-roll bar connecting link to the left-hand lower suspension arm, then the two bolts securing the tie bar to the lower suspension arm.

26 Extract the split pins and undo the nuts securing the steering gear track rod end balljoint and the left-hand lower suspension arm balljoint to the swivel hub. Remove the nuts and release the balljoint tapered shanks using a universal balljoint separator.

27 Insert a suitable flat bar in between the left-hand inner constant velocity joint and gearbox housing, then carefully lever the joint out of position, whilst taking great care not to damage the gearbox housing.

28 Withdraw the left-hand inner constant velocity joint from the gearbox and support the driveshaft to avoid damaging the constant velocity joints or gaiters. Repeat the operations described in paragraphs 25 to 28 for the right-hand driveshaft.

29 On K8 engines, the cylinder head has a tapped hole provided at the right-hand rear end (above the dipstick tube) and at the left-hand front end (behind the spark plug lead clips). On K16 engine cylinder heads, the right-hand end hole is in the same place but at the left-hand end, the air intake duct support bracket mounting points must be used. Attach lifting brackets to the engine at these points **(see illustrations)**. Take the weight of the engine/gearbox unit on the engine hoist.

30 From underneath the vehicle, unscrew the two bolts securing the rear engine/gearbox mounting bracket to the gearbox, then slacken the connecting link-to-body through-bolt and pivot the mounting away from the gearbox.

31 Slacken and remove the two bolts securing the left-hand gearbox bracket to the mounting. Lower the gearbox slightly then undo the four bolts securing the mounting to the body and manoeuvre the mounting out of position.

32 Raise the gearbox again then slacken and remove the right-hand engine/gearbox mounting through-bolt and nut. Unscrew the two nuts securing the mounting to the engine bracket and remove it, noting the rubber washers which are fitted on each side of the bracket.

33 Make a final check that all components have been removed or disconnected that will prevent removal of the engine/gearbox unit from the vehicle and ensure that components such as the gearchange linkage link rods are secured so that they cannot be damaged on removal.

34 Lift the engine/gearbox unit out of the vehicle, ensuring that nothing is trapped or damaged. Once the unit is high enough, lift it

2B

4.29a Right-hand engine lifting bracket ...

4.29b ... and left-hand engine lifting bracket - K16 engine

out over the front of the body and lower the unit to the ground **(see illustration)**.

35 To separate the engine and gearbox, first remove the starter motor.

36 Unbolt the flywheel front, lower and rear cover plates, then unscrew the four bolts securing the gearbox to the engine and gently prise the gearbox off the two locating dowels (at the front and rear of the main bearing ladder). Move the gearbox squarely away from the engine, ensuring that the clutch components are not damaged.

37 If the engine is to be overhauled, remove the clutch.

Refitting

38 Refitting is the reverse of removal, following where necessary the instructions given in the other Chapters of this Manual. Note the following additional points:

a) *Overhaul and lubricate the clutch components before refitting.*

b) *When the gearbox, starter motor and flywheel cover plates have been refitted, lift the engine/gearbox unit and lower it into the engine compartment so that it is slightly tilted (gearbox down). Engage both driveshafts then return the unit to the horizontal and refit the engine/gearbox mountings.*

c) *Remove the lifting brackets and refit any components removed to enable them to be fitted.*

d) *Tighten all nuts and bolts to the specified torque wrench settings.*

e) *Adjust the choke and/or accelerator cable(s).*

f) *Refill the engine and gearbox with oil.*

g) *Refill the cooling system.*

5 Engine overhaul - dismantling sequence

Note: *When removing external components from the engine, pay close attention to details that may be helpful or important during refitting. Note the fitted position of gaskets, seals, spacers, pins, washers, bolts and other small items.*

1 It is much easier to work on the engine if it is mounted on a portable engine stand. These stands can often be hired from a tool hire shop. Before the engine is mounted on a stand, the flywheel should be removed so that the stand bolts can be tightened into the end of the cylinder block/crankcase (not the main bearing ladder).

2 If a stand is not available, it is possible to dismantle the engine with it blocked up on a sturdy workbench or on the floor. Be extra careful not to tip or drop the engine when working without a stand.

3 If you are going to obtain a reconditioned engine, all external components must be removed for transference to the replacement engine (just as if you are doing a complete

4.34 Lifting out engine/gearbox unit

engine overhaul yourself). These components include the following:

a) *Alternator mounting brackets.*

b) *Power steering pump and air conditioning compressor brackets (where fitted).*

c) *Distributor, HT leads and spark plugs.*

d) *Thermostat and housing, coolant rail, coolant outlet elbow.*

e) *Dipstick tube.*

f) *Carburettor/fuel injection system components.*

g) *All electrical switches and sensors.*

h) *Inlet and exhaust manifolds.*

i) *Oil filter.*

j) *Fuel pump.*

k) *Engine mountings.*

l) *Flywheel.*

4 If you are obtaining a short motor (which consists of the engine cylinder block/crankcase and main bearing ladder, crankshaft, pistons and connecting rods all assembled), then the cylinder head, sump, oil pump, and timing belt will have to be removed also.

5 If you are planning a complete overhaul, the engine can be dismantled and the internal components removed in the following order:

a) *Inlet and exhaust manifolds.*

b) *Timing belt, sprockets, tensioner and timing belt inner cover.*

c) *Cylinder head.*

d) *Flywheel.*

e) *Sump.*

f) *Oil pump.*

g) *Piston/connecting rod assemblies.*

h) *Crankshaft.*

6.3a Using a valve spring compressor to release split collets

6 Before beginning the dismantling and overhaul procedures, make sure that you have all of the correct tools necessary. Refer to the introductory pages at the beginning of this Manual for further information.

6 Cylinder head - dismantling

Note: *New and reconditioned cylinder heads are available from the manufacturer and from engine overhaul specialists. Due to the fact that some specialist tools are required for dismantling and inspection, and new components may not be readily available, it may be more practical and economical for the home mechanic to purchase a reconditioned head rather than dismantle, inspect and recondition the original.*

1 Remove the camshaft(s) and hydraulic tappets.

2 Remove the cylinder head.

3 Using a valve spring compressor, compress each valve spring in turn until the split collets can be removed. Release the compressor and lift off the spring retainer and spring, then use a pair of pliers to extract the spring bottom seat/stem seal **(see illustrations)**.

> **HAYNES HiNT** *If, when the valve spring compressor is screwed down, the spring retainer refuses to free and expose the split collets, gently tap the top of the tool directly over the retainer with a light hammer. This will free the retainer.*

4 Withdraw the valve through the combustion chamber.

5 It is essential that each valve is stored together with its collets, retainer and spring, and that all valves are kept in their correct sequence, unless they are so badly worn that they are to be renewed. If they are going to be kept and used again, place each valve assembly in a labelled polythene bag or

6.3b Extracting a valve spring bottom seat/stem seal

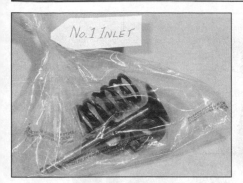

6.5 Use a labelled plastic bag to keep together and identify valve components

7.6a Checking a cylinder head gasket surface for warpage

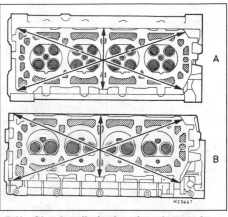

7.6b Check cylinder head gasket surface for warpage along paths shown

A K16 engine   B K8 engine

similar small container (see illustration). Note that No 1 valve is nearest to the timing belt end of the engine.

7 Cylinder head and valves - cleaning and inspection

Note: *If the engine has been severely overheated, it is best to assume that the cylinder head is warped and to check carefully for signs of this.*
Note: *Be sure to perform all the following inspection procedures before concluding that the services of a machine shop or engine overhaul specialist are required. Make a list of all items that require attention.*
1 Thorough cleaning of the cylinder head and valve components, followed by a detailed inspection, will enable you to decide how much valve service work must be carried out during the engine overhaul.

Cleaning
2 Scrape away all traces of old gasket material and sealing compound from the cylinder head.
3 Scrape away all carbon from the combustion chambers and ports, then wash the cylinder head thoroughly with paraffin or a suitable solvent.
4 Scrape off any heavy carbon deposits that may have formed on the valves, then use a power-operated wire brush to remove deposits from the valve heads and stems.

Inspection
Cylinder head
5 Inspect the head very carefully for cracks, evidence of coolant leakage and other damage. If cracks are found, a new cylinder head should be obtained.
6 Use a straight-edge and feeler gauge blade to check that the cylinder head surface is not distorted (see illustrations). If it is, it may be possible to resurface it, provided that the specified reface limit is not exceeded in so doing, or that the cylinder head is not reduced to less than the specified height.
7 Examine the valve seats in each of the combustion chambers. If they are severely

pitted, cracked or burned, then they will need to be renewed or re-cut by an engine overhaul specialist. If they are only slightly pitted, this can be removed by grinding-in the valve heads and seats with fine valve-grinding compound as described below. To check for excessive wear, refit each valve and measure the installed height of the stem tip above the cylinder head upper surface (see illustration). If the measurement is above the specified limit, repeat the test using a new valve. If the measurement is still excessive, renew the seat insert.
8 If the valve guides are worn, indicated by a side to side motion of the valve, new guides must be fitted. Measure the diameter of the existing valve stems (see below) and the bore of the guides, then calculate the clearance and compare the result with the specified value. If the clearance is excessive, renew the valves or guides as necessary.
9 Valve guide renewal is best carried out by an engine overhaul specialist. If the work is to be carried out at home, then use a stepped, double-diameter drift to drive out the worn guide towards the combustion chamber. On fitting the new guide, place it first in a deep-freeze for one hour, then drive it into the cylinder head bore from the camshaft side until it projects the specified amount above the spring bottom seat/stem seal surface.

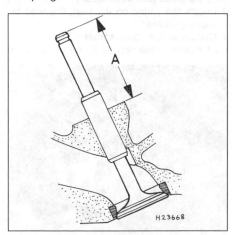

7.7 Check valve seat wear by measuring valve stem installed height (A)

10 If the valve seats are to be re-cut, this must be done only after the guides have been renewed.

Valves
11 Examine the head of each valve for pitting, burning, cracks and general wear, then check the valve stem for scoring and wear ridges. Rotate the valve and check for any obvious indication that it is bent. Look for pits and excessive wear on the tip of each valve stem. Renew any valve that shows any such signs of wear or damage.
12 If the valve appears satisfactory at this stage, measure the valve stem diameter at several points by using a micrometer (see illustration). Any significant difference in the readings obtained indicates wear of the valve stem. Should any of these conditions be apparent, the valve(s) must be renewed.
13 If the valves are in satisfactory condition they should be ground (lapped) into their respective seats to ensure a smooth gas-tight seal. If the seat is only lightly pitted, or if it has been re-cut, fine grinding compound only should be used to produce the required finish. Coarse valve-grinding compound should not be used unless a seat is badly burned or deeply pitted. If this is the case, the cylinder head and valves should be inspected by an expert to decide whether seat re-cutting or

2B

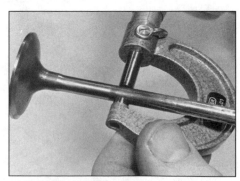

7.12 Measuring valve stem diameter

7.15 Grinding-in a valve seat

7.19 Measuring valve spring free length

even the renewal of the valve or seat insert is required.

14 Valve grinding is carried out as follows. Place the cylinder head upside down on a bench.

15 Smear a trace of (the appropriate grade of) valve-grinding compound on the seat face and press a suction grinding tool onto the valve head. With a semi-rotary action, grind the valve head to its seat, lifting the valve occasionally to redistribute the grinding compound **(see illustration)**. A light spring placed under the valve head will greatly ease this operation.

16 If coarse grinding compound is being used, work only until a dull, matt even surface is produced on both the valve seat and the valve, then wipe off the used compound and repeat the process with fine compound. When a smooth unbroken ring of light grey matt finish is produced on both the valve and seat, the grinding operation is complete. Do not grind in the valves any further than absolutely necessary, or the seat will be prematurely sunk into the cylinder head.

17 To check that the seat has not been over-ground, measure the valve stem installed height, as described in paragraph 7.

18 When all the valves have been ground-in, carefully wash off all traces of grinding compound using paraffin or a suitable solvent.

Valve components

19 Examine the valve springs for signs of

damage and discoloration and also measure their free length using vernier calipers or by comparing each existing spring with a new component **(see illustration)**.

20 Stand each spring on a flat surface and check it for squareness. If any of the springs are damaged, distorted or have lost their tension, then obtain a complete new set of springs.

21 Check the hydraulic tappets as described in Part A of this Chapter.

8 Cylinder head - reassembly

1 Lubricate the valve stems with clean engine oil and insert each valve into its original location. If new valves are being fitted, insert them into the locations to which they have been ground.

2 Working on the first valve, dip the spring bottom seat/stem seal in clean engine oil then carefully locate it over the valve and onto the guide. Take care not to damage the seal as it is passed over the valve stem. Use a suitable socket or metal tube to press the seal firmly onto the guide **(see illustration)**.

3 Locate the spring on the seat, followed by the spring retainer.

4 Compress the valve spring and locate the split collets in the recess in the valve stem.

Use a little grease to hold the collets in place. Release the compressor, then repeat the procedure on the remaining valves.

5 With all the valves installed, place the cylinder head flat on the bench and, using a hammer and interposed block of wood, tap the end of each valve stem to settle the components.

6 Refit the hydraulic tappets and camshaft(s) as described in Part A of this Chapter.

9 Piston/connecting rod assembly - removal

Note: *Due to the design of the engine, it will become very difficult, almost impossible, to turn the crankshaft once the cylinder head bolts have been slackened. The manufacturer accordingly states that the crankshaft will be 'tight' and should not be rotated more than absolutely necessary once the head has been removed. If the crankshaft cannot be rotated, then it must be removed for overhaul work to proceed. With this in mind, during any servicing or overhaul work the crankshaft must always be rotated to the desired position before the bolts are disturbed.*

Removal - without removing crankshaft

1 Remove the timing belt, the camshaft sprocket(s) and tensioner, and the timing belt inner cover.

2 Remove the camshaft(s) and hydraulic tappets, being careful to store the hydraulic tappets correctly.

3 If the flywheel has been removed, temporarily refit the crankshaft pulley and apply a spanner to the bolt to rotate the crankshaft.

4 Rotate the crankshaft until Nos 1 and 4 cylinder pistons are at the top of their stroke.

5 Remove the cylinder head. The crankshaft cannot now be rotated.

6 Slacken and remove the two dipstick tube retaining bolts and remove the tube from the cylinder block/crankcase **(see illustrations)**.

8.2 Using a socket to install valve stem seal

9.6a Dipstick tube mounting bolts (arrowed)

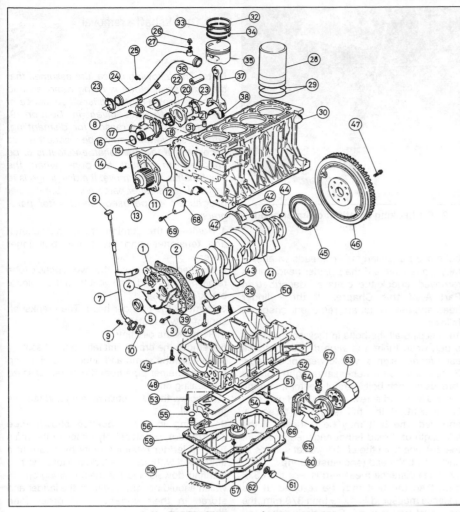

9.6b Engine bottom end components

1 Oil pump	27 Sealing washer	51 Stud
2 Gasket	28 Liner	52 Oil rail
3 Bolt	29 O-rings	53 Bolt
4 Bolt	30 Cylinder block/crankcase	54 Nut
5 Oil seal	31 Dowel	55 O-ring
6 Engine oil level dipstick	32 Top compression ring	56 Oil pump pick-up/
7 Dipstick tube	33 Second compression	strainer pipe
8 Bolt	ring	57 Bolt
9 Bolt	34 Oil control ring	58 Sump
10 Gasket	35 Piston	59 Gasket
11 Coolant pump	36 Gudgeon pin *	60 Bolt
12 O-ring	37 Connecting rod	61 Engine oil drain plug
13 Pillar bolt	38 Big-end bearing shell	62 Sealing washer
14 Bolt	39 Big-end bearing cap	63 Oil filter
15 Dowel pin	40 Big-end bearing cap bolt	64 Oil filter adaptor
16 O-ring	41 Crankshaft	65 Bolt
17 Thermostat housing	42 Crankshaft thrustwasher	66 Gasket
18 Gasket	43 Crankshaft main bearing	67 Oil pressure switch
19 Thermostat	shell	68 Blanking plate -
20 Thermostat housing	44 Dowel	carburettor engines
21 Bolt	45 Oil seal	69 Screw
22 Coolant hose	46 Flywheel (with reluctor	
23 Hose clip	ring)	*Note: Main bearing ladder is
24 Coolant rail	47 Flywheel bolt	supplied only with cylinder
25 Screw	48 Main bearing ladder *	block/crankcase assembly.
26 Cooling system bleed	49 Bolt	Gudgeon pin is supplied only
screw	50 Dowel	with piston assembly

7 Remove the sump and unbolt the oil pump pick-up/strainer pipe from the oil rail. Discard the sealing ring (**see illustration**).

8 Unscrew the two retaining nuts and remove the oil rail (**see illustration**).

9 Using a hammer and centre punch, paint or similar, mark each connecting rod big-end bearing cap with its respective cylinder number on the flat, machined surface provided. If the engine has been dismantled before, note carefully any identifying marks made previously (**see illustration**). Note that No 1 cylinder is at the timing belt end of the engine.

10 Unscrew and remove the big-end bearing cap bolts and withdraw the cap, complete with bearing shell, from the connecting rod. If only the bearing shells are being attended to,

9.7 Removing oil pump pick-up/strainer pipe from oil rail - renew O-ring (arrowed)

9.8 Removing oil rail to reach big-end bearings

9.9 Mark big-end bearing caps before removal - No 4 cylinder cap shown

2B

push the connecting rod up and off the crankpin, ensuring that the connecting rod big-ends do not mark the cylinder bore walls, then remove the upper bearing shell. Keep the cap, bolts and (if they are to be refitted) the bearing shells together in their correct sequence.

11 With Nos 2 and 3 cylinder big-ends disconnected, repeat the procedure (exercising great care to prevent damage to any of the components) to remove Nos 1 and 4 cylinder bearing caps.

12 Remove the ridge of carbon from the top of each cylinder bore. Push each piston/connecting rod assembly up and remove it from the top of the bore, and ensure that the connecting rod big-ends do not mark the cylinder bore walls.

13 Note that the number stamped by you on each bearing cap should match the cylinder number stamped on the front (alternator bracket side) of each connecting rod. If any connecting rod number does not match its correct cylinder, mark or label it immediately so that each piston/connecting rod assembly can be refitted to its original bore.

HAYNES HINT *Fit the bearing cap, shells and bolts to each removed piston/connecting rod assembly, so that they are all kept together as a matched set.*

Removal - alternative methods

14 If the engine is being completely dismantled and the cylinder head has been removed, either unbolt the main bearing ladder so that the crankshaft can be rotated with care, or remove the crankshaft completely and then remove the connecting rods and pistons.

Cylinder head bolts - condition check

15 Check the condition of the cylinder head

9.16 Checking length of cylinder head bolts

bolts and particularly their threads whenever they are removed. If the cylinder head only is removed, check the bolts as described in Part A of this Chapter. If the cylinder head and the oil rail are removed, check as follows.

16 Keeping all the bolts in their correct fitted order, wash them and wipe dry, then check each for any sign of visible wear or damage. Renew any bolt if necessary. Lightly oil the threads of each bolt, carefully enter it into the original hole and screw it in, by hand only until finger-tight. If the full length of thread is engaged, the bolt may be re-used. If the full length of thread is not engaged, measure the distance from the oil rail gasket surface to under the bolt head **(see illustration)**.

17 If the distance measured is less than 378 mm, then the bolt may be re-used. If the distance measured is more than 378 mm, the bolt must be renewed. Considering the task these bolts perform and the pressures they must withstand, owners should consider renewing all the bolts as a matched set if more than one of the originals fail inspection or are close to the limit set.

18 Note that if any of the cylinder head bolt threads in the oil rail are found to be damaged, then the oil rail must be renewed. Thread inserts are not an acceptable repair in this instance.

10 Crankshaft - removal

Note: *The following procedure assumes that the crankshaft alone is being removed and therefore uses a slightly different sequence of operations to that given in Section 9. Depending on the reason for dismantling, either sequence may be adapted as necessary. If the crankshaft endfloat is to be checked, this must be done when the crankshaft is free to move. If a dial gauge is to be used, check after paragraph 1, but if feeler gauges are to be used, check after paragraph 9.*

1 Remove the timing belt, sprocket(s) and tensioner, and the timing belt inner cover.

2 Slacken and remove the two dipstick tube retaining bolts and remove it from the cylinder block/crankcase.

3 Remove the cylinder head. The crankshaft cannot now be rotated.

4 Remove the oil pump.

5 Remove the crankshaft left-hand oil seal.

6 Remove the sump and unbolt the oil pump pick-up/strainer pipe from the oil rail. Discard the sealing ring.

7 Unscrew the two retaining nuts and remove the oil rail.

8 Working in the sequence shown **(see illustration)**, progressively unscrew the main bearing ladder retaining bolts by a turn at a time, then withdraw the ladder. Note the two locating dowels and the main bearing shells, which should be removed from the ladder and stored in their correct fitted order **(see illustration)**.

9 Mark the big-end bearing caps, then unscrew and remove the big-end bearing cap bolts and withdraw the cap, complete with the lower bearing shell, from each of the four connecting rods **(see illustration)**. Push the connecting rods up and off their crankpins, then remove the upper bearing shell. Keep the cap, bolts and (if they are to be refitted) the bearing shells together in their correct sequence.

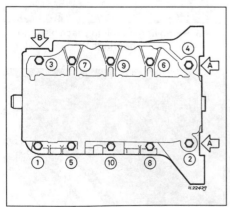

10.8a Crankshaft main bearing ladder bolt slackening sequence

A Bolts hidden in ladder flanges
B Location of single longer bolt

10.8b Removing main bearing ladder (two locating dowels arrowed)

10.9 Removing No 1 cylinder big-end bearing cap and lower bearing shell

10.10 Removing the crankshaft

10 Remove the crankshaft (see illustration).
11 Withdraw the two thrustwashers from the No 3 main bearing upper location. Noting the position of the grooved shells, remove the upper main bearing shells, which must be kept with their correct respective partners from the main bearing ladder so that all shells can be identified and (if necessary) refitted in their original locations.
12 Check the condition of the cylinder head bolts, as described in Section 9.

11 Cylinder block/crankcase - cleaning and inspection

Warning: Wear eye protection when using compressed air!

Note: *During any cleaning operations, take care not to score the mating surfaces of the cylinder block/crankcase, bearing ladder and oil rail. It may be necessary to use a foam action gasket remover.*

Cleaning

1 For complete cleaning, remove the cylinder liners, all external components and all electrical switches/sensors.
2 Scrape all traces of gasket from the cylinder block/crankcase, bearing ladder and oil rail, taking care not to damage the gasket/sealing surfaces.
3 Remove all oil gallery plugs (where fitted). The plugs are usually very tight and may have to be drilled out and the holes re-tapped. Use new plugs when the engine is reassembled.
4 If any of the castings are extremely dirty, all should be steam cleaned.
5 After the castings are returned, clean all oil holes and oil galleries one more time. Flush all internal passages with warm water until the water runs clear, then dry thoroughly and apply a light film of oil to all liner surfaces to prevent rusting. If you have access to compressed air, use it to speed up the drying process and to blow out all the oil holes and galleries.
6 If the castings are not very dirty, you can do an adequate cleaning job with hot soapy water and a stiff brush. Take plenty of time

and do a thorough job. Regardless of the cleaning method used, be sure to clean all oil holes and galleries very thoroughly and to dry all components well. Protect the liners as described above to prevent rusting.
7 All threaded holes must be clean to ensure accurate torque readings during reassembly. To clean all threads **except** those of the flywheel retaining bolts, run the proper size tap into each of the holes to remove rust, corrosion, thread sealant or sludge and to restore damaged threads. If possible, use compressed air to clear the holes of debris produced by this operation. A good alternative is to inject aerosol-applied water-dispersant lubricant into each hole, using the long spout usually supplied. Always wear eye protection when cleaning out holes in this way. The flywheel retaining bolt threads must be cleaned by using the procedure described in Section 18, in Part A of this Chapter. Now is a good time to check the condition of the cylinder head bolts.
8 Apply suitable sealant to the new oil gallery plugs and insert them into the holes in the block. Tighten them securely.
9 If the engine is not going to be reassembled right away, cover it with a large plastic bag to keep it clean. Protect the liners as described above to prevent rusting.

Inspection

10 Inspect all castings for cracks and corrosion. Look for stripped threads. If there has been any history of internal coolant leakage, it may be worthwhile having an engine overhaul specialist check the cylinder block/crankcase with special equipment. If defects are found, have them repaired, if possible, or renew the assembly.
11 Check the bore of each cylinder liner for scuffing and scoring.
12 Measure the diameter of each cylinder liner bore 60 mm from the top of the bore, both parallel to the crankshaft axis and at right angles to it.
13 Compare the diameter with that specified. If any measurement exceeds the service limit then the liner must be renewed.
14 Measure the piston diameter at right angles to the gudgeon pin axis, 16 mm up from the bottom of the skirt. Compare the results with those specified.
15 To measure the piston-to-bore clearance, either measure the bore and piston skirt as described above and subtract the skirt diameter from the bore measurement, or insert each piston into the original bore, select a feeler gauge and slip it into the bore along with the piston. The piston must be aligned exactly in its normal attitude and the feeler gauge must be between the piston and bore on one of the thrust faces, 20 mm up from the bottom of the bore.
16 If the clearance is excessive, then a new piston will be required. If the piston binds at the lower end of the bore and is loose towards the top, then the bore is tapered. If

tight spots are encountered as the piston/feeler gauge is rotated in the bore, then the bore is out-of-round.
17 Repeat this procedure for the remaining pistons and cylinder liners.
18 If the cylinder liner walls are badly scuffed or scored, or if they are excessively worn, out-of-round or tapered, obtain new cylinder liners. New pistons will also be required.
19 If the bores are in reasonably good condition and not worn to the specified limits, and if the piston-to-bore clearances can be maintained properly, then it may only be necessary to renew the piston rings.
20 If this is the case, the bores should be honed to allow the new rings to bed in correctly and provide the best possible seal. The conventional type of hone has spring-loaded stones and is used with a power drill. You will also need some paraffin, or honing oil, and rags. The hone should be moved up and down the bore to produce a crosshatch pattern and plenty of honing oil should be used. Ideally the crosshatch lines should intersect at approximately a 60° angle. Do not take off more material than is necessary to produce the required finish. If new pistons are being fitted, the piston manufacturers may specify a finish with a different angle, so their instructions should be followed. Do not withdraw the hone from the bore while it is still being turned, but stop it first. After honing a bore, wipe out all traces of the honing oil. If equipment of this type is not available, or if you are not sure whether you are competent to undertake the task yourself, an engine overhaul specialist will carry out the work at moderate cost.

12 Cylinder liners - removal and refitting

Removal

1 Invert the cylinder block/crankcase and support it on blocks of wood, then use a hard wood drift to tap out each liner from the crankshaft side. When all the liners are released, tip the cylinder block/crankcase on its side and remove each liner from the cylinder head side. Discard the two sealing rings from the base of each. If the liners are to be re-used, mark each one by sticking masking tape on its right-hand (timing belt) face and writing the cylinder number on the tape.

Refitting

2 To install the liners, thoroughly clean the liner mating surfaces in the cylinder block/crankcase and use fine abrasive paper to polish away any burrs or sharp edges which might damage the liner sealing rings. Clean the liners and wipe dry, then fit new sealing rings to the two grooves at the base of each liner and apply a thin film of oil to the

2B

12.2 Renew liner O-rings

12.3 Tap liner onto locating shoulder - ensuring O-rings are not displaced

13.1 Measuring piston diameter

rings and to the liner surface on each side of the rings **(see illustration)**.

3 If the original liners are being refitted, use the marks made on removal to ensure that each is refitted the same way round into its original bore. Insert each liner into the cylinder block/crankcase, taking great care not to displace or damage the sealing rings, and press it home as far as possible by hand. Using a hammer and a block of wood, tap each liner lightly but fully onto its locating shoulder **(see illustration)**. Wipe clean, then lightly oil all exposed liner surfaces to prevent rusting.

13 Piston/connecting rod assembly - inspection

1 Examine all pistons for ovality, scoring and scratches, and for wear of the piston ring grooves. Use a micrometer to measure the pistons **(see illustration)**.

2 If the pistons or connecting rods are to be renewed, it is necessary to have this work carried out by a Rover dealer or suitable engine overhaul specialist who will have the necessary tooling to remove and install the gudgeon pins.

3 If new rings are to be fitted to the original pistons, expand the old rings over the top of the pistons. The use of two or three old feeler gauge blades will be helpful in preventing the

rings dropping into empty grooves **(see illustration)**.

4 When the original piston rings have been removed, ensure that the ring grooves in the piston are free of carbon by cleaning them with a ring cleaning tool or an old ring. Break a ring in half to do this.

5 When measuring new rings, lay out each piston set with a piston/connecting rod assembly and keep them together as a matched set from now on.

6 Check the ring-to-groove clearance by inserting each ring from the outside together with a feeler gauge blade between the ring's top surface and the piston land. Check the ring end gaps by inserting each ring into the cylinder bore and pushing it in with the piston crown to ensure that it is square in the bore, 20 mm from the top. Use feeler gauges to measure the gap **(see illustrations)**.

7 If the end gap of a new ring is found to be too large or too small, double-check to ensure that you have the correct rings. If the end gap is still too small, it must be opened up by careful filing of the ring ends using a fine file. If it is too large, this is not as serious unless the specified service limit is exceeded, in which case very careful checking is required of the dimensions of all components as well as of the new parts.

8 Note that each piston should be considered as being matched to its respective liner and they must not be interchanged.

14 Crankshaft - inspection

⚠️ *Warning: Wear eye protection when using compressed air! Be sure to clean oil holes with a pipe cleaner or similar probe.*

Checking endfloat

1 If crankshaft endfloat is to be checked, this must be done when the crankshaft is still installed in the cylinder block/crankcase but is free to move.

2 Check endfloat by using a dial gauge in contact with the end of the crankshaft. Push the crankshaft fully one way and then zero the gauge. Push the crankshaft fully the other way and check the endfloat. The result can be compared with the specified amount and will give an indication as to whether new thrustwashers are required.

3 If a dial gauge is not available, feeler gauges can be used. First push the crankshaft fully towards the flywheel end of the engine, then use feeler gauges to measure the gap between the web of No 3 crankpin and the thrustwasher.

Inspection

4 Clean the crankshaft and dry it with compressed air, if available.

5 Check the main and crankpin (big-end)

13.3 Removing piston rings with feeler blades

13.5a Measuring piston ring-to-groove clearance

13.5b Measuring piston ring end gap

14.6 Using a penny to check crankshaft journal condition

14.8 Measuring crankshaft journal diameter

bearing journals for uneven wear, scoring, pitting and cracking.

6 Rub a penny across each journal several times. If a journal picks up copper from the penny, it is too rough **(see illustration)**.

7 Remove any burrs from the crankshaft oil holes with a stone, file or scraper.

8 Using a micrometer, measure the diameter of the main bearing and crankpin (big-end) journals and compare the results with those specified **(see illustration)**. Check carefully that each journal's diameter is within the tolerances of the size grade corresponding to the code number on the crankshaft right-hand web (main bearing) or indicated by the code letter on the left-hand web (crankpin/big-end bearing). If any diameter measured is incorrect for the grade indicated, re-check the measurement carefully. If the journal is fit for further service, the correct grade code should be substituted when selecting new bearing shells.

9 By measuring the diameter at a number of points around each journal's circumference,

you will be able to determine whether or not the journal is out-of-round. Take the measurement at each end of the journal (near the webs) to determine if the journal is tapered.

10 If the crankshaft journals are damaged, tapered, out-of-round or worn beyond the limits specified, the crankshaft must be renewed unless an engine overhaul specialist can be found who will regrind it and supply the necessary undersize bearing shells.

11 Check the oil seal journals at each end of the crankshaft for wear and damage. If either seal has worn an excessive groove in its journal, consult an engine overhaul specialist who will be able to advise whether a repair is possible or whether a new crankshaft is necessary.

15 Main and big-end bearings - inspection

1 Even though the main and big-end bearings should be renewed during the engine overhaul, the old bearings should be retained for close examination, as they may reveal valuable information about the condition of the engine. The bearing shells are graded by thickness, the grade of each shell being indicated by the colour code marked on it.

2 Bearing failure occurs because of lack of lubrication, the presence of dirt or other foreign particles, overloading the engine and corrosion. Regardless of the cause of bearing failure, it must be corrected before the engine is reassembled to prevent it from happening again **(see illustration)**.

3 When examining the bearing shells, remove them from the cylinder block/crankcase, the main bearing ladder, the connecting rods and the connecting rod big-end bearing caps, then lay them out on a clean surface in the same general position as their location in the engine. This will enable you to match any bearing problems with the corresponding crankshaft journal. Do not touch any shell's

bearing surface with your fingers while checking it, or the delicate surface may be scratched.

4 Dirt and other foreign particles get into the engine in a variety of ways. It may be left in the engine during assembly, or it may pass through filters or the crankcase ventilation system. It may get into the oil and from there into the bearings. Metal chips from machining operations and normal engine wear are often present. Abrasives are sometimes left in engine components after reconditioning, especially when parts are not thoroughly cleaned by using the proper cleaning methods. Whatever the source, these foreign objects often end up embedded in the soft bearing material and are easily recognized. Large particles will not embed in the bearing but will score or gouge the bearing and journal. The best prevention for this cause of bearing failure is to clean all parts thoroughly and keep everything spotlessly clean during engine assembly. Frequent and regular engine oil and filter changes are also recommended.

5 Lack of lubrication (or lubrication breakdown) has a number of interrelated causes. Excessive heat (which thins the oil), overloading (which squeezes the oil from the bearing face) and oil leakage (from excessive bearing clearances, worn oil pump or high engine speeds) all contribute to lubrication breakdown. Blocked oil passages, which usually are the result of misaligned oil holes in a bearing shell, will also oil starve a bearing and destroy it. When lack of lubrication is the cause of bearing failure, the bearing material is wiped or extruded from the steel backing of the bearing. Temperatures may increase to the point where the steel backing turns blue from overheating.

6 Driving habits can have a definite effect on bearing life. Full throttle, low speed operation (labouring the engine) puts very high loads on bearings, which tends to squeeze out the oil film. These loads cause the bearings to flex, which produces fine cracks in the bearing face (fatigue failure). Eventually, the bearing material will loosen in pieces and tear away from the steel backing. Short-distance driving leads to corrosion of bearings because insufficient engine heat is produced to drive off the condensed water and corrosive gases. These products collect in the engine oil, forming acid and sludge. As the oil is carried to the engine bearings, the acid attacks and corrodes the bearing material.

7 Incorrect bearing installation during engine assembly will lead to bearing failure as well. Tight fitting bearings leave insufficient bearing running clearance and will result in oil starvation. Dirt or foreign particles trapped behind a bearing shell result in high spots on the bearing which lead to failure. Do not touch any shell's bearing surface with your fingers during reassembly as there is a risk of scratching the delicate surface or of depositing particles of dirt on it.

2B

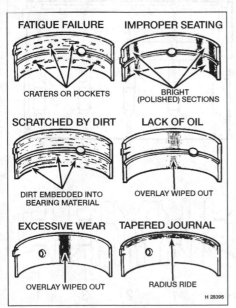

FATIGUE FAILURE

IMPROPER SEATING

CRATERS OR POCKETS

BRIGHT (POLISHED) SECTIONS

SCRATCHED BY DIRT

LACK OF OIL

DIRT EMBEDDED INTO BEARING MATERIAL

OVERLAY WIPED OUT

EXCESSIVE WEAR

TAPERED JOURNAL

OVERLAY WIPED OUT

RADIUS RIDE

H 28395

15.2 Typical bearing shell failures

16 Engine overhaul - reassembly sequence

1 Before reassembly begins, ensure that all new parts have been obtained and that all necessary tools are available. Read through the entire procedure to familiarise yourself with the work involved and to ensure that all items necessary for reassembly of the engine are at hand. In addition to all normal tools and materials, it will be necessary to obtain the Rover sealant kit LVV 10002. Carefully read the instructions supplied with the sealant kit and take care not to allow the sealant to contact the fingers, as it will bond skin.

2 In order to save time and avoid problems, engine reassembly can be carried out in the following order:
a) *Crankshaft.*
b) *Piston/connecting rod assemblies.*
c) *Oil pump.*
d) *Sump.*
e) *Flywheel.*
f) *Cylinder head.*
g) *Timing belt inner cover, tensioner and sprockets, and timing belt.*
h) *Engine external components.*

3 At this stage, all engine components should be absolutely clean and dry, with all faults

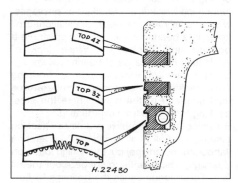

17.3 Piston ring fitting details and top surface markings

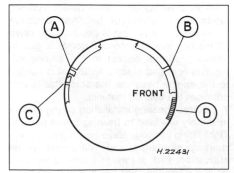

17.4 Piston ring end gap locations

A *Top compression ring*
B *Second compression ring*
C *Oil control ring*
D *Oil control ring spring*

repaired, and should be laid out (or in individual containers) on a completely clean work surface.

17 Piston rings - refitting

1 Refer to Section 13 for inspection details.
2 Once all rings have been checked, they can be installed. Ensure that each ring is refitted only to its matched piston and bore.
3 Install the new rings by fitting them over the top of the piston, starting with the oil control ring spring. Note that all rings must be fitted with the word TOP uppermost **(see illustration)**.
4 With all the rings in position, space the ring gaps as shown **(see illustration)**, noting that the FRONT marking shown is usually in fact an arrow mark on the piston crown and indicates the timing belt end of the engine.

18 Crankshaft - refitting and main bearing running clearance check

Selection of bearing shells

1 The main bearing running clearance is controlled in production by selecting one of three grades of bearing shell. The grades are indicated by a colour-coding marked on the edge of each shell which governs the shell's thickness, as follows:
a) *Green - Thin.*
b) *Blue - Intermediate.*
c) *Red - Thick.*

2 If shells of differing grades are to be fitted to the same journal, the thicker shell must always be fitted to the main bearing ladder location. Bear this carefully in mind when ordering replacement shells for Nos 2, 3 and 4 bearings.
3 If the bearing shells are to be renewed, first check and record the main bearing code letters stamped on the right-hand front face of the main bearing ladder **(see illustration)**. The letters are read with the ladder inverted, No 1 bearing's code letter then being at the top and the remainder following in order from the engine's timing belt end.
4 Secondly, check and record the crankshaft journal code numbers stamped on the crankshaft's right-hand web, No 1 journal's code number being the first. If the original crankshaft is to be re-used, the size grade can be checked by direct measurement, as described in Section 14.
5 Note that if the crankshaft is found to be excessively worn, then it must be renewed and the code numbers of the new component must be used instead to select a new set of bearing shells.
6 Matching the codes noted to the following table, select a new set of bearing shells.

Ladder code letter	Crankshaft code number	Shells
A	1	Blue, Blue
A	2	Red, Blue
A	3	Red, Red
B	1	Blue, Green
B	2	Blue, Blue
B	3	Red, Blue
C	1	Green, Green
C	2	Blue, Green
C	3	Blue, Blue

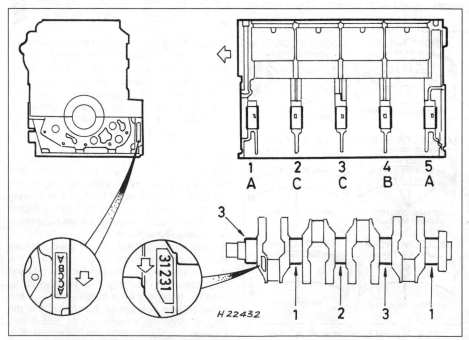

18.3 Crankshaft main bearing size code locations

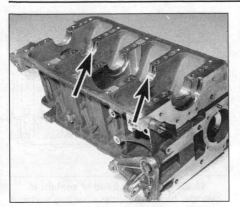

18.9 Ensure grooved bearing shells (arrowed) are installed exactly as described in text - early engine shown

18.14 Lay length of Plastigauge on journal to be measured, parallel to crankshaft centre-line

18.18 Using scale on Plastigauge envelope to check (at widest point) width of crushed Plastigauge

Main bearing running clearance check

7 Clean the backs of the bearing shells and the bearing locations in both the cylinder block/crankcase and the main bearing ladder.

8 Press the bearing shells into their locations, ensuring that the tab on each shell engages in the notch in the cylinder block/crankcase or main bearing ladder location. Take care not to touch any shell bearing surface with your fingers.

9 Press the bearing shells with the oil grooves into the upper locations (in the cylinder block/crankcase). Note the following points **(see illustration)**:

a) *On all engines, grooved bearing shells are fitted to Nos 2, 3 and 4 upper bearing locations. Note the central locating tabs of the grooved shells.*

b) *On early engines, grooved bearing shells were fitted only to Nos 2 and 4 upper bearing locations at the factory. On reassembly of one of these units, a grooved shell must be fitted at No 3 upper bearing location as well, instead of the plain item originally used. Note, however, that this will require a grooved shell with an offset locating tab instead of the central tab that is used on all other grooved shells. See your Rover dealer for details.*

c) *If bearing shells of differing grades are to be fitted to the same journal, the thicker shell must always be fitted to the main bearing ladder location (see paragraph 1).*

d) *On all engines, if the original main bearing shells are being re-used, these must be refitted to their original locations in the cylinder block/crankcase and main bearing ladder.*

10 The main bearing running clearance should be checked if there is any doubt about the amount of crankshaft wear that has taken place, if the crankshaft has been reground and is to be refitted with non-Rover undersized bearing shells, or if non-genuine

bearing shells are to be fitted. If the original crankshaft or a Rover replacement part is to be installed, the shell selection procedure given above will produce the correct clearances and a further check will not be necessary. If the clearance is to be checked, it can be done in either of two ways.

11 The first method (which will be difficult to achieve without a range of internal micrometers or internal/external expanding calipers) is to refit the main bearing ladder to the cylinder block/crankcase, with bearing shells in place. With the ladder retaining bolts tightened to the specified torque, refit the oil rail and the cylinder head, then measure the internal diameter of each assembled pair of bearing shells. If the diameter of each corresponding crankshaft journal is measured and then subtracted from the bearing internal diameter, the result will be the main bearing running clearance.

12 The second (and more accurate) method is to use product known as Plastigauge. This consists of a fine thread of perfectly round plastic which is compressed between the bearing shell and the journal. When the shell is removed, the plastic is deformed and can be measured with a special card gauge supplied with the kit. The running clearance is determined from this gauge. Plastigauge is sometimes difficult to obtain but enquiries at one of the larger specialist quality motor factors should produce the name of a stockist in your area. The procedure for using Plastigauge is as follows.

13 With the main bearing upper shells in place, carefully lay the crankshaft in position. Do not use any lubricant. The crankshaft journals and bearing shells must be perfectly clean and dry.

14 Cut several lengths of the appropriate size Plastigauge (they should be slightly shorter than the width of the main bearings) and place one length on each crankshaft journal axis **(see illustration)**.

15 With the main bearing lower shells in position, refit the main bearing ladder (see below) and the oil rail, tightening the fasteners

to the specified torque wrench settings. Take care not to disturb the Plastigauge.

16 Refit the cylinder head (using the original gasket, to save over-compressing the new one). Tighten the bolts to the specified torque in the approved sequence. **Do not** rotate the crankshaft at any time during this operation.

17 Remove the cylinder head, the oil rail and the main bearing ladder. Do not disturb the Plastigauge or rotate the crankshaft.

18 Compare the width of the crushed Plastigauge on each journal to the scale printed on the Plastigauge envelope to obtain the main bearing running clearance **(see illustration)**.

19 If the clearance is not as specified, the bearing shells may be the wrong grade (or excessively worn if the original shells are being re-used). Before deciding that different grade shells are needed, make sure that no dirt or oil was trapped between the bearing shells and the ladder or cylinder block/crankcase when the clearance was measured. If the Plastigauge was wider at one end than at the other, the journal may be tapered.

20 Carefully scrape away all traces of the Plastigauge material from the crankshaft and bearing shells using a fingernail or other object which is unlikely to score the shells.

Final crankshaft refitting

21 Carefully lift the crankshaft out of the cylinder block once more.

22 Using a little grease, stick the thrustwashers to each side of the No 3 main bearing upper location. Ensure that the oilway grooves on each thrustwasher face outwards.

23 Place the bearing shells in their locations, as described in paragraphs 7 to 9. If new shells are being fitted, ensure that all traces of the protective grease are cleaned off using paraffin. Wipe dry the shells and connecting rods with a lint-free cloth. Liberally lubricate each bearing shell in the cylinder block/crankcase, then lower the crankshaft into position so that Nos 2 and 3 cylinder crankpins are at TDC.

24 Refit the piston/connecting rod

2B

18.24a If piston/connecting rod assemblies are refitted before main bearing ladder . . .

18.24b . . . care is required to hold crankshaft steady while connecting rod big-end cap bolts are tightened

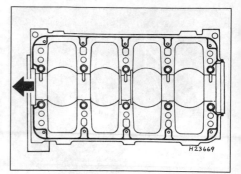

18.25 Apply thin bead of sealant to cylinder block/crankcase mating surface along paths shown by heavy black lines, then spread to an even film

assemblies **(see illustrations)**. Leave No 1 and 4 cylinders at the TDC position

25 Thoroughly degrease the mating surfaces of the cylinder block/crankcase and the main bearing ladder. Apply the special Rover sealant to the mating surface of the cylinder block/crankcase as shown **(see illustration)**. Carefully follow the instructions supplied with the sealant kit. If the Rover sealant is being used, assembly must be completed as soon as possible after the sealant has been applied (maximum of 20 minutes). If another sealant is being used, follow the manufacturer's instructions.

26 Lubricate the bearing shells, then refit the main bearing ladder, ensuring that the shells are not displaced and that the locating dowels engage correctly. Working progressively, by a turn at a time and in the sequence shown **(see illustration)**, tighten the ladder bolts to the specified torque wrench setting. The crankshaft cannot now be rotated.

27 Thoroughly degrease the mating surfaces of the oil rail and the main bearing ladder. Apply the special Rover sealant to the oil rail mating surface as shown **(see illustration)**. Carefully follow the instructions supplied with the sealant kit.

28 Refit the oil rail, tightening the nuts to the specified torque wrench setting.

29 Using a new sealing ring, refit the oil pump pick-up/strainer pipe to the oil rail, then refit the sump. Tighten all nuts and bolts to the specified torque wrench settings.

30 Fit a new crankshaft left-hand oil seal, then refit the flywheel **(see illustrations)**.

31 Refit the oil pump and install a new crankshaft right-hand oil seal **(see illustrations)**.

32 Refit the cylinder head. Rotate the crankshaft to the 90° BTDC position so that the crankshaft sprocket timing marks align.

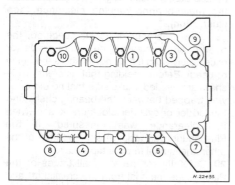

18.26 Crankshaft main bearing ladder bolt tightening sequence

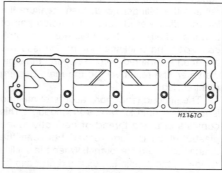

18.27 Apply thin bead of sealant to oil rail mating surface as shown by heavy black lines, then spread to an even film

18.30a Fitting a new crankshaft left-hand oil seal

18.30b Always use new bolts when refitting flywheel

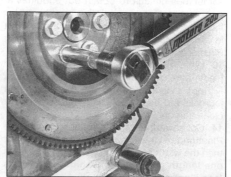

18.30c Use fabricated tool to lock flywheel while slackening or tightening flywheel bolts

18.31a Use grease to stick new gasket in place when refitting oil pump

18.31b Fitting a new crankshaft right-hand oil seal

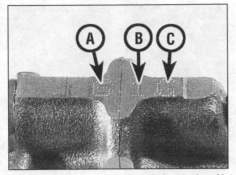

19.3 Big-end bearing size code number (A - on cap) piston/connecting rod assembly cylinder number (B) and connecting rod weight code letter (C)

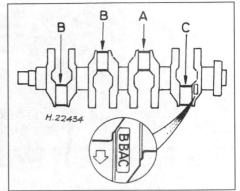

19.4 Crankpin (big-end) journal size code location

33 Refit the dipstick tube to the cylinder block/crankcase, tightening the bolts to the specified torque wrench setting.

34 Refit the timing belt inner cover, the sprocket(s) and tensioner, and the belt itself.

35 Using a torque wrench, check that the amount of force required to rotate the crankshaft does not exceed 31 Nm. If the effort required is greater than this, the engine must be dismantled again to trace and rectify the cause. This value takes into account the increased friction of a new engine and is much higher than the actual pressure required to rotate a run-in engine, so do not make allowances for tight components.

19 Piston/connecting rod assembly - refitting and big-end bearing running clearance check

Selection of bearing shells

1 The big-end bearing running clearance is controlled in production by selecting one of three grades of bearing shell. The grades are indicated by a colour-coding marked on the edge of each shell which governs the shell's thickness, as follows:
a) Yellow - Thin.
b) Blue - Intermediate.
c) Red - Thick.

2 If shells of differing grades are to be fitted to the same journal, the thicker shell must always be fitted to the big-end bearing cap location.

3 If the bearing shells are to be renewed, first check and record the codes stamped on the front face of each big-end bearing cap and connecting rod. The number stamped on the big-end bearing cap is the bearing size code, the number stamped on the connecting rod is the piston/rod assembly's cylinder number and the letter stamped on the connecting rod is the weight code **(see illustration)**.

4 Secondly, check and record the crankpin/big-end journal code letters stamped on the crankshaft's left-hand web **(see illustration)**, No 1 journal's code letter

being the first. If the original crankshaft is to be re-used, the code letter can be checked by direct measurement.

5 If the crankshaft is found to be excessively worn, then it must be renewed and the code letters of the new component must be used instead to select a new set of bearing shells.

6 Matching the codes noted to the following table, select a new set of bearing shells:

Cap code number	Crankshaft code letter	Shells
5	A	Blue, Blue
5	B	Red, Blue
5	C	Red, Red
6	A	Blue, Yellow
6	B	Blue, Blue
6	C	Red, Blue
7	A	Yellow, Yellow
7	B	Blue, Yellow
7	C	Blue, Blue

Big-end bearing running clearance check

7 The big-end bearing running clearance should be checked if there is any doubt about the amount of crankshaft wear that has taken place, if the crankshaft has been reground and is to be refitted with non-Rover undersized bearing shells, or if non-genuine bearing shells are to be fitted. If the original crankshaft or a Rover replacement part is to be installed, the shell selection procedure given above will produce the correct clearances and a further check will not be necessary. If the clearance is to be checked, it can be done in either of two ways.

8 The first method is to refit the big-end bearing cap to the connecting rod, with bearing shells in place. With the cap retaining bolts tightened to the specified torque, use an internal micrometer or vernier caliper to measure the internal diameter of each assembled pair of bearing shells. If the diameter of each corresponding crankshaft journal is measured and then subtracted from the bearing internal diameter, the result will be the big-end bearing running clearance.

9 The second method is to use Plastigauge. Place a strand of Plastigauge on each

(cleaned) crankpin journal and refit the (clean) piston/connecting rod assemblies, shells and big-end bearing caps, tightening the bolts to the specified torque wrench settings. Take care not to disturb the Plastigauge. Dismantle the assemblies without rotating the crankshaft and use the scale printed on the Plastigauge envelope to obtain the big-end bearing running clearance. On completion of the measurement, carefully scrape off all traces of Plastigauge from the journal and shells using a fingernail or other object which will not score the components.

Final piston/connecting rod assembly refitting

10 Note that the following procedure assumes that the cylinder liners have been refitted to the cylinder block/crankcase and that the crankshaft and main bearing ladder are in place. It is of course possible to refit the piston/connecting rod assemblies to the cylinder bores, to refit the crankshaft and to reassemble the piston/connecting rods on the crankshaft before refitting the main bearing ladder (see Section 18).

11 Clean the backs of the bearing shells and the bearing recesses in both the connecting rod and the big-end bearing cap. If new shells are being fitted, ensure that all traces of the protective grease are cleaned off using paraffin. Wipe dry the shells and connecting rods with a lint-free cloth.

12 Press the bearing shells into their locations, ensuring that the tab on each shell engages in the notch in the connecting rod or big-end bearing cap and taking care not to touch any shell's bearing surface with your fingers. Note the following points:
a) If bearing shells of differing grades are to be fitted to the same journal, the thicker shell must always be fitted to the big-end bearing cap location (see paragraph 1).
b) On all engines, if the original big-end bearing shells are being re-used, these must be refitted to their original locations in the connecting rod and big-end bearing cap.

2B

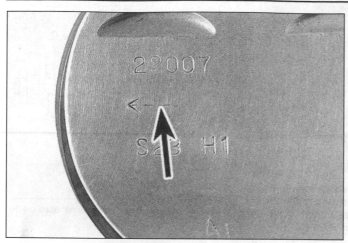

19.15a Arrow or FRONT marking (arrowed) on piston crown must point to timing belt end of engine

18.15b Using piston ring compressor to clamp piston rings

13 Lubricate the cylinder bores, the pistons and piston rings, then lay out each piston/connecting rod assembly in its respective position.

14 Starting with assembly No 1, make sure that the piston rings are still correctly spaced, then clamp them in position with a piston ring compressor.

15 Insert the piston/connecting rod assembly into the top of liner No 1, ensuring that the arrow (or FRONT marking) on the piston crown faces the timing belt end of the engine. Note that the stamped marks on the connecting rod and big-end bearing cap should face the front (alternator bracket side) of the engine. Using a block of wood or hammer handle against the piston crown, tap the assembly into the liner until the piston crown is flush with the top of the liner (see illustrations).

16 Ensure that the bearing shell is still correctly installed. Taking care not to mark the liner bores, liberally lubricate the crankpin and both bearing shells, then pull the piston/connecting rod assembly down the bore and onto the crankpin. Noting that the faces with the stamped marks must match (which means that the bearing shell locating tabs abut each other), refit the big-end bearing cap, tightening the bolts finger-tight at first.

17 Use a torque wrench to tighten the bolts evenly to the (first stage) torque wrench setting specified, then use an angular torque gauge to tighten the bolts evenly through the (second stage) angle specified (see illustrations).

18 Repeat the procedure for the remaining three piston/connecting rod assemblies, but do not attempt to rotate the crankshaft.

19 Thoroughly degrease the mating surfaces of the oil rail and the main bearing ladder. Apply the special Rover sealant to the oil rail mating surface (see illustration 18.27). Carefully follow the instructions supplied with the sealant kit.

20 Refit the oil rail, tightening the nuts to the specified torque wrench setting.

21 Refit the oil pump pick-up/strainer pipe and sump.

22 Refit the cylinder head. Rotate the crankshaft to the 90° BTDC position so that the crankshaft sprocket timing marks align.

23 Refit the dipstick tube to the cylinder block/crankcase, tightening the bolts to the specified torque wrench setting.

24 Refit the hydraulic tappets and camshaft(s).

25 Refit the timing belt inner cover, sprocket(s) and tensioner, and the belt itself.

26 Using a torque wrench, check that the amount of force required to rotate the crankshaft does not exceed 31 Nm. If the effort required is greater than this, the engine must be dismantled again to trace and rectify the cause. This value takes into account the increased friction of a new engine and is much higher than the actual pressure required to rotate a run-in engine, so do not make allowances for tight components.

19.17a Tighten connecting rod big-end bearing cap bolts to specified torque wrench setting (first stage) . . .

19.17b . . . then use angular torque gauge to tighten bolts through angle specified (second stage)

20 Engine - initial start-up after overhaul

1 With the engine refitted in the vehicle, double-check the engine oil and coolant levels. Make a final check that everything has been reconnected and that there are no tools or rags left in the engine compartment.

2 With the spark plugs removed and the ignition system disabled by earthing the ignition HT coil distributor spark plug (HT) lead with a jumper lead, turn the engine over on the starter until the oil pressure warning lamp goes out.

3 Refit the spark plugs and connect all the spark plug (HT) leads.

4 Start the engine, noting that this may take a little longer than usual due to the fuel system components being empty.

5 While the engine is idling, check for fuel, coolant and oil leaks. Do not be alarmed if there are some odd smells and smoke from parts getting hot and burning off oil deposits. If the hydraulic tappets have been disturbed, some valve gear noise may be heard at first; this should disappear as the oil circulates fully around the engine and normal pressure is restored in the tappets.

6 Keep the engine idling until hot coolant is felt circulating through the top hose, check the ignition timing and idle speed and mixture (as appropriate), then switch it off.

7 After a few minutes, recheck the oil and coolant levels and top up as necessary.

8 If they were tightened as described, there is no need to re-tighten the cylinder head bolts once the engine has first run after reassembly.

9 If new pistons, rings or crankshaft bearings have been fitted, the engine must be run-in for the first 500 miles (800 km). Do not operate the engine at full throttle or allow it to labour in any gear during this period. It is recommended that the oil and filter be changed at the end of this period.

2B

Notes

Chapter 3
Cooling, heating and ventilation systems

Contents

Degrees of difficulty

Easy, suitable for novice with little experience	Fairly easy, suitable for beginner with some experience	Fairly difficult, suitable for competent DIY mechanic	Difficult, suitable for experienced DIY mechanic	Very difficult, suitable for expert DIY or professional 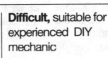

Specifications

System
Type .... Pressurised, pump-assisted thermo-syphon with front mounted radiator and thermostatically-controlled electric cooling fan

Thermostat
Type .... Wax
Start to open temperature .... 76 to 80°C
Fully open temperature .... 82 or 88°C (actual value stamped in unit end)
Full lift height .... 9.0 mm

Expansion tank
Cap pressure .... 0.9 to 1.0 bar

Cooling fan
Operating temperature .... 88 to 92°C

Torque wrench settings

	Nm	lbf ft
Cooling system		
Fan motor nuts	5	4
Temperature gauge sender unit	15	11
Thermostat housing cover bolts	9	7
Thermostat housing/dipstick tube-to-cylinder block/crankcase bolt ...	9	7
Coolant rail-to-cylinder block/crankcase bolts	9	7
Coolant pump-to-timing belt upper left-hand (inner) cover bolt	9	7
Coolant pump-to-cylinder block/crankcase bolts	10	7
Heating system		
Heater lower mounting nut	21	15
Heater blower motor mounting bolts	10	7
Air conditioning system		
Compressor mounting bolts	45	33
Condenser unions	17	13
Evaporator inlet union (from receiver drier)	17	13
Evaporator outlet union	33	24
Receiver drier union	17	13
Trinary switch	12	9

3

1 General information and precautions

General information

The cooling system is of the pressurised, pump-assisted thermo-syphon type. It consists of the front-mounted radiator, a translucent expansion tank mounted on the right-hand inner wing, a thermostatically-controlled electric cooling fan mounted on the rear of the radiator, a thermostat and a centrifugal coolant pump, as well as the connecting hoses **(see illustration)**. The coolant pump is driven by the engine timing belt.

The system is of the by-pass type, allowing coolant to circulate around the engine while the thermostat is closed. With the engine cold, the thermostat closes off the coolant feed from the bottom radiator hose. Coolant is then drawn into the engine via the heater matrix, inlet manifold and from the top of the cylinder block. This allows some heat transfer, by convection, to the radiator through the top hose whilst retaining the majority of heat within the cylinder block.

The siting of the thermostat in the intake rather than the outlet side of the system ensures that the engine warms up quickly by circulating a small amount of coolant around a shorter tract. This also prevents temperature build-up in the cylinder head prior to the thermostat opening.

When the coolant reaches a predetermined temperature, the thermostat opens and the coolant is allowed to flow freely through the top hose to the radiator. As the coolant circulates through the radiator, it is cooled by the inrush of air when the vehicle is in forward motion. Airflow is supplemented by the action of the electric cooling fan when necessary. Upon reaching the bottom of the radiator, the coolant is now cooled and the cycle is repeated.

With the engine at normal operating temperature, the coolant expands and some of it is displaced into the expansion tank. This coolant collects in the tank and is returned to the radiator when the system cools.

The electric cooling fan mounted behind the radiator is controlled by a thermostatic switch located in the radiator side tank. At a predetermined coolant temperature the switch contacts close, thus actuating the fan.

Precautions

Cooling system

Do not attempt to remove the expansion tank filler cap or to disturb any part of the cooling system whilst it or the engine is hot, as there is a very great risk of scalding. If the expansion tank filler cap must be removed before the engine and radiator have fully cooled down (even though this is not recommended) the pressure in the cooling system must first be released. Cover the cap with a thick layer of cloth, to avoid scalding, and slowly unscrew the filler cap until a hissing sound can be heard. When the hissing has stopped, showing that pressure is released, slowly unscrew the filler cap until it can be removed. If more hissing sounds are heard, wait until they have stopped before unscrewing the cap completely. At all times keep well away from the filler opening.

Do not allow antifreeze to come in contact with your skin or painted surfaces of the vehicle. Rinse off spills immediately with plenty of water. Never leave antifreeze lying around, it is fatal if ingested.

If the engine is hot, the electric cooling fan may start rotating even if the engine is not running, so be careful to keep hands, hair and loose clothing well clear when working in the engine compartment.

Air conditioning system

On models equipped with an air conditioning system, it is necessary to observe special precautions whenever dealing with any part of the system, its associated components and any items which necessitate disconnection of the system. If for any reason the system must be disconnected, entrust this task to your Rover dealer or a refrigeration engineer.

Refrigerant must not be allowed to come in contact with a naked flame, otherwise a poisonous gas will be created. Do not allow the fluid to come in contact with the skin or eyes.

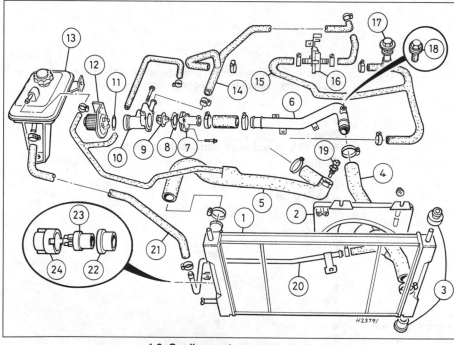

1.0 Cooling system components

1 Radiator	9 Thermostat	18 Cooling system bleed screw
2 Cooling fan and cowling	10 Thermostat housing	
3 Radiator mounting rubbers	11 O-ring	19 Engine overheat switch - where fitted
4 Bottom hose	12 Coolant pump	
5 Top hose	13 Expansion tank	20 Coolant pipe - expansion tank to bottom hose
6 Coolant pipe - bottom hose to thermostat housing	14 Hose - heater matrix and manifold return	21 Hose - expansion tank return
	15 Hose - heater matrix and manifold feed	22 Sealing ring
7 Thermostat housing cover	16 Heater temperature control valve	23 Cooling fan thermostatic switch
8 Gasket	17 Coolant filler stem	24 Locking ring

2 Cooling system - draining, flushing and refilling

Refer to Chapter 1.

3 Cooling system - general inspection

Refer to "Weekly Checks" and Chapter 1.

4 Cooling system hoses - renewal

HAYNES HiNT *Never work on the cooling system when it is hot. Release any pressure from the system by loosening the expansion tank cap, having first covered it with a cloth to avoid any possibility of scalding.*

1 If inspection of the cooling system reveals a faulty hose, then it must be renewed as follows.

2 First drain the cooling system. If the coolant is not due for renewal, it may be re-used if collected in a clean container.

3 To disconnect any hose, use a screwdriver to slacken the clips then move them along the hose clear of the outlet. Carefully work the hose off its outlets. Do not attempt to disconnect any part of the system when still hot.

4 Note that the radiator hose outlets are fragile. Do not use excessive force when attempting to remove the hoses. If a hose proves stubborn, try to release it by rotating it on its outlets before attempting to work it off. If all else fails, cut the hose with a sharp knife then slit it so that it can be peeled off in two pieces. While expensive, this is preferable to buying a new radiator.

5 When refitting a hose, first slide the clips onto the hose then work the hose onto its outlets. If the hose is stiff, use soap as a lubricant or soften it by first soaking it in boiling water whilst taking care to prevent scalding.

6 Work each hose end fully onto its outlet, check that the hose is settled correctly and is properly routed, then slide each clip along the hose until it is behind the outlet flared end before tightening it securely.

7 Refill the system with coolant.

8 Check carefully for leaks as soon as possible after disturbing any part of the cooling system.

5 Radiator and expansion tank - removal, inspection and refitting

Removal
Radiator

1 Drain the cooling system.

2 On models equipped with air conditioning, remove the condenser fan, then undo the two bolts securing the air conditioning pipes to the bonnet platform.

3 Remove the air cleaner metal intake duct and intake hose.

4 Disconnect the radiator cooling fan wiring connector, then slacken and remove the bolt

securing the earth leads to the bonnet platform. Disconnect the wiring from the thermostatic switch(es) which are fitted to the right-hand side of the radiator (see illustrations).

5 Slacken the bottom hose retaining clip and disconnect the hose from the radiator.

6 Slacken the retaining clips and disconnect the top hose from both the radiator and engine coolant elbow (see illustrations). Position the hose clear of the radiator so that it does not hinder removal.

7 Undo the two bolts securing the upper mounting brackets to the bonnet platform and remove the brackets from the radiator. Disengage the radiator from its lower mounting points and carefully manoeuvre it out of the engine compartment (see illustrations).

5.4a Disconnect cooling fan wiring connector then remove earth lead retaining bolt (arrowed)

5.4b Disconnecting wiring connector from radiator switch

5.6a Slacken clips and disconnect top hose from radiator . . .

5.6b . . . and engine coolant elbow

5.7a Undo radiator mounting bolts . . .

5.7b . . . remove mounting brackets . . .

5.7c . . . and manoeuvre radiator out of engine compartment

3

Expansion tank

8 Slacken and remove the three bolts securing the expansion tank to the body. Unscrew the expansion tank cap and tip out its contents into a suitable container.

9 Slacken the retaining clips then disconnect both the hoses from the expansion tank and remove the tank from the vehicle.

Inspection

Radiator

10 If the radiator was removed because of clogging (causing overheating) then try reverse flushing or, in severe cases, use a radiator cleanser strictly in accordance with the manufacturer's instructions. Ensure that the cleanser is suitable for use in a copper/brass radiator. Refer to Chapter 1 for further information

11 Use a soft brush and an air line or garden hose to clear the radiator matrix of leaves, insects etc.

 HAYNES HiNT *Minor leaks from the radiator can be cured using a suitable sealant with the radiator in situ.*

12 Major leaks or extensive damage should be repaired by a specialist, or the radiator should be renewed or exchanged for a reconditioned unit.

13 Examine the mounting rubbers for signs of damage or deterioration and renew if necessary.

Expansion tank

14 Empty any remaining coolant from the tank and flush it with fresh water to clean it. If the tank is leaking it must be renewed but it is worth first attempting a repair using a proprietary sealant or suitable adhesive.

15 The expansion tank cap should be cleaned and checked whenever it is removed. Check that its sealing surfaces and threads are clean and undamaged and that they mate correctly with those of the expansion tank.

16 The cap's performance can only be checked by using a cap pressure-tester (cooling system tester) with a suitable adaptor. On applying pressure, the cap's pressure relief valve should hold until the specified pressure is reached, at which point the valve should open.

17 If there is any doubt about the cap's performance, then it must be renewed. Ensure that the replacement is of the correct type and rating.

Refitting

Radiator

18 Refitting is the reverse of the removal procedure whilst noting the following:
a) *Ensure that the radiator is seated correctly and without strain on its mountings.*
b) *Ensure that the radiator hoses are securely held by the retaining clips.*
c) *Ensure that all wiring connectors are correctly routed so that they are clear of the cooling fan and are retained by any necessary clips or ties.*
d) *Refill the cooling system as described in Chapter 1.*

Expansion tank

19 Refitting is the reverse of the removal procedure whilst noting the following:
a) *Ensure that all hoses are correctly routed with no kinks or sharp bends and are securely held by the retaining clips.*
b) *Top up the expansion tank as described in Chapter 1.*

6 Thermostat - removal, testing and refitting

Removal

1 Note that access to the thermostat is very limited. Depending on the tools available, it may be easier to raise the front of the vehicle and to work from underneath, ensuring that the vehicle is securely supported on axle stands. In most cases, access is better if the air cleaner and carburettor (or throttle body on SPi engines) are removed and is best if the complete inlet manifold is removed. If the inlet manifold is removed, the thermostat housing

6.1 Thermostat can be removed without disturbing housing if inlet manifold is first removed

cover can be unbolted to remove the thermostat without disturbing the housing itself **(see illustration)**. Whichever method is used, first drain the cooling system.

2 On carburettor models equipped with a catalytic converter, either remove the thermostatically-operated vacuum switch or disconnect the vacuum pipes from the switch so that it can be removed with the thermostat housing.

3 Unbolt the coolant rail from the rear of the cylinder block/crankcase, then slacken the clips and disconnect the coolant rail hose and heater/inlet manifold return hose from the thermostat housing **(see illustration)**.

4 Undo the thermostat housing/dipstick tube-to-cylinder block/crankcase bolt and remove the thermostat housing from the cylinder block/crankcase. Remove the housing O-ring which must be renewed whenever it is disturbed **(see illustrations)**.

5 Slacken and remove the three thermostat housing cover bolts and lift off the housing cover. Discard the gasket and remove the thermostat.

Testing

6 If the thermostat remains in the open position at room temperature, then it is faulty and must be renewed.

7 To test it fully, suspend the (closed) thermostat on a length of string in a container of cold water, with a thermometer beside it.

6.3 Disconnect coolant rail and heater/inlet manifold hoses (arrowed) . . .

6.4a . . . unscrew dipstick tube retaining bolt . . .

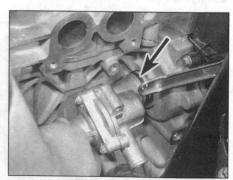

6.4b . . . and withdraw thermostat housing (O-ring arrowed) – inlet manifold removed for clarity

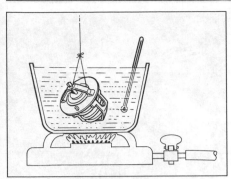

6.7 Testing the thermostat

6.8 Note temperature specification stamped on thermostat end

6.10 Thermostat housing and coolant hoses refitted

Ensure that neither touches the side of the container **(see illustration)**.

8 Heat the water and check the temperature at which the thermostat begins to open. Compare this value with that specified. Continue to heat the water until the thermostat is fully open. The temperature at which this should happen is stamped in the unit's end **(see illustration)**. Remove the thermostat and measure the height of the fully opened valve, then allow the thermostat to cool down and check that it closes fully.

9 If the thermostat does not open and close as described, if it sticks in either position, or if it does not open at the specified temperature, then it must be renewed.

Refitting

10 Refitting is the reverse of the removal procedure, noting the following **(see illustration)**:

a) *Clean the thermostat housing, housing cover and cylinder block/crankcase mating surfaces thoroughly.*

b) *Always fit a new housing cover gasket and O-ring. Smear the O-ring with grease to aid refitting.*

c) *Tighten all bolts to their specified torque wrench settings (where given).*

d) *Ensure the coolant hose clips are positioned so that they do not foul any other component, then tighten them securely.*

e) *Refit any components removed for improved access.*

f) *Refill the cooling system as described in Chapter 1.*

7.5 Removing the coolant pump

7 Coolant pump - removal and refitting

Removal

1 Coolant pump failure is usually indicated by coolant leaking from the gland behind the pump bearing, or by rough and noisy operation, usually accompanied by excessive pump spindle play. If the pump shows any of these symptoms then it must be renewed as follows.

2 Drain the cooling system.

3 Remove the timing belt.

4 Noting the location of the pillar bolt(s), unscrew the five bolts securing the coolant pump to the cylinder block/crankcase, then unscrew the single bolt securing the pump to the timing belt upper left-hand (inner) cover.

5 Withdraw the coolant pump and discard its sealing ring which should be renewed whenever it is disturbed. Carefully clean the cylinder block/crankcase mating surface and the pump socket **(see illustration)**.

Refitting

6 On refitting, install the pump using a new sealing ring and tighten all bolts to the specified torque wrench settings.

7 The remainder of the refitting procedure is the reverse of removal.

8 Electric cooling fan - testing, removal and refitting

Note: *On models equipped with air conditioning, there are two switches fitted to the right-hand side of the radiator, the lower of these is the cooling fan switch.*

Testing

1 The cooling fan motor is supplied with current via the ignition switch, fuse 4 and the cooling fan relay. The relay is energised by the radiator-mounted thermostatic switch which is fed via fuse number 15.

2 If the fan does not appear to work, first check that both fuses are in good condition and have not blown. Run the engine until normal operating temperature is reached, then allow it to idle. If the fan does not cut in within a few minutes, switch off the ignition and disconnect the two wires from the thermostatic switch. Bridge these two wires with a length of spare wire and switch on the ignition. If the fan now operates, the thermostatic switch is probably faulty and must be tested further as described in Section 9.

3 If the fan still fails to operate, check that full battery voltage is available at the switch's light green and grey wire terminal. If not, check the feed for a blown fuse or other fault such as a broken wire. If the feed is good, check the cooling fan relay, see Chapter 12. If the relay operates correctly, check for continuity between the fan motor black wire terminal and a good earth point on the body. If not, then the earth connection is faulty and must be remade. The circuit earth connection is one of those at earth header 1, attached to the left-hand inner wing panel next to the battery.

4 If the switch and wiring are in good condition, the fault must be in the motor itself. This can be checked by disconnecting it from the wiring loom and connecting a 12 volt supply directly to it. If the motor does not work then it must be renewed.

Removal

5 Drain the cooling system, then jack up the front of the vehicle and support it securely on axle stands.

6 From underneath the front of the vehicle, slacken and remove the three bolts securing the bumper flange to the body. Remove the seven bolts securing the front undercover panel to the body and remove the panel.

7 Remove the air cleaner metal intake duct and intake hose.

8 Slacken the retaining clips and disconnect the top hose from both the radiator and engine. Position the hose clear of the radiator so that it does not hinder removal.

9 Disconnect the radiator cooling fan wiring connector.

3

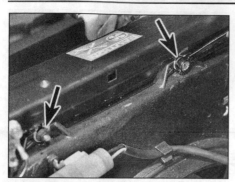

8.10a Undo cooling fan cowling retaining nuts (2 arrowed) . . .

8.10b . . . and remove fan assembly

8.11 Cooling fan motor retaining nuts (arrowed)

10 Undo the four nuts securing the cooling fan cowling to the rear of the radiator and manoeuvre the fan assembly out of the engine compartment **(see illustrations)**.

11 To dismantle the assembly, first prise off the fan retaining circlip, then lift the fan off the motor spindle. Undo the three nuts which secure the motor assembly to the cowling then release the motor wiring and connector and separate the motor and cowling **(see illustration)**.

Refitting

12 Refitting is a reverse of the removal procedure, noting the following:

a) If necessary, reassemble the fan motor, cowling and fan, then tighten the motor retaining nuts to the specified torque. Ensure that the motor wiring is securely retained by the cowling clips.

b) Ensure that the radiator hose is securely held by its retaining clips.

c) On completion, refill the cooling system as described in Chapter 1.

9 Cooling system electrical switches - testing, removal and refitting

Note: On models equipped with air conditioning, there are two switches fitted to the right-hand side of the radiator, the lower of these is the cooling fan switch.

Testing

Cooling fan thermostatic switch

1 Refer to Section 8 for details of a quick test which should eliminate most faulty switches. If the switch is to be renewed, or to be tested thoroughly, it must be removed.

2 To carry out a thorough test of the switch, use two spare wires to connect to it either a multimeter (set to the resistance function) or a battery and bulb test circuit. Suspend the switch in a pan of water which is being heated. Measure the temperature of the water with a thermometer. Do not let either the switch or the thermometer touch the pan itself **(see illustration)**.

3 The switch contacts should close to the ON position (ie: continuity should exist) when the water reaches the temperature specified. Stop heating the water and allow it to cool down. The switch contacts should open.

4 If the switch's performance is significantly different from that specified, or if it does not work at all, then it must be renewed.

Coolant temperature gauge sender unit

5 The coolant temperature gauge mounted in the instrument panel is fed with a stabilised 10 volt supply from the instrument panel feed (via the ignition switch and fuse 1), its earth being controlled by the sender unit.

6 The sender unit is screwed into the coolant outlet elbow mounted on the left-hand end of the cylinder head, underneath the distributor **(see illustration)**. It contains a thermistor, which is an element whose electrical resistance decreases at a predetermined rate as its temperature rises. Thus, when the coolant is cold, the sender's resistance is high, current flow through the gauge is reduced and the gauge needle points to the C (cold) end of the scale. If the unit is faulty it must be renewed.

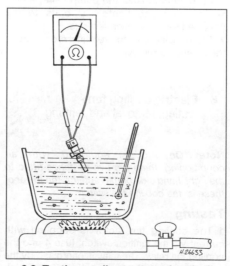

9.2 Testing cooling system electrical switch

7 If the gauge develops a fault, check first the other instruments. If they do not work at all, check the instrument panel feed. If the readings are erratic, there may be a fault in the voltage stabiliser which will necessitate the renewal of the gauge unit or printed circuit. If the fault is in the temperature gauge alone, check it as follows.

8 If the gauge needle remains at the C end of the scale, disconnect the sender unit wire and earth it to the cylinder head. If the needle then deflects when the ignition is switched on, then the sender unit is proven faulty and must be renewed. If the needle still does not move, remove the instrument panel and check the continuity of the green/blue wire between the gauge and the sender unit and the feed to the gauge unit. If continuity is shown and the fault still exists, then the gauge is faulty and the gauge unit must be renewed.

9 If the gauge needle remains at the H end of the scale, disconnect the sender unit wire. If the needle then returns to the C end of the scale when the ignition is switched on, then the sender unit is proven faulty and must be renewed. If the needle still does not move, check the remainder of the circuit as described above.

Inlet manifold pre-heater temperature switch - carburettor engines

10 The switch screwed into the underside of the inlet manifold on carburettor engines

9.6 Coolant temperature gauge sender unit

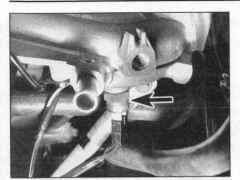

9.10 Inlet manifold pre-heater temperature switch (carburettor engines)

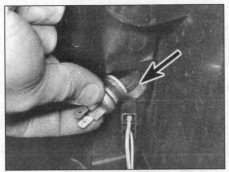

9.20 Remove cooling fan thermostatic switch and withdraw sealing ring (arrowed)

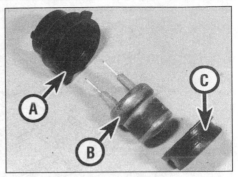

9.27 Cooling fan switch locking ring (A) thermostatic switch (B) and sealing ring (C)

controls the inlet manifold heater circuit **(see illustration)**.

11 The switch contacts should be closed to the ON position (ie: continuity should exist) only at temperatures below 50°C. Remove the switch and test it as described in paragraphs 2 to 4.

Thermostatically-operated vacuum switch - carburettor engines equipped with catalytic converters

12 This switch is screwed into the thermostat housing.

13 To test the switch, fit two suitable lengths of hose to the switch and suspend the switch in a pan of water which is being heated. Measure the temperature of the water with a thermometer. Do not let either the switch or the thermometer touch the pan itself.

14 Blow down one of the hoses attached to the switch. The switch should be closed (ie: passes no air) when the water temperature is below 70°C. Above 70°C, the switch should open and air should flow freely through the hoses. Stop heating the water then allow the water to cool down and check that the switch closes at 70°C or just below.

15 If the switch performance is significantly different from that specified, or if it does not work at all, then it must be renewed.

Coolant temperature sensor - fuel injected engines

16 This sensor, which is screwed into the underside of the inlet manifold (SPi engines), or located in the coolant pipe adjacent to the foward top edge of the timing belt cover (MPi engines), is a thermistor (see paragraph 6) which is supplied with approximately 5 volts by the engine management system ECU. The ECU also controls the sensor's earth path and, by measuring the amount of current in the sensor circuit, determines the engine's temperature. This information is used, in conjunction with other inputs, to control idle speed, injector opening time duration and ignition timing.

17 If the sensor circuit should fail to provide adequate information, the ECU's back-up

facility assumes a value corresponding to 60°C. The sensor itself can be tested only by having a Rover dealer check the complete system using the correct diagnostic equipment. Do not attempt to test the circuit using any other equipment, or the ECU will be damaged.

Removal

Cooling fan thermostatic switch

18 With the engine and radiator cold, either drain the cooling system down to the level of the sender unit, or unscrew the expansion tank filler cap to release any remaining pressure and have a suitable plug ready that can be used to stop the escape of coolant while the switch is removed.

19 Disconnect the battery negative lead.

20 Disconnect the wiring connector from the switch then rotate the locking ring to release it. Withdraw the switch and sealing ring from the radiator **(see illustration)**.

Coolant temperature gauge sender unit

21 With the engine and radiator cold, either drain the cooling system down to the level of the switch, or unscrew the expansion tank filler cap to release any remaining pressure and have a suitable plug ready that can be used to stop the escape of coolant while the unit is removed.

22 Disconnect the battery negative lead.

23 Disconnect the unit's wiring connector and unscrew the unit from the coolant outlet elbow.

Inlet manifold pre-heater temperature switch - carburettor engines

24 Refer to Chapter 4.

Thermostatically-operated vacuum switch - carburettor engines equipped with catalytic converters

25 Refer to Chapter 5.

Coolant temperature sensor - fuel injected engines

26 Refer to Chapter 4.

Refitting

Cooling fan thermostatic switch

27 On refitting, renew the sealing ring if it is worn or compressed and carefully clean the radiator seat before pressing in the sealing ring and switch **(see illustration)**. Refit the locking ring and rotate it to tighten it securely. Reconnect the switch and battery, then replenish the cooling system.

Coolant temperature gauge sender unit

28 On refitting, apply a suitable sealant to the unit threads and tighten it to its specified torque wrench setting. Reconnect the unit and battery, then replenish the cooling system.

Inlet manifold pre-heater temperature switch - carburettor engines

29 Refer to Chapter 4.

Thermostatically-operated vacuum switch - carburettor engines equipped with catalytic converters

30 Refer to Chapter 5.

Coolant temperature sensor - fuel injected engines

31 Refer to Chapter 4.

10 Heater components - removal and refitting

Removal

Heater unit

1 Drain the cooling system.

2 Working in the engine compartment, slacken the hose clips and disconnect the heater feed and return hoses from the matrix outlets on the bulkhead. Disconnect the cable inner from the heater valve and free the cable outer from its retaining clip. Slacken and

3

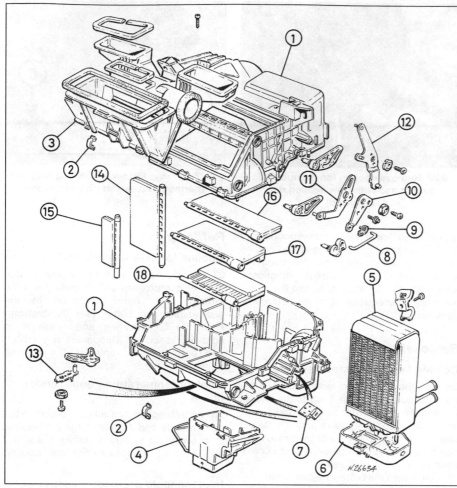

10.2b Disconnect heater feed and return hoses . . .

10.2c . . . and free heater valve cable from retaining clip

10.2d Slacken and remove heater unit lower mounting nut

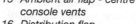

10.2a Heater unit components

1 Heater case	8 Floor level flap operating lever	15 Ambient air flap - centre console vents
2 Heater case clip		
3 Face level/windscreen duct	9 Clip	16 Distribution flap - windscreen
4 Floor level duct	10 Floor level flap idler lever	
5 Heater matrix	11 Face level flap idler lever	17 Distribution flap - face level vents
6 Heater matrix cover	12 Flap operating lever	
7 Cable retaining clip	13 Air mix flap operating lever	18 Distribution flap - floor level vents
	14 Air mix flap	

remove the heater lower mounting nut which is situated just to the left of the matrix outlets **(see illustrations)**.

3 Working inside the vehicle, remove the facia.

4 Slacken and remove the two retaining screws and remove the blower motor-to-heater unit duct **(see illustration)**. On models equipped with air conditioning, the evaporator unit is fitted in place of the duct. It may be possible to gain the necessary clearance required to disengage the evaporator from the heater unit by removing the mounting brackets and nuts. If not, the evaporator must be removed.

5 Undo the screw securing the right-hand heater duct to the mounting bracket, then move the duct to the right to disengage it from the heater unit **(see illustrations)**.

6 Undo the inertia switch retaining nut and disengage the switch from the steering column support bracket.

10.4 Remove blower motor-to-heater unit duct

7 Release the wiring block connector from the right-hand end of the steering column support bracket and undo the fusebox

10.5a Undo right-hand duct retaining screw (arrowed) . . .

10.5b . . . and disengage duct from heater unit

10.7a Release wiring connector from steering column support bracket and remove fusebox nut (arrowed)

10.7b Remove mounting bolts and manoeuvre steering column mounting bracket out of position

retaining nut. Slacken and remove the five support bracket retaining bolts and remove the bracket from the vehicle (see illustrations).

8 Disconnect the air recirculation cable inner from the flap and free the cable outer from the blower motor.

9 Prise out the stud securing the rear heater duct sleeve to the bottom of the heater unit, then slide the sleeve down to disengage it from the unit (see illustration).

10 Disconnect the wiring connectors from the heater control panel, then remove the two upper heater unit retaining nuts and carefully manoeuvre the heater unit out of the vehicle (see illustrations).

Heater matrix

11 Remove the heater unit.

12 Undo the screw securing the matrix outlet pipe bracket to the heater unit and remove the bracket (see illustration).

13 Slacken and remove the two matrix cover retaining screws, then remove the cover and withdraw the matrix from the heater unit (see illustrations).

14 If the matrix is leaking, it is best to obtain a new or reconditioned unit as home repairs are seldom successful. If it is blocked, it can sometimes be cleared by reverse flushing using a garden hose. Use a proprietary radiator cleaning product if absolutely necessary.

10.9 Remove retaining stud and disengage rear heater duct sleeve from heater unit

10.10a Disconnect wiring from heater control panel . . .

10.10b . . . and remove heater retaining nuts

10.12 Undo retaining screw and remove matrix outlet pipe bracket

3

10.13a Undo two matrix cover retaining screws . . .

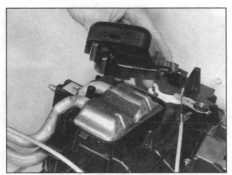

10.13b . . . then remove cover . . .

10.13c . . . and withdraw matrix from heater unit

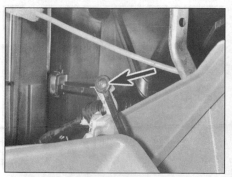

10.15 Glovebox damper retaining screw (arrowed)

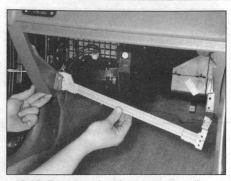

10.16 Remove glovebox support rail . . .

10.17 . . . then remove blower motor-to-heater unit duct

Heater blower motor

15 Undo the two glovebox retaining screws then partially withdraw the glovebox until access can be gained to the glovebox damper to facia screw. Undo the damper screw and remove the glovebox and damper **(see illustration)**.

16 Slacken and remove the four glovebox support rail mounting bolts and remove the rail **(see illustration)**.

17 Slacken and remove the two retaining screws and remove the blower motor-to-heater unit duct **(see illustration)**. On models equipped with air conditioning, the evaporator unit is fitted in place of the duct. It may be possible to gain the necessary clearance required to disengage the evaporator and remove the blower motor by removing the mounting brackets and nuts. If not, the evaporator must be removed.

18 Disconnect the air recirculation cable inner from the flap and free the cable outer from the blower motor. Disconnect the two blower motor wiring connectors **(see illustration)**.

19 Slacken and remove the three blower motor mounting bolts and manoeuvre the blower unit out from underneath the facia **(see illustrations)**.

20 To remove the motor from the unit, undo the four motor cover retaining screws, then disconnect the breather hose and lift off the cover. Slacken and remove the three motor retaining bolts and withdraw the motor assembly from the blower unit. Undo the fan retaining nut and separate the fan and motor, noting the seal fitted between the two components **(see illustrations)**.

Heater blower motor resistor

21 Remove the glovebox as described in paragraphs 15 and 16.

22 Disconnect the wiring connector, then undo the two retaining screws and remove the resistor from the front of the motor assembly.

Heater valve

23 Working in the engine compartment, disconnect the cable inner from the heater

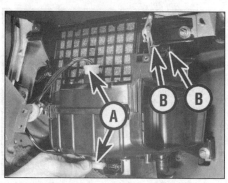

10.18 Disconnect motor wiring connectors (A) and air recirculation cable (B)

10.19a Undo three blower motor mounting bolts (arrowed) . . .

10.19b . . . and remove unit from behind facia

10.20a Remove motor cover retaining screws (arrowed) . . .

10.20b . . . and disconnect breather hose

10.20c Undo motor retaining bolts and withdraw motor from unit

10.20d Remove fan retaining nut . . .

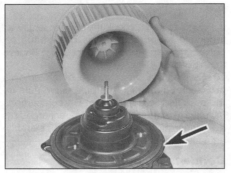

10.20e . . . and lift off fan (seal arrowed)

valve and free the cable outer from the retaining clip.
24 Slacken and remove the bolt securing the heater valve mounting bracket to the engine compartment bulkhead.
25 Either drain the cooling system or clamp the coolant hoses on each side of the coolant valve to minimise the loss of coolant.
26 Slacken the hose retaining clips, then disconnect both hoses from the coolant valve and remove the valve from the engine compartment. Mop up any spilt coolant immediately.

Refitting

Heater unit

27 Refitting is a reverse of the removal procedure, noting the following:
a) Ensure that the heater ducts are securely connected to the unit so that there are no air leaks or gaps.
b) Check the operation of all heater cables before refitting the facia, ensuring that the relevant component moves smoothly from the fully open to the fully closed position. If necessary, adjustments can be made by releasing the relevant retaining clip and repositioning the cable outer.
c) Ensure that the heater hoses are correctly reconnected and are securely held by the retaining clips.
d) Tighten the heater lower mounting nut to the specified torque setting.
e) Refill the cooling system as described in Chapter 1.

12.2a Disconnect control cables from heater unit . . .

Heater matrix

28 Refitting is a reverse of the removal procedure.

Heater blower motor

29 Refitting is a reversal of the removal sequence, noting the following:
a) Ensure that the foam rubber seal is refitted correctly so that the blower motor-to-bulkhead aperture is closed off.
b) Tighten the blower motor mounting bolts to the specified torque setting.
c) Ensure that the air recirculation cable and flap functions correctly before refitting the glovebox. If necessary, adjust by releasing the cable retaining clip and repositioning the cable outer.

Heater blower motor resistor

30 Refitting is a reverse of the removal procedure.

Heater valve

31 Refitting is a reversal of the removal procedure. On completion, check the heater cable operates smoothly and replenish the cooling system.

11 Heater ducts and vents - removal and refitting

Removal

Facia ducts

1 Remove the facia.

12.2b . . . and remove heater control panel with cables

2 The ducts are mounted on the facia assembly and can be removed individually, once the retaining screws have been removed.

Heater unit ducts

3 The left-hand heater unit to blower motor duct is removed as described in paragraphs 15 to 17 of Section 10.
4 To remove the right-hand duct, first remove the facia. Slacken and remove the retaining screw which secures the right-hand end of the duct to the mounting bracket and release the radio aerial from the retaining clips on the underside of the duct. The duct can then be manoeuvred out of position.
5 Removal of the lower ducts which supply air to the rear passenger footwells is a complex job, requiring the removal of the front seats, centre console and the various trim panels so that the floor carpet can be peeled back, and is therefore not recommended.

Centre console vents

6 Remove the centre console.
7 The vents can then be unclipped from the rear of the front console section and removed.

Facia vents

8 The adjustable face-level vents can be removed by prising them gently out of the facia until the clips are released, taking care not to mark the facia.
9 The door window demister vents, fitted to the sides of the facia, can also be prised out of position once the relevant door has been opened.

Refitting

10 Refitting is a reverse of the removal procedure.

12 Heater controls - removal, refitting and adjustment

Removal

1 Remove the heater unit.
2 Disconnect the heater control cables from the heater unit and unclip the control panel. Remove the panel assembly complete with cables **(see illustrations)**.

Refitting and adjustment

3 Refit the heater control panel to the heater unit and reconnect the necessary control cables to their original positions.
4 Check the operation of the control cables, ensuring that they operate smoothly and move the necessary component from the fully open to the fully closed position. Adjustments can be made by releasing the cable retaining clip and repositioning the cable outer.
5 Once the necessary control cables are functioning correctly, refit the heater unit.

3

13 Air conditioning compressor drivebelt - inspection, adjustment and renewal

Refer to Chapter 1 (alternator drivebelt check).

14 Air conditioning refrigerant - level check

Refer to Chapter 1.

15 Air conditioning system components - removal and refitting

Warning: The air conditioning system must be professionally discharged before carrying out any of the following work. Cap or plug the pipe lines as soon as they are disconnected to prevent the entry of moisture.

Compressor

Removal

1 Remove the alternator/air conditioning compressor drivebelt as described in Chapter 1.
2 Disconnect the air conditioning pipes from the compressor **(see illustration)**.
3 Slacken and remove the four bolts securing the compressor to the mounting bracket and manoeuvre it downwards and away from the engine.

Refitting

4 Refitting is a reverse of the removal sequence, tightening the compressor mounting bolts to the specified torque setting. Ensure that the compressor pipe unions are securely tightened then refit and adjust the drivebelt as described in Chapter 1. On completion, have the air conditioning system recharged by a refrigeration specialist or suitably-equipped Rover dealer.

Condenser

Removal

5 Remove the front bumper.
6 Slacken and remove the bolts securing the power steering oil cooler to the body, then undo the bonnet lock mounting bracket bolts and position the lock assembly clear of the condenser unit.
7 Unscrew the air conditioning pipe union nuts from the condenser unit then disconnect the pipes. Discard the union pipe O-rings as these must be renewed whenever they are disturbed.
8 Slacken and remove the four retaining bolts and withdraw both the condenser upper mounting brackets. Release the condenser from its lower mounting points and manoeuvre it away from the vehicle.

Refitting

9 Prior to refitting, check the condenser lower mounting rubbers for signs of damage or deterioration and renew as necessary. Renew the pipe union O-rings.
10 Refitting is a direct reversal of the removal procedure, tightening the pipe union nuts to the specified torque setting. On completion, have the air conditioning system recharged by a refrigeration specialist or a suitably equipped Rover dealer.

Condenser cooling fan

Removal

11 Drain the cooling system.
12 Disconnect the wiring connector from the engine overheat switch, located in the top coolant hose, then slacken the clips securing the hose to the radiator and engine. Disconnect the hose from the radiator and engine and position it clear of the condenser so that it does not hinder removal.
13 Disconnect the condenser fan electrical wiring connector then undo the four fan cowling retaining nuts and manoeuvre the assembly out of the engine compartment.

14 To dismantle the assembly, first undo the fan retaining nut then lift the fan off the motor spindle. Undo the two screws which secure the motor assembly to the cowling then release the motor wiring and connector and separate the motor and cowling.

Refitting

15 Refitting is a reverse of the removal procedure, noting the following points:
a) *Ensure that the motor wiring is securely retained by the cowling clips and is clear of the condenser fan.*
b) *Ensure that the radiator hose is securely held by its retaining clips.*
c) *On completion, refill the cooling system.*

Evaporator

Removal

16 Undo the three bolts which secure the washer system reservoir to the engine compartment bulkhead and move the reservoir to gain access to the two evaporator union nuts. Slacken both the union nuts and disconnect the pipes from the evaporator. Remove the O-rings from the union nuts and discard them.

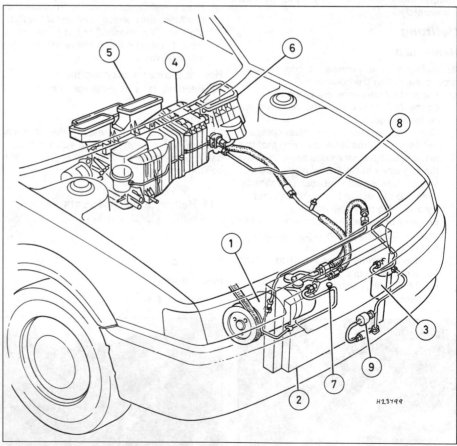

15.2 Air conditioning system layout

1 Compressor
2 Condenser
3 Receiver drier
4 Evaporator
5 Heater unit
6 Blower unit
7 High pressure servicing connection
8 Low pressure servicing connection
9 Trinary switch

17 Working from inside the vehicle, undo the two glovebox retaining screws, then partially withdraw the glovebox until access can be gained to the glovebox damper-to-facia screw. Undo the damper screw and remove the glovebox and damper.

18 Slacken and remove the four glovebox support rail mounting bolts and remove the rail.

19 Undo the two evaporator bracket retaining bolts and remove both the brackets.

20 Disconnect the wiring connector from the right-hand side of the evaporator.

21 Slacken and remove the two evaporator mounting nuts and manoeuvre the unit out of position.

Refitting

22 Refitting is a reverse of the removal procedure noting the following:

a) *Ensure that the evaporator is correctly joined to the heater unit and blower motor, so that there are no air leaks or gaps, then tighten the retaining nuts and bracket bolts securely.*

b) *Fit new O-rings to the pipe unions and tighten the union nuts to the specified torque setting.*

c) *On completion, have the system recharged by a refrigeration specialist or a suitably-equipped Rover dealer.*

Receiver drier

Removal

23 Remove the left-hand headlamp and the battery and battery tray.

24 Undo the two screws securing the air intake grille to the body. Disengage the grille from the resonator and remove it from the vehicle. Move the resonator to one side to gain access to the receiver drier.

25 Slacken the union nuts and disconnect the pipes from the receiver drier noting the O-rings which are fitted to the pipe unions. Discard the O-rings as they must be renewed whenever they are disturbed. The receiver drier unit unions must be capped immediately after they are disconnected and must remain capped until they are to be reconnected. If the receiver drier unit is left uncapped for any period of time it must be renewed.

26 Slacken the receiver drier clamp bolt then slide the unit out of the retaining clamp and remove it from the engine compartment.

Refitting

27 Refitting is a direct reversal of the removal sequence, tightening the pipe union nuts to the specified torque setting. On completion, have the system recharged by a refrigeration specialist or suitably-equipped Rover dealer.

Trinary switch

Removal

28 Remove the front bumper.

29 Disconnect the wiring connector and unscrew the switch from the air conditioning pipe. Remove the O-ring from the switch and discard it.

Refitting

30 Refitting is a reverse of the removal procedure. Fit a new O-ring to the switch and tighten it to the specified torque setting. On completion, have the system recharged by a refrigeration specialist or suitably-equipped Rover dealer.

3

Notes

Chapter 4 Part A
Fuel and exhaust systems - carburettor engines

Contents

Degrees of difficulty

Easy, suitable for novice with little experience	**Fairly easy,** suitable for beginner with some experience	**Fairly difficult,** suitable for competent DIY mechanic 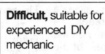	**Difficult,** suitable for experienced DIY mechanic	**Very difficult,** suitable for expert DIY or professional

Specifications

Fuel pump

Type . . . .   Mechanical, driven by eccentric on camshaft

Carburettor

Type . . . .   Hobourn-SU constant-depression/variable choke
Designation . . . .   KIF 44
Carburettor number:
  Without catalytic converter . . . .   MAC 10004 or 10025
  With catalytic converter . . . .   MAC 10011 or 10027
Throttle bore diameter . . . .   44.0 mm
Piston spring colour code . . . .   Red
Damper . . . .   LZX 2337
Jet size . . . .   ZX 2237 (0.100 in)
Needle identification . . . .   BGZ
Needle valve seat . . . .   LZX 1756
Fast idle speed - at choke control first detent . . . .   1200 rpm
Idle speed . . . .   850 ± 50 rpm
CO level at idle speed - engine at normal operating temperature:
  Without catalytic converter . . . .   2.0 to 3.0 %
  With catalytic converter - at gas sampling pipe . . . .   1.0 to 3.0 %
Choke type . . . .   Manual

Recommended fuel

Minimum octane rating:
  Without catalytic converter . . . .   95 RON unleaded (ie: unleaded Premium) or 97 RON leaded
      (ie: 4-star)
  With catalytic converter . . . .   95 RON unleaded (ie: unleaded Premium)

Torque wrench settings

	Nm	lbf ft
Fuel system		
Carburettor retaining screws	10	7
Carburettor vent and air bleed pipe mounting nuts and bolts	9	7
Needle retaining (grub) screw	1.7 to 2.3	1.3 to 1.7
Throttle disc retaining screws	0.80 to 1.14	0.59 to 0.84
Fuel pump mounting nuts	10	7
Fuel tank hose retaining clip and union nuts	9	7
Manifold temperature sensor	15	11
Inlet manifold nuts and bolts	25	18
Inlet manifold support stay bolts	25	18
Exhaust system		
Manifold retaining nuts	45	33
Manifold shroud screws	6	4
System flange nuts:		
Manifold-to-front pipe joint	50	37
All other joints	45	33
Front pipe mounting bolts	15	11

1 General information and precautions

General information

The fuel system consists of a fuel tank mounted under the rear of the vehicle, a mechanical fuel pump and a carburettor. The fuel pump is operated by an eccentric on the camshaft and is mounted on the rear of the cylinder head. The air cleaner contains a disposable paper filter element and incorporates a flap valve air temperature control system which allows cold air from the outside of the vehicle and warm air from around the exhaust manifold to enter the air cleaner in the correct proportions.

The carburettor is the Hobourn SU-manufactured KIF type, a development by Rover of the previous HIF instrument. To reduce emissions and to improve driveability when the engine is cold, the inlet manifold is heated by the cooling system coolant and by an electric pre-heater system. Mixture enrichment for cold starting is by a manually-operated choke control.

The exhaust system consists of three sections which are the front pipe and front silencer box, the intermediate pipe and middle silencer box, and the tailpipe and main silencer box. The system is suspended throughout its entire length by rubber mountings. If a catalytic converter is fitted, the exhaust system consists of four sections, the catalytic converter being situated between the front pipe and the (much shorter) intermediate pipe.

Precautions

Fuel warning

Many of the procedures in this Chapter require the removal of fuel lines and connections which may result in some fuel spillage. Before carrying out any operation on the fuel system, refer to the precautions given in *Safety first!* at the beginning of this Manual and follow them implicitly. Petrol is a highly dangerous and volatile liquid and the precautions necessary when handling it cannot be overstressed.

Unleaded petrol - usage

The information given in this Chapter is correct at the time of writing and applies only to petrol currently available in the UK. If updated information is required, check with a Rover dealer. If travelling abroad, consult one of the motoring organisations (or a similar authority) for advice on petrol types available and their suitability for your vehicle

The fuel recommended by Rover for the 214 and 414 models is given in Specifications, followed by the equivalent petrol currently on sale in the UK. RON and MON are different testing standards. RON stands for Research Octane Number (also written as RM); MON stands for Motor Octane Number (also written as MM, which is a different name for the same octane scale).

All Rover 214 and 414 models are designed

3.2 Note colour-coding of thermac switch vacuum pipes before disconnecting

to run on 95 (RON) octane petrol. Super/Super Plus (unleaded) petrols can be used without modification. If nothing else is available, 4-star (leaded) petrol can only be used if the vehicle is **not** fitted with a catalytic converter. The only vehicles which **must** use unleaded petrol at all times are those with catalytic converters.

Catalytic coverters

Before attempting work on these items, carefully read the precautions listed in Part D of this Chapter.

2 Air cleaner filter element - renewal

Refer to Chapter 1.

3 Air cleaner assembly - removal and refitting

Removal

1 Release the two clips securing the air intake duct to the assembly, then undo the four screws securing the assembly to its mounting bracket.

2 Release the assembly from the intake duct and withdraw it until the thermac switch vacuum pipes can be reached. Make a note of the correct fitted positions of the pipes to ensure that they are correctly connected on refitting (yellow to the temperature control valve, red to the inlet manifold) then disconnect them and withdraw the air cleaner assembly **(see illustration)**.

3 Check the condition of the O-ring around the carburettor inlet and renew it if worn or damaged.

3.4 Slacken clamp to disconnect intake hose from air cleaner assembly metal intake duct

4.4 Disconnect vacuum pipe from control valve to check operation of system components

4.9 Thermac switch is clipped into air cleaner assembly

4 To remove the metal intake duct, disconnect the vacuum pipe from the air temperature control valve and slacken the intake hose retaining clamp **(see illustration)**. Undo the fastener securing the duct to its mounting bracket and remove the metal duct, taking care not to lose the hot air intake connector hose which connects the duct to the exhaust manifold shroud.

5 To remove the air intake hose, it will first be necessary to remove the left-hand headlamp assembly so as to gain access to the two retaining screws. Remove the retaining screws securing the front of the hose to the body front panel then release the clip securing the ignition HT lead to the hose. If the metal intake duct is still in position, slacken the hose clamp then remove the hose from the engine compartment.

6 A resonator chamber is fitted to the intake hose to reduce the amount of induction noise. To remove the chamber, first remove the battery and battery tray. Disconnect the intake hose and release any relevant retaining clips from the resonator then remove the resonator from the engine compartment.

Refitting

7 Refitting is the reverse of the removal procedure. Ensure that the vacuum pipes are correctly reconnected and are not trapped as the assembly is refitted, then check that the assembly sits properly on the carburettor inlet before tightening the screws securely.

---

4 Air cleaner air temperature control system - inspection and component renewal

---

Inspection

1 The system is controlled by a thermac switch mounted in the air cleaner assembly. When the engine is started from cold, the switch is closed to allow inlet manifold depression to act on the air temperature control valve in the intake duct. This raises a vacuum servo in the valve assembly and draws a flap valve across the cold air intake,

thus allowing only (warmed) air from around the exhaust manifold to enter the air cleaner.

2 As the temperature of the exhaust-warmed air in the air cleaner rises, a bi-metallic strip in the thermac switch deforms and opens the switch to shut off the depression in the air temperature control valve assembly. The flap is lowered gradually across the hot air intake until, when the engine is fully warmed-up to normal operating temperature, only cold air from the front of the vehicle is entering the air cleaner.

3 To check the system, allow the engine to cool down completely, then slacken the intake hose retaining clamp and disconnect the hose from the metal intake duct. The flap valve in the duct should be securely seated across the hot air intake. Start the engine. The flap should immediately rise to close off the cold air intake and should then lower steadily as the engine warms up, until it is eventually seated across the hot air intake again.

4 To check the thermac switch, disconnect the vacuum pipe from the control valve when the engine is running and place a finger over the pipe end **(see illustration)**. When the engine is cold, full inlet manifold vacuum should be present in the pipe. When the engine is at normal operating temperature, there should be no vacuum in the pipe.

5 To check the air temperature control valve, slacken the intake hose retaining clamp and disconnect the hose from the metal intake duct. The flap valve should be securely seated

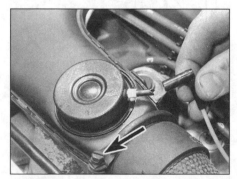

4.11 Disconnecting vacuum pipe from air temperature control valve - intake hose-to-metal intake duct securing clamp (arrowed)

across the hot air intake. Disconnect the vacuum pipe and suck hard at the control valve stub. The flap should rise to shut off the cold air intake.

6 If any component is faulty then it must be renewed.

Thermac switch - renewal

7 Remove the air cleaner assembly.

8 Release the lid retaining clips then remove the lid and withdraw the air cleaner filter element.

9 Bend up the tags on the switch clip and remove the clip, then withdraw the switch and its seal **(see illustration)**.

10 Refitting is the reverse of the removal procedure. Ensure that the switch mating surfaces are clean and that the switch and seal are correctly located before fastening the clip.

Air temperature control valve - renewal

11 Disconnect the vacuum pipe from the air temperature control valve, then slacken the intake hose retaining clamp and disconnect the hose from the metal intake duct **(see illustration)**.

12 Release the two clips securing the air intake duct to the air cleaner assembly and undo the fastener securing the duct to its mounting bracket. Withdraw the duct, taking care not to lose the hot air intake connector hose which connects the duct to the manifold shroud **(see illustration)**.

4A

4.12 Do not lose hot air intake connector hose when removing air cleaner metal intake duct

6.3 Plug fuel hoses after disconnection - pump inlet hose disconnected, outlet hose arrowed

6.5 Removing fuel pump and insulating block

7 Fuel gauge sender unit - removal and refitting

13 The air temperature control valve can be renewed only with the complete intake duct assembly. If a new intake duct assembly is being fitted, undo the four screws securing the hot air intake adaptor plate to the bottom of the duct and transfer the adaptor plate to the new duct.

14 Refitting is the reverse of the removal procedure.

5 Fuel system - inspection

Refer to Chapter 1.

6 Fuel pump - testing, removal and refitting

Testing

1 To test the fuel pump on the engine, temporarily disconnect the outlet pipe which leads to the carburettor and hold a wad of rag over the pump outlet while an assistant spins the engine on the starter. Keep your hands away from the electric cooling fan. Regular spurts of fuel should be ejected as the engine turns.

2 The pump can also be tested by removing it. With the pump outlet pipe disconnected but the inlet pipe still connected, hold a wad

of rag by the outlet. Operate the pump lever by hand, moving it in and out. If the pump is in a satisfactory condition, a strong jet of fuel should be ejected.

Removal

3 Identify the pump inlet and outlet hoses then, using a pair of pliers, release the retaining clips and disconnect them from the pump. Place wads of rag beneath the hose unions to catch any spilled fuel and plug the hose ends to minimise fuel loss (see illustration).

4 Slacken and remove the nuts and washers securing the pump to the cylinder head.

5 Withdraw the fuel pump from the engine and remove the insulating block (see illustration).

Refitting

6 Refitting is the reverse of the removal procedure. Clean the mating surfaces and renew the insulating block if its sealing surfaces are marked or damaged. Tighten the pump mounting nuts to the specified torque wrench setting.

Removal

1 Disconnect the battery negative lead.

2 On 214 models, open the tailgate and remove the parcel tray shelf. Fold the rear seats fully forwards then raise the luggage compartment carpet to gain access to the fuel sender unit access cover.

3 On 414 models, open the boot lid and lift up the luggage compartment carpet to gain access to the fuel sender unit access cover.

4 On all models, undo the three screws and remove the access cover from the floor (see illustration).

5 Remove the sender unit wiring connector rubber cover and disconnect the connector from the sender.

6 Unscrew the sender unit retaining ring by turning it in an anti-clockwise direction and remove it from the fuel tank. In the absence of the special Rover ring spanner, Service tool number 18G 1595 (see illustration), a pair of slip-jointed pliers will serve as an adequate substitute to slacken the ring.

7 Carefully lift the sender unit, taking great care not to bend or damage the sender float, and remove the sealing ring. Examine the sealing ring and renew it if it is worn or damaged.

Refitting

8 Refitting is the reverse of the removal procedure. Ensure that the tab on the sender unit is correctly engaged with the cutout in the fuel tank.

8 Fuel tank - removal and refitting

⚠ Warning: Do not under any circumstances attempt to solder or weld a fuel tank.

Removal

1 Before removing the fuel tank, all fuel must be drained from the tank. Since a fuel tank drain plug is not provided, it is therefore preferable to carry out the removal operation when the tank is nearly empty. Before proceeding, disconnect the battery negative lead and syphon or hand pump the remaining fuel from the tank.

2 Chock the front wheels, then jack up the rear of the vehicle and support it on axle stands. Remove the left-hand rear roadwheel.

3 Undo the bolt then slacken and remove the two screws securing the cover fitted to the left-hand side of the fuel tank. Prise out the screw retaining plugs and remove the cover to

7.4 Undo three screws to remove fuel gauge sender unit access cover

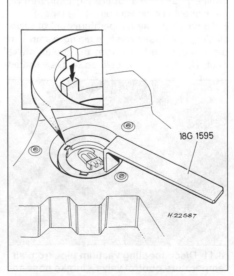

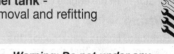

7.6 Using Rover special tool to remove fuel gauge sender unit

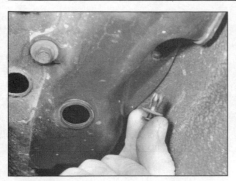

8.3 Removing cover retaining bolt (arrowed) and screw retaining plugs

8.4 Fuel tank return pipe retaining clip (A) and feed pipe union nut (B)

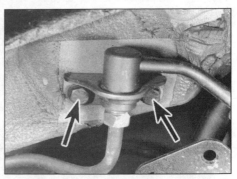

8.5 Feed pipe union mounting bolts (arrowed)

gain access to the fuel tank feed and return pipes **(see illustration)**.

4 Using a suitable pair of pliers, release the retaining clip and disconnect the small section of return pipe hose from the fuel tank **(see illustration)**.

5 Slacken the fuel feed pipe union nut and disconnect the pipe from the union. Undo the two union mounting bolts and free the union from the body **(see illustration)**.

6 Disconnect the fuel tank wiring block connector from the main wiring harness. If the block connector cannot yet be reached, it may be disconnected as the tank is lowered out of position.

7 Slacken the clamp securing the filler neck hose to the tank and use a pair of pliers to release the filler neck breather pipe retaining clip **(see illustration)**. Disconnect both the filler neck hose and breather pipe from the fuel tank.

8 Release the fuel tank breather, situated directly above the filler neck hose, from the vehicle body.

9 Slacken the tank retaining strap locknuts, then unscrew the lower locknuts and remove the straps whilst supporting the tank **(see illustration)**.

10 Lower the fuel tank out of position and remove it from under the vehicle.

11 If the tank is contaminated with sediment or water, remove the sender unit and swill the tank out with clean fuel. If the tank is damaged or leaks, it should be repaired by a

specialist or alternatively renewed. Do not under any circumstances attempt to solder or weld a fuel tank.

Refitting

12 Refitting is the reverse of the removal procedure. Tighten all nuts and bolts to their specified torque wrench settings and ensure that all hoses are correctly routed and securely fastened so that there can be no risk of fuel leakage.

9 Accelerator cable - removal, refitting and adjustment

Removal

1 Unscrew the four windscreen wiper motor mounting bolts to free the motor from the engine compartment bulkhead.

2 Slacken the accelerator cable locknuts and free the cable outer from its mounting bracket on the carburettor. Release the cable inner from the accelerator cam **(see illustration)**.

3 Work back along the cable outer and release it from any retaining clamps and ties.

4 Working from inside the vehicle, undo the five right-hand lower facia panel retaining screws and remove the panel.

5 Release the cable from the upper end of the accelerator pedal and withdraw the cable from the engine compartment.

Refitting

6 Refitting is the reverse of the removal procedure. Tighten the windscreen wiper motor retaining bolts to the specified torque (Chapter 12). Prior to tightening the cable locknuts, adjust the cable as follows.

Adjustment

7 Slacken both locknuts then gently pull up on the cable outer until all free play is removed from the cable and the accelerator cam just starts to move.

8 Holding the cable in position, screw the upper locknut down until there is a gap of approximately 5.0 mm between the lower edge of the nut and the cable mounting bracket. Release the cable then have an assistant depress the accelerator pedal fully and check that the throttle opens fully and returns to the at-rest position when the pedal is released. If the throttle operation is correct, hold the upper locknut stationary and tighten the lower locknut securely.

10 Accelerator pedal - removal and refitting

Removal

1 Working from inside the vehicle, undo the five right-hand lower facia panel retaining screws and remove the panel.

4A

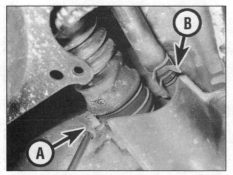

8.7 Slacken filler neck hose retaining clamp (A) and disconnect breather pipe (B)

8.9 Fuel tank mounting strap retaining locknut

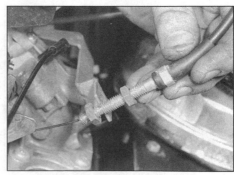

9.2 Disconnecting accelerator cable from carburettor

2 Release the accelerator cable from the upper end of the pedal and, using a pair of pliers, unhook the accelerator pedal return spring.

3 Prise off the circlip from the pedal pivot and withdraw the accelerator pedal from the mounting bracket.

Refitting

4 Refitting is a reverse of the removal procedure. Apply a smear of multi-purpose grease to the pedal pivot. On completion, adjust the accelerator cable.

11 Accelerator pedal switch - removal and refitting

Removal

1 Working from inside the vehicle, undo the five right-hand lower facia panel retaining screws and remove the panel.

2 Using a suitable pair of pliers, unhook the accelerator pedal return spring from the pedal then disconnect the accelerator cable from the pedal.

3 Disconnect the wiring connectors from the accelerator pedal switch then prise off the C-clip and remove the switch from the mounting bracket. Note the wave washer fitted between the switch and bracket.

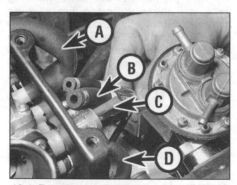

13.4 Breather hose (A), float chamber vent and full load air bleed hoses (B), idle bypass solenoid wiring (C) and fuel pump outlet hose (D)

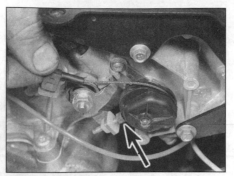

12.2 Releasing clip to disconnect choke cable from carburettor - fast idle adjusting screw arrowed

Refitting

4 Refitting is a reversal of the removal procedure.

12 Choke cable - removal, refitting and adjustment

Removal

1 Remove the air cleaner assembly.

2 Free the choke cable outer from its retaining clip on the carburettor and disconnect the cable inner from the choke cam **(see illustration)**.

3 Work back along the cable outer and release it from any retaining clamps and ties. Prise the cable grommet out of the engine compartment bulkhead.

4 Working inside the vehicle, undo the five right-hand lower facia panel retaining screws and remove the panel.

5 Using a suitable small screwdriver, slacken and remove the choke knob grub screw then pull the knob off the cable.

6 Unscrew the choke cable retaining nut then release the cable from the facia and disconnect the choke switch wiring connectors. The cable can then be withdrawn from the engine compartment and removed from the vehicle.

Refitting

7 Refitting is a reverse of the removal procedure. On completion adjust as follows.

Adjustment

8 Have an assistant pull the choke control knob fully out and check that the choke cam opens fully. Push the choke knob fully in and check that the choke cam returns to the fully-off position so that there is clearance between the cam and the fast idle adjusting screw. Providing that the choke cam returns fully, there should be no free play present in the cable.

9 The cable is adjusted by releasing the carburettor clip and repositioning the cable outer.

13 Carburettor - removal and refitting

Removal

1 Remove the air cleaner assembly.

2 Slacken the accelerator cable locknuts and free the cable outer from its mounting bracket on the carburettor. Release the cable inner from the accelerator cam.

3 Free the choke cable outer from its retaining clip on the carburettor and disconnect the cable inner from the choke cam.

4 Make a note of the correct fitted positions of the two small bore vacuum pipes, to ensure they are correctly positioned on refitting, then disconnect them from the carburettor **(see illustration)**.

5 Using pliers, release the retaining clip and disconnect the fuel feed hose from the carburettor. Place wads of rag around the union to catch any spilled fuel and plug the hose as soon as it is disconnected to minimise fuel loss.

6 Make a note of the correct fitted positions of the breather hoses then, where necessary, release the retaining clips and disconnect the three breather hoses from the carburettor.

7 Disconnect the wiring connector from the carburettor idle bypass solenoid **(see illustration)**.

8 Unscrew the four Torx screws securing the carburettor manifold adaptor to the inlet manifold and remove the carburettor assembly from the vehicle **(see illustrations)**. Remove the gasket and discard it, as a new one must be used on refitting. Plug the inlet

13.7 Note connections before disconnecting idle bypass solenoid wiring

13.8a Unscrew upper-to-lower inlet manifold Torx screws ...

13.8b ... and remove carburettor assembly

port with a wad of clean cloth to prevent the possible entry of foreign matter.

Refitting

9 Refitting is the reverse of the removal procedure, noting the following:
a) *Ensure the carburettor and inlet manifold sealing faces are clean and flat. Fit a new gasket and tighten the carburettor retaining screws to the specified torque.*
b) *Use the notes made on dismantling to ensure all hoses are refitted to their original positions and, where necessary, are securely held by their retaining clips.*
c) *Adjust the choke cable and accelerator cables.*
d) *Adjust the idle speed and mixture settings.*

14 Carburettor - diagnosis, overhaul and adjustments

Diagnosis

1 The SU carburettor does not usually suffer from jet blockages and wear is usually only found between the needle and jet, although it is worth checking the fit of the piston in the suction chamber whenever the carburettor is dismantled. If the idle speed is too high and cannot be reduced by normal adjustment, it is worth checking the throttle disc overrun valve spring (if fitted). If this spring has weakened, the throttle disc must be renewed.
2 If a carburettor fault is suspected, always check first the following:
a) *That the ignition timing is accurate.*
b) *That the spark plugs are in good condition and correctly gapped.*
c) *That the accelerator and choke cables are correctly adjusted.*
d) *That the carburettor piston damper is topped-up.*
e) *That the float chamber vent hose and (especially if the mixture is very rich) the full load air bleed hose are clear.*
f) *That the air cleaner filter element is clean.*
3 If the engine is running very roughly, check the compression pressures, bearing in mind the possibility that one of the hydraulic tappets might be faulty, thereby producing an incorrect valve clearance.
4 If careful checking of all of the above produces no improvement, the carburettor must be removed for cleaning and overhaul.

Overhaul

5 A complete strip-down of a carburettor is unlikely to cure a fault which is not immediately obvious without introducing new problems. If persistent carburation problems are encountered, it is recommended that the advice of a Rover dealer or carburettor specialist is sought. Most dealers will be able to provide carburettor re-jetting and servicing facilities and if necessary, it should be

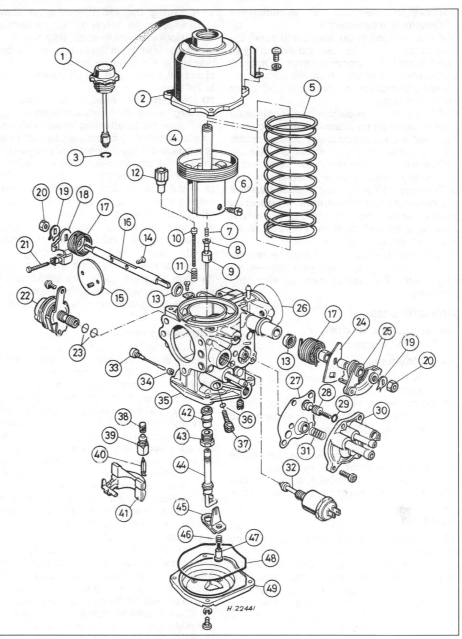

14.8 SU KIF carburettor assembly

1 Piston damper	16 Throttle spindle	33 Float pivot
2 Suction chamber	17 Return spring	34 Pivot seal
3 C-clip	18 Fast idle lever	35 Carburettor body
4 Piston	19 Lockwasher	36 O-ring
5 Piston spring	20 Nut	37 Jet adjusting screw
6 Needle retaining (grub) screw	21 Fast idle adjusting screw	38 Fuel strainer
7 Needle spring	22 Choke assembly	39 Float needle seat
8 Needle	23 O-ring	40 Float needle
9 Needle guide	24 Throttle return spring lever	41 Float
10 Idle speed screw	25 Throttle lever	42 Jet bearing
11 Spring	26 O-ring	43 Jet bearing nut
12 Idle speed adjusting knob	27 Diaphragm	44 Jet
13 Throttle spindle seal	28 Idle air bypass screw	45 Bi-metal lever assembly
14 Screw	29 O-ring	46 Spring
15 Throttle disc - with overrun valve	30 Full load enrichment device	47 Jet retaining screw
	31 Spring	48 O-ring
	32 Idle bypass solenoid	49 Float chamber cover

4A

possible to purchase a reconditioned carburettor of the relevant type.

6 If it is decided to go ahead and service a carburettor, check the cost and availability of spare parts before commencement. Obtain a carburettor repair kit, which will contain the necessary gaskets, diaphragms and other renewable items.

7 When working on carburettors, scrupulous cleanliness must be observed and care must be taken not to introduce any foreign matter into components. Carburettors are delicate instruments and care should be taken not to disturb any components unnecessarily.

8 Referring to the relevent exploded view of the carburettor **(see illustration on previous page)**, remove each component part whilst making a note of its fitted position. Make alignment marks on linkages, etc.

9 Reassemble the carburettor in the reverse order to dismantling, using new gaskets, O-rings, etc. Be careful not to kink any diaphragms.

Adjustments

Idle speed and mixture

10 Refer to Chapter 1.

Fast idle speed

11 Check the accelerator and choke cables are correctly adjusted.

12 Warm the engine up to normal operating temperature and check that the idle speed and mixture are correctly set.

13 Pull out the choke control to the first detent position and check that the engine speed increases to the specified amount.

14 If adjustment is required, screw the fast idle adjusting screw in or out until the engine speed is correct.

Fuel level

15 The carburettor fuel level is adjusted by bending the float arm to alter the float height, usually measured with the carburettor inverted. However, since the necessary information is not provided by the manufacturer, the vehicle should be taken to a Rover dealer or SU carburettor specialist if the fuel level is thought to be incorrect.

Jet adjustment

16 Accurate jet adjustment is not easy for the inexperienced and can only be carried out using an exhaust gas analyser. If the jet adjustment is thought to be incorrect or is to be checked, owners without the required equipment and the skill to use it are advised to have the work carried out by a Rover dealer or SU carburettor specialist, otherwise proceed as follows.

17 Warm the engine up to normal operating temperature and check that the ignition timing, idle speed and mixture are correctly set and that the carburettor piston damper is topped-up, see Chapter 1.

18 Remove the tamperproof cap from the jet adjusting screw recess at the front left-hand corner of the carburettor body.

19 Counting the exact number of turns required to do so, screw the idle air bypass screw clockwise until it seats lightly, then start the engine, switch on the headlamps, heated rear window and heater blower motor (first speed only) and adjust the idle speed to 700 to 750 rpm.

20 Connect the exhaust gas analyser following its manufacturer's instructions.

21 Turning the jet adjusting screw either way (clockwise to richen the mixture) by half a turn at a time and waiting for the analyser reading to respond and stabilise before making a further alteration, set the mixture to a base CO level of 5.5 % ± 0.5 %. When the analyser reading is steady at the correct level, switch off all electrical loads.

22 Screw the idle air bypass screw anti-clockwise by the number of turns previously noted to return it to its original setting, then set the true idle mixture to the specified value.

23 Stop the engine when the adjustment is correct, disconnect the test equipment and fit a new tamperproof cap to the jet adjusting screw recess.

Idle bypass system

24 As well as the carburettor idle air bypass passage and screw, the system incorporates the solenoid and the accelerator pedal switch.

25 When the accelerator is closed and the ignition is switched on the solenoid is energised, its plunger being retracted to open the bypass passage. This allows air to bypass the carburettor piston and thus makes the idle mixture independent of the needle metering. Screwing in (clockwise) the idle air bypass screw reduces the amount of air bypassing the piston and richens the idle mixture.

26 As soon as the accelerator pedal is depressed, the accelerator pedal switch opens, the solenoid is de-energised and the bypass passage is shut off.

27 To check the system, listen closely by the carburettor while an assistant switches on the ignition and depresses and releases the accelerator pedal several times. The solenoid should be heard to be clicking in and out.

28 If no clicking is heard, remove the air cleaner assembly and use a meter or similar to check the solenoid earth and feed, see Chapter 12.

Use a meter to check that the accelerator pedal switch contacts open and close. If the solenoid or switch is faulty, then it must be renewed. Note that if trouble is encountered with an ignition system fuse blowing repeatedly, and the fault cannot otherwise be traced, the solenoid may be at fault.

15 Inlet manifold pre-heater - operation, removal and refitting

Operation

1 The system incorporates the manifold PTC (Positive Temperature Coefficient) heater, the relay and the manifold temperature switch.

2 When the ignition is switched on and the engine is cold (coolant below 50°C), the relay-energising current flows through the closed manifold temperature switch contacts, which then closes the relay contacts and allows current to flow from the battery to the heater. This ensures that the inlet manifold is warm enough, even before the effect of the coolant heating becomes apparent, to prevent fuel droplets condensing in the manifold, thus improving driveability and reducing exhaust emissions when the engine is cold.

3 As soon as the engine warms up to temperatures above 50°C, the switch contacts open and the relay cuts off the power supply to the manifold heater.

4 If the engine suddenly develops flat spots when cold, the system may be faulty.

PTC heater

Removal

5 Drain the cooling system.

6 Apply the handbrake then jack up the front of the vehicle and support it on axle stands. Access to the PTC heater can then be gained from underneath the vehicle, via the gap between the engine and engine compartment bulkhead.

7 Disconnect the wiring connector from the heater terminal then extract the heater retaining circlip. Withdraw the heater from the underside of the manifold **(see illustrations)**.

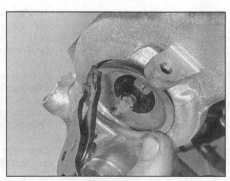

15.7a Extract circlip . . .

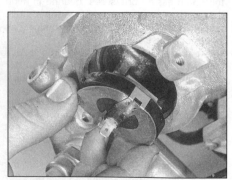

15.7b . . . and remove PTC heater from inlet manifold - manifold removed for clarity

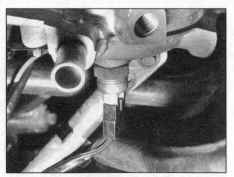

15.9 Inlet manifold pre-heater temperature switch location

16.11a Inlet manifold support stay upper end bolt (arrowed)

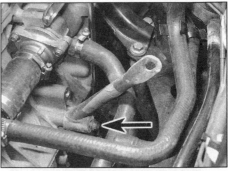

16.11b Inlet manifold support stay lower end bolt (arrowed)

Inspect the heater rubber seal for signs of damage or deterioration and renew if necessary.

Refitting

8 Refitting is the reverse of the removal procedure. Ensure that the heater locating projection is correctly engaged in the manifold recess. On completion, lower the vehicle to the ground and refill the cooling system.

Pre-heater temperature switch

Removal

9 The pre-heater temperature switch is fitted to the underside of the inlet manifold (see illustration). Either drain the cooling system or be prepared for some loss of coolant as the switch is unscrewed.
10 Release the wire retaining clip and disconnect the wiring connector from the switch.
11 Unscrew the switch from the manifold and withdraw it, then plug the opening to prevent the entry of dirt. If the cooling system has not been drained, work quickly to minimise coolant loss.

Refitting

12 Wipe clean the threads of the switch and of the thermostat housing. If a sealing washer is fitted, renew it whenever it is disturbed to prevent leaks. If no sealing washer is fitted, apply a smear of sealant to the switch threads.
13 Refit the switch, working quickly if the

cooling system was not drained, and tighten it. Reconnect the wiring connector.
14 Replenish the cooling system.

Manifold heater relay

15 Refer to Chapter 12.

16 Inlet manifold - removal and refitting

Note: *The following procedure describes removal of the manifold with the carburettor. Access to some of the components concerned is much improved if the carburettor is first removed separately and if this is done, the following procedure should be amended as required.*

Removal

1 Disconnect the battery negative terminal.
2 Remove the air cleaner assembly.
3 Drain the cooling system.
4 Disconnect the accelerator and choke cables.
5 Slacken the retaining clamps and disconnect the coolant hoses from the inlet manifold.
6 Trace the float chamber vent hose and the full load air bleed hose from the carburettor down to their metal pipes then unscrew the nut and bolts securing the pipes to the cylinder block/crankcase.
7 Using pliers, release the retaining clip and

disconnect the fuel feed hose from the carburettor. Place wads of rag around the union to catch any spilled fuel and plug the hose as soon as it is disconnected to minimise fuel loss.
8 Disconnect the vacuum pipe from the distributor vacuum diaphragm unit and disconnect the breather hose from the cylinder head cover.
9 Slacken and remove the brake vacuum servo unit hose union bolt and disconnect the hose. Discard the hose union sealing washers which must be renewed whenever they are disturbed.
10 Disconnect the idle bypass solenoid wiring, making notes of the connections so that they can be correctly reconnected, then disconnect the wiring from the manifold pre-heater switch and heater which are situated on the underside of the manifold.
11 Undo the single bolt which secures each manifold support stay to the cylinder block/crankcase and slacken the bolts which secure the stays to the inlet manifold (see illustrations).
12 Make a final check that all the necessary fuel/breather hoses have been disconnected from the carburettor/manifold then unscrew the nuts and bolts securing the manifold to the cylinder head. Manoeuvre the manifold out of the engine compartment and discard its gasket.

Refitting

13 Refitting is the reverse of the removal procedure, noting the following (see illustrations):
a) Ensure that the manifold and cylinder

16.13a Fit a new manifold gasket . . .

16.13b . . . and fit inlet manifold - less carburettor

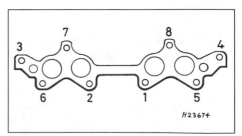

16.13c Inlet manifold tightening sequence - K8 engine

4A

head mating surfaces are clean and dry, then fit a new manifold gasket.
b) Working in the sequence shown, tighten the manifold retaining nuts and bolts evenly to the specified torque wrench setting.
c) Ensure all relevant hoses are reconnected to their original positions and are securely held (where necessary) by their retaining clips.
d) Renew the vacuum servo unit vacuum hose banjo union sealing washers and tighten the union bolt.
e) Adjust the accelerator and choke cables.
f) On completion, refill the cooling system.

17 Exhaust manifold - removal and refitting

Removal

1 Disconnect the battery negative terminal.
2 Remove the air cleaner metal intake duct assembly.
3 Firmly apply the handbrake then jack up the front of the vehicle and support it on axle stands.
4 Unscrew the nuts securing the exhaust front pipe to the manifold, then disconnect the pipe and collect the gasket.
5 Remove the four exhaust manifold shroud retaining screws and remove the shroud.
6 Unscrew the nuts securing the manifold to the cylinder head, then manoeuvre it out of the engine compartment. Remove the manifold gasket and discard it.
7 Examine all the exhaust manifold studs for signs of damage and corrosion. Remove all traces of corrosion and repair or renew any damaged studs.

Refitting

8 Refitting is the reverse of the removal procedure, noting the following **(see illustrations)**:
a) Ensure that the manifold and cylinder head sealing faces are clean and flat, then fit a new manifold gasket.
b) Working in the sequence shown, tighten the manifold retaining nuts evenly to the specified torque wrench setting.
c) Tighten all other disturbed nuts and bolts to their specified torque wrench settings (where given).

18 Exhaust system - inspection, removal and refitting

Note: If a catalytic converter is fitted to the exhaust system, remember that it is FRAGILE. Do not use hammers, mallets, etc. to strike any part of the system and take care not to drop it or strike the converter against anything while handling it.

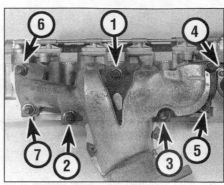

17.8a Refitting exhaust manifold with new gasket

17.8b Exhaust manifold tightening sequence - K8 engine

1 On models not equipped with a catalytic converter the exhaust system is in three sections. All exhaust sections are joined by a flanged joint. If a catalytic converter is fitted, it is situated between the front pipe and the intermediate pipe, with a flanged joint at each end. The front pipe then has a gas-sampling take off point which is fitted to permit mixture checks using an exhaust gas analyser **(see illustrations)**.

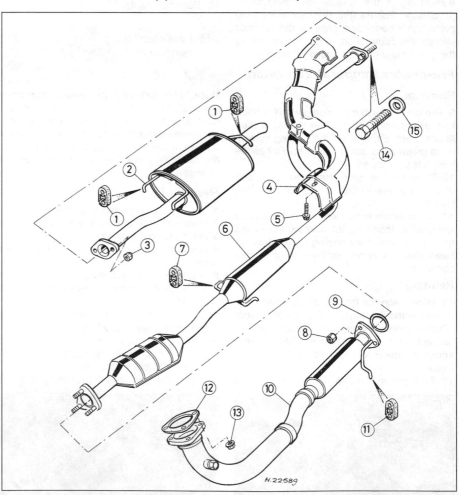

18.1a Exhaust system components - without catalytic converter

1 Mounting rubber	7 Mounting rubber	12 Gasket - front pipe to exhaust manifold
2 Tailpipe	8 Nut	
3 Nut	9 Gasket - front pipe to intermediate pipe	13 Nut
4 Heatshield	10 Front pipe	14 Bolt (stud replacement)
5 Bolt	11 Mounting rubber	15 Plain washer
6 Intermediate pipe		

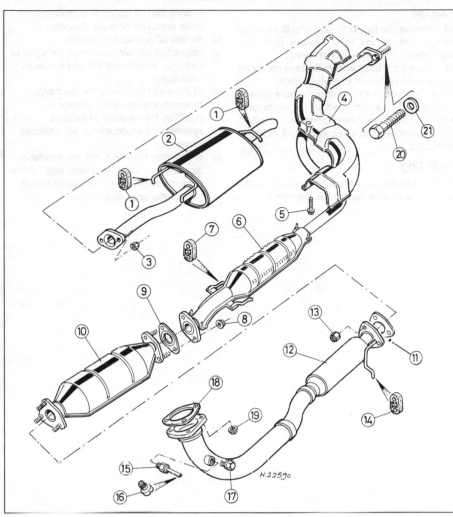

18.1b Exhaust system components - with catalytic converter

1	Mounting rubber	10	Catalytic converter	16	Gas sampling pipe sealing
2	Tailpipe	11	Gasket - front pipe to		screw - open loop system
3	Nut		catalytic converter	17	Blanking plug - closed
4	Heatshield	12	Front pipe		loop system
5	Bolt	13	Nut	18	Gasket - front pipe to
6	Intermediate pipe	14	Mounting rubber		exhaust manifold
7	Mounting rubber	15	Gas sampling pipe - open	19	Nut
8	Nut		loop system	20	Bolt (stud replacement)
9	Gasket - catalytic converter			21	Plain washer
	to intermediate pipe				

2 The exhaust system is suspended throughout its entire length by rubber mountings **(see illustration)**.

Inspection

3 Refer to Chapter 1.

Removal

4 Each exhaust section can be removed individually or, alternatively, the complete system can be removed as a unit once the front pipe has been unbolted from the manifold and the system has been freed from all its mounting rubbers.

5 To remove the system or any part of the system, first jack up the front or rear of the vehicle and support it on axle stands. Alternatively position the vehicle over an inspection pit or on car ramps.

Front pipe

6 Remove the three nuts securing the front pipe flange joint to the manifold and, where necessary, the two bolts securing the front pipe to its mounting bracket. Separate the flange joint and collect the gasket **(see illustration)**.

7 Free the pipe from its mounting rubber then undo the three nuts securing the front pipe to the intermediate pipe/catalytic converter (as applicable) and manoeuvre the front pipe out from under the vehicle **(see illustration)**.

Catalytic converter

8 Slacken and remove the two nuts securing the catalytic converter to the intermediate pipe, then separate the flange joint and recover the gasket.

9 Undo the three nuts securing the converter to the front pipe then remove it from the vehicle.

Intermediate pipe

10 Slacken the two nuts securing the tailpipe flange joint to the intermediate pipe and separate the flange joint.

11 Undo the three nuts securing the intermediate pipe to the front pipe, or the two nuts securing the pipe to the catalytic converter (as applicable).

12 Free the intermediate pipe from all its mounting rubbers and manoeuvre it out from under the vehicle.

4A

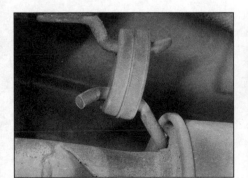

18.2 Exhaust system rubber mounting

18.6 Front pipe-to-manifold flange joint

18.7 Front pipe-to-intermediate pipe flange joint and mounting rubber

18.13 Tailpipe-to-intermediate flange joint

Tailpipe

13 Remove the two nuts securing the tailpipe flange joint to the intermediate pipe and separate the joint **(see illustration)**.

14 Unhook the tailpipe from its three mounting rubbers and remove it from the vehicle.

15 If the threads of the intermediate pipe to tailpipe studs are damaged, or the studs snap when the nuts are being undone, the studs can be knocked out of position and replaced with bolts.

Refitting

16 Each section is refitted by a reverse of the removal sequence, noting the following:

a) Ensure that all traces of corrosion have been removed from the flanges.

b) Renew all necessary gaskets.

c) Inspect all rubber mountings for signs of damage or deterioration and renew as necessary.

d) Tighten all flange nuts by hand only to locate the disturbed section in position, then ensure all exhaust system rubber mountings are correctly seated.

e) Check that there is adequate clearance between the exhaust system and vehicle underbody before tightening all flange nuts to the specified torque.

Chapter 4 Part B Fuel and exhaust systems - single-point fuel injection engines

Contents

Degrees of difficulty

| Easy, suitable for novice with little experience | Fairly easy, suitable for beginner with some experience | Fairly difficult, suitable for competent DIY mechanic | Difficult, suitable for experienced DIY mechanic | Very difficult, suitable for expert DIY or professional |

Specifications

System
Type .... Rover/Motorola Modular Engine Management System, using ECU-controlled single-point injection (MEMS-SPi) and speed/density method of airflow measurement

MEMS-SPi system data
Fuel pump type .... Electric, immersed in fuel tank
Fuel pump pressure:
  Maximum - at 16 volts .... 2.7 bar
  Regulated constant pressure .... 1.0 to 1.2 bar
Injector/pressure regulator assembly .... JZX 3028
Throttle potentiometer voltage:
  Throttle closed .... 0 to 1 volt
  Throttle open .... 4 to 5 volts
Idle speed - nominal value given for reference purposes only .... 850 ± 50 rpm
CO level at idle speed - engine at normal operating temperature:
  Without catalytic converter - at tailpipe .... 0.5 to 2.0 %
  With catalytic converter - at gas-sampling pipe .... 0.5 to 2.0 %

Recommended fuel
Minimum octane rating:
  Without catalytic converter .... 95 RON unleaded (ie: unleaded Premium) or 97 RON leaded (ie: 4-star)
  With catalytic converter .... 95 RON unleaded (ie: unleaded Premium)

Torque wrench settings

	Nm	lbf ft
Fuel system		
Injector housing fuel pipe union nuts	24	18
Injector housing fuel pipe adaptors	24	18
Injector housing screws	5	4
Throttle housing retaining nuts	18	13
Fuel system pressure release bolt - models without catalytic converter	12	9
Fuel pump retaining nuts	9	7
Vent valve and hose retaining nuts	9	7
ECU retaining nuts	9	7
Intake air temperature sensor	7	5
Coolant temperature sensor	15	11
Inlet manifold nuts and bolts	25	18
Inlet manifold support stay bolts	25	18
Exhaust system		
Oxygen (lambda) sensor	55	41
Exhaust manifold retaining nuts	45	33
Exhaust manifold shroud screws	6	4
Exhaust system flange nuts:		
Manifold-to-front pipe joint	50	37
All other joints	45	33
Exhaust front pipe mounting bolts	15	11

1 General information and precautions

General information

The fuel system consists of a fuel tank mounted under the rear of the vehicle with an electric fuel pump immersed in it, a fuel filter, fuel feed and return lines and the throttle body assembly (which incorporates the single fuel injector and the fuel pressure regulator), as well as the Engine Management Electronic Control Unit (ECU) and the various sensors, electrical components and related wiring. The ECU fully controls both the ignition system and the fuel injection system, integrating the two in a complete engine management system **(see illustration)**. Refer to Chapter 5 for information on the ignition side of the system.

The Rover/Motorola Modular Engine Management System uses ECU-controlled single-point injection (MEMS-SPi) and the speed/density method of airflow measurement. The whole system is best explained if considered as three sub-systems which are, the fuel delivery, air metering and electrical control systems.

The fuel delivery system incorporates the fuel tank with an electric fuel pump, which is immersed in a swirl pot to prevent aeration of the fuel, inside it. When the ignition is switched on, the pump is supplied with current via the fuel pump relay, under the control of the ECU. The pump feeds petrol via a non-return valve (to prevent fuel draining out of the system components and back to the tank when the pump is not working) to the fuel filter and from the filter to the injector. Fuel pressure is controlled by the pressure regulator, which lifts to allow excess fuel to

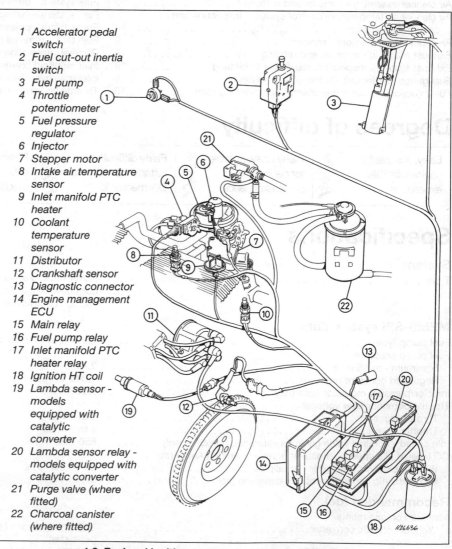

1 Accelerator pedal switch
2 Fuel cut-out inertia switch
3 Fuel pump
4 Throttle potentiometer
5 Fuel pressure regulator
6 Injector
7 Stepper motor
8 Intake air temperature sensor
9 Inlet manifold PTC heater
10 Coolant temperature sensor
11 Distributor
12 Crankshaft sensor
13 Diagnostic connector
14 Engine management ECU
15 Main relay
16 Fuel pump relay
17 Inlet manifold PTC heater relay
18 Ignition HT coil
19 Lambda sensor - models equipped with catalytic converter
20 Lambda sensor relay - models equipped with catalytic converter
21 Purge valve (where fitted)
22 Charcoal canister (where fitted)

1.0 Fuel and ignition system components - MEMS-SPi

return to the tank swirl pot, where a venturi causes the returning fuel to draw cool fuel from the tank into the swirl pot. In the event of sudden deceleration (ie: an accident) an inertia switch cuts off the power to the pump so that the risk of fire is minimised from fuel spraying out of broken fuel lines under pressure.

The air metering system includes the intake air temperature control system and the air cleaner, but the main components are in the throttle body assembly. This incorporates the injector, which sprays fuel onto the back of the throttle disc, the throttle potentiometer, which is linked to the throttle disc spindle and sends the ECU information on the rate of throttle opening by transmitting a varying voltage, and the stepper motor, which is controlled by the ECU and operates the throttle disc spindle lever via a cam and pushrod to provide idle speed control. Note that there is no provision for adjustment of the idle speed except by reprogramming the ECU using Rover diagnostic equipment. If checking idle speed, remember that it will vary constantly under ECU control.

The electrical control system consists of the ECU, with all the sensors that provide it with information, and the actuators by which it controls the whole system's operation. The ECU's manifold absolute pressure sensor is connected, by hoses and a fuel (vapour) trap mounted in the air cleaner assembly, to the inlet manifold. Variations in manifold pressure are converted into graduated electrical signals which are used by the ECU to determine the load on the engine. The intake air temperature sensor is self-explanatory, the crankshaft sensor gives it the engine speed and crankshaft position, the coolant temperature sensor gives it the engine temperature and the accelerator pedal switch tells it when the accelerator is closed. The throttle potentiometer is explained above and the lambda sensor (where fitted) in Part D of this Chapter. In addition, the ECU senses battery voltage (adjusting the injector pulse width to suit and using the stepper motor to increase the idle speed and, therefore, the alternator output if it is too low), incorporates short-circuit protection and diagnostic capabilities and can both receive and transmit information

via the diagnostic connector, thus permitting engine diagnosis and tuning by Rover diagnostic equipment. If either the coolant temperature sensor, the intake air temperature sensor or the manifold absolute pressure sensor circuits should fail to provide adequate information, the ECU has a back-up facility which assumes a value corresponding to a coolant temperature of 60°C, an intake air temperature of 35°C and an engine load based on the engine speed and throttle position. These are used to implement a back-up air/fuel mixture ratio.

All these signals are compared by the ECU, using digital techniques, with set values pre-programmed (mapped) into its memory. Based on this information, the ECU selects the response appropriate to those values and controls the ignition HT coil (varying the ignition timing as required), the fuel injector (varying its pulse width - the length of time the injector is held open - to provide a richer or weaker mixture, as appropriate), the stepper motor (controlling the idle and fast idle speeds), the fuel pump relay (controlling the fuel delivery), the manifold heater relay (controlling the inlet manifold pre-heater system) and the main relay, the purge control valve (where fitted) and the lambda sensor and relay (where fitted) accordingly. The mixture, idle speed and ignition timing are constantly varied by the ECU to provide the best settings for cranking, starting and engine warm-up (with either a hot or cold engine), idle, cruising and acceleration. A rev-limiter circuit is built into the ECU which switches off the injector earth (ie: the fuel supply) if engine speed exceeds 6860 rpm, switching it back on at 6820 rpm. The injector earth is also switched off on the overrun (coolant temperature above 80°C, throttle pedal switch contacts closed, engine speed above 1500 rpm) to improve fuel economy and reduce exhaust emissions.

The ECU idle control is an adaptive system which learns the engine load and wear characteristics over a period of time and adjusts the idle speed to suit. If the ECU is renewed, or one from another vehicle is fitted, it will take a short period of normal driving for

the new ECU to learn the engine's characteristics and restore full idle control.

To reduce emissions and to improve driveability when the engine is cold, the inlet manifold is heated by the cooling system coolant and by an electric pre-heater system. Mixture enrichment for cold starting is a pre-programmed function of the system.

The air cleaner contains a disposable paper filter element and incorporates a flap valve air temperature control system which allows cold air from the outside of the vehicle and warm air from the exhaust manifold to enter the air cleaner in the correct proportions.

The exhaust system is as described in Part A of this Chapter.

Precautions

Fuel injection system

Residual pressure will remain in the fuel lines long after the vehicle was last used, therefore extra care must be taken when disconnecting a fuel line hose. Loosen any fuel hose slowly to avoid a sudden release of pressure which may cause fuel spray. As an added precaution, place a rag over each union as it is disconnected to catch any fuel which is forcibly expelled.

Fuel usage

Refer to Part A of this Chapter.

Catalytic converters

Before attempting work on these items, carefully read the precautions listed in Part D of this Chapter.

---

2   Air cleaner filter element - renewal

Refer to Chapter 1.

---

3   Air cleaner assembly - removal and refitting

Removal

1 Release the two clips securing the air intake duct to the assembly, then undo the three screws securing the assembly to the throttle body **(see illustration)**.

2 Release the assembly from the intake duct and withdraw it, collecting the throttle housing seal and the intake duct sealing ring (where fitted), then disconnect the following **(see illustration)**:

a) *The thermac switch vacuum pipes. These are colour-coded (yellow to the temperature control valve, red to the inlet manifold).*

b) *The ECU manifold absolute pressure sensor fuel trap vacuum hoses. These are colour-coded (green to the ECU, white to the inlet manifold).*

c) *The intake air temperature sensor wiring.*

3.1 Releasing clips to separate intake duct from air cleaner

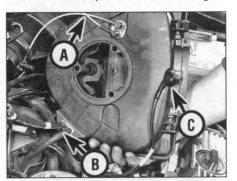

3.2 Thermac switch vacuum pipes (A), fuel trap vacuum hoses (B), intake air temperature sensor wiring (C) and throttle housing seal (D)

3.6a Remove T-piece . . .

3.6b . . . then remove resonator

3 Check the condition of the throttle housing seal and the intake duct O-ring (where fitted). Renew either if worn or damaged.

4 To remove the metal intake duct, refer to Section 4, paragraphs 3 and 4.

5 To remove the air intake hose it will first be necessary to remove the left-hand headlamp assembly, to gain access to the two retaining screws. Remove the two retaining screws and disconnect the duct from the body front panel, release the clip securing the ignition HT lead, then slacken the retaining clamp and unfasten the rubber strap to separate the cold air duct from the intake duct. Release the intake hose from the resonator T-piece and remove it from the engine compartment.

6 A resonator chamber is fitted to the intake hose to reduce the amount of induction noise. To remove the chamber, first remove the battery and battery tray. Disconnect the intake hose from the T-piece then remove the resonator T-piece. Release any relevant retaining clips from the resonator, then remove the resonator from the engine compartment **(see illustrations)**.

Refitting

7 Refitting is the reverse of the removal procedure. Ensure that the vacuum pipes and hoses are correctly reconnected and are not trapped as the assembly is refitted, then check that the assembly sits properly on the throttle body before tightening the screws securely.

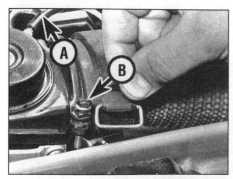

4.3 Unfastening cold air intake duct rubber strap - vacuum pipe (A) and clamp screw (B)

4 Air cleaner air temperature control system - inspection and component renewal

Inspection

1 Refer to Section 4 in Part A of this Chapter.

Thermac switch - renewal

2 Refer to Section 4 in Part A of this Chapter, removing the air cleaner assembly as described in the previous Section.

Air temperature control valve - renewal

3 Disconnect the vacuum pipe from the air temperature control valve, then slacken the intake hose retaining clamp. Release the intake hose rubber retaining strap and disconnect the hose from the metal intake duct **(see illustration)**.

4 Release the two clips securing the air intake duct to the air cleaner assembly and undo the bolt securing the duct to its mounting bracket **(see illustration)**. Withdraw the duct, taking care not to lose the hot air intake connector hose which connects the duct to the exhaust manifold shroud.

5 The air temperature control valve can be renewed only with the complete intake duct assembly. If a new intake duct assembly is being fitted, undo the three screws securing

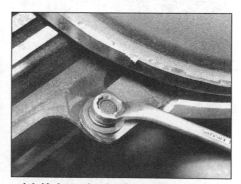

4.4 Unfastening intake duct-to-support bracket retaining bolt

the hot air intake adaptor plate to the bottom of the duct and transfer the adaptor plate to the new duct.

6 Refitting is the reverse of the removal procedure.

5 Fuel system - inspection

Refer to Chapter 1.

6 Fuel system - depressurisation

> ⚠ **Warning: The following procedure will merely relieve the pressure in the fuel system. Remember that fuel will still be present in the system components and take precautions accordingly before disconnecting any of them.**

1 The fuel system referred to in this Section is defined as the tank-mounted fuel pump, the fuel filter, the fuel injector and the pressure regulator in the injector housing, and the metal pipes and flexible hoses of the fuel lines between these components. All these contain fuel which will be under pressure while the engine is running and/or while the ignition is switched on. The pressure will remain for some time after the ignition has been switched off and must be relieved before any of these components are disturbed for servicing work.

Models with a catalytic converter

2 On models equipped with a catalytic converter, the system is depressurised via the small bolt fitted to the fuel filter inlet (feed) union nut.

3 Position wads of rag around the union to catch the spilled fuel and slowly slacken the bolt.

4 Once all pressure has been released, remove the bolt. Inspect the sealing washer for signs of wear or damage and renew if necessary.

5 Refit the bolt and sealing washer to the union nut and tighten it securely.

Models without a catalytic converter

6 On models not fitted with a catalytic converter, the system is depressurised via the bolt in the metal fuel filter outlet pipe.

7 Position wads of rag around the pipe to catch the spilled fuel as the bolt is removed. Carefully slacken the bolt whilst holding the fuel pipe boss with an open-ended spanner to

6.7 Slackening pressure release bolt to depressurise fuel system - non-catalyst system

prevent any undue strain being placed on the fuel pipe **(see illustration)**.

8 Once all pressure has been relieved, remove the bolt and inspect the sealing washer for signs of wear or damage and renew if necessary.

9 Refit the bolt and washer to the fuel pipe and tighten it to the specified torque wrench setting whilst using a spanner to counter-hold the pipe boss, to prevent the pipe or filter being damaged.

7 Fuel system - pressure check

1 The following procedure is based on the use of the Rover pressure gauge and adaptor (Service tool numbers 18G 1500 and 18G 1500/3).

2 Depressurise the fuel system.

3 Unscrew the pressure release bolt and screw in the adaptor, then connect the pressure gauge.

4 Turn the engine over on the starter motor. The pressure should reach the specified

value. Stop cranking the engine and watch the gauge. The pressure drop in the first minute should not exceed 0.7 bar.

5 If the pressure first recorded was too high, renew the pressure regulator, which means renewing the complete injector housing assembly.

6 If the pressure first recorded was too low or if it falls too quickly, check the system carefully for leaks. If no leaks are found, check the pump by substituting a new one, then recheck the pressure. If the pressure does not improve, the fault is in the pressure regulator and the complete injector housing assembly must be renewed. If this is the case, it is worth dismantling the regulator to check that the fault is not due to its being jammed open with dirt.

8 Fuel pump - removal and refitting

Removal

1 Remove the fuel tank.

2 Release the clips securing the tank vent hose to the fuel tank breather and fuel cut-off valve, then disconnect the hose. Undo the vent hose and valve retaining nuts, then disconnect the vent valve hose from the fuel pump and remove the vent hose and valve assembly from the tank **(see illustration)**.

3 Disconnect the wiring connector from the fuel pump.

4 Slacken and remove the six fuel pump retaining nuts. Carefully withdraw the fuel pump assembly from the tank and remove the pump seal.

Refitting

5 Refitting is a reversal of the removal sequence, noting the following:

a) Renew the pump seal if there is any doubt as to its condition.
b) Tighten all retaining nuts to the specified torque setting.
c) Ensure that the vent hoses are correctly connected and are securely held by any necessary retaining clips.

9 Fuel gauge sender unit - removal and refitting

Refer to Section 7 in Part A of this Chapter.

10 Fuel tank - removal and refitting

1 Refer to Section 8 in Part A of this Chapter. Note that the fuel system must be depressurised before any fuel hose is disconnected.

11 Accelerator cable - removal, refitting and adjustment

Removal

1 Remove the four windscreen wiper motor mounting bolts to free the motor from the engine compartment bulkhead.

2 Slacken the accelerator cable locknuts and free the cable outer from its mounting bracket. Release the cable inner from the throttle cam **(see illustration)**.

3 Work back along the cable outer and release it from any retaining clamps.

4 Working inside the vehicle, undo the five right-hand lower facia panel retaining screws and remove the panel.

5 Release the cable from the upper end of the accelerator pedal and withdraw the cable from the engine compartment.

Refitting

6 Refitting is the reverse of the removal procedure. Tighten the windscreen wiper motor retaining bolts to the specified torque

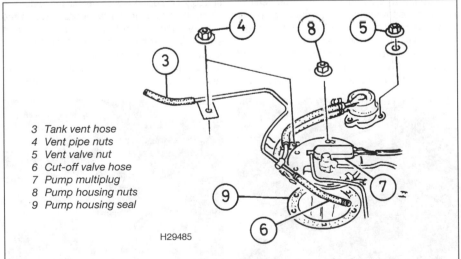

3 Tank vent hose
4 Vent pipe nuts
5 Vent valve nut
6 Cut-off valve hose
7 Pump multiplug
8 Pump housing nuts
9 Pump housing seal

H29485

8.2 Fuel pump connections

11.2 Disconnecting accelerator cable from throttle cam pulley

4B

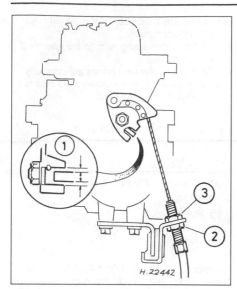

11.7 Accelerator cable adjustment

1 *Throttle lever to lost motion link clearance should be equal on each side*
2 *Adjuster nut*
3 *Adjuster locknut*

(Chapter 12) and prior to tightening the cable locknuts, adjust the cable as follows.

Adjustment

7 With the pedal fully released, check that there is equal clearance on each side of the throttle lever at the lost motion link **(see illustration)** and no slack in the cable. Have an assistant fully depress the pedal and check that the throttle cam opens fully, then check that it returns to the at-rest position when released.

8 To adjust the cable, switch on the ignition and position the stepper motor by moving the cam only to open, and fully close the throttle. Note that it is essential for accurate positioning of the stepper motor that the accelerator pedal switch contacts remain closed, so that the ECU recognises the throttle movement as a command and indexes the stepper motor to 25 steps.

9 Slacken the adjuster locknut (upper nut), then tighten the adjuster (lower) nut until the clearance is equal on each side of the throttle

lever at the lost motion link. Tighten the locknut without disturbing this setting. Recheck the adjustment and switch off the ignition.

12 Accelerator pedal - removal and refitting

Refer to Section 10 in Part A of this Chapter.

13 Throttle housing - removal and refitting

Removal

1 Depressurise the fuel system.
2 Disconnect the battery negative terminal and remove the air cleaner assembly.
3 Examine the injector housing fuel pipe feed and return unions for signs of leakage, then wipe them clean.
4 Using a spanner to hold each adaptor, unscrew the pipe union nuts and release the fuel feed and return pipes from the adaptors. Plug each pipe and adaptor to minimise the loss of fuel and prevent the entry of dirt into the system.
5 Release the wire retaining clips then disconnect the wiring connectors from the injector housing, the throttle potentiometer and the stepper motor.
6 Slacken the accelerator cable locknuts and free the cable outer from its mounting bracket. Release the cable inner from the throttle cam.
7 Using a suitable pair of pliers, release the retaining clips and disconnect the breather hoses from the throttle housing **(see illustration)**.
8 Slacken and remove the four nuts securing the throttle housing to the inlet manifold, then remove the throttle housing from the vehicle. Remove the throttle housing insulating spacer and examine it for signs of wear or damage, renewing it if necessary **(see illustrations)**.
9 If leakage was detected from the feed and return pipes or their union nuts, check the sealing surfaces of the nuts and adaptors and

renew the adaptor or the pipe assembly, as necessary.
10 If leakage is detected from the adaptors, unscrew each through one turn with a spanner, then through two turns by hand. If the adaptor is still a tight fit in the housing, the threads are damaged and the housing and adaptors must be renewed as a set. If the threads are sound, fit new sealing washers to the adaptors and refit them, tightening them to their specified torque wrench setting.

Refitting

11 Refitting is a reverse of the removal sequence, noting the following:
a) *Ensure that the mating surfaces of the throttle housing and inlet manifold are clean then fit the insulating spacer.*
b) *Tighten the throttle housing and fuel pipe union nuts to their specified torque settings.*
c) *On completion, reconnect and adjust the accelerator cable.*

14 Fuel injection system components - testing

1 If a fault appears in the engine management (ignition/fuel injection) system, first ensure that the fault is not due to poor maintenance. That is, check that the air cleaner filter element is clean, the spark plugs are in good condition and correctly gapped, and that the engine breather hoses are clear and undamaged. Also check that the throttle cable is correctly adjusted. If the engine is running very roughly, check its compression pressures, bearing in mind that possibly one of the hydraulic tappets might be faulty, producing an incorrect valve clearance.
2 If these checks fail to reveal the cause of the problem, the vehicle should be taken to a suitably-equipped Rover dealer for testing. A wiring block connector is incorporated in the engine management circuit into which a special electronic diagnostic tester can be plugged. The tester will locate the fault quickly and simply, thereby alleviating the need to test all the system components individually

13.7 Disconnecting breather hoses from throttle housing

13.8a Lift throttle body assembly away from inlet manifold . . .

13.8b . . . and remove throttle body gasket spacer

15.1 Disconnecting fuel feed and return pipes from injector housing

15.2 Disconnecting wiring connector from injector housing

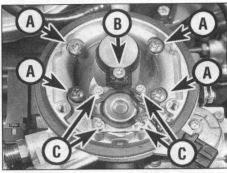

15.3a Injector housing-to-throttle body screws (A), connector cap screw (B) and pressure regulator screws (C)

which is a time consuming operation that carries a high risk of damaging the ECU.

3 If necessary, the system wiring and wiring connectors can be checked as described in Chapter 12. Ensure that the ECU wiring connectors have first been disconnected.

15 Fuel injection system components - removal and refitting

Injector housing

Removal

1 Carry out the operations described in paragraphs 1 to 4 of Section 13 (see illustration).
2 Release the wire retaining clip and disconnect the wiring connector from the injector housing (see illustration).
3 Remove the four screws securing the injector housing to the throttle body, then lift off the injector housing and remove the gasket (see illustrations).
4 If leakage was detected from the fuel feed and/or return pipes, perform the checks described in paragraph 9 of Section 13.

Refitting

5 Refitting is a reversal of the removal procedure, noting the following:

a) Ensure the injector and throttle housing mating surfaces are clean, then fit a new gasket.
b) Apply thread locking compound (Rover recommend Loctite Screwlock or Nutlock) to the threads of the injector housing screws, then tighten them to the specified torque.
c) Tighten the fuel pipe union nuts to the specified torque setting.

Fuel injector

Removal

6 Note that as a Rover replacement part, the injector is available only as part of the injector housing. Commence removal by depressurising the fuel system.
7 Disconnect the battery negative terminal then remove the air cleaner assembly.
8 Slacken and remove the injector connector cap retaining screw and lift off the connector cap. The injector can then be lifted out of the housing (see illustrations).

Refitting

9 Refitting is the reverse of the removal procedure. Ensure that the connector cap makes good contact with the injector pins.

Fuel pressure regulator

10 The fuel pressure regulator is available

15.3b Remove injector housing from throttle body - noting gasket

only as part of the injector housing assembly. Refer to paragraphs 1 to 5 for details on removal and refitting.

Stepper motor

Removal

11 Remove the injector housing as described in paragraphs 1 to 4.
12 Release the retaining clip and disconnect the stepper motor wiring connector (see illustration).
13 Remove the four stepper motor retaining screws and remove the stepper motor assembly from the throttle housing (see

4B

15.8a Remove screw then lift off injector connector cap . . .

15.8b . . . and withdraw injector

15.12 Disconnecting stepper motor wiring connector

15.13a Undo stepper motor retaining screws (arrowed) . . .

15.13b . . . and remove stepper motor assembly

15.17 Disconnecting throttle potentiometer wiring connector (mounting screws arrowed)

illustrations). Do not attempt to dismantle the assembly.

Refitting

14 Refitting is the reverse of the removal procedure. Ensure that the throttle housing and motor mating surfaces are clean and on completion, adjust the throttle cable to ensure that the stepper motor is correctly indexed.

Throttle potentiometer

Removal

15 Although not strictly necessary, access is greatly improved if the air cleaner assembly is first removed.

15.19 Ensure potentiometer tongue engages correctly with throttle lever (spacer arrowed)

16 Disconnect the battery negative lead.
17 Release the wire retaining clip and disconnect the potentiometer wiring connector (see illustration).
18 Remove the two screws and remove the potentiometer from the throttle housing, noting how its tongue engages with the throttle disc spindle lever. Withdraw the spacer if required.

Refitting

19 Refitting is the reverse of the removal procedure, noting the following (see illustration):
a) Carefully clean the mating surfaces of the throttle body, the spacer and the potentiometer, then refit the spacer.
b) Refit the potentiometer so that its tongue engages FORWARD of (ie: inside) the throttle disc spindle lever, then rotate the throttle cam to check the action of the lever and tongue.
c) Securely tighten the potentiometer screws then recheck the potentiometer operation before reconnecting the wiring connector.

Engine management (ignition/fuel injection) ECU

Removal

20 Disconnect the battery negative terminal and unplug the wiring connector(s) from the ECU (see illustration).

21 Disconnect the absolute pressure sensor vacuum hose from the unit, then undo the three retaining nuts and remove the ECU from the engine compartment (see illustrations).

Refitting

22 Refitting is a reverse of the removal sequence. Tighten the ECU retaining nuts to the specified torque. Due to the nature of the ECU, if a new or different ECU has been fitted, it may take a short while for full idle control to be restored.

Manifold absolute pressure sensor

23 This is part of the ECU and is removed and refitted as described above.
24 The sensor's vacuum hose runs from the inlet manifold to the ECU via a fuel (vapour) trap mounted in the air cleaner assembly.
25 To remove the fuel trap, remove the air cleaner assembly cover, release the clips and disconnect the hoses, then remove the single retaining screw and withdraw the trap.
26 On refitting, note that the hoses are colour-coded (green to the ECU, white to the inlet manifold) to ensure correct reconnection (see illustration).

Intake air temperature sensor

Removal

27 Disconnect the battery negative lead.

15.20 Disconnect wiring connector . . .

15.21a . . . and absolute pressure sensor vacuum hose from ECU . . .

15.21b . . . then undo ECU mounting nuts (arrowed) and remove unit

15.26 Absolute pressure sensor fuel trap hoses are colour-coded to ensure correct refitting

15.28 Remove air cleaner metal intake duct to gain access to intake air temperature sensor

15.32 Coolant temperature sensor (arrowed)

28 Remove the air cleaner metal intake duct **(see illustration)**.
29 Release the wire clip and disconnect the sensor wiring.
30 Unscrew the sensor and remove it from the air cleaner housing.

Refitting

31 Refitting is the reverse of the removal procedure. Tighten the sensor to its specified torque wrench setting.

Coolant temperature sensor

Removal

32 The coolant temperature sensor is fitted to the underside of the inlet manifold **(see illustration)**. Either drain the cooling system or be prepared for some loss of coolant as the sensor is unscrewed.
33 Release the wire retaining clip and disconnect the wiring connector from the sensor.
34 Unscrew the sensor from the manifold and withdraw it, then plug the opening to prevent the entry of dirt. If the cooling system has not been drained, work quickly to minimise coolant loss.

Refitting

35 Wipe clean the threads of the sensor and of the thermostat housing. If a sealing washer is fitted, renew it whenever it is disturbed to

prevent leaks. If no sealing washer is fitted, apply a smear of sealant to the sensor threads.
36 Refit the sensor, working quickly if the cooling system was not drained, and tighten it to the specified torque. Reconnect the wiring connector.
37 Replenish the cooling system.

Accelerator pedal switch

38 Refer to Section 11 in Part A of this Chapter.

Fuel cut-off inertia switch

39 The fuel cut-off inertia switch is located behind the centre console where it is mounted on the steering column support bracket. If the switch has tripped, it can be reset by pressing in the plunger situated at the top of the switch **(see illustration)**.

Removal

40 Remove the centre console.
41 Disconnect the wiring connector, then undo the switch mounting bracket retaining nut and remove the switch **(see illustrations)**.

Refitting

42 Refitting is a reverse of the removal sequence. Before installing the centre console, reset the inertia switch by pressing in the plunger.

15.39 Reset fuel cut-off inertia switch by depressing plunger

Relays

43 Refer to Chapter 12 for further information.

---

16 Inlet manifold pre-heater - operation, removal and refitting

1 Refer to Section 15 in Part A of this Chapter. Note that there is no separate manifold pre-heater temperature switch. The ECU uses the information sent from the coolant temperature sensor **(see illustration)**.

15.41a Undo inertia switch retaining nut . . .

15.41b . . . and remove switch

16.1 Inlet manifold partially removed to show manifold PTC heater and coolant temperature sensor (arrowed)

4B

17.3 Disconnect coolant hoses (arrowed) . . .

17.4 . . . and brake servo vacuum hose from inlet manifold

17.6a Ensure all vacuum pipes and hoses are disconnected

17.6b Remove inlet manifold and withdraw gasket

17 Inlet manifold -
removal and refitting

Removal

1 Remove the throttle housing.
2 Drain the cooling system.
3 Slacken the retaining clamps and disconnect the coolant hoses from the inlet manifold (see illustration).
4 Slacken and remove the brake vacuum servo unit hose union bolt and disconnect the hose (see illustration). Discard the hose union sealing washers which must be renewed whenever they are disturbed.
5 Undo the single bolt securing each manifold support stay to the cylinder block/crankcase and slacken the bolts which secure the stays to the inlet manifold.
6 Make a final check that all the necessary vacuum hoses have been disconnected from the manifold then unscrew the nuts and bolts securing the manifold to the cylinder head.

Manoeuvre the manifold out of the engine compartment and discard the manifold gasket (see illustrations).

Refitting

7 Refitting is the reverse of the removal procedure, noting the following (see illustration):
a) Ensure that the manifold and cylinder head mating surfaces are clean and dry, then fit a new manifold gasket.
b) Working in the sequence shown, tighten the manifold retaining nuts and bolts evenly, to the specified torque wrench setting.
c) Ensure all relevant hoses are reconnected to their original positions and are securely held (where necessary) by the retaining clips.
d) Renew the vacuum servo unit vacuum hose banjo union sealing washers and tighten the union bolt securely.
e) On completion, refill the cooling system.

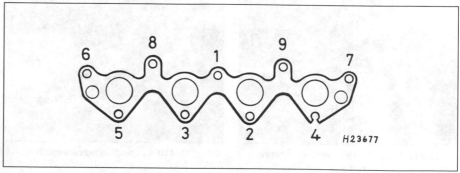

17.7 Inlet manifold tightening sequence - K16 engine

18 Exhaust manifold - removal and refitting

Removal

1 Disconnect the battery negative lead. Firmly apply the handbrake then jack up the front of the vehicle and support it on axle stands.

2 Remove the air cleaner metal intake duct. Undo the two bolts securing the duct mounting bracket to the cylinder head cover and remove the bracket.

3 Undo the two bolts securing the upper radiator mountings to the bonnet platform, then remove the mountings and tilt the radiator forward to gain the clearance necessary to remove the manifold.

4 Unscrew the nuts securing the exhaust front pipe to the manifold, then disconnect the pipe and collect the gasket.

5 Undo the five nuts securing the exhaust manifold to the cylinder head, then carefully manoeuvre the manifold out of the engine compartment. Remove the manifold gasket and discard it.

6 Examine all the exhaust manifold studs for signs of damage and corrosion. Remove all traces of corrosion and repair or renew any damaged studs.

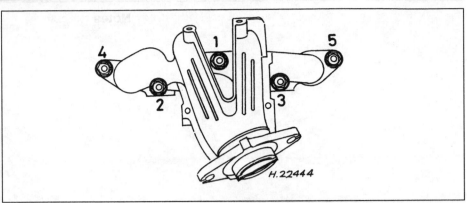

18.7 Exhaust manifold tightening sequence - K16 engine

Refitting

7 Refitting is the reverse of the removal procedure, noting the following **(see illustration)**:

a) *Ensure that the manifold and cylinder head sealing faces are clean and flat, then fit a new manifold gasket.*

b) *Working in the sequence shown, tighten the manifold retaining nuts evenly to the specified torque wrench setting.*

c) *Tighten all other disturbed nuts and bolts to their specified torque wrench settings (where given).*

19 Exhaust system - inspection, removal and refitting

1 Refer to Section 18 in Part A of this Chapter. Note that on models fitted with a closed-loop catalytic converter, the lambda sensor must be removed or its wiring disconnected whenever the exhaust system front pipe is disconnected from the manifold.

4B

Notes

Chapter 4 Part C
Fuel and exhaust systems - multi-point fuel injection engines

Contents

Degrees of difficulty

Easy, suitable for novice with little experience	Fairly easy, suitable for beginner with some experience	Fairly difficult, suitable for competent DIY mechanic 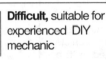	Difficult, suitable for experienced DIY mechanic 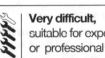	Very difficult, suitable for expert DIY or professional

Specifications

System

Type . . . . Rover/Motorola Modular Engine Management System, using ECU-controlled multi-point injection (MEMS-MPi) and speed/density method of airflow measurement

MEMS-MPi system data

Fuel pump type . . . . Electric, immersed in fuel tank
Fuel pressure . . . . 3.0 ± 0.2 bar constant
MEMS - ECU assembly:
    Alloy inlet manifold . . . . MNE 101470
    Plastic inlet manifold . . . . MKC 101730
Injectors . . . . MJY 10015
Throttle potentiometer voltage:
    Throttle closed . . . . 0 to 1 volt
    Throttle open . . . . 4 to 5 volt
Idle speed - nominal value given for reference purposes only . . . . 850 ± 50 rpm
CO level at idle speed — engine at normal operating temperature . . . . 0.5 %

Recommended fuel

Minimum octane rating . . . . 95 RON unleaded (ie: unleaded Premium) only

Torque wrench settings

	Nm	lbf ft
Fuel system		
ECU mounting bracket nuts	9	7
Vent valve-to-fuel tank nut	9	7
Vent pipe-to-fuel tank nuts	9	7
Fuel pump-to-fuel tank nuts	9	7
Fuel filter pressure release union	38	28
Fuel feed hose union-to-body bolts	9	7
Fuel feed hose bolts	10	7
Fuel rail bolts	10	7
Fuel rail support bracket bolts - alloy manifold	10	7
Intake air temperature sensor	7	5
Coolant temperature sensor	15	11
Crankshaft sensor bolts	6	4

4C

Torque wrench settings

	Nm	lbf ft
Fuel system (continued)		
Throttle housing-to-alloy manifold nuts	8	6
Throttle housing-to-plastic manifold bolts	4	3
Throttle potentiometer screws - plastic manifold	1.5	1.1
Stepper motor screws - plastic manifold	1.5	1.1
Pressure regulator-to-fuel rail bolts - alloy manifold	10	8
Pressure release bolt	12	9
Inlet manifold mounting nuts and bolts	25	18
Exhaust system		
Oxygen (lambda) sensor	55	40
Exhaust manifold retaining nuts	45	33
Exhaust manifold shroud screws	6	4
Exhaust system flange nuts:		
Manifold-to-front pipe joint	50	37
All other joints	45	33
Exhaust front pipe mounting bolts	15	11

1 General information and precautions

General information

The fuel system comprises a fuel tank which is mounted under the rear of the vehicle with an electric fuel pump immersed in it, a fuel filter, fuel feed and return lines which service four fuel injectors interlinked by a rail, as well as the Electronic Control Unit (ECU) and the various sensors, electrical components and related wiring which make up the system as a whole (see illustration). Inlet manifolds of either alloy or plastic construction are fitted.

The air cleaner assembly contains a disposable paper filter element and is mounted on the side of the battery tray.

To reduce emissions and to improve driveability when the engine is cold, the inlet manifold is heated by the coolant. Mixture enrichment for cold starting is a pre-programmed function of the system.

The ECU fully controls both the ignition system and the fuel injection system, integrating the two in a complete engine management system (MEMS-MPi). System operation is similar to that described for the single-point fuel injection system (MEMS-SPi) in Part B of this Chapter, any differences being made clear in the following Sections. Refer to Chapter 5 for information on the ignition side of the system and to Chapter 12 for details of the system relays.

The exhaust system consists of four main components which are the front downpipe, the catalytic converter, the intermediate pipe and middle silencer box, and the tailpipe and main silencer box. The system is suspended throughout its entire length by rubber mountings.

Precautions

Fuel injection system

Residual pressure will remain in the fuel lines long after the vehicle was last used,

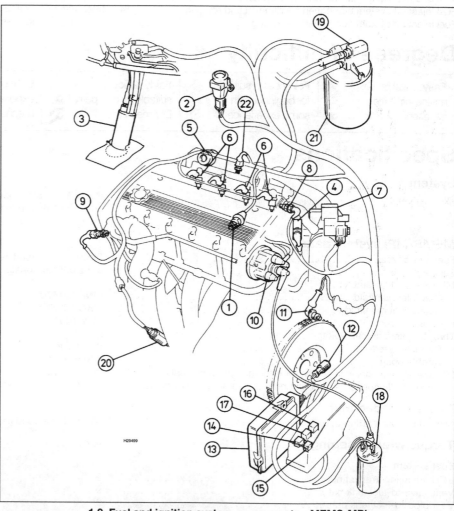

1.0 Fuel and ignition system components - MEMS-MPi

2 Fuel cut-out inertia switch	9 Coolant temperature sensor	15 Fuel pump relay
3 Fuel pump		16 Lambda sensor relay
4 Throttle potentiometer	10 Distributor	17 Starter relay
5 Fuel pressure regulator	11 Crankshaft sensor	18 Ignition HT coil
6 Injectors	12 Diagnostic connector	19 Purge valve
7 Stepper motor	13 Engine management ECU	20 Lambda sensor
8 Intake air temperature sensor	14 Main relay	21 Charcoal canister
		22 Fuel temperature sensor

H29499

3.2 Releasing throttle housing-to-air cleaner securing clips

3.3 Removing battery tray-to-air cleaner securing bolts (arrowed)

3.4 Releasing HT coil-to-distributor cap lead from air cleaner

therefore extra care must be taken when disconnecting a fuel line hose. Loosen any fuel hose slowly to avoid a sudden release of pressure which may cause fuel spray. As an added precaution, place a rag over each union as it is disconnected to catch any fuel which is forcibly expelled.

Fuel usage

Refer to Part A of this Chapter.

Catalytic coverters

Before attempting work on these items, carefully read the precautions listed in Part D of this Chapter.

2 Air cleaner filter element - renewal

Refer to Chapter 1.

3 Air cleaner assembly - removal and refitting

Removal

1 For improved access, remove the battery.
2 Release the two securing clips and detach the connecting hose from between the throttle housing and air cleaner **(see illustration)**. Note that on engines fitted with a plastic inlet manifold, the hose is secured to the throttle housing with a spring clip.
3 Remove the two battery tray-to-air cleaner securing bolts **(see illustration)**.
4 Disconnect the HT coil-to-distributor cap lead at the cap and from its retaining clip on the air cleaner **(see illustration)**.
5 Pull the air cleaner assembly free of its mounting bracket, release it from its inlet hose, then remove it from the vehicle.

Refitting

6 Refitting is the reverse of the removal procedure. Ensure that all rubber mounting grommets and hoses are free of splits or perishing and that all hose clips are securely tightened.

4 Fuel system - inspection

Refer to Chapter 1.

5 Fuel system - depressurisation

Note: *The following procedure will merely relieve pressure in the fuel system. Remember that fuel will still be present in the system components and take precautions accordingly before disconnecting any of them.*

1 The fuel system is defined as the tank-mounted fuel pump, the fuel filter, the fuel injectors and the metal pipes and flexible hoses of the fuel lines between these components. All these contain fuel which will be under pressure while the engine is running and/or while the ignition is switched on. The pressure will remain for some time after the ignition has been switched off and must be relieved before any of these components are disturbed for servicing work.
2 The fuel system is depressurised by loosening the fuel filter pipe union.
3 Position wads of rag around the union to catch spilled fuel. Carefully loosen the union whilst holding the fuel pipe with an open-ended spanner to prevent any undue strain being placed upon it **(see illustration)**.
4 Once all pressure has been released, retighten the union to the specified torque setting whilst using a spanner to counter-hold the pipe.

6 Fuel system - pressure check

1 Fuel system testing will involve the use of specialist Rover tools. Consult your Rover dealer as to the availability of these tools and refer to Section 7 in Part B of this Chapter and to the figures given in the Specifications Section before proceeding.

7 Fuel pump - removal and refitting

Refer to Section 8 in Part B of this Chapter.

8 Fuel gauge sender unit - removal and refitting

Refer to Section 9 in Part A of this Chapter.

9 Fuel tank - removal and refitting

1 Refer to Section 10 in Part A of this Chapter but depressurise the fuel system before disconnecting any of the fuel lines.

10 Accelerator cable - removal, refitting and adjustment

Note: *Before proceeding with any adjustment of the accelerator cable, ensure that it is correctly routed. Do not attempt to adjust the cable by means of the throttle stop screw.*

Removal

1 Detach the cable adjuster nut from its abutment bracket and disengage the cable

5.3 Loosening fuel filter pipe union

4C

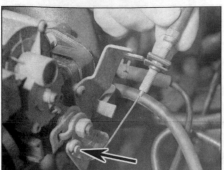

10.1 Remove accelerator cable adjuster nut from abutment bracket and disengage cable end nipple from throttle cam (arrowed)

10.2 Releasing accelerator cable from retaining clip on engine compartment bulkhead

10.5 Release accelerator cable from bulkhead by turning retaining clip (arrowed)

end nipple from the throttle cam **(see illustration)**.

2 On vehicles with an alloy inlet manifold, release the cable from its retaining clip on the engine compartment bulkhead **(see illustration)**.

3 On vehicles with a plastic inlet manifold, release the cable from its retaining clip on the manifold.

4 It may be necessary to remove the windscreen wiper motor to gain access to where the cable passes through the bulkhead.

5 Release the cable outer from the bulkhead by turning its retaining clip **(see illustration)**.

6 Remove the cable inner-to-throttle pedal securing clip and detach the cable from the pedal.

7 Withdraw the cable from the vehicle.

Refitting

8 Refitting is the reverse of the removal procedure. Adjust the cable as follows:

Adjustment

Alloy inlet manifold only

9 Ensure that the throttle potentiometer and stepper motor are synchronised.

10 Turn the ignition on and wait for 10 seconds before turning the ignition off to

ensure that the stepper motor is in the setting position.

Alloy and plastic inlet manifolds

11 Detach the cable adjuster nut from its abutment bracket and reposition the cable outer in the bracket.

12 Turn the cable adjuster nut until it just makes contact with the top of the abutment bracket.

Alloy inlet manifold only

13 Hold the cam in the "throttle closed" position and ensure that the screw is in contact with the stepper motor pin. Turn the cable adjuster nut until all slack is removed from the cable inner. Any linkage gap must be removed without opening the throttle **(see illustration)**.

Plastic inlet manifold only

14 Hold the throttle cam in contact with the throttle stop screw and turn the cable adjuster nut until all slack is removed from the cable inner. This must be achieved without opening the throttle.

Alloy and plastic inlet manifolds

15 Check that there is no free play in the cable outer and refit the cable adjuster nut into its abutment bracket.

16 Operate the throttle pedal, checking that the throttle opens to its stop.

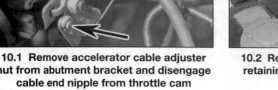

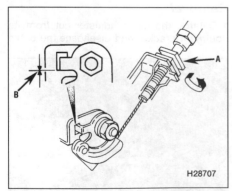

10.13 Turn accelerator cable adjuster nut (A) until all slack is removed from cable inner. Any linkage gap (B) must be removed without opening throttle

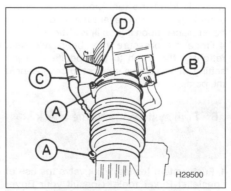

12.2 Release hose securing clips (A), disconnect stepper motor multiplug (B), throttle potentiometer multiplug (C) and breather hose (D)

11 Accelerator pedal -
removal and refitting

Refer to Section 10 in Part A of this Chapter.

12 Throttle housing -
removal and refitting

Alloy inlet manifold

1 Disconnect the battery earth lead.

2 Release the two securing clips and detach the connecting hose from between the throttle housing and air cleaner **(see illustration)**.

3 Disconnect the stepper motor and throttle potentiometer multiplugs.

4 Disconnect the breather hose from the throttle housing.

5 Pull the accelerator cable adjuster nut from its abutment bracket and release the cable inner from the throttle cam.

6 Remove the four nuts securing the throttle housing to its mounting and remove the housing from the vehicle.

7 Refitting is the reverse of the removal procedure, noting the following:

a) Thoroughly clean all component parts, paying particular attention to the mating surfaces.

b) Examine the throttle housing mounting for splits or damage and renew if necessary.

c) Tighten the housing securing nuts to the specified torque wrench settings.

d) Check all hose connections are secure.

e) Check accelerator cable adjustment.

Plastic inlet manifold

8 Disconnect the battery earth lead.

9 Release the two securing clips and

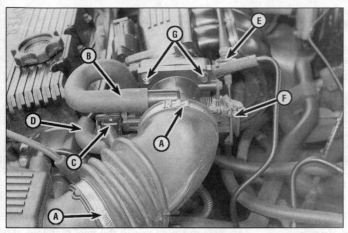

12.9 Throttle housing assembly - plastic inlet manifold

A   Hose securing clips
B   Stepper motor hose
C   Throttle potentiometer
    multiplug
D   Throttle housing breather
    hose
E   Throttle cable adjuster
F   Throttle cam
G   Throttle housing securing
    bolts (two shown)

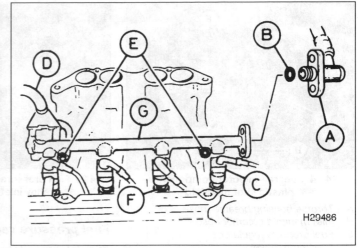

14.4 Fuel rail/injector assembly - alloy inlet manifold

A   Fuel feed hose connection
B   O-ring
C   Injector multiplug (1 of 4)
D   Fuel pressure regulator
E   Fuel rail securing bolts
F   Fuel injector (1 of 4)
G   Fuel rail

detach the connecting hose from between the throttle housing and air cleaner **(see illustration)**.
10 Loosen the stepper motor hose-to-throttle housing retaining clip and detach the hose from the housing.
11 Disconnect the multiplug from the throttle potentiometer.
12 Disconnect the breather hose from the throttle housing after loosening its retaining clip.
13 Pull the accelerator cable adjuster nut from its abutment bracket and release the cable inner from the throttle cam.
14 Remove the four bolts securing the throttle housing to the inlet manifold, detach the throttle housing from the manifold and discard the sealing ring.
15 Refitting is the reverse of the removal procedure, noting the following.
a) *Thoroughly clean all component parts, paying particular attention to the mating surfaces.*
b) *Fit a new throttle housing sealing ring, lubricating it with silicone grease.*

c) *Tighten the housing securing bolts to the specified torque wrench settings.*
d) *Check all hose connections are secure.*
e) *Check accelerator cable adjustment.*

13 Fuel injection system components - testing

Refer to Section 14 in Part B of this Chapter.

14 Fuel injection system components - removal and refitting

Fuel rail/injectors

Alloy inlet manifold

1 Disconnect the battery earth lead.
2 Depressurise the fuel system.
3 Detach the inlet manifold chamber and discard the gasket.

4 Remove the two bolts securing the fuel feed hose to the fuel rail and release the hose from the rail, discarding the O-ring **(see illustration)**.
5 Disconnect the four injector multiplugs.
6 Release the retaining clip and disconnect the hose from the fuel pressure regulator.
7 Remove the two bolts securing the fuel rail to the inlet manifold.
8 Pull each injector from its location in the inlet manifold and remove the fuel rail, complete with injectors and pressure regulator, from the vehicle, placing it on a clean surface.
9 Remove and discard the O-ring fitted to the base of each injector, then cover the exposed end of each injector to prevent the ingress of dirt or moisture **(see illustration)**.
10 To remove the injectors from the fuel rail, first remove the spring clip which secures each injector to the rail **(see illustration)**. Pull each injector from the rail and discard the O-ring fitted to its upper end. Again, cover the exposed end of each injector to prevent the ingress of dirt or moisture.
11 Refitting of the injectors and rail is the reverse of the removal procedure, noting the following:
a) *Thoroughly clean all component parts, paying particular attention to the mating surfaces.*
b) *Fit new O-rings, lubricating them with clean fuel.*
c) *Where applicable, tighten all securing bolts to the specified torque wrench settings.*

Plastic inlet manifold

12 Disconnect the battery earth lead.
13 Depressurise the fuel system.
14 Loosen the throttle housing breather

4C

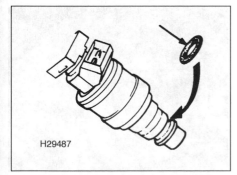

14.9 Discard O-ring (arrowed) fitted to injector base

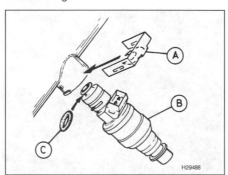

14.10 Remove spring clip (A), pull injector (B) from rail and discard O-ring (C)

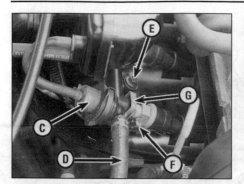

14.14 Fuel rail/injector components - plastic inlet manifold

A Throttle housing breather hose
B Inlet manifold breather hose
C Fuel pressure regulator
D Fuel return hose
E Fuel rail securing bolt (1 of 2)
F Fuel injector multiplug (1 of 4)
G Fuel injecdtor securing clip (1 of 4)

hose-to-camshaft cover retaining clip and detach the hose **(see illustration)**.
15 Disconnect the multiplug from the stepper motor.
16 Disconnect the inlet manifold breather hose from the camshaft cover.
17 Disconnect the vacuum pipe from the fuel pressure regulator.
18 Loosen the retaining clip and disconnect the fuel return hose from the fuel rail.
19 Remove the two bolts which secure the fuel feed pipe to the fuel rail and release the pipe from the rail, discarding the O-ring **(see illustration 14.4).**
20 Disconnect each injector multiplug and securing clip.
21 Remove the two bolts securing the fuel rail to the inlet manifold and detach the rail from the manifold, together with the fuel pressure regulator.
22 Note that the rail and regulator are serviced as an assembly and should not be separated. If unions are to be left disconnected for any length of time, then plug them with clean cloth to prevent the ingress of dirt or moisture into the system.
23 To remove the injectors, pull each one from its location in the inlet manifold and discard both of its O-rings. If leaving the injectors for any length of time, cover their exposed ends to prevent the ingress of dirt or moisture.
24 Refitting of the injectors and rail is the reverse of the removal procedure, noting the following:
a) *Thoroughly clean all component parts, paying particular attention to the mating surfaces.*
b) *Fit new O-rings, lubricating them with silicone grease.*
c) *Where applicable, tighten all securing bolts to the specified torque wrench settings.*

14.25 Fuel pressure regulator location - alloy inlet manifold

Fuel pressure regulator

Alloy inlet manifold

25 The fuel pressure regulator is secured to the end of the fuel rail by two bolts **(see illustration)**.
26 With fuel system pressure released and the fuel hose disconnected from the regulator (see fuel rail removal above), remove the securing bolts and detach the regulator from the rail.
27 Remove the spacer and O-ring, discarding the O-ring.
28 Refitting the regulator is the reverse of the removal procedure. Thoroughly clean the mating surfaces and fit a new O-ring, lubricating it with clean fuel.

Plastic inlet manifold

29 The fuel pressure regulator is available only as part of the fuel rail and should not be separated from the same.

Stepper motor

Alloy inlet manifold

30 The stepper motor fitted to this type of manifold is an integral part of the throttle housing and as a consequence, cannot be removed.

Plastic inlet manifold

31 Disconnect the multiplug from the stepper motor **(see illustration)**.
32 Remove the two Torx screws which

14.35 Disconnecting potentiometer multiplug - alloy inlet manifold

14.31 Disconnect stepper motor multiplug (A) and remove Torx screws (B - one hidden)

secure the motor to the inlet manifold and remove the motor, discarding its O-ring.
33 Refitting is the reverse of the removal procedure, noting the following:
a) *Thoroughly clean the mating surfaces.*
b) *Fit a new O-ring to the motor, lubricating it with silicone grease.*
c) *Tighten the motor securing bolts to the specified torque wrench setting.*

Throttle potentiometer

Alloy inlet manifold

34 Disconnect the battery earth lead.
35 Disconnect the multiplug from the potentiometer **(see illustration)**.
36 Remove the two securing screws and detach the potentiometer from the throttle housing.
37 Refitting is the reverse of the removal procedure, noting the following:
a) *Thoroughly clean the mating surfaces.*
b) *Ensure correct engagement of the potentiometer before fitting the securing screws.*

Plastic inlet manifold

38 Disconnect the potentiometer multiplug **(see illustration)**.
39 Remove and discard the two securing screws and wavewashers and remove the clamping plate.
40 Pull the potentiometer off the throttle spindle being carefull not to apply leverage or twist the potentiometer.

14.38 Potentiometer multiplug (arrowed) - plastic inlet manifold

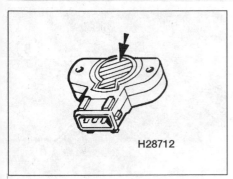

14.41 When pressing potentiometer onto spindle, apply finger pressure only to shaded area

41 Refitting is the reverse of the removal procedure, noting the following:
a) *Carefully clean the mating surfaces of the throttle housing and potentiometer.*
b) *Refit the potentiometer so that the flat on the spindle is aligned with the mating portion of the potentiometer.*
c) *When pressing the potentiometer onto the spindle, apply finger pressure only to the shaded area shown (see illustration).*
d) *Rotate the potentiometer anti-clockwise only to align the fixing holes.*
e) *Tighten the potentiometer screws to their specified torque wrench setting.*
f) *Operate the throttle cam 2 or 3 times and ensure that full travel exists between the throttle open and closed positions.*

Engine management (ignition/fuel injection) ECU

42 Remove the battery.
43 Undo the three nuts securing the ECU to its mounting bracket (see illustration).
44 Unplug the two multiplug connectors from the ECU.
45 Release the securing clip and pull the vacuum hose from the ECU.
46 Remove the ECU from the vehicle.
47 Refitting the ECU is the reverse of the removal procedure. If a new or different ECU has been fitted, it may take a short while for full idle control to be restored.

14.53 Coolant temperature sensor multiplug (arrowed)

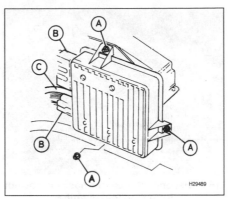

14.43 ECU connection points

A *Mounting nuts*
B *Multiplug connectors*
C *Vacuum hose*

Intake air temperature sensor

48 Disconnect the battery earth lead.
49 Disconnect the sensor multiplug and unscrew the sensor from the inlet manifold (see illustration).
50 Refitting is the reverse of the removal procedure, noting the following:
a) *Thoroughly clean the sensor threads and mating surfaces.*
b) *Tighten the sensor to the specified torque wrench setting.*

Coolant temperature sensor

51 Disconnect the battery earth lead.
52 Either drain the cooling system or be prepared for some loss of coolant as the sensor is unscrewed.
53 Disconnect the sensor multiplug (see illustration).
54 Unscrew the sensor and withdraw it, then plug the opening to prevent any entry of dirt. If the cooling system has not been drained, work quickly to minimise coolant loss.
55 Refitting is the reverse of the removal procedure, noting the following:
a) *Thoroughly clean the sensor threads and mating surfaces.*
b) *If a sealing washer is fitted, renew it. If no sealing washer is fitted, apply a smear of sealant to the sensor threads.*

16.6 Disconnecting stepper motor multiplug

14.49 Intake air temperature sensor multiplug (arrowed)

c) *Tighten the sensor to the specified torque wrench setting.*
d) *On completion, replenish the cooling system.*

Accelerator pedal switch

56 Refer to Section 11 in Part A of this Chapter.

Fuel cut-off inertia switch

57 Refer to Section 15 in Part B of this Chapter.

Relays

58 Refer to Chapter 12 for further information.

15 Inlet manifold pre-heater - operation, removal and refitting

1 Refer to Section 15 in Part A of this Chapter. Note that there is no separate manifold pre-heater temperature switch. The ECU uses the information sent from the coolant temperature sensor.

16 Inlet manifold - removal and refitting

Alloy inlet manifold

Removal

1 Disconnect the battery earth lead.
2 Depressurise the fuel system.
3 Disconnect the hose from the fuel filter, covering the open connections to prevent any ingress of dirt.
4 Refer to Chapter 1 and drain the cooling system.
5 Release the securing clip and detach the throttle housing-to-air cleaner hose from the throttle housing.
6 Disconnect the stepper motor and throttle potentiometer multiplugs (see illustration).
7 Disconnect the breather hose from the throttle housing.

4C

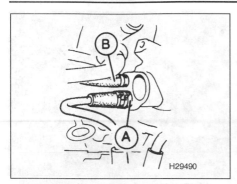

16.8 Disconnect breather pipe (A) from manifold chamber

B Manifold chamber breather hose (1 of 3)

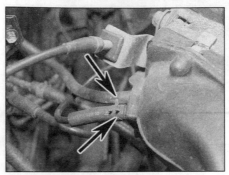

16.9 Disconnect breather hoses (arrowed) from manifold chamber

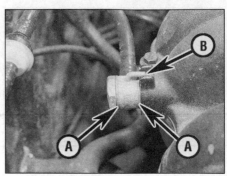

16.10 Brake servo line banjo union

A Sealing washers
B Union alignment tang in manifold chamber slot

8 Release the retaining clip and disconnect the breather pipe from the manifold chamber (see illustration).

9 Release the retaining clips and disconnect the three breather hoses from the manifold chamber (see illustration, also illustration 16.8).

10 Unscrew the brake servo line banjo bolt from the manifold chamber, discarding both sealing washers (see illustration).

11 Remove the five bolts securing the manifold chamber to the inlet manifold.

12 Remove the support stay to manifold chamber securing bolt.

13 Detach the manifold chamber from the inlet manifold and discard its gasket.

14 Remove the engine oil dipstick, covering the open pipe to prevent any ingress of dirt.

15 Disconnect the four fuel injector multiplugs and the intake air temperature sensor multiplug.

16 Release the coolant hose from the inlet manifold (see illustration).

17 Remove the two nuts and three bolts securing the upper face of the inlet manifold to the cylinder head, loosening each one a little at a time.

18 Remove the two bolts securing the engine wiring harness brackets to the inlet manifold.

19 Release the two clips which secure the fuel return hose.

20 Remove the bolt securing the support stay to the inlet manifold.

21 Remove the four bolts securing the lower face of the inlet manifold to the cylinder head, loosening each one a little at a time.

22 Remove the inlet manifold, discarding the gasket.

Refitting

23 Refitting is the reverse of the removal procedure, noting the following:

a) Thoroughly clean all component parts, paying particular attention to the mating surfaces.

b) Always fit a new manifold gasket.

c) Working in the sequence shown (see illustration), tighten the manifold retaining nuts and bolts evenly to the specified torque wrench setting.

d) Tighten all disturbed fasteners to their specified torque wrench settings (where given).

e) Renew all sealing washers and O-rings.

f) Remove all masking materials.

g) Ensure all hose connections are securely remade.

h) Ensure the brake servo line banjo union alignment tang is located in the manifold chamber slot.

i) Refill the cooling system and check the coolant level, then wash off any spilt coolant.

Plastic inlet manifold

Removal

24 Disconnect the battery earth lead.

25 Depressurise the fuel system.

26 Refer to Chapter 1 and drain the cooling system.

27 Release the securing clip and detach the throttle housing-to-air cleaner hose from the air cleaner.

28 Release the retaining clip and detach the purge hose from the inlet manifold (see illustration).

29 Disconnect the breather hose from the throttle housing after loosening its retaining clip.

30 Disconnect the multiplug from the throttle potentiometer.

31 Loosen the stepper motor hose-to-abutment retaining clip and detach the hose, moving it to one side.

32 Release the accelerator cable from its retaining clip on the right-hand side of the manifold.

33 Remove the four bolts securing the throttle housing to the inlet manifold.

34 Detach the throttle housing from the manifold and discard its sealing ring.

35 Disconnect the multiplug from the stepper motor.

36 Release the breather hose from the inlet manifold and depress the plastic collar of the brake servo hose quick-fit connector to

16.16 Releasing coolant hose from inlet manifold

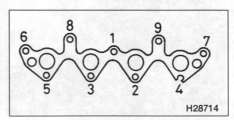

16.23 Alloy inlet manifold tightening sequence

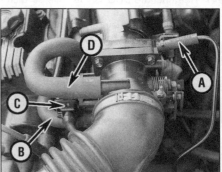

16.28 Throttle housing connections - plastic inlet manifold

A Purge hose
B Breather hose
C Throttle potentiometer
D Stepper motor hose

16.36a Release breather hose (arrowed) . . .

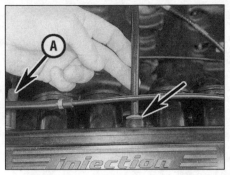

16.36b . . . and depress plastic collar (arrowed) of brake servo hose quick-fit connector to release from manifold

A ECU vacuum pipe

16.38 Disconnect fuel return hose (A) and expansion tank hose (B)

release it from the manifold (see illustrations).

37 Disconnect the ECU vacuum pipe from the manifold.

38 Loosen the retaining clip and disconnect the fuel return hose from the fuel rail, covering the open connections to prevent any ingress of dirt **(see illustration)**.

39 Disconnect the coolant system expansion tank hose from the inlet manifold.

40 Release the fuel return hose from its retaining clips.

41 Disconnect the injector harness and air temperature sensor multiplugs.

42 Remove the two bolts which secure the fuel feed pipe to the fuel rail and release the pipe from the rail. Discard the O-ring and cover the open connections to prevent any ingress of dirt.

43 Working from the centre of the manifold outwards, progressively loosen the manifold securing nuts and bolts. Remove the manifold, discarding the gasket.

Refitting

44 Refitting is the reverse of the removal procedure, noting the following:

a) *Thoroughly clean all component parts, paying particular attention to the mating surfaces.*

b) *Ensure that a metal insert is located in each manifold stud or bolt hole.*

c) *Always fit a new manifold gasket (see illustration).*

d) *Working in the sequence shown (see illustration), tighten the manifold*

retaining nuts and bolts evenly to the specified torque wrench setting.

e) *Tighten all disturbed fasteners to their specified torque wrench settings (where given).*

f) *Fit new O-rings, lubricating them with silicone grease.*

g) *Remove all masking materials.*

h) *Ensure all hose connections are securely remade.*

i) *Refill the cooling system and check the coolant level, then wash off any spilt coolant.*

17 Exhaust manifold - removal and refitting

Removal

1 Disconnect the battery negative lead.

2 Remove the air cleaner assembly.

3 Remove the alternator.

4 Referring to Part D of this Chapter, release the lambda sensor multiplug from the gearbox bracket and disconnect the plug from the sensor.

5 Firmly apply the handbrake then jack up the front of the vehicle and support it on axle stands.

6 Unscrew the nuts securing the exhaust front pipe to the manifold, then disconnect the pipe and collect the gasket.

7 Undo the five nuts securing the exhaust manifold to the cylinder head, then carefully manoeuvre the manifold out of the engine compartment. Remove the manifold gasket and discard it.

8 Examine all the exhaust manifold studs for signs of damage and corrosion. Remove all traces of corrosion and repair or renew any damaged studs.

Refitting

9 Refitting is the reverse of the removal procedure, noting the following:

a) *Ensure that the manifold and cylinder head sealing faces are clean and flat, then fit a new manifold gasket.*

b) *Working in the sequence shown (see illustration), tighten the manifold retaining nuts evenly to the specified torque wrench setting.*

c) *Tighten all other disturbed nuts and bolts to their specified torque wrench settings (where given).*

18 Exhaust system - inspection, removal and refitting

1 Refer to Section 18 in Part A of this Chapter. Note that on models fitted with a closed-loop catalytic converter, the lambda sensor must be removed or its wiring disconnected whenever the exhaust system front pipe is disconnected from the manifold.

4C

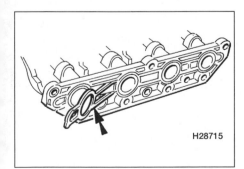

16.44a Fit a new inlet manifold gasket (arrowed)

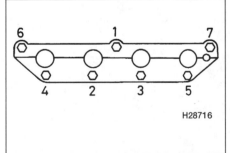

16.44b Plastic inlet manifold tightening sequence

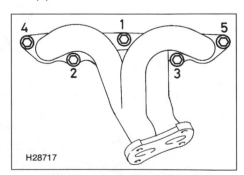

17.9 Exhaust manifold tightening sequence

Notes

Chapter 4 Part D
Emission control systems

Contents

Degrees of difficulty

Easy, suitable for novice with little experience	Fairly easy, suitable for beginner with some experience	Fairly difficult, suitable for competent DIY mechanic	Difficult, suitable for experienced DIY mechanic	Very difficult, suitable for expert DIY or professional

Specifications

Torque wrench settings	Nm	lbf ft
Lambda sensor	55	41

4D

1 General information

Apart from their ability to use unleaded petrol and the various features which help to minimise emissions and are built into the fuel system, all models have at least the crankcase emission-control system described below. Models equipped with a catalytic converter are also fitted with the exhaust and evaporative emission control system.

Crankcase emission control

To reduce the emission of unburned hydrocarbons from the crankcase into the atmosphere, the engine is sealed and the blow-by gases and oil vapour are drawn from the crankcase, through a wire mesh oil separator in the cylinder head cover, into the inlet tract to be burned by the engine during normal combustion. On carburettor engines, a single breather hose connects the cylinder head cover to the carburettor continuous-depression area. On fuel-injected engines, a small-bore breather hose connects the cylinder head cover to the throttle body downstream of the throttle disc, while a larger-bore hose is connected above the throttle disc so that the same effect is obtained at all states of manifold depression.

Under conditions of high manifold depression (idling, deceleration), the gases will be sucked positively out of the crankcase. Under conditions of low manifold depression (acceleration, full-throttle running), the gases are forced out of the crankcase by the (relatively) higher crankcase pressure. If the engine is worn, the raised crankcase pressure (due to increased blow-by) will cause some of the flow to return under all manifold conditions.

Evaporative emission control

To minimise the escape into the atmosphere of unburned hydrocarbons, an evaporative emissions control system is fitted to models equipped with a catalytic converter. The fuel tank filler cap is sealed and a charcoal canister is mounted in the engine compartment to collect the petrol vapours generated in the tank when the vehicle is parked. It stores them until they can be cleared from the canister (under the control of the fuel-injection/ignition system ECU via the purge control valve) into the inlet tract to be burned by the engine during normal combustion.

To ensure that the engine runs correctly when it is cold and/or idling and to protect the catalytic converter from the effects of an over-rich mixture, the purge control valve is not opened by the ECU until the engine has warmed up to above 70∞C, the engine speed exceeds 1500 rpm and manifold absolute pressure is below 30 kPa. The valve solenoid is then modulated on and off to allow the stored vapour to pass into the inlet tract.

Exhaust emission control

To minimise the amount of pollutants which escape into the atmosphere, some models are fitted with a catalytic converter in the exhaust system. Either an open-loop control system, which has no feedback from the converter to the fuel system, or a closed-loop control system, in which the lambda sensor in the exhaust system provides the fuel-injection/ignition system ECU with constant feedback (which enables it to adjust the mixture to provide the best possible conditions for the converter to operate) may be fitted.

If a lambda sensor is fitted, it has a heating element built-in that is controlled by the ECU through the lambda sensor relay to quickly bring the sensor's tip to an efficient operating temperature. The sensor's tip is sensitive to oxygen and sends the ECU a varying voltage depending on the amount of oxygen in the exhaust gases. If the intake air/fuel mixture is too rich, the exhaust gases are low in oxygen so the sensor sends a low-voltage signal, the voltage rises as the mixture weakens and the amount of oxygen rises in the exhaust gases. Peak conversion efficiency of all major pollutants occurs if the intake air/fuel mixture is maintained at the chemically-correct ratio for the complete combustion of petrol of 14.7 parts (by weight) of air to 1 part of fuel (the stoichiometric ratio). The sensor output voltage alters in a large step at this point, the ECU using the signal change as a reference point and correcting the intake air/fuel mixture accordingly by altering the fuel injector pulse width.

2 Catalytic converters - general information and precautions

The catalytic converter is a reliable and simple device which needs no maintenance in itself but there are some facts of which an owner should be aware if the converter is to function properly for its full service life.

a) DO NOT use leaded petrol in a vehicle equipped with a catalytic converter.
b) Always keep the ignition and fuel systems well-maintained in accordance with the manufacturer's schedule.
c) If the engine develops a misfire, do not drive the vehicle at all (or at least as little as possible) until the fault is cured.

d) DO NOT push-start or tow-start the vehicle.
e) DO NOT switch off the ignition at high engine speeds.
f) DO NOT use fuel or engine oil additives.
g) DO NOT continue to use the vehicle if the engine burns oil to the extent of leaving a visible trail of blue smoke.
h) Remember that the catalytic converter operates at very high temperatures, hence the heat shields on the vehicle's underbody, and the casing will become hot enough to ignite combustible materials which brush against it. DO NOT, therefore, park the vehicle in dry undergrowth, over long grass or piles of dead leaves.
i) Remember that the catalytic converter is FRAGILE. DO NOT strike it with tools during servicing work, take great care when working on the exhaust system, ensure that the converter is well clear of any jacks or other lifting gear used to raise the vehicle and do not drive the vehicle over rough ground, road humps, etc. in such a way as to ground the exhaust system.
j) In some cases, particularly when the vehicle is new and/or is used for stop/start driving, a sulphurous smell (like that of rotten eggs) may be noticed from the exhaust. Once the vehicle has covered a few thousand miles the problem should disappear. In the meantime, a change of driving style or of the brand of petrol used may effect a solution.
k) The catalytic converter, used on a well-maintained and well-driven vehicle, should last for between 50 000 and 100 000 miles.

3 Emission control system components - testing and renewal

Crankcase emission control

1 The components of this system require no attention other than to check that all hoses

3.1 Clean oil separators whenever cylinder head cover is removed

are clear and that the wire mesh oil separators are flushed clean with a suitable solvent whenever the cylinder head cover is removed (see illustration).

Evaporative emission control

Testing

2 If the system is thought to be faulty, disconnect the hoses from the charcoal canister and purge control valve and check that they are clear by blowing through them. If the purge control valve or charcoal canister are thought to be faulty, they must be renewed. Note that the purge control valve may either be separate from, or mounted on top of, the charcoal canister.

Charcoal canister (purge valve separate) - renewal

3 Disconnect the battery negative lead.
4 Note the fitted positions of the canister hoses, then use a suitable pair of pliers to release the retaining clips (where fitted) and disconnect all the hoses from the canister (see illustration).
5 Lift the canister up to free it from its mounting bracket then remove it from the engine compartment.
6 Refitting is the reverse of the removal procedure. Ensure that all hoses are correctly refitted and, where necessary, securely held by their retaining clips.

Charcoal canister/purge valve assembly - renewal

7 Disconnect the battery negative lead.

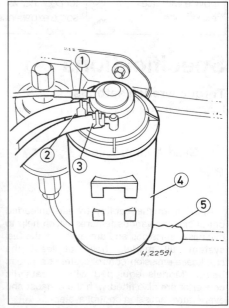

3.4 Charcoal canister hose connections

1   Vacuum hose
2   Outlet hose - canister to purge valve
3   Inlet hose - fuel tank to canister
4   Charcoal canister
5   Drain hose

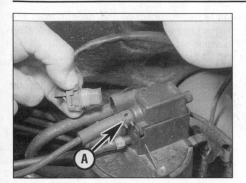

3.8 Disconnecting multiplug from purge valve

A Hose securing clip

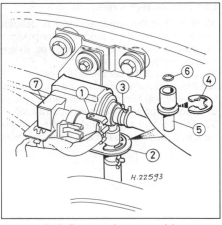

3.13 Purge valve assembly

1 *Wiring connector*
2 *Inlet hose - charcoal canister to purge valve*
3 *Outlet hose - purge valve to throttle housing*
4 *C-clip*
5 *Inlet hose connector*
6 *O-ring*
7 *Purge valve*

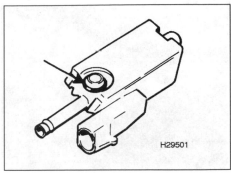

3.21 Renew purge valve O-ring (arrowed)

8 Disconnect the multiplug from the purge valve **(see illustration)**.
9 Release the securing clip and disconnect the hose from the purge valve.
10 Note the fitted positions of the canister fuel and vent hoses, then use a suitable pair of pliers to release the retaining clips (where fitted) and disconnect both hoses from the canister.
11 Release the securing strap and remove the canister/purge valve assembly.
12 Refitting is the reverse of the removal procedure. Ensure that all hoses are correctly refitted and, where necessary, securely held by their retaining clips.

Purge valve (charcoal canister separate) - renewal

13 Disconnect the battery negative terminal then disconnect the wiring connector from the purge valve **(see illustration)**.
14 Release the retaining clips and disconnect the inlet and outlet hoses from the valve.
15 Prise out the C-clip which secures the inlet hose adaptor to the mounting bracket, then withdraw the adaptor, noting the O-ring which is fitted between the adaptor and purge valve. Discard the O-ring which must be renewed.
16 Undo the bolt securing the purge valve to its mounting bracket and remove the valve from the vehicle.
17 Refitting is a reverse of the removal procedure. Use a new inlet hose adaptor O-ring.

Purge valve (on charcoal canister) - renewal

18 Disconnect the battery negative lead.
19 Disconnect the multiplug from the purge valve.
20 Release the securing clip and disconnect the hose from the purge valve.
21 Pull the valve from its location on the canister and discard its O-ring **(see illustration)**.
22 Refitting the valve is the reverse of the removal procedure, noting the following:
a) *Thoroughly clean the mating surfaces.*
b) *Fit a new O-ring to the valve.*
c) *Ensure all connections are secure.*

Exhaust emission control

23 If the CO level reading is too high (or if any other symptom is encountered which causes you to suspect a fault in the exhaust emission control system), always check first that the air cleaner filter element is clean, the spark plugs are in good condition and correctly gapped, that the engine breather and vacuum hoses are clear and undamaged, and that the accelerator cable is correctly adjusted. If the engine is running very roughly, check its compression pressures, bearing in mind the possibility that one of the hydraulic tappets might be faulty, producing an incorrect valve clearance. Check also that all wiring is in good condition, with securely-fastened connectors, that the fuel filter (fuel-injected engines only) has been renewed at the recommended intervals and that the exhaust system is entirely free of air leaks which might upset the operation of the catalytic converter. Only when all these have been checked and found to be in serviceable condition should the converter be suspected.

Testing - open-loop system

24 The performance of the catalytic converter can be checked only by using a good-quality, carefully-calibrated exhaust gas analyser.
25 Check that the CO level is as specified at the gas-sampling pipe when the engine is fully warmed-up to normal operating temperature. If not, check the fuel and ignition systems until the fault is found and the level is restored to its correct value.
26 Once the CO level is known to be correct upstream of the catalytic converter, take the vehicle on a brisk 4-mile road test and check the CO level at the tailpipe immediately on return. It should be significantly lower than the level at the gas-sampling pipe (below 0.5 % approximately on fuel-injected engines, slightly higher on carburettor engines).
27 If the tailpipe CO level is little different from that at the gas-sampling pipe, repeat the check ensuring that it is made immediately on return from road test or the converter may not be at normal operating temperature and will not have reached its peak conversion efficiency. If the results are the same, the catalytic converter is proven faulty and must be renewed.

Testing - closed-loop system

28 The performance of the catalytic converter can be checked only by using a good-quality, carefully-calibrated exhaust gas analyser.
29 Where a gas-sampling pipe is fitted, the test described above can be carried out. If the CO level at the tailpipe is little different from that at the gas-sampling pipe, the catalytic converter is probably faulty and must be renewed, once the fuel-injection and ignition systems have been checked thoroughly using Rover diagnostic equipment and are known to be free from faults.
30 If a gas-sampling pipe is not fitted and the CO level at the tailpipe is too high, the complete fuel-injection and ignition systems must be checked thoroughly by using Rover diagnostic equipment. Once these have been checked and are known to be free from faults, the fault must be in the catalytic converter, which must be renewed.

Catalytic converter - renewal

31 Refer to Section 18 in Part A of this Chapter.

Lambda (oxygen) sensor - operational check

32 The manufacturer's maintenance schedule calls for regular checks of the lambda sensor's operation. This can be done only by attaching Rover diagnostic equipment to the sensor wiring and checking that the voltage varies from low to high values when the engine is running. Do not attempt to test any part of the system with anything other than the correct test equipment.

4D

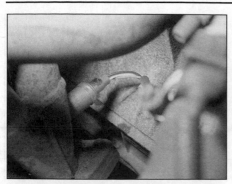

3.35 Lambda sensor viewed from above

Lambda sensor - renewal

33 Note that the lambda sensor is delicate and will not work if it is dropped or knocked, if its power supply is disrupted, or if any cleaning materials are used on it.

34 Disconnect the battery earth lead.

35 Release the sensor's wiring connector from the bracket on the gearbox and unplug it to disconnect the sensor **(see illustration)**.

36 Raising and supporting the front of the vehicle, if required, to remove the sensor from underneath, unscrew the sensor from the exhaust system front pipe. Retain its sealing washer.

37 On refitting, clean the sealing washer and renew it if it is damaged or worn, then refit the sensor, tightening it to its specified torque wrench setting. Reconnect the wiring and refit the connector plug.

Lambda sensor relay - general

38 Refer to Chapter 12.

Chapter 5 Part A
Ignition system - carburettor engines

Contents

Degrees of difficulty

Easy, suitable for novice with little experience	Fairly easy, suitable for beginner with some experience	Fairly difficult, suitable for competent DIY mechanic 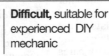	Difficult, suitable for experienced DIY mechanic 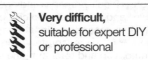	Very difficult, suitable for expert DIY or professional

Specifications

General
System type . . . . Lucas constant energy inductive
Firing order . . . . 1-3-4-2 (No 1 cylinder at timing belt end)
Direction of crankshaft rotation . . . . Clockwise (viewed from right-hand side of vehicle)

Distributor
Type . . . . Lucas 67 DM4, incorporating centrifugal and vacuum advance mechanisms and externally-mounted amplifier module
Identification:
  With catalytic converter . . . . NJC 10026
  Without catalytic converter . . . . NJC 10033
Direction of rotor arm rotation . . . . Anti-clockwise (viewed from left-hand side of vehicle)
Pick-up coil resistance . . . . 950 to 1150 ohms
Vacuum diaphragm unit identification:
  With catalytic converter 80-200-8
  Without catalytic converter 80-200-6
Vacuum advance commences . . . . 107 mbar (80 mm Hg)
Maximum vacuum advance:
  With catalytic converter . . . . 16° @ 267 mbar (200 mm Hg)
  Without catalytic converter . . . . 12° @ 267 mbar (200 mm Hg)
Deceleration check - vacuum disconnected . . . . 4° to 8° @ 2500 rpm
Note: *Degree and speed values to be measured at crankshaft*

HT coil
Type . . . . AUU 1326 or ADU 8779
Manufacturer . . . . Bosch, Ducellier or Rudi Cajavec
Current consumption - average . . . . 0.25 to 0.75 amps @ idle speed
Winding resistances:
  Primary . . . . 0.3 to 0.5 ohms @ 20°C
  Secondary . . . . 5 to 15 K ohms @ 20°C

Ignition timing
At 1500 rpm (vacuum pipe disconnected) . . . . 9° ± 1° BTDC

5A

Torque wrench settings

	Nm	lbf ft
Spark plugs	25	18
Distributor cap screws	2	21
Amplifier module-to-distributor body (hex-head) screws	5	4
Distributor mounting bolts	25	18
Ignition HT coil mounting bolts	7	5

---

1 General information and precautions

General information

The ignition system is fully-electronic in operation and of the inductive type, incorporating a contact-less distributor (driven off the camshaft left-hand end) and an amplifier module, as well as the spark plugs, HT leads, ignition HT coil and associated wiring.

The system is divided into two circuits, which are the primary (low tension/LT) and secondary (high tension/HT). The primary circuit consists of the battery, ignition switch, ignition HT coil primary windings, amplifier module and distributor pick-up coil and wiring. The secondary circuit consists of the ignition HT coil secondary windings, the distributor cap and rotor arm, the spark plugs and HT leads.

The distributor incorporates features which advance the ignition timing both mechanically and by vacuum operation. Its shaft, driven by the camshaft, incorporates a reluctor which has four shaped poles and is mounted on the centre of a centrifugal advance assembly, whose two weights move outwards under centrifugal force as engine speed rises, thus rotating the reluctor on the shaft and advancing or retarding the spark, the amount of movement being controlled by light springs. A pick-up coil generates a weak magnetic field whenever the ignition is switched on. As the engine rotates the reluctor poles pass the coil, disturbing the field each time and sending a signal current to the amplifier module. Whenever this signal exceeds a threshold level determined by engine speed, a high-voltage transistor in the amplifier is switched on, thus allowing HT coil current to flow. When this current has reached the required level, it is held constant until the transistor is switched off, thus triggering the spark. The pick-up coil is clamped to a stator pack that is able to rotate under the control of the vacuum diaphragm unit mounted on the side of the distributor. The unit consists of a diaphragm, one side of which is connected via a small-bore pipe to the carburettor and the other side to the stator pack. Inlet manifold depression, which varies with engine speed and throttle position, causes the diaphragm to move, thus rotating the stator pack and advancing or retarding the spark.

Models fitted with catalytic converters have a thermostatically-operated vacuum switch screwed into the cooling system thermostat housing. The switch is connected into the vacuum hose linking the carburettor to the distributor vacuum diaphragm unit. At coolant temperatures below 70ºC, the switch cuts off the vacuum supply to the diaphragm and prevents the unit from advancing the ignition timing. This causes the exhaust gas temperatures to rise, due to the retarded ignition timing, and brings the catalytic converter swiftly up to its efficient operating temperature. Once coolant temperature rises above 70ºC, the switch opens and allows the vacuum to reach the diaphragm unit, thus restoring normal advance and retard of the ignition timing.

Precautions

General

It is necessary to take extra care when working on the electrical system to avoid damage to semi-conductor devices (diodes and transistors), and to avoid the risk of personal injury. In addition to the precautions given in the *"Safety first!"* Section at the beginning of this manual, take note of the following points when working on the system.

Always remove rings, watches, etc. before working on the electrical system. Even with the battery disconnected, capacitive discharge could occur if a component live terminal is earthed through a metal object. This could cause a shock or nasty burn.

Do not reverse the battery connections. Components such as the alternator or any other having semi-conductor circuitry could be irreparably damaged.

If the engine is being started using jump leads and a slave battery, connect the batteries *positive to positive* and *negative to negative*. This also applies when connecting a battery charger.

Never disconnect the battery terminals, or alternator multi-plug connector, when the engine is running.

The battery leads and alternator multi-plug must be disconnected before carrying out any electric welding on the car.

Never use an ohmmeter of the type incorporating a hand cranked generator for circuit or continuity testing.

Ignition and engine management systems

The HT voltage generated by an electronic ignition system is extremely high, and in certain circumstances could prove fatal. Take care to avoid receiving electric shocks from the HT side of the ignition system. *Persons with surgically-implanted cardiac pacemaker devices should keep well clear of the ignition circuits, components and test equipment.*

Do not handle HT leads, or touch the distributor or coil when the engine is running. If tracing faults in the HT circuit, use well insulated tools to manipulate live leads.

Engine management modules are very sensitive components. Certain precautions must be taken to avoid damage to the module when working on a vehicle equipped with an engine management system, as follows.

When carrying out welding operations on the vehicle using electric welding equipment, the battery and alternator should be disconnected.

Although underbonnet-mounted modules will tolerate normal underbonnet conditions, they can be adversely affected by excess heat or moisture. If using welding equipment or pressure washing equipment in the vicinity of the module, take care not to direct heat, or jets of water or steam at the module. If this cannot be avoided, remove the module from the vehicle, and protect its wiring plug with a plastic bag.

Before disconnecting any wiring, or removing components, always ensure that the ignition is switched off.

On models with underbonnet-mounted modules, do not run the engine with the module detached from the body panel, as the body acts as an effective heat sink and the module may be damaged due to internal overheating.

Do not attempt to improvise fault diagnosis procedures using a test lamp or multimeter, as irreparable damage could be caused to the module.

After working on ignition/engine management system components, ensure that all wiring is correctly reconnected before reconnecting the battery or switching on the ignition.

2 Spark plugs - renewal

Refer to Chapter 1.

3 HT leads, distributor cap and rotor arm - inspection and renewal

Refer to Chapter 1.

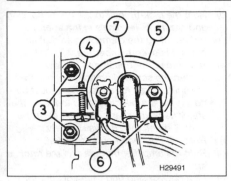
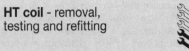
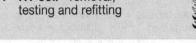

4.4 HT coil connections

3 *Mounting bolts*   6 *LT connections*
4 *Clamp screw*   7 *HT connection*
5 *HT coil*

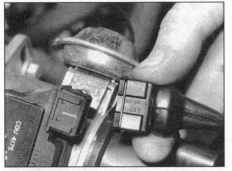

5.2 Disconnecting wiring connector from ignition amplifier module

5.3 Disconnecting vacuum pipe from distributor vacuum diaphragm unit

4 HT coil - removal, testing and refitting

Removal

1 The coil is mounted on the left-hand side of the engine compartment, between the battery and the left-hand headlamp unit.
2 Disconnect the battery negative terminal.
3 To improve access to the coil, remove the headlamp bulb cover.
4 Peel back the end cover, then disconnect the HT lead from the coil. Note which terminals they are connected to and disconnect the two pairs of LT wires from the coil **(see illustration)**.
5 Remove the two coil mounting bolts and withdraw the coil from the engine compartment. If necessary, slacken the clamp screw and separate the coil from its mounting bracket.

Testing

6 Test the coil by using a multimeter, set to its resistance function, to check the primary (LT + to – terminals) and secondary (LT + to HT

lead terminal) windings for continuity. The resistance of either winding can be checked and compared with the specified value. Note that the resistance of the coil windings will vary slightly according to the coil temperature.
7 Using an ohmmeter or continuity tester, check that there is no continuity between the HT lead terminal and the coil body.
8 If the coil is faulty it must be renewed.

Refitting

9 Refitting is the reverse of the removal procedure.

5 Distributor - removal, overhaul and refitting

Removal

1 Disconnect the battery negative terminal.
2 Release the wire retaining clip and unplug the wiring connector from the ignition amplifier module **(see illustration)**.
3 Disconnect the vacuum pipe from the vacuum diaphragm unit **(see illustration)**.
4 Position the engine so that No 1 cylinder is at TDC on the compression stroke.
5 Mark the relationship of the distributor body

5.5 Making alignment marks on distributor body and cylinder head

to the cylinder head, as a guide for refitting **(see illustration)**.
6 Unscrew the distributor mounting bolts and withdraw the distributor **(see illustration)**. Do not disturb the crankshaft setting while the distributor is removed.
7 Remove the distributor body sealing ring which must be renewed whenever it is disturbed **(see illustration)**.

Overhaul

8 Remove the distributor cap and withdraw the rotor arm, if not already removed **(see illustration)**.

5A

5.6 Unscrew distributor mounting bolts (remaining bolt arrowed) . . .

5.7 . . . then remove distributor (O-ring arrowed)

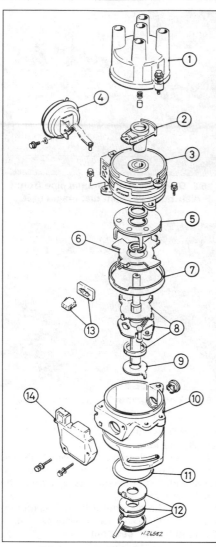

5.8 Lucas 67 DM4 distributor

1 Distributor cap
2 Rotor arm
3 Upper housing
4 Vacuum diaphragm unit
5 Stator pack including thrustwasher(s) and circlip
6 Pick-up coil
7 Clamp ring
8 Distributor shaft, including reluctor and advance assembly
9 Thrustwasher
10 Lower housing
11 O-ring
12 Drive coupling, including thrustwasher, spring and roll pin
13 Connector and gasket
14 Amplifier module

9 Undo the two bolts securing the amplifier module to the body, then carefully remove the gasket and withdraw the connector.
10 Remove the screws and separate the upper housing from the lower.
11 Remove the clamp ring and pick-up coil from the upper housing.

12 Remove the circlip (and first thrustwasher, if fitted) from the underside of the upper housing, disengage the stator pack from the vacuum diaphragm unit arm and withdraw the stator pack, followed by the (second) thrustwasher.
13 Remove the retaining screw and withdraw the vacuum diaphragm unit from the distributor.
14 Check the distributor shaft endfloat and if it seems excessive, seek expert advice.
15 Remove the spring from the distributor drive coupling, then use a scriber or similar to mark the relationship of the coupling to the shaft. It is essential that the coupling is refitted correctly in relationship to the rotor arm on refitting. Release the distributor shaft by driving out the retaining roll pin and removing the coupling, noting the toothed thrustwasher which is fitted behind it.
16 Withdraw the shaft, noting the toothed thrustwasher underneath the centrifugal advance assembly. Be very careful not to bend any of the reluctor poles and do not attempt to remove it from the shaft.
17 The advance assembly and shaft can be lubricated but if any part of the assembly is found to be worn or damaged, then the complete distributor must be renewed. Individual replacement parts are not available.
18 Clean and examine all components. If any are found to be worn or damaged, seek expert advice. A repair kit of sundry parts is available separately, also the coupling assembly, the pick-up coil and vacuum diaphragm unit, as well as the rotor arm and the distributor cap. If any other parts are worn or damaged, the complete distributor must be renewed.
19 In addition to the checks in Chapter 1, use an ohmmeter or continuity tester to check that there is no continuity between any of the cap's terminal segments. Similarly, check that there is no continuity between the rotor arm body and its brass segment. Note that the arm has a built-in resistance.
20 Reassembly is the reverse of the dismantling procedure, noting the following:
a) Apply a few drops of suitable oil to the advance assembly pivots and springs, also to the shaft, upper housing and stator pack bearing surfaces.
b) Using the marks made on dismantling, be very careful to ensure that the coupling is located correctly on the shaft end (in relationship to the rotor arm) before driving in the roll pin to secure it, then ensure that the spring is fitted over the roll pin ends.
c) Grease the vacuum diaphragm unit arm before refitting it and use grease to stick the thrustwasher to the underside of the upper housing. Refit the stator pack, ensuring it engages correctly with the vacuum diaphragm unit arm peg, followed by the (remaining thrustwasher, if fitted, and) circlip. Tighten the unit retaining screw securely.

d) Refit the pick-up coil to the upper housing and centre its terminals in the aperture before fitting the clamp ring so that its cut-out is over the aperture.
e) Refit the upper housing to the lower, tighten the screws lightly and check that the shaft is free to rotate. There must be no sign of the reluctor poles touching the stator pack arms, as either can easily be bent. Tighten the screws securely.
f) Refit the connector and its gasket.
g) Refit the amplifier module and the rotor arm.
h) Fit a new sealing ring to the distributor body.

Refitting

Original distributor

21 Ensure that No 1 cylinder is at TDC, then rotate the rotor arm to align with the distributor cap's No 1 terminal. Fit a new sealing ring to the distributor body and lubricate it with a smear of engine oil.
22 Align the marks made on removal and refit the distributor to the cylinder head. If necessary, rotate the rotor arm very slightly to help the distributor drive dogs locate in the camshaft slots; they are offset and so will fit only one way. Refit the distributor mounting bolts and tighten them to the specified torque.
23 Refit the spark plugs.
24 Refit the distributor cap, ensuring it is correctly located, and tighten its retaining screws to the specified torque. Reconnect the HT leads to the relevant spark plugs.
25 Reconnect the vacuum pipe to the vacuum diaphragm unit and the wiring connector to the ignition amplifier module.
26 Check and, if necessary, adjust the ignition timing.

New distributor

27 If a new distributor is to be fitted (or no marks were made on removal), the following procedure will produce a basic setting which will enable the engine to start and run while the ignition timing is accurately set.
28 Position the engine so that No 1 cylinder is at TDC on the compression stroke.
29 Rotate the crankshaft slightly anti-clockwise until the pulley notch is positioned in the 9° BTDC position (between the 8 and 12 marks on the timing scale).
30 Rotate the distributor rotor arm to align with the distributor cap's No 1 terminal. This terminal is marked with a K which is cast on the outside of the distributor cap. Fit a new sealing ring to the distributor body and lubricate it with a smear of engine oil.
31 Fit the distributor to the cylinder head and refit its mounting bolts. Positioning the distributor body so that the mounting bolts are in the middle of their respective slots then tighten the bolts finger-tight only.
32 Perform the operations given in paragraphs 23 to 25.
33 Check and adjust the ignition timing.

6 Ignition amplifier module - removal and refitting

⚠️ *Warning: Do not attempt to open or repair the ignition amplifier module. If faulty, it must be renewed.*

Removal

1 Disconnect the battery negative terminal.
2 Releasing its wire clip, unplug the wiring connector from the amplifier module.
3 Remove the two bolts and withdraw the module, taking care not to damage the terminal pins.
4 Check carefully that the mating surfaces of the module and distributor are completely clean and unmarked and that the pick-up coil terminal pins are clean and a secure fit in the module. If in doubt, it is permissible to remove the connector and its gasket and to gently squeeze together the female terminals to improve the fit.
5 The pick-up coil-to-connector and connector-to-module connections must be checked with particular care if the module is thought to be faulty. Similarly, check, clean and tighten (if necessary) the distributor wiring connector-to-module terminals. It is essential that there is good electrical contact between the module and the distributor and at all four LT wiring connections mentioned above.

Refitting

6 On refitting, apply a smear of heat-conducting silicone grease to the mating surfaces of the module and distributor. The correct grease can be obtained from Rover dealers under Part Number BAU 5812 but if this is not available, either a heat-sink compound or an anti-seize compound (such as Holt's Copaslip), will serve as an adequate substitute.
7 Check that the terminal pins are not bent or damaged and that they engage correctly with the module's connections.
8 Tighten the module retaining bolts to the specified torque wrench setting, then reconnect the distributor wiring and battery.

7 Thermostatically-operated vacuum switch - removal and refitting

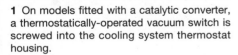

1 On models fitted with a catalytic converter, a thermostatically-operated vacuum switch is screwed into the cooling system thermostat housing.

Removal

2 Either drain the cooling system or be prepared for some loss of coolant as the switch is unscrewed.
3 Access to the thermostat housing is possible with the inlet manifold and carburettor in place, but is made much easier if these are first removed.
4 Disconnect and plug the switch vacuum pipes.
5 Unscrew the switch and withdraw it, then plug the opening to prevent the entry of dirt. If the cooling system has not been drained, work quickly to minimise coolant loss.
6 If required, the switch can be tested as described in Chapter 3.

Refitting

7 Refitting is the reverse of the removal procedure, noting the following:
a) *Wipe clean the threads of the switch and thermostat housing.*
b) *If a sealing washer is fitted, renew it whenever it is disturbed so as to prevent leaks. If no sealing washer is fitted, apply a smear of sealant to the switch threads.*
c) *Tighten the switch securely and reconnect the vacuum pipes.*
d) *Refit any components removed to improve access.*
e) *Replenish the cooling system.*

8 Ignition timing - checking and adjustment

Refer to Chapter 1.

9 Ignition system - testing

Note: *Always switch off the ignition before disconnecting or connecting any system component and when using a multi-meter to check resistances. Any voltmeter or multi-meter used to test ignition system components must have an impedance of 10 Mohms or greater.*

General

1 The components of electronic ignition systems are normally very reliable. Most faults are likely to be due to loose or dirty connections or to 'tracking' of HT voltage due to dirt, dampness or damaged insulation, than to the failure of any of the system's components. Always check all wiring thoroughly before condemning an electrical component and work methodically to eliminate all other possibilities before deciding that a particular component is faulty.
2 The old practice of checking for a spark by holding the live end of an HT lead a short distance away from the engine is not recommended. Not only is there a high risk of a powerful electric shock but the HT coil or amplifier module will be damaged. Never try to diagnose misfires by pulling off one HT lead at a time.

Engine will not start

3 If the engine will not turn over at all or only turns very slowly, check the battery and starter motor. Connect a voltmeter across the battery terminals (meter positive probe to battery positive terminal), disconnect the ignition coil HT lead from the distributor cap and earth it, then note the voltage reading obtained while turning over the engine on the starter for (no more than) ten seconds. If the reading obtained is less than approximately 9.5 volts, check the battery, starter motor and charging system.
4 If the engine turns over at normal speed but will not start, check the HT circuit by connecting a timing light (following the manufacturer's instructions) and turning the engine over on the starter motor. If the light flashes then voltage is reaching the spark plugs, so these should be checked first. If the light does not flash, check the HT leads themselves followed by the distributor cap, carbon brush and rotor arm.
5 If there is a spark, check the fuel system for faults.
6 If there is still no spark, check the voltage at the ignition HT coil + terminal. It should be the same as the battery voltage (ie: at least 11.7 volts). If the voltage at the coil is more than 1 volt less than that at the battery, check the feed back through the fusebox and ignition switch to the battery and its earth until the fault is found.
7 If the feed to the HT coil is sound, check the coil's primary and secondary winding resistance. Renew the coil if faulty but be careful to carefully check the condition of the LT connections themselves before doing so, to ensure that the fault is not due to dirty or poorly-fastened connectors.
8 If the HT coil is in good condition, the fault is probably within the amplifier module or distributor pick-up coil. So that the operation of these two can be checked quickly, Rover dealers have a neon indicator, which when connected across the HT coil's LT terminals, flashes every time the amplifier triggers an HT pulse in the coil if the ignition is switched on and the engine is turned over on the starter. Owners can substitute a low-wattage bulb. If the bulb flickers or flashes when the engine is turned over, the amplifier and distributor are sound.
9 If the amplifier and distributor are sound, and the entire LT circuit is in good condition, the fault, if it lies in the ignition system, must be in the HT circuit components. These should be checked carefully, as outlined above.
10 If the indicator or bulb does not flash, the fault is in either the distributor pick-up coil or the amplifier module. Owners should note that by far the commonest cause of failure of either of these is a poor connection, either between the amplifier module and the distributor body or in the LT circuit wiring connections themselves. If a voltmeter or

5A

multi-meter is available, check the feed to the amplifier (the voltage reading obtained should be the same as that measured at the HT coil LT + terminal), then check that there is no measurable resistance between the amplifier module fixing screws and engine earth and that there is no continuity between either module terminal and earth. If any doubt exists as to the condition of the connections, remove the module, clean and check carefully the module earth and the connections and, if necessary, improve their fit. If these checks fail to correct the fault, measure the resistance of the pick-up coil, comparing it with the specified value. Renew the coil if the reading obtained differs significantly from that given. If

the fault still exists, the only solution is to try the effect of renewing the amplifier module.

Engine misfires

11 An irregular misfire suggests either a loose connection or intermittent fault on the primary circuit, or an HT fault on the coil side of the rotor arm.
12 With the ignition switched off, check carefully through the system ensuring that all connections are clean and securely fastened. If the equipment is available, check the LT circuit as described in paragraphs 6 to 10 above.
13 Check that the HT coil, the distributor cap and the HT leads are clean and dry. Check the leads themselves and the spark

plugs (by substitution, if necessary), then check the distributor cap, carbon brush and rotor arm.
14 Regular misfiring is almost certainly due to a fault in the distributor cap, HT leads or spark plugs. Use a timing light to check whether HT voltage is present at all leads.
15 If HT voltage is not present on any particular lead, the fault will be in that lead or in the distributor cap. If HT is present on all leads, the fault will be in the spark plugs. Check and renew them if there is any doubt about their condition.
16 If no HT is present, check the HT coil as its secondary windings may be breaking down under load.

Chapter 5 Part B
Ignition system - fuel injection engines

Contents

Degrees of difficulty

Easy, suitable for novice with little experience	**Fairly easy,** suitable for beginner with some experience	**Fairly difficult,** suitable for competent DIY mechanic 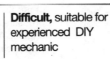	**Difficult,** suitable for experienced DIY mechanic	**Very difficult,** suitable for expert DIY or professional

Specifications

General
System types . . . . Rover/Motorola Modular Engine Management System (MEMS), fully electronic, controlled by ECU. Either single-point (SPi) or multi-point (MPi) fuel injection.

Firing order . . . . 1-3-4-2 (No 1 cylinder at timing belt end)
Direction of crankshaft rotation . . . . Clockwise (viewed from right-hand side of vehicle)

Distributor
Type . . . . Spark distribution only (ignition timing controlled by ECU)
Direction of rotor arm rotation . . . . Anti-clockwise (viewed from left-hand side of vehicle)
Distributor cap:
  SPi . . . . AUU 1186
  MPi . . . . NJD 10010
Rotor arm . . . . AUU 1641 (resistive type)

Engine management Electronic Control Unit (ECU)
SPi:
  With catalytic converter . . . . MNE 10008, MNE 10023 or MNE 10042
  Without catalytic converter . . . . MNE 10011, MNE 10013 or MNE 10051
MPi:
  Alloy inlet manifold . . . . MNE 101470
  Plastic inlet manifold . . . . MKC 101730

Ignition timing @ idle speed (ECU-controlled)
SPi with catalytic converter - by ECU number (vacuum pipe connected) :
  MNE 10008 . . . . 13° ± 2° BTDC
  MNE 10023, MNE 10042 . . . . 14° ± 2° BTDC
SPi without catalytic converter - by ECU number (vacuum pipe connected) :
  MNE 10011 . . . . 13 ± 2° BTDC
  MNE 10013, MNE 10051 . . . . 14 ± 2° BTDC
MPi - by ECU number (vacuum pipe connected) :
  MNE 101470, MKC 101730 . . . . 10 ± 5° BTDC
Note: *Nominal value given for checking purposes only - not adjustable and may vary under ECU control*

5B

Crankshaft sensor

Type . . . .   ADU 7340

HT coil

Type:
  SPi . . . .   NEC 10002 or NEC 10003
  MPi . . . .   NEC 10002, NEC 10003 or NEC 10004
Manufacturer . . . .   Bosch, Ducellier or Rudi Cajavec
Current consumption - average . . . .   0.25 to 0.75 amps @ idle speed
Winding resistances:
  Primary:
    Spi . . . .   0.3 to 0.5 ohms @ 20ºC
    Mpi . . . .   0.7 to 0.8 ohms @ 20ºC
  Secondary . . . .   5 to 15 K ohms @ 20ºC

Torque wrench settings

	Nm	lbf ft
Spark plugs	25	18
Distributor cap screws	2	1
Distributor rotor arm grub screw	10	7
Reluctor ring to flywheel setscrews	3	2
Ignition HT coil mounting screws	7	5
Crankshaft sensor mounting screws	6	4
Crankshaft sensor lead-to-flywheel cover plate screw	6	4

1 General information and precautions

General information

The ignition system is fully electronic in operation, incorporating an Electronic Control Unit (mounted on the engine compartment bulkhead), a distributor (driven off the inlet camshaft left-hand end) and a crankshaft sensor (mounted in the left-hand rear end of the engine cylinder block/crankcase) which registers with the reluctor ring fixed to the flywheel. The system also incorporates spark plugs, HT leads, an ignition HT coil and associated wiring.

The system is divided into two circuits, which are the primary (low tension/LT) and secondary (high tension/HT) circuits. The primary circuit consists of the battery, ignition switch, ignition HT coil primary windings, ECU and wiring. The secondary circuit consists of the ignition HT coil secondary windings, the distributor cap and rotor arm, the spark plugs and the interconnecting HT leads.

The ECU controls both the ignition system and the fuel injection system, integrating the two in a complete engine management system. Refer to Chapter 4 for information on any part of the system not given in this Chapter.

As far as the ignition system is concerned, the ECU receives information in the form of electrical impulses or signals from the crankshaft sensor (which gives it the engine speed and crankshaft position), from the coolant temperature sensor (which gives it the engine temperature), from the throttle pedal switch (which tells it when the throttle is closed) and from the manifold absolute pressure sensor (which gives it the load on the engine). All these signals are compared by the ECU, using digital techniques, with set values pre-programmed (mapped) into its memory. Based on this information, the ECU selects the ignition timing appropriate to those values and controls the ignition HT coil accordingly.

This means that the distributor is just that, a distributor of the HT pulse to the appropriate spark plug. It has no effect whatsoever on the ignition timing. Also, the system is so sensitive that, at idle speed, the ignition timing may be constantly changing. This should be remembered if trying to check the ignition timing.

Precautions

Refer to Part A of this Chapter.

2 Spark plugs - renewal

Refer to Chapter 1.

3 HT leads, distributor cap and rotor arm - inspection and renewal

1 Refer to Chapter 1. Note the anti-flash shield fitted beneath the rotor arm.

4 HT coil - removal, testing and refitting

1 Refer to Section 4 in Part A of this Chapter.

5 Distributor - removal and refitting

Removal

1 Disconnect the battery negative terminal.
2 Disconnect the HT leads from the spark plugs.
3 Undo the two distributor cap retaining screws and remove the cap and leads as an assembly.
4 Slacken and remove the grub screw securing the rotor arm to the camshaft end then pull off the rotor arm (see illustration).
5 Remove the distributor cap insulating plate from the cylinder head.
6 Examine each components for signs of wear or damage and renew as necessary.

Refitting

7 Refitting is a reverse of the removal procedure. Tighten the rotor arm grub screw and distributor cap screws to the specified torque settings.

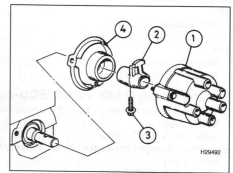

5.4 Distributor assembly

1 Distributor cap
2 Rotor arm
3 Grub screw
4 Insulating plate

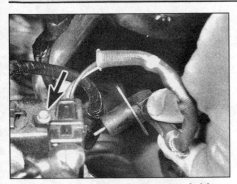

6.3 Removing crankshaft sensor (wiring lead screw arrowed)

6.6 Reluctor ring-to-flywheel screws (arrowed)

6 Crankshaft sensor and reluctor ring - removal and refitting

Removal

Crankshaft sensor

1 Disconnect the battery negative terminal.
2 Disconnect the sensor wiring at its connector plug on the flywheel rear cover plate, then undo the retaining screw to release the wiring lead.
3 Remove the two retaining screws and withdraw the sensor from the cylinder block/crankcase **(see illustration)**.
4 Inspect the sensor for obvious signs of wear or damage and renew it if necessary. No data is available to enable the sensor to be tested. If thought to be faulty, it can be checked only by substitution with a new component.

Reluctor ring

5 Remove the flywheel.
6 Undo the two screws securing the reluctor ring to the rear of the flywheel and withdraw it **(see illustration)**.

7 Check the ring for obvious signs of wear or damage and renew it if necessary.

Refitting

Crankshaft sensor

8 Ensure that the sensor and cylinder block/crankcase mating surfaces are clean then refit the sensor and tighten its retaining screws to the specified torque.
9 Connect the sensor wiring connector and tighten the connector mounting screw to the specified torque.
10 Reconnect the battery negative terminal.

Reluctor ring

11 Refitting is a reversal of the removal procedure. Tighten the reluctor retaining screws to the specified torque.

7 Engine management electronic control unit (ECU) - removal and refitting

Refer to Chapter 4.

8 Ignition timing - checking and adjustment

Refer to Chapter 1.

9 Ignition system - testing

1 If a fault appears in the engine management (ignition/fuel) system, first ensure that the fault is not due to poor maintenance. Check that the air cleaner filter element is clean, the spark plugs are in good condition and correctly gapped, and that the engine breather hoses are clear and undamaged. Also check that the accelerator cable is correctly adjusted. If the engine is running very roughly, check the compression pressures, bearing in mind that possibly one of the hydraulic tappets might be faulty, producing an incorrect valve clearance.
2 If these checks fail to reveal the cause of the problem, the vehicle should be taken to a suitably-equipped Rover dealer for testing. A wiring block connector is incorporated in the engine management circuit into which a special electronic diagnostic tester can be plugged. The tester will locate the fault quickly and simply, alleviating the need to test all the system components individually, which is a time-consuming operation that carries a high risk of damaging the ECU.
3 The only ignition system checks which can be carried out by the home mechanic are those described for the spark plugs, HT leads, rotor arm and distributor cap (Chapter 1), and the Ignition HT coil (this Chapter). If necessary, the system wiring and wiring connectors can be checked as described in Chapter 12, ensuring that the ECU wiring connectors have first been disconnected.

5B

Notes

Chapter 5 Part C
Starting and charging systems

Contents

Degrees of difficulty

Easy, suitable for novice with little experience 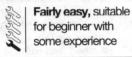	Fairly easy, suitable for beginner with some experience 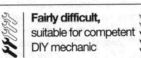	Fairly difficult, suitable for competent DIY mechanic	Difficult, suitable for experienced DIY mechanic	Very difficult, suitable for expert DIY or professional

Specifications

System

Type . . . . 12 volt, negative earth

Battery

Type . . . . Maintenance-free (sealed for life) lead-acid
Lucas code:
   Standard equipment 063
   Cold climates 063S

Performance:

	Cold cranking	Reserve capacity
063	360 amps	60 amps
063S	405 amps	70 amps

Alternator

Type . . . . Lucas/Magneti Marelli A127-65
Output - @ 14 volts and 6000 rpm . . . . 65 amps
Regulated voltage . . . . 14 volts maximum
Brush minimum protrusion . . . . 5.0 mm approx.
Voltage regulator . . . . Lucas 21TR

Starter motor

Type . . . . Lucas M79
Rating . . . . 0.8 kW
Brush minimum length . . . . 3.5 mm approx.

Torque wrench settings	Nm	lbf ft
Alternator		
Pulley retaining nut	25	18
Mounting/pivot/adjusting arm bolts	25	18
Starter motor		
Motor-to-gearbox bolts	45	33
Motor support bracket fasteners:		
Bracket front half-to-motor nuts	25	18
Bracket front half-to-rear half bolt	45	33
Bracket rear half-to-gearbox bolts	25	18

5C

1 General information and precautions

General information

The electrical system is of the 12 volt negative earth type and comprises a 12 volt battery, alternator with integral voltage regulator, starter motor and related electrical accessories, components and wiring. The battery is charged by an alternator which is belt-driven.

The starter motor is of the pre-engaged type incorporating an integral solenoid. On starting, the solenoid moves the drive pinion into engagement with the flywheel ring gear before the starter motor is energised. Once the engine has started, a one-way clutch prevents the motor armature being driven by the engine until the pinion disengages from the flywheel.

Precautions

It is necessary to take extra care when working on the electrical system to avoid damage to semi-conductor devices (diodes and transistors), and to avoid the risk of personal injury. In addition to the precautions given in the *"Safety first!"* Section at the beginning of this manual, take note of the following points when working on the system.

Always remove rings, watches, etc before working on the electrical system. Even with the battery disconnected, capacitive discharge could occur if a component live terminal is earthed through a metal object. This could cause a shock or nasty burn.

Do not reverse the battery connections. Components such as the alternator or any other having semi-conductor circuitry could be irreparably damaged.

If the engine is being started using jump leads and a slave battery, connect the batteries *positive to positive* and *negative to negative*. This also applies when connecting a battery charger.

Always ensure that the battery negative lead is disconnected when working on the electrical system.

Do not allow the engine to turn the alternator when the alternator is not connected.

Never test for alternator output by 'flashing' the output lead to earth.

Never disconnect the battery terminals, or alternator multi-plug connector, when the engine is running.

The battery leads and alternator multi-plug must be disconnected before carrying out any electric welding on the vehicle.

Never use an ohmmeter of the type incorporating a hand cranked generator for circuit or continuity testing.

2 Battery - maintenance

Refer to Chapter 1 and *"Weekly Checks"*.

3 Battery - testing and charging

⚠ **Warning: Specially rapid 'boost' charges which are claimed to restore the power of a battery in 1 to 2 hours are not recommended as they can cause serious damage to the battery plates through overheating.**

⚠ **Warning: During battery electrolyte replenishment, never add water to sulphuric acid otherwise it will explode. Always pour the acid slowly onto the water.**

⚠ **Warning: The battery will be emitting significant quantities of highly inflammable hydrogen gas during charging and for approximately 15 minutes afterwards. Do not allow sparks or naked flames near the battery or it may explode.**

Testing

1 In normal use, the battery should not require charging from an external source unless very heavy use is made of electrical equipment over a series of journeys that are too short to allow the charging system to keep pace with demand. Otherwise, a need for regular recharging points to a fault either in the battery or in the charging system.

2 If the vehicle is laid up for long periods (in excess of thirty days at a time) the battery will lose approximately 1% of its charge per week. This figure is for a disconnected battery. If the battery is left connected, circuits such as the clock (where fitted) will drain it at a faster rate. To prevent this happening, always disconnect the battery negative lead whenever the vehicle is to be laid up for a long period. To keep the battery fully charged, it should be given regular 'refresher' charges every six weeks or so. This is particularly important on 'maintenance-free' batteries, which will suffer permanent reduction of charge capacity if allowed to become fully discharged.

3 If a discharged battery is suspected, the simplest test for most owners is as follows. Leave the battery disconnected for at least two hours, then measure the (open circuit, or no-load) voltage using a sensitive voltmeter connected across the battery terminals. Compare the reading obtained with the following:

Voltmeter reading	Charge condition
0.50 volts	Fully discharged - battery scrap
12.30 volts	50% charged
12.48 volts	75% charged
12.66 volts or more	Fully charged

4 If frequent topping-up is required and the battery case is not fractured, then the battery is being over-charged and the voltage regulator will have to be checked.

5 If the vehicle covers a very small annual mileage, it is worthwhile checking the specific gravity of the electrolyte every three months to determine the state of charge of the battery. Use a hydrometer to make the check and compare the results with the following table:

	Normal climates	Tropics
Discharged	1.120	1.080
Half charged	1.200	1.160
Fully charged	1.280	1.230

6 If the battery condition is suspect, first check the specific gravity of electrolyte in each cell. A variation of 0.040 or more between any cells indicates loss of electrolyte or deterioration of the internal plates.

7 A further test can be made only by a battery specialist using a battery heavy discharge meter. Alternatively, connect a voltmeter across the battery terminals and operate the starter motor with the ignition coil HT lead disconnected from the distributor and earthed, and with the headlamps, heated rear window and heater blower switched on. If the voltmeter reading remains above approximately 9.5 volts, the battery condition is satisfactory. If the voltmeter reading drops below 9.5 volts and the battery has already been charged, it is proven faulty.

Charging

8 In winter when heavy demand is placed on the battery (starting from cold and using more electrical equipment), it is a good idea occasionally to have the battery fully charged from an external source. The battery's bench charge rate depends on its code (see a Rover dealer or Lucas agent for details). For most owners, the best method will be to use a trickle-charger overnight, charging at a rate of 1.5 amps. Rapid 'boost' charges which are claimed to restore the power of the battery in 1 to 2 hours are not recommended, as they can cause serious damage to the battery plates through overheating and may cause a sealed battery to explode.

9 Ideally, the battery should be removed from the vehicle before charging and moved to a well-ventilated area. As a minimum precaution, both battery terminal leads must be disconnected (negative lead first) before connecting the charger leads.

10 Continue to charge the battery until all cells are gassing vigorously and no further rise in specific gravity or increase in no-load voltage is noted over a four-hour period. When charging is complete, turn the charger off before disconnecting the leads from the battery.

4.4 Battery clamp bolt

4.6a Battery tray retaining bolts (arrowed)

4.6b Battery tray mounting bracket retaining bolts (viewed from underneath)

4 Battery - removal and refitting

Removal

1 First check that all electrical components are switched off to avoid a spark occurring as the negative lead is disconnected. If the radio/cassette unit has a security code, de-activate the code temporarily and re-activate it when the battery is re-connected. Refer to the instructions and code supplied with the unit.

2 Slacken the terminal clamp nut then lift the clamp and negative (–) lead from the terminal. This is the terminal to disconnect before working on any electrical component on the vehicle. If the terminal is tight, carefully ease it off by moving it from side to side.

3 Raise the plastic cover from the positive (+) terminal clamp and slacken the clamp nut, then lift the clamp and lead from the terminal.

4 Unscrew the clamp bolt and remove the clamp from the battery tray (see illustration).

5 Lift the battery from the tray, keeping it upright and taking care not to allow it to contact your clothing.

6 If the battery tray is to be removed, first release any relevant wiring harness clips from the tray. Unscrew the six bolts securing the battery tray in position and remove the tray. If necessary, undo the two bolts securing the battery tray mounting bracket to the body and remove the bracket (see illustrations).

7 Clean the battery terminal posts, clamps, tray and battery casing. If the bodywork is rusted as a result of battery acid spilling onto it, clean it thoroughly and re-paint.

8 Whenever the battery is removed, check it for cracks and leakage.

Refitting

9 Refitting is the reverse of the removal procedure. Ensure that the terminal posts and leads are cleaned before re-connection. Smear petroleum jelly on the terminals after reconnecting the leads. Always connect the positive terminal clamp first and the negative terminal clamp last.

5 Charging system - testing

1 If the ignition warning lamp fails to light when the ignition is switched on, first check the alternator wiring connections for security. If satisfactory, check that the warning lamp bulb has not blown and is secure in its holder. If the lamp still fails to light, check the continuity of the warning lamp feed wire from the alternator to the bulbholder. If all is satisfactory, the alternator is at fault and should be renewed or taken to an auto-electrician for testing and repair.

2 If the ignition warning lamp lights when the engine is running, stop the engine and check that the drivebelt is correctly tensioned and that the alternator connections are secure. If all is satisfactory, check the alternator brushes and commutator. If the fault persists, the alternator should be renewed or taken to an auto-electrician for testing and repair.

3 If the alternator output is suspect, even though the warning lamp functions correctly, the regulated voltage may be checked as follows.

4 Connect a voltmeter across the battery terminals and start the engine.

5 Increase engine speed until the voltmeter reading remains steady. This should be approximately 12 to 13 volts and no more than 14 volts.

6 Switch on as many electrical accessories (eg: the headlamps, heated rear window and heater blower) as possible and check that the alternator maintains the regulated voltage at around 13 to 14 volts.

7 If the regulated voltage is not as stated, the fault may be due to worn brushes, weak brush springs, a faulty voltage regulator, a faulty diode, a severed phase winding or a worn or damaged commutator. The brushes and commutator may be checked but if the fault persists, the alternator should be renewed or taken to an auto-electrician for testing and repair.

6 Alternator drivebelt - inspection, adjustment and renewal

Refer to Chapter 1.

7 Alternator brush holder and voltage regulator - renewal

Note: *The vast majority of actual alternator faults are due to the voltage regulator or brushes being defective. If the renewal of either assembly does not cure the fault, then the advice of an expert should be sought. For most owners, the best course of action will be to renew the alternator as a complete unit. In many cases, overhaul will not be viable on economic grounds alone.*

Removal

1 While it is physically possible to remove the voltage regulator and brush holder assembly with the alternator in place on the vehicle, owners are advised to remove the alternator so that it can be serviced in clean working conditions.

2 Unscrew the screws securing the voltage regulator and brush holder assembly to the alternator. Lift off the regulator/brush holder, disconnect the electrical lead and remove the regulator/brush holder from the alternator (see illustration).

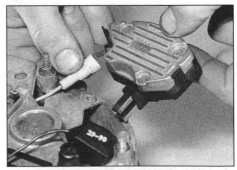

7.2 Remove voltage regulator/brush holder from alternator and disconnect wiring lead

5C

7.3 Alternator brush wear limit marks (arrowed)

8.8a Remove cover from rear of alternator . . .

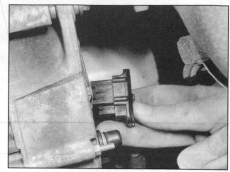

8.8b . . . and disconnect wiring connector

Inspection

3 In most cases, the brushes will have wear limit marks in the form of a groove etched along one face of each brush. When these marks are erased by wear, the brushes are worn out **(see illustration)**. If no marks are provided, measure the protrusion of each brush from the brush holder end to the tip of the brush. No dimension is given by Rover but as a rough guide, 5.0 mm should be regarded as a minimum. If either brush is worn to or below this amount, renew the voltage regulator and brush holder assembly. If the brushes are still serviceable, clean them with a solvent-moistened cloth. Check that the brush spring pressure is equal for both brushes and holds the brushes securely against the slip rings. If in doubt about the condition of the brushes and springs, compare them with new components.

4 Clean the slip rings with a solvent-moistened cloth, then check for signs of scoring, burning or severe pitting. If worn or damaged, the slip rings should be attended to by an auto-electrician.

Refitting

5 Refitting is the reverse of the removal procedure.

8 Alternator - removal and refitting

Removal

1 Disconnect the battery negative lead.

2 Firmly apply the handbrake then jack up the front of the vehicle and remove the right-hand front roadwheel.

3 From underneath the front of the vehicle, slacken and remove the three bolts securing the bumper flange to the body. Remove the seven bolts securing the front undercover panel to the body and remove the panel.

Models with air conditioning

4 Undo the two bolts and washers securing the heat shield to the rear of the alternator,

then remove the nut securing the heat shield to the engine and lift the shield out of the engine compartment.

5 Disconnect the wiring connector from the rear of the alternator.

6 Slacken the adjuster pulley retaining nut, then turn the pulley adjusting bolt until sufficient drivebelt free play is obtained to be able to disengage the drivebelt from the alternator pulley.

7 Slacken and remove the three bolts securing the alternator to its mounting bracket then manoeuvre the alternator out of the engine compartment.

Models without air conditioning

8 Unscrew the three nuts and washers securing the rear cover to the alternator and remove the cover. Release the wire retaining clip and disconnect the alternator wiring connector **(see illustrations)**.

9 Slacken the lower alternator-to-adjusting arm bolt and the two upper alternator pivot bolts, then slacken the drivebelt adjusting bolt until sufficient free play is obtained to disengage the drivebelt from the alternator pulley **(see illustrations)**.

10 Remove the alternator adjusting arm and upper pivot bolts and manoeuvre the alternator out of the engine compartment.

Refitting

11 If a new alternator is being fitted, it will be necessary to remove the pulley and cooling fan from the old unit. To do this, slacken the

pulley retaining nut whilst preventing it from rotating by using a suitable Allen key to retain the alternator shaft, or by clamping the pulley firmly in a vice equipped with soft jaws. Remove the pulley, cooling fan and fan washer from the old alternator and, ensuring that the pulley and shaft mating surfaces are clean, fit them to the new unit. Tighten the pulley retaining nut to the specified torque whilst using the method employed on removal to retain the pulley.

Models with air conditioning

12 Manoeuvre the alternator into position then refit its mounting bolts and tighten them to the specified torque.

13 Locate the drivebelt on the alternator pulley then adjust drivebelt tension as described in Chapter 1.

14 Reconnect the wiring connector to the rear of the alternator then refit the heat shield, tightening its retaining nut and bolts securely. Reconnect the battery.

Models without air conditioning

15 Manoeuvre the alternator into position then refit the adjusting arm and pivot bolts and tighten them lightly.

16 Locate the drivebelt on the alternator pulley and adjust drivebelt tension as described in Chapter 1.

17 Reconnect the wiring connector to the rear of the alternator then refit the rear cover, tightening its retaining nuts securely. Reconnect the battery.

8.9a Slacken upper pivot mounting bolts . . .

8.9b . . . and lower adjusting arm bolt (A) then rotate adjuster bolt (B) to slacken drivebelt tension

9 Starting system - testing

1 If the starter motor fails to operate when the switch is operated, the following may be the cause:
a) *The battery is faulty.*
b) *The electrical connections between the ignition switch, solenoid, battery and starter motor are somewhere failing to pass the necessary current from the battery through the starter to earth.*
c) *The solenoid is faulty.*
d) *The starter relay is faulty.*
e) *The starter motor is mechanically or electrically defective.*

2 To check the battery, switch on the headlamps. If they dim after a few seconds then the battery is discharged. Recharge or renew the battery. If the lamps glow brightly, operate the ignition switch and see what happens to the lamps. If they dim, then you know that power is reaching the starter motor, therefore the motor must be removed and renewed or overhauled to cure the fault. If the lamps stay bright (and no clicking sound can be heard from the solenoid), there is a fault in the circuit or solenoid. If the starter turns slowly when switched on, but the battery is in good condition, then either the starter must be faulty or there is considerable resistance in the circuit.

3 If the circuit is suspected, disconnect the battery terminals (including the earth connection to the body), the starter/solenoid wiring and the engine/gearbox unit earth lead, thoroughly clean their connections and refit them, then use a meter or test lamp to check that full battery voltage is available at the solenoid terminal of the battery positive lead and that the earth is sound. Smear petroleum jelly around the battery terminals to prevent corrosion. Corroded connections are the most frequent cause of electrical system malfunctions.

4 If the battery and all connections are in good condition, check the circuit first by disconnecting the wire from the solenoid blade terminal. Connect a meter or test lamp between the wire end and the terminal and check that the wire is live when the ignition switch is operated. If it is, then the circuit is sound. If not, proceed to paragraph 7.

5 The solenoid contacts can be checked by putting a voltmeter or test lamp across the main cable connection on the starter side of the solenoid and earth. When the switch is operated, there should be a reading or lighted bulb. If there is no reading or lighted bulb, the solenoid is faulty and should be renewed.

6 If the circuit and solenoid are proved sound, the fault must be in the starter motor. Remove the motor and check its brushes. If the fault does not lie in the brushes, the motor windings must be faulty. In this event, the motor must be renewed, unless an auto-electrical specialist can be found who will overhaul the unit at a cost significantly less than that of a new or exchange starter motor.

7 If the circuit is thought to be faulty, first check the starter relay which is situated in the engine compartment fusebox. A simple test is to temporarily replace it with one of the other relays from the fusebox, such as the cooling fan relay, which is known to be in a good condition. If this resolves the fault, then the starter relay is faulty and must be renewed. If not, check the ignition switch and wiring.

10 Starter motor - removal and refitting

Removal

1 Disconnect the battery negative lead.
2 Firmly apply the handbrake then jack up the front of the vehicle and support it on axle stands. Remove the right-hand front roadwheel.
3 From underneath the front of the vehicle, slacken and remove the three bolts securing the bumper flange to the body. Remove the seven bolts securing the front undercover panel to the body and remove the panel.
4 Undo the nut and disconnect the battery cable from the main solenoid terminal. Carefully disconnect the spade connector from the solenoid **(see illustration)**.
5 Unscrew the two bolts securing the starter motor support bracket to the gearbox **(see illustration)**.
6 Slacken and remove the three starter motor mounting bolts, noting the earth strap which is fitted to the upper bolt, and manoeuvre the starter motor out from underneath the vehicle **(see illustrations)**.

Refitting

7 Refitting is a reverse of the removal sequence, tightening all nuts and bolts to their specified torque settings.

5C

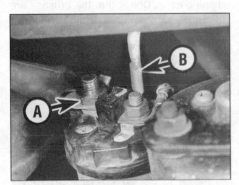
10.4 Starter solenoid main terminal nut (A) and spade connector (B)

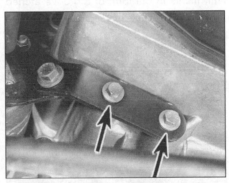
10.5 Starter motor support bracket-to-gearbox bolts

10.6a Starter motor lower mounting bolts viewed from underneath

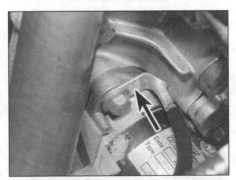
10.6b Starter motor upper mounting bolt and earth strap (arrowed) - viewed from above

10.6c Removing the starter motor

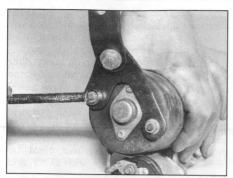

11.2 Undo retaining nuts and remove support bracket from starter motor

11.3 Remove cover to gain access to armature C-clip

11 Starter motor - brush and solenoid renewal

1 Remove the starter motor.

Brushes

Removal

2 Undo the two nuts securing the support bracket to the rear of the starter motor and remove the bracket **(see illustration)**.
3 Undo the two screws and remove the small cover and gasket from the centre of the starter motor end cover **(see illustration)**. Prise out the C-clip and withdraw any thrustwashers fitted to the armature end.
4 Noting the alignment marks between the end cover or grommet and the yoke, unscrew the two through-bolts and withdraw the end cover **(see illustrations)**.
5 Carefully prise off the negative (field coil) brush retaining caps from the brush holder assembly then remove the springs and slide the brushes out of the holder.
6 Remove the nut and spring washer securing the positive brush lead to the solenoid terminal and slide the brush holder assembly off the end of the commutator. Withdraw the plastic insulating plate then remove the positive brush retaining caps and springs and remove the positive brushes from the holder **(see illustrations)**.

Inspection

7 In most cases, the brushes will have wear limit marks in the form of a groove etched along one face of each brush. When the brushes are worn down to these marks, they are worn out and must be renewed. If no marks are provided, measure the length of each brush **(see illustration)**. No dimension is given by Rover but as a rough guide 3.5 mm should be regarded as a minimum. If any brush is worn below this amount, renew the brushes as a set. If the brushes are still serviceable, clean them with a solvent-moistened cloth. Check that the brush spring pressure is equal for all brushes and holds the brushes securely against the commutator. If in doubt about the condition of the brushes and springs, compare them with new components.
8 Clean the commutator with a solvent-moistened cloth, then check for signs of scoring, burning, excessive wear or severe pitting. If worn or damaged, the commutator should be attended to by an auto-electrician.

Refitting

9 On refitting, slot the positive brushes into position in the brush holder then refit the insulating plate, ensuring that the small threaded brackets are correctly positioned on the brush holder and locate with the pins on the insulating plate.
10 Fit the brush holder assembly to the commutator and slot the negative (field coil) brushes into position in the brush holder. With all the brushes in position, fit the brush springs and secure them in position with the retaining caps. Check that the brushes are

11.4a Note alignment marks between yoke and grommet . . .

11.4b . . . then remove through-bolts and withdraw end cover

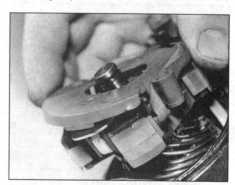

11.6a Remove plastic insulating plate . . .

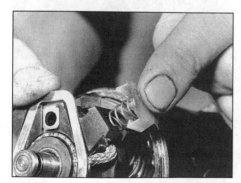

11.6b . . . remove brush spring caps and springs . . .

11.6c . . . and remove positive brush assembly from motor

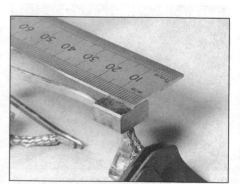

11.7 Measuring starter motor brush length

11.14 Unscrew nut and disconnect starter motor lead from solenoid terminal

11.15 Remove solenoid retaining bolts (one arrowed) . . .

11.16 . . . then release solenoid plunger from lever and remove assembly from motor

free to move in their holders against spring pressure.

11 Refit the starter motor end cover, engaging it with the grommet, and aligning the marks noted on removal. Tighten the cover through-bolts securely.

12 Refit any necessary thrustwashers to the end of the armature and secure them in position with the C-clip. Refit the gasket and small cover to the end cover and tighten its retaining screws securely. Connect the positive brush lead to the solenoid terminal and tighten the nut securely.

13 Refit the support bracket to the motor and tighten its retaining nuts to the specified torque.

Solenoid

Removal

14 Slacken and remove the nut and spring washer securing the starter motor (positive brush) lead to the solenoid and disconnect the lead from the solenoid terminal **(see illustration)**.

15 Unscrew the two bolts and spring washers securing the solenoid to the starter

motor drive end bracket **(see illustration)**.

16 Release the solenoid plunger from the starter engaging lever, then withdraw the solenoid, noting the spring which is fitted to the plunger **(see illustration)**.

Refitting

17 Refitting is the reverse of the removal procedure. Ensure that the solenoid, its plunger and the motor/solenoid mating surfaces are clean and lubricate the plunger/starter engaging lever surfaces with a smear of grease (Rover recommend Shell Alvania).

5C

Notes

Chapter 6
Clutch

Contents

Degrees of difficulty

Easy, suitable for novice with little experience	Fairly easy, suitable for beginner with some experience	Fairly difficult, suitable for competent DIY mechanic	Difficult, suitable for experienced DIY mechanic	Very difficult, suitable for expert DIY or professional 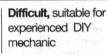

Specifications

Clutch

Type .... Single dry plate with diaphragm spring, cable-operated, self-adjusting

Friction plate

Diameter .... 190 mm
Friction material total thickness - AP plate only:
  New plate .... 8.00 to 8.40 mm
  Service limit .... 6.30 mm
Rivet depth - distance from friction material surface to rivet heads:
  New plate:
    AP .... 1.3 mm minimum
    Valeo .... 0.9 mm minimum
  Service limit:
    AP .... 0.2 mm
    Valeo .... 0.1 mm
Maximum run-out - at outer edge of friction material:
  AP .... 1.3 mm
  Valeo .... 1.0 mm

Pressure plate

Diaphragm spring finger maximum clearance:
  AP .... 0.65 mm
  Valeo .... 1.00 mm
Diaphragm spring finger height above flywheel surface:
  New plate:
    AP .... 27.6 to 33.1 mm
    Valeo .... 29.1 to 32.0 mm
  Service limit:
    AP .... 39.4 mm
    Valeo .... 36.5 mm
Maximum warpage of machined surface:
  AP .... 0.08 mm
  Valeo .... 0.20 mm

Torque wrench settings	Nm	lbf ft
Pressure plate-to-flywheel bolts	18	13
Release bearing guide sleeve-to-bellhousing bolts	5	4

6

1 General information and precautions

General information

The clutch consists of a friction plate, a pressure plate assembly, a release bearing and a release mechanism. All of these components are contained in the large cast aluminium alloy bellhousing sandwiched between the engine and gearbox. The release mechanism is mechanical, being operated by cable **(see illustrations)**.

The friction plate is fitted between the flywheel and the clutch pressure plate and is allowed to slide on the gearbox input shaft splines. It consists of two circular facings of friction material riveted in position to provide the clutch bearing surface, and a spring-cushioned hub to damp out transmission shocks.

The pressure plate assembly is bolted to the flywheel and is located by three dowel pins. It comprises the clutch cover, the diaphragm spring and the pressure plate. When the engine is running, drive is transmitted from the crankshaft via the flywheel and clutch cover to the friction plate (these last three components being clamped securely together by the pressure plate and diaphragm spring) and from the friction plate to the gearbox input shaft.

To interrupt the drive, the spring pressure must be relaxed. This is achieved by a sealed release bearing fitted concentrically around the gearbox input shaft. When the driver depresses the clutch pedal, the release bearing is pressed against the fingers at the centre of the diaphragm spring. Since the spring is held by rivets between two annular fulcrum rings, the pressure at its centre causes it to deform so that it flattens and thus releases the clamping force it exerts, at its periphery, on the pressure plate.

Depressing the clutch pedal pulls the control cable inner wire and this in turn rotates the release fork by acting on the lever at the fork's upper end, above the bellhousing. The fork itself is clipped to the left of the release bearing.

As the friction plate facings wear, the pressure plate moves towards the flywheel. This causes the diaphragm spring fingers to push against the release bearing, thus reducing the clearance which must be present in the mechanism. To ensure correct operation, the clutch cable incorporates a spring-loaded self-adjusting mechanism, eliminating the need for periodic adjustments.

Precautions

The clutch friction and pressure plates are manufactured by two suppliers, Automotive Products (AP) and Valeo. Both the friction plate and the pressure plate must come from the same supplier as they are not interchangeable

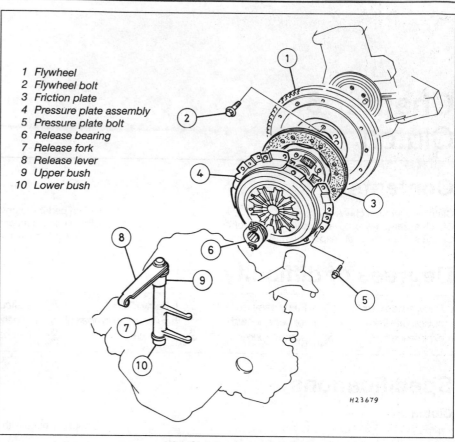

1 Flywheel
2 Flywheel bolt
3 Friction plate
4 Pressure plate assembly
5 Pressure plate bolt
6 Release bearing
7 Release fork
8 Release lever
9 Upper bush
10 Lower bush

1.0a Clutch components

between the two. Apart from the manufacturer's name which may be stamped on either component, AP components can be identified by the part number being applied with white paint, while on Valeo components the part number is applied either with green paint or with black paint with a green spot. All other clutch components are the same, irrespective of supplier.

Dust, created by clutch wear and deposited on the clutch components, may contain asbestos which is a health hazard. DO NOT blow it out with compressed air or inhale any of it. DO NOT use petrol or petroleum-based solvents to clean off the dust. Brake system cleaner or methylated spirit should be used to flush the dust into a suitable receptacle. After the clutch components are wiped clean with rags, dispose of the contaminated rags and cleaner in a sealed, marked container.

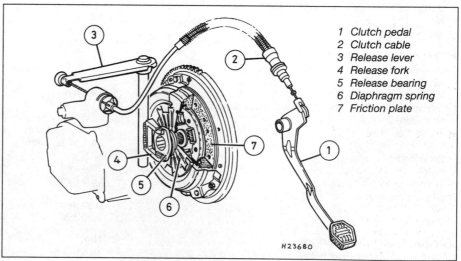

1 Clutch pedal
2 Clutch cable
3 Release lever
4 Release fork
5 Release bearing
6 Diaphragm spring
7 Friction plate

1.0b Clutch release mechanism

3.1a Compress clutch cable spring then remove C-clip

3.1b Unhook cable from clutch release lever and withdraw càble from gearbox bracket

3.4 Disconnect clutch cable from clutch pedal hook

2 Clutch - operation check

Refer to Chapter 1.

3 Clutch cable - removal, inspection and refitting

Removal

1 Working in the engine compartment, compress the cable spring and remove the C-clip, then unhook the cable end fitting from the release fork lever (see illustrations).
2 Release the cable from the gearbox bracket(s) and free it from any relevant cable ties or clamps.
3 Working inside the vehicle, undo the five retaining screws and remove the right-hand lower facia panel.
4 Unhook the cable from the pedal upper end (see illustration).
5 Return to the engine compartment and withdraw the cable through the bulkhead.

Inspection

6 Examine the cable, looking for worn end fittings or a damaged outer casing and for signs of fraying of the inner wire.
7 Check cable operation. The inner wire should move smoothly and easily through the outer casing. A cable that appears serviceable when tested off the vehicle may well be much heavier in operation when fitted into its working position.
8 Renew the cable if it shows any signs of excessive wear or of damage.

Refitting

9 Refitting is the reverse of the removal procedure. Apply a thin smear of multi-purpose grease to the cable end fittings. Align the slot in the inner wire's end with the pedal hook and smear petroleum jelly on the cable

outer's rubber bush before hooking the cable onto the pedal. Press the bush firmly into the bulkhead so that the steel washer butts firmly against the bulkhead boss.
10 Ensure that the cable is routed correctly, with no sharp bends or kinks, also that it is retained by any necessary clamps or ties.
11 When the cable is refitted, depress the pedal several times through its full travel, releasing it fully at each stroke, to enable the self-adjusting mechanism to set itself. Check that clutch operation is correct.

4 Clutch pedal - removal, inspection and refitting

Removal

1 Disconnect the clutch cable from the pedal.
2 Using a pair of pliers, carefully unhook the clutch pedal return spring from the pedal and remove it (see illustration).
3 Slacken and remove the clutch pedal pivot nut and slide the pedal off the pivot.

Inspection

4 Carefully clean all components and renew any that are worn or damaged
5 Check the bearing surfaces of the pivot bushes and shaft with particular care.

4.2 Clutch pedal return spring and pivot nut (arrowed)

The bushes can be renewed separately if worn.

Refitting

6 Refitting is the reverse of the removal procedure. Apply a thin smear of multi-purpose grease to the pedal pivot bearing surfaces.

5 Clutch assembly - removal, inspection and refitting

Warning: Dust created by clutch wear and deposited on the clutch components may contain asbestos, which is a health hazard. DO NOT blow asbestos with compressed air or inhale any of it. DO NOT use petrol or petroleum-based solvents to clean off dust. Brake system cleaner or methylated spirit should be used to flush dust into a suitable receptacle. After the clutch components are wiped clean with rags, dispose of the contaminated rags and cleaner in a sealed, marked container.

Note: Due to the amount of work necessary to remove and refit clutch components, it is usually considered good practice to renew the clutch friction plate, pressure plate assembly and release bearing as a matched set, even if only one of these is actually worn enough to require renewal.

Removal

1 Unless the complete engine/gearbox unit is to be removed from the vehicle and separated for major overhaul, the clutch can be reached by removing just the gearbox.
2 Before disturbing the clutch, use chalk or a felt-tip pen to mark the relationship of the pressure plate assembly to the flywheel.
3 Working in a diagonal sequence, slacken the pressure plate bolts by half a turn at a time until the spring pressure is released and the bolts can be unscrewed by hand.
4 Prise the pressure plate assembly off its

6

5.4 Note locating dowels (two arrowed) and friction plate fitted position

5.8 Measuring friction plate rivet depth

5.9 Measuring friction plate total thickness

locating dowels and collect the friction plate, noting which way round the friction plate is fitted **(see illustration)**.

Inspection

5 Remove the clutch assembly.
6 Remove dust from the clutch components by using a clean, dry cloth. Work in a well-ventilated space.
7 Check the friction plate facings for signs of wear, damage or oil contamination. If the friction material is cracked, burnt, scored or damaged, or if it is contaminated with oil or grease (shown by shiny black patches), the friction plate must be renewed.
8 If the depth from the friction material surface to any of the rivets is worn to the specified service limit or less, the friction plate must be renewed **(see illustration)**.
9 If the friction plate is an AP item, the total thickness of friction material can be measured and compared with that specified **(see illustration)**. If the plate is excessively worn, or even close to the service limit, it must be renewed.
10 If the friction material is still serviceable, check that the centre boss splines are unworn, that the torsion springs are in good condition and securely fastened and that all the rivets are tightly fastened. If any wear or damage is found, the friction plate must be renewed.

11 If the friction material is fouled with oil, this will be due to an oil leak, either from the crankshaft left-hand oil seal, the sump to main bearing ladder joint, the main bearing ladder-to-cylinder block/crankcase joint or from the gearbox input shaft. Renew the seal or repair the joint, as appropriate.
12 Check the pressure plate assembly for obvious signs of wear or damage. Shake it to check for loose rivets or worn or damaged fulcrum rings and check that the drive straps securing the pressure plate to the cover do not show signs (such as a deep yellow or blue discoloration) of overheating. If the diaphragm spring is worn or damaged, or if its pressure is in any way suspect, the pressure plate assembly should be renewed.
13 To check the condition of the diaphragm spring, place a circular piece of flat plate across the tips of the spring fingers and use feeler gauges to measure the clearance between each finger's tip and the plate **(see illustration)**. If any finger is distorted so that the clearance between its tip and the plate is at the specified service limit or greater, the pressure plate must be renewed.
14 To check the condition of the pressure plate, refit it to the flywheel, without the friction plate. Measure the height of each diaphragm spring finger from the flywheel's machined bearing surface. If any finger's

height is at the service limit specified or greater, the pressure plate assembly must be renewed.
15 Examine the machined bearing surfaces of the pressure plate and of the flywheel. They should be clean, completely flat and free from scratches or scoring. If either is discoloured from excessive heat or shows signs of cracks then it should be renewed, although minor damage of this nature can sometimes be polished away using emery paper. Use a straight-edge, placed across the pressure plate surface at four different points, and feeler gauges to check the pressure plate surface, comparing any warpage found with the specified service limit.
16 Check the release bearing as described in Section 6.

Refitting

17 Ensure that the bearing surfaces of the flywheel and pressure plate are completely clean, smooth and free from oil or grease. Use solvent to remove any protective grease from new components.
18 Fit the friction plate so that the longer part of its central, splined, boss is towards the flywheel and so that its spring hub assembly faces away from the flywheel. There may also be a mark showing which way round the plate is to be refitted **(see illustration)**.
19 Refit the pressure plate assembly, aligning the marks made on dismantling (if the original pressure plate is re-used) and locating the pressure plate on its three locating dowels. Fit the pressure plate bolts, tightening them only finger-tight so that the friction plate can still be moved.
20 The friction plate must now be centralised so that, when the gearbox is refitted, its input shaft will pass through the splines at the centre of the friction plate.
21 Centralisation can be achieved by passing a screwdriver or other long bar through the friction plate and into the hole in the crankshaft. The friction plate can then be moved around until it is centred on the crankshaft hole. Alternatively, a clutch aligning tool can be used to eliminate the guesswork

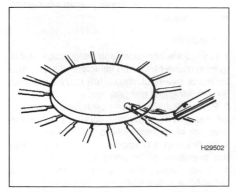

5.13 Measuring diaphragm spring finger clearance

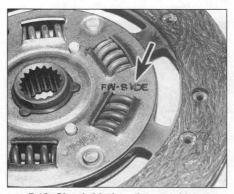

5.18 Check friction plate markings (arrowed) - this side must face flywheel

5.21 Using clutch aligning tool to centralise friction plate

6.3 Drive out roll pin and remove release fork lever

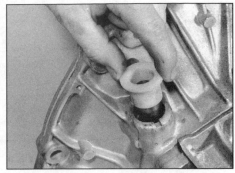

6.4 Removing release fork upper bush

(see illustration). This can be obtained from most accessory shops or can be made up from a length of metal rod or wooden dowel which fits closely inside the crankshaft hole, and has insulating tape wound around it to match the diameter of the friction plate splined hole.

22 When the friction plate is centralised, tighten the pressure plate bolts evenly and in a diagonal sequence to the specified torque setting.

23 Apply a thin smear of molybdenum disulphide grease to the splines of the friction plate and the gearbox input shaft, also to the release bearing bore and release fork shaft.

24 Refit the gearbox.

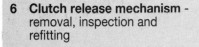

6 Clutch release mechanism -
removal, inspection and refitting

Removal

1 Unless the complete engine/gearbox unit is to be removed from the vehicle and separated for major overhaul, the clutch release mechanism can be reached only by removing the gearbox.

2 Disengaging the release bearing from the fork ends, pull the release bearing off its guide sleeve.

3 Drive out the roll pin from the top of the release fork by using a hammer and a parallel punch, then remove the lever **(see illustration)**.

4 Using a suitable flat-bladed screwdriver, carefully prise the release fork upper bush out

of the gearbox housing. Withdraw the release fork then prise out the lower bush **(see illustration)**.

Inspection

5 Check the release mechanism, renewing any component which is worn or damaged. Carefully check all bearing surfaces and points of contact.

6 When checking the release bearing itself, note that it is often considered worthwhile to renew it as a matter of course. Check that the contact surface rotates smoothly and easily, with no sign of noise or roughness and that the surface itself is smooth and unworn, with no signs of cracks, pitting or scoring. If there is any doubt about its condition, the bearing must be renewed.

7 When cleaning clutch components, do not use solvents on the release bearing as it is packed with grease which may be washed out if care is not taken.

Refitting

8 Reassembly is the reverse of the dismantling procedure, noting the following **(see illustrations)**:

a) When refitting the release fork bushes, ensure that each bush's locating tags engage in the bellhousing slots. Apply a smear of molybdenum disulphide grease to the release fork shaft's bearing surfaces before refitting it and use a new roll pin (if required) to secure the release fork lever.

b) Clean the release bearing bore and guide sleeve, then apply a smear of molybdenum disulphide grease to both bearing surfaces before engaging the bearing on the fork ends and sliding it onto the sleeve.

c) Move the fork up and down to check that it fits correctly against the bearing, then move the release lever to check that the fork and bearing operate properly before refitting the gearbox.

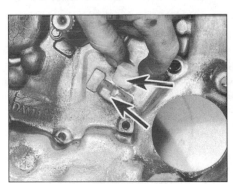

6.8a Align bush locating tabs with bellhousing slots (arrowed) . . .

6.8b . . . and ensure release bearing hooks are correctly engaged with fork

6

Notes

Chapter 7
Gearbox

Contents

Degrees of difficulty

Easy, suitable for novice with little experience	Fairly easy, suitable for beginner with some experience	Fairly difficult, suitable for competent DIY mechanic	Difficult, suitable for experienced DIY mechanic	Very difficult, suitable for expert DIY or professional

Specifications

Gearbox

Type	Manual, five forward speeds and reverse. Synchromesh on all forward speeds
Designation	Rover R65
Code	5C 39W

Lubrication

Gearchange linkage grease	Rover grease containing 3% molybdenum disulphide – Part No. AFU1500.1509

Torque wrench settings

	Nm	lbf ft
Oil filler/level and drain plugs	25	18
Clutch release bearing guide sleeve bolts	5	4
Flywheel cover plate bolts	8	6
Gearbox-to-engine bolts	85	63
Anti-beaming bracket-to-support bracket bolt	45	33
Engine/gearbox left-hand mounting:		
Mounting-to-body bolts	45	33
Mounting-to-gearbox bracket bolts	60	44
Gearbox bracket bolts	100	74
Engine/gearbox rear mounting:		
Mounting bracket-to-gearbox bolts	100	74
Connecting link-to-gearbox bracket bolt	60	44
Connecting link-to-subframe bracket bolt	85	63
Subframe mounting bracket bolts	63	46

7

1 General information

The transmission unit is contained in a cast aluminium alloy casing which is bolted to the engine's left-hand end. It comprises the gearbox and final drive differential, often called a transaxle.

Drive is transmitted from the crankshaft via the clutch to the gearbox input shaft, which has a splined extension to accept the clutch friction plate and rotates in sealed ball-bearings. From the input shaft, drive is transmitted to the output shaft, which rotates in a roller bearing at its right-hand end and a sealed ball-bearing at its left-hand end. From the output shaft, drive is transmitted to the differential crownwheel, which rotates with the differential case and planetary gears, thus driving the sun gears and driveshafts. The rotation of the planetary gears on their shaft allows the inner roadwheel to rotate at a slower speed than the outer roadwheel when the vehicle is cornering.

The gearbox input and output shafts are arranged side by side, parallel to the crankshaft and driveshafts, so that their gear pinion teeth are in constant mesh. In the neutral position, the output shaft gear pinions rotate freely so that drive cannot be transmitted to the crownwheel.

Gear selection is by a floor-mounted lever acting through a remote control linkage on the selector mechanism. The selector mechanism causes the appropriate selector fork to move its respective synchro-sleeve along the shaft to lock the gear pinion to the synchro-hub. Since the synchro-hubs are splined to the output shaft, this locks the pinion to the shaft so that drive can be transmitted. To ensure that gear changing can be made quickly and quietly, a synchromesh system is fitted to all forward gears, consisting of baulk rings and spring-loaded fingers as well as the gear pinions and synchro-hubs. The synchromesh cones are formed on the mating faces of the baulk rings and gear pinions.

2 Gearbox oil - level check

Refer to Chapter 1.

3 Gearbox oil - renewal

Draining

1 This operation is much quicker and more efficient if the vehicle is first taken on a journey of sufficient length to warm the gearbox up to normal operating temperature.

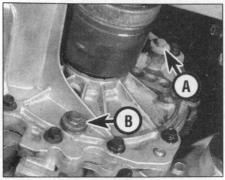

3.3 Gearbox oil filler/level plug (A) and drain plug (B)

2 Park the vehicle on level ground, switch off the ignition and apply the handbrake firmly. For improved access, jack up the front of the vehicle and support it securely on axle stands.
3 Unscrew the filler/level plug, then position a suitable container under the drain plug at the rear of the gearbox (below the left-hand driveshaft inner constant velocity joint). Unscrew the drain plug (see illustration).
4 Allow the oil to drain completely into the container. If the oil is hot, take precautions against scalding.
5 Clean both the filler/level and the drain plugs, being especially careful to wipe any metallic particles off the magnetic inserts. Discard the original sealing washers as they should be renewed whenever disturbed.
6 When the oil has finished draining, clean the drain plug threads and those of the gearbox casing, fit a new sealing washer and refit the drain plug, tightening it to the specified torque wrench setting. If the vehicle was raised for the draining operation, now lower it to the ground.

Filling

7 Filling the gearbox is an extremely awkward operation. Above all, allow plenty of time for the oil level to settle properly before checking it. Note that the vehicle must be parked on flat level ground when checking the oil level.
8 Refill the gearbox with the exact amount of the specified type of oil, see "Lubricants and Fluids". Allow time for the oil to settle.

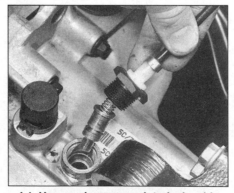

4.1 Unscrewing reverse interlock cable from gearbox

9 Check the oil level. If the correct amount was poured into the gearbox and a large amount flows out on checking the level, refit the filler/level plug and take the vehicle on a short journey so that the new oil is distributed fully around the gearbox components, then check the level again.
10 On completion, fit a new sealing washer and refit the filler/level plug, tightening it to the specified torque wrench setting.
11 Dispose of old oil safely. Do not pour it down a drain.

4 Reverse interlock cable - removal and refitting

Note: On later models (from VIN XW 408115 onwards) or earlier models which have been fitted with a Unipart replacement gearbox and/or gearbox housing, there is no provision for the reverse interlock cable. Therefore the reverse interlock cable is no longer needed and, if already fitted, can be removed.

Removal

1 Working from within the engine compartment, unscrew the reverse interlock cable nut from the top of the gearbox housing (see illustration). In the absence of the special spanner (Rover service tool number 18G 1591), use a close fitting spanner to unscrew the plastic nut whilst being aware that it is easily damaged. Plug the gearbox orifice to prevent the entry of dirt.
2 Firmly apply the handbrake then jack up the front of the vehicle and support it on axle stands.
3 From underneath the vehicle, trace the cable back along its entire length and free it from all the retaining clips securing it to the subframe and gearchange linkage control rod.
4 From inside the vehicle remove the centre console assembly.
5 With the console removed, prise off the rubber cover from the base of the gearchange lever and slide the cover off the lever (see illustration).
6 Release the cable outer from its abutment and disconnect the cable inner from the

4.5 Remove rubber cover . . .

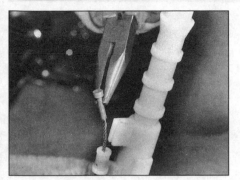

4.6 . . . and disconnect cable from gearchange lever

gearchange lever reverse slide **(see illustration)**. The cable can now be removed from underneath the vehicle.

Refitting

7 Refitting is the reverse of the removal procedure. Ensure that the cable is securely retained by all the necessary ties. On completion, check that the cable functions correctly before taking the vehicle on the road.

5 Gearchange linkage - adjustment

1 If a stiff, sloppy or imprecise gearchange leads you to suspect that a fault exists within the linkage, first dismantle it completely and check for wear or damage, then reassemble it, applying a smear of the approved grease to all bearing surfaces **(see illustration)**.
2 If this does not cure the fault, the vehicle should be examined by an expert, as the fault must lie within the gearbox itself. There is no adjustment as such in the linkage. While the length of the link rods can be altered, this is for initial setting-up only and is not intended to provide a form of compensation for wear.
3 If the link rods have been renewed, or the length of the originals is incorrect, adjust them as follows.

4 Ensure that the vehicle is parked on level ground, with the ignition switched off, the handbrake firmly applied and neutral selected. Remembering that the selector mechanism is spring-loaded so that the gearchange lever rests naturally between the third and fourth gear positions, have an assistant hold the gearchange lever in its normal position.
5 Working in (or under) the engine compartment, slacken the locknut at the bellcrank end of the rod to be adjusted. If not already done, disconnect the rod from the gearbox selector levers.
6 Check that the selector lever concerned is in its neutral position, with no signs of free play or damage, then hold the rod end socket over the lever ball and alter the length of the rod by screwing the rod end socket in or out (as applicable).
7 When the length of the rod is correct, tighten the locknut securely whilst retaining the socket.
8 Press the link rod socket firmly onto the selector lever and check that all gears can be selected, with the gearchange lever returning properly to its correct at-rest position.

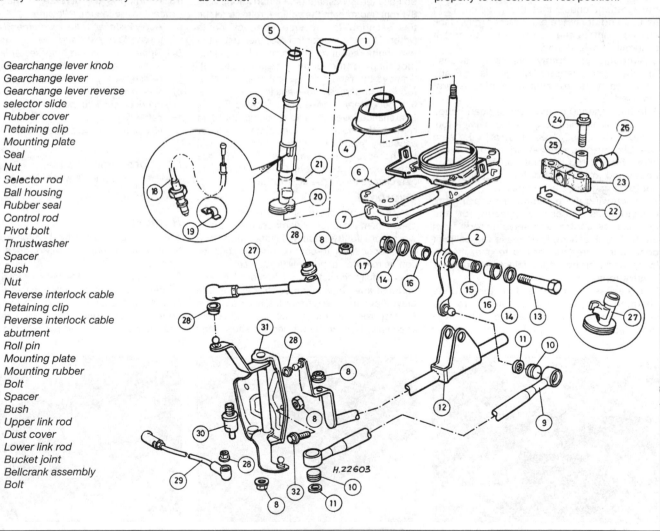

1 Gearchange lever knob
2 Gearchange lever
3 Gearchange lever reverse selector slide
4 Rubber cover
5 Retaining clip
6 Mounting plate
7 Seal
8 Nut
9 Selector rod
10 Ball housing
11 Rubber seal
12 Control rod
13 Pivot bolt
14 Thrustwasher
15 Spacer
16 Bush
17 Nut
18 Reverse interlock cable
19 Retaining clip
20 Reverse interlock cable abutment
21 Roll pin
22 Mounting plate
23 Mounting rubber
24 Bolt
25 Spacer
26 Bush
27 Upper link rod
28 Dust cover
29 Lower link rod
30 Bucket joint
31 Bellcrank assembly
32 Bolt

5.1 Gearchange linkage assembly

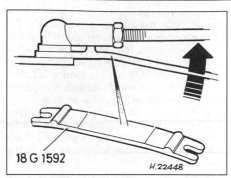

6.3 Using Rover special tool to disconnect gearchange linkage link rod balljoint

6.4a Disconnect gearchange linkage rods from bellcrank . . .

6.4b . . . and selector rod from gearchange lever

6 Gearchange linkage - removal, overhaul and refitting

Removal

1 Park the vehicle on level ground, switch off the ignition, check that the gearbox is in neutral and apply the handbrake firmly. Jack up the front of the vehicle and support it securely on axle stands.
2 Although not strictly necessary, access to the gearchange linkage is greatly improved if the exhaust front pipe is first removed.
3 In the absence of the special gearchange linkage balljoint separator (Rover service tool number 18G 1592) **(see illustration)**, use a suitable flat-bladed screwdriver to carefully lever the link rod balljoints off the gearbox upper and lower selector levers, taking care not to damage the balljoint gaiters.
4 Unscrewing the nuts and/or releasing the balljoints as necessary, disconnect the gearchange control and selector rods from the bellcrank assembly. Release the balljoint connecting the selector rod to gearchange lever and remove the selector rod **(see illustrations)**.
5 If necessary, remove the three bolts securing the bellcrank assembly to the suspension front subframe and remove it from the vehicle.

6 Working inside the vehicle, remove the centre console assembly.
7 With the console removed, carefully prise the rubber cover off the base of the gearchange lever and slide the cover off the lever to gain access to the control rod pivot bolt. Slacken the nut and remove the pivot bolt and thrustwashers **(see illustration)**.
8 From underneath the vehicle, release all the ties securing the reverse interlock cable (where fitted) to the control rod, then undo the two bolts securing the control rod rear mounting to the body **(see illustration)**. Remove the mounting assembly and control rod from underneath the vehicle.
9 If necessary, slacken and remove the six gearchange lever housing retaining nuts and remove the seal, mounting plate and lever assembly from the vehicle, noting that it will be necessary to disconnect the reverse interlock cable (where fitted) from the gearchange lever **(see illustration)**.

Overhaul

10 Thoroughly clean all components and check them for wear or damage, renewing all worn or faulty items. Note that the gearchange lever-to-control rod pivot bushes can be renewed separately if necessary.
11 Carefully check the condition of all linkage joints. If any show signs of stiffness or free play, they must be renewed. Check also the control rod mounting rubber and bush assembly. Renew the rubber if it shows any

sign of cracks, splits or other deterioration and renew the bush if it is a sloppy fit on the control rod end.
12 The bellcrank assembly must be renewed complete if it is worn or damaged.

Refitting

13 Refitting is the reverse of the removal procedure, noting the following:
a) *Apply a smear of the recommended grease to all pivot and bearing surfaces.*
b) *Tighten all nuts and bolts securely and ensure that all gearchange linkage balljoints are pressed firmly together.*
c) *Where necessary, secure the reverse interlock cable to the control rod with the cable ties.*
d) *Check the linkage for correct adjustment.*

7 Speedometer drive - removal and refitting

Removal

1 Firmly apply the handbrake then jack up the front of the vehicle and support it on axle stands.
2 From underneath the vehicle, pull out the rubber retaining pin which secures the lower end of the speedometer cable to the gearbox housing. Withdraw the cable from the speedometer drive and remove the O-rings

6.7 Removing control rod pivot bolt

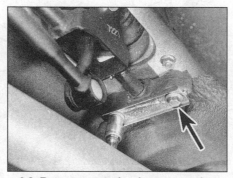

6.8 Remove control rod rear mounting retaining bolts (remaining one arrowed)

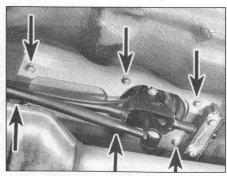

6.9 Gearchange lever housing retaining nut locations (arrowed)

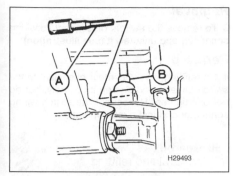

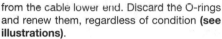

7.2a Remove rubber retaining pin (A) and withdraw speedometer cable (B) from drive

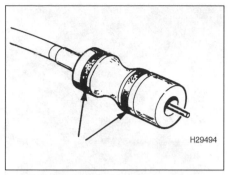

7.2b Renew O-rings (arrowed) on speedometer cable lower end

7.3 Removing speedometer drive housing

from the cable lower end. Discard the O-rings and renew them, regardless of condition **(see illustrations)**.

3 Undo the speedometer drive housing retaining bolt then withdraw the housing and driven gear pinion from the gearbox. Separate the pinion and housing and remove the oil seal and O-ring from the pinion housing. Discard the oil seal and O-ring as both must be renewed as a matter of course whenever they are disturbed **(see illustration)**.

4 Renew the pinion if its teeth are worn or damaged and check the housing for cracks or damage. Note that the speedometer drive gear pinion can be checked visually with the pinion assembly removed by shining a torch into the aperture. If any of the gear teeth are damaged, then the gearbox must be removed from the vehicle and dismantled so that the gear can be renewed. It is pressed onto the differential case.

Refitting

5 On reassembly, fit the new oil seal and O-ring into the pinion housing, then refit the pinion, applying a smear of grease to all components before installation. Insert the assembly into the gearbox, rotating the driven pinion until it is felt to engage the teeth of the drive gear pinion, then press the housing into place. Do not use excessive force or the drive components may be damaged.

6 When the drive is correctly refitted, tighten the retaining bolt securely.

7 Apply a smear of engine oil to the speedometer cable O-rings, then refit the cable to the gearbox and secure it in position with the rubber retaining pin. Lower the vehicle to the ground.

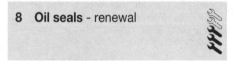

8 Oil seals - renewal

Driveshaft seal

Removal

1 Chock the rear wheels of the vehicle, firmly apply the handbrake then jack up the front of the vehicle and support it on axle stands. Remove the appropriate front roadwheel.

2 Drain the gearbox oil.

3 Slacken and remove the bolt and washer securing the anti-roll bar connecting link to the lower suspension arm, and the two bolts securing the tie bar to the lower suspension arm.

4 Extract the split pins and undo the nuts securing the steering gear track rod end balljoint and the lower suspension arm balljoint to the swivel hub. Remove the nuts and release the balljoint tapered shanks by using a universal balljoint separator.

5 Insert a suitable flat bar in between the inner constant velocity joint and gearbox housing then carefully lever the joint out of

position, taking great care not to damage the gearbox housing.

6 Withdraw the inner constant velocity joint from the gearbox and support the driveshaft to avoid damaging the constant velocity joints or gaiters.

7 Carefully prise the oil seal out of the gearbox with a large flat-bladed screwdriver **(see illustration)**.

Fitting

8 Remove all traces of dirt from the area around the oil seal aperture then apply a smear of grease to the outer lip of the new oil seal. Fit the new seal into its aperture and drive it squarely into position by using a suitable tubular drift (such as a socket) which bears only on the hard outer edge of the seal, until it abuts its locating shoulder **(see illustration)**.

9 Prior to refitting the driveshaft, check that the inner constant velocity joint shoulder is smooth and free of burrs and scratches. Small burrs or scratches can be removed using emery cloth, however larger imperfections may require the renewal of the joint. Regardless of its apparent condition, renew the circlip which is fitted to the groove in the inner constant velocity joint splines.

10 Thoroughly clean the driveshaft splines and apply a thin film of grease to the oil seal lips and to the inner constant velocity joint splines and shoulder.

11 Ensure that the circlip is located securely in its groove, then locate the joint splines with those of the differential sun gear whilst taking great care not to damage the oil seal. Push the joint fully into the gearbox and check that it is securely retained by the circlip by pulling the hub assembly outwards.

12 Insert the lower suspension arm and track rod balljoints into their respective locations in the swivel hub and tighten their retaining nuts to the specified torque. Secure both nuts with new split pins.

13 Refit the bolts securing the trailing arm and anti-roll bar connecting link to the lower suspension arm and tighten them to the specified torque.

14 Refit the roadwheel then lower the vehicle to the ground and tighten the wheel nuts to the specified torque.

7

8.7 Prising old seal out of position with large flat-bladed screwdriver

8.8 Using a suitably-sized socket to tap new seal into position

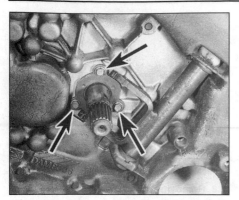

8.17 Clutch release bearing guide sleeve retaining bolts (arrowed)

9.3 Disconnecting reversing lamp wiring connector

Removal

3 To remove the switch, disconnect its wiring connector and unscrew it **(see illustration)**.

Refitting

4 On refitting, apply a smear of sealant to the switch threads and tighten it securely, but do not overtighten. Reconnect the switch wiring connector and test circuit operation.

10 Gearbox -
removal and refitting

Removal

1 Drain the gearbox oil then refit the drain and filler plugs, tightening them to the specified torque.
2 Remove the battery.
3 Unscrew the plastic nut securing the reverse interlock cable to the top of the gearbox housing and plug the gearbox orifice to prevent the entry of dirt.
4 Trace the clutch cable back from the clutch release lever to the bulkhead and remove the C-clip which retains the cable outer spring in position. Unhook the cable inner from the release lever and free the cable outer from its mounting bracket, positioning it clear of the gearbox **(see illustration)**.
5 Disconnect the wiring connector from the reversing lamp switch.
6 Firmly apply the handbrake and chock the rear wheels, then jack up the front of the vehicle and support it on axle stands. Remove both front roadwheels.
7 Undo the three bolts securing the front bumper flange to the body then remove the seven front undercover panel retaining bolts and remove the panel from underneath the front of the vehicle.
8 Remove the starter motor.
9 In the absence of the special gearchange linkage balljoint separator (Rover service tool number 18G 1592), use a suitable flat-bladed screwdriver to carefully lever the link rod balljoints off the selector upper and lower selector levers, taking care not to damage the balljoint gaiters. Move the gearbox selector lever fully towards the engine so that it will clear the subframe.
10 Release the driveshaft inner constant velocity joints from the gearbox, with reference to Section 8, paragraphs 3 to 6 **(see illustration)**.
11 Withdraw the rubber retaining pin which secures the speedometer cable in position in the gearbox and withdraw the cable. Remove the O-rings from the lower end of the cable and discard them, as they must be renewed whenever disturbed.
12 Where necessary, slacken and remove the two bolts securing the exhaust front pipe to its mounting bracket.
13 Undo the lower flywheel cover and front flywheel cover retaining bolts and remove

15 Refill the gearbox with the correct type and quantity of oil.

Input shaft seal

Removal

16 Remove the gearbox from the vehicle, then remove the clutch release fork.
17 Undo the three bolts securing the clutch release bearing guide sleeve in position and slide the guide off the input shaft **(see illustration)**. Discard the bolts as they must be renewed whenever they are disturbed.
18 Carefully lever the oil seal out of the guide by using a suitable flat-bladed screwdriver.

Fitting

19 Before fitting a new seal, check the input shaft's seal rubbing surface for signs of burrs, scratches or other damage which may have caused the seal to fail in the first place. It may be possible to polish away minor faults of this sort using fine abrasive paper, however, more serious defects will require the renewal of the input shaft.
20 Clean any thread locking material from the bellhousing threads using Loctite Chisel and a suitable tap, then degrease thoroughly. Ensure that the input shaft is clean and greased to protect the seal lips on refitting.
21 Dip the new seal in clean oil and fit it to

the guide sleeve. Carefully slide the guide sleeve into position then fit the new retaining bolts and tighten them to the specified torque wrench setting.
22 Reassemble and lubricate the clutch release mechanism, then wipe off any surplus oil or grease and refit the gearbox to the vehicle.

9 Reversing lamp switch -
testing, removal and refitting

Testing

1 The reversing lamp circuit is controlled by a plunger-type switch that is screwed into the top of the gearbox casing. If a fault develops in the circuit, first ensure that the circuit fuse has not blown.
2 To test the switch, disconnect its wires and use a multimeter (set to the resistance function) or a battery and bulb test circuit to check that there is continuity between the switch terminals only when reverse gear is selected. If this is not the case and there are no obvious breaks or other damage to the wires, the switch is faulty and must be renewed.

10.4 Disconnect clutch cable and free it from gearbox bracket

10.10 Lever out both driveshaft inner CV joints from gearbox

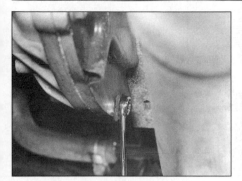

10.13a Undo flywheel lower cover plate . . .

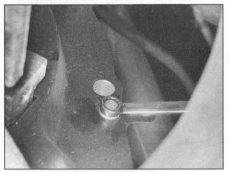

10.13b . . . and front flywheel cover plate retaining bolts

10.14 Clutch cable/wiring harness support bracket-to-gearbox bolts (arrowed)

both covers from the engine/gearbox unit **(see illustrations)**.

14 Unscrew the two bolts securing the clutch cable/wiring harness support bracket to the gearbox and remove the bracket **(see illustration)**.

15 Remove the two rear flywheel cover retaining bolts and remove the cover from the engine/gearbox unit **(see illustration)**.

16 Place a jack with interposed block of wood beneath the engine to take the weight of the engine. Alternatively, attach lifting eyes to the engine and fit a hoist or support bar to take the weight of the engine **(see illustration)**.

17 Place a jack and block of wood beneath the gearbox.

18 Undo the two bolts securing the engine/gearbox unit rear mounting assembly bracket to the gearbox. Slacken the bolt securing the connecting link to the subframe bracket and pivot the assembly away from the gearbox **(see illustrations)**.

19 Slacken and remove the bolt securing the anti-beaming bracket in position and remove the bracket **(see illustration)**.

20 Undo the two bolts securing the gearbox bracket to the engine/gearbox unit left-hand mounting, then lower the gearbox. Undo the four engine/gearbox unit mounting-to-body bolts and remove the mounting to gain access to the bolts securing the mounting bracket to the gearbox. Remove the two bracket

retaining bolts and remove the bracket from the gearbox **(see illustrations)**.

21 On models equipped with air conditioning, remove the bolt securing the air conditioning pipe to the top of the gearbox.

22 Remove all remaining gearbox housing-to-engine bolts then make a final check that all necessary components have been disconnected.

23 Lower the engine/gearbox unit slightly, then release the gearbox from the engine. It may initially be tight owing to the locating dowels. Once the gearbox is free, lower the jack and remove the gearbox out from under the vehicle.

10.15 Removing rear flywheel cover plate

10.16 Using a support bar to take engine weight

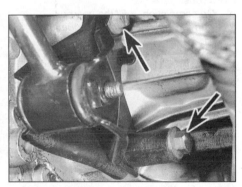

10.18a Unbolt rear mounting-to-gearbox bolts (arrowed) . . .

10.18b . . . then slacken connecting link-to-subframe bracket bolt

10.19 Anti-beaming bracket retaining bolt (arrowed)

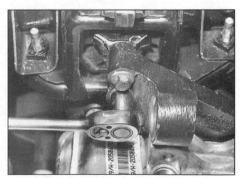

10.20a Remove gearbox bracket-to-mounting bolts . . .

7

10.20b ... then lower gearbox and remove four left-hand mounting-to-body bolts (arrowed) ...

10.20c ... and manoeuvre mounting out of position

10.20d Gearbox bracket is retained by two bolts

Refitting

24 The gearbox is refitted by a reversal of the removal procedure, bearing in mind the following:

a) *Ensure the dowels are correctly positioned prior to installation.*

b) *Apply a little high melting point grease to the splines of the gearbox input shaft. Do not apply too much otherwise there is a possibility of the grease contaminating the clutch friction plate.*

c) *Renew the driveshaft inner constant velocity joint circlips and install the driveshafts.*

d) *Tighten all nuts and bolts to the specified torque.*

e) *On completion, refill the gearbox with the specified type and quantity of oil.*

11 Gearbox - overhaul

Overhauling a gearbox is a difficult and involved job for the DIY home mechanic. In addition to dismantling and reassembling many small parts, clearances must be precisely measured and, if necessary, changed by selecting shims and spacers. Internal gearbox components are also often difficult to obtain and in many instances, extremely expensive. Because of this, if the gearbox develops a fault or becomes noisy, the best course of action is to have the unit overhauled by a specialist repairer or to obtain an exchange reconditioned unit.

Nevertheless, it is not impossible for the more experienced mechanic to overhaul the gearbox if the special tools are available and the job is done in a deliberate step-by-step manner so that nothing is overlooked.

The tools necessary for an overhaul include internal and external circlip pliers, bearing pullers, a slide hammer, a set of pin punches, a dial test indicator and possibly a hydraulic press. In addition, a large, sturdy workbench and a vice will be required.

During dismantling of the gearbox, make careful notes of how each component is fitted to make reassembly easier and accurate.

Before dismantling the gearbox, it will help if you have some idea what area is malfunctioning. Certain problems can be closely related to specific areas in the gearbox which can make component examination and replacement easier. Refer to the *"Fault finding"* Section at the end of this Manual for more information.

Chapter 8
Driveshafts

Contents

Degrees of difficulty

Easy, suitable for novice with little experience	**Fairly easy,** suitable for beginner with some experience	**Fairly difficult,** suitable for competent DIY mechanic	**Difficult,** suitable for experienced DIY mechanic	**Very difficult,** suitable for expert DIY or professional

Specifications
Specifications

Driveshafts

Type .... Unequal-length solid steel shafts, splined to inner and outer constant velocity joints, dynamic damper on both shafts

Torque wrench setting	**Nm**	**lbf ft**
Driveshaft retaining nut	185	137

1 General information and precautions

General information

Drive is transmitted from the differential to the front wheels by means of two unequal length, solid steel driveshafts.

Both driveshafts are splined at their outer ends to accept the wheel hubs and are threaded so that each hub can be fastened by a large nut. The inner end of each driveshaft is splined to accept the differential sun gear and has a groove to accept the circlip which secures the driveshaft to the sun gear **(see illustration).**

Constant velocity (CV) joints are fitted to both ends of each driveshaft to ensure the smooth and efficient transmission of drive at all possible angles as the roadwheels move up and down with the suspension and as they turn from side to side under steering. Both inner and outer CV joints are of the ball-and-cage type.

A dynamic damper is fitted to each driveshaft to reduce harmonic vibrations and resonance.

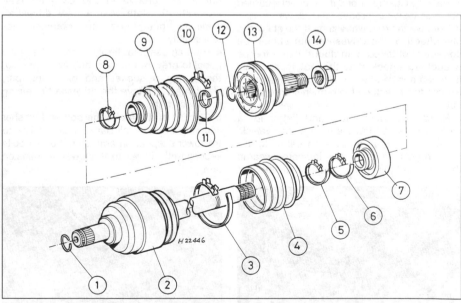

1.0 Driveshaft assembly

1	Circlip	5	Small gaiter retaining clip	10	Large gaiter retaining clip
2	Inner joint and shaft assembly	6	Damper clip	11	Stopper ring
3	Large gaiter retaining clip	7	Dynamic damper	12	Circlip
4	Gaiter	8	Small gaiter retaining clip	13	Outer joint assembly
		9	Gaiter	14	Driveshaft retaining nut

8

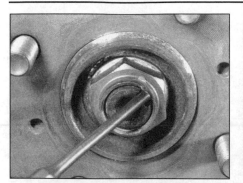

3.3 Using a hammer and punch to release driveshaft nut staking

3.6 Using a universal balljoint separator to separate balljoint shanks

3.7 Pull swivel hub outwards and disengage driveshaft outer CV joint

Precautions

The driveshaft retaining nuts are very tight, ensure the car is securely supported when slackening and tightening them.

The only replacement parts listed are the inner CV joint and shaft assemblies, the outer CV joint assemblies and the rubber gaiters. The gaiters are supplied in a kit with the necessary sachets of grease and clips.

If any CV joint is worn or damaged, it cannot be reconditioned but must be renewed. In the case of the inner joints, this means that the complete joint/shaft assembly must be renewed.

2 Driveshaft rubber gaiters and constant velocity joints - inspection

1 Refer to Chapter 1 and if the checks carried out indicate wear, proceed as follows.
2 Remove the roadwheel trim. If the staking is still effective, the driveshaft nut should be correctly tightened. If in doubt, use a torque wrench to check that the nut is securely fastened and re-stake it. Refit the wheel trim. Repeat this check on the remaining driveshaft nut.
3 Road test the vehicle and listen for a metallic clicking from the front as the vehicle is driven slowly in a circle on full lock. If a clicking noise is heard, this indicates wear in the outer CV joint. This means that the joint

must be renewed as reconditioning is not possible.
4 If vibration, consistent with road speed, is felt through the vehicle when accelerating, there is a possibility of wear in the inner CV joints.

3 Driveshafts - removal and refitting

Removal

1 Chock the rear wheels, firmly apply the handbrake then jack up the front of the vehicle and support it on axle stands. Remove the appropriate front roadwheel.
2 Drain the gearbox oil.
3 Using a hammer and suitable punch, tap up the staking securing the driveshaft retaining nut to the groove in the CV joint (see illustration). Note that a new driveshaft retaining nut must be obtained for reassembly.
4 Have an assistant firmly depress the brake pedal to prevent the front hub from rotating, then using a socket and extension bar, slacken and remove the driveshaft retaining nut. Discard the nut.
5 Slacken and remove the bolt and washer securing the anti-roll bar connecting link to the lower suspension arm, then the two bolts securing the tie bar to the lower suspension arm.

6 Extract the split pins and undo the nuts securing the steering gear track rod end balljoint and the lower suspension arm balljoint to the swivel hub. Remove the nuts and release the balljoint tapered shanks using a universal balljoint separator (see illustration).
7 Carefully pull the swivel hub assembly outwards and withdraw the driveshaft outer CV joint from the hub assembly (see illustration). If necessary, the shaft can be tapped out of the hub using a soft-faced mallet.
8 To release the inner CV joint, insert a suitable flat bar in between the joint and gearbox housing, then carefully lever the joint out of position, whilst taking great care not to damage the driveshaft oil seal (see illustration).
9 Support the inner CV joint whilst withdrawing it from the gearbox to ensure the oil seal is not damaged, then remove the driveshaft from the vehicle.

Refitting

10 Before fitting the driveshaft, examine the gearbox housing driveshaft oil seal for signs of damage or deterioration and, if necessary, renew it. Similarly, inspect the oil seal which is fitted to the outer CV joint for damage or deterioration and renew if necessary. Regardless of its apparent condition, renew the circlip which is fitted to the groove in the inner CV joint splines as a matter of course (see illustrations).

3.8 Carefully lever driveshaft inner CV joint out of housing

3.10a Inspect outer CV joint oil seal (arrowed)

3.10b Inner CV joint circlip (arrowed) must be renewed

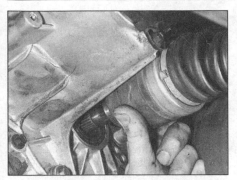

3.12 Refit driveshaft inner CV joint, taking care not to damage driveshaft oil seal . . .

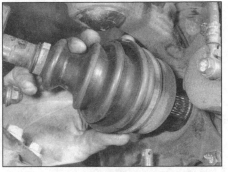

3.13 . . . and engage outer CV joint with swivel hub

3.16 Stake driveshaft retaining nut firmly into CV joint groove

11 Thoroughly clean the driveshaft splines and the apertures in the gearbox and hub assembly. Apply a thin film of grease to the oil seal lips and to the driveshaft splines and shoulders. Check that all gaiter clips are securely fastened.

12 Ensure that the circlip fitted to the inner CV joint is located securely in its groove, then locate the joint splines with those of the differential sun gear, taking great care not to damage the oil seal. Push the joint fully into the gearbox (see illustration). Check that the joint is securely retained by the circlip by pulling the shaft outwards.

13 Locate the outer CV joint splines with those of the swivel hub and slide the joint back into position in the hub (see illustration).

14 Insert the lower suspension arm and track rod balljoints into their respective locations in the swivel hub and tighten the retaining nuts to the specified torque. Secure both nuts in position using new split pins.

15 Refit the bolts securing the trailing arm and anti-roll bar connecting link to the lower suspension arm and tighten them to the specified torque.

16 Fit the new driveshaft retaining nut and tighten it to the specified torque setting whilst an assistant firmly depresses the brake pedal. Release the brake, check that the hub rotates freely, then stake the nut firmly into the groove on the CV joint using a suitable punch (see illustration).

17 Refit the roadwheel then lower the vehicle to the ground. Tighten the wheel nuts to the specified torque.

18 Refill the gearbox with the correct type and quantity of oil.

4 Driveshaft rubber gaiters - renewal

Outer joint

Removal

1 Remove the driveshaft from the vehicle.

2 Secure the driveshaft in a vice equipped with soft jaws and release the two rubber gaiter retaining clips by raising the locking tangs with a screwdriver and then raising the end of the clip with pliers. If necessary, the gaiter retaining clips can be cut to release them (see illustration).

3 Slide the rubber gaiter down the shaft to expose the outer CV joint.

4 Using a soft-faced mallet, sharply strike the inner member of the joint to drive it off the end of the shaft (see illustration). The outer joint is retained on the driveshaft by a circular section circlip and striking the joint in this manner forces the circlip into its groove, so allowing the joint to slide off.

5 Once the joint assembly has been removed, remove the circlip from the groove in the driveshaft splines and discard it. A new circlip must be fitted on reassembly.

6 Withdraw the rubber gaiter from the driveshaft.

7 With the CV joint removed from the driveshaft, thoroughly clean the joint using paraffin or a suitable solvent and dry it thoroughly. Inspect the joint as follows.

8 Move the inner splined driving member from side to side to expose each ball in turn at the top of its track. Examine the balls for cracks, flat spots or signs of surface pitting.

9 Inspect the ball tracks on the inner and outer members. If the tracks have widened, the balls will no longer be a tight fit. At the same time check the ball cage windows for wear or cracking between the windows.

10 If on inspection any of the CV joint components are found to be worn or damaged, it will be necessary to renew the complete joint assembly, since no components are available separately. If the joint is in satisfactory condition, obtain a repair kit consisting of a new gaiter, retaining clips and the correct type and quantity of grease.

Fitting

11 Tape over the splines on the end of the driveshaft, then fit the small retaining clip onto the gaiter and carefully slide the gaiter onto the shaft.

12 Remove the tape then, ensuring that the stopper ring is securely located in its groove, fit a new circlip to the groove in the driveshaft splines (see illustration). Engage the help of an assistant for the following operations.

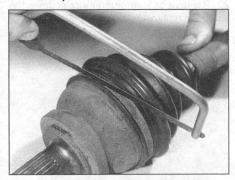

4.2 Cutting gaiter clips to release them

4.4 Driving outer CV joint off driveshaft end

4.12 Ensure stopper ring and new circlip are correctly located before fitting outer CV joint

8

4.17 Using correct tool to tighten gaiter clip - side cutters can be used if care is exercised

13 Position the CV joint over the splines on the driveshaft until it abuts the circlip.

14 Using two small screwdrivers placed one either side of the circlip, compress the clip and at the same time have your assistant firmly strike the end of the joint with a soft faced mallet. This should not require an undue amount of force. If the joint does not spring into place, remove it, reposition the circlip and try again. Do not force the joint, otherwise the circlip will be damaged.

15 Check that the circlip holds the joint securely on the driveshaft end then pack the joint with the grease supplied. Work the grease well into the ball tracks whilst twisting the joint and fill the rubber gaiter with any excess.

16 Ease the gaiter over the joint and place the large retaining clip in position. Ensure that

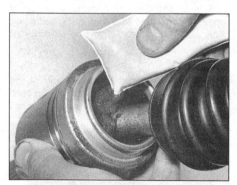

4.25 Pack inner CV joint with grease supplied in gaiter kit

4.22 Cutting inner CV joint clip to release it

the gaiter is correctly located in the grooves on both the driveshaft and CV joint.

17 Using pliers, pull the large retaining clip and fold it over until the end locates between the two raised tangs. Hold the clip in this position and bend the tangs over to lock the clip in position. Remove any slack in the gaiter retaining clip by carefully compressing the raised section of the clip. In the absence of the special tool, a pair of side cutters may be used **(see illustration)**. Secure the small retaining clip using the same procedure.

18 Check that the CV joint moves freely in all directions, then refit the driveshaft.

Inner joint
Removal

19 Remove the outer CV joint and gaiter as described in paragraphs 1 to 5.

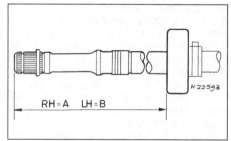

4.28 Position dynamic damper specified distance from outer end of driveshaft

Right-hand driveshaft - 405 to 411 mm
Left-hand driveshaft - 148 to 154 mm

20 Tape over the splines on the driveshaft and carefully remove the outer CV joint rubber gaiter.

21 Release the dynamic damper retaining clip and slide the damper off the end of the driveshaft. Use liquid soap if necessary to aid damper removal and clean off any rust deposits or similar using emery cloth.

22 Release the inner joint gaiter retaining clips and slide the gaiter off the shaft **(see illustration)**.

23 Thoroughly clean the joint using paraffin, or a suitable solvent, and dry it thoroughly. Inspect the joint as described in paragraphs 8 and 9.

24 If on inspection the CV joint components are found to be worn or damaged, it will be necessary to renew the complete joint and shaft assembly, since the joint is not available separately. If the joint is in satisfactory condition, obtain a repair kit consisting of a new gaiter, retaining clips and the correct type and quantity of grease. Although not strictly necessary, it is also recommended that the outer CV joint gaiter is renewed, regardless of its apparent condition.

Fitting

25 Pack the joint with the grease supplied in the gaiter kit. Work the grease well into the ball tracks whilst twisting the joint **(see illustration)**.

26 Clean the shaft, using emery cloth to remove any rust or sharp edges which may damage the gaiter, then slide the inner joint gaiter along the driveshaft.

27 Locate the gaiter in the grooves on the joint and shaft and fit both the large and small retaining clips. Secure the clips in position as described in paragraph 17 and check that the joint moves freely in all directions.

28 Lubricate the shaft and position a new retaining clip on the dynamic damper flange. Slide the dynamic damper onto the shaft so that its clip flange is innermost (faces the inner CV joint). Position the damper as shown **(see illustration)**, then secure it in position with the retaining clip.

29 Remove any surplus lubricant from the shaft and refit the outer CV joint.

Chapter 9
Braking system

Contents

Degrees of difficulty

Easy, suitable for novice with little experience	**Fairly easy,** suitable for beginner with some experience	**Fairly difficult,** suitable for competent DIY mechanic 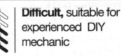	**Difficult,** suitable for experienced DIY mechanic	**Very difficult,** suitable for expert DIY or professional

Specifications

Brake system

Type . . . . Dual hydraulic circuit, split diagonally on models without ABS and front to rear on models with ABS. Disc front brakes. Drum rear brakes except on models with ABS which have rear disc brakes. Vacuum servo-assistance on all models. Cable-operated handbrake on rear brakes

Front brakes

Type	Disc, with single piston sliding caliper
Disc diameter:	
Non-ABS	238 mm
ABS	262 mm
Disc thickness:	
New:	
Non-ABS	12.80 mm
ABS	21.60 mm
Minimum thickness after machining:	
Non-ABS	10.70 mm
ABS	19.00 mm
Maximum disc run-out	0.02 mm
Brake pad friction material minimum thickness	3.0 mm

9

Rear brakes

Non-ABS

Type	Single leading shoe drum
Drum diameter:	
New	200 mm
Maximum diameter after machining	204 mm
Maximum drum ovality	0.012 mm
Brake shoe friction material minimum thickness	2.0 mm

ABS

Type	Disc, with single piston sliding caliper
Disc diameter	239 mm
Disc thickness:	
New	10 mm
Minimum thickness after machining	8 mm
Maximum disc run-out	0.06 mm
Brake pad friction material minimum thickness	3.0 mm

Torque wrench settings

	Nm	lbf ft
Servo vacuum hose-to-inlet manifold union bolt	50	37
Brake hose union bolt	38	28
Master cylinder-to-servo unit nuts	17	13
Master cylinder brake pipe union nuts	24	18
Brake caliper guide pin bolt	32	24
Brake disc retaining screws	12	9
Front brake caliper bracket-to-hub bolts	81	60
Pressure regulating valve union nuts	14	10
Rear brake drum retaining screws	10	7
Rear wheel cylinder-to-backplate bolts	10	7
Rear brake caliper bracket-to-trailing arm bolts	40	30
Handbrake cable-to-underbody retaining bolts	22	16
ABS modulator mounting nuts	7	5
ABS modulator brake pipe union nuts:		
Upper union nuts	15	11
Lower union nuts	24	18
ABS front wheel sensor retaining bolts	25	18
ABS rear wheel sensor retaining bolts	10	7
ABS wheel sensor wiring bracket bolts	10	7
ABS rear wheel sensor cover and cover strap bolts	10	7
Roadwheel nuts	100	74

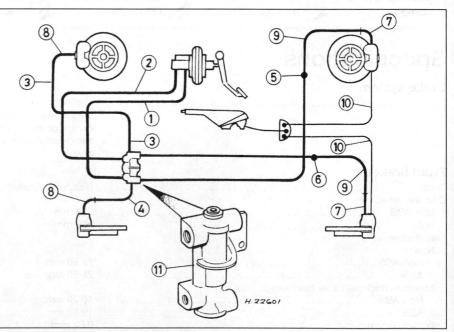

1 Primary hydraulic circuit
2 Secondary hydraulic circuit
3 Brake pipe - pressure regulating valve to right-hand front hose
4 Brake pipe - pressure regulating valve to left-hand front hose
5 Brake pipe - pressure regulating valve to right-hand rear hose
6 Brake pipe - pressure regulating valve to left-hand rear hose
7 Brake pipe - hose to rear wheel cylinder
8 Brake flexible hose - brake pipe to front brake caliper
9 Brake flexible hose - rear wheel
10 Handbrake cable
11 Pressure regulating valve

1.0a Non-ABS braking system component layout

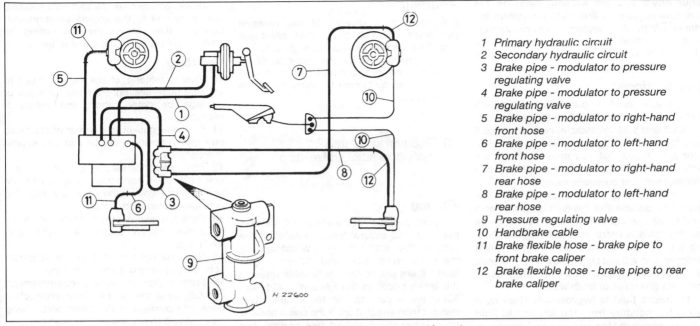

1 Primary hydraulic circuit
2 Secondary hydraulic circuit
3 Brake pipe - modulator to pressure
   regulating valve
4 Brake pipe - modulator to pressure
   regulating valve
5 Brake pipe - modulator to right-hand
   front hose
6 Brake pipe - modulator to left-hand
   front hose
7 Brake pipe - modulator to right-hand
   rear hose
8 Brake pipe - modulator to left-hand
   rear hose
9 Pressure regulating valve
10 Handbrake cable
11 Brake flexible hose - brake pipe to
   front brake caliper
12 Brake flexible hose - brake pipe to rear
   brake caliper

1.0b ABS braking system component layout

1 General information and precautions

General information

The braking system is of the servo-assisted, dual circuit hydraulic type. The arrangement of the hydraulic system is such that each circuit operates one front and one rear brake from a tandem master cylinder. Under normal circumstances both circuits operate in unison. However, in the event of hydraulic failure in one circuit, full braking force will still be available at two wheels **(see illustrations)**.

On models not equipped with an Anti-lock Braking System (ABS), a pressure regulating valve is also incorporated in the hydraulic circuit to regulate the pressure applied to the rear brakes and reduce the possibility of the rear wheels locking under heavy braking. On models equipped with ABS, the pressure regulating valve is fitted is but it is non-operational.

All models are fitted with front disc brakes. Models equipped with ABS are fitted with ventilated discs, whereas non-ABS models are fitted with solid discs. The disc brakes are actuated by single piston sliding type calipers which ensure that equal pressure is applied to each disc pad.

Non-ABS models are fitted with rear drum brakes, incorporating leading and trailing shoes which are actuated by twin piston wheel cylinders. A self-adjust mechanism is incorporated to automatically compensate for brake shoe wear. As the brake shoe linings

wear, the footbrake operation automatically operates the adjuster mechanism quadrant which effectively lengthens the shoe strut and repositions the brake shoes to remove the lining-to-drum clearance.

ABS models are equipped with rear disc brakes. The disc brakes are actuated by a single piston sliding caliper which incorporates a mechanical handbrake mechanism.

On all models, the handbrake provides an independent mechanical means of rear brake application. Full details of ABS system operation are as follows.

Anti-lock Braking System (ABS) - operation

ABS is available as an option on all models covered in this Manual. The system comprises a modulator block which contains an ABS Electronic Control Unit (ECU), hydraulic solenoid valves and accumulators, and an electrically-driven return pump. One sensor is fitted to each roadwheel. The purpose of this system is to prevent wheel locking during heavy braking. This is achieved by automatic release of the brake on the relevant wheel, followed by reapplication of the brake.

The solenoids are controlled by the ECU which receives signals from the four roadwheel sensors, which in turn monitor the speed of rotation of each wheel. By comparing these speed signals from the four wheels, the ECU can determine the speed at which the vehicle is travelling. It can then use this speed to determine when a wheel is decelerating at an abnormal rate compared to the speed of the vehicle and therefore predict when a wheel is about to lock. During normal

operation, the system functions in the same way as a non-ABS braking system.

If the ECU senses that a wheel is about to lock, the ABS system enters the 'pressure maintain' phase. The ECU operates the relevant solenoid valve in the modulator block which then isolates the brake caliper on the wheel which is about to lock from the master cylinder, effectively sealing in the hydraulic pressure.

If the speed of rotation of the wheel continues to decrease at an abnormal rate, the ABS system then enters the 'pressure decrease' phase, where the electrically-driven return pump operates and pumps the hydraulic fluid back into the master cylinder, releasing pressure on the brake caliper so that the brake is released. Once the speed of rotation of the wheel returns to an acceptable rate, the pump stops and the solenoid valve opens thereby allowing the hydraulic master cylinder pressure to return to the caliper which then reapplies the brake. This cycle can be carried out at up to 10 times a second.

The action of the solenoid valves and return pump creates pulses in the hydraulic circuit. When the ABS system is functioning, these pulses can be felt through the brake pedal.

The solenoid valves connected to the front calipers operate independently, but the valve connected to the rear calipers, together with the pressure regulating valve, operates both calipers simultaneously.

Operation of the ABS system is entirely dependent on electrical signals. To prevent the system responding to any inaccurate signals, a built-in safety circuit monitors all signals received by the ECU. If an inaccurate signal or low battery voltage is detected, the ABS system is automatically

9

shut down and the warning lamp on the instrument panel is illuminated to inform the driver that the ABS system is not operational.

If a fault does develop in the ABS system the vehicle must be taken to a Rover dealer for fault diagnosis and repair.

Precautions

Hydraulic fluid is poisonous. Wash off immediately and thoroughly in the case of skin contact and seek immediate medical advice if any fluid is swallowed or gets into the eyes. Certain types of hydraulic fluid are inflammable and may ignite when allowed into contact with hot components.

When servicing any hydraulic system, it is safest to assume that the fluid is inflammable and to take precautions against the risk of fire as though it is petrol that is being handled. Hydraulic fluid is also an effective paint stripper and will attack plastics. If any is spilt, it should be washed off immediately using copious quantities of fresh water.

Hydraulic fluid is hygroscopic, that is, it absorbs moisture from the air, so old fluid may be contaminated and unfit for further use. When topping-up or renewing fluid, always use the recommended type and ensure that it comes from a freshly-opened sealed container.

When working on brake components, take care not to disperse brake dust into the air, or to inhale it, since it may contain asbestos which is injurious to health.

When servicing any part of the system, work carefully and methodically. Also observe scrupulous cleanliness when overhauling any part of the hydraulic system. Always renew components (in axle sets, where applicable) if in doubt about their condition and use only genuine Rover replacement parts, or at least those of known good quality.

2 Brake pedal - removal and refitting

Removal

1 Working inside the vehicle, undo the five screws and remove the right-hand lower facia panel.
2 Extract the R-clip and clevis pin securing the servo unit pushrod to the brake pedal.
3 Using pliers, carefully unhook the brake pedal return spring from the pedal to release all the spring tension.
4 Slacken and remove the nut and washers (as applicable) from the brake pedal pivot bolt then withdraw the pivot bolt and remove the brake pedal and return spring.
5 Examine all brake pedal components for signs of wear, paying particular attention to the pedal bushes, pivot bolt and return spring, renewing as necessary.

Refitting

6 Refitting is a reverse of the removal procedure. Lubricate the bushes, pivot bolt and clevis pin with multi-purpose grease.
7 On completion, check the operation of the pedal and ensure that it returns smoothly to its at rest position under the pressure of the return spring.

3 Vacuum servo unit - testing, removal and refitting

Testing

1 To test operation of the servo unit, depress the footbrake several times to exhaust the vacuum, then start the engine whilst keeping the pedal firmly depressed. As the engine starts, there should be a noticeable 'give' in the brake pedal as the vacuum builds up. Allow the engine to run for at least two minutes then switch it off. If the brake pedal is now depressed it should feel normal, but further applications should result in the pedal felling firmer, with the pedal stroke decreasing with each application.
2 If the servo does not operate as described, inspect the servo unit check valve, see Section 4.
3 If the servo unit still fails to operate satisfactorily, the fault lies within the unit itself. Repairs to the unit are possible but special tools are required and the work should be entrusted to a suitably equipped Rover dealer.

Removal

4 Remove the air cleaner assembly.
5 Remove the master cylinder.
6 Disconnect the vacuum hose connection from the grommet on the servo unit, taking great care not to damage or displace the sealing grommet **(see illustration)**.
7 Working inside the vehicle, undo the five retaining screws and remove the right-hand lower facia panel.
8 Extract the R-clip and clevis pin securing the servo unit pushrod to the brake pedal **(see illustration)**.

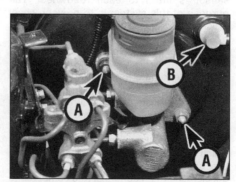

3.6 Master cylinder mounting nuts (A) and servo vacuum hose connection (B)

9 Slacken and remove the four nuts securing the servo unit to the engine compartment bulkhead then remove the unit, noting the gasket which is fitted to the rear of the unit.

Refitting

10 Prior to refitting, check the servo unit to vacuum hose sealing grommet for signs of damage or deterioration and renew if necessary.
11 Fit a new gasket to the rear of the servo unit and reposition the unit in the engine compartment.
12 From inside the vehicle, ensure the servo unit pushrod is correctly engaged with the brake pedal then refit the servo unit mounting nuts and tighten them securely.
13 Refit the servo unit pushrod to brake pedal clevis pin and secure it in position with the R-clip.
14 Refit the right-hand lower facia panel, tightening its retaining screws securely.
15 From inside the engine compartment, carefully ease the vacuum hose connection back into position in the servo unit, taking care not to displace the sealing grommet.
16 Refit the air cleaner assembly and master cylinder.
17 On completion, start the engine and check for air leaks at the vacuum hose to servo unit connection and the operation of the braking system.

4 Vacuum servo unit check valve - removal, testing and refitting

Note: *The vacuum servo unit check valve is only available as part of the vacuum hose assembly. Do not try to remove the valve, the servo unit connection, or the inlet manifold union from the hose or air leaks may ensue, necessitating renewal of the hose assembly.*

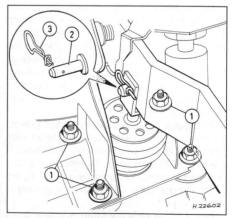

3.8 Vacuum servo unit and pushrod attachments
1 Servo unit mounting nuts
2 Pushrod clevis pin
3 R-clip

Removal

1 Carefully unplug the hose connection from the vacuum servo unit taking care not to damage the sealing grommet.

2 Unscrew the union bolt securing the vacuum hose assembly to the inlet manifold and withdraw the hose assembly from the engine compartment. Remove the union bolt from the hose end and discard the sealing washers.

Testing

3 Examine the hose for damage, splits, cracks or general deterioration. Make sure that the check valve inside the hose is working correctly by blowing through the hose from the servo unit connection end. Air should flow in this direction but not when blown through from the inlet manifold union. Renew the hose and check valve assembly if at all suspect.

4 Examine the servo unit sealing grommet for signs of damage or deterioration and renew if necessary.

Refitting

5 Position a new sealing washer on each side of the hose union and refit the hose-to-inlet manifold union bolt. Ensure that the hose union locating pin is correctly situated between the lugs on the manifold then tighten the union bolt to the specified torque setting **(see illustration)**.

6 Carefully ease the hose connection into the servo unit sealing grommet, taking care not to displace or damage the grommet.

7 On completion, start the engine and check the vacuum hose-to-servo unit connection for signs of air leaks.

5 Hydraulic fluid - level check and renewal

Refer to *"Weekly Checks"* and Chapter 1.

6 Hydraulic system - bleeding

 Hydraulic fluid is an effective paint stripper and will attack plastics. If any is spilt, it should be washed off immediately using copious quantities of fresh water.

General

1 The correct operation of any hydraulic system is only possible after removal of all air from the components and circuit. This is achieved by bleeding the system.

2 During the bleeding procedure, add only clean, unused hydraulic fluid of the

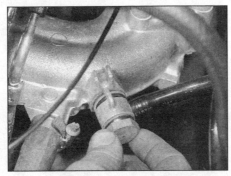
4.5 Ensure hose union locating pin is correctly located between lugs on inlet manifold

recommended type. Never re-use fluid that has already been bled from the system. Ensure that sufficient fluid is available before starting work.

3 If there is any possibility of incorrect fluid being already in the system, the brake components and circuit must be flushed completely with uncontaminated, correct fluid and new seals should be fitted to the various components.

4 If hydraulic fluid has been lost from the system, or air has entered because of a leak, then ensure that the fault is cured before proceeding further.

5 Park the vehicle on level ground, switch off the engine and select first or reverse gear, then chock the wheels and release the handbrake.

6 Check that all pipes and hoses are secure, unions tight and bleed screws closed. Clean any dirt from around the bleed screws.

7 Unscrew the master cylinder reservoir cap and top the master cylinder reservoir up to the MAX level line. Refit the cap loosely and remember to maintain the fluid level at least above the MIN level line throughout the procedure or there is a risk of further air entering the system.

8 There are a number of one-man, do-it-yourself brake bleeding kits currently available from motor accessory shops. It is recommended that one of these kits is used whenever possible as they greatly simplify the bleeding operation and also reduce the risk of expelled air and fluid being drawn back into the system. If such a kit is not available, then the basic (two-man) method must be used which is described in detail below.

9 If a kit is to be used, prepare the vehicle as described previously and follow the kit manufacturer's instructions as the procedure may vary slightly according to the type being used. Generally, they are as outlined below in the relevant sub-section.

10 Whichever method is used, the same sequence must be followed (paragraphs 11 and 12) to ensure the removal of all air from the system.

Bleeding sequence

11 If the system has been only partially disconnected and suitable precautions were

taken to minimise fluid loss, it should be necessary only to bleed that part of the system (ie: the primary or secondary circuit).

12 If the complete system is to be bled, then it should be done working in the following sequence:

Non-ABS models

Left-hand front brake.
Right-hand rear brake.
Right-hand front brake.
Left-hand rear brake.

ABS models

Left-hand front brake.
Right-hand front brake.
Left-hand rear brake.
Right-hand rear brake.

Bleeding - basic (two-man) method

13 Collect a clean glass jar, a suitable length of plastic or rubber tubing which is a tight fit over the bleed screw and a ring spanner to fit the screw. The help of an assistant will also be required.

14 Remove the dust cap from the first screw in the sequence. Fit the spanner and tube to the screw, place the other end of the tube in the jar and pour in sufficient fluid to cover the end of the tube.

15 Ensure that the master cylinder reservoir fluid level is maintained at least above the MIN level line throughout the procedure.

16 Have the assistant fully depress the brake pedal several times to build up pressure, then maintain it on the final stroke.

17 While pedal pressure is maintained, unscrew the bleed screw (approximately one turn) and allow the fluid and air to flow into the jar. The assistant should maintain pedal pressure, following it down to the floor if necessary and should not release it until instructed to do so. When the flow stops, tighten the bleed screw again, release the pedal slowly and recheck the reservoir fluid level.

18 Repeat the steps given in paragraphs 16 and 17 until the fluid emerging from the bleed screw is free from air bubbles. If the master cylinder has been drained and refilled and air is being bled from the first screw in the sequence, allow approximately five seconds between cycles for the master cylinder passages to refill.

19 When no more air bubbles appear, tighten the bleed screw securely, remove the tube and spanner and refit the dust cap. Do not overtighten the bleed screw.

20 Repeat the procedure on the remaining screws in the sequence until all air is removed from the system and the brake pedal feels firm again.

Bleeding - using a one-way valve kit

21 As their name implies, these kits consist of a length of tubing with a one-way valve

9

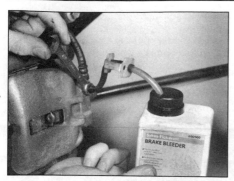

6.21 Using a one-way valve kit to bleed braking system

fitted to prevent expelled air and fluid being drawn back into the system. Some kits include a translucent container which can be positioned so that the air bubbles can be more easily seen flowing from the end of the tube (see illustration).

22 The kit is connected to the bleed screw, which is then opened. The user returns to the driver's seat and depresses the brake pedal with a smooth, steady stroke and slowly releases it. This sequence is repeated until the expelled fluid is clear of air bubbles.

23 Note that these kits simplify work so much that it is easy to forget the master cylinder reservoir fluid level. Ensure that this is maintained at least above the MIN level line at all times.

Bleeding - using a pressure bleeding kit

24 These kits are usually operated by the reservoir of pressurised air contained in the spare tyre, although note that it will probably be necessary to reduce the pressure to a lower limit than normal. Refer to the instructions supplied with the kit.

25 By connecting a pressurised, fluid-filled container to the master cylinder reservoir, bleeding can be carried out simply by opening each screw in turn (in the specified sequence) and allowing the fluid to flow out until no more air bubbles can be seen in the expelled fluid.

26 This method has the advantage that the large reservoir of fluid provides an additional safeguard against air being drawn into the system during bleeding.

27 Pressure bleeding is particularly effective when bleeding 'difficult' systems or when bleeding the complete system at the time of routine fluid renewal.

All methods

28 When bleeding is complete and firm pedal feel is restored, wash off any spilt fluid, tighten the bleed screws securely and refit their dust caps.

29 Check the hydraulic fluid level and top up if necessary.

30 Discard any hydraulic fluid that has been bled from the system as it will not be fit for re-use.

31 Check the feel of the brake pedal. If it

feels at all spongy, air must still be present in the system and further bleeding is required. Failure to bleed satisfactorily after a reasonable repetition of the bleeding procedure may be due to worn master cylinder seals.

7 Hydraulic pipes and hoses - inspection

Refer to Chapter 1, Section 6.

8 Hydraulic pipes and hoses - renewal

1 If any pipe or hose is to be renewed, minimise fluid loss by removing the master cylinder reservoir cap and then tightening it down onto a piece of polythene (taking care not to damage the sender unit) to obtain an airtight seal. Alternatively, flexible hoses can be sealed by using a proprietary brake hose clamp, while metal brake pipe unions can be plugged (if care is taken not to allow dirt into the system) or capped immediately they are disconnected (see illustration). Place a wad of rag under any union that is to be disconnected to catch any spilt fluid.

2 If a flexible hose is to be disconnected, unscrew the brake pipe union nut before removing the spring clip which secures the hose to its mounting bracket.

3 To unscrew the union nuts it is preferable to obtain a brake pipe spanner of the correct size. These spanners are available from most large motor accessory shops (see illustration). Failing this, a close-fitting open-ended spanner will be required, though if the nuts are tight or corroded, their flats may be rounded-off if the spanner slips. In such a case, a self-locking wrench is often the only way to unscrew a stubborn union but it follows that the pipe and the damaged nuts must be renewed on reassembly. Always clean a union and surrounding area before disconnecting it. If disconnecting a component with more than one union, make a careful note of the connections before disturbing any of them.

4 If a brake pipe is to be renewed, then it can be obtained from Rover dealers, cut to length and with the union nuts and end flares in place. All that is then necessary is to bend it to shape, following the line of the original, before fitting it to the vehicle. Alternatively, most motor accessory shops can make up brake pipes from kits but this requires very careful measurement of the original to ensure that the replacement is of the correct length. The safest answer is usually to take the original to the shop as a pattern.

5 On refitting, do not overtighten the union nuts. The specified torque wrench settings, where given, are not high and it is not necessary to exercise brute force to obtain a sound joint. When refitting flexible hoses, always renew any sealing washers used.

6 Ensure that the pipes and hoses are correctly routed with no kinks and that they are secured in the clips or brackets provided. After fitting, remove the polythene from the reservoir and bleed the hydraulic system. Wash off any spilt fluid and check carefully for fluid leaks.

9 Master cylinder - removal, overhaul and refitting

> ⚠️ **Warning: Do not syphon brake fluid by mouth as it is poisonous.**

Note: Before attempting to overhaul the master cylinder, check the price and availability of individual components and compare this with the price of a new or reconditioned unit, as overhaul may not be viable on economic grounds alone.

Removal

1 Remove the master cylinder reservoir cap, having disconnected the sender unit wiring connector, and syphon all hydraulic fluid from the reservoir. Do not syphon the fluid by mouth as it is poisonous but use a syringe or an old poultry baster. Alternatively, open any convenient bleed screw in the system and gently pump the brake pedal to expel the fluid through a plastic tube connected to the screw.

8.1 Using a brake hose clamp to minimise fluid loss

8.3 Using a brake pipe spanner to unscrew a union nut

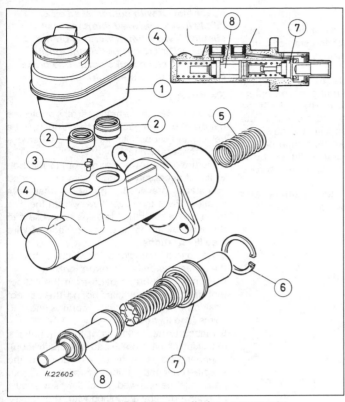

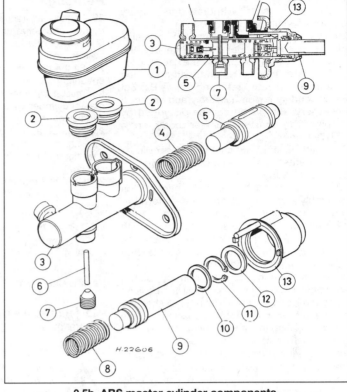

9.5a Non-ABS master cylinder components

1 Master cylinder reservoir	5 Spring
2 Mounting seals	6 Circlip
3 Secondary piston stop pin	7 Primary piston
4 Master cylinder body	8 Secondary piston

9.5b ABS master cylinder components

1 Master cylinder reservoir	4 Spring	9 Primary piston
2 Mounting seals	5 Secondary piston	10 Washer
3 Master cylinder body	6 Retaining pin	11 Circlip
	7 Grub screw	12 Flat washer
	8 Spring	13 Dust cap

2 Wipe clean the area around the brake pipe unions on the side of the master cylinder and place absorbent rags beneath the pipe unions to catch any surplus fluid. Unscrew the two union nuts and carefully withdraw the pipes. Plug or tape over the pipe ends and master cylinder orifices to minimise loss of brake fluid and to prevent the entry of dirt into the system. Wash off any spilt fluid immediately with cold water.

3 Slacken and remove the two nuts and washers securing the master cylinder to the vacuum servo unit then withdraw the unit from the engine compartment. Remove the O-ring from the rear of the master cylinder and discard it.

Overhaul

4 Remove the master cylinder from the vehicle as described above and clean it thoroughly.

5 Carefully prise the reservoir from the master cylinder body and remove the two mounting seals **(see illustrations)**.

6 Prepare a clean working surface and proceed as follows.

Non-ABS system

7 Using a wooden dowel, press the primary piston in as far as possible and extract the

secondary piston stop pin from the reservoir inlet port, then remove the retaining circlip.

8 Noting the order of removal and the direction of fitting of each component, withdraw the piston assemblies with their springs and seals, tapping the body on to a clean wooden surface to dislodge them. If necessary, clamp the master cylinder body in a vice (fitted with soft jaw covers) and use compressed air of low pressure (applied through the secondary circuit fluid port) to assist the removal of the secondary piston assembly.

9 Thoroughly clean all components using only methylated spirit, isopropyl alcohol or clean hydraulic fluid as a cleaning medium. Never use mineral-based solvents such as petrol or paraffin which will attack the hydraulic system's rubber components. Dry the components immediately using compressed air or a clean, lint-free cloth.

10 Check all components and renew any that are worn or damaged. Check particularly the cylinder bores and pistons. The complete assembly should be renewed if these are scratched, worn or corroded. If there is any doubt about the condition of the assembly or of any of its components, renew it. Check that the body's inlet and bypass ports are clear.

11 If the assembly is fit for further use, obtain a repair kit. Renew all seals and O-rings disturbed on dismantling, never re-use them. Renew also any other items included in the repair kit.

12 On reassembly, soak the pistons and new seals in clean hydraulic fluid. Smear clean fluid into the cylinder bore.

13 Fit the new seals to their pistons, using only the fingers to manipulate them into the grooves.

14 Insert the pistons into the bore by using a twisting motion to avoid trapping the seal lips. Ensure that all components are refitted in the correct order and the right way round.

15 Press the secondary piston assembly fully up into the bore using a clean wooden dowel, then refit the stop pin.

16 Refit the primary piston assembly, then secure it in position with a new circlip.

17 Press the new mounting seals into the master cylinder body and carefully refit the reservoir ensuring that it is pressed fully into position.

ABS system

18 Carefully prise out the dust cap from the rear of the master cylinder body and remove the flat washer.

19 Using a wooden dowel, press the primary

9

piston in as far as possible and extract the circlip and washer. Withdraw the primary piston assembly and spring.

20 Undo the grub screw from the underside of the master cylinder body then use the wooden dowel to press the secondary piston into the body and withdraw the secondary piston retaining pin. Extract the secondary piston assembly and spring. If necessary, the piston can be dislodged by tapping the master cylinder body on a wooden block.

21 Examine and overhaul the master cylinder components as described above in paragraphs 9 to 14.

22 Fit the spring to the secondary piston assembly and use a clean wooden dowel to press the assembly fully into the master cylinder bore. Align the slot in the piston with the retaining pin hole then insert the secondary piston retaining pin. Refit the grub screw and tighten it securely.

23 Fit the spring to the primary piston assembly and press the assembly into position using the wooden dowel. Refit the washer and secure the piston assembly in position with the circlip, ensuring that it is correctly located in its groove in the master cylinder bore.

24 Fit the flat washer and refit the dust cap to the rear of the master cylinder body.

25 Align the lugs on the new mounting seals with the slots in the master cylinder body and press them into position. Carefully refit the reservoir, ensuring that it is pressed fully into the master cylinder body.

Refitting

26 Remove all traces of dirt from the master cylinder and servo unit mating surfaces, then fit a new O-ring to the groove on the master cylinder body.

27 Fit the master cylinder to the servo unit, ensuring that the servo unit pushrod enters the master cylinder bore centrally. Refit the master cylinder washers and mounting nuts and tighten them to the specified torque.

28 Wipe clean the brake pipe unions then refit them to the master cylinder ports and tighten them to the specified torque setting.

29 Refill the master cylinder reservoir with new fluid and bleed the hydraulic system.

10 Front brake pads - inspection

Refer to Chapter 1.

11 Front brake pads - renewal

⚠️ *Warning: Renew both sets of front brake pads at the same time. Never renew the pads on only one wheel as uneven braking may result. The dust created by pad wear may contain asbestos, which is a health hazard.*

Never blow it with compressed air or inhale it. An approved filtering mask should be worn when working on the brakes. DO NOT use petroleum-based solvents to clean brake parts. Use brake cleaner or methylated spirit only.

Removal

1 Chock the rear wheels, firmly apply the handbrake then jack up the front of the vehicle and support it on axle stands. Remove both front roadwheels.

2 Remove the lower caliper guide pin bolt whilst, if necessary, using a slim open-ended spanner to prevent the guide pin itself from rotating. Pivot the caliper away from the disc to gain access to the brake pads and tie it to the suspension strut using a piece of wire **(see illustrations)**.

3 Remove the circular shim which is fitted to the caliper piston **(see illustration)**.

4 Remove the brake pads from the caliper mounting bracket whilst noting the correct position of the pad retainer springs and pad shims **(see illustration)**.

5 Measure the thickness of friction material remaining on each brake pad **(see illustration)**. If either pad is worn at any point to the specified minimum thickness or less, all four pads must be renewed. Also, the pads should be renewed if any are fouled with oil or grease as there is no satisfactory way of degreasing friction material once contaminated. If any of the brake pads are worn unevenly or fouled with oil or grease, trace and rectify the cause before reassembly. New brake pad kits are available from Rover dealers and include new shims and pad retainer springs.

6 If the brake pads are still serviceable, carefully clean them using a clean, fine wire brush or similar, paying particular attention to the sides and back of the metal backing. Clean out the grooves in the friction material (where applicable) and pick out any large embedded particles of dirt or debris. Carefully clean the pad retainer springs and the pad locations in the caliper body and mounting bracket.

Fitting

7 Prior to fitting the pads, check that the guide pins are free to slide easily in the caliper

11.2a Remove lower caliper guide pin bolt . . .

11.2b . . . and pivot caliper away from disc

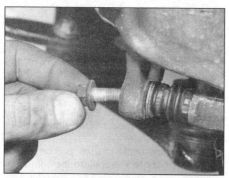

11.3 Removing circular shim from caliper piston

11.4 Removing pads with springs and shims

11.5 Measuring thickness of brake pad friction material

11.7 Check condition of guide pins and gaiters before refitting pads

11.8 Fit pad retainer springs to caliper bracket . . .

11.9 . . . and fit shims on pads

bracket and check that the rubber guide pin gaiters are undamaged **(see illustration)**. Brush the dust and dirt from the caliper and piston but **do not** inhale it as it is injurious to health. Inspect the dust seal around the piston for damage and the piston for evidence of fluid leaks, corrosion or damage. Renew as necessary.

8 On refitting, first fit the pad retainer springs to the caliper mounting bracket **(see illustration)**.

9 Apply a thin smear of high-temperature brake grease (silicone- or PBC/Poly Butyl Cuprysil-based) or anti-seize compound (eg Holts Copaslip) to the sides and back of each pad's metal backing and to those surfaces of the caliper body and mounting bracket which bear on the pads. Fit the shims to the back of both pads and apply a thin smear of lubricant to the back of each shim. Do not allow the lubricant to foul the friction material **(see illustration)**.

10 Install the brake pads in the caliper mounting bracket, ensuring that the friction material is against the disc.

11 If new brake pads have been fitted, the caliper piston must be pushed back into the cylinder to make room for them. Either use a G-clamp or similar tool, or use suitable pieces of wood as levers. Provided that the master cylinder reservoir has not been overfilled with hydraulic fluid there should be no spillage but keep a careful watch on the fluid level while retracting the piston. If the fluid level rises above the MAX level line at any time, the surplus should be syphoned off or ejected via a plastic tube connected to the bleed screw.

12 Apply a thin smear of the recommended lubricant (see above) to the circular shim and fit the shim to the caliper piston. Pivot the caliper body down over the brake pads then refit the bottom guide pin bolt and tighten it to the specified torque wrench setting.

13 Check that the caliper body slides smoothly in the mounting bracket, then depress the brake pedal repeatedly until the pads are pressed into firm contact with the brake disc and normal (non-assisted) pedal pressure is restored.

14 Repeat the above procedure on the remaining front brake caliper.

15 Refit the roadwheels, then lower the vehicle to the ground and tighten the roadwheel nuts to the specified torque setting.

16 On completion, check the hydraulic fluid level.

12 Front brake caliper - removal, overhaul and refitting

> ⚠ **Warning: Brake hydraulic fluid may be under considerable pressure in a pipeline, take care not to allow hydraulic fluid to spray into the face or eyes when loosening a connection.**

Removal

1 Chock the rear wheels, firmly apply the handbrake, jack up the front of the vehicle and support on axle stands. Remove the appropriate front roadwheel.

2 Minimise fluid loss either by removing the master cylinder reservoir cap and then tightening it down onto a piece of polythene to obtain an airtight seal (taking care not to damage the sender unit), or by using a brake hose clamp, a G-clamp or a similar tool to clamp the flexible hose.

3 Clean the area around the union, then undo the brake hose union bolt and disconnect the hose from the caliper. Plug the end of the hose and the caliper orifice to prevent dirt entering the hydraulic system. Discard the sealing washers as they must be renewed whenever disturbed.

4 Unscrew the two caliper guide pin bolts whilst, if necessary, using a slim open-ended spanner to prevent the guide pins themselves from rotating **(see illustration)**.

5 Carefully lift the caliper assembly off the brake pads and remove the circular shim from

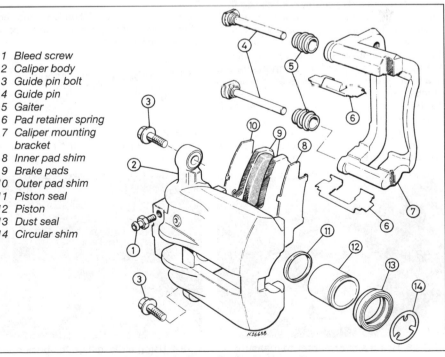

1 Bleed screw
2 Caliper body
3 Guide pin bolt
4 Guide pin
5 Gaiter
6 Pad retainer spring
7 Caliper mounting bracket
8 Inner pad shim
9 Brake pads
10 Outer pad shim
11 Piston seal
12 Piston
13 Dust seal
14 Circular shim

12.4 Front brake caliper components

the caliper piston. Note that the brake pads need not be disturbed and can be left in position in the caliper mounting bracket.

Overhaul

6 With the caliper on the bench, wipe away all traces of dust and dirt. Avoid inhaling the dust as it is injurious to health.

7 Withdraw the piston from the caliper body and remove the dust seal. The piston can be withdrawn by hand or if necessary, pushed out by applying compressed air to the union bolt hole. Only low pressure should be required such as is generated by a foot pump.

8 Using a small screwdriver, extract the piston hydraulic seal whilst taking great care not to damage the caliper bore.

9 Withdraw the guide pins from the caliper mounting bracket and remove the guide pin gaiters.

10 Thoroughly clean all components using only methylated spirit, isopropyl alcohol or clean hydraulic fluid as a cleaning medium. Never use mineral-based solvents such as petrol or paraffin which will attack the hydraulic system's rubber components. Dry the components immediately using compressed air or a clean, lint-free cloth. Use compressed air to blow clear the fluid passages.

11 Check all components and renew any that are worn or damaged. Check particularly the cylinder bore and piston. These should be renewed (note that this means the renewal of the complete body assembly) if they are scratched, worn or corroded in any way. Similarly, check the condition of the guide pins and their bores in the mounting bracket. Both guide pins should be undamaged and (when cleaned) a reasonably tight sliding fit in the mounting bracket bores. If there is any doubt about the condition of any component, renew it.

12 If the assembly is fit for further use, obtain the appropriate repair kit. Components are available from Rover dealers in various combinations.

13 Renew all rubber seals, dust covers and caps. Also the sealing washers disturbed on dismantling.

14 On reassembly, ensure that all components are absolutely clean and dry.

15 Soak the piston and the new piston (fluid) seal in clean hydraulic fluid. Smear clean fluid on the cylinder bore surface.

16 Fit the new piston (fluid) seal using only the fingers to manipulate it into the cylinder bore groove. Fit the new dust seal to the piston and refit it to the cylinder bore using a twisting motion, ensuring that the piston enters squarely into the bore. Press the piston fully into the bore, then secure the dust seal to the caliper body.

17 Apply the grease supplied in the repair kit, or a good quality high-temperature brake grease (silicone- or PBC/Poly Butyl Cuprysil-based) or anti-seize compound (eg Holts Copaslip), to the guide pins and fit the new gaiters. Fit the guide pins to the caliper mounting bracket, ensuring that the gaiters are correctly located in the grooves on both the guide pin and mounting bracket.

Refitting

18 Refit the circular shim to the piston and carefully slide the caliper into position over the brake pads. Refit the caliper guide pin bolts and tighten them to the specified torque setting.

19 Position a new sealing washer on each side of the hose union and refit the brake hose union bolt. Ensure that the brake hose union is correctly positioned between the lugs on the caliper then tighten the union bolt to the specified torque setting.

20 Remove the brake hose clamp, where fitted, and bleed the hydraulic system. Providing the precautions described were taken to minimise brake fluid loss, it should only be necessary to bleed the relevant front brake.

21 Refit the roadwheel then lower the vehicle to the ground and tighten the roadwheel nuts to the specified torque.

13 Front brake disc - inspection, removal and refitting

Note: *If either brake disc requires renewal, both should be renewed at the same time to ensure even and consistent braking.*

Inspection

1 Chock the rear wheels, firmly apply the handbrake, jack up the front of the vehicle and support on axle stands. Remove the appropriate front roadwheel.

2 Slowly rotate the brake disc so that the full area of both sides can be checked. Remove the brake pads if better access is required to the inboard surface. Light scoring is normal in the area swept by the brake pads but if heavy scoring is found, then the disc must be renewed. The only alternative to this is to have the disc surface-ground until it is flat again, but this must not reduce the disc to less than the minimum thickness specified.

3 It is normal to find a lip of rust and brake dust around the disc's perimeter. This can be scraped off if required. If, however, a lip has formed due to excessive wear of the brake pad swept area, then the disc's thickness must be measured by using a micrometer **(see illustration)**. Take measurements at four places around the disc at the inside and outside of the pad swept area. If the disc has worn at any point to the specified minimum thickness or less, then it must be renewed.

4 If the disc is thought to be warped, it can be checked for run-out (at a point 6.0 mm in from the disc's outer edge) by either using a dial gauge mounted on any convenient fixed point, while the disc is slowly rotated, or by using feeler gauges to measure (at several points all around the disc) the clearance between the disc and a fixed point, such as the caliper mounting bracket **(see illustration)**. If the measurements obtained are at the specified maximum or beyond, the disc is excessively warped and must be renewed. However, it is worth checking first that the hub bearing is in good condition. Also, try the effect of removing the disc and turning it through 180° to reposition it on the hub. If run-out is still excessive the disc must be renewed.

5 Check the disc for cracks, especially around the stud holes, and any other wear or damage. Renew it if any of these are found.

Removal

6 Unscrew the two bolts securing the caliper mounting bracket to the swivel hub and slide the caliper assembly off the disc **(see illustration)**.

13.3 Using a micrometer to measure brake disc thickness

13.4 Using a dial gauge to check brake disc run-out

13.6 Removing caliper assembly

13.7a Removing disc retaining screws (jacking holes arrowed)

13.7b Drawing off a disc using two 8 mm bolts

Using a piece of wire or string, tie the caliper to the front suspension coil spring to avoid placing any strain on the hydraulic brake hose.

7 Use chalk or paint to mark the relationship of the disc to the hub, then remove the two screws securing the brake disc to the hub and remove the disc. If the disc is a tight fit on the hub it can be drawn off by screwing two bolts into the jacking holes provided **(see illustrations)**.

Refitting

8 Refitting is the reverse of the removal procedure, noting the following:

a) *Ensure that the mating surfaces of the disc and hub are clean and flat.*

b) *Align (if applicable) the marks made on removal.*

c) *If a new disc has been fitted, use a suitable solvent to wipe any preservative coating from the disc before refitting the caliper.*

d) *Tighten the disc retaining screws, caliper bracket bolts and roadwheel nuts to their specified torque wrench settings.*

14 Pressure regulating valve - testing, removal and refitting

Testing

1 The pressure regulating valve is mounted on the right-hand side of the engine compartment bulkhead.

2 Specialist equipment is required to check valve performance. If the valve is thought to be faulty, the vehicle should be taken to a suitably equipped Rover dealer for testing. However, in the event of an internal failure, brake fluid will seep from the plug on the front face of the valve which is situated directly above the lower two hose unions **(see illustration)**. Repairs are not possible and, if faulty, the valve must be renewed.

Removal

3 Disconnect the sender unit wiring connector and unscrew the master cylinder reservoir filler cap. Place a piece of polythene over the filler neck and securely refit the cap (taking care not to damage the sender unit). This will minimise brake fluid loss during subsequent operations. As an added precaution, place absorbent rags beneath the pressure regulating valve brake pipe unions.

4 Wipe clean the area around the brake pipe unions on the pressure regulating valve, then make a note of how the pipes are arranged for reference on refitting. Unscrew the union nuts and carefully withdraw the pipes. Plug or tape over the pipe ends and valve orifices to minimise the loss of brake fluid and to prevent the entry of dirt into the system. Wash off any spilt fluid immediately with cold water.

5 Slacken the two bolts which secure the valve to the bulkhead and remove it from the engine compartment.

Refitting

6 Refit the pressure regulating valve to the bulkhead and tighten its mounting bolts securely.

7 Wipe the brake pipe unions clean and refit them to the valve, using the notes made on

14.2 In the event of failure, fluid will seep from pressure regulating valve plug (arrowed)

dismantling to ensure they are correctly positioned. Tighten the union nuts to the specified torque.

8 Remove the polythene from the master cylinder reservoir filler neck and bleed the complete hydraulic system.

15 Rear brake shoes - inspection

Refer to Chapter 1.

16 Rear brake shoes - renewal

Warning: Brake shoes must be renewed on both rear wheels at the same time. Never renew the shoes on only one wheel as uneven braking may result.

Removal

1 Remove the brake drum.

2 Working carefully and noting all precautions, remove all traces of brake dust from the brake drum, backplate and shoes.

3 Measure the thickness of friction material remaining on each brake shoe at several points. If either shoe is worn at any point to the specified minimum thickness or less, all four shoes must be renewed as a set. Also, the shoes should be renewed if any are fouled with oil or grease as there is no satisfactory way of degreasing friction material once contaminated.

4 If any of the brake shoes are worn unevenly or fouled with oil or grease, trace and rectify the cause before reassembly.

5 To remove the brake shoes, first remove the shoe retainer springs and pins, using a pair of pliers to press in each retainer clip until it can be rotated through 90° and released. Ease the shoes out one at a time from the

9

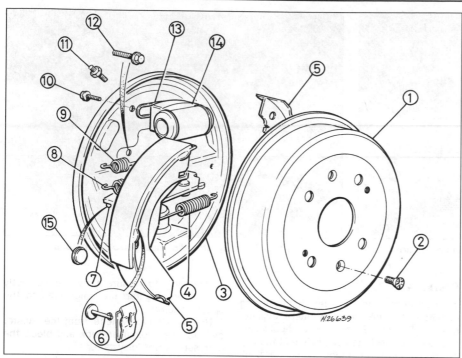

16.5a Rear drum brake assembly

1 Brake drum
2 Drum retaining screw
3 Backplate
4 Lower return spring
5 Brake shoe
6 Retainer pin and spring
7 Adjuster strut
8 Strut spring
9 Upper return spring
10 Wheel cylinder retaining bolt
11 Bleed screw
12 Backplate mounting bolt
13 Seal
14 Wheel cylinder
15 Grommet

16.5b Remove brake shoe retainer springs . . .

16.5c . . . unhook lower return spring . . .

16.5d . . . and manoeuvre shoe and adjuster strut assembly away from backplate

16.6 Correct fitted positions of adjuster strut and springs

16.10 Ensure handbrake stop lever is correctly located

lower pivot point to release the tension of the return spring, then disconnect the lower return spring from both shoes. Ease the upper end of both shoes out from their wheel cylinder locations, taking great care not to damage the wheel cylinder seals, and disconnect the handbrake cable from the trailing shoe. The brake shoe and adjuster strut assembly can now be manoeuvred out of position and away from the backplate **(see illustrations)**. Do not depress the brake pedal until the brakes are reassembled. Wrap a strong elastic band around the wheel cylinder pistons to retain them.

6 With the brake shoe assembly on the worksurface, make a note of the fitted positions of the adjuster strut and springs to use as guide on reassembly **(see illustration)**. Carefully ease the adjuster strut from its slot in the trailing shoe and remove the short spring which secures the two components together. Detach the upper return spring and separate the shoes and strut.

7 Examine the adjuster strut assembly for signs of wear or damage, paying particular attention to the adjuster quadrant and knurled wheel. If damaged, the strut assembly must be renewed. Renew all the brake shoe return springs regardless of their apparent condition.

8 Peel back the rubber protective caps and check the wheel cylinder for fluid leaks or other damage. Check that both cylinder pistons are free to move easily.

Fitting

9 Prior to fitting, clean the backplate and apply a thin smear of high-temperature brake grease (silicone- or PBC/Poly Butyl Cuprysil-based) or anti-seize compound (eg Holts Copaslip) to all those surfaces of the backplate which bear on the shoes, particularly the adjuster and the wheel cylinder pistons. Do not allow lubricant to foul the friction material.

10 Ensure the handbrake lever stop on the trailing shoe is correctly engaged with the lever and is pressed tight against the brake shoe **(see illustration)**.

11 Fully extend the adjuster strut quadrant and fit the leading brake shoe into the adjuster strut slot, ensuring that the strut spring and

16.14 Reset adjuster strut prior to refitting drum

knurled wheel are situated on the underside of the strut assembly. Using a screwdriver, move the quadrant away from the knurled wheel and set it in the minimum adjustment position.
12 Fit the upper return spring to its respective location on the leading shoe. Fit the trailing shoe to the upper return spring and carefully ease the shoe into position in the adjuster strut slot. Once in position, fit the small spring which secures the trailing shoe to the strut assembly.
13 Remove the elastic band fitted to the wheel cylinder and manoeuvre the shoe and strut assembly into position on the backplate. Locate the upper end of both shoes with the wheel cylinder pistons and fit the handbrake cable to the trailing shoe operating lever. Fit the lower return spring to both shoes and ease the shoes into position on the lower pivot point.
14 Tap the shoes to centralise them with the backplate, then refit the shoe retainer pins and springs and secure them in position with the retainer clips. Check that the adjuster quadrant is still in the minimum adjuster position and if necessary, reset as follows. Place a block of wood between the trailing shoe and hub, to prevent the shoe moving forwards, then lever the leading shoe away from the hub to release the brake shoe return spring pressure on the adjuster quadrant With the shoe held in this position, reset the quadrant to the minimum adjustment setting **(see illustration)**. Once the adjuster strut is correctly set, ease the leading shoe back into position then remove the block of wood and check that the shoes are still central.

17.3 Removing brake drum retaining screws (jacking holes arrowed)

15 Refit the brake drum and repeat the above operation on the remaining rear brake assembly.
16 On completion, apply the footbrake repeatedly to set the shoe-to-drum clearance, until normal (non-assisted) brake pedal operation returns.
17 Check handbrake cable operation and, if necessary, adjust as described in Chapter 1.
18 Refit the roadwheels then lower the vehicle to the ground and tighten the roadwheel nuts to the specified torque.
19 Check the hydraulic fluid level.

17 Rear brake drum - removal, inspection and refitting

Note: *If either brake drum requires renewal, both should be renewed at the same time to ensure even and consistent braking.*

Removal

1 Chock the front wheels then jack up the rear of the vehicle and support it on axle stands. Remove the appropriate rear wheel.
2 Use chalk or paint to mark the relationship of the drum to the hub.
3 With the handbrake firmly applied to prevent drum rotation, unscrew the drum retaining screws **(see illustration)**. Fully release the handbrake cable and withdraw the drum.
4 If the drum will not pull away, first check that the handbrake is fully released. If the drum will still not come away, remove the grommet from the rear of the backplate and, using a small screwdriver, disengage the handbrake lever stop from behind the lever to increase the shoe to drum clearance. If removal still proves troublesome, the brake drum can be drawn off by screwing two bolts into the jacking holes provided **(see illustrations)**.

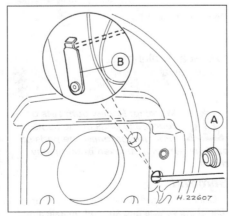

17.4a Releasing handbrake mechanism stop lever

Remove rubber grommet (A) and use small screwdriver to depress handbrake lever stop (B)

Inspection

5 Working carefully, remove all traces of brake dust from the drum. Avoid inhaling the dust as it is injurious to health.
6 Scrub clean the outside of the drum and check it for obvious signs of wear or damage such as cracks around the road-wheel stud holes. Renew the drum if necessary.
7 Examine carefully the inside of the drum. Light scoring of the friction surface is normal but if heavy scoring is found, the drum must be renewed. It is usual to find a lip on the drum's inboard edge which consists of a mixture of rust and brake dust. This should be scraped away to leave a smooth surface which can be polished with fine (120 to 150 grade) emery paper. If, however, the lip is due to the friction surface being recessed by excessive wear, then the drum must be renewed.
8 If the drum is thought to be excessively worn or oval, its internal diameter must be measured at several points by using an internal micrometer. Take measurements in pairs, the second at right angles to the first, and compare the two to check for signs of ovality. Provided that it does not enlarge the drum to beyond the specified maximum diameter, it may be possible to have the drum refinished by skimming or grinding but if this is not possible, the drums on both sides must be renewed
.

Refitting

9 Refitting is the reverse of the removal procedure, noting the following:
a) *On fitting a new brake drum, use a suitable solvent to remove any preservative coating that may have been applied to its interior.*
b) *Use a clean wire brush to remove all traces of dirt, brake dust and corrosion from the mating surfaces of the drum and the hub flange.*
c) *Align (if applicable) the marks made on removal.*
d) *Tighten the drum retaining screws and the roadwheel nuts to their specified torque wrench settings.*

17.4b Brake drum can be drawn off hub by using two 8 mm bolts

9

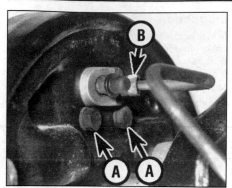

18.3 Wheel cylinder retaining bolts (A) and brake pipe union nut (B)

18 Rear wheel cylinder - removal, overhaul and refitting

Note: *Before attempting to overhaul a rear wheel cylinder, check the price and availability of individual components and the price of a new or reconditioned unit, as overhaul may not be viable on economic grounds alone.*

Removal

1 Remove the brake shoes.
2 Minimise fluid loss by removing the master cylinder reservoir cap and then tightening it down onto a piece of polythene to obtain an airtight seal (taking care not to damage the sender unit), or by using a brake hose clamp, a G-clamp or a similar tool to clamp the flexible hose.
3 Wipe away all traces of dirt around the brake pipe union at the rear of the wheel cylinder and unscrew the union nut. Carefully ease the pipe out of the wheel cylinder and plug or tape over its end to prevent dirt entry **(see illustration)**.
4 Unscrew the two wheel cylinder retaining bolts from the rear of the backplate and remove the cylinder, noting the rubber sealing ring which is fitted between the cylinder and backplate.

Overhaul

5 Remove the wheel cylinder from the vehicle and clean it thoroughly.
6 Mount the wheel cylinder in a soft-jawed vice and remove the rubber protective caps. Extract the piston assemblies.
7 Thoroughly clean all components using only methylated spirit, isopropyl alcohol or clean hydraulic fluid as a cleaning medium. Never use mineral-based solvents such as petrol or paraffin which will attack the hydraulic system's rubber components. Dry the components immediately using compressed air or a clean, lint-free cloth.
8 Check all components and renew any that are worn or damaged. Check particularly the cylinder bore and pistons. The complete assembly must be renewed if these are

scratched, worn or corroded. If there is any doubt about the condition of the assembly or of any of its components, renew it. Remove the bleed screw and check that the fluid entry port and bleed screw passages are clear.
9 If the assembly is fit for further use, obtain a repair kit. Renew the rubber protective caps, dust caps and seals disturbed on dismantling, these should never be re-used. Renew also any other items included in the repair kit.
10 On reassembly, soak the pistons and the new seals in clean hydraulic fluid. Smear clean fluid on the cylinder bore surface.
11 Fit the new seals to their pistons using only the fingers to manipulate them into the grooves. Ensure that all components are refitted in the correct order and the right way round.
12 Insert the pistons into the bore using a twisting motion to avoid trapping the seal lips. Apply a smear of rubber lubricant to each piston before fitting the new rubber protective caps.

Refitting

13 Fit a new sealing ring to the rear of the wheel cylinder and place the cylinder in position on the backplate.
14 Refit the wheel cylinder retaining bolts and tighten them to the specified torque.
15 Tighten the brake pipe union nut and, if necessary, remove the clamp from the brake hose.
16 Refit the brake shoes.
17 Bleed the hydraulic braking system. If precautions were taken to minimise fluid loss, it should only be necessary to bleed the relevant rear brake. On completion, check that both footbrake and handbrake function correctly before taking the vehicle on the road.

19 Rear brake pads - inspection

Refer to Chapter 1.

20 Rear brake pads - renewal

 Warning: Renew both sets of rear brake pads at the same time. Never renew the pads on only one wheel as uneven braking may result.

Removal

1 Chock the front wheels then jack up the rear of the vehicle and support on axle stands. Remove the rear roadwheels.
2 Undo the two bolts securing the caliper shield in position and remove the shield from the rear of the caliper.
3 Remove both caliper guide pin bolts whilst,

if necessary, using a slim open-ended spanner to prevent the guide pins from rotating. Lift the caliper away from the disc, noting the upper pad spring which is fitted to the roof of the caliper. Tie the caliper to the suspension strut using a piece of wire to avoid straining the hydraulic hose **(see illustration)**.
4 Remove the brake pads from the caliper mounting bracket whilst noting the correct fitted positions of the brake pads, pad retainer springs and pad shims.
5 Inspect the pads as described for the front brake pads and, if necessary, renew as a complete axle set.

Fitting

6 Fit the pad retainer springs to the caliper mounting bracket.
7 Apply a thin smear of Molykote M77 compound to the sides and back of each pad's metal backing and to those surfaces of the caliper body and mounting bracket which bear on the pads. In the absence of the specified lubricant, a good quality high-temperature brake grease (silicone- or PBC/Poly Butyl Cuprysil-based) or anti-seize compound (eg Holts Copaslip) may be used. Fit the shims to the back of both pads, noting that the smaller shim must be fitted to the piston side pad, and apply a thin smear of lubricant to the back of each shim. Do not allow lubricant to foul the friction material.
8 Install the brake pads in the caliper mounting bracket, ensuring that the friction material is against the disc and the pad with the smaller shim attached is fitted on the inside.
9 If new pads have been fitted, it will be necessary to retract the piston fully into the caliper bore by rotating it in a clockwise direction. This can be achieved by using a suitable pair of circlip pliers as a peg spanner or by fabricating a peg spanner for the task. Provided that the master cylinder reservoir has not been overfilled with hydraulic fluid, there should be no spillage, but keep a careful watch on the fluid level while retracting the piston. If the fluid level rises above the MAX level line at any time, the surplus should be syphoned off or ejected via a plastic tube connected to the bleed screw.
10 Ensure the upper pad spring is still in position in the caliper then slide the caliper into position in its mounting bracket. When fitting the caliper, ensure that the lug on the rear of the piston side pad is located in one of the piston slots. Refit the caliper guide pin bolts and tighten them to the specified torque setting.
11 Depress the footbrake to bring the piston into contact with the pads then check that the lug on the piston side pad is located in one of the piston slots. If necessary, remove the caliper and adjust the piston position as described above. Refit the shield to the rear of the caliper.
12 Repeat the above procedure on the remaining rear brake caliper.

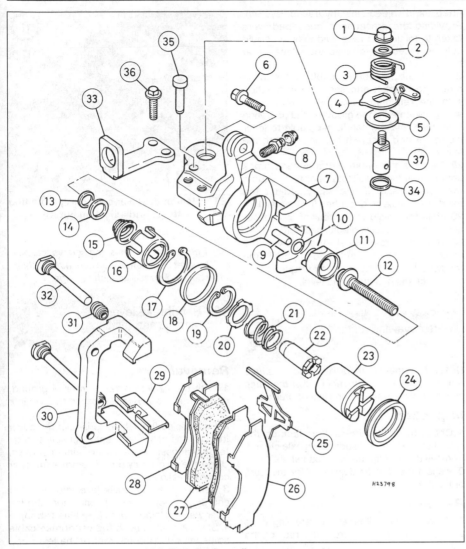

20.3 Rear brake caliper components

1 Handbrake lever retaining nut	13 Bearing	26 Inner pad shim
2 Washer	14 Spring seat	27 Brake pads
3 Return spring	15 Spring	28 Outer pad shim
4 Handbrake operating lever	16 Spring cover	29 Pad spring
5 Dust seal	17 Circlip	30 Caliper mounting bracket
6 Guide pin bolt	18 Piston seal	31 Gaiter
7 Caliper body	19 Circlip	32 Guide pin
8 Bleed screw	20 Thrustwasher	33 Handbrake cable mounting bracket
9 Pushrod	21 Spring	34 Cam washer
10 O-ring	22 Adjuster nut	35 Pin
11 Adjusting bolt piston	23 Piston	36 Bolt
12 Adjusting bolt	24 Dust seal	37 Handbrake mechanism cam
	25 Pad spring	

13 Once both calipers have been done, repeatedly depress the brake pedal until normal (non-assisted) pedal operation returns, then repeatedly apply the handbrake to set handbrake adjustment. Check the operation of the handbrake and, if necessary, adjust the cable as described in Chapter 1.

14 Refit the roadwheels, then lower the vehicle to the ground and tighten the roadwheel nuts to the specified torque.

15 Check the hydraulic fluid level.

21 Rear brake caliper - removal, overhaul and refitting

Removal

1 Chock the front wheels, then jack up the rear of the vehicle and support on axle stands. Remove the rear wheel.

2 Undo the two bolts securing the caliper

shield in position and remove the shield from the rear of the caliper.

3 Extract the spring clip and clevis pin securing the handbrake cable to the caliper handbrake lever, then remove the clip securing the outer cable to its mounting bracket and detach the handbrake cable from the caliper.

4 Minimise fluid loss by removing the master cylinder reservoir cap and then tightening it down onto a piece of polythene to obtain an airtight seal (taking care not to damage the sender unit), or by using a brake hose clamp, a G-clamp or a similar tool to clamp the flexible hose.

5 Clean the area around the hose union, then undo the brake hose union bolt and disconnect the hose from the caliper. Plug the end of the hose and the caliper orifice to prevent dirt entering the hydraulic system. Discard the sealing washers as they must be renewed whenever disturbed.

6 Remove both the caliper guide pin bolts whilst, if necessary, using a slim open-ended spanner to prevent the guide pins from rotating, then lift the caliper away from the disc, noting the upper pad spring which is fitted to the roof of the caliper. Note that the brake pads need not be disturbed and can be left in position in the caliper mounting bracket.

Overhaul

7 With the caliper on the bench, wipe away all traces of dust and dirt. Avoid inhaling the dust as it is injurious to health.

8 Using a small screwdriver, carefully prise out the dust seal from the caliper bore.

9 Remove the piston from the caliper bore by rotating it in an anti-clockwise direction. This can be achieved using a suitable pair of circlip pliers as a peg spanner or by fabricating a peg spanner for the task. Once the piston turns freely but does not come out any further, then it can be withdrawn by hand, or if necessary, pushed out by applying compressed air to the union bolt hole. Only low pressure should be required such as is generated by a foot pump.

10 With the piston removed, extract the circlip from inside the piston and withdraw the thrustwasher, spring and adjuster nut.

11 Remove the piston (fluid) seal whilst taking great care not to scratch the caliper bore.

12 Extract the circlip from the caliper bore and withdraw the spring cover, spring, spring seat, bearing and adjusting bolt. Then remove the adjusting bolt piston, noting the O-ring fitted to the rear of the piston, and withdraw the small pushrod.

13 Slacken and remove the handbrake lever retaining nut and washer and remove the return spring, lever and dust seal. Withdraw the handbrake mechanism cam from the caliper and remove the cam washer.

14 Withdraw the guide pins from the caliper mounting bracket and remove the guide pin gaiters.

9

15 Inspect all the caliper components as described for the front brake caliper and renew as necessary.

16 On reassembly ensure that all components are absolutely clean and dry.

17 Apply a good quality high-temperature brake grease (silicone- or PBC/Poly Butyl Cuprysil-based) or anti-seize compound (eg Holts Copaslip) to the handbrake mechanism cam and refit the cam washer and cam to the caliper. Fit the dust seal, lever, return spring and washer and tighten the handbrake lever retaining nut securely.

18 Fit a new O-ring to the adjusting bolt piston then insert the small pushrod into the rear of the piston and install the adjusting bolt piston assembly in the caliper bore. Operate the handbrake lever and check that the piston is free to move smoothly then refit the adjusting bolt, followed by the bearing and spring seat. Fit the spring, so that its tapered end is innermost, then install the spring cover. Secure all the above components in position with the circlip, ensuring that it is correctly seated in the groove in the caliper bore.

19 Locate the adjusting nut with the cutout on the inside of the caliper piston and refit the spring, thrustwasher and circlip. Ensure the circlip is correctly located in its groove.

20 Soak the piston and the new piston (fluid) seal in clean hydraulic fluid. Smear clean fluid on the cylinder bore surface.

21 Fit the new piston (fluid) seal using only the fingers to manipulate it into the cylinder bore groove and refit the piston assembly. Turn the piston in a clockwise direction, using the method employed on dismantling, until it is fully retracted into the caliper bore.

22 Fit the dust seal to the caliper ensuring that it is correctly located in the caliper and also the groove on the piston.

23 Apply the grease supplied in the repair kit, or a good quality high-temperature brake grease (silicone- or PBC/Poly Butyl Cuprysil-based) or anti-seize compound (eg Holts Copaslip), to the guide pins and fit the new gaiters. Fit the guide pins to the caliper mounting bracket, ensuring that the gaiters are correctly located in the grooves on both the guide pin and mounting bracket.

Refitting

24 Ensure the upper pad spring is still in position in the caliper then slide the caliper into position in its mounting bracket. When fitting the caliper, ensure that the lug on the rear of the piston side pad is located in the centre of the caliper piston at the point where the two piston slots cross. Refit the caliper guide pin bolts and tighten them to the specified torque setting.

25 Position a new sealing washer on each side of the hose union and refit the brake hose union bolt. Ensure that the brake hose union is correctly positioned between the lugs on the caliper then tighten the union bolt to the specified torque setting.

26 Remove the brake hose clamp, where

fitted, and bleed the hydraulic system. Providing the precautions described were taken to minimise brake fluid loss, it should only be necessary to bleed the relevant rear brake.

27 Refit the handbrake cable outer to its mounting bracket and secure it in position with the retaining clip. Ensure the return spring is located in the groove in the operating lever then refit the handbrake cable to lever clevis pin and secure it in position with the spring clip.

28 Depress the brake pedal several times until normal (non-assisted) operation returns then check and, if necessary, adjust the handbrake cable as described in Chapter 1.

29 Refit the shield to the rear of the caliper and tighten its retaining bolts securely.

30 Refit the roadwheel, then lower the vehicle to the ground and tighten the roadwheel nuts to the specified torque.

31 Check the hydraulic fluid level.

---

22 Rear brake disc - inspection, removal and refitting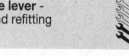

Note: *If either rear brake disc requires renewal, both should be renewed at the same time to ensure even and consistent braking.*

Inspection

1 Chock the front wheels, then jack up the rear of the vehicle and support on axle stands. Remove the appropriate rear roadwheel.

2 Inspect the disc as described for the front brake disc.

Removal

3 Undo the two caliper shield retaining bolts and remove the shield from the rear of the caliper.

4 Undo the two bolts securing the caliper mounting bracket to the trailing arm assembly and slide the caliper assembly off the disc. Using a piece of wire or string, tie the caliper to the rear suspension coil spring to avoid placing any strain on the hydraulic brake hose.

5 Use chalk or paint to mark the relationship of the disc to the hub, then remove the two screws securing the brake disc to the hub and remove the disc. If the disc is a tight fit on the hub, it can be drawn off by screwing two bolts into the jacking holes provided.

Refitting

6 Refitting is the reverse of the removal procedure, noting the following:
a) *Ensure that the mating surfaces of the disc and hub are clean and flat.*
b) *Align (if applicable) the marks made on removal.*
c) *If a new disc has been fitted, use a suitable solvent to wipe any preservative coating from the disc before refitting the caliper.*

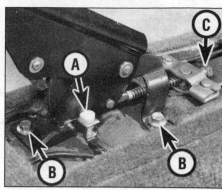

23.3 Handbrake lever switch (A), mounting bolts (B) and adjusting nut (C)

d) *Tighten the disc retaining screws, caliper bracket bolts and roadwheel nuts to their specified torque wrench settings.*

---

23 Handbrake lever - removal and refitting

Removal

1 With the vehicle parked on level ground, chock the roadwheels so that the vehicle cannot move.

2 From inside the vehicle, prise out the cover from the top of the rear centre console section to gain access to the two retaining screws. Undo the two screws and remove the rear console section.

3 Remove the handbrake lever rubber gaiter and disconnect the wiring connector from the lever warning lamp switch **(see illustration)**.

4 Slacken and remove the handbrake cable adjusting nut from the rear of the lever and undo the bolts securing the handbrake lever assembly to the floorpan **(see illustration opposite)**.

5 Lift the handbrake assembly out of position, noting the spring which is fitted to the lever adjusting rod.

Refitting

6 Refitting is a reverse of the removal procedure. Prior to refitting the handbrake lever rubber gaiter, adjust the handbrake cable as described in Chapter 1.

---

24 Handbrake cables - removal and refitting

Removal

1 Firmly chock the front wheels then jack up the rear of the vehicle and support it on axle stands. The handbrake cable consists of two sections (right and left-hand), which are linked to the lever assembly by an equalizer plate. Each section can be removed individually.

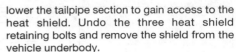

lower the tailpipe section to gain access to the heat shield. Undo the three heat shield retaining bolts and remove the shield from the vehicle underbody.

8 Work along the length of the cable section and remove all bolts securing the cable outer to the vehicle underbody and trailing arm. Once free, withdraw the cable from underneath the vehicle and, if necessary, repeat the procedure for the remaining cable section.

Refitting

9 Refitting is a reversal of the removal sequence noting the following:
a) Lubricate all exposed linkages and cable pivots with a good quality multi-purpose grease.
b) Ensure the cable outer grommet is correctly located in the floorpan and that all retaining bolts are tightened to the specified torque.
c) On non-ABS models, relocate the trailing shoe and refit the brake drum.
d) Prior to refitting the rear centre console section, adjust the handbrake cable as described in Chapter 1.

25 Stop lamp switch - removal, refitting and adjustment

Removal

1 Working inside the vehicle, undo the five screws and remove the right-hand lower facia panel.
2 Disconnect the wiring connector from the stop lamp switch (see illustration).
3 Slacken the stop lamp switch locknut and unscrew the switch from its mounting bracket.

Refitting and adjustment

4 Screw the switch back into position in the mounting bracket.
5 Connect an ohmmeter across the stop lamp switch terminals and screw the switch in until an open circuit is present between the switch terminals. Gently depress the pedal and check that continuity exists between the

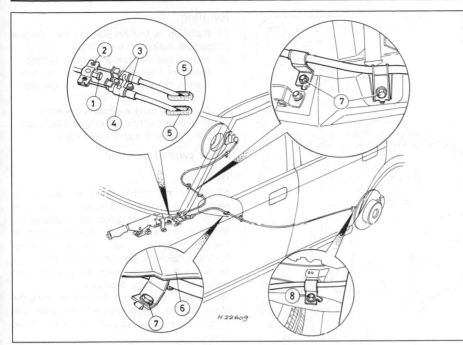

23.4 Handbrake mechanism layout

1 Handbrake cable adjuster nut
2 Equalizer plate
3 Bolts
4 Cable retaining plate
5 Grommet
6 Exhaust heatshield
7 Bolts - cable to body
8 Bolts - cable to trailing arm

2 From inside the vehicle, prise out the cover from the top of the rear centre console section to gain access to the two retaining screws. Undo the two screws and remove the rear console section.
3 Slacken and remove the handbrake cable adjusting nut from the rear of the lever and disconnect the equalizer plate, noting the spring which is fitted to the lever adjusting rod.
4 Undo the two bolts securing the cable outer retaining plate to the floor pan (see illustration). Remove the retaining plate then detach the relevant cable inner from the equalizer plate and release the cable grommet from the floorpan.
5 On models equipped with ABS, working from underneath the vehicle, remove the two brake caliper shield retaining bolts and remove the shield from the caliper. Extract the

spring clip and clevis pin securing the handbrake cable to the caliper handbrake lever then remove the clip securing the cable outer to its mounting bracket and detach the handbrake cable from the caliper.
6 On non-ABS models, remove the relevant rear brake drum. Remove the trailing shoe retainer spring and pin, using a pair of pliers to press in the retainer clip until it can be rotated through 90° and released. Ease the trailing shoe out of the lower pivot point to release the tension of the return spring, then disconnect the lower return spring from both shoes. Disconnect the handbrake cable from the trailing shoe then use a 12 mm spanner to compress the handbrake cable retaining tangs and withdraw the cable from the rear of the backplate (see illustration).
7 On all models, release the main silencer from its three rubber mountings and carefully

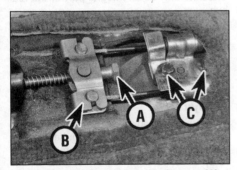

24.4 Handbrake cable adjusting nut (A), equalizer plate (B) and cable outer retaining plate bolts (C)

24.6 Using a 12 mm spanner to compress cable outer retaining tangs

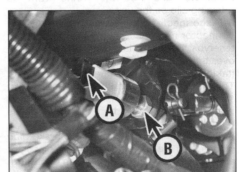

25.2 Stop lamp switch wiring connector (A) and locknut (B)

9

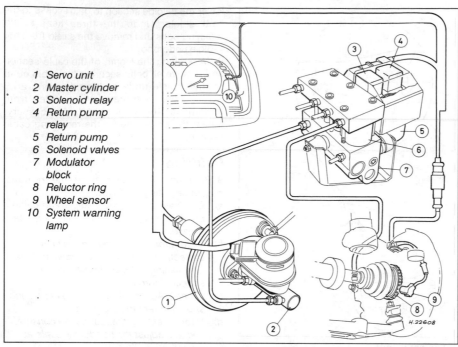

1 Servo unit
2 Master cylinder
3 Solenoid relay
4 Return pump relay
5 Return pump
6 Solenoid valves
7 Modulator block
8 Reluctor ring
9 Wheel sensor
10 System warning lamp

26.1 ABS system components

switch terminals as soon as the pedal is depressed. If necessary, reposition the switch until it operates as specified.

6 Once the stop lamp switch is correctly adjusted, hold the switch stationary and tighten the locknut securely.

7 Connect the wiring connector to the switch and refit the lower facia panel.

26 Anti-lock Braking system (ABS) - component removal and refitting

Modulator block

Removal

1 Disconnect the battery negative terminal then undo the screw and remove the modulator relay cover **(see illustration)**.

2 Disconnect the wiring connectors from the modulator and free the wiring from its retaining clip on the unit.

3 Disconnect the sender unit wiring connector and unscrew the master cylinder reservoir filler cap. Place a piece of polythene over the filler neck and securely refit the cap (taking care not to damage the sender unit). This will minimise brake fluid loss during subsequent operations. As an added precaution, place absorbent rags beneath the modulator brake pipe unions.

4 Wipe clean the area around the brake pipe unions then make a note of how the pipes are arranged for reference when refitting. Unscrew the union nuts and carefully withdraw the pipes. Plug or tape over the pipe ends and valve orifices to minimise the loss of

brake fluid and to prevent the entry of dirt into the system. Wash off any spilt fluid immediately with cold water.

5 Undo the earth lead retaining nut and slacken the modulator block mounting nuts. Disconnect the earth lead and remove the modulator assembly from the engine compartment. Do not attempt to dismantle the modulator block assembly. Overhaul of the unit is a complex job and should be entrusted to a Rover dealer.

Refitting

6 Refitting is the reverse of the removal procedure, noting the following:
a) *Tighten the modulator block mounting nuts to the specified torque.*
b) *Refit the brake pipes to their respective unions and tighten the union nuts to the specified torque.*
c) *On completion, bleed the braking system.*

Front wheel sensor

Removal

7 Chock the rear wheels, firmly apply the handbrake, jack up the front of the vehicle and support on axle stands. Remove the appropriate front roadwheel.

8 From inside the engine compartment, disconnect the relevant sensor wiring connector and displace the sensor wiring grommet.

9 From underneath the vehicle, pull the sensor wiring lead through the wing valance then undo the sensor lead bracket retaining bolts and remove the brackets.

10 Slacken and remove the two bolts securing the sensor unit to the wheel hub then remove the sensor and lead assembly.

Refitting

11 Refitting is the reverse of the removal procedure, noting the following:
a) *Ensure that the sensor and hub sealing faces are clean then refit the sensor and tighten its retaining bolts to the specified torque.*
b) *Ensure the sensor wiring is correctly routed and all bracket retaining bolts are tightened to the specified torque.*

Rear wheel sensor

Removal

12 Chock the front wheels then jack up the rear of the vehicle and support it on axle stands. Remove the appropriate roadwheel.

13 Trace the wiring back from the sensor to the wiring connector then free the connector from its retaining clips and disconnect it.

14 Undo the sensor lead bracket retaining bolts and remove the brackets.

15 Slacken and remove the bolt securing the strap to the sensor cover then undo the sensor cover retaining bolts and remove the cover.

16 Undo the two bolts securing the sensor to the rear hub assembly and remove it from the vehicle, along with the shim which is fitted behind it.

Refitting

17 Refitting is the reverse of the removal procedure, noting the following:
a) *Ensure the sensor and hub sealing faces are clean, then install the sensor and shim and tighten the sensor retaining bolts to the specified torque.*
b) *Refit the sensor cover, cover strap retaining bolt and sensor lead brackets, then tighten all retaining bolts to the specified torque.*
c) *Reconnect the sensor lead wiring connector and refit the connector to its retaining clip.*

Reluctor rings

18 The reluctor rings are not available as separate items. The front rings are available only as an integral part of the outer constant velocity joint assembly and the rear rings are available only as an integral part of the rear hub.

19 The front reluctor rings are situated on the outer constant velocity joint and the rear reluctor rings are part of the stub axle assembly. Examine the rings for signs of damage such as chipped or missing teeth and renew as necessary.

Relays

20 Both the solenoid relay and return pump relay are located in the modulator block assembly. To gain access to them, undo the relay cover retaining screw and lift off the cover. Either relay can then be simply pulled out of position. Refer to Chapter 12 for further information on relays.

Chapter 10
Suspension and steering

Contents

Degrees of difficulty

Easy, suitable for novice with little experience	**Fairly easy,** suitable for beginner with some experience	**Fairly difficult,** suitable for competent DIY mechanic	**Difficult,** suitable for experienced DIY mechanic	**Very difficult,** suitable for expert DIY or professional

Specifications

Front suspension

Type . . . . Fully independent, by MacPherson struts with coil springs and integral shock absorbers. Anti-roll bar mounted onto both lower suspension arms

Rear suspension

Type . . . . Fully independent double wishbone type, by trailing arms with transverse lateral links, suspension struts with coil springs and integral shock absorbers

Steering

Type . . . . Rack and pinion, power-assisted steering available as an option
Turns lock-to-lock:
    Manual 4.0
    Power-assisted 3.4

10

Wheel alignment and steering angles

All measurements are with vehicle at kerb weight

Toe-out in turns	Inside roadwheel 17° 17'
	Outside roadwheel 16° 21' ± 2'
Camber angle:	
Front	0° 20' negative ± 0° 10'
Rear	0° 50' negative to 0° 50' positive
Castor angle:	
Front	1° 59' positive ± 0° 30'
Rear	N/A
Steering axis inclination (SAI) or kingpin inclination (KPI)	12°
Toe setting:	
Front	0° 10' ± 0° 15' toe-out
Rear	0° 11' ± 0° 7.5' toe-in

Roadwheels

Type:	
214 GSi	Steel (alloy optional)
All other models	Steel
Size:	
214 S without ABS	4.5 x 13
214 S with ABS, 214, 414 Si and SLi	5 x 14
214 GSi:	
Standard (steel wheels)	5 x 14
Optional (alloy wheels)	5.5 x 14

Tyres

Type	Tubeless, steel-braced radial	
Size:		
214 S without ABS	155 SR 13	
214 S with ABS, 214, 414 Si and SLi	175/65 TR 14	
214 GSi:		
Standard (steel wheels)	175/65 TR 14	
Optional (alloy wheels)	185/60 HR 14	
Pressures (cold) - 155 SR 13 tyres:	**Front**	**Rear**
Normal driving conditions	2.1 bar (30 psi)	2.1 bar (30 psi)
Loads in excess of four persons	2.1 bar (30 psi)	2.3 bar (34 psi)
Speeds in excess of 100 mph - all loads	2.2 bar (32 psi)	2.2 bar (32 psi)
Pressures (cold) - 175/65 TR 14 tyres:	**Front**	**Rear**
All loads - up to 100 mph	2.1 bar (30 psi)	2.1 bar (30 psi)
All loads - over 100 mph	2.2 bar (32 psi)	2.2 bar (32 psi)
Pressures (cold) - 185/60 HR 14 tyres:	**Front**	**Rear**
All loads - up to 100 mph	2.1 bar (30 psi)	2.1 bar (30 psi)
All loads - over 100 mph	2.5 bar (36 psi)	2.5 bar (36 psi)

Note: *Pressures apply only to original equipment tyres and may vary if any other make or type is fitted. Check with the tyre manufacturer or supplier for correct pressures if necessary*

Torque wrench settings

	Nm	lbf ft
Front suspension		
Driveshaft retaining nut	185	137
Front suspension strut:		
Upper mounting nuts	32	24
Swivel hub pinch-bolt	100	74
Brake hose clamp bolt	25	18
Upper mounting plate retaining nut	40	30
Anti-roll bar:		
Mounting clamp bolts	15	11
Connecting link bolts	45	33
Tie bar:		
Lower suspension arm bolts	80	59
Retaining nut	55	41
Lower arm:		
Balljoint retaining nut	60	44
Body pivot bolt	45	33

Torque wrench settings (continued)

	Nm	lbf ft
Rear suspension		
Rear hub nut	185	137
Drum brake backplate-to-trailing arm bolts	65	48
Disc brake shield-to-trailing arm bolts	15	11
Brake hose bracket-to-trailing arm bolts	15	11
Handbrake cable-to-trailing arm bolts	22	16
Stub axle:		
Retaining nut	170	125
Trailing arm bolts	55	41
Rear suspension strut:		
Upper mounting nuts	32	24
Lower mounting bolt	45	33
Upper mounting plate retaining nut	40	30
Lateral link pivot bolts	45	33
Trailing arm mounting bolts	83	61
Steering		
Steering wheel nut:		
Without airbag	52	39
With airbag	45	32
Steering column:		
Lower mounting bolt and nut	20	15
Upper mounting bolts	20	15
Upper mounting nuts	13	10
Universal joint pinch-bolts	30	22
Steering gear mounting bolts	42	31
Steering gear mounting nuts	25	18
Power-assisted steering gear:		
Feed pipe union nut	39	29
Return pipe union nut	31	23
Track rod balljoint:		
Retaining nut	44	32
Locknut	55	41
Power steering pump:		
Mounting bolts	48	35
Outlet pipe union nut	55	41
Pulley retaining bolts	9	7
Power steering oil cooler mounting bolts	9	7
Roadwheels		
Roadwheel nuts	100	74

1 General information and precautions

General information

The independent front suspension is of the MacPherson strut type, incorporating coil springs and integral telescopic shock absorbers. The MacPherson struts are located by transverse lower suspension arms, which utilize rubber inner mounting bushes and incorporate a balljoint at the outer ends, and forward facing longitudinal tie bars. Both lower suspension arms are connected to an anti-roll bar via a small connecting link. The front swivel hubs, which carry the wheel bearings, brake calipers and the hub/disc assemblies, are bolted to the MacPherson struts and connected to the lower arms via the balljoints.

The fully independent rear suspension is of double wishbone type, utilising pressed steel trailing arms which have the roadwheel stub axles bolted into their rear ends. These are located longitudinally on the vehicle underbody via a large rubber bush which is situated towards the centre of each arm. Each trailing arm assembly is located transversely by three lateral links, which utilize rubber mounting bushes at both their inner and outer ends. The rear suspension struts incorporate coil springs and integral telescopic shock absorbers and are mounted onto the rear lower lateral link via a rubber mounting bush.

The steering wheel is of the energy-absorbing type (to protect the driver in the event of an accident) and is attached by a deeply-recessed nut to the steering column which is also collapsible. In the event of an impact, such as in an accident, the lower steering column clamp and the upper column mounting, fitted with energy absorbing bending plates, is designed to allow the column to slide downwards. The downwards movement of the column bends the mounting plates which absorb some of the energy, so lessening the force transmitted to the driver via the steering wheel.

An airbag is available as an option and, when fitted, is mounted in the centre of the steering wheel. See Chapter 12 for full details.

The steering column has a universal joint fitted towards the lower end of its length and its bottom end is clamped to a second universal joint, which is in turn clamped to the steering gear pinion.

The steering gear is mounted onto the engine compartment bulkhead and is connected by two track rods, with balljoints at their outer ends, to the steering arms projecting rearwards from the hub carriers. The track rod ends are threaded to facilitate adjustment.

Power-assisted steering is available as an

10

option on all models. The main components being a rack and pinion steering gear unit, a hydraulic pump which is belt-driven off the crankshaft and the hydraulic feed and return lines between the pump and steering gear.

Precautions

The driveshaft hub and stub axle nuts are very tight – ensure the car is securely supported when loosening and tightening them.

A number of precautions must be observed when working on the steering components of vehicles equipped with airbags, these are listed in Chapter 12.

2 Front swivel hub assembly - removal and refitting

Removal

1 Chock the rear wheels, firmly apply the handbrake then jack up the front of the vehicle and support it on axle stands. Remove the appropriate front roadwheel.

2 Using a hammer and suitable chisel nosed tool, tap up the staking securing the driveshaft retaining nut to the groove in the outer constant velocity joint **(see illustration)**.

3 Have an assistant firmly depress the footbrake, then using a socket and extension bar, slacken and remove the driveshaft retaining nut. Discard the nut. A new nut must be obtained for reassembly.

4 If the hub bearings are to be disturbed, remove the brake disc. If not, undo the two bolts securing the caliper mounting bracket to the hub and slide the caliper off the disc. Tie the caliper to the suspension strut to avoid placing any strain on the brake hose.

5 On models equipped with ABS, remove the front wheel sensor.

6 Slacken and remove the bolt and washer securing the anti-roll bar connecting link to the lower suspension arm and undo the two bolts securing the tie bar to the lower suspension arm.

7 Extract the split pins and undo the nuts securing the steering gear track rod and lower suspension arm balljoints to the swivel hub. Release both the balljoints from the swivel hub by using a suitable balljoint separator, taking great care not to damage the balljoint gaiters.

8 Slacken the swivel hub-to-suspension strut clamp bolt then carefully ease the hub off the strut. Once free, pull the hub outwards to free it from the constant velocity joint splines, then remove it from the vehicle **(see illustration)**. Whilst the hub is removed, support the driveshaft by tying it to the suspension strut to avoid damaging the inner constant velocity joint or gaiter.

2.2 Front suspension components

1 Rubber cover	17 Flanged washer	32 Lower arm pivot bush
2 Self-locking nut	18 Mounting bush	33 Lower arm pivot bolt
3 Washer	19 Spacer	34 Anti-roll bar connecting
4 Strut upper mounting nut	20 Driveshaft retaining nut	link
5 Upper mounting plate	21 Brake disc	35 Bolt
6 Bearing	22 Disc retaining screw	36 Nut
7 Upper spring seat	23 Hub	37 Bolt - anti-roll bar
8 Dust cover	24 Disc shield	connecting link to lower
9 Coil spring	25 Bolt	arm
10 Washer	26 Circlip	38 Anti-roll bar
11 Rubber damper stop	27 Hub bearing	39 Mounting rubber
12 Strut	28 Swivel hub	40 Mounting clamp
13 Strut lower clamp bolt	29 Driveshaft	41 Bolt
14 Tie bar	30 Lower suspension arm	42 Split pin
15 Bolt - tie bar to lower arm	31 Balljoint retaining nut	43 Track rod balljoint
16 Nut - tie bar to subframe		

2.8 Removing swivel hub assembly

Refitting

9 Refitting is reversal of the removal procedure noting the following:
a) *Ensure that the lug on the base of the suspension strut correctly engages with the slot in the swivel hub assembly clamp.*
b) *Tighten all nuts and bolts to the specified torque.*
c) *Where necessary, refit the brake disc and/or ABS wheel sensor as described in Chapter 9.*
d) *Use new split pins to secure the track rod and lower suspension arm balljoint retaining nuts in position.*
e) *When fitting the new driveshaft retaining nut, tighten it to the specified torque then stake it firmly into the groove in the constant velocity joint by using a suitable punch.*

3 Front hub bearings - removal and refitting

Note: *The front hub bearing is a sealed, pre-adjusted and pre-lubricated, double-row roller type, and is intended to last the vehicle's entire service life without maintenance or attention. Do not attempt to remove the bearing unless absolutely necessary, as it will probably be damaged during the removal operation. Never overtighten the driveshaft nut beyond the specified torque wrench setting in an attempt to 'adjust' the bearing.*
Note: *A press will be required to dismantle and rebuild the hub assembly. If such a tool is not available, a large bench vice and suitable spacers (such as large sockets) will serve as an adequate substitute. The service tool numbers for the special Rover mandrels are given in the accompanying illustrations. The bearing's inner races are an interference fit on the hub. If the outboard inner race remains on the hub when it is pressed out of the hub carrier, a proprietary knife-edged bearing puller will be required to remove it.*

Removal

1 Remove the swivel hub assembly, then undo the brake disc shield retaining screws and remove the shield from the hub.
2 Press the hub out of the swivel hub using a tubular spacer **(see illustration)**. If the bearing's outboard inner race remains on the hub, remove it using a suitable bearing puller.
3 Extract both circlips from the swivel hub and discard them as they should be renewed whenever disturbed.
4 Press the bearing out of the swivel hub by using a suitable tubular spacer **(see illustration)**.
5 Thoroughly clean the hub and swivel hub, removing all traces of dirt and grease. Polish away any burrs or raised edges which might hinder reassembly. Check both for cracks or any other signs of wear or damage and renew

the hub if necessary. The bearing and its circlips must be renewed whenever they are disturbed. A replacement bearing kit is available from Rover dealers which consists of the bearing and both circlips.
6 Check the condition of the roadwheel studs in the hub flange. If any are sheared off, stretched or have damaged threads, they can be pressed out of the hub providing that its flange is fully supported. On refitting, support the hub flange and press in the new stud until it seats fully.

Refitting

7 On reassembly, check (if possible) that the new bearing is packed with grease and fit the new circlip to the swivel hub outboard groove. Apply a light film of oil to the bearing inner and outer races and to the matching surfaces in the hub and swivel hub to aid fitting of the bearing.
8 Support the swivel hub outboard face and, using a suitable tubular spacer which bears only on the bearing's outer race, press in the new bearing until it seats against the circlip **(see illustration)**. Secure the bearing in position by fitting the second new circlip to the swivel hub's inboard groove.
9 Fully supporting the bearing inner race, press the hub into the bearing and swivel hub until the hub shoulder seats against the bearing's inner race **(see illustration)**. Wipe off any surplus oil or grease.

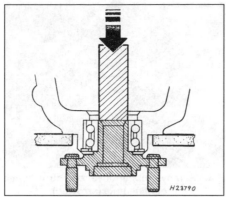
3.2 **Pressing out hub from swivel hub**

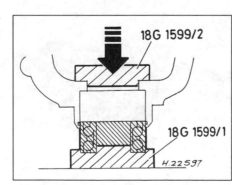
3.8 **Pressing new hub bearing into swivel hub**

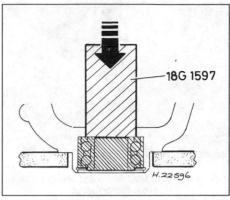
3.4 **Pressing hub bearing out of swivel hub**

10 Refit the brake disc shield to the swivel hub and tighten its retaining screws securely.
11 Refit the swivel hub assembly.

4 Suspension - inspection

Refer to Chapter 1.

5 Front suspension strut - removal and refitting

Removal

1 Chock the rear wheels, firmly apply the handbrake, then jack up the front of the vehicle and support on axle stands. Remove the appropriate roadwheel.
2 Extract the split pin and undo the nut securing the steering gear track rod balljoint to the swivel hub. Release the balljoint shank, using a suitable balljoint separator tool whilst taking care not to damage the balljoint gaiter.
3 Slacken and remove the bolt and washer securing the anti-roll bar connecting link to the lower suspension arm, then undo the two

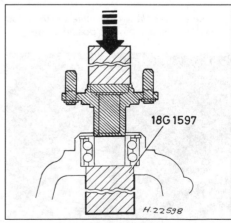
3.9 **Pressing hub into swivel hub - note support for bearing inner race**

5.4 Removing bolt securing brake hose to suspension strut

5.6a Remove rubber cover and strut upper mounting nuts (arrowed)

5.6b Removing a front suspension strut

bolts securing the tie bar to the lower suspension arm.

4 Undo the bolt securing the brake hose retaining clamp to the strut, then remove the clamp and free the flexible hose **(see illustration)**.

5 Slacken the swivel hub-to-suspension strut clamp bolt, then carefully ease the swivel hub assembly off the end of the strut.

6 Working in the engine compartment, remove the rubber suspension strut cover. Use chalk or a dab of paint to mark the relative positions of the suspension strut upper mounting and body. Undo the three strut upper mounting nuts and manoeuvre the strut out from under the wheelarch whilst noting the seal which is fitted between the upper mounting plate and vehicle body **(see illustrations)**.

Refitting

7 Refitting is a reversal of the removal procedure, noting the following **(see illustration)**:

a) *Ensure that the marks made on removal are aligned when fitting the strut.*
b) *Ensure that the lug on the base of the suspension strut correctly engages with the slot in the swivel hub assembly.*
c) *Tighten all nuts and bolts to the specified torque.*
d) *Use a new split pin to secure the track rod balljoint retaining nut in position.*

---

6 Front suspension strut - dismantling, inspection and reassembly

Note: *Before attempting to dismantle the front suspension strut, a suitable tool to hold the coil spring in compression must be obtained. Adjustable coil spring compressors are readily available and are recommended for this operation. Any attempt to dismantle the strut without such a tool is likely to result in damage or personal injury.*

Dismantling

1 With the strut removed from the vehicle, clean away all external dirt then mount it upright in a vice.

2 Fit the spring compressor and compress the coil spring until all tension is relieved from the upper mounting plate **(see illustration)**.

3 Slacken the upper mounting retaining nut whilst retaining the strut piston with an Allen key **(see illustration)**.

4 Remove the nut and washer followed by the mounting plate, bearing and upper spring seat. Lift off the coil spring and damper piston dust cover and separate the two components. Slide the washer and rubber damper stop off the strut piston.

Inspection

5 With the strut assembly completely dismantled, examine all components for wear,

damage or deformation and check the bearing for smoothness of operation. Renew any of the components, as necessary.

6 Examine the strut for signs of fluid leakage. Check the strut piston for signs of pitting along its entire length and check the strut body for signs of damage. Test the operation of the strut, while holding it in an upright position, by moving the piston through a full stroke and then through short strokes of 50 to 100 mm. In both cases the resistance felt should be smooth and continuous. If the resistance is jerky, or uneven, or if there is any visible sign of wear or damage to the strut, renewal is necessary.

7 If any doubt exists about the condition of the coil spring, carefully remove the spring compressors and check the spring for distortion and signs of cracking. Since no minimum free length is specified by Rover, the only way to check the tension of the spring is to compare it to a new component. Renew the spring if it is damaged or distorted or there is any doubt as to its condition.

8 Inspect all other components for signs of damage or deterioration and renew any that are suspect.

Reassembly

9 Reassembly is a reversal of dismantling. Ensure that the spring ends are correctly located in the upper and lower seats and that the upper mounting plate retaining nut is tightened to the specified torque.

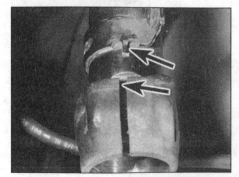

5.7 Align suspension strut lug with slot in swivel hub (arrowed)

6.2 Compress coil spring with suitable pair of spring compressors . . .

6.3 . . . and remove upper mounting nut whilst retaining piston with Allen key

7.4 Slacken and remove anti-roll bar-to-connecting link bolts

7.5 Correct position of anti-roll bar mounting bush split (arrowed)

7 Front anti-roll bar - removal and refitting

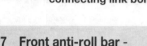

Removal

1 Chock the rear wheels, firmly apply the handbrake then jack up the front of the vehicle and support it on axle stands. Remove both front roadwheels.

2 From underneath the vehicle, undo the bolts securing the gearchange control rod rear rubber mounting to the vehicle underbody. Remove the rubber mounting assembly and bolts, noting the correct fitted positions of the mounting rubber spacers and mounting plate.

3 Release the exhaust system from its front rubber mountings, then undo the three gearchange linkage bellcrank assembly retaining bolts and lower the gearchange linkage assembly down onto the exhaust system.

4 Slacken and remove the nuts and washers securing each end of the anti-roll bar to the connecting links and remove the bolts **(see illustration)**.

5 Mark the location of the clamp bushes on the bar, then undo the mounting clamp retaining bolts and remove the clamps. Make a note of the fitted position of the rubber bush splits to ensure that they are positioned correctly on refitting **(see illustration)**. Manoeuvre the anti-roll bar out over the gearchange linkage and exhaust system and remove it from the right-hand side of the vehicle.

6 Carefully examine the anti-roll bar components for signs of wear, damage or deterioration, paying particular attention to the mounting rubbers. Inspect the gearchange mechanism control rod mounting rubber and bush for signs of wear or deterioration. Renew worn components as necessary.

Refitting

7 Manoeuvre the anti-roll bar into position from the right-hand side of the vehicle and refit the connecting link bolts. Refit the

washers and tighten the nuts, finger tight only.

8 Lubricate the mounting clamp bushes with a solution of soapy water then lever the bar down and slide them into position on the anti-roll bar. Ensure that the splits are on the right side of the bushes then align them with the marks made on dismantling.

9 Refit the anti-roll bar mounting clamps and tighten the retaining bolts to the specified torque setting, then tighten the anti-roll bar-to-connecting link bolts to the specified torque.

10 Refit the front gearchange mechanism linkage mounting plate assembly retaining bolts and tighten them securely.

11 Apply a smear of grease to the gearchange control rod bush and refit the rear mounting rubber assembly. Tighten the mounting bolts to the specified torque setting and check that the gearchange mechanism operates smoothly. Refit the exhaust system to the front mounting rubbers.

12 Refit the roadwheels then lower the vehicle to the ground and tighten the roadwheel nuts to the specified torque.

8 Front anti-roll bar connecting link - removal and refitting

Removal

1 Chock the rear wheels, firmly apply the handbrake, jack up the front of the vehicle

8.2 Anti-roll bar connecting link

and support on axle stands. Remove the appropriate front roadwheel.

2 From underneath the vehicle, slacken and remove the bolt and washer securing the connecting link to the lower suspension arm **(see illustration)**.

3 Remove the nut and washer securing the connecting link to the anti-roll bar, then withdraw the bolt and remove the connecting link from under the vehicle.

4 Inspect the connecting link rubber mounting bushes for signs of damage and renew them if they are cracked, worn, split or perished. The bushes are a press fit in the connecting link and can be pressed out and in using a vice and two suitable sized tubular drifts, such as sockets (one bearing on the hard outer edge of the bush and another bearing against the edge of the connecting link).

Refitting

5 Refitting is the reverse of the removal sequence. Tighten both the connecting link bolts to the specified torque setting.

9 Front suspension tie bar - removal and refitting

Removal

1 Chock the rear wheels, firmly apply the handbrake, jack up the front of the vehicle and support on axle stands. Remove the appropriate front roadwheel.

2 From underneath the front of the vehicle, slacken and remove the three bolts securing the bumper flange to the body. Remove the seven bolts securing the front undercover panel to the body and remove the panel.

3 Undo the nut securing the front of the tie bar to the front subframe then remove the flanged washer and mounting bush, noting which direction the flange is facing **(see illustration)**.

4 Undo the two bolts securing the tie bar to the lower suspension arm, then remove the rod from the vehicle and slide the spacer,

9.3 Tie bar retaining nut is accessed from front of subframe

10

9.4 Tie bar-to-lower suspension arm bolts

9.5 Renew tie bar mounting bushes if damaged (arrowed)

9.6 Fit flange washer, spacer and mounting bush onto tie bar . . .

mounting bush and flanged washer off the tie bar **(see illustration)**.

5 Examine all the components for signs of wear or damage, paying particular attention to the mounting bushes and tie bar threads. Renew components as necessary **(see illustration)**.

Refitting

6 Slide the flange washer, mounting bush and spacer onto the tie bar threads. Ensure that the flange of the washer is facing away from the mounting bush and that the rounded surface of the bush is facing the washer **(see illustration)**.

7 Refit the tie bar to the front subframe and fit the second mounting bush and flanged washer. Ensure the flat surface of the mounting bush is facing the subframe and that the flange of the washer is facing away from the mounting bush, then refit the tie bar nut, tightening it finger tight **(see illustration)**.

8 Refit the tie bar-to-lower suspension arm bolts and tighten them to the specified torque, then tighten the tie bar retaining nut to the specified torque setting.

9 Refit the front undercover panel and tighten all the panel and bumper flange bolts securely.

10 Refit the roadwheel then lower the vehicle to the ground and tighten the roadwheel nuts to the specified torque.

10 Front suspension lower arm - removal, overhaul and refitting

Note: *The lower arm balljoint is an integral part of the lower arm assembly and is not available separately. If renewal of the balljoint is necessary, then the complete lower arm assembly must be renewed.*

Removal

1 Chock the rear wheels, firmly apply the handbrake, jack up the front of the vehicle and support on axle stands. Remove the appropriate front roadwheel.

2 Slacken and remove the bolt and washer securing the anti-roll bar connecting link to the lower suspension arm and undo the two bolts securing the tie bar to the lower suspension arm.

3 Extract the split pin and undo the nut securing the lower arm balljoint to the swivel hub. Release the balljoint shank by using a

9.7 . . . then refit tie bar to subframe and install second mounting bush and flange washer

suitable balljoint separator tool whilst taking care not to damage the balljoint gaiter.

4 Undo the lower suspension arm-to-body pivot bolt and withdraw the lower arm from the vehicle **(see illustrations)**.

Overhaul

5 Thoroughly clean the lower arm and the area around the arm mountings, removing all traces of dirt and underseal if necessary, then check carefully for cracks, distortion or any other signs of wear or damage. Check that the

10.4a Release balljoint from swivel hub assembly . . .

10.4b . . . then remove pivot bolt (arrowed) and withdraw lower suspension arm

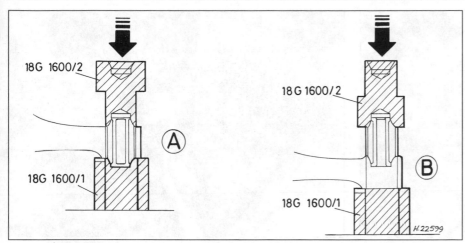

10.6 Using special Rover mandrels to renew lower suspension arm bush

A Removing old bush   B Fitting new bush

lower arm balljoint moves freely without any sign of roughness and that the balljoint gaiter shows no sign of deterioration and is free from cracks and splits. Examine the shank of the pivot bolt for signs of wear or scoring. Renew worn components, as necessary.

6 Check the lower arm inner pivot bush and renew it if worn, cracked, split or perished. Bush renewal is best left to a Rover dealer as a press, a special bush removal/refitting mandrel and a support are required (Rover Service Tool Numbers 18G 1600/2 and 18G 1600/1 respectively). While the old bush can be extracted using a strong bench vice and suitable sockets, it is unlikely that new bushes can be installed successfully without the shaped mandrel **(see illustration)**.

Refitting

7 Offer up the lower arm and fit the arm to body pivot bolt. Tighten the bolt by hand only at this stage.
8 Insert the lower arm balljoint shank into the swivel hub and tighten its retaining bolt to the specified torque. Secure the balljoint nut in position with a new split pin.
9 Refit the tie bar and anti-roll bar connecting link to lower arm bolts and tighten them to the specified torque.

10 Refit the roadwheel, then lower the vehicle to the ground and tighten the roadwheel nuts to the specified torque.
11 With the vehicle standing on its wheels, rock the suspension to settle the lower arm bush in position then tighten the lower arm-to-body pivot bolt to the specified torque setting.
12 Check and, if necessary, adjust front wheel alignment.

11 Rear hub and bearings - removal and refitting

Note: *The bearing is a sealed, pre-adjusted and pre-lubricated, double-row tapered-roller type and is intended to last the vehicle's entire service life without maintenance or attention. Never overtighten the hub nut beyond the specified torque wrench setting in an attempt to 'adjust' the bearings.*
Note: *The bearing is an integral part of the hub and can not be purchased separately. If renewal of the bearing is necessary, the complete hub assembly must be renewed as a unit. The only component which is available separately are roadwheel studs.*

Removal

1 Chock the front wheels, then jack up the rear of the vehicle and support it on axle stands. Remove the appropriate rear roadwheel.
2 Prise out the cap from the centre of the hub assembly and, using a hammer and suitable chisel nosed tool, tap up the staking securing the hub retaining nut to the groove in the stub axle **(see illustration)**.
3 Have an assistant firmly depress the footbrake then, using a socket and extension bar, slacken but do not remove the hub retaining nut.
4 Remove the brake drum or disc, as applicable.
5 Once the brake drum/disc has been removed, remove the hub nut and toothed washer and pull the hub assembly off the stub axle. If necessary, the hub can be drawn off the stub axle using a three-legged puller. Discard the nut, noting that a new hub retaining nut must be obtained for reassembly.
6 Check that there is no sign of free play in the hub bearing and that the bearing inner race rotates smoothly and easily without any sign of roughness. If there is any sign of wear or damage to the hub assembly or bearing, the complete hub assembly must be renewed as a unit.
7 Check the condition of the roadwheel studs in the hub flange. If any are sheared off, stretched or have damaged threads, they can be pressed out of the hub providing that its flange is fully supported. On refitting, support the hub flange and press in the new stud until it seats fully.

Refitting

8 Prior to refitting the hub, inspect the stub axle for signs of wear or scoring and, if necessary, renew it.
9 Apply a thin smear of grease to the hub bearing seal and refit the hub assembly. Refit the toothed washer, ensuring that its tooth locates with the groove in the stub axle. Install the new hub nut, tightening it by hand only **(see illustrations)**.
10 Refit the brake drum or disc (as applicable) but do not refit the roadwheel.

10

11.2 Prise off centre cap to gain access to rear hub nut

11.9a Refit the hub . . .

11.9b . . . and washer, ensuring its tooth engages with stub axle groove

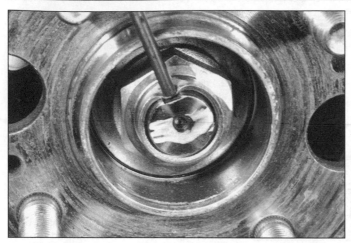

11.11 Stake hub retaining nut firmly into stub axle groove

12.2a Using 12 mm spanner to compress handbrake cable retaining tangs

11 Have an assistant firmly apply the footbrake, then tighten the hub retaining nut to the specified torque. Release the brake and check that the hub rotates smoothly then stake the hub retaining nut fully into the stub axle groove **(see illustration)**. Refit the hub centre cap.

12 Refit the roadwheel, then lower the vehicle to the ground and tighten the roadwheel nuts to the specified torque.

13 Check and, if necessary, adjust rear wheel alignment.

12 Rear stub axle - removal and refitting

Removal

1 Remove the rear hub assembly.

2 On models fitted with rear drum brakes, remove the lower brake shoe return spring, then disconnect the handbrake cable from the

trailing shoe. Undo the bolts securing the handbrake cable and brake hose brackets to the trailing arm, then use a 12 mm ring spanner to compress the handbrake cable retaining clip and withdraw the cable from the backplate. Remove the four bolts securing the backplate to the trailing arm and carefully ease the backplate assembly outwards and off the end of the stub axle **(see illustrations)**. Position the backplate assembly out of the way of the stub axle and tie it to the rear suspension unit coil spring using a piece of wire.

3 On models fitted with rear disc brakes, undo the four disc shield retaining bolts and remove the shield from the trailing arm.

4 On all models, using a socket and extension bar, undo the large stub axle retaining nut from the rear of the trailing arm assembly **(see illustration)**.

5 Slacken and remove the four Torx bolts securing the stub axle mounting plate to the trailing arm assembly, then withdraw the stub axle and remove it from the vehicle.

6 Examine the stub axle spindle and mounting plate for signs of wear or damage such as scoring or cracking. If damaged, the stub axle must be renewed.

Refitting

7 Refitting is a reverse of the removal procedure, tightening all nuts and bolts to the specified torque settings.

13 Rear suspension strut - removal and refitting

Removal

1 Chock the front wheels, then jack up the rear of the vehicle and support it on axle stands. Remove the appropriate rear roadwheel.

2 Slacken and remove both pivot bolts securing the rear lower lateral link to the body

12.2b Backplate retaining bolts (arrowed)

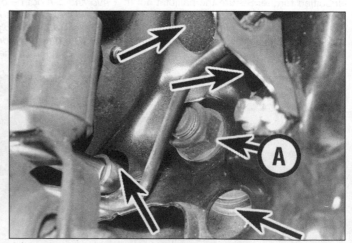

12.4 Stub axle retaining nut (A) - Torx bolts are accessed via four holes (arrowed)

1 Self-locking nut
2 Washer
3 Seal
4 Mounting rubber
5 Strut upper mounting nut
6 Upper mounting plate
7 Spacer
8 Mounting rubber
9 Rubber damper
10 Dust seal
11 Dust cover
12 Coil spring
13 Stop plate
14 Rubber stop
15 Strut
16 Strut lower mounting bolt
17 Strut lower mounting bush
18 Rear upper lateral link outer bush
19 Rear upper lateral link
20 Rear upper lateral link inner bush
21 Bolt - rear upper link to body
22 Pivot bolt - rear upper link to trailing arm
23 Front lateral link
24 Front lateral link bush
25 Trailing arm
26 Trailing arm mounting bush
27 Bolt - trailing arm to body
28 Pivot bolt - front link to trailing arm
29 Pivot bolt - rear lower link to trailing arm
30 Rear lower lateral link
31 Rear lower lateral link outer bush
32 Rear lower lateral link inner bush
33 Pivot bolt - rear lower link to body
34 Rear hub
35 Washer
36 Rear hub retaining nut
37 Hub cap

38 Brake drum
39 Drum retaining screw
40 Backplate assembly
41 Backplate mounting bolt
42 Disc retaining screw
43 Disc shield
44 Disc shield mounting bolt
45 Brake disc
46 Pivot bolt
47 Washer

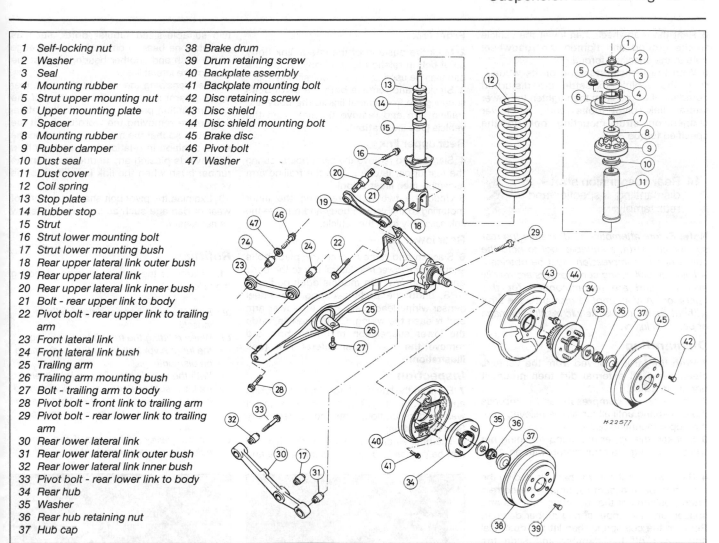

13.2 Rear suspension components

and trailing arm **(see illustration)**. On models equipped with ABS, undo the bolts securing the wheel sensor wiring load bracket to the lower arm and release the wiring. On all models, undo the lower suspension strut mounting bolt and remove the rear lower lateral link.

3 On 214 models, from inside the luggage compartment, prise off the trim cap to gain access to the rear suspension strut upper mounting nuts. On 414 models, remove the relevant luggage compartment side trim panel to gain access **(see illustration)**.

4 Remove the rubber cover and use chalk or a dab of paint to mark the relative positions of the suspension strut upper mounting and body. Undo the two suspension strut upper mounting nuts and manoeuvre the strut out from under the wheelarch, noting the seal fitted between the upper mounting plate and vehicle body **(see illustration)**.

Refitting

5 Prior to refitting, examine the rear lower lateral link mounting bushes and renew any which are worn or damaged.

6 Ensure the rubber seal is in position on the upper mounting plate then refit the suspension strut, aligning the marks made on removal (where necessary). Refit the upper mounting nuts. Tighten the nuts to the specified torque setting and refit the rubber cover and trim cap/panel.

13.3 Remove luggage compartment side trim to gain access to strut upper mounting nuts - 414 models

7 Offer up the lower lateral link and refit the lower suspension strut mounting bolt followed by both the lower lateral link pivot bolts. Tighten the bolts loosely. On models equipped with ABS, refit the wheel sensor wiring bracket retaining bolts and tighten them securely.

13.4 Removing rear suspension strut

10

8 Refit the roadwheel, then lower the vehicle to the ground and tighten the roadwheel nuts to the specified torque.
9 With the vehicle standing on its wheels, rock the vehicle to settle the disturbed components in position then tighten the lower lateral link pivot bolts and the lower suspension strut mounting bolt to the specified torque.

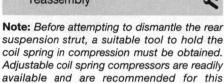

14 Rear suspension strut - dismantling, inspection and reassembly

Note: *Before attempting to dismantle the rear suspension strut, a suitable tool to hold the coil spring in compression must be obtained. Adjustable coil spring compressors are readily available and are recommended for this operation. Any attempt to dismantle the strut without such a tool is likely to result in damage or personal injury.*

Dismantling

1 With the strut removed from the vehicle, clean away all external dirt then mount it upright in a vice.
2 Fit the spring compressor and compress the coil spring until all tension is relieved from the upper mounting plate.
3 Slacken the upper mounting retaining nut whilst retaining the strut piston with an Allen key.
4 Remove the nut and washer followed by the mounting plate assembly, noting the correct fitted positions of the mounting rubbers and spacer, and the upper spring rubber damper. Remove the coil spring then lift the dust seal and cover off the damper and slide the damper stop plate and rubber stop off the strut piston.

Inspection

5 Examine all the rear suspension strut components, using the information given for the front suspension strut.

Reassembly

6 Reassembly is a reversal of the removal procedure. Ensure that the spring ends are correctly located in the upper and lower seats and that the upper mounting plate retaining nut is tightened to the specified torque setting.

15 Rear suspension lateral links - removal, inspection and refitting

Removal

1 Chock the front wheels, then jack up the rear of the vehicle and support it on axle stands. Remove the appropriate rear roadwheel.

Front link

2 Mark the position of the lateral link body pivot bolt in relation to the body. This mark can then be used as a guide on refitting.
3 Slacken and remove both the pivot bolts securing the front lateral link to the body and trailing arm and remove the link from the vehicle **(see illustration)**.

Rear upper link

4 Slacken and remove the pivot bolt securing the rear upper lateral link to the trailing arm assembly **(see illustration)**.
5 Undo the two bolts securing the inner mounting to the vehicle body and remove the link assembly from the vehicle.

Rear lower link

6 Slacken and remove both the pivot bolts securing the lower rear lateral link to the body and trailing arm. On models equipped with ABS, undo the bolts securing the wheel sensor wiring lead bracket to the lower arm and release the wiring. On all models, undo the lower suspension mounting bolt and remove the rear lower lateral link **(see illustration)**.

Inspection

7 Examine the lateral link for signs of cracking and check the mounting bushes for signs of wear or deterioration, renewing as necessary **(see illustration)**.
8 The bushes are a press fit in the link and can be pressed out and in using a vice and

two suitable-sized tubular drifts, such as sockets (one bearing on the hard outer edge of the bush and another bearing against the edge of the lateral link).
9 When renewing the inner bush on the rear upper lateral link, mark the position of the bush mounting plate in relation to the lateral link before removing the worn bush. Fit the new bush so that the mounting plate is in the same position in relation to the lateral link. This avoids placing any undue strain on the rubber bush when the link is refitted to the vehicle.
10 Examine the pivot bolt shanks for signs of wear or damage such as scoring and renew as necessary.

Refitting

11 Refitting is the reverse of removal, noting the following:

a) *Refit the pivot bolts and tighten them loosely.*
b) *When refitting the front lateral link, align the inner pivot bolt using the marks made on dismantling.*
c) *With the vehicle standing on its wheels, rock the suspension to settle all disturbed components in position then tighten all the disturbed pivot bolts to the specified torque.*
d) *On completion, check and, if necessary, adjust rear wheel alignment.*

15.3 Front lateral link to body mounting bolt (arrowed) is slotted to permit rear wheel alignment

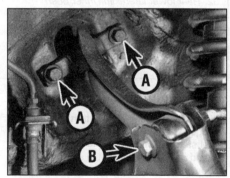

15.4 Rear upper lateral link to body bolts (A) and trailing arm pivot bolt (B)

15.6 Removing rear lower lateral link

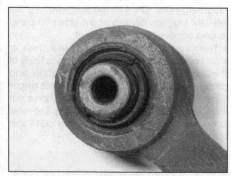

15.7 Examine lateral link bushes for signs of wear and renew if necessary

16.3 Remove retaining clip and free brake hose from trailing arm

16.8 Trailing arm mounting bolts (arrowed)

16 Rear suspension trailing arm - removal and refitting

Removal

1 Chock the front wheels then jack up the rear of the vehicle and support it on axle stands. Remove the appropriate rear roadwheel, then follow the procedure under the relevant sub heading.

Non-ABS models

2 Remove the rear hub assembly.
3 Undo the bolts and remove the clips securing the handbrake cable and brake hose brackets to the trailing arm (see illustration). Remove the four bolts securing the backplate to the trailing arm and carefully ease the backplate assembly outwards and off the end of the stub axle. Position the backplate out of the way of the stub axle and tie it to the rear suspension unit coil spring using a piece of wire.

ABS models

4 Remove the two brake caliper shield retaining screws and remove the shield from the caliper.
5 Slacken and remove the bolts securing the handbrake cable and brake hose retaining clamps to the trailing arm. Undo the two bolts securing the caliper mounting bracket to the trailing arm and slide the caliper off the disc. Tie the caliper to the rear suspension strut coil spring to avoid placing any strain on the hydraulic hose or handbrake cable.
6 Remove the ABS rear wheel sensor.

All models

7 Slacken and remove the three pivot bolts securing the front lateral link, rear lower lateral link and rear upper lateral link to the trailing arm.
8 Remove the two bolts securing the trailing arm mounting bracket to the vehicle body, then manoeuvre the trailing arm assembly out of position and away from the vehicle (see illustration).

9 Inspect the trailing arm for signs of damage such as cracks, paying particular to the areas around the mounting bolt holes, and examine the mounting bush for signs of damage and deterioration. If either the arm or bush show signs of wear or damage, the trailing arm and bush assembly must be renewed as a unit since neither component is available separately.

Refitting

10 Refitting is the reverse of removal, noting the following:

a) *Manoeuvre the trailing arm into position and tighten its mounting bolts to the specified torque.*
b) *Refit all the pivot bolts and tighten them only loosely.*
c) *On non-ABS models, tighten the backplate retaining bolts to the specified torque then refit the hub.*
d) *On ABS models, tighten the brake caliper mounting bracket bolts to the specified torque and refit the wheel sensor.*
e) *With the vehicle standing on its wheels, rock the suspension to settle all the suspension components in position then tighten all the disturbed pivot bolts to their specified torque setting.*
f) *On completion, check and, if necessary, adjust rear wheel alignment.*

18.2a Remove horn button from steering wheel . . .

17 Steering - inspection

Refer to Chapter 1.

18 Steering wheel - removal and refitting

Models without airbag (SRS)

Removal

1 Set the front wheels in the straight-ahead position. The steering wheel spokes should be horizontal.
2 Carefully prise out the horn button from the centre of the steering wheel. Disconnect the wires from the button terminals and remove the button (see illustrations).
3 Using a socket, unscrew and remove the steering wheel retaining nut.
4 Mark the steering wheel and steering column shaft in relation to each other then lift the steering wheel off the column splines. If it is tight, tap it up near the centre, using the palm of your hand, or twist it from side to side whilst pulling upwards to release it from the shaft splines.

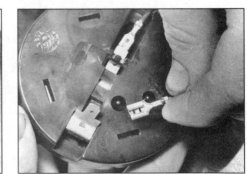

18.2b . . . and disconnect wiring from button terminals

10

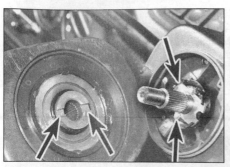

18.6a Ensure steering wheel cut-outs are correctly engaged with indicator cancelling cam tabs (arrowed) . . .

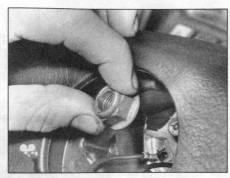

18.6b . . . then refit wheel retaining nut

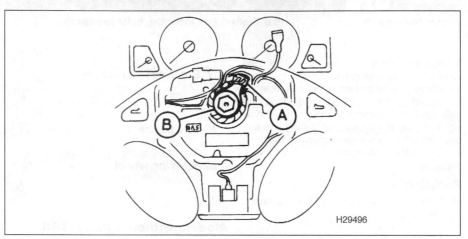

18.10 Detach SRS harness multiplug (A) from slip ring and unscrew steering wheel retaining nut (B)

Refitting

5 Before refitting, check that the steering column splines are clean.

6 Refit the wheel, entering the cut-outs on its lower surface with the direction indicator cancelling cam tabs and aligning the marks made on dismantling. This should leave the wheel positioned as described in paragraph 1 **(see illustrations)**.

7 Tighten the steering wheel nut to the specified torque wrench setting, then reconnect the horn wiring to the horn terminals and press the horn into position in the centre of the wheel.

Models with airbag (SRS)
Removal

8 Remove the ignition key and wait at least ten minutes to allow the SRS system backup circuit to fully discharge. Disconnect both battery leads, earth lead first, to avoid accidental detonation of the airbag.

9 Remove the airbag unit, see Chapter 12.

10 Detach the SRS harness multiplug from the slip ring **(see illustration)**.

11 Set the steering in the straight-ahead position and, using a socket, unscrew the steering wheel retaining nut until its top is flush with the end of the column shaft.

12 Mark the steering wheel and steering column shaft in relation to each other then lift the steering wheel off the column splines. If it is tight, tap it up near the centre, using the palm of your hand, to release it from the shaft splines.

13 Remove and discard the steering wheel retaining nut. A new self-locking nut must be obtained for reassembly.

14 Remove the steering wheel from the column.

Refitting

15 Refit the steering wheel by reversing the removal procedure, noting the following:

a) *Before refitting, check that the steering column splines are clean.*

b) *Enter the cut-outs on the lower surface of the wheel with the direction indicator cancelling cam tabs and align the marks made on dismantling. This should leave the wheel in the same position as before removal.*

c) *Take care to ensure that wiring is not trapped between mating surfaces.*

d) *Fit a new wheel retaining nut and tighten it to the specified torque wrench setting*

e) *Refit the airbag unit, carrying out the system check given in Chapter 12.*

f) *When reconnecting the battery leads, fit the negative lead last*

19 Steering column - removal and refitting

Models without airbag
Removal

1 Insert the key to ensure the steering column is unlocked, then release the column tilt lever and position the steering wheel at the lowest possible position. Remove the steering wheel.

2 Disconnect the battery negative terminal then undo the five right-hand lower facia panel retaining screws and remove the panel from the facia.

3 Prise the large snap-ring which secures the two halves of the steering column shroud together from the top of the shrouds and remove the ignition key. Undo the three screws securing the lower shroud to the steering column and remove both the upper and lower steering column shrouds **(see illustrations)**.

19.3a Prise off snap-ring . . .

19.3b . . . undo lower shroud retaining screws (arrowed) . . .

19.3c . . . and remove lower and upper shrouds

19.5 Combination switch assembly is retained by two screws (arrowed)

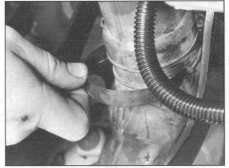

19.7a Remove retaining clips . . .

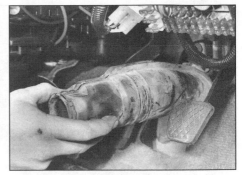

19.7b . . . and withdraw lower steering column cover

4 Lift the indicator cancelling cam off the steering column and disconnect the wiring connectors from the rear of the steering column combination switch assembly.

5 Undo the two combination switch retaining screws and slide the assembly off the end of the steering column (see illustration).

6 Trace the ignition switch wiring back to its wiring connectors and disconnect them from the main wiring loom.

7 Pull back the driver's footwell carpet and remove the two studs securing the lower column cover to the floor. Remove the two retaining clips from the upper end of the cover and withdraw the cover (see illustrations).

8 Using a hammer and punch, white paint or similar, mark the exact relationship between the steering column shaft and shaft-to-steering gear universal joint, then slacken and remove the pinch-bolt securing the joint to the column shaft.

9 Undo the nut and bolt securing the lower steering column mounting clamp in position and remove the clamp (see illustration). Slacken and remove the two nuts and bolts securing the upper mounting assembly to the vehicle then disengage the column from its mounting studs and universal joint then remove it from the vehicle.

Refitting

10 Before refitting the steering column, closely examine the upper mounting assembly for damage or misalignment.

11 Align the marks made on dismantling and engage the steering column shaft splines with those of the universal joint.

12 Locate the upper mounting bracket assembly over its mounting studs and refit the upper mounting nuts and bolts. Refit the lower mounting clamp and tighten its retaining nut and bolt to the specified torque setting, then tighten the upper mounting nuts and bolts to their specified torque settings.

13 Refit the universal joint to steering column pinch-bolt and tighten it to the specified torque. Refit the lower cover over the steering column and secure it in position with the retaining clips and studs.

14 Refit the combination switch to the column and tighten its screws securely. Refit the indicator cancelling cam to the steering column, ensuring that it is correctly located with the switch assembly, and reconnect the combination and ignition switch wiring connectors (see illustration). Ensure that the wiring is correctly routed and secured by any relevant clips.

15 Offer up the two halves of the steering column shroud and refit the three retaining screws to the lower shroud. Ensure the shroud halves are clipped firmly together, then refit the snap ring to its groove.

16 Refit the lower facia panel, tightening its retaining screws securely, then refit the steering wheel.

Models with airbag (SRS)
Removal

17 Remove the ignition key and wait at least ten minutes to allow the SRS system backup circuit to fully discharge. Disconnect both battery leads, earth lead first, to avoid accidental detonation of the airbag.

18 Set the steering in the straight-ahead position then lock the steering column in its lowest position.

19 Remove the airbag unit, see Chapter 12.

20 Remove the steering wheel.

21 Remove the steering column combination switch, see Chapter 12.

22 Disconnect the combination switch and ignition switch multiplugs, then release the cable tie securing the wiring harness to the steering column (see illustration).

23 Carry out the sequence given in paragraphs 7 to 9 inclusive.

Refitting

24 Carry out the sequence given in paragraphs 10 to 13 inclusive.

25 Reconnect the combination switch and ignition switch multiplugs, then secure the wiring harness to the steering column.

26 Refit the steering column combination switch, see Chapter 12.

27 Refit the steering wheel, then refit the airbag unit, see Chapter 12.

19.9 Steering column lower mounting clamp components

19.14 Ensure that indicator cancelling cam is correctly engaged with combination switch assembly

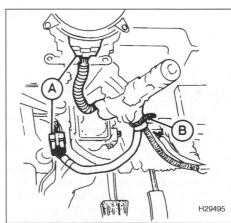

19.22 Disconnect switch multiplugs (A) then release cable tie (B)

10

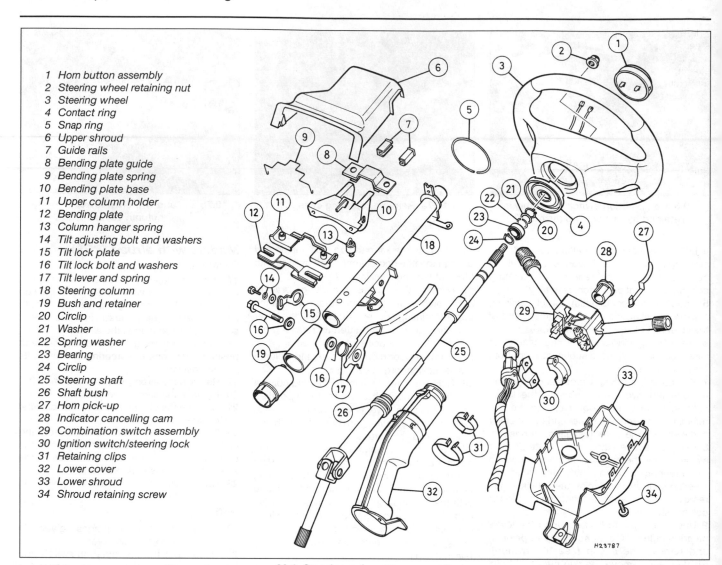

1 Horn button assembly
2 Steering wheel retaining nut
3 Steering wheel
4 Contact ring
5 Snap ring
6 Upper shroud
7 Guide rails
8 Bending plate guide
9 Bending plate spring
10 Bending plate base
11 Upper column holder
12 Bending plate
13 Column hanger spring
14 Tilt adjusting bolt and washers
15 Tilt lock plate
16 Tilt lock bolt and washers
17 Tilt lever and spring
18 Steering column
19 Bush and retainer
20 Circlip
21 Washer
22 Spring washer
23 Bearing
24 Circlip
25 Steering shaft
26 Shaft bush
27 Horn pick-up
28 Indicator cancelling cam
29 Combination switch assembly
30 Ignition switch/steering lock
31 Retaining clips
32 Lower cover
33 Lower shroud
34 Shroud retaining screw

H23787

20.1 Steering column components

20 Steering column - overhaul

1 With the steering column removed from the vehicle, fit the ignition key and check that the steering lock is off. Remove the circlip from the upper end of the column shaft and lift off the washer and spring washer **(see illustration)**.
2 Carefully withdraw the steering shaft from the lower end of the steering column. Note the inner circlip fitted to the shaft upper end.
3 Inspect the steering shaft for straightness and for signs of impact and damage to the collapsible portion. Check for signs of wear, such as scoring, on the shaft bush and check the steering shaft universal joint for signs of damage or roughness in the joint bearings. If any damage or wear is found on the steering shaft, shaft bush or universal joint, the shaft must be renewed as an assembly.

4 Inspect the steering column for signs of damage and renew if necessary. Closely examine the column upper mounting and tilt assembly for signs of damage or distortion, paying particular attention to the upper mounting bending plate and its spring retainer. The bending plate is designed to distort in the event of an impact hitting the steering wheel and must be renewed, along with its spring retainer, if it is not completely straight. Renew other components as necessary.
5 If renewal of any of the upper mounting or steering column tilt assembly components is necessary, make a note of the correct fitted positions of all components before dismantling the assembly. Use this as a guide when reassembling all the components to ensure they are correctly fitted. Ensure that the ends of the bending plate spring retainer are correctly located in the holes in the mounting bracket and the retainer is hooked over the claw situated in the centre of the bracket **(see illustration)**.

6 Apply a smear of grease to the steering shaft and column bearing surfaces and to the shaft bush. If a new steering shaft is being installed, transfer the inner circlip from the old shaft onto the second groove in the upper end of the new shaft.

20.5 Fitted positions of upper mounting assembly components

7 Insert the steering shaft into position in the steering column and refit the spring washer and flat washer to the upper end of the steering shaft, securing them in position with the circlip. Ensure that the circlip is correctly located in its groove and check that the shaft rotates freely in the column. Remove the ignition key and check that the steering lock functions correctly.

8 Before installing the column assembly, check the steering shaft-to-steering gear universal joint for signs of wear or damage and smoothness of operation. If there is any sign of roughness in the joint bearing, it must be renewed before refitting the steering column.

21 Steering lock/ignition switch - removal and refitting

 Warning: Before attempting removal of the ignition switch, read carefully the precautions listed in Chapter 12, appertaining to vehicles equipped with airbags (SRS).

Note: The steering lock/ignition switch is secured by two shear-head bolts. Although new bolts are supplied with replacement steering lock assemblies, always ensure that the bolts themselves are available before beginning work.

Removal

1 Remove the steering column.
2 Securely clamp the column assembly in a vice equipped with soft jaws, taking great care not to overtighten the vice and distort the steering column.
3 Centre-punch the two steering lock shear bolts then drill off the heads of the bolts. Note that new shear bolts must be obtained for refitting.
4 Withdraw the steering lock/ignition switch, then unscrew the remains of the shear bolts by using a self-locking wrench or similar on the exposed ends.

Refitting

5 On refitting, carefully align the assembly on the steering column, lightly tighten the bolts and check that the steering lock works smoothly.
6 Tighten the shear bolts evenly until their heads shear off.
7 Refit the steering column.

22 Steering gear rubber gaiters - renewal

1 Remove the track rod balljoint and unscrew the locknut from the track rod end **(see illustration)**.
2 Using a pair of pliers, release the outer steering gear gaiter retaining clip and slide it off the track rod end. Remove the inner gaiter retaining clip by cutting it, then slide the gaiter off the end of the track rod.
3 Thoroughly clean the track rod and the steering gear housing, using fine abrasive paper to polish off any corrosion, burrs or sharp edges which might damage the new gaiter's sealing lips on fitting. Repair kits which consist of new gaiters and retaining clips are available from Rover dealers.
4 Fit the new rubber gaiter, ensuring that it is correctly seated in the grooves in the steering gear housing and track rod.
5 Check that the gaiter is not twisted or dented then secure it in position using new retaining clips.
6 Refit the locknut and balljoint onto the track rod end.

23 Steering gear - removal, overhaul and refitting

Removal

1 Chock the rear wheels, firmly apply the handbrake, jack up the front of the vehicle and support on axle stands. Remove the appropriate front roadwheel.
2 Working inside the vehicle, peel back the driver's footwell carpet and remove the studs securing the lower steering column cover to the floor. Remove the two retaining clips from the upper end of the cover and withdraw the cover.
3 Mark the relative positions of the steering gear pinion and joint to use as a guide when refitting, then slacken and remove the two universal joint pinch-bolts **(see illustration)**. Slide the universal joint up the steering

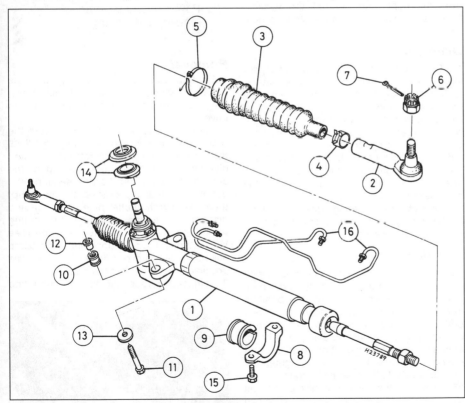

22.1 Steering gear components

1 Steering rack	8 Mounting clamp	13 Washer
2 Track rod balljoint	9 Mounting bush	14 Washers
3 Steering rack gaiter	10 Mounting bush	15 Steering rack mounting clamp bolt
4 Gaiter outer retaining clip	11 Steering rack mounting bolt	16 Power steering fluid pipes (where fitted)
5 Gaiter inner retaining clip	12 Spacer	
6 Balljoint retaining nut		
7 Split pin		

23.3 Steering column universal joint pinch-bolts (arrowed)

10

23.7 Gearchange linkage bellcrank mounting bolts (arrowed)

23.9 Power steering pipes and steering gear right-hand mounting bolts (arrowed)

column shaft splines until it is free from the steering gear pinion.

4 Extract the split pins and undo the nuts securing the steering gear track rod balljoints to the swivel hubs. Release the balljoint shanks by using a suitable balljoint separator tool whilst taking care not to damage the balljoint gaiters.

5 From underneath the vehicle, slacken and remove the bolt securing the rear engine/gearbox unit mounting connecting link to the subframe bracket, then remove the three subframe bracket retaining bolts and remove the bracket, releasing it from the exhaust mounting rubber. Undo the two bolts securing the connecting link and bracket assembly to the gearbox housing and remove the assembly from the vehicle.

6 Undo the three front exhaust pipe to manifold retaining nuts and, where necessary, the two bolts securing the front pipe mounting bracket to the vehicle. Release the intermediate exhaust section from its mountings and lower the front of the exhaust system.

7 In the absence of the special gearchange linkage balljoint separator (Rover service tool Number 18G 1592), use a suitable flat-bladed screwdriver to carefully lever the lower gearchange rod balljoint off the gearchange linkage bellcrank assembly. Remove the three bolts securing the assembly to the subframe **(see illustration)**.

8 Using a suitable stout bar, lever down on the rear of the engine/gearbox unit and insert a block of wood between the gearbox and subframe to hold it in position. This is necessary to gain the required clearance to remove the steering gear.

9 On models equipped with power-assisted steering, remove the bolt securing the feed and return pipe mounting bracket to the subframe. Mark the pipe union bolts to ensure they are correctly positioned on reassembly, then unscrew the pipe to steering gear union nuts **(see illustration)**. Be prepared for fluid spillage and position a suitable container beneath the pipes whilst unscrewing the union nuts. This fluid must be disposed of and new fluid of the specified type used when refilling. Plug the pipe ends and steering gear orifices to prevent excessive fluid

leakage and entry of dirt into the hydraulic system.

10 On all models, fully extend the left-hand track rod then undo the two left-hand steering gear mounting bolts and remove the mounting bracket. Undo the two right-hand mounting bolts, noting the mounting bushes and spacers, and free the steering gear pinion from its cutout.

11 Initially move the steering gear to the left, to free the right-hand track rod from the subframe, then manoeuvre the assembly out from the right-hand side of the vehicle. Remove the washers from the steering gear pinion.

Overhaul

12 Examine the steering gear assembly for signs of wear or damage and check that the rack moves freely throughout the full length of its travel with no signs of roughness or excessive free play between the steering gear pinion and rack. The steering gear is available only as a complete assembly with no individual components, the exception being the track rod balljoints and rubber gaiters. Therefore, if worn, the complete assembly must be renewed.

13 Inspect the steering gear mounting bushes for signs of damage or deterioration and renew as necessary.

Refitting

14 Refit the washers to the pinion and, with the left-hand track rod fully extended, manoeuvre the steering gear into position from the right-hand side of the vehicle. Once both the track rods are located in the subframe cutouts, refit the mounting clamp and bolts, ensuring that the mounting bushes and spacers are correctly positioned. Tighten the mounting bolts to the specified torque.

15 Centralise the steering gear rack so that both track rods are protruding by an equal distance.

16 On models equipped with power-assisted steering, wipe clean the feed and return pipe unions then refit them to their respective positions on the steering gear and tighten the union nuts to the specified torque. Refit the bolt securing the pipe retaining bracket to the subframe and tighten securely.

17 The remainder of the refitting procedure is direct reversal of removal, noting the following:
a) Tighten all nuts and bolts to the specified torque settings.
b) Secure the track rod balljoint retaining nuts in position with new split pins.
c) When refitting the universal joint to the steering gear pinion splines, ensure that the front wheels are pointing in the straight-ahead direction then, if necessary, align the marks made on dismantling and check that the steering wheel spokes are horizontal.
d) On completion, check and, if necessary, adjust front wheel alignment.
e) On models equipped with power-assisted steering, bleed the hydraulic system.

24 Power steering pump drivebelt - inspection and adjustment

Refer to Chapter 1.

25 Power steering pump - removal and refitting

Removal

1 Slacken, but do not remove, the three power steering pump pulley retaining bolts, then remove the power steering pump drivebelt.

2 Position a suitable container beneath the power steering pump to catch any spilt fluid, then slacken the inlet hose retaining clip and disconnect the hose from the top of the steering pump. Undo the bolt securing the outlet pipe retaining bracket to the pump, then unscrew the outlet pipe union nut and disconnect the pipe from the pump, noting the O-ring which is fitted to the union **(see illustrations)**. Plug the hose ends and pump unions to prevent excessive fluid loss and the possible entry of dirt into the system.

3 Remove the reservoir from its mounting

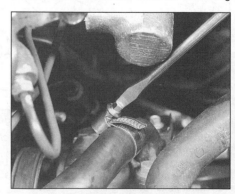

25.2a Slacken retaining clamp and disconnect inlet hose from pump

25.2b Remove outlet pipe bracket retaining bolt . . .

25.2c . . . and unscrew outlet pipe union nut from pump

25.3 Removing power steering fluid reservoir from retaining clamp

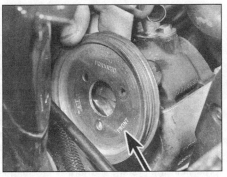

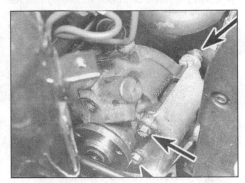

25.4a Remove pulley retaining bolts (arrowed) . . .

25.4b . . . and withdraw pulley. Note FRONT mark on pulley face (arrowed)

25.5a Unscrew power steering pump mounting bolts (three arrowed) . . .

bracket and position it clear of the pump assembly **(see illustration)**.

4 Unscrew the pump pulley retaining bolts and remove the pulley. Check that the front face of the pulley is marked FRONT and if not, mark it by using a dab of white paint. This mark can then be used to ensure that the pulley is correctly refitted **(see illustrations)**.

5 Undo the five bolts (three on the right-hand side of the pump, and two on the left) securing the power steering pump to the mounting bracket and remove the pump from the engine **(see illustrations)**.

6 The power steering pump is a sealed unit and cannot be repaired. If faulty the pump assembly must be renewed.

Refitting

7 Refitting is a reverse of the removal procedure, noting the following **(see illustration)**:

a) *Tighten the pump mounting bolts to the specified torque.*

b) *Fit a new O-ring to the pump outlet pipe union and tighten the union nut to the specified torque.*

c) *Ensure the pulley is correctly installed and lightly tighten its mounting bolts.*

d) *Refit and adjust the drivebelt, then tighten the pulley mounting bolts to the specified torque.*

e) *On completion, bleed the hydraulic system.*

26 Power steering oil cooler - removal and refitting

Removal

1 Remove the right-hand headlamp assembly.

2 Remove the bonnet lock.

3 Position a suitable container beneath the power steering oil cooler hose connections to catch any spilt fluid, then slacken the hose retaining clips and disconnect both hoses **(see illustration)**. Plug the hose and oil cooler ends to prevent excessive fluid loss and possible entry of dirt into the system.

25.5b . . . and remove pump

25.7 Always renew outlet pipe O-ring (arrowed)

26.3 Slacken clamps and disconnect hoses from power steering oil cooler

10

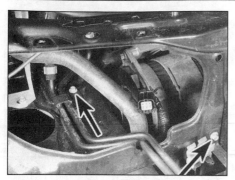

26.4a Power steering oil cooler upper mounting bolts (arrowed)

26.4b Oil cooler lower mounting bolt can be accessed via bumper grille

4 Undo the three oil cooler mounting bracket retaining bolts, then manoeuvre the oil cooler assembly out from between the front bumper and body (see illustrations).

Refitting

5 Refitting is the reverse of the removal procedure. On completion, bleed the system.

27 Power steering system - bleeding

Warning: Avoid holding the steering at full lock for long periods of time. Failure to do so could lead to overheating, and possible damage, of the power steering pump and steering gear.

1 Remove the cap from the power steering fluid reservoir and fill the reservoir with the specified fluid.
2 Disconnect the distributor wiring to prevent the engine from starting, then turn the engine over for approximately 5 seconds to prime the power steering pump.
3 Reconnect the distributor wiring, then check the reservoir fluid level is between the MAX and MIN level markings on the side of the reservoir, topping up if necessary.
4 Start the engine and allow it to idle for approximately 30 seconds with the front wheels

pointing in the straight-ahead position. After 30 seconds, turn the steering onto full lock in one direction, hold it there for a few seconds, then turn it onto full lock in the opposite direction and hold it there for a few seconds. Return the front wheels to the straight-ahead position. Repeat this procedure until air bubbles cease to appear in the fluid reservoir.
5 If, when turning the steering, an abnormal noise is heard from the fluid lines, it indicates that there is still air in the system. Check this by turning the wheels to the straight-ahead position and switching off the engine. If the fluid level in the reservoir rises, then air is present in the system and further bleeding is necessary.
6 Once all traces of air have been removed from the power steering hydraulic system, turn the engine off and allow the system to cool. Once cool, check that fluid level is up to the MAX mark on the power steering fluid reservoir. Top up if necessary.

28 Track rod balljoint - removal and refitting

Removal

1 Apply the handbrake, then jack up the front of the vehicle and support it on axle stands. Remove the appropriate front roadwheel.

2 If the balljoint is to be re-used, use a straight-edge and a scriber, or similar, to mark its relationship to the track rod.
3 Holding the balljoint, unscrew its locknut by one quarter of a turn.
4 Extract the split pin and undo the nut securing the steering gear track rod balljoint to the swivel hub. Release the balljoint shank by using a suitable balljoint separator tool whilst taking care not to damage the balljoint gaiter (see illustration).
5 Unscrew the balljoint from the track rod, counting the exact number of turns necessary to do so. If the locknut is to be removed, mark its position on the track rod and count the number of turns required to remove it so that it can be returned exactly to its original position on reassembly.
6 Carefully clean the balljoint and the threads. Renew the balljoint if its movement is sloppy or too stiff, if it is excessively worn, or if it is damaged in any way. Carefully check the stud taper and threads. No grease leakage should be visible.

Refitting

7 If necessary, screw the locknut onto the track rod by the number of turns noted on removal. This should align the locknut with the mark made on dismantling.
8 Screw the balljoint onto the track rod by the number of turns noted on removal. This should bring the balljoint to within a quarter of a turn from the locknut, with the alignment marks that were made (if applicable) on removal lined up.
9 Refit the balljoint shank to the swivel hub and tighten its retaining nut to the specified torque setting. Use a new split pin to secure the retaining nut in position (see illustration).
10 Refit the roadwheel, then lower the vehicle to the ground and tighten the roadwheel nuts to the specified torque setting.
11 Check and, if necessary, adjust front wheel alignment.

28.4 Using a universal balljoint separator to free track rod balljoint from swivel hub

28.9 Secure balljoint retaining nut in position with new split pin

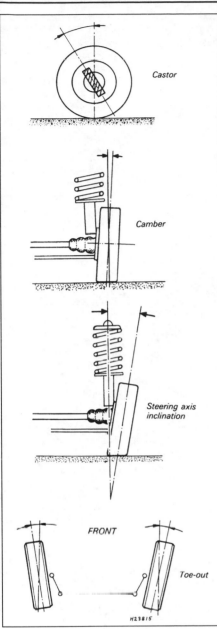

29.1 Wheel alignment and steering angles

29 Wheel alignment and steering angles

1 A vehicle's steering and suspension geometry is defined in five basic settings. All angles are expressed in degrees and the steering axis is defined as an imaginary line drawn through the centres of the front suspension upper and lower balljoints, extended where necessary to contact the ground **(see illustration)**.

Camber

2 Camber is the angle between each roadwheel and a vertical line drawn through its centre and tyre contact patch when viewed from the front or rear of the vehicle. Positive camber is when the roadwheels are tilted outwards from the vertical at the top. Negative camber is when they are tilted inwards.

3 Camber is not adjustable and given for reference only. While it can be checked using a camber checking gauge, If the figure obtained is significantly different from that specified, then the vehicle must be taken for careful checking by a professional, as the fault can only be caused by wear or damage to the body or suspension components.

Castor

4 Castor is the angle between the steering axis and a vertical line drawn through each roadwheel's centre and tyre contact patch when viewed from the side of the vehicle. Positive castor is when the steering axis is tilted so that it contacts the ground ahead of the vertical. Negative castor is when it contacts the ground behind the vertical.

5 Castor is not adjustable and is given for reference only. While it can be checked using a castor checking gauge, if the figure obtained is significantly different from that specified, then the vehicle must be taken for careful checking by a professional, as the fault can only be caused by wear or damage to the body or suspension components.

Steering axis inclination/SAI

6 Also known as kingpin inclination/KPI, this is the angle between the steering axis and a vertical line drawn through each roadwheel's centre and tyre contact patch when viewed from the front or rear of the vehicle.

7 SAI/KPI is not adjustable and is given for reference only.

Toe

8 Toe is the difference, viewed from above, between lines drawn through the roadwheel centres and the vehicle's centre-line. Toe-in is when the roadwheels point inwards, towards each other at the front. Toe-out is when they splay outwards from each other at the front.

9 At the front, toe setting is adjusted by screwing the track rods in or out of their balljoints to alter the effective length of the track rod assemblies.

10 At the rear, toe setting is adjusted by slackening the front lateral link-to-body pivot bolt and repositioning the bolt in its mounting slot, thereby altering the position of the trailing arm assembly.

Toe-out on turns

11 Also known as turning angles or Ackermann angles, this is the difference, viewed from above, between the angles of rotation of the inside and outside front roadwheels when they have been turned through a given angle.

12 Toe-out on turns is set in production and is not adjustable as such, but can be upset by altering the length of the track rods unequally. It is essential, therefore, to ensure that the track rod lengths are exactly the same and that they are turned by the same amount whenever the toe setting is altered.

Checking and adjustment

13 Due to the special measuring equipment necessary to check wheel alignment and the skill required to use it properly, checking and adjustment of the aforementioned settings is best left to a Rover dealer or similar expert. Note that most tyre-fitting shops now possess sophisticated checking equipment.

Notes

Chapter 11
Bodywork and fittings

Contents

Degrees of difficulty

Easy, suitable for novice with little experience	Fairly easy, suitable for beginner with some experience	Fairly difficult, suitable for competent DIY mechanic	Difficult, suitable for experienced DIY mechanic	Very difficult, suitable for expert DIY or professional

Specifications

Torque wrench settings	Nm	lbf ft
Front bumper mounting bolts	10	7
Rear bumper:		
Mounting nuts	22	16
Mounting bolt	10	7
Bonnet hinge mounting bolts	10	7
Bonnet lock mounting bolts	10	7
Bonnet release lever mounting bolts	10	7
Wheelarch liner screws	10	7
Door glass regulator and top slide bolts	6	4
Door glass-to-regulator bolts	6	4
Door glass channel nut and bolt	6	4
Door hinge bolts	24	18
Boot lid hinge bolts	10	7
Boot lid lock retaining bolts	10	7
Boot lid lock cylinder retaining bolt	10	7
Tailgate hinge nuts and bolts	10	7
Front seat slide mounting bolts	45	33
Rear seat hinge bolts:		
214 models	25	18
414 models	10	7
Seat belt fastenings:		
Mounting bolts - front and rear	32	24
Front belt upper mounting nut	25	18
Inertia reel upper mounting bolt	9	7
Inertia reel lower mounting bolt	32	24
Rear side belt guide retaining bolts	32	24
Seat belt pretensioners:		
Pretensioner to seat frame	20	15
Belt retainer to seat frame	30	22
Facia mounting bolts	9	7

1 General information and precautions

General information

The vehicle bodyshell is made of pressed-steel sections in three and five-door Hatchback and four-door Saloon versions. Most components are welded together but some use is made of structural adhesives. The front wings are bolted on.

The bonnet, door, tailgate and some other vulnerable panels are made of zinc-coated metal. Once assembled, the entire body is given an eight-stage pretreatment process including a high-pressure wash before painting. The first coat of primer is applied by cathodic electro-deposition, followed by four coats of paint and two of lacquer. An anti-stone chip coating (finished in matt black, where exposed) is applied to the outer faces of the sills and the corresponding surfaces of the front and rear wings. A PVC coating is applied to the underbody, followed by a coating of protective wax. All chassis members, box-sections and sills are injected with liquid cavity wax.

Several of the body cavities are filled with 'expand-in-place' foam. This process features a two-part liquid silicon foam and hardener mix which is injected into the cavities after the body has been painted and wax treated. The foam improves the noise insulation of the vehicle and is flame retardant. The foam is also hydrophobic, that is, it repels water.

Extensive use is made of plastic materials, mainly on the interior but also in exterior components such as the wheelarch liners to improve the body's resistance to corrosion.

Precautions

Airbag unit

When cleaning the interior of the vehicle, do not allow the airbag unit in the centre of the steering wheel to become flooded with detergents or water and do not clean with petrol or furniture cream and polishes. Clean the unit sparingly with a damp cloth and upholstery cleaner. Failure to observe these precautions may result in the airbag inflating, with the subsequent risk of personal injury.

Seat belt pretensioners

When removing or fitting a front seat which is equipped with a seat belt pretensioner, note the following:

a) *Once activated (after a serious frontal impact) both pretensioners must be renewed. Note that the seat belts will still function as restraints.*

b) *The red service key must be inserted into the pretensioner slot whenever the seat or pretensioner is removed.*

c) *The red service key must not be removed from the pretensioner slot until the seat is securely fitted in the vehicle. Failure to*

remove the key will prevent the pretensioner from activating.

d) *The pretensioner is a shock sensitive device and must be handled with extreme care.*

e) *Do not fit a pretensioner that has been dropped.*

f) *Do not attempt to dismantle a pretensioner. This will cause the unit to activate with the likelihood of personal injury.*

g) *Never carry a pretensioner by its cable or tube and always with both hands.*

h) *Never slide a seat with a pretensioner fitted across the floor or subject it to similar rough treatment.*

2 Vehicle exterior and interior - maintenance and inspection

Vehicle exterior

1 The general condition of a vehicle's bodywork is the one thing that significantly affects its value. Maintenance is easy but needs to be regular. Neglect, particularly after minor damage, can lead quickly to further deterioration and costly repair bills. It is important also to keep watch on those parts of the vehicle not immediately visible, for instance the underbody, inside all the wheelarches and the lower part of the engine compartment.

2 The basic maintenance routine for the bodywork is washing - preferably with a lot of water, from a hose. This will remove all the loose solids which may have stuck to the vehicle. It is important to flush these off in such a way as to prevent grit from scratching the finish. The wheelarches and underbody need washing in the same way to remove any accumulated mud which will retain moisture and tend to encourage rust, particularly in winter when it is essential that any salt (from that put down on the roads) is washed off. Paradoxically enough, the best time to clean the underbody and wheelarches is in wet weather when the mud is thoroughly wet and soft. In very wet weather the underbody is usually cleaned automatically of large accumulations; this is therefore a good time for inspection.

3 If the vehicle is very dirty, especially underneath or in the engine compartment, it is tempting to use one of the pressure washers or steam cleaners available on garage forecourts. Whilst these are quick and effective, especially for the removal of the accumulation of oily grime which sometimes is allowed to become thick in certain areas, their usage does have some disadvantages. If caked-on dirt is simply blasted off the paintwork, its finish soon becomes scratched and dull and the pressure can allow water to penetrate door and window seals and the lock mechanisms. If the full force of such a jet is

directed at the vehicle's underbody, the wax-based protective coating can easily be damaged and water (with whatever cleaning solvent is used) could be forced into crevices or components that it would not normally reach. Similarly, if such equipment is used to clean the engine compartment, water can be forced into the components of the fuel and electrical systems and the protective coating can be removed that is applied to many small components during manufacture; this may therefore actually promote corrosion (especially inside electrical connectors) and initiate engine problems or other electrical faults. Also, if the jet is pointed directly at any of the oil seals, water can be forced past the seal lips and into the engine or transmission. Great care is required, therefore, if such equipment is used and, in general, regular cleaning by such methods should be avoided.

4 A much better solution in the long term is just to flush away as much loose dirt as possible using a hose alone, even if this leaves the engine compartment looking dirty. If an oil leak has developed, or if any other accumulation of oil or grease is to be removed, there are one or two excellent grease solvents available, which can be brush applied. The dirt can then be simply hosed off. Take care to replace the wax-based protective coat, if this was affected by the solvent.

5 Normal washing of the bodywork is best carried out using cold or warm water with a proprietary car shampoo. Tar spots can be removed by using white spirit, followed by soapy water to remove all traces of spirit. Try to keep water out of the bonnet air intakes and check afterwards that the heater air inlet box drain tube is clear so that any water has drained out of the box.

6 After washing the paintwork, wipe off with a chamois leather to give an unspotted clear finish. A coat of clear protective wax polish will give added protection against chemical pollutants in the air. If the paintwork sheen has dulled or oxidised, use a cleaner/polisher combination to restore the brilliance of the shine. This requires a little effort, but such dulling is usually caused because regular washing has been neglected. Care needs to be taken with metallic paintwork, as special non-abrasive cleaner/polisher is required to avoid damage to the finish.

7 Brightwork should be treated in the same way as paintwork.

8 Windscreens and windows can be kept clear of the smeary film which often appears, by the use of proprietary glass cleaner. Never use any form of wax or other body or chromium polish on glass.

Vehicle interior

9 Mats and carpets should be brushed or vacuum cleaned regularly to keep them free of grit. If they are badly stained remove them from the vehicle for scrubbing or sponging and make quite sure they are dry before refitting.

10 Where leather upholstery is fitted it should be cleaned only if necessary, using either a mild soap (such as saddle soap) or a proprietary leather cleaner; do not use strong soaps, detergents or chemical cleaners. If the leather is very stained, seek the advice of a Rover dealer. Fabric-trimmed seats and interior trim panels can be kept clean by wiping with a damp cloth and a suitable cleaner. If they do become stained (which can be more apparent on light coloured upholstery) use a little liquid detergent and a soft nail brush to scour the grime out of the grain of the material. Do not forget to keep the headlining clean in the same way as the (fabric) upholstery.

11 When using liquid cleaners of any sort inside the vehicle, do not over-wet the surfaces being cleaned. Excessive damp could get into the seams and padded interior causing stains, offensive odours or even rot. If the inside of the vehicle gets wet accidentally it is worthwhile taking some trouble to dry it out properly, particularly where carpets are involved. Do not leave oil or electric heaters inside the vehicle for this purpose.

12 Do not allow the airbag unit in the centre of the steering wheel to become flooded with detergents or water and do not clean with petrol or furniture cream and polishes. Clean the unit sparingly with a damp cloth and upholstery cleaner. Failure to observe these precautions may result in the airbag inflating, with the subsequent risk of personal injury.

3 Minor body damage - repair

Repairs of minor scratches in bodywork

If the scratch is very superficial, and does not penetrate to the metal of the bodywork, repair is very simple. Lightly rub the area of the scratch with a paintwork renovator, or a very fine cutting paste, to remove loose paint from the scratch, and to clear the surrounding bodywork of wax polish. Rinse the area with clean water.

Apply touch-up paint to the scratch using a fine paint brush; continue to apply fine layers of paint until the surface of the paint in the scratch is level with the surrounding paintwork. Allow the new paint at least two weeks to harden, then blend it into the surrounding paintwork by rubbing the scratch area with a paintwork renovator or a very fine cutting paste. Finally, apply wax polish.

Where the scratch has penetrated right through to the metal of the bodywork, causing the metal to rust, a different repair technique is required. Remove any loose rust from the bottom of the scratch with a penknife, then apply rust-inhibiting paint to prevent the formation of rust in the future. Using a rubber or nylon applicator, fill the scratch with

bodystopper paste. If required, this paste can be mixed with cellulose thinners to provide a very thin paste which is ideal for filling narrow scratches. Before the stopper-paste in the scratch hardens, wrap a piece of smooth cotton rag around the top of a finger. Dip the finger in cellulose thinners, and quickly sweep it across the surface of the stopper-paste in the scratch; this will ensure that the surface of the stopper-paste is slightly hollowed. The scratch can now be painted over as described earlier in this Section.

Repairs of dents in bodywork

When deep denting of the vehicle's bodywork has taken place, the first task is to pull the dent out, until the affected bodywork almost attains its original shape. There is little point in trying to restore the original shape completely, as the metal in the damaged area will have stretched on impact, and cannot be reshaped fully to its original contour. It is better to bring the level of the dent up to a point which is about 3 mm below the level of the surrounding bodywork. In cases where the dent is very shallow anyway, it is not worth trying to pull it out at all. If the underside of the dent is accessible, it can be hammered out gently from behind, using a mallet with a wooden or plastic head. Whilst doing this, hold a suitable block of wood firmly against the outside of the panel, to absorb the impact from the hammer blows and thus prevent a large area of the bodywork from being "belled-out".

Should the dent be in a section of the bodywork which has a double skin, or some other factor making it inaccessible from behind, a different technique is called for. Drill several small holes through the metal inside the area - particularly in the deeper section. Then screw long self-tapping screws into the holes, just sufficiently for them to gain a good purchase in the metal. Now the dent can be pulled out by pulling on the protruding heads of the screws with a pair of pliers.

The next stage of the repair is the removal of the paint from the damaged area, and from an inch or so of the surrounding "sound" bodywork. This is accomplished most easily by using a wire brush or abrasive pad on a power drill, although it can be done just as effectively by hand, using sheets of abrasive paper. To complete the preparation for filling, score the surface of the bare metal with a screwdriver or the tang of a file, or alternatively drill small holes in the affected area. This will provide a really good "key" for the filler paste.

To complete the repair, see the Section on filling and respraying.

Repairs of rust holes or gashes in bodywork

Remove all paint from the affected area, and from an inch or so of the surrounding "sound" bodywork, using an abrasive pad or a wire brush on a power drill. If these are not

available, a few sheets of abrasive paper will do the job most effectively. With the paint removed, you will be able to judge the severity of the corrosion, and therefore decide whether to renew the whole panel (if this is possible) or to repair the affected area. New body panels are not as expensive as most people think, and it is often quicker and more satisfactory to fit a new panel than to attempt to repair large areas of corrosion.

Remove all fittings from the affected area, except those which will act as a guide to the original shape of the damaged bodywork (eg headlight shells etc). Then, using tin snips or a hacksaw blade, remove all loose metal and any other metal badly affected by corrosion. Hammer the edges of the hole inwards, in order to create a slight depression for the filler paste.

Wire-brush the affected area to remove the powdery rust from the surface of the remaining metal. Paint the affected area with rust-inhibiting paint, if the back of the rusted area is accessible, treat this also.

Before filling can take place, it will be necessary to block the hole in some way. This can be achieved by the use of aluminium or plastic mesh, or aluminium tape.

Aluminium or plastic mesh, or glass-fibre matting, is probably the best material to use for a large hole. Cut a piece to the approximate size and shape of the hole to be filled, then position it in the hole so that its edges are below the level of the surrounding bodywork. It can be retained in position by several blobs of filler paste around its periphery.

Aluminium tape should be used for small or very narrow holes. Pull a piece off the roll, trim it to the approximate size and shape required, then pull off the backing paper (if used) and stick the tape over the hole; it can be overlapped if the thickness of one piece is insufficient. Burnish down the edges of the tape with the handle of a screwdriver or similar, to ensure that the tape is securely attached to the metal underneath.

Bodywork repairs - filling and respraying

Before using this Section, see the Sections on dent, deep scratch, rust holes and gash repairs.

Many types of bodyfiller are available, but generally speaking, those proprietary kits which contain a tin of filler paste and a tube of resin hardener are best for this type of repair. A wide, flexible plastic or nylon applicator will be found invaluable for imparting a smooth and well-contoured finish to the surface of the filler.

Mix up a little filler on a clean piece of card or board - measure the hardener carefully (follow the maker's instructions on the pack), otherwise the filler will set too rapidly or too slowly. Using the applicator, apply the filler paste to the prepared area; draw the applicator across the surface of the filler to

11

achieve the correct contour and to level the surface. As soon as a contour that approximates to the correct one is achieved, stop working the paste - if you carry on too long, the paste will become sticky and begin to "pick-up" on the applicator. Continue to add thin layers of filler paste at 20-minute intervals, until the level of the filler is just proud of the surrounding bodywork.

Once the filler has hardened, the excess can be removed using a metal plane or file. From then on, progressively-finer grades of abrasive paper should be used, starting with a 40-grade production paper, and finishing with a 400-grade wet-and-dry paper. Always wrap the abrasive paper around a flat rubber, cork, or wooden block - otherwise the surface of the filler will not be completely flat. During the smoothing of the filler surface, the wet-and-dry paper should be periodically rinsed in water. This will ensure that a very smooth finish is imparted to the filler at the final stage.

At this stage, the "dent" should be surrounded by a ring of bare metal, which in turn should be encircled by the finely "feathered" edge of the good paintwork. Rinse the repair area with clean water, until all of the dust produced by the rubbing-down operation has gone.

Spray the whole area with a light coat of primer - this will show up any imperfections in the surface of the filler. Repair these imperfections with fresh filler paste or bodystopper, and once more smooth the surface with abrasive paper. Repeat this spray-and-repair procedure until you are satisfied that the surface of the filler, and the feathered edge of the paintwork, are perfect. Clean the repair area with clean water, and allow to dry fully.

If bodystopper is used, it can be mixed with cellulose thinners to form a really thin paste which is ideal for filling small holes.

The repair area is now ready for final spraying. Paint spraying must be carried out in a warm, dry, windless and dust-free atmosphere. This condition can be created artificially if you have access to a large indoor working area, but if you are forced to work in the open, you will have to pick your day very carefully. If you are working indoors, dousing the floor in the work area with water will help to settle the dust which would otherwise be in the atmosphere. If the repair area is confined to one body panel, mask off the surrounding panels; this will help to minimise the effects of a slight mis-match in paint colours. Bodywork fittings (eg chrome strips, door handles etc) will also need to be masked off. Use genuine masking tape, and several thicknesses of newspaper, for the masking operations.

Before commencing to spray, agitate the aerosol can thoroughly, then spray a test area (an old tin, or similar) until the technique is mastered. Cover the repair area with a thick coat of primer; the thickness should be built up using several thin layers of paint, rather than one thick one. Using 400-grade wet-and-dry paper, rub down the surface of the primer until it is really smooth. While doing this, the work area should be thoroughly doused with water, and the wet-and-dry paper periodically rinsed in water. Allow to dry before spraying on more paint.

Spray on the top coat, again building up the thickness by using several thin layers of paint. Start spraying at one edge of the repair area, and then, using a side-to-side motion, work until the whole repair area and about 2 inches of the surrounding original paintwork is covered. Remove all masking material 10 to 15 minutes after spraying on the final coat of paint.

Allow the new paint at least two weeks to harden, then, using a paintwork renovator, or a very fine cutting paste, blend the edges of the paint into the existing paintwork. Finally, apply wax polish.

Plastic components

With the use of more and more plastic body components by the vehicle manufacturers (eg bumpers, spoilers, and in some cases major body panels), rectification of more serious damage to such items has become a matter of either entrusting repair work to a specialist in this field, or renewing complete components. Repair of such damage by the DIY owner is not really feasible, owing to the cost of the equipment and materials required for effecting such repairs. The basic technique involves making a groove along the line of the crack in the plastic, using a rotary burr in a power drill. The damaged part is then welded back together, using a hot-air gun to heat up and fuse a plastic filler rod into the groove. Any excess plastic is then removed, and the area rubbed down to a smooth finish. It is important that a filler rod of the correct plastic is used, as body components can be made of a variety of different types (eg polycarbonate, ABS, polypropylene).

Damage of a less serious nature (abrasions, minor cracks etc) can be repaired by the DIY owner using a two-part epoxy filler repair material. Once mixed in equal proportions, this is used in similar fashion to the bodywork filler used on metal panels. The filler is usually cured in twenty to thirty minutes, ready for sanding and painting.

If the owner is renewing a complete component himself, or if he has repaired it with epoxy filler, he will be left with the problem of finding a suitable paint for finishing which is compatible with the type of plastic used. At one time, the use of a universal paint was not possible, owing to the complex range of plastics encountered in body component applications. Standard paints, generally speaking, will not bond to plastic or rubber satisfactorily. However, it is now possible to obtain a plastic body parts finishing kit which consists of a pre-primer treatment, a primer and coloured top coat. Full instructions are normally supplied with a kit, but basically, the method of use is to first apply the pre-primer to the component concerned, and allow it to dry for up to 30 minutes. Then the primer is applied, and left to dry for about an hour before finally applying the special-coloured top coat. The result is a correctly-coloured component, where the paint will flex with the plastic or rubber, a property that standard paint does not normally possess.

4 Major body damage - repair

Note: *Where serious damage has occurred to a vehicle, any repair is best left to a professional or a Rover agent with specialist equipment.*

Where serious damage has occurred, or large areas need renewal due to neglect, it means that complete new panels will need welding in. This is best left to professionals. If the damage is due to impact, it will also be necessary to check completely the alignment of the bodyshell. This can only be carried out accurately by a Rover dealer using special jigs. If the body is left misaligned, it is primarily dangerous as the vehicle will not handle properly and secondly, uneven stresses will be imposed on the steering, suspension and possibly transmission, causing abnormal wear or complete failure, particularly to items such as the tyres.

5 Body exterior trim panels - renewal

1 The exterior body and door trim strips are held in position with a special adhesive tape. Removal requires the trim to be heated, to soften the adhesive, and then cut away from the door surface. Due to the high risk of damage to the vehicles paintwork during this operation, it is recommended that work is entrusted to a Rover dealer.

6 Hinges, latches and locks - lubrication

Refer to Chapter 1.

7 Bumpers - removal and refitting

Front
Removal

1 Firmly apply the handbrake then jack up the front of the vehicle and support it on axle stands.

7.4 Front bumper mounting plate-to-bracket bolts

7.16 Remove rubber grommet to gain access to bumper mounting nut

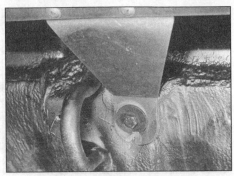

7.17 Rear bumper centre mounting bracket-to-body bolt - 414 models

2 Remove the headlamps.
3 Remove the four screws securing the bumper to the right-hand wheelarch liner, then undo the three screws securing the top of the liner to the body and prise out the screw retaining plugs. Free the right-hand wheelarch liner from the front bumper and repeat the complete procedure for the left-hand wheelarch.
4 Undo the three bolts securing the bumper to the front undercover panel, followed by the four bolts securing the bumper mounting plates to the body mounting brackets **(see illustration)**.
5 Release both the left and right-hand bumper slides from their retaining studs and pull the bumper fowards, away from the vehicle.
6 If necessary, the bumper mounting plates, trim strip and number plate can be removed from the bumper and the bumper mountings can be unbolted from the vehicle. Renew the components as necessary and/or transfer them to the new bumper.

Refitting

7 Refitting is a reverse of the removal sequence. Ensure that the bumper mounting bolts are tighten to the specified torque.

Rear

Removal - 214 models

8 Chock the front wheels then jack up the rear of the vehicle and support it on axle stands.
9 From underneath the vehicle, undo the four screws securing the undercover panel to the left-hand side of the bumper and remove the panel.
10 Remove the screw securing the left-hand wheelarch liner to the body, then the screw securing the right-hand wheelarch liner to the bumper.
11 Undo the bolt, situated next to the towing hook, securing the underside of the bumper to the vehicle.
12 Open the tailgate and from inside the luggage compartment, prise out the two circular grommets to gain access to the bumper mounting nuts, then undo both nuts and remove the flat washers.
13 Release both the left and right-hand bumper slides from their mountings and pull the bumper

rearwards, away from the vehicle. Note the sealing washer and two flat washers which are fitted to each of the bumper mounting studs.
14 If a new bumper is being fitted, transfer the trim strip and mounting stud washers.

Removal - 414 models

15 Chock the front wheels then jack up the rear of the vehicle and support it on axle stands.
16 Open the boot lid and, from inside the luggage compartment, prise out the two circular grommets to gain access to the bumper mounting nuts, then undo both nuts and remove the flat washers **(see illustration)**.
17 From underneath the vehicle, slacken and remove the two nuts and washers securing the bumper mounting brackets to the body, then undo the bolt securing the bumper centre mounting bracket to the body **(see illustration)**.
18 Remove the screw securing the left-hand wheelarch liner to the wheelarch.
19 Release both the left and right-hand bumper slides from their mountings and pull the bumper rearwards, away from the vehicle. Note the sealing washers which are fitted to each of the bumper mounting studs.
20 If necessary, the bumper mounting brackets and trim strip can be removed from the bumper and either renewed or transferred to a new bumper.

Refitting

21 Refitting is a reverse of the removal sequence. Ensure that the bumper mounting

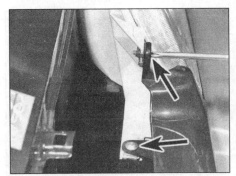

8.1 Radiator grille left-hand retaining screws (arrowed)

nuts and bolts are tightened to their specified torque settings.

8 Radiator grille - removal and refitting

Removal

1 Open the bonnet. Remove the four screws securing the radiator grille to the headlamp assemblies and remove the grille from the vehicle **(see illustration)**.

Refitting

2 Fit the grille into position between the headlamps and tighten its retaining screws securely.

9 Bonnet - removal, refitting and adjustment

Removal

1 Open the bonnet and have an assistant support it. Mark the outline of each bonnet hinge to use as a guide when refitting.
2 Disconnect the windscreen washer supply pipe from the T-piece, then undo the bonnet retaining bolts and, with the help of an assistant, carefully lift the bonnet clear. Note any shims which may be fitted between the bonnet and hinge **(see illustrations)**. Store the bonnet out of the way in a safe place.

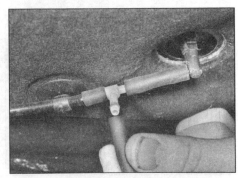

9.2a Disconnect washer supply pipe . . .

9.2b . . . and remove bonnet

9.3 Bonnet retaining bolts

Refitting and adjustment

3 Offer up the bonnet to the vehicle, position the shims (where fitted) between the bonnet and hinges, then loosely fit the retaining bolts (see illustration). Align the hinges with the marks made on removal (where applicable) then tighten the retaining bolts securely and reconnect the windscreen washer supply pipe.
4 Close the bonnet and check for alignment with the adjacent panels. If necessary, slacken the hinge bolts and realign the bonnet to suit. Once the bonnet is correctly aligned, tighten the hinge bolts to the specified torque.
5 Check that the bonnet height is correct with that of the front wings and, if necessary, adjust by altering the height of the bonnet rubber stops.

10.2 Mudflap retaining screws (arrowed)

6 Once the bonnet is correctly aligned, check that the bonnet fastens and releases in a satisfactory manner. If adjustment is necessary, remove the plastic lock cover then slacken the bonnet lock retaining bolts and adjust the position of the lock to suit. Once the lock is operating correctly, tighten its retaining bolts to the specified torque and refit the lock cover.

10 Bonnet release cable - removal and refitting

Removal

1 With the bonnet open, carefully prise off the plastic lock cover, then disconnect the cable inner from the lock operating mechanism and release the cable outer from the lock bracket.
2 Undo the three screws securing the right-hand mudflap to the wheelarch and remove the mudflap (see illustration).
3 Remove the four screws securing the right-hand wheelarch liner to the front bumper, then undo the six screws securing the liner to the wheel arch and prise out the screw retaining plugs. Manoeuvre the liner out from under the wheelarch (see illustration).
4 Release the cable from its retaining clips in the engine compartment and under the right-hand wing. Pull the cable through from under the right wheelarch (see illustration).
5 From inside the vehicle, undo the two bolts

securing the bonnet release lever to the vehicle then release the cable sealing grommet from under the facia panel. Pull the cable through from inside the vehicle and remove it from the vehicle.

Refitting

6 Feed the cable through from inside the vehicle until the bonnet release lever is in position. Tighten the lever mounting bolts to the specified torque and refit the sealing grommet.
7 From under the right-hand wheelarch, feed the cable through into the engine compartment then fit the cable to the two retaining clips situated under the wheelarch.
8 Ensure the cable is correctly routed around the engine compartment and retained by all the necessary retaining clips, then connect the cable to the bonnet lock.
9 Refit the right-hand wheelarch liner and press the six screw retaining plugs back into position. Refit the retaining screws and the liner to bumper screws and tighten all screws to the specified torque. Refit the mudflap.
10 Check that the bonnet fastens and releases in a satisfactory manner. If adjustment is necessary, slacken the bonnet lock retaining bolts and adjust the position of the lock to suit. Once the lock is operating correctly, tighten its retaining bolts to the specified torque and refit the lock cover.

11 Bonnet lock - removal, refitting and adjustment

Removal

1 Remove the radiator grille.
2 Carefully prise off the plastic cover from the lock then mark the outline of the bonnet lock on the body to use as a guide when refitting (see illustration).
3 Slacken and remove the three bonnet lock retaining bolts then withdraw the lock and disconnect the cable inner from the lock operating mechanism. Release the cable

10.3 Remove right-hand wheelarch liner . . .

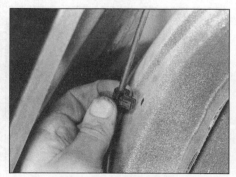

10.4 . . . and release cable retaining clips from wheelarch

11.2 Remove plastic bonnet lock cover . . .

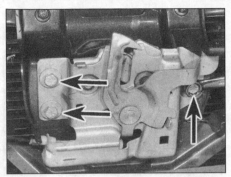

11.3a ... and undo three retaining bolts (arrowed) ...

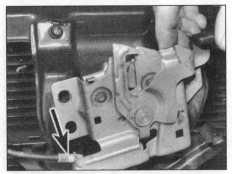

11.3b ... then remove lock and disconnect release cable (arrowed)

outer from the lock bracket and remove the lock from the vehicle (see illustrations).

Refitting and adjustment

4 Refit the release cable to the lock operating mechanism then align the lock with the marks made on removal and tighten the lock retaining bolts to the specified torque.

5 Check that the bonnet fastens and releases in a satisfactory manner. If adjustment is necessary, slacken the bonnet lock retaining bolts and adjust the position of the lock to suit. Once the lock is operating correctly, tighten its retaining bolts to the specified torque and refit the lock cover and radiator grille.

12 Door lock, lock cylinder and handles - removal and refitting

Removal

Front door lock

1 Remove the front door window glass then the lock cylinder, see paragraph 15.

2 Position the window sealing strip clear of the lock assembly and, where necessary, release the wiring retaining clips from the door panel.

3 Remove the three screws securing the interior handle to the door panel and free the operating rod from the retaining clips (see illustration).

4 Undo the two bolts securing the exterior handle to the door then remove the three door lock retaining screws (see illustration).

5 Partially withdraw the lock and handle assembly, then disconnect the interior and exterior handle connecting rods from the lock and remove both handles from the door. Disconnect the inner lock button operating rod from the lock and remove the button.

6 Disconnect the wiring connector from the central locking motor (where fitted) and manoeuvre the lock assembly out of the door.

Rear door lock

7 Remove the rear door window glass.

8 Remove the screw securing the inner lock button pivot to the door panel then release the button operating rod from its retaining clips. Disconnect the operating rod from the lock assembly and remove the inner button assembly from the door.

9 Free the interior handle operating rod from its retaining clips and disconnect the rod from the lock.

10 Undo the two bolts securing the exterior handle to the door then remove the three door lock retaining screws.

11 Partially withdraw the lock assembly, then disconnect the exterior handle operating rod and remove the exterior handle and lock assembly from the door.

Front door lock cylinder

12 Ensure the window glass is fully up then remove the door inner trim panel.

13 Where necessary, disconnect the wiring connectors from the central locking (left-hand door) or electric window (right-hand door) control unit, then undo the unit retaining screws and remove it from the door panel. Disconnect the wiring from the central locking motor and release any relevant retaining clips from the door panel.

14 Undo the two armrest support bracket retaining screws then remove the bracket and carefully peel back the polythene watershield to gain access to the lock components.

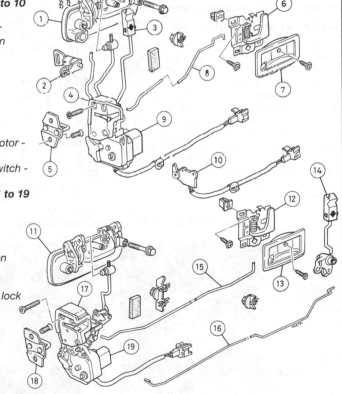

Front door - items 1 to 10
1 Exterior handle
2 Door lock cylinder
3 Interior lock button
4 Lock assembly
5 Lock striker
6 Interior handle
7 Interior handle escutcheon
8 Link rod - interior handle to lock
9 Central locking motor - passenger door *
10 Central locking switch - drivers door *

Rear door - items 11 to 19
11 Exterior handle
12 Interior handle
13 Interior handle escutcheon
14 Interior lock button
15 Link rod - interior handle to lock
16 Link rod - interior lock button to lock
17 Lock assembly
18 Lock striker
19 Central locking motor *
* Not fitted to all models

12.3 Door lock and handle components

12.4 Door lock retaining screws (Torx type)

11

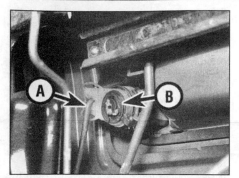

12.15 Front door lock cylinder operating rod (A) and circlip (B)

12.17 Interior handle retaining screws (arrowed)

12.19 Exterior handle retaining bolts (arrowed)

15 Disconnect the operating rod from the lock cylinder retaining clip then remove the circlip and withdraw the cylinder from the door **(see illustration)**.

Interior handle

16 Remove the inner trim panel.
17 Undo the screws securing the interior handle to the door, then disconnect the handle from its operating rod and remove it from the vehicle **(see illustration)**.

Exterior handle

18 Remove the inner trim panel and carefully peel back the polythene watershield to gain access to the exterior handle retaining bolts.
19 Disconnect the operating rod from the handle, then undo the two retaining bolts and remove the handle from the door **(see illustration)**.

Refitting

20 Refitting is the reverse of the removal sequence, noting the following:
a) *Ensure that all operating rods are securely held in position by the retaining clips.*
b) *Apply grease to all lock and operating rod pivot points.*
c) *Before fitting the inner trim panel, thoroughly check the operation of all the door lock handles and, where necessary, the central locking system. Ensure that the polythene watershield is securely stuck to the door.*

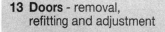

13 Doors - removal, refitting and adjustment

Note: *If there is insufficient slack in the wiring to be able to withdraw the wiring connectors from the door panel, then it will be necessary to remove the inner trim panel and peel back the polythene watershield to gain further access.*

Removal

1 Open the door and peel back the wiring gaiter, or displace the wiring grommet from the front edge of the door panel. Carefully withdraw the wiring from the door until the wiring connector(s) emerge. Disconnect the

block connector(s) and tape the door side of the connectors to the door frame to prevent them falling back into the door panel.
2 Mark the outline position of each door hinge to use as a guide when refitting.
3 Remove the retaining clip and extract the pin securing the door check link to the door pillar.
4 Have an assistant support the door and undo the nuts which secure the upper and lower hinges to the door, then remove the door from the vehicle.
5 If necessary, the hinges can now be unbolted and removed from the door pillar, having first marked the position of the hinge on the pillar. To gain access to the front door hinge bolts, it will first be necessary to remove the wheelarch liner **(see illustration)**.

Refitting and adjustment

6 The door is refitted by a reverse of the removal procedure. Align the hinges with the marks made on removal and tighten the bolts to the specified torque.
7 On completion, shut the door and check that the door is correctly aligned with all surrounding bodywork with an equal clearance all around. If necessary, adjustment can be made by slackening the hinge bolts and moving the door. Once the door is positioned correctly, tighten the hinge bolts to the specified torque.
8 With the door correctly aligned, check that it closes easily, is flush with the adjacent panels and does not rattle when closed. If not,

13.5 Remove wheel archliner to gain access to front door hinge retaining bolts (arrowed)

slacken the door striker retaining screws and reposition the striker. Once door operation is satisfactory, tighten the striker retaining screws securely.

14 Door inner trim panel - removal and refitting

Removal

1 Open the door and carefully prise out and remove either the mirror inner trim panel (front door) or window inner trim panel (rear door).
2 Undo the door inner handle escutcheon retaining screw and remove the escutcheon **(see illustrations)**.

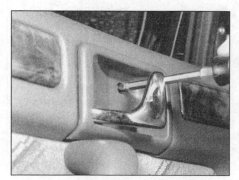

14.2a Undo retaining screw . . .

14.2b . . . and remove inner door handle escutcheon

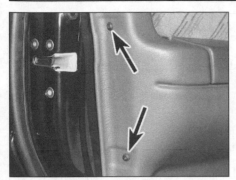

14.4a Front door trim panel retaining screws (arrowed)

14.4b Removing front armrest retaining screw

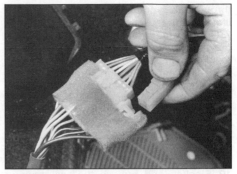

14.5 Disconnect wiring connectors as trim panel is removed - electrically-operated windows

3 On models equipped with manually-operated windows, remove the window regulator handle horseshoe clip **(see illustration 14.6)** by hooking it out with a screwdriver or bent piece of wire, then pull the handle off the spindle and remove the regulator escutcheon.

4 Remove the screws securing the inner trim panel and armrest to the door. Note that on certain models, the armrest mounting screws may be hidden behind trim caps **(see illustrations)**.

5 Release the door trim panel studs by carefully levering between the panel and door with a suitable flat-bladed screwdriver. With all the studs released, lift the panel upwards and away from the door. Note that on models with electrically-operated windows, it will be necessary to disconnect the switch wiring connector(s) as the panel is removed **(see illustration)**.

Refitting

6 Refitting the trim panel is the reverse of removal, noting the following **(see illustration)**:

a) *Check the trim panel retaining studs for breakage and renew as necessary.*

b) *When refitting the window regulator handle (where fitted), fit the clip to the handle first then push the handle onto the regulator spindle.*

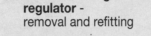

15 Door window glass and regulator - removal and refitting

Removal

Front door window glass and regulator

1 Remove the front door inner trim panel.

2 Undo the four screws securing the speaker to the door then withdraw the speaker and disconnect its wiring connectors.

3 Undo the two armrest support bracket retaining screws and remove the bracket from the door **(see illustration)**.

4 On models equipped with electrically-operated windows, temporarily connect the window switch wiring connector(s) and position the glass so that access can be gained to both glass retaining bolts via the cutaway in the door panel. If work is being carried out on the right-hand door, unplug the wiring connectors from the window control unit then undo the control unit mounting screws and remove the unit from the door panel **(see illustration)**. Release any relevant wiring retaining clips from the door.

5 On models equipped with central locking,

14.6 Fit horseshoe clip (arrowed) to handle before refitting handle to regulator

disconnect the wiring connectors from the door lock motor unit and release the wiring retaining clips from the door panel. If work is being carried out on the left-hand door, unplug the wiring connectors from the central locking control unit then undo the control unit mounting screws and remove the unit from the door panel **(see illustration)**.

6 On models equipped with manually-operated windows, temporarily refit the regulator handle and position the glass so that its retaining bolts can be accessed

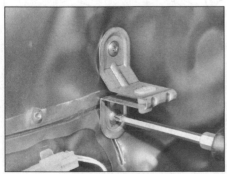

15.3 Armrest support bracket is retained by two screws

15.4 Control unit for electrically-operated windows must be removed when working on right-hand door

15.5 Central locking control unit must be removed when working on left-hand door

11

through the cutaway in the door (see illustration).

7 On all models, carefully peel back the polythene watershield to gain access to the regulator components (see illustration).

8 Slacken and remove the bolt securing the front glass channel to the door then carefully disengage the channel from the window glass.

9 Undo the two bolts securing the window glass to the regulator then lift up the glass and manoeuvre it out of the door (see illustration).

10 Slacken and remove the six regulator assembly retaining bolts and manoeuvre the assembly out through the door panel cutaway.

Rear door window glass and regulator

11 Remove the rear door inner trim panel.

12 Where necessary, disconnect the wiring from the central locking motor and free any relevant wiring clips from the door panel.

13 Temporarily refit the regulator handle or reconnect the switch wiring connector (as applicable) and position the window glass so the retaining bolts can be accessed through the cutaway in the door panel (see illustration).

14 Undo the two arm rest support bracket retaining screws then remove the bracket from the door and carefully peel back the polythene watershield.

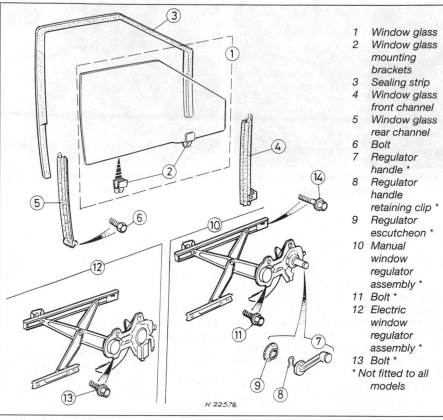

1 Window glass
2 Window glass mounting brackets
3 Sealing strip
4 Window glass front channel
5 Window glass rear channel
6 Bolt
7 Regulator handle *
8 Regulator handle retaining clip *
9 Regulator escutcheon *
10 Manual window regulator assembly *
11 Bolt *
12 Electric window regulator assembly *
13 Bolt *
* Not fitted to all models

15.6 Front door window glass and regulator components

15.7 Carefully peel back polythene watershield to gain access to regulator components

15.9 Undo window-to-regulator retaining bolts

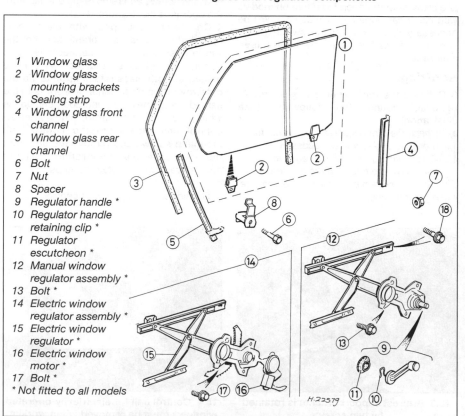

1 Window glass
2 Window glass mounting brackets
3 Sealing strip
4 Window glass front channel
5 Window glass rear channel
6 Bolt
7 Nut
8 Spacer
9 Regulator handle *
10 Regulator handle retaining clip *
11 Regulator escutcheon *
12 Manual window regulator assembly *
13 Bolt *
14 Electric window regulator assembly *
15 Electric window regulator *
16 Electric window motor *
17 Bolt *
* Not fitted to all models

15.13 Rear door window glass and regulator components

15 Undo the window outer rear trim panel retaining screw and remove the panel from the door.

16 Remove the screw securing the outer window sealing strip to the rear of the door then carefully prise the strip out of the door panel and remove it from the vehicle.

17 Slacken and remove the bolt securing the lower end of the rear window glass channel to the door panel and recover the spacer, through which the bolt passes, from inside the door panel. Undo the nut securing the channel to the door then release the rear channel from the window glass and rubber sealing strip and remove it from the door.

18 Undo the two bolts securing the window glass to the regulator then lift up the glass and manoeuvre it out of the door.

19 Slacken and remove the six regulator assembly retaining bolts and manoeuvre the assembly out through the door panel cutaway.

Refitting

Front door window glass and regulator

20 Refit the regulator to the door panel and lightly tighten its retaining bolts. Operate the regulator mechanism, either using the handle or by connecting the switch, to align the top slide then tighten the retaining bolts to the specified torque.

21 Install the window glass and tighten the glass to regulator bolts to the specified torque.

22 Refit the front glass channel, ensuring that it is correctly located in position, then tighten its retaining bolt lightly. Operate the regulator mechanism a few times to align the channel with the window glass, checking that the window travels up and down smoothly, then tighten the channel bolt to the specified torque.

23 Refit the polythene watershield to the door ensuring that it is securely stuck down around the edges. The remainder of refitting is a reversal of the removal procedure.

Rear door window glass and regulator

24 Refit the regulator and glass as described in paragraphs 20 and 21.

16.2a Removing mirror glass - electrically-operated mirrors

25 Relocate the rear window glass channel with the rubber sealing strip and window glass, then refit its retaining nut. Position the spacer inside the door panel then refit the channel lower bolt, ensuring it passes through the spacer, then tighten both the channel retaining nut and bolt lightly. Operate the regulator mechanism a few times to align the channel with the window glass, checking that the window travels up and down smoothly, then tighten the channel retaining nut and bolt to the specified torque setting.

26 Refit the polythene watershield to the door ensuring that it is securely stuck down around the edges. The remainder of refitting is a reversal of the removal procedure.

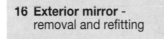

16 Exterior mirror - removal and refitting

Removal

Mirror glass

1 On models equipped with manually-operated mirrors, heat the mirror glass with a hairdryer to soften the adhesive used to stick the glass to its mounting plate. Once warm, the mirror glass can be levered out of position.

2 On models equipped with electrically-operated mirrors, position the mirror so that

16.2b Disconnect wiring connectors (arrowed) and remove mirror glass - electrically-operated mirrors

access can be gained to the rear of the outer edge of the glass. Using a piece of welding rod or other suitable wire, bend the end of the rod into a hook. Locate the hook with the spring clip on the rear of the mirror glass and pull the clip outwards to release the mirror **(see illustration)**. Disconnect the wiring from the mirror heating element and remove the glass from the vehicle **(see illustration)**.

Mirror assembly

3 Carefully prise the mirror inner trim panel from the door **(see illustration)**.

4 Disconnect the mirror wiring connector (where necessary) then slacken and remove the three screws and mounting plate securing the mirror to the door and remove the mirror assembly **(see illustrations)**.

Refitting

Mirror glass

5 On models equipped with manually-operated mirrors, first ensure that all traces of old adhesive are removed from the mounting plate. Remove the backing from the new mirror, then press the glass firmly into place and adjust to the required position.

6 On models equipped with electrically-operated mirrors, connect the wiring connectors to the heating element terminals then align the mirror spring clip with the motor mounting point. Press the mirror glass firmly onto the motor and check that it is securely

16.3 Remove mirror inner trim panel . . .

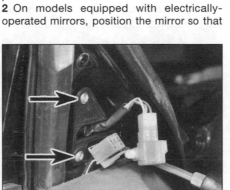

16.4a . . . disconnect wiring connector then undo mirror retaining screws (remaining two arrowed) . . .

16.4b . . . and remove mirror assembly from door

retained by the spring clip, then adjust the mirror to the required position.

Mirror assembly

7 Refitting is a reverse of the removal procedure.

17 Boot lid - removal, refitting and adjustment

Removal

1 Open the boot lid then disconnect the release cable outer from the lock bracket and release the cable inner from the lock operating mechanism.
2 Disconnect the wiring connectors from the boot lid lock warning lamp switch.
3 Remove the access cover from the left-hand side of the boot lid and free the release cable from all its retaining clips and ties on the boot lid and hinge. Tie a piece of string to the end of the cable then withdraw the cable from the boot lid. Untie the string from the cable end and leave it in position in the boot lid. The string can then be used when refitting to draw the cable into position.
4 Remove the right-hand access cover from the boot lid and repeat the operation described in paragraph 3 for the warning lamp wiring, again leaving the string in position in the boot lid.
5 Mark the outline of each hinge on the boot lid.
6 With the aid of an assistant, undo the four hinge retaining bolts and lift the boot lid away from the vehicle.

Refitting and adjustment

7 Offer up the boot lid, aligning the hinges with the marks made on dismantling. Fit and tighten the hinge bolts securely. Tie the left-hand piece of string to the boot release cable and use the string to draw the cable through the boot lid, then repeat the procedure using the right-hand piece of string to draw the warning lamp switch wiring through the lid, then untie both pieces of string. If a new

boot lid is being installed, it will be necessary to centralise the boot lid on its hinges then feed the release cable and wiring through the boot lid.
8 Connect the release cable inner to the lock operating mechanism and refit the cable outer to its position on the lock. Secure the release cable to the boot lid hinge using the necessary retaining clips.
9 Connect the warning connectors to the boot lock warning lamp switch and secure the wiring to the right-hand hinge, using all the necessary retaining clips.
10 Refit both the left- and right-hand access covers to the boot lid.
11 Close the boot lid then check that is correctly aligned with all surrounding bodywork, with an equal clearance all around. If necessary, adjustment can be made by slackening the hinge bolts and repositioning the boot lid. Once correctly positioned, tighten the hinge bolts to the specified torque.
12 Once the boot lid is correctly aligned, ensure that it closes without slamming and is securely retained. If not, slacken the boot lid striker retaining bolts and reposition the striker. Once boot lid operation is satisfactory, tighten the striker retaining bolts securely.

18 Boot lid lock and lock cylinder - removal and refitting

Removal

Boot lid lock

1 Open the boot lid and disconnect the release cable outer from the lock bracket, then release the cable inner from the lock operating mechanism.
2 Disconnect the wiring connectors from the boot lid lock warning lamp switch **(see illustration)**.
3 Carefully prise off the boot lid lock cover then undo the three bolts securing the lock to the boot lid.
4 Partially withdraw the lock, then disconnect the lock cylinder operating rod from the rear

of the assembly and remove the lock from the vehicle.
5 If necessary, remove the right-hand access cover from the boot lid, then disconnect the operating rod from the lock cylinder and remove it from the vehicle.

Boot lid lock cylinder

6 Open the boot lid and remove the right-hand access cover.
7 Detach the operating rod from the lock cylinder and remove the bolt securing the cylinder to the boot lid **(see illustration)**.
8 Manoeuvre the lock cylinder out of the boot lid. Remove the lock cylinder gasket and discard it. A new gasket should be used on refitting.

Refitting

Boot lid lock

9 Refitting is a reversal of the removal sequence. Tighten the lock retaining bolts to the specified torque. On completion, check that the boot lid closes without slamming and is securely retained when shut. If not, slacken the boot lid striker retaining bolts and reposition the striker. Once boot lid operation is satisfactory, tighten the striker retaining bolts securely.

Boot lid lock cylinder

10 Refitting is a reverse of the removal procedure. Ensure that a new gasket is fitted to the cylinder and the cylinder retaining bolt is tightened to the specified torque.

19 Boot lid/tailgate and fuel filler flap release cables - removal and refitting

Removal

1 Remove the driver's seat and rear seats.
2 Undo the right-hand front sill finisher and carpet retainer screws, then remove the sill finisher and carpet retainer from the vehicle **(see illustration)**.
3 Remove the boot lid/tailgate and fuel filler release lever handles, then lift the flap situated

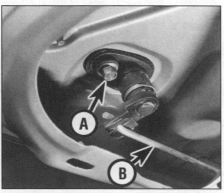

18.2 Boot lid lock release cable (A), warning lamp wiring connectors (B) and retaining bolts (C)

18.7 Boot lid lock cylinder retaining bolt (A) and operating rod (B)

19.2 Removing right-hand sill finisher

19.3a Remove release lever handles . . .

19.3b . . . then undo lever cover retaining screw

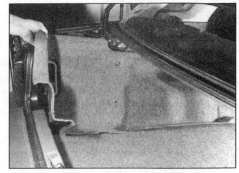

19.8 Removing left-hand luggage compartment trim panel - 414 models

on the top of the release lever cover to gain access to the retaining screw. Undo the screw and lift off the release lever cover (see illustrations).

4 On four and five-door models, open the right-hand rear door and undo the two screws securing the sill finisher to the floor, then remove the sill finisher and carpet retainer. Carefully prise out the lower trim panels from the centre and rear door pillars.

5 On three-door models, remove the four screws securing the right-hand lower rear seat side trim panel to the luggage compartment carpet, then carefully peel the front door sealing strip away from the door pillar so that the front edge of the trim panel is freed. The panel can then be released by carefully prising it away from the body, using a large flat-bladed screwdriver to release its retaining clips.

6 On all models, remove the cap from the driver's seat belt lower anchorage bolt then undo the bolt and free the belt from the floor. Release the trim clips securing the carpet to the floor and peel back the carpet to gain access to the release cables.

7 Open the boot lid/tailgate, prise out the screw caps (where necessary) and undo the screws securing the luggage compartment rear inner trim panel in position. Remove the panel from the vehicle. Release any relevant retaining clips and remove the luggage compartment carpet.

8 Closely examine the luggage compartment left-hand side trim panel and remove any relevant retaining screws. Carefully prise the panel away from the body and remove it from the luggage compartment (see illustration).

Boot lid/tailgate release cable

9 On 414 models, release the cable outer from the boot lid lock bracket then release the cable inner from the lock/striker operating mechanism. Remove the left-hand access cover from the boot lid and the release cable from all its retaining clips and ties on the boot lid and hinge. Tie a piece of string to the end of the cable then withdraw the cable from the boot lid. Untie the string from the cable end and leave it in position in the boot lid. The string can then be used when refitting to draw the cable into position.

10 On 214 models, undo the tailgate striker retaining screws then withdraw the striker and detach the release cable.

11 On all models, release the cable from all the retaining clips in the luggage compartment then, from inside, pull the cable through into the vehicle. Work back along the length of the cable and free it from any retaining clips. Disconnect the cable outer from the release lever mounting bracket then detach the cable inner from the lever and withdraw the cable from the vehicle (see illustration).

Fuel filler release cable

12 Detach the fuel filler release cable from the left-hand side of the luggage

compartment (see illustration). The cable can then be removed as described in paragraph 11.

Refitting

13 Refitting is a reversal of the removal procedure, noting the following:
a) Ensure the cable is correctly routed and retained by any relevant clips, then check the release lever operates satisfactorily before proceeding further.
b) Where possible, renew any broken trim panel retaining clips.
c) Ensure all carpets and trim panels are properly located and securely retained by all necessary clips and screws.
d) Tighten the lower seat belt anchorage bolt to the specified torque setting.

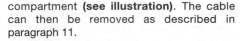

20 Tailgate - removal, refitting and adjustment

Removal

1 Open the tailgate and undo the two screws securing the tailgate inner trim panel to the tailgate, then carefully prise out the screw retaining plugs.

2 Using a large flat-bladed screwdriver, work around the outside of the trim panel and carefully prise it away from the tailgate to free all the retaining clips. Once all the retaining clips have been freed, remove the trim panel.

3 Disconnect the two wiring block connectors, situated on the right-hand side of the tailgate, which connect the tailgate electrical components to the main wiring loom. Tie a piece of string around the wiring side of the block connector, then displace the grommet from the upper right-hand corner of the tailgate and withdraw the wiring. Once free, untie the string from the end of the wiring and leave it in place in the tailgate. The string can then be used to draw the wiring back into position when refitting.

4 Disconnect the washer hose from the tailgate grommet.

5 Mark the positions of the hinges on the tailgate.

19.11 Detach relevant cable from release lever and withdraw from vehicle
A Fuel filler release cable
B Boot lid release cable

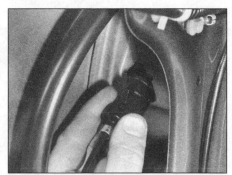

19.12 Disconnecting fuel filler release cable - 414 models

11

6 Have an assistant support the tailgate then raise the spring clips and pull the support struts off their balljoint mountings on the tailgate. Undo the four hinge retaining bolts and remove the tailgate from the vehicle, noting any shims which may be fitted between the hinge and tailgate.

Refitting and adjustment

7 Offer up the tailgate, positioning any shims necessary between the hinge and tailgate. Refit the hinge bolts. Press the support struts firmly onto the balljoint mountings and clip the spring clips back into position. Align the hinges with the marks made on removal, or centralise the hinges, and tighten the retaining bolts to the specified torque.

8 Tie the string around the end of the tailgate wiring and draw the wiring back into position. Untie the string, then reconnect the wiring connectors and relocate the grommet in the tailgate.

9 Renew any broken retaining clips, then refit the inner trim panel to the tailgate. Ensure the panel is securely clipped in position then refit the screw retaining plug and tighten the screws securely. Reconnect the washer hose to the tailgate grommet.

10 On completion, shut the tailgate and check that it is correctly aligned with the surrounding bodywork. If adjustment is necessary, slacken the hinge bolts and reposition the tailgate as necessary. Once alignment is correct, tighten the hinge bolts to the specified torque.

11 If correct alignment is not possible by repositioning the tailgate, it will be necessary to alter the hinge-to-body position. To do this, peel away the tailgate sealing strip from the top edge of the body and carefully prise the top of the right and left-hand tailgate pillar trim panels until the headlining can be peeled back sufficiently to gain access to the hinge retaining nuts. Slacken the hinge nuts and reposition the tailgate noting that, as a guide, Rover state there should be a gap of approximately 7 mm along the top edge of the tailgate. Once correctly positioned, tighten the retaining nuts to the specified torque then relocate the headlining, trim panels and tailgate sealing strip.

12 Adjust the height of the tailgate by screwing the rubber stop in or out, as necessary, then check that the tailgate closes easily and does not rattle when closed. If adjustment is necessary, slacken the tailgate striker retaining screws and reposition the striker as necessary. Once tailgate operation is satisfactory, tighten the striker retaining bolts securely.

21 Tailgate support strut - removal and refitting

Removal

1 Support the tailgate in the open position by using a stout piece of wood, or with the help of an assistant.

2 Raise the spring clip and pull the support strut off its balljoint mounting on the tailgate (see illustration). Repeat the procedure for the strut-to-body mounting and remove the strut from the vehicle.

Refitting

3 Refitting is the reverse sequence of removal. Ensure that the strut is pressed firmly onto each of its balljoints and the spring clips are correctly positioned.

22 Tailgate lock and lock cylinder - removal and refitting

Removal

Tailgate lock

1 Open the tailgate and undo the two screws securing the tailgate inner trim panel to the tailgate, then carefully prise out the screw retaining plugs (see illustration).

2 Using a large flat-bladed screwdriver, work around the outside of the trim panel and carefully prise it away from the tailgate to free all the retaining clips. Once all the clips have been freed, remove the trim panel.

3 Disconnect the operating rod from the lock and then remove the plastic cover from outside of the lock (see illustration). Mark the position of the lock assembly on the tailgate.

4 Undo all the tailgate lock retaining bolts and remove the lock assembly from the vehicle.

Tailgate lock cylinder

5 Open the tailgate and remove the right-hand access panel from the tailgate trim.

6 Disconnect the operating rod from the lock cylinder, then undo the retaining bolt and remove the cylinder from the tailgate.

Refitting

Tailgate lock

7 Refitting is a reverse of the removal sequence. Align the lock with the marks made on dismantling.

8 On completion, check that the tailgate closes easily and does not rattle when closed. If adjustment is necessary, slacken the tailgate striker retaining screws and reposition the striker as necessary (see illustration). Once tailgate operation is satisfactory, tighten the striker retaining bolts securely.

Tailgate lock cylinder

8 Refitting is a reverse of the removal procedure.

21.2 Raising tailgate support strut spring clip to release mounting

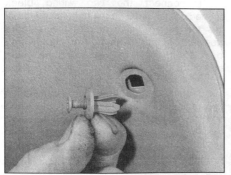

22.1 Tailgate inner trim panel retaining screw and plug

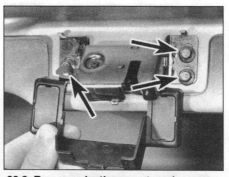

22.3 Remove plastic cover to gain access to tailgate lock retaining bolts (arrowed)

22.8 Tailgate striker retaining screws (Torx type)

23 Quarterlight glass (3-door Hatchback) - removal and refitting

Removal

1 Remove the rear window parcel shelf, then fold the rear seat cushion fully forwards and remove the rear seat back. Remove the rubber seal from the rear seat back retaining catch.

2 Remove the four screws securing the rear seat side trim panel to the luggage compartment carpet and carefully peel the front door sealing strip away from the door pillar, so that the front edge of the trim panel is freed. The panel can then be released by carefully prising it away from the body and using a large flat-bladed screwdriver to release the retaining clips.

3 Remove the single retaining screw securing the rear quarterlight trim panel in position, then carefully prise the panel away from the body and remove it from the vehicle.

4 Remove the seat belt upper mounting cover then undo the retaining nut and remove the seat belt from its mounting point.

5 Undo the upper door pillar trim panel retaining screw and peel the door sealing strip away from the front edge of the panel. Release all the panel retaining clips and remove it from the vehicle.

6 Mark the position of the quarterlight rear catch on the body, then remove the three hinge retaining screws.

7 Support the window glass then undo the front hinge retaining screws and remove the glass from the vehicle.

8 Examine the window seal for signs of damage or deterioration and renew if necessary. To renew the seal, first undo the two nuts securing the door pillar trim panel in position and remove the panel. The old seal can then be removed and the new seal installed. With the seal correctly positioned, refit the trim panel and tighten its retaining screws securely.

Refitting

9 Refitting is a reverse of the removal sequence, noting the following:

a) Align the rear window catch with the marks made on dismantling and lightly tighten the retaining screws.

b) Close the window and check that it is correctly aligned with the surrounding bodywork. Adjust, if necessary, by repositioning the hinge, then tighten all the hinge retaining screws securely.

c) Where possible, renew any broken trim panel retaining clips.

d) Tighten the seat belt upper mounting nut to the specified torque.

e) On completion, ensure all trim panels are securely retained and the door sealing strip is correctly located on the pillar.

24 Windscreen, fixed rear quarterlight and tailgate/rear window glass

1 These areas of glass are secured by the tight fit of the weatherstrip in the body aperture. Although they are not fixed by the direct-bonding method used on many modern vehicles, removal and refitting of these areas of fixed glass is still difficult, messy and time-consuming for the inexperienced. It is also difficult, unless one has plenty of practice, to obtain a secure, waterproof fit. Furthermore, the task carries a high risk of breakage. This applies especially to the laminated glass windscreen. In view of this, owners are strongly advised to have this sort of work carried out by one of the many specialist windscreen fitters.

25 Sunroof - repair

1 A sunroof is available as an option on all models, both electrically-operated and manually-operated sunroofs being available. Due to the complexity of the sunroof mechanism, considerable expertise is needed to repair or replace sunroof components successfully. Removal of the sunroof requires the headlining to be removed, which is a complex and tedious operation and not a task

to be undertaken lightly. Any problems with the sunroof should therefore be referred to a Rover dealer.

2 On models equipped with an electrically-operated sunroof, if the sunroof motor fails to operate, first check the relevant fuse. If the fault cannot be traced and rectified, then the sunroof can be opened and closed manually by using a suitable torx wrench or Allen key. Use a coin to unscrew the circular access cover in the panel in the headlining, situated between the sun visors, and insert the wrench into the drive spindle. Rotate the key to move the sunroof to the required position. A suitable wrench is supplied with the vehicle and should be in the luggage compartment where it is stowed next to the wheel trim remover.

26 Seats - removal and refitting

Note: *Before attempting any work on a model with pretensioners, read carefully the precautions listed at the beginning of this Chapter.*

Removal

Front seats - without pretensioners

1 Slide the seat fully backwards, then slacken and remove the two Torx bolts securing the front of the seat slides to the floor **(see illustration)**.

2 Slide the seat fully forwards, then undo the two Torx bolts securing the rear of the seat slides to the floor and remove the seat from the vehicle.

Front seats - with pretensioners

3 Slide the seat fully backwards, then slacken and remove the two Torx bolts securing the front of the seat slides to the floor.

4 Slide the seat fully forwards and remove the seat belt pretensioner cover retaining screw **(see illustration)**. Remove the pretensioner cover.

5 Remove the red service key from the end of the pretensioner and insert it into the pretensioner slot, pushing it firmly into position **(see illustration)**. Note that the

26.1 Front seat slides are secured to floor by Torx bolts

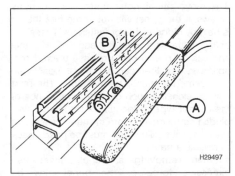

26.4 Seat belt pretensioner cover (A) and retaining screw (B)

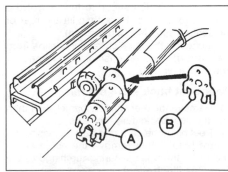

26.5 Remove service key from end of pretensioner (A) and insert into pretensioner slot (B)

11

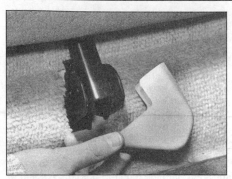

26.7 Remove seat cushion hinge covers to gain access to retaining bolts - 214 models

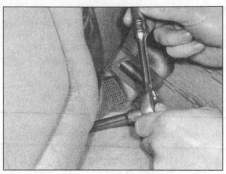

26.8 Removing rear seat cushion retaining bolt - 414 models

26.11 Rear seat back centre hinge retaining bolts - 214 models

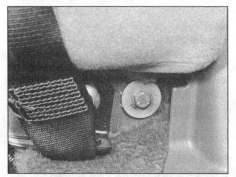

26.14 Rear seat back retaining bolt - 414 models

service key **must** be fitted to prevent accidental firing of the pretensioner.
6 Remove the two Torx bolts securing the rear of the seat slides to the floor and remove the seat from the vehicle. Handle the seat gently once removed, to avoid any chance of the service key becoming dislodged.

Rear seat cushion - 214 models
7 Carefully prise off the hinge covers from the front of the seat cushion, then undo the two Torx bolts securing the hinges to the floor. The cushion can then be lifted out of position and removed from the vehicle **(see illustration)**.

Rear seat cushion - 414 models
8 Remove the bolt securing the rear of the cushion to the seat back then lift the rear of the seat cushion **(see illustration)**.
9 Disengage the cushion retaining clips from the front of the seat cushion and remove it from the vehicle.

Rear seat back - 214 models
10 Remove the rear window parcel shelf then fold the seat backs fully forwards.
11 Peel back the carpet to gain access to the centre hinge, then remove the hinge cover and undo the bolts securing the hinge to the floor **(see illustration)**.
12 Disengage the rear seat back pivot pins from the body and remove the assembly from the vehicle.

Rear seat back - 414 models
13 Remove the rear seat cushion.
14 Remove the three bolts securing the bottom of the seat back to the body, then pull the seat back forwards to release it from its retaining clips and remove it from the vehicle **(see illustration)**.

Refitting
15 Refitting is the reverse of removal, noting the following:
a) *Tighten seat or hinge mounting bolts (as applicable) to the specified torque setting.*
b) *Where applicable, with the front seat secured in position, remove the red service key from the pretensioner slot and refit it to the end of the pretensioner, then refit the pretensioner cover.*

27 Interior trim - removal and refitting

Interior trim panels
1 The interior trim panels are secured either by screws or by various types of trim fasteners, usually studs or clips.
2 Check that there are no other panels overlapping the one to be removed. Usually there is a sequence that has to be followed that will become obvious on close inspection.
3 Remove all obvious fasteners, such as screws. If the panel will not come free then it is held by hidden clips or fasteners. These are usually situated around the edge of the panel and can be prised up to release them. Note, however, that they can break quite easily so replacements should be available. The best way of releasing such clips in the absence of the correct type of tool, is to use a large flat-bladed screwdriver. Note in many cases that the adjacent sealing strip must be prised back to release a panel.
4 When removing a panel, never use excessive force or the panel may be damaged. Always check carefully that all fasteners have been removed or released before attempting to withdraw a panel.

5 Refitting is the reverse of the removal procedure. Secure the fasteners by pressing them firmly into place and ensure that all disturbed components are correctly secured to prevent rattles. If adhesives were found at any point on removal, use white spirit to remove all traces of old adhesive, then wash off all traces of spirit using soapy water. Use a suitable trim adhesive (a Rover dealer should be able to recommend a proprietary product) on reassembly.

Carpets
6 The passenger compartment floor carpet is in one piece and is secured at its edges by screws or clips, usually the same fasteners used to secure the various adjoining trim panels.
7 Carpet removal and refitting is reasonably straightforward but very time-consuming due to the fact that all adjoining trim panels must be removed first, as must components such as the seats, the centre console and seat belt lower anchorages.

Headlining
8 The headlining is clipped to the roof and can be withdrawn once all fittings such as the grab handles, sun visors, sunroof (if fitted), windscreen and rear quarterlights and related trim panels have been removed and the door, tailgate and sunroof aperture sealing strips have been prised clear.
9 Note that headlining removal requires considerable skill and experience if it is to be carried out without damage and is therefore best entrusted to an expert.

28 Seat belts - removal and refitting

Removal

Front seat belt - 4 and 5-door models
1 Carefully prise the lower door pillar trim panel out of position and remove it from the vehicle.

28.2 Removing cover to reveal front seat belt upper mounting nut

28.3 Prise off trim cap and remove front seat belt lower mounting bolt

28.4 Front seat belt inertia reel retaining bolts (arrowed)

2 Remove the cover from the belt upper mounting, undo the seat belt retaining nut and detach the belt **(see illustration)**.

3 Remove the cap from the seat belt lower mounting bolt then undo the bolt and detach the belt from the floor **(see illustration)**.

4 Undo the two bolts securing the inertia reel to the door pillar and remove the reel and belt assembly from the vehicle **(see illustration)**.

Front seat belt - 3-door models

5 Remove the rear window parcel shelf then fold the rear seat cushion fully forwards and remove the rear seat back. Remove the rubber seal from the rear seat back mounting catch.

6 Prise out the seat belt lower mounting point cover then slacken and remove the lower

mounting bolt and detach the belt from the body.

7 Remove the four screws securing the rear seat side trim lower panel to the luggage compartment carpet and carefully peel the front door sealing strip away from the door pillar so that the front edge of the trim panel is freed. The panel can then be released by carefully prising it away from the body, using a large flat-bladed screwdriver to release its retaining clips.

8 Prise off the cover from the seat belt upper mounting then undo the nut securing the belt to the inertia reel and detach the belt.

9 Prise off the covers from the seat belt lower mounting bar bolts then undo both bolts. Disengage the mounting bar from the belt and remove it from the vehicle.

10 Release the seat belt from its door pillar guide, then slacken and remove the two inertia reel retaining bolts and remove the belt and inertia reel from the vehicle.

Front seat belt stalk - all models

11 Remove the seat from the vehicle, undo the seat belt stalk-to-seat mounting bolt and remove the stalk.

Rear seat side belt - 5-door models

12 Remove the rear window parcel shelf and fold the rear seats fully forwards.

13 Carefully examine the luggage compartment side trim panel and remove all its retaining screws. If the right-hand panel is being removed, prise out the luggage compartment lamp from the trim panel, disconnect the lamp wiring and remove it from the vehicle. Release the trim panel and remove it from the luggage compartment.

14 Remove the cover from the seat belt lower mounting point then undo the mounting bolt and detach the belt from the body **(see illustration)**.

15 Prise off the cover from the seat belt upper guide point and undo the two seat belt guide retaining bolts **(see illustrations)**.

16 Undo the six screws securing the rear door pillar trim panel in position and remove the rubber seal from the rear seat back mounting catch. Remove the trim panel to gain access to the inertia reel **(see illustrations)**.

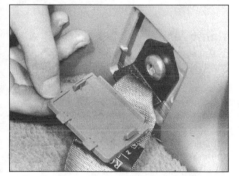

28.14 Remove cover to gain access to rear seat belt lower retaining bolt

28.15a Prise off cover . . .

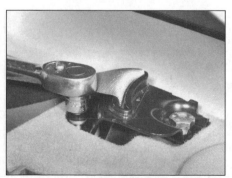

28.15b . . . and remove seat belt guide retaining bolts

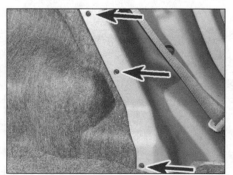

28.16a Remove rear door pillar trim panel retaining screws (arrowed) . . .

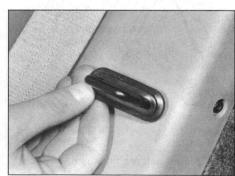

28.16b . . . and remove seat catch rubber seal

11

17 Undo the two bolts securing the inertia reel to the body and remove the belt and reel assembly from the vehicle.

Rear seat side belt - 4-door models

18 Remove the rear seat cushion and back.
19 Carefully examine the luggage compartment side trim panel and remove all its retaining screws. Release the trim panel and remove it from the luggage compartment.
20 Remove the seat belt lower mounting bolt and detach the belt from the body (see illustration).
21 Prise off the cover from the seat belt upper guide point and undo the two seat belt guide retaining bolts.
22 Undo the two bolts securing the inertia reel to the body and remove the belt and reel assembly from the vehicle (see illustration).

Rear seat side belt - 3-door models

23 Remove the rear window parcel shelf then fold the rear seat fully forwards and remove the rear seat back. Remove the rubber seal from the seat back mounting catch.
24 Carry out the operations described in paragraphs 13 to 15.
25 Carefully peel the front door sealing strip away from the door pillar so that the front edge of the rear seat side trim panel is freed. Release the panel by carefully prising it away from the body, using a large flat-bladed screwdriver, then remove it from the vehicle to gain access to the inertia reel.
26 Undo the two bolts securing the inertia reel to the body and remove the seat bolt and inertia reel assembly from the vehicle.

Rear seat centre belt and buckles

27 On 214 models, fold the rear seat cushion fully forwards. On 414 models, remove the rear seat cushion.
28 The centre belt and/or buckle assembly can now be removed by freeing the buckle(s) from the rear seat back and removing the mounting bolt(s).

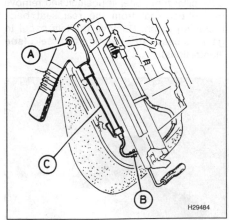

29.2 Seat belt pretensioner assembly

A   Torx screw
B   Cable retaining clip
C   Pretensioner unit

28.20 Rear seat side belt lower mounting bolt . . .

Refitting

29 Refitting is the reversal of removal, noting the following:
a) *Tighten all the seat belt, seat belt guide, seat belt stalk and inertia reel mounting nuts and bolts (as applicable) to the specified torque setting.*
b) *Where possible, renew any broken trim panel retaining clips.*
c) *On completion, ensure all trim panels are securely held by their retaining clips and, if disturbed, the door sealing strips are correctly located.*

29 Seat belt pretensioners - removal and refitting

Note: *Before attempting any work on a seat belt pretensioner, read carefully the precautions listed at the beginning of this Chapter.*

Removal

1 Remove the front seat from the vehicle, turn it upside down and place it on a clean, level work surface.
2 Remove the Torx screw securing the seat belt retainer to the seat frame (see illustration).
3 Release the pretensioner cable from the clip on the seat frame.

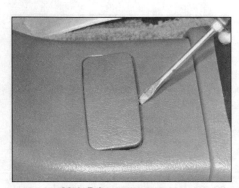

30.1 Prise out cover . . .

28.22 . . . and inertia reel retaining bolts (arrowed) - 4-door models

4 Remove the Torx screw securing the pretensioner to the seat frame.
5 Using both hands, carefully lift the pretensioner assembly away from the seat frame.

Refitting

6 Refitting is a reversal of the removal procedure, noting the following:
a) *Tighten all retaining screws to the specified torque settings.*
b) *Ensure the pretensioner cable is correctly routed and secured in position.*

30 Centre console - removal and refitting

Removal

1 Prise out the cover, situated just in front of the handbrake lever, from the rear centre console section to gain access to the two retaining bolts (see illustration).
2 Undo the two bolts, then slide the rear console section backwards to free it from the retaining bracket and front console section, then remove it from the vehicle (see illustrations).
3 Unscrew the gearchange lever knob, then prise off the reverse gear selector slide

30.2a . . . then undo retaining bolts . . .

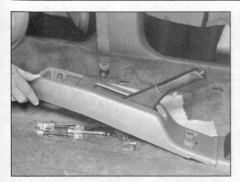

30.2b ... and remove centre console rear section (front seats removed for clarity)

30.3 Prise off reverse gear selector slide retaining clip ...

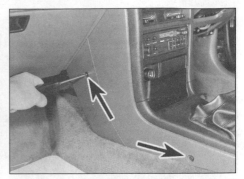

30.4a ... then remove front console section retaining screws ...

30.4b ... and remove console section from vehicle

31.5 Right-hand lower facia panel retaining screws (arrowed)

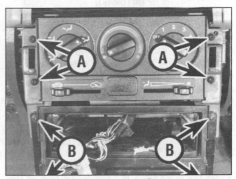

31.7a Heater control panel retaining screws (A) and lower central facia panel retaining screws (B)

retaining clip and disengage the slide from the gearchange lever (see illustration).
4 Remove the four front console section retaining screws and remove it from the vehicle (see illustrations).

Refitting

5 Refitting is a reversal of the removal procedure.

31 Facia - removal and refitting

> **Warning: Read carefully the precautions listed in Chapter 12, appertaining to vehicles**

equipped with airbags (SRS) before disturbing the steering column.

Removal

1 Disconnect the battery negative terminal. From within the engine compartment, unscrew the union nuts and separate the two halves of the speedometer cable.
2 Remove the centre console.
3 Slide the front seats rearwards and remove the radio/cassette player.
4 Working on the passenger side of the facia, remove the mat from the facia tray, then carefully prise out the clock mounting trim panel. Disconnect the wiring connector from the rear of the clock and remove the trim panel.
5 Undo the five right-hand lower facia panel

retaining screws and remove the panel (see illustration).
6 Remove the nuts and bolts securing the steering column assembly to the body and remove the lower mounting clamp. Carefully lower the column assembly away from facia, releasing the wiring from any necessary retaining clips, and rest it on the driver's seat taking great care to ensure that no strain is placed on any of the column wiring.
7 Slacken and remove the four screws securing the heater control panel to the facia, then undo the four screws securing the lower central panel to the facia. Partially withdraw the lower central facia panel then disconnect the wiring and remove the cigar lighter and ashtray illumination bulbs. Remove the lower central panel from the vehicle (see illustrations).

31.7b Withdraw central facia panel ...

31.7c ... disconnect wiring connectors ...

31.7d ... and remove ashtray illumination bulb

11

31.9 Slacken two facia mounting bolts and remove relay module mounting bracket (arrowed)

31.11a Remove door demister duct . . .

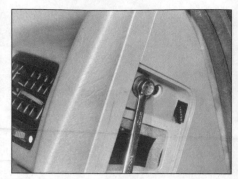

31.11b . . . then slacken and remove facia right-hand upper . . .

8 With the panel removed, disconnect the two block connectors from the relay module and release the wiring retaining clip from the facia mounting bracket. Use a screwdriver to release the retaining clip and remove the relay module.

9 Slacken the two bolts securing the facia to the mounting bracket on the transmission tunnel, then remove the bolts along with the relay module mounting bracket **(see illustration)**.

10 Open the glovebox and remove the door demister duct from the left-hand end of the facia. Slacken and remove the two left-hand facia mounting bolts then close the glovebox.

11 Remove the door demister duct from the right-hand end of the facia and undo the two right-hand facia mounting bolts **(see illustrations)**.

12 Slacken and remove the centre facia mounting bolt, which is accessed through the clock aperture. Partially withdraw the facia until access can be gained to the wiring block connectors (situated behind the right-hand end of the facia) and the speedometer cable **(see illustrations)**.

13 Reach behind the facia and press in the speedometer cable retaining clip, then disconnect the cable from the instrument panel.

14 Disconnect the facia/instrument panel wiring block connectors and carefully manoeuvre the facia assembly out of the vehicle.

Refitting

15 Offer up the facia and reconnect the four wiring connectors. Refit the speedometer

cable to the instrument panel, ensuring it is clipped securely in position.

16 Manoeuvre the panel into position, ensuring that the heater control panel is correctly positioned, then refit the facia mounting bolts and tighten them to the specified torque.

17 The remainder of the refitting procedure is a reversal of removal, noting the following:

a) *Tighten the steering column mounting nuts and bolts to the specified torque, noting that the lower clamp nut and bolt should be tightened first.*

b) *On completion, reconnect the battery and check that all electrical components and switches function correctly.*

31.11c . . . and lower mounting bolts

31.12a Facia centre mounting bolt is accessed via clock aperture

31.12b Removing facia assembly

Chapter 12
Body electrical systems

Contents

Degrees of difficulty

| Easy, suitable for novice with little experience | Fairly easy, suitable for beginner with some experience | Fairly difficult, suitable for competent DIY mechanic | Difficult, suitable for experienced DIY mechanic | Very difficult, suitable for expert DIY or professional |

Specifications

System
Type .... 12 volt, negative earth

Relays and control units

Component	Location
Starter relay	Engine compartment fusebox, centre relay of right-hand three
Intake manifold heater relay	Engine compartment fusebox, rear relay of right-hand three
Main relay	Engine compartment fusebox, front relay of right-hand three
Fuel pump relay	Engine compartment fusebox, front relay of left-hand two
Cooling fan relay	Engine compartment fusebox, rear relay of left-hand two
Direction indicator relay	Behind right-hand lower facia panel (square relay)
Heated rear window relay	Behind right-hand lower facia panel (circular relay)
Cigar lighter relay, fog lamp relay, horn relay and main beam relay	Part of relay module, mounted on transmission tunnel behind lower central facia panel
Electric window relay	Behind lower central facia panel
Electric window control unit	Behind right-hand front door inner trim panel
Central locking control unit	Behind left-hand front door inner trim panel
Air conditioning relay	Mounted on left-hand side of engine compartment bulkhead
Dim-dip relay	Behind right-hand lower facia panel
Windscreen wiper relay	Behind right-hand lower facia panel
Sunroof relay	Behind right-hand lower facia panel
Lambda sensor relay - catalytic converter models only	Engine compartment fusebox, next to fusible links
Tailgate wiper relay	Behind right-hand luggage compartment trim

12

Fuses

Fuse	Rating (amps)	Circuit(s) protected
1	10	Clock, instruments, direction indicators and dim-dip unit
2	10	Starter signal
3	15	Central locking
4	10	Cigar lighter
5	10	Dim-dip resistor
6	30	Sunroof
7	10	Right-hand sidelamps, tail lamp and number plate lamps
8	10	Left-hand sidelamps, tail lamp and interior lamps
9	10	Fog lamps
10	10	Left-hand headlamp dipped beam
11	10	Right-hand headlamp dipped beam
12	15	Radio/cassette memory, clock and interior lamps
13	15	Front windscreen washers and wipers
14	10	Engine management system
15	15	Cooling fan, tailgate washer and wiper
16	15	Reversing lamps, stop lamps and electric windows
17	10	Cigar lighter, Multi-function unit and radio/cassette player
18	10	Electric door mirrors
19	15	Headlamp dim-dip
20	15	Fuel pump
21	15	Right-hand headlamp main beam
22	15	Left-hand headlamp main beam
23	25	Heated rear window and heated door mirrors
24	20	Heater blower motor
25	15	ABS system
26	15	Left-hand rear electric window
27	15	Right-hand rear electric window
28	15	Left-hand front electric window
29	15	Right-hand front electric window
Additional		Airbag (SRS). **Do not remove**

Note: Fuse locations are typical and may vary slightly according to model type. Refer to vehicle handbook.

Fusible links

Link	Rating (amps)	Circuit(s) protected
1	40	ABS pump
2	40	Lighting and cigar lighter
3	40	Ignition switch
4	40	Electric window relay, sunroof, central locking and heated rear window
5	40	Ignition switch
6	60	Main relay, fuel pump relay and lambda sensor relay

Bulbs

	Fitting	Wattage
Headlamps:		
Dip/main beam bulb	H4	60/55
Individual main beam bulb	H1	55
Front sidelamps	Capless	5
Direction indicator lamps	Bayonet	21
Direction indicator side repeater lamps	Capless	5
Interior lamp	Festoon	5
Instrument panel warning and illumination	Integral with holder*	14V 1.4 or 3W
Glovebox lamp	Festoon	5
Luggage compartment lamp	Bayonet	10
Reversing lamps	Bayonet	21
Tail lamps	Capless	5
Stop lamps	Bayonet	21
Rear foglamps	Bayonet	21
Number plate lamps	Capless	5

* With exception of rear illumination panel bulb which is capless

Torque wrench settings

	Nm	lbf ft
Wiper arm spindle nut	14	10
Wiper motor mounting bolts	9	6
Windscreen wiper linkage spindle assembly bolts	9	6
Airbag-to-steering wheel (Torx) screws	8	6
Airbag control unit-to-steering wheel (Torx) screws	3	2

1 General information and precautions

General information

The electrical system is of the 12-volt negative earth type and comprises a 12-volt battery, an alternator with integral voltage regulator, a starter motor and related electrical accessories, components and wiring. The battery is of the maintenance-free (sealed for life) type and is charged by the alternator, which is belt-driven from a crankshaft-mounted pulley.

While some repair procedures are given, the usual course of action is to renew a defective component. The owner whose interest extends beyond mere component renewal should obtain a copy of the *Automobile Electrical & Electronic Systems Manual*, available from the publishers of this Manual.

Precautions

It is necessary to take extra care when working on the electrical system to avoid damage to semi-conductor devices (diodes and transistors) and to avoid the risk of personal injury. In addition to the precautions given in "*Safety first!*" at the beginning of this Manual, observe the following when working on the system:

a) *Always remove rings, watches, etc. before working on the electrical system. Even with the battery disconnected, capacitive discharge could occur if a component's live terminal is earthed through a metal object. This could cause a shock or nasty burn.*

b) *Do not reverse the battery connections. Components such as the alternator, fuel injection/ignition system ECU, or any other having semi-conductor circuitry could be irreparably damaged.*

c) *If the engine is being started using jump leads and a slave battery, connect the batteries positive-to-positive and negative-to-negative. This also applies when connecting a battery charger.*

d) *Never disconnect the battery terminals, the alternator, any electrical wiring or any test instruments when the engine is running.*

e) *Do not allow the engine to turn the alternator when the alternator is not connected.*

f) *Never test for alternator output by 'flashing' the output lead to earth.*

g) *Never use an ohmmeter of the type incorporating a hand-cranked generator for circuit or continuity testing.*

h) *Always ensure that the battery negative lead is disconnected when working on the electrical system.*

i) *Before using electric-arc welding equipment on the vehicle, disconnect the*

battery, alternator and components such as the fuel injection/ignition system ECU to protect them.

A number of additional precautions must be observed when working on vehicles equipped with airbags (SRS), they are as follows:

a) *When cleaning the interior of the vehicle, do not allow the airbag unit to become flooded with detergents or water and do not clean with petrol or furniture cream and polishes. Clean the unit sparingly with a damp cloth and upholstery cleaner.*

b) *Before working on any part of the system, remove the ignition key and wait at least ten minutes to allow the system backup circuit to fully discharge. Disconnect both battery leads, earth lead first, to avoid accidental detonation of the airbag.*

c) *Make no attempt to splice into any of the electric cables in the SRS wiring harness as this may affect the operation of the SRS. Never fit electronic equipment such as mobile telephones, radios, etc. into the harness and ensure that the harness is routed so that it cannot be trapped.*

d) *Avoid hammering or causing any harsh vibration at the front of the vehicle, particularly in the engine bay, as this may trigger the crash sensors and activate the SRS.*

e) *Do not use ohmmeters or any other device capable of supplying current on any of the SRS components, as this may cause accidental detonation. Use only a digital circuit tester.*

f) *Always use new replacement parts. Never fit parts that are from another vehicle or show signs of damage through being dropped or improperly handled*

g) *Airbags are classed as pyrotechnical devices and must be stored and handled according to the relevant laws in the country concerned. In general, do not leave these components disconnected from their electrical cabling any longer than is absolutely necessary as in this state they are unstable and the risk of accidental detonation is introduced. Rest a disconnected airbag unit with the pad surface facing upwards and never rest anything on the pad. Store it on a secure flat surface, away from flammable materials, high heat sources, oils, grease, detergents or water, and never leave it unattended.*

h) *The SRS indicator light should extinguish 3 seconds after the ignition switch is turned to position "II". If this is not the case, check the electrical system connections as soon as possible.*

i) *The airbag control unit and slip ring are non-serviceable components and no attempt should be made to carry out repairs or modifications to them.*

j) *Only use the recommended special bolts when fitting the airbag assembly. Do not use any other type of bolt.*

k) *Never invert the airbag unit.*

l) *Renew the airbag unit and slip ring every ten years, regardless of condition.*

m) *Return an unwanted airbag unit to your Rover dealer for safe disposal. Do not endanger others by careless disposal of a unit.*

2 Electrical fault finding - general information

1 A typical electrical circuit consists of an electrical component, any switches, relays, motors, fuses, fusible links or circuit breakers related to that component and the wiring and connectors that link the component to both the battery and the chassis. To help you pinpoint an electrical circuit problem, wiring diagrams are included at the end of this Chapter.

2 Before tackling any troublesome electrical circuit, first study the appropriate wiring diagrams to get a complete understanding of what components are included in that individual circuit. Trouble spots, for instance, can be narrowed down by noting if other components related to the circuit are operating properly. If several components or circuits fail at one time, then the problem is probably in a fuse or earth connection, because several circuits are often routed through the same fuse and earth connections.

3 Electrical problems usually stem from simple causes, such as loose or corroded connections, a blown fuse, a melted fusible link or a faulty relay. Inspect the condition of all fuses, wires and connections in a problem circuit before testing the components. Use the diagrams to note which terminal connections will need to be checked in order to pinpoint the trouble spot.

4 The basic tools needed for electrical fault finding include a circuit tester or voltmeter (a 12-volt bulb with a set of test leads can also be used), a continuity tester, a battery and set of test leads, and a jumper wire, preferably with a circuit breaker incorporated, which can be used to bypass electrical components. Before attempting to locate a problem with test instruments, use the wiring diagram to decide where to make the connections.

Voltage checks

5 Voltage checks should be performed if a circuit is not functioning properly. Connect one lead of a circuit tester to either the negative battery terminal or a known good earth. Connect the other lead to a connector in the circuit being tested, preferably nearest to the battery or fuse. If the bulb of the tester lights then voltage is present, which means that the part of the circuit between the connector and the battery is problem free. Continue checking the rest of the circuit in the same fashion. When you reach a point at which no voltage is present, the problem lies between that point and the last test point with

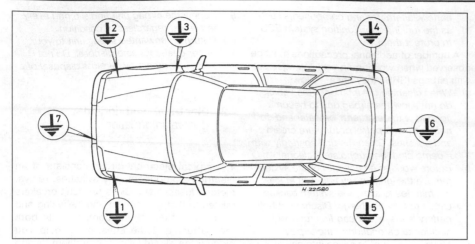

2.9 Electrical system earth points

1 Behind left-hand headlamp - E1
2 Behind right-hand headlamp - E2
3 Base of right-hand front door pillar - E3
4 Beneath right-hand rear lamp cluster - E4
5 Beneath left-hand rear lamp cluster - E5
6 Centre of tailgate/boot lid - E6
7 Bonnet lock platform - E7

voltage. Most problems can be traced to a loose connection. Bear in mind that some circuits are only live when the ignition switch is switched to a particular position.

Finding a short circuit

6 One method of finding a short circuit is to remove the fuse and connect a test light or voltmeter to the fuse terminals with all the relevant electrical components switched off. There should be no voltage present in the circuit. Move the wiring from side to side while watching the test light. If the bulb lights up, there is a short to earth somewhere in that area, probably where the insulation has rubbed through. The same test can be performed on each component in the circuit, even a switch.

Earth check

7 Perform an earth test to check whether a component is properly earthed. Disconnect the battery and connect one lead of a self-powered test light, known as a continuity tester, to a known good earth point. Connect the other lead to the wire or earth connection being tested. If the bulb lights up, the earth is good. If not, the earth is faulty.
8 If an earth connection is thought to be faulty, dismantle the connection and clean back to bare metal both the bodyshell and the wire terminal or the component's earth connection mating surface. Be careful to remove all traces of dirt and corrosion, then use a knife to trim away any paint, so that a clean metal-to-metal joint is made. On reassembly, tighten the joint fasteners securely; if a wire terminal is being refitted, use serrated washers between the terminal and the bodyshell to ensure a clean and secure connection. When the connection is remade, prevent the onset of corrosion in the future by applying a coat of petroleum jelly or silicone-based grease or by spraying on a proprietary ignition sealer or a water dispersant lubricant at regular intervals.
9 The vehicle's wiring harness has seven multiple-earth connections, each one being identified in the wiring diagrams by a reference number (E1 to E7). Each of these earth connections serves several circuits and are located as follows **(see illustration)**:

E1 Behind left-hand headlamp.
E2 Behind right-hand headlamp.
E3 Base of right-hand front door pillar.
E4 Beneath right-hand rear lamp cluster.
E5 Beneath left-hand rear lamp cluster.
E6 Centre of tailgate/boot lid.
E7 Bonnet lock platform.

Continuity check

10 A continuity check is necessary to determine if there are any breaks in a circuit. With the circuit off (ie: no power in the circuit), a self-powered continuity tester can be used to check the circuit. Connect the test leads to both ends of the circuit, or to the positive end and a good earth. If the test light comes on, the circuit is passing current properly. If the light does not come on, there is a break somewhere in the circuit. The same

procedure can be used to test a switch, by connecting the continuity tester to the switch terminals. With the switch turned on, the test light should come on.

Finding an open circuit

11 When checking for possible open circuits, it is often difficult to locate them by sight because oxidation or terminal misalignment are hidden by the connectors. Merely moving a connector on a sensor or in the wiring harness may correct the open circuit condition. Remember this when an open circuit is indicated when fault finding in a circuit. Intermittent problems may also be caused by oxidized or loose connections.

General

12 Electrical fault finding is simple if you keep in mind that all electrical circuits are basically electricity flowing from the battery, through the wires, switches, relays, fuses and fusible links to each electrical component (light bulb, motor, etc.) and to earth, from which it is passed back to the battery. Any electrical problem is an interruption in the flow of electricity from the battery.

3	Fuses, fusible links and relays - location and renewal	

Fuses

1 Most of the fuses are located behind the panel in the right-hand lower facia panel, with a few odd fuses being located in the fusebox on the left-hand side of the engine compartment.
2 Access to the fuses is gained by removing the fusebox lid/cover. Symbols on the reverse of the lid/cover indicate the circuits protected by the fuses and five spare fuses are supplied, together with plastic tweezers to remove and fit them **(see illustration)**. Further details on fuse ratings and circuits protected are given in the Specifications.
3 On vehicles equipped with airbags, the fuse protecting the airbag circuit is located on the side of the main fuse box **(see illustration)**.

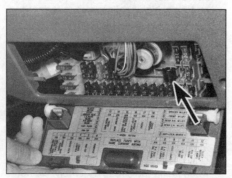

3.2 Remove fuses with plastic tweezers supplied (arrowed)

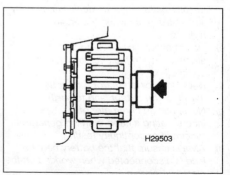

3.3 Airbag circuit fuse (arrowed) is located on side of main fusebox

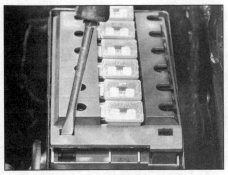
3.10a Unclip plastic cover . . .

3.10b . . . then undo retaining screws and remove fusible link

3.15a Use a screwdriver to release relay module retaining clip . . .

Under no circumstances should this fuse be removed as this may cause inflation of the airbag. Refer to your Rover dealer if you think fuse renewal is necessary.

4 To remove a fuse, first switch off the circuit concerned (or the ignition), then fit the tweezers and pull the fuse out of its terminals. Slide the fuse sideways from the tweezers. The wire within the fuse is clearly visible. If the fuse is blown, the wire will be broken or melted.

5 Always renew a fuse with one of an identical rating. Never use a fuse with a different rating from the original or substitute anything else. The fuse rating is stamped on top of the fuse. Fuses are also colour-coded for easy recognition.

6 If a new fuse blows immediately, find the cause before renewing it again. A short to earth as a result of faulty insulation is the most likely cause. Where a fuse protects more than one circuit, try to isolate the defect by switching on each circuit in turn (if possible) until the fuse blows again.

7 If any of the spare fuses are used, always replace them so that a spare of each rating is available.

Fusible links

8 The fusible links are located in the rear of the fusebox, situated on the left-hand side of the engine compartment. Unclip the lid to gain access to them.

9 Details of link ratings and circuits protected are given in the Specifications. All links are numbered on the rear of the fusebox lid.

10 To remove a fusible link, first ensure that the circuit concerned is switched off then prise off the plastic cover. Slacken the two link retaining screws then lift the fusible link out of the fusebox **(see illustrations)**. The wire within the fusible link is clearly visible. If the fuse is blown, it will be broken or melted. A blown fusible link indicates a serious wiring or system fault which must be diagnosed before the link is renewed.

11 Always renew a fusible link with one of an identical rating. Never use a link with a different rating from the original or substitute anything else. On refitting, tighten the link

retaining screws securely and refit the link cover.

Relays

12 The Specifications Section gives full information on the location and function of the various relays fitted. Refer to the relevant wiring diagram for details of wiring connections.

13 If a circuit or system controlled by a relay develops a fault and the relay is suspect, operate the system. If the relay is functioning, it should be possible to hear it click as it is energized. If this is the case, the fault lies with the components or wiring of the system. If the relay is not being energized, then either the relay is not receiving a main supply or a switching voltage, or the relay itself is faulty. Testing is by the substitution of a known good unit but be careful as some relays are identical in appearance, but perform different functions.

14 To renew a relay, ensure that the ignition switch is off, then simply pull direct from the socket and press in the new relay.

15 Certain relays are contained in the relay module which is situated behind the lower central facia panel. To remove this, first remove the lower central panel from the facia. Disconnect its two wiring block connectors then release its retaining clip and slide to the left to withdraw it from the mounting bracket **(see illustrations)**. The complete module must be renewed, even if only one of the relays is faulty.

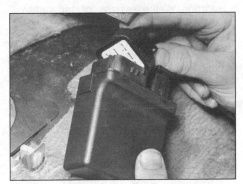
3.15b . . . then slide module out of position and disconnect its wiring connectors

Steering column combination switch

Models without airbag (SRS)

2 Remove the steering wheel and steering column shrouds, then disconnect the switch wiring, as described in Chapter 10.

3 Each individual switch can be removed by unscrewing its two retaining screws and sliding the switch out of the housing **(see illustrations)**.

4 To remove the complete switch assembly, slacken and remove the two retaining screws and slide the assembly off the steering column.

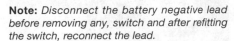

4 Switches - removal and refitting

Note: *Disconnect the battery negative lead before removing any switch and after refitting the switch, reconnect the lead.*

Ignition switch

1 Refer to Chapter 10 for details of switch removal and refitting. A Rover dealer will be able to tell you whether the switch can be obtained separately from the steering lock.

4.3a Individual combination switches can be removed by slackening retaining screws . . .

4.3b . . . and sliding switch out of main assembly

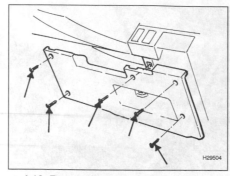

4.10 Remove fusebox cover securing screws (arrowed)

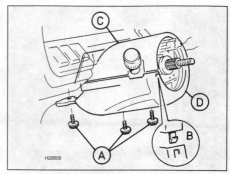

4.11 Remove screws (A), release clips (B) and separate two halves of shroud (C and D)

5 Refitting is the reverse of the removal procedure.

Models with airbag (SRS)

6 Remove the ignition key and wait at least ten minutes to allow the SRS system backup circuit to fully discharge. Disconnect both battery leads, earth lead first, to avoid accidental detonation of the airbag.

7 Set the steering in the dead-ahead position then lock the steering column in its lowest position.

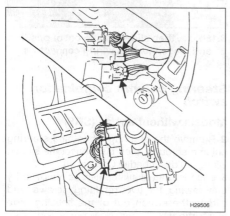
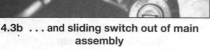

4.12 Disconnect four multiplugs (arrowed) from combination switch

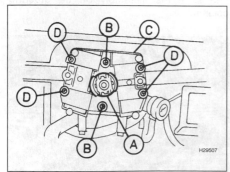

4.14 Steering column switch assembly

A Indicator cancelling cam
B Column switch screws
C Column switch assembly
D Combination switch screws

8 Remove the airbag unit.
9 Remove the steering wheel, see Chapter 10.
10 Remove the five fusebox cover securing screws and release the cover from the facia (see illustration).
11 Remove the three screws securing the lower half of the steering column shroud, release the two clips securing the front of the shroud, then separate the two halves of the shroud, manoeuvring each one clear of the column (see illustration).
12 Disconnect the four multiplugs from the combination switch (see illustration).
13 Remove the four screws securing the slip ring to the combination switch, remove the ring from the column and place it to one side whilst taking care not to allow it to hang from its wiring.
14 Remove the indicator cancelling cam (see illustration).
15 Each individual switch can be removed by unscrewing its two retaining screws and sliding the switch out of the housing.
16 To remove the complete combination switch, slacken and remove the two retaining screws and slide the switch off the steering column.
17 Refitting is the reverse of the removal procedure.
18 Upon completion of refitting the airbag unit, reconnect both battery leads, negative lead last, and turn the ignition switch to the

"II" position. Check the condition of the system by observing the SRS warning light located in the steering wheel centre pad. The light should stay illuminated for 3 seconds whilst the system performs a self-diagnosis test. If the test is satisfactory, the light will extinguish. If the test is unsatisfactory, the light will remain on or fail to illuminate at all, denoting that the system must be serviced as soon as possible.

Instrument panel and facia switches

19 Check that the switch is in the off position, then taking great care not to scratch or damage the switch or its surround, prise it out using a suitable flat-bladed screwdriver. Withdraw the switch until the connector plug appears then disconnect the wiring connector and remove the switch (see illustrations). Tie a piece of string to the wiring connector to prevent it from falling behind the facia panel.
20 On refitting, connect the wiring connector to the switch and press the switch into position until the retaining clips click into place.

Electrically-operated window switches

21 Remove the door inner trim panel.

4.19a Carefully prise facia switches out of position . . .

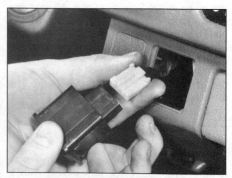

4.19b . . . and disconnect wiring connectors

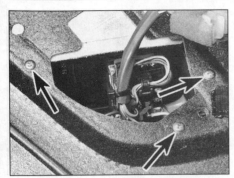

4.22 Driver's side window switch retaining screws (arrowed)

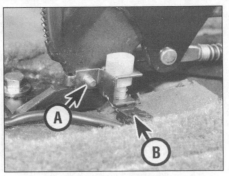

4.28 Handbrake warning lamp switch retaining screw (A) and wiring connector (B)

4.30 Prise horn button from steering wheel . . .

22 Undo the retaining screws and remove the switch from the trim panel **(see illustration)**.
23 On refitting tighten the switch screws securely.

Courtesy lamp switches

24 With the door open, undo the two screws securing the switch to the body. Pull out the switch and tie a piece of string to the wiring to prevent it dropping into the body.
25 Disconnect the switch and remove it from the vehicle.
26 Refitting is a reverse of removal.

Handbrake warning lamp switch

27 From inside the vehicle, carefully prise out the cover from the top of the centre console rear section to gain access to the two retaining screws. Undo the two screws and remove the rear centre console section.
28 Disconnect the wiring connector from the switch, then slacken and remove the retaining screw and remove the switch from the handbrake lever quadrant **(see illustration)**.
29 Refitting is a reverse of the removal procedure.

Horn push switch

Models without airbag (SRS)

30 Using the flat of a screwdriver, carefully prise the horn button out of the centre of the steering wheel **(see illustration)**.
31 Disconnect the wire from each button terminal and remove the button **(see illustration)**.
32 Refitting is a reverse of the removal procedure. Test the horn on completion.

Models with airbag (SRS)

33 Remove the airbag unit, noting all precautions.
34 Detach the earth wire from the steering wheel **(see illustration)**.
35 Disconnect the Lucar connector from the steering wheel connection.
36 Remove each horn button by carefully using the flat blade of a small screwdriver to lever it from position.

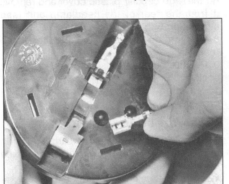

4.31 . . . and disconnect wire from each button terminal

37 Detach the two electrical connectors from the button and remove it.
38 Refitting is the reversal of removal, noting the following:
a) Take care to ensure that wiring is not trapped between mating surfaces.
b) Refit the airbag unit, carrying out the system check.
c) Test the horn after refitting each button.

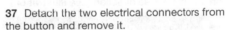

5 Bulbs (exterior lamps) - renewal

General

1 Whenever a bulb is renewed, note the following:
a) Disconnect the battery negative lead before starting work.
b) Remember that if the lamp has just been in use, the bulb may be extremely hot.
c) Always check the bulb contacts and holder, ensuring that there is clean metal-to-metal contact between the bulb and its live contacts and earth. Clean off any corrosion or dirt before fitting a new bulb.
d) Wherever bayonet-type bulbs are fitted, ensure that the live contacts bear firmly against the bulb contact.
e) Always ensure that the new bulb is of the

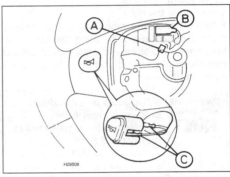

4.34 Disconnect earth wire (A) and Lucar connector (B), then lever button from position and detach electrical connectors (C)

correct rating and that it is completely clean before fitting. This applies particularly to headlamp bulbs.

Headlamp

2 Working in the engine compartment, twist off the relevant circular plastic cover and remove it from the rear of the headlamp unit **(see illustration)**.
3 Unplug the wiring connector, then press together the ears of the bulb retaining clip and

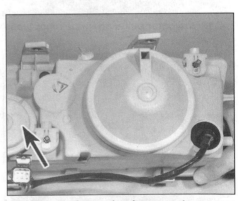

5.2 Remove large circular cover to access dip/main beam bulb and sidelamp bulbs and smaller cover (arrowed) to access individual main beam bulb

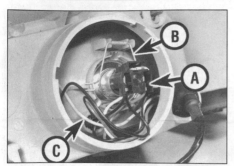

5.3 Headlamp dip/main beam bulb wiring connector (A), retaining clip (B) and sidelamp bulbholder (C)

5.11 Remove retaining screw . . .

5.12 . . . then withdraw indicator lamp and twist bulbholder free

release it from the rear of the lamp **(see illustration)**.
4 Withdraw the bulb.
5 When handling a new bulb, use a tissue or clean cloth to avoid touching the glass with the fingers. Moisture and grease from the skin can cause blackening and rapid failure of this type of bulb.

 HAYNES HiNT *If the glass of a headlamp bulb is accidentally touched, wipe it clean using methylated spirit.*

6 Refitting is the reverse of the removal procedure. Ensure that the new bulbs locating tabs are correctly located in the lamp cutouts.

Front sidelamp

7 Working in the engine compartment, twist

off the large circular plastic cover and remove it from the rear of the headlamp unit **(see illustration 5.2)**.
8 Pull the bulbholder from the headlamp reflector.
9 Pull the capless (push fit) bulb out of its socket.
10 Refitting is the reverse of the removal procedure.

Front direction indicator

11 Working in the engine compartment, undo the indicator lamp upper retaining screw and withdraw the lamp **(see illustration)**.
12 Twist the bulbholder in an anti-clockwise direction to free it from the lamp and remove it from the lamp unit **(see illustration)**.
13 The bulb is a bayonet fit in the holder and can be removed by pressing it and twisting in an anti-clockwise direction **(see illustration)**.

14 Refitting is a reverse of the removal procedure.

Front direction indicator side repeater

15 Push the lamp unit towards the right to free its retaining clips then withdraw it from the wing **(see illustration)**.
16 Pull the bulbholder out of the lamp unit then pull the capless (push fit) bulb out of its holder **(see illustration)**.
17 Refitting is a reverse of the removal procedure.

Rear lamp cluster

18 From inside the luggage compartment, remove the relevant rear cover from the lamp.
19 Depress the catches and withdraw the bulb panel from the lens unit **(see illustration)**.
20 The relevant bulb can then be removed from the panel. The tail lamp bulb is of the capless (push fit) type, whereas all other bulbs have a bayonet fitting **(see illustrations)**.
21 Refitting is the reverse of the removal sequence. Note that the rubber seal must be renewed if damaged.

Number plate lamps

22 Undo the two mounting screws and remove the number plate lamp lens and seal.
23 Withdraw the lamp and remove the clip

5.13 Indicator bulbs are of bayonet type

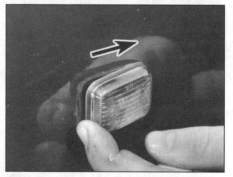

5.15 Push indicator side repeater lamp to right . . .

5.16 . . . then withdraw lamp and pull out bulbholder

5.19 Depress catches and withdraw rear lamp bulb panel

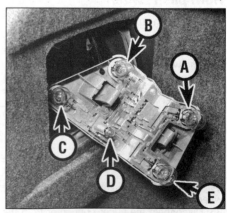

5.20a Rear lamp cluster

A   Direction indicator   D   Tail lamp
B   Reversing lamp   E   Stop lamp
C   Foglamp

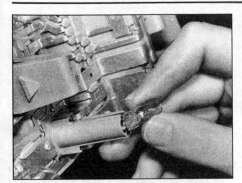

5.20b Rear cluster tail lamp bulb is of capless type . . .

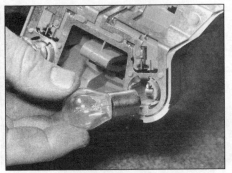

5.20c . . . whereas all other bulbs have bayonet type fitting

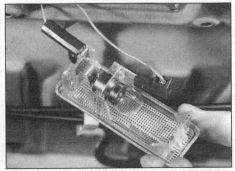

6.9 Luggage compartment lamp bulb is of bayonet type

from the top of the lamp body to gain access to the bulb.

24 The bulb is of the capless (push fit) type and can be pulled out of the lamp unit.

25 Refitting is a reverse of the removal procedure.

6 Bulbs (interior lamps) - renewal

General

1 Refer to Section 5.

Courtesy lamps

2 Carefully prise the lens off the lamp unit then remove the festoon bulb from its end contacts.

3 Fit the new bulb using a reversal of the removal procedure. Check the tension of the spring contacts and if necessary, bend them so that they firmly contact the bulb end caps.

Glovebox lamp

4 Open up the glovebox and undo the two switch/lamp assembly retaining screws. Disconnect the wiring connector and remove the switch/lamp unit from the glovebox.

5 Depress the lens retaining lug and remove the lens assembly from the unit.

6 Release the festoon bulb from its contacts and remove it from the lens.

7 Fit the new bulb using a reversal of the removal procedure. Check the tension of the spring contacts and if necessary, bend them so that they firmly contact the bulb end caps.

Luggage compartment lamp

8 Carefully prise the lamp out of the trim panel using a suitable flat-bladed screwdriver.

9 The bulb is a bayonet fit and can be removed by pressing it in and twisting anti-clockwise **(see illustration)**.

10 Refitting is a reverse of the removal procedure.

Instrument panel illumination and warning lamps

11 Remove the instrument panel.

12 Twist the relevant bulbholder **(see illustration)** anti-clockwise and withdraw it from the rear of the panel.

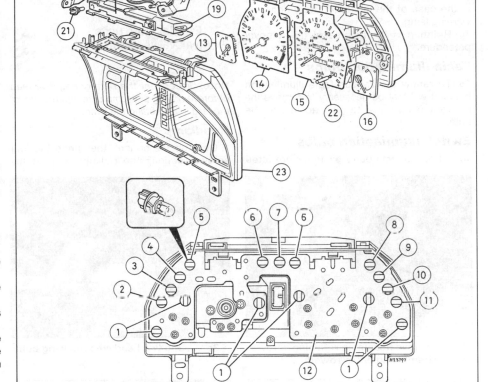

6.12 Instrument panel assembly

1 Panel rear illumination bulbs
2 ABS warning lamp bulb (where fitted)
3 Boot open warning lamp bulb
4 Hazard warning lamp bulb
5 Brake fail/handbrake warning lamp bulb
6 Direction indicator warning lamp bulb
7 Main beam warning lamp bulb
8 Oil pressure warning lamp bulb
9 Ignition/charging lamp warning bulb
10 Choke warning lamp bulb - carburettor models
11 Caravan/trailer indicator warning lamp bulb
12 Printed circuit
13 Coolant temperature gauge
14 Tachometer
15 Speedometer
16 Fuel gauge
17 Left-hand support bracket
18 Right-hand support bracket
19 Illumination panel cover
20 Illumination panel printed circuit
21 Panel front illumination bulb
22 Tripmeter reset knob
23 Instrument panel cover
24 Instrument panel case

6.13a Instrument panel illumination bulbholder is a twist fit in panel . . .

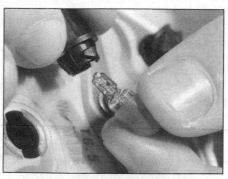

6.13b . . . bulb being of capless type

13 All bulbs, with the exception of the main panel illumination bulb, are integral with their holders. The main panel illumination bulb is of the capless type and is a push fit in its holder (see illustrations). Be very careful to ensure that the new bulbs are of the same rating as those removed as this is especially important in the case of the ignition/battery charging warning lamp.

14 Refitting is the reverse of the removal procedure.

Facia illumination bulbs

15 To renew the various facia illumination bulbs, it will first be necessary to remove the relevant facia panel to gain access to the bulb.

Switch illumination bulbs

16 All of the facia panel switches are fitted

with illuminating bulbs. Some are also fitted with a bulb to show when the circuit concerned is operating. These bulbs are an integral part of the switch assembly and cannot be obtained separately. Bulb replacement will therefore require renewal of the complete switch assembly.

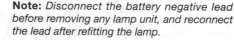

7 Exterior lamp units - removal and refitting

Note: *Disconnect the battery negative lead before removing any lamp unit, and reconnect the lead after refitting the lamp.*

Headlamp

1 Open up the bonnet, then undo the four screws securing the radiator grille to the

headlamps and remove the grille from the vehicle.

2 Remove the screw securing the indicator lamp assembly to the wing and position the lamp unit clear of the headlamp assembly.

3 Undo the two headlamp retaining screws situated behind the indicator lamp and undo the two upper headlamp retaining bolts (see illustrations).

4 Disconnect the headlamp wiring connector (see illustration).

5 Gently pull the headlamp upwards to release it from its lower retainer, then remove the headlamp and lower finisher trim panel assembly from the vehicle.

6 If necessary, the lower finisher can be removed from the headlamp by removing the retaining screw and releasing the two retaining clips.

7 Refitting is a reversal of the removal procedure. On completion adjust the headlamp beam.

Front direction indicator

8 Open up the bonnet and remove the indicator lamp upper retaining screw.

9 Withdraw the lamp unit from the wing, then twist the bulbholder in an anti-clockwise direction to free it from the lamp and remove the lamp unit from the vehicle.

10 Refitting is the reverse of the removal procedure.

Front direction indicator side repeater

11 Push the lamp unit towards the right to free its retaining clips then withdraw it from the wing.

12 Pull the bulbholder out and remove the lamp from the vehicle.

13 Refitting is a reverse of the removal procedure.

Rear lamp cluster

14 Working from within the luggage compartment, remove the relevant rear lamp cover and disconnect the lamp wiring connector (see illustration).

15 Undo the four nuts securing the lamp unit to the body and remove the unit from the vehicle. Note the rubber seal which is fitted between the lamp unit and body (see illustration).

7.3a Remove headlamp retaining screws (remaining one arrowed) . . .

7.3b . . . and two headlamp retaining bolts

7.4 Disconnecting headlamp wiring connector

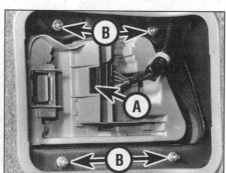

7.14 Disconnect wiring connector (A) and remove rear lamp unit retaining nuts (B)

7.15 Withdraw rear lamp unit noting rubber seal

16 Refitting is a reversal of the removal procedure. The rubber seal must be renewed if damaged.

Number plate lamps

17 Undo the two mounting screws and remove the number plate lamp lens and seal.
18 Withdraw the lamp unit until the wiring connector appears then disconnect the connector and remove the unit from the vehicle.
19 Refitting is the reverse of the removal procedure. The rubber seal must be renewed if damaged.

8 Headlamp beams - alignment

Refer to Chapter 1.

9 Dim-dip headlamp system - operation

1 This system comprises the dim-dip unit (mounted behind the right-hand lower facia panel) and a resistor (situated behind the left-hand headlamp assembly).
2 The dim-dip unit is supplied with current from the sidelamp circuit and energised by a feed from the ignition switch. When energised, the unit allows battery voltage to pass through the resistor to the headlamp

10.2a Carefully prise left-hand switch assembly out of instrument panel shroud . . .

dipped-beam circuits. This lights the headlamps with approximately one-sixth of their normal power so that the vehicle cannot be driven using sidelamps alone.

10 Instrument panel - removal and refitting

Removal

1 Working in the engine compartment, disconnect the battery negative lead, then unscrew the union nut which secures the upper and lower sections of the speedometer cable together.
2 Position the steering column in its lowest possible height setting then, using a suitable flat-bladed screwdriver, carefully prise out the switch assembly from the left-hand side of the

10.2b . . . then withdraw assembly and disconnect wiring connectors

instrument panel shroud. Disconnect the switch wiring connector and remove the switch assembly **(see illustrations)**.
3 On models equipped with an electrically-operated sunroof, repeat the above operation for the sunroof switch.
4 On models without an electrically-operated sunroof, carefully prise out the cover from the right-hand lower corner of the instrument shroud **(see illustration)**.
5 Remove the four instrument panel shroud retaining screws and remove the shroud from the facia **(see illustrations)**.
6 Undo the four screws securing the instrument panel to the facia and carefully withdraw the panel until access can be gained to the rear of the panel. Release the speedometer cable retaining clip then disconnect the cable and three wiring block connectors from the panel **(see illustrations)**.

10.4 On models without electric sunroof, remove cover from right-hand side of instrument panel shroud

10.5a Instrument panel shroud lower retaining screws are accessed through switch apertures

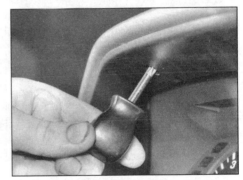

10.5b Remove upper retaining screws . . .

10.5c . . . then withdraw instrument panel shroud

10.6a Remove instrument panel upper (arrowed) and lower retaining screws . . .

10.6b . . . then disconnect speedometer cable . . .

12

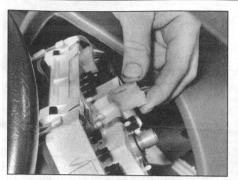

10.6c . . . and wiring connectors . . .

10.7 . . . and withdraw instrument panel from facia

Instruments

Removal

5 Remove the instrument illumination panel.
6 Release the instrument panel cover retaining clips and lift the cover off the instrument panel case **(see illustration)**.
7 Individual instruments can now be removed separately by unscrewing their retaining screws **(see illustrations)**. When removing the speedometer, note the foam washer which is fitted around the base of the instrument stalk.

Refitting

8 Refitting is a reversal of the removal procedure.

7 Remove the instrument panel from the facia **(see illustration)**.

Refitting

8 Refitting is a reverse of the removal procedure. On completion, check the operation of all panel warning lamps and instrument shroud switches to ensure that they are functioning correctly.

---

11 Instrument panel components - removal and refitting

1 Remove the instrument panel then proceed as described under the relevant sub heading.

Instrument illumination panel

Removal

2 Remove the screws securing the right and left-hand upper mounting brackets to the panel assembly and remove both brackets **(see illustrations)**.
3 Release the rear illumination panel bulbholder by twisting it in an anti-clockwise direction, then remove the illumination panel from the top of the instruments **(see illustration)**.

Refitting

4 Refitting is a reversal of the removal procedure.

Printed circuit

Removal

9 Remove the speedometer, tachometer, fuel gauge and temperature gauge from the meter case as described in paragraphs 5 to 7.
10 Remove all bulbholders from the rear of the case by twisting them in an anti-clockwise direction, then release the printed circuit from its retaining pins and remove it from the case.

Refitting

11 Refitting is a reverse of the removal sequence.

11.2a Unscrew retaining screws . . .

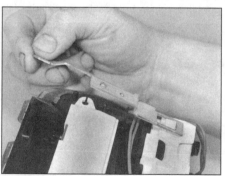

11.2b . . . and remove upper mounting brackets from instrument panel

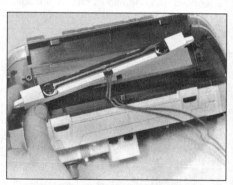

11.3 Removing instrument illumination panel

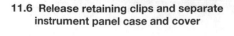

11.6 Release retaining clips and separate instrument panel case and cover

11.7a Remove retaining screws (remaining two arrowed) . . .

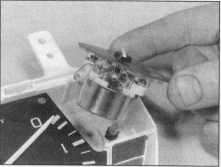

11.7b . . . and remove relevant instrument from panel case (temperature gauge shown)

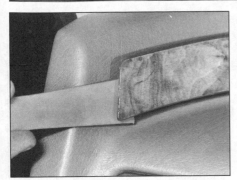

13.2a Carefully prise out clock mounting trim strip . . .

13.2b . . . and disconnect clock wiring connector

13.3 Removing clock retaining screws (remaining one arrowed)

12 Cigar lighter -
removal and refitting

Removal

1 Disconnect the battery negative lead.
2 Remove the lighter element, then carefully prise out the metal surround, followed by the plastic body. Note the wiring connections before disconnecting them and tie a piece of string around the connector to prevent the wire from falling back inside the facia.

Refitting

3 Refitting is the reverse of the removal procedure.

13 Clock -
removal and refitting

Removal

1 Disconnect the battery negative lead.
2 Using a suitable flat-bladed instrument, carefully prise out the clock mounting trim strip from the facia. Withdraw the trim and disconnect the wiring connector from the rear of the clock. Tie a piece of string around the connector to prevent it from falling back inside the facia (see illustrations).
3 Undo the two clock retaining screws and

remove the clock from the trim strip (see illustration).

Refitting

4 Refitting is a reversal of the removal procedure.

14 Multi-function unit -
operation, removal and refitting

Operation

1 The multi-function unit (MFU) is mounted onto the rear of the fusebox, which is located behind the right-hand lower facia panel. The unit controls the following functions:
a) Front and rear wiper system delay intervals.
b) Heated rear window timer.
c) Courtesy lamp delay.
d) Lamps-on warning bleeper.
2 The MFU also has a self diagnostic mode where it checks out all the relevant circuits it controls.
3 To start the diagnostic sequence, press the heated rear window switch and turn on the ignition switch on simultaneously. Release the heated rear window switch as soon as the ignition switch is turned on, the MFU should then bleep to indicate it has entered its diagnostic mode, then press the heated rear window switch for a second time. Subsequent

operations of the interior lamp switches, wiper switches and headlamp switch will result in a bleep from the MFU as it receives a signal. If the unit does not bleep, a fault is indicated in the relevant circuit. A third press on the heated rear window switch will enter the MFU into the second stage of its diagnostic sequence. The MFU will now operate each of its functions in turn starting with the heated rear window, followed by the front and rear wipers and finally the courtesy lamp will operate for approximately two seconds if there are no faults. When all checks are complete, turn the ignition switch off to take the MFU out of its diagnostic sequence.
4 If a fault appears in one of the circuits controlled by the MFU, then check the relevant relay (where fitted) and wiring. If this fails to locate the fault, it is likely that the MFU is at fault. The MFU is a sealed unit and must be renewed even if only one of its control functions is faulty.

Removal

5 Disconnect the battery negative terminal.
6 Undo the five retaining screws and remove the right-hand lower facia panel (see illustration).
7 Release the left-hand fuse panel from the side of the main fusebox and disconnect the two wiring block connectors from the front of the fusebox (see illustrations).
8 Remove the two fusebox retaining nuts then partially withdraw the fusebox until the

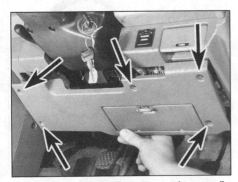

14.6 Remove retaining screws (arrowed) and withdraw right-hand lower facia panel

14.7a Release left-hand fuse panel . . .

14.7b . . . and disconnect wiring connectors from front of fusebox

12

14.8 Fusebox retaining nuts (arrowed)

14.9a Release Multi-Function Unit from rear of fusebox . . .

14.9b . . . and disconnect wiring connector

upper wiring block connector(s) can be disconnected **(see illustration)**.

9 Carefully turn the fusebox assembly around and disconnect the block connector from the MFU. Release the MFU from the rear of the fusebox and remove it from the vehicle **(see illustrations)**.

Refitting

10 Refitting is a reversal of the removal procedure. Ensure that all wiring connectors are correctly refitted. On completion, reconnect the battery terminal and check that all electrical circuits function correctly.

15 Supplementary Restraint System (SRS) - operation

1 At vehicle start-up, a warning light located in the steering wheel centre pad will illuminate when the system electrical circuits are activated by turning the ignition switch to position "II" and will stay illuminated for 3 seconds whilst the system performs a self-diagnosis test. If this test is satisfactory, the light will extinguish. If the test is unsatisfactory, the light will remain on or fail to illuminate at all, denoting that the system must be serviced as soon as possible. System operation is as follows:

2 Upon the vehicle suffering a frontal impact over a specified force, a sensor inside the airbag control unit, which is located in the steering wheel centre, activates the system. A sensor (fitted to discriminate between actual impact and driving on rough road surfaces, etc.) is also activated and power is supplied to the airbag ignitor from the battery or a backup circuit, causing the airbag to inflate within 30 milliseconds.

3 As the driver of the vehicle is thrown foward into the inflated airbag it immediately discharges its contents through a vent, thereby providing a progressive deceleration and reducing the risk of injury from contact with the steering wheel, facia or windscreen. The total time taken from the start of airbag inflation to its complete deflation is approximately 0.1 seconds.

16 Supplementary Restraint System (SRS) - component removal and refitting

⚠️ **Warning: Under no circumstances, attempt to diagnose problems with SRS components using standard workshop equipment.**

Note: *For safety reasons, owners are strongly advised against attempting to diagnose problems with the SRS using standard workshop equipment. The information in this Section is therefore limited to those components in the SRS which must be removed to gain access to other components on the vehicle. Read carefully the precautions given in Section 1 of this Chapter before commencing work on any part of the system.*

Note: *All SRS system wiring can be identified by its yellow protective covering.*

Airbag unit

Removal

1 Remove the ignition key and wait at least ten minutes to allow the system backup circuit to fully discharge. Disconnect **both** battery leads, earth lead first, to avoid accidental detonation of the airbag.

2 Remove the two airbag unit retaining screws which are accessed from behind the steering wheel **(see illustration)**.

3 Carefully prise the airbag unit away from the steering wheel to gain access to its wiring behind. Do not allow the unit to hang from its wiring.

4 Unplug the wiring connector from the rear of the airbag unit and carefully remove the unit from the vehicle, placing it in safe storage.

Refitting

5 Refit the airbag unit by reversing the removal procedure, noting the following:

a) *The cable connector must face uppermost when refitted to the airbag unit.*

b) *Observe the specified torque wrench setting when tightening the airbag retaining screws (TX30 Torx type) and take care not to cross-thread them.*

c) *With the airbag unit in position, press either side of the steering wheel to allow the ridge on the wheel to engage in the groove of the airbag unit.*

d) *Reconnect both battery leads, negative lead last, and turn the ignition switch to the "II" position. Check the condition of the system by observing the SRS warning light located in the steering wheel centre pad. The light should stay illuminated for 3 seconds whilst the system performs a self-diagnosis test. If the test is satisfactory, the light will extinguish. If the test is unsatisfactory, the light will remain on or fail to illuminate at all, denoting that the system must be serviced as soon as possible.*

Airbag control unit

Removal

6 Remove the airbag unit.

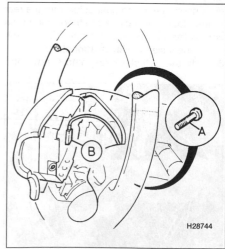

16.2 Remove retaining screws (A) to release airbag unit (B)

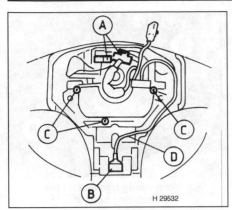

16.7 Disconnect Lucar connection and multiplug (A), SRS warning light (B), remove control unit securing screws (C) and release SRS warning light wiring harness (D)

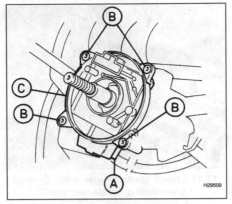

16.15 Disconnect SRS wiring harness multiplug (A), remove slip ring securing screws (B) and remove slip ring (C)

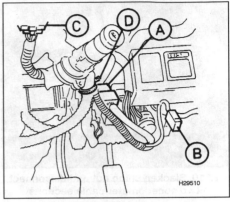

16.23 Disconnect SRS multiplug from main harness (A), SRS fuse (B), SRS multiplug from slip ring (C) and cable tie (D)

7 Disconnect the control unit multiplug and Lucar connection **(see illustration)**.

8 Detach the SRS warning light from the steering wheel.

9 Remove the three screws securing the control unit to the steering wheel.

10 Release the SRS warning light wiring harness and remove the control unit.

Refitting

11 Refit the control unit by reversing the removal procedure, noting the following:

a) *If the control unit is to be renewed, then the bar code on the new item must be recorded by your Rover dealer.*

b) *Take care to ensure that wiring is not trapped between mating surfaces.*

c) *Observe the specified torque wrench setting when tightening the control unit retaining screws (TX20 Torx type) and take care not to cross-thread them.*

d) *Refit the airbag unit, carrying out the system check.*

Slip ring

Removal

12 Set the steering in the straight-ahead position.

13 Remove the airbag unit.

14 Refer to Chapter 10 and remove the steering wheel, followed by the steering column nacelle.

15 Disconnect the airbag wiring harness multiplug from the underside of the slip ring **(see illustration)**.

16 Remove the four screws securing the ring to the column switch assembly and remove the ring from the vehicle.

Refitting

17 Refit the slip ring by reversing the removal procedure, noting the following:

a) *If the slip ring is to be renewed, then the bar code on the new item must be recorded by your Rover dealer.*

b) *Take care to ensure that wiring is not trapped between mating surfaces.*

c) *Refit the airbag unit, carrying out the system check.*

Airbag link harness

Removal

18 Remove the ignition key and wait at least ten minutes to allow the SRS system backup circuit to fully discharge. Disconnect **both** battery leads, earth lead first, to avoid accidental detonation of the airbag.

19 Remove the airbag unit.

20 Set the steering in the straight-ahead position then lock the steering column in its lowest position.

21 Remove the five fusebox cover securing screws and release the cover from the facia.

22 Remove the three screws securing the lower half of the steering column shroud and manoeuvre the lower half of the shroud clear of the column.

23 Disconnect the SRS multiplug from the main wiring harness **(see illustration)**.

24 Release the SRS fuse from the side of the main fusebox.

25 Detach the SRS harness multiplug from the slip ring.

26 Release the cable tie securing the wiring harness to the steering column and remove the harness from the vehicle.

Refitting

27 Refit the harness by reversing the removal procedure, noting the following:

a) *Take care to ensure that the harness is correctly routed and not trapped between mating surfaces.*

b) *Check all wiring connectors are firmly fastened*

c) *Refit the airbag unit, carrying out the system check.*

17 Speedometer drive cable - removal and refitting

1 The speedometer drive cable is in two parts. The lower cable runs from the gearbox to a point just below the fuel filter, while the upper cable runs from that point to the rear of the instrument panel.

Upper cable

Removal

2 Remove the instrument panel and make a note of the correct routing of the speedometer cable.

3 Working in the engine compartment, release the cable sealing grommet from the engine compartment bulkhead and withdraw the cable section from the bulkhead.

Refitting

4 If a new cable is being fitted, transfer the grommet from the old cable to the new item.

5 Have an assistant feed the cable in through the engine compartment bulkhead whilst checking from inside the vehicle that the cable is following the correct route behind the demister duct, over the pedal mounting bracket and through the steering column support bracket.

6 With the cable correctly routed, refit the sealing grommet to the bulkhead then draw the cable through until the coloured tape on the outer cable abuts the sealing grommet.

7 Refit the instrument panel then reconnect the speedometer cable sections and tighten the union nut securely.

Lower cable

Removal

8 Apply the handbrake then jack up the front of the vehicle and support it on axle stands to improve access to the lower end of the cable.

12

17.10 Slacken union nut and disconnect two speedometer cable sections

17.11 Lower speedometer cable O-rings (arrowed) must be renewed

18.3 Horn wiring connectors (A) and retaining bolt (B)

9 Pull out the rubber retaining pin which secures the lower end of the cable in position then withdraw the cable from the gearbox.

10 Slacken the union nut securing the upper and lower cable sections together, then disconnect the two cable sections **(see illustration)**.

11 Release the lower cable from any relevant retaining clips or ties and remove it from the vehicle. Remove the O-rings from the lower end of the cable and discard them as these should be renewed whenever disturbed **(see illustration)**.

Refitting

12 Lubricate the cable lower end fitting O-rings with engine oil and insert the end fitting into the gearbox. Refit the rubber retaining pin to secure the cable in position.

13 Ensure the cable section is correctly routed and is retained by any necessary clamps or ties.

14 Connect the upper cable to the lower cable and tighten the union nut securely. Lower the vehicle to the ground.

18 Horn - removal and refitting

Removal

1 Disconnect the battery negative terminal.

2 Remove the front bumper.

3 Disconnect the horn wiring connectors and unbolt the horn(s) from the body **(see illustration)**.

Refitting

4 Refitting is a reversal of the removal procedure.

19 Windscreen/tailgate wiper blades and arms - inspection and renewal

Refer to *"Weekly Checks"*.

20 Windscreen/headlamp washer system - inspection and adjustment

Refer to *"Weekly Checks"*.

21 Windscreen/tailgate washer system components - removal and refitting

1 The windscreen washer reservoir is situated in the rear left-hand corner of the engine compartment, with the washer system pump being mounted on the side of the reservoir. On 214 models, the reservoir is also used to supply the tailgate washer system via a second pump **(see illustration)**.

Removal

2 To remove the washer reservoir and pump(s), unscrew the mounting nut and bolts and lift the reservoir from the left-hand corner of the engine compartment.

3 Disconnect the wiring connector(s) from the pump(s) then disconnect the plastic tubing from the reservoir and remove the assembly from the vehicle.

1 *Windscreen washer tube T-piece connector*
2 *Windscreen washer tube*
3 *Reservoir cap*
4 *Reservoir mounting nut*
5 *Reservoir mounting bolt*
6 *Washer pump retaining clip*
7 *Reservoir mounting bolt*
8 *Wiring connector*
9 *Windscreen washer pump*
10 *Seal*
11 *Washer reservoir*
12 *Wiring connector**
13 *Tailgate washer pump**
14 *Seal**
15 *Tailgate washer tube**
16 *Non-return valve**
* *Fitted to 214 models only*

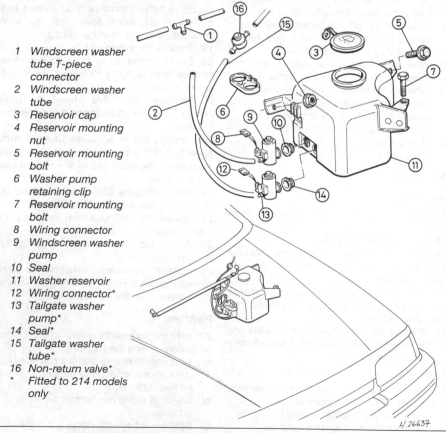

21.1 Windscreen/tailgate washer system components

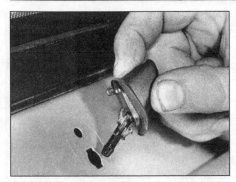

21.5 Removing tailgate washer jet - 214 models

22.3a Slacken spindle nuts . . .

22.3b . . . and remove wiper arms from spindles

4 Empty the reservoir of any remaining fluid then undo the retaining screws and separate the pump(s) and reservoir.

5 If necessary, the windscreen washer nozzles can carefully be prised out of the ventilation grille and disconnected from the tubing. On 214 models, prise the washer jet out and remove it from the tailgate **(see illustration)**.

6 If trouble is experienced at any time with the flow to the tailgate washer, check that the non-return valve is not blocked. The valve is fitted in the tube next to the reservoir and should allow fluid to pass only outwards to the jet.

Refitting

7 Refitting is a reversal of removal. Ensure that the washer tubes are not trapped when refitting the reservoir and note that the connectors for the pumps are colour-coded to aid correct reconnection on reassembly.

22 Windscreen wiper motor and linkage - removal and refitting

Removal

1 Operate the wiper motor then switch it off so that the wiper blades return to the rest position.

2 Stick a piece of masking tape on the windscreen alongside the edge of each wiper blade to use as an alignment aid on refitting, then open the bonnet.

3 Slacken and remove the wiper arm spindle nuts and pull the arms off their spindles **(see illustrations)**. If necessary, the arms can be levered off their spindles by using a large flat-bladed screwdriver.

4 Carefully prise out the seven trim caps from the ventilation grille to gain access to the grille retaining screws. Slacken and remove all the retaining screws then release the eight retaining clips situated along the front edge of the grille and remove the grille from the vehicle **(see illustration)**.

5 Using a large flat-bladed screwdriver,

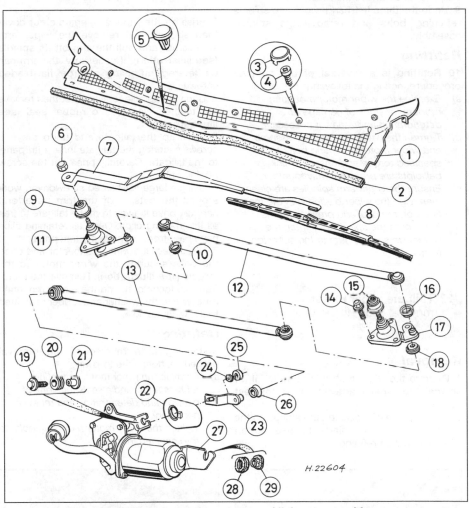

22.4 Windscreen wiper motor and linkage assembly

1 Ventilation grille
2 Sealing strip
3 Trim cap
4 Screw
5 Retaining clip
6 Wiper arm spindle nut
7 Wiper arm
8 Wiper blade
9 Spindle cap
10 Dust seal
11 Right-hand spindle

assembly
12 Connecting rod
13 Operating rod
14 Bolt
15 Spindle cap
16 Dust seal
17 Left-hand spindle assembly
18 Dust seal
19 Wiper motor mounting bolt

20 Mounting rubber
21 Spacer
22 Water shield
23 Wiper motor crank arm
24 Spring washer
25 Nut
26 Dust seal
27 Wiper motor
28 Mounting rubber
29 Spacer

H.22604

12

carefully lever the wiper linkage arm off the wiper motor crank arm balljoint.

6 Disconnect the wiring connector from the wiper motor and remove the four bolts securing the motor to the bulkhead, then remove the motor from the engine compartment taking care not to lose its mounting rubbers (see illustration).

7 Remove the three bolts securing the right-hand wiper arm spindle in position then, using a large flat-bladed screwdriver, disconnect the linkage rod from the spindle balljoint and remove the spindle assembly.

8 Disconnect the two linkage rods from the left-hand wiper arm spindle assembly balljoints and remove the rods.

9 Undo the three left-hand wiper arm spindle retaining bolts and remove the spindle assembly.

Refitting

10 Refitting is a reversal of the removal procedure, noting the following:
a) Examine the wiper motor mounting rubbers for signs of damage or deterioration and renew if necessary.
b) Tighten the wiper arm spindle assembly and wiper motor mounting bolts to the specified torque and ensure all linkage balljoints are pressed firmly together.
c) Ensure the wiper arm spindles are clean then align the wiper blades with the tape fitted on removal and press the arms firmly onto the spindles. Tighten the wiper arm spindle nuts to the specified torque.

23 Tailgate wiper motor - removal and refitting

Removal

1 Operate the wiper motor, then switch it off so that the wiper blade returns to the rest position.

2 Stick a piece of masking tape alongside the edge of the wiper blade to use as an alignment aid on refitting.

22.6 Windscreen wiper motor mounting bolts (arrowed - lower bolt hidden)

3 Prise off the wiper arm spindle nut cover then slacken and remove the wiper arm spindle nut and pull the arm off its spindle (see illustration). If necessary, the arm can be levered off using a large flat-bladed screwdriver.

4 Undo the spindle retaining nut then remove the toothed washer and rubber seal (see illustrations).

5 Open up the tailgate and undo the two screws securing the tailgate inner trim panel to the tailgate. Carefully prise out the screw retaining plugs.

6 Using a large flat-bladed screwdriver, work around the outside of the trim panel and carefully prise it away from the tailgate to free all its retaining clips. Once all retaining clips have been freed, remove the trim panel.

7 Disconnect the wiring connector and undo the bolts securing the wiper motor to the tailgate (see illustration). Remove the motor from the tailgate, noting the motor mounting rubbers and the washer and rubber seal fitted to the wiper spindle.

Refitting

8 Refitting is a reverse of the removal procedure, noting the following:
a) Examine the wiper motor mounting rubbers and spindle seals for signs of damage and deterioration and renew if necessary.
b) Tighten the wiper motor mounting bolts to the specified torque.

23.3 Removing cover to reveal tailgate wiper arm spindle nut

c) Ensure the wiper arm spindle is clean, then align the wiper blade with the tape fitted on removal and press the arm firmly onto the spindle. Tighten the wiper arm spindle nut to the specified torque and refit the nut cover.

24 Radio/cassette player - removal and refitting

Note: The following removal and refitting procedure is for the range of radio/cassette units which Rover fit as standard equipment. Removal and refitting procedures of non-standard units may differ slightly.

Removal

1 Referring to the instructions supplied with the radio/cassette unit, temporarily de-activate the security code.

2 Disconnect the battery negative lead.

3 To remove the unit, two standard DIN extraction tools are required. These are two U-shaped rods which are inserted into the four small holes in the front of the unit to release the unit retaining clips. The tools may possibly be obtained from a Rover dealer or any audio accessory outlet, or can be made out of 3.0 mm wire rod, such as welding rod. Using the tools, push back the clamps on the left and right-hand sides, withdraw the unit

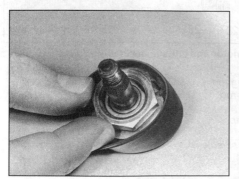

23.4a Unscrew wiper spindle retaining nut . . .

23.4b . . . and withdraw toothed washer and rubber seal

23.7 Tailgate wiper motor mounting bolts (arrowed)

24.3a Use DIN tools to release retaining clips . . .

24.3b . . . then withdraw radio/cassette unit and disconnect aerial and wiring connectors

connections and undo the three nuts securing the speaker to the parcel shelf **(see illustration)**.

7 The speaker can then be lifted away from the parcel shelf from inside the vehicle.

Refitting

8 Refitting is a reverse of the removal procedure.

and disconnect the wiring plugs and aerial **(see illustrations)**.

Refitting

4 Refitting is the reverse of the removal procedure. On completion, connect the battery negative terminal and reactivate the security code.

25 Speakers -
removal and refitting

Removal

Front speaker

1 Remove the front door inner trim panel.
2 Undo the three speaker retaining screws

then withdraw the speaker. Disconnect the speaker wiring connectors and remove the speaker from the door **(see illustrations)**.

Rear speaker - 214 models

3 Prise off the trim cap from the rear seat belt upper mounting point, then slacken and remove the two seat belt guide retaining bolts.
4 Open up the tailgate, then remove the four screws securing the speaker grille panel and position the panel clear of the speaker **(see illustration)**.
5 Undo the four speaker retaining screws then lift out the speaker. Disconnect the wiring connectors and remove the speaker from the vehicle **(see illustration)**.

Rear speaker - 414 models

6 Working from inside the luggage compartment, disconnect the speaker wiring

26 Radio aerial -
removal and refitting

Removal

1 Remove the radio/cassette player.
2 Undo the five screws securing the right-hand lower facia panel and remove the panel to gain access to the relay mounting bracket. Remove the relay mounting bracket retaining bolt.
3 Trace the aerial lead back along its length and free it from any retaining clips or ties. Tie a long piece of string around the aerial end plug.
4 Undo the two screws securing the aerial to the roof and remove the aerial and sealing rubber. Carefully withdraw the aerial lead until the plug comes out of the aerial aperture then untie the string and leave it in position in the vehicle.

Refitting

5 Securely tie the string around the aerial lead plug and fit the rubber seal to the aerial.
6 From inside the vehicle, gently pull the string through the radio aperture whilst feeding the aerial lead in through the roof. When the aerial lead plug emerges on the inside of the vehicle, untie the string.
7 Ensure the rubber seal is correctly located on the base of the aerial then tighten the aerial retaining screws securely.
8 Refit the aerial lead to the necessary retaining clips and ties then refit the relay mounting bracket and right-hand lower facia panel. Tighten all retaining screws and bolts securely.
9 Refit the radio/cassette unit.

25.2a Slacken three retaining screws . . .

25.2b . . . withdraw speaker from door and disconnect wiring connectors

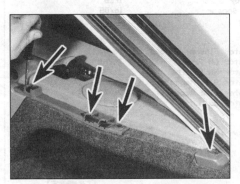

25.4 Rear speaker grille panel retaining screws (arrowed) - 214 models

25.5 Rear speakers are retained by four screws - 214 models

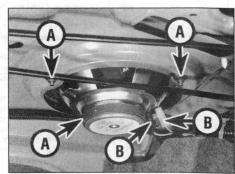

25.6 Rear speaker retaining nuts (A) and wiring connectors (B) - 414 models

12

NOTES:

1. All diagrams are divided into numbered circuits depending on function e.g. Diagram 2: Exterior lighting.
2. Items are arranged in relation to a plan view of the vehicle.
3. Items may appear on more than one diagram so are found using a grid reference e.g. 2/A1 denotes an item on diagram 2 grid location A1.
4. Complex items appear on the diagrams as blocks and are expanded on the internal connections page.
5. Feed wire colour varies dependant on the circuit supplied but all earth wires are coloured black or have a black tracer.
6. Not all items are fitted to all models.

ENGINE COMPARTMENT FUSEBOX

FUSE	RATING	CIRCUIT
3	10A	Hazard Warning Lamps
4	25A	Cooling Fan Relay
7	15A	Horn

ENGINE COMPARTMENT FUSEBOX

FUSE-LINK	RATING	CIRCUIT
FL1	40A	ABS Pump
FL2	40A	Lighting, Cigar Lighter
FL3	40A	Ignition Switch
FL4	40A	Electric Window Relay, Sunroof, Central Door Locking, Heated Rear Window
FL5	40A	Ignition Switch
FL6	60A	Main Relay, Fuel Pump Relay, Lambda Sensor Relay

PASSENGER COMPARTMENT FUSEBOX

FUSE	RATING	CIRCUIT
1	10A	Clock, Instruments, Direction Indicators, Dim/Dip Unit
2	10A	Starter Signal
3	15A	Central Locking
4	10A	Cigar Lighter
5	10A	Dim/Dip Resistor
6	30A	Sunroof
7	10A	RH Side, Tail, Number Plate Lamps
8	10A	LH Side, Tail, Interior Illumination
9	10A	Fog Lamps
10	10A	LH Headlamp Dipped Beam
11	10A	RH Headlamp Dipped Beam
12	15A	Clock, Interior Lamps, Radio Memory
13	15A	Front Wash/Wipe
14	10A	Engine Management System
15	15A	Cooling Fan, Rear Wash/Wipe
16	15A	Reversing Lamps, Stop Lamps, Electric Windows
17	10A	Cigar Lighter, Multi-Function Unit, Radio Cassette Unit
18	10A	Electric Door Mirrors
19	15A	Headlamp Dim/Dip
20	15A	Fuel Pump
21	15A	RH Headlamp Main Beam
22	15A	LH Headlamp Main Beam
23	25A	Heated Rear Window, Heated Door Mirrors
24	20A	Heater Blower Motor
25	15A	Anti-lock Braking System
26	15A	LH Rear Electric Window
27	15A	RH Rear Electric Window
28	15A	LH Front Electric Window
29	15A	RH Front Electric Window

ITEM	DESCRIPTION	DIAGRAM/GRID REF.
1	ABS Electronic Control Unit	4/F5
2	ABS Pump	4/F7
3	ABS Pump Relay	4/F7
4	ABS Solenoid Relay	4/E7
5	ABS Solenoid Valve LH Front	4/F5
6	ABS Solenoid Valve Rear	4/F6
7	ABS Solenoid Valve RH Front	4/F5
8	Alternator	1/A2
9	Ashtray Illumination	2b/F5
10	Battery	1/B6, 1a/B6, 2/B6, 2a/B6, 2b/A7, 3/B7, 3a/B7, 4/B7, 5/B6
11	Canister Purge Solenoid (Cat. Only)	1a/G3
12	Central Locking Control Unit	3a/H1
13	Central Locking Motor LH Front	3a/J8
14	Central Locking Motor LH Rear	3a/M8
15	Central Locking Motor RH Rear	3a/M1
16	Central Locking Switch	3a/J1
17	Choke Switch	1/K4
18	Cigar Lighter	2b/F6
19	Cigar Lighter Relay	2b/E4
20	Clock	2b/D5
21	Coolant Temp. Gauge Sender Unit	1/C1
22	Coolant Temp. Sensor	1a/D4
23	Cooling Fan Motor	1/A4
24	Cooling Fan Switch	1/A3
25	Cooling Fan Relay	1/E8
26	Crank. Position Sensor	1a/B5
27	Dim/Dip Resistor	2/A5
28	Dim/Dip Unit	2/J2
29	Dimmer Unit	2b/J1
30	Direction Indicator Flasher Relay	2a/F2
31	Direction Indicator LH Front	2a/A8
32	Direction Indicator RH Front	2a/A1
33	Direction Indicator Side Repeater LH	2a/C8
34	Direction Indicator Side Repeater RH	2a/C1
35	Direction Indicator Switch	2a/J3
36	Distributor	1/C4, 1a/B3
37	Electric Door Mirror LH	3a/E8

Notes, fuses and key to wiring diagrams

H24200

T.H.MARKE

ITEM	DESCRIPTION	DIAGRAM/GRID REF.	ITEM	DESCRIPTION	DIAGRAM/GRID REF.
38	Electric Door Mirror RH	3a/E1	86	Lamp Cluster LH Rear	2/M8, 2a/M8
39	Electric Door Mirror Switch	3a/F2	87	Lamp Cluster RH Rear	2/M1, 2a/M1
40	Electric Window Control Unit	3a/H8	88	Light Switch	2/J3, 2a/J4, 2b/J3, 5/J4
41	Electric Window Motor LH Front	3a/G8			
42	Electric Window Motor LH Rear	3a/L8			
43	Electric Window Motor RH Front	3a/H1	89	Low Brake Fluid Sender Unit	1/E2
44	Electric Window Motor RH Rear	3a/L1	90	Luggage Comp. Lamp	2b/L5
45	Electric Window Relay	3a/E5	91	Luggage Comp. Lamp Switch	2b/M4
46	Electric Window Switch LH Front	3a/G7	92	Main Beam Relay	2/E5
47	Electric Window Switch LH Rear	3a/L7	93	Main Relay	1a/F6
48	Electric Window Switch RH Front	3a/J4	94	Manifold Heater	1/F4, 1a/F3
49	Electric Window Switch RH Rear	3a/L2	95	Manifold Heater Relay	1/F7, 1a/H6
50	Foglamp Relay	2a/G6			
51	Foglamp Switch	2a/J5, 2b/J4	96	Manifold Temp. Switch	1/E4
52	Fuel Gauge Sender Unit	1/M4	97	MEMS Unit	1a/C7
53	Fuel Injector	1a/F3	98	Multi-Function Unit	2b/D2, 3/E2
54	Fuel Pump	1a/M4			
55	Fuel Pump Relay	1a/F8	99	Number Plate Lamp	2/M4, 2/M5
56	Glove Box Lamp	2b/E7			
57	Glove Box Lamp Switch	2b/E7	100	Oil Pressure Switch	1/C2
58	Handbrake Warning Switch	1/L5	101	Radio/Cassette Unit	5/F5
59	Hazard Warning Lamp Switch	2a/J5, 2b/J5	102	Reversing Lamp Switch	2a/C5
60	Headlamp Unit LH	2/A7	103	Spark Plugs	1/C3, 1a/B3
61	Headlamp Unit RH	2/A2	104	Speaker LH Front	5/F8
62	Heated Rear Window	3/L4	105	Speaker LH Rear	5/M8
63	Heated Rear Window Relay	3/F1	106	Speaker RH Front	5/F1
64	Heated Rear Window Switch	2b/J5, 3/J5	107	Speaker RH Rear	5/M1
65	Heater Blower Motor	3/G7	108	Starter Motor	1/A5
66	Heater Blower Resistor Pack	3/G7	109	Starter Relay	1/D7, 1a/G6
67	Heater Blower Switch	3/J7	110	Stepper Motor	1a/E3
68	Heater Blower Switch Illumination	2b/E6	111	Stop-Lamp Switch	2a/E4, 4/D3
69	Horn	3/A1, 3/A8	112	Sunroof Control Switch	5/J2
70	Horn Relay	3/G5	113	Sunroof Control Unit	5/H5
71	Horn Switch	3/K3	114	Sunroof Microswitch	5/K5
72	Idle Solenoid	1/F4	115	Sunroof Motor	5/K4
73	Ignition Amplifier Module	1/C4	116	Sunroof Relay	5/H6
74	Ignition Coil	1/A7, 1a/A7	117	Throttle Pedal Switch	1/G3, 1a/H3
75	Ignition Switch	1/K1, 1a/L1, 2/J1, 2a/J1, 2b/K1, 3/J1, 3a/F2, 4/J1, 5/J1	118	Throttle Potentiometer	1a/E2
			119	Washer Pump Front	3/E6
			120	Washer Pump Rear	3/E6
			121	Wheel Sensor LH Front	4/D8
76	Inertia Switch	1a/L4	122	Wheel Sensor LH Rear	4/L8
77	Instrument Cluster	1/J3, 1a/K3, 2/G4, 2a/G3, 2b/G3, 4/J3	123	Wheel Sensor RH Front	4/D1
			124	Wheel Sensor RH Rear	4/L1
			125	Wiper Motor Front	3/C3
			126	Wiper Motor Rear	3/M4
			127	Wiper Relay Front	3/D1
			128	Wiper Relay Rear	3/M1
78	Intake Air Temp. Sensor	1a/E3	129	Wiper Switch Front	3/J3
79	Interior Lamp	2b/J4	130	Wiper Switch Rear	3/K3
80	Interior Lamp Door Switch LH Front	2b/H8			
81	Interior Lamp Door Switch LH Rear	2b/L8			
82	Interior Lamp Door Switch RH Front	2b/H1			
83	Interior Lamp Door Switch RH Rear	2b/L1			
84	Lambda Sensor (Cat. Only)	1a/A4			
85	Lambda Sensor Relay (Cat. Only)	1a/H8			

Key to wiring diagrams (continued)

H24201
T.M.MARKE

INTERNAL CONNECTION DETAILS

INTERNAL CONNECTIONS FOR ITEM 39

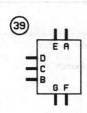

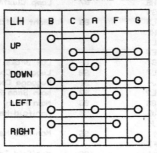

LH	B	C	A	F	G
UP					
DOWN					
LEFT					
RIGHT					

RH	B	C	A	F	G
UP					
DOWN					
LEFT					
RIGHT					

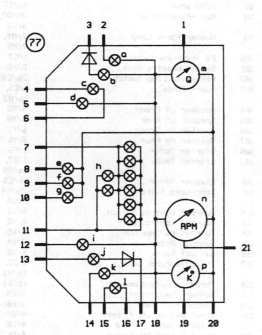

KEY TO INSTRUMENT CLUSTER (ITEM 77)

a = ABS Warning Lamp
b = Tailgate Open Warning Lamp
c = Hazard Warning Lamp
d = Handbrake/Low Brake Fluid Warning Lamp
e = RH Direction Indicator Lamp
f = Main Beam Warning Lamp
g = LH Direction Indicator Lamp
h = Instrument Illumination
i = Oil Pressure Warning Lamp
j = Ignition Warning Lamp
k = Choke Warning Lamp
l = Trailer Warning Lamp
m = Fuel Gauge
n = Tachometer
p = Coolant Temperature Gauge

WIRE COLOURS

B	Blue	R	Red
Bk	Black	Rs	Pink
Bn	Brown	S	Grey
LGn	Light Green	V	Violet
Gn	Green	W	White
O	Orange	Y	Yellow
P	Purple		

KEY TO SYMBOLS

PLUG-IN CONNECTOR

EARTH

BULB

LINE CONNECTOR

DIODE

FUSE/ FUSIBLE LINK

EARTH POINT

E4

Internal connection details, wire colours and key to symbols

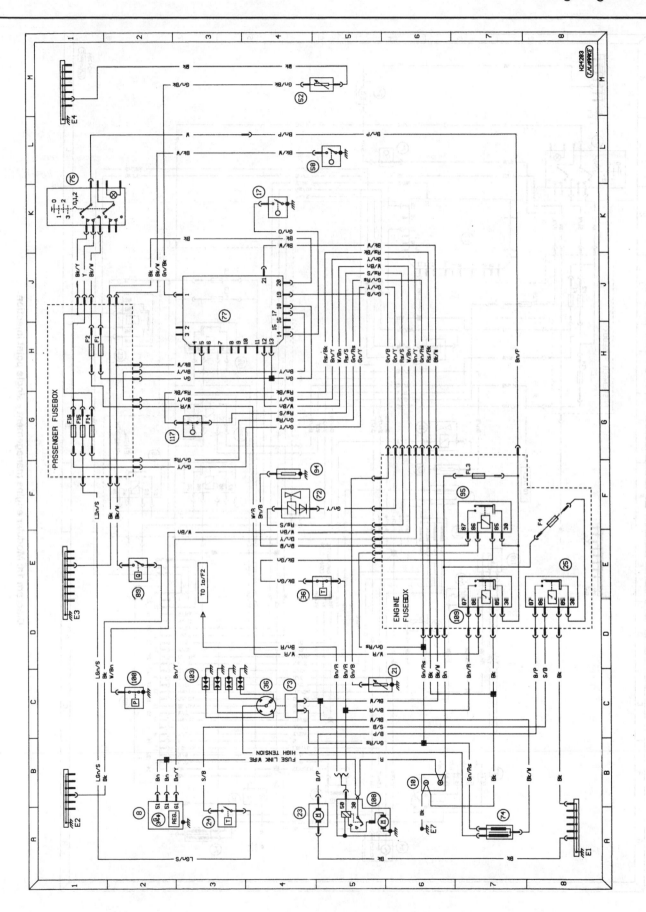

Diagram 1: Starting, charging, ignition (carburettor models), cooling fan, warning lamps and gauges. All models

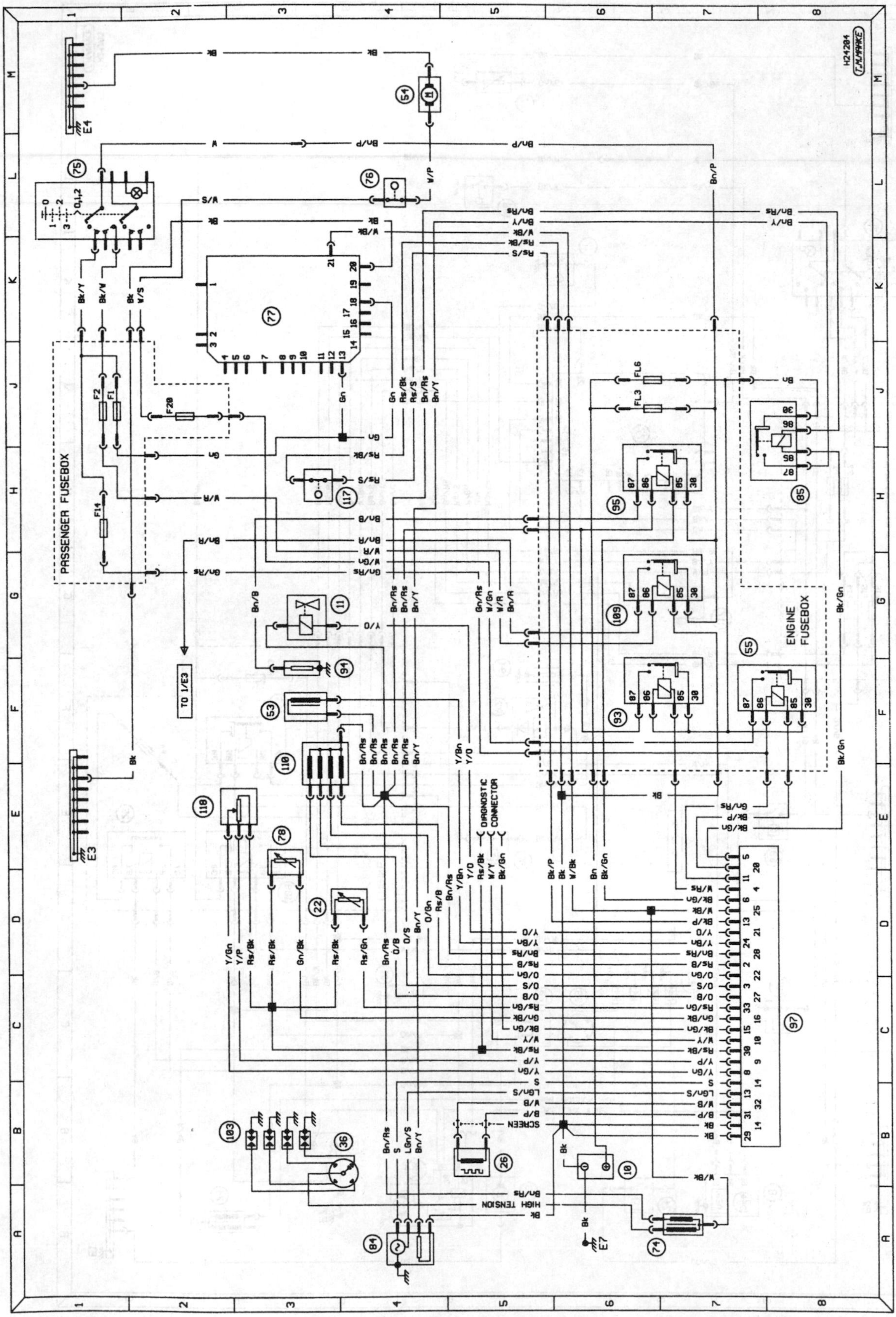

Diagram 1a: Modular engine management - single point injection

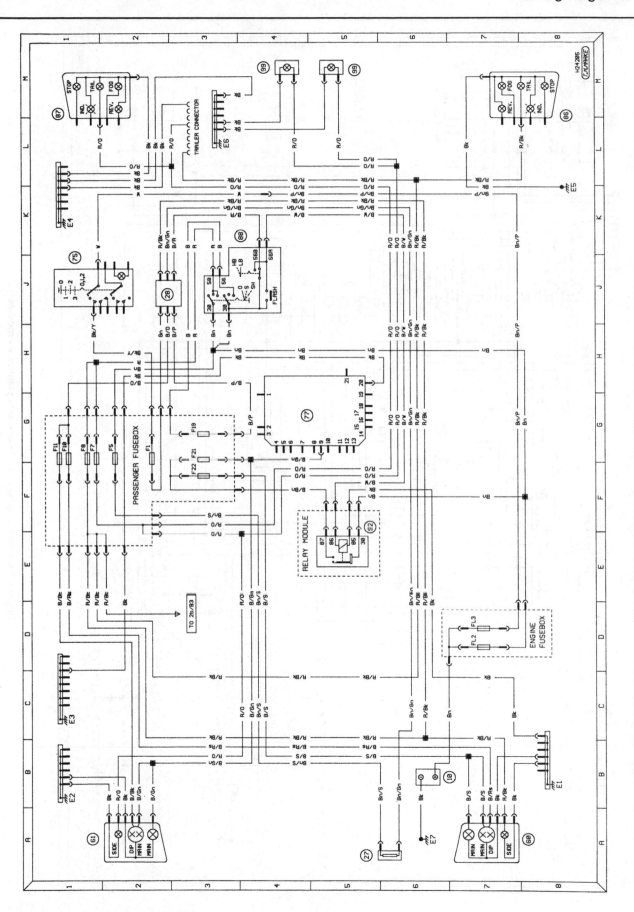

Diagram 2: Exterior lighting - sidelamps and headlamps. All models

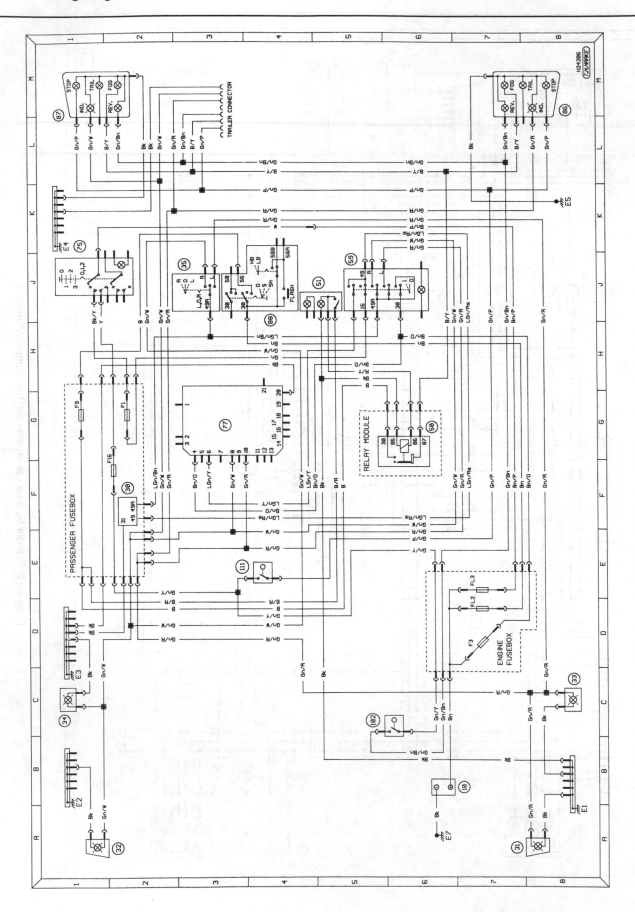

Diagram 2a: Exterior lighting - signal/warning lamps. All models

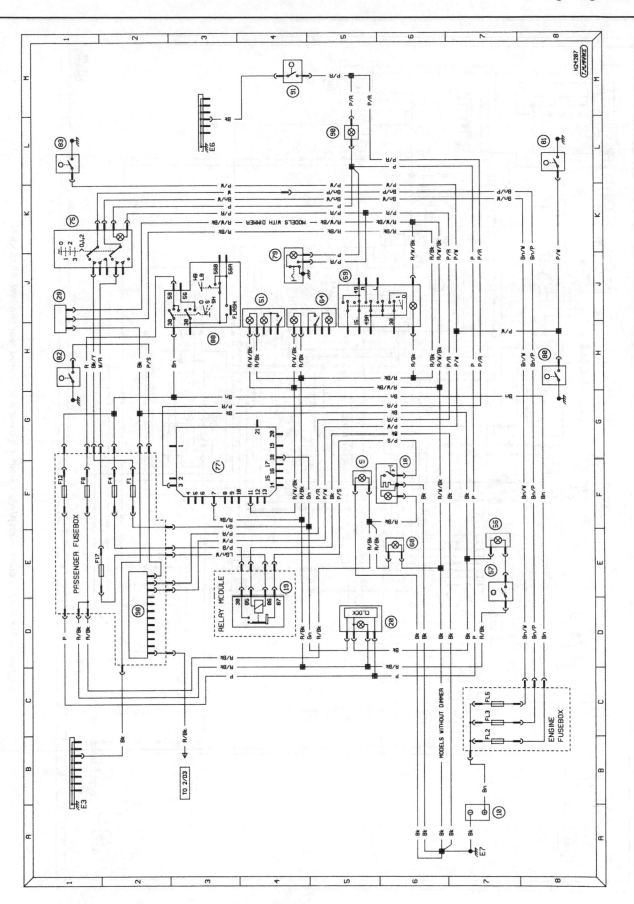

Diagram 2b: Interior lighting and associated circuits. All models

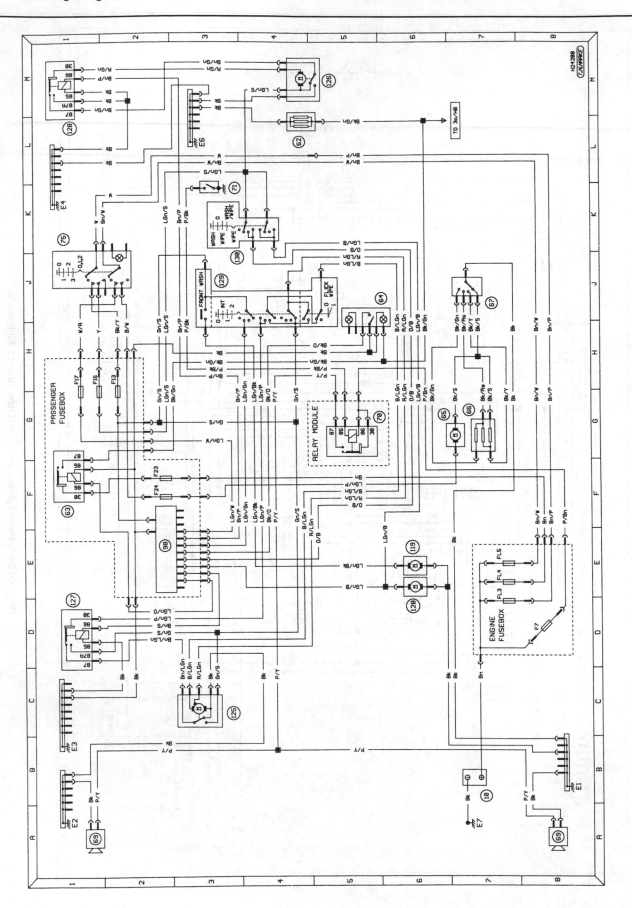

Diagram 3: Ancillary circuits - wash/wipe, heater blower and heated rear window. All models

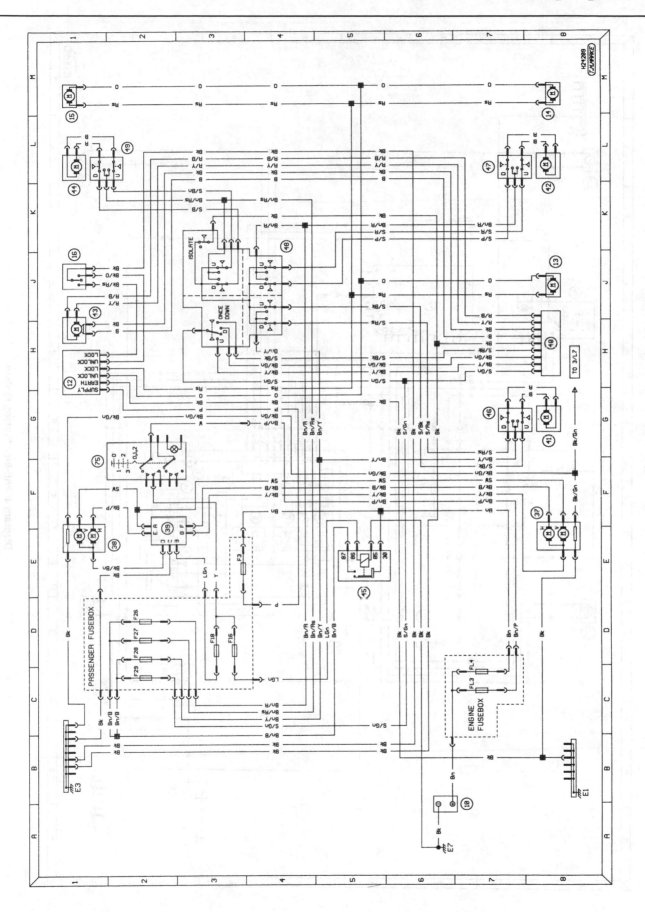

Diagram 3a: Ancillary circuits - electric windows, mirrors and central locking

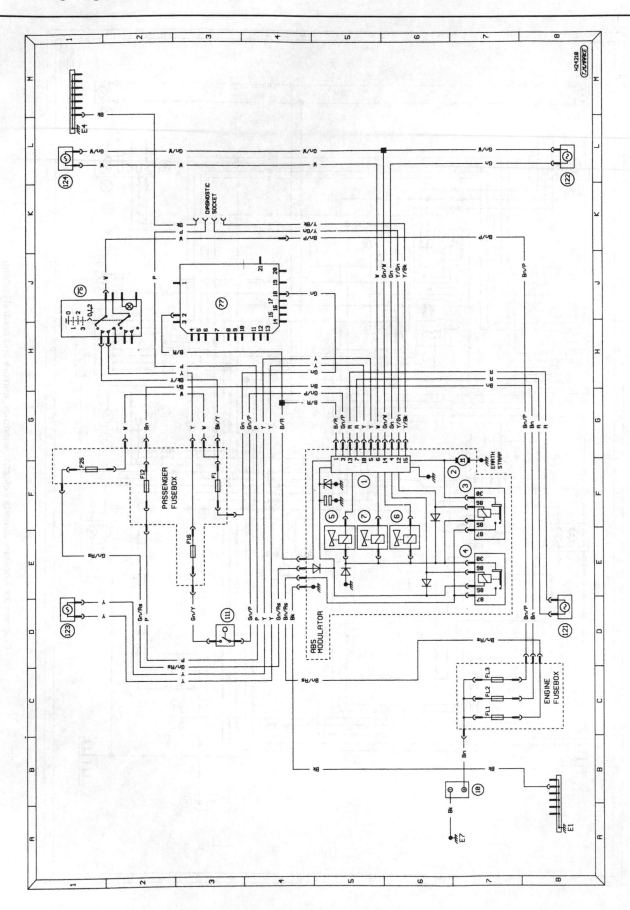

Diagram 4: Anti-lock braking system

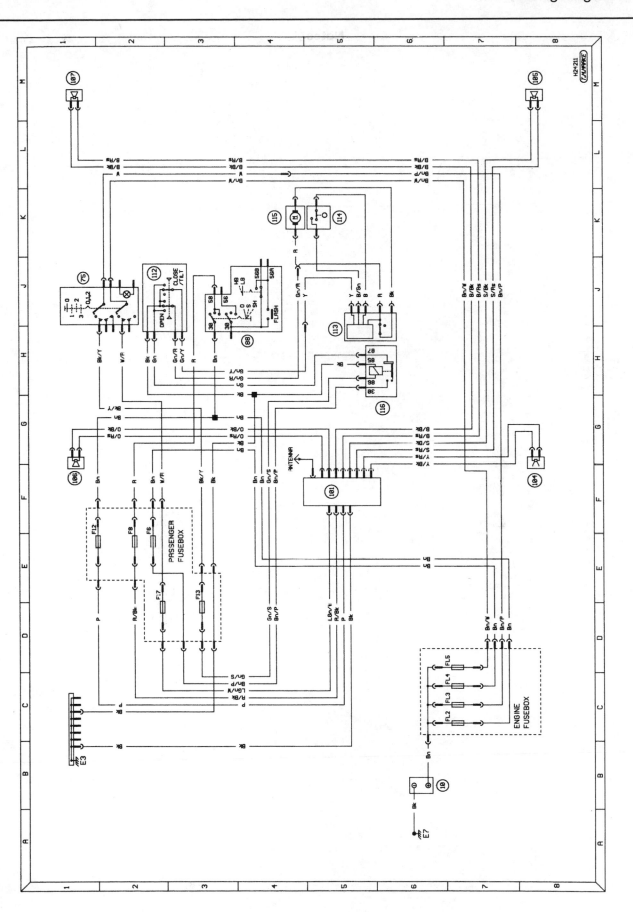

Diagram 5: In-car entertainment and electric sunroof

Notes

Dimensions and weights

Dimensions

Overall length:
- 214 models . . . . 4220 mm
- 414 models . . . . 4370 mm

Overall width (including mirrors) . . . . 1940 mm
Overall height (at kerb weight) . . . . 1400 mm
Wheelbase . . . . 2550 mm
Turning circle . . . . 10 200 mm

Weights

Kerb weight:*
- 214 S - 3-door . . . . 995 kg
- 214 Si - 3-door . . . . 1020 kg
- 214 S - 5-door . . . . 1025 kg
- 214 Si - 5-door . . . . 1030 kg
- 214 SLi - 5-door . . . . 1050 kg
- 214 GSi - 5-door . . . . 1065 kg
- 414 Si - 4-door . . . . 1020 kg
- 414 SLi - 4-door . . . . 1040 kg

Maximum gross vehicle weight . . . . 1580 kg
Maximum roof rack load . . . . 65 kg
Maximum towing weight with braked trailer:
- 214 S models . . . . 900 kg
- All other models . . . . 1000 kg

Towing hitch downward load . . . . 50 kg

*Vehicle unladen, less options, with full fuel tank, coolant and all fluids, tools and spare wheel. Add 5 kg if catalytic converter is fitted

Conversion Factors

Length (distance)

Inches (in)	x 25.4	= Millimetres (mm)	x 0.0394	= Inches (in)
Feet (ft)	x 0.305	= Metres (m)	x 3.281	= Feet (ft)
Miles	x 1.609	= Kilometres (km)	x 0.621	= Miles

Volume (capacity)

Cubic inches (cu in; in^3)	x 16.387	= Cubic centimetres (cc; cm^3)	x 0.061	= Cubic inches (cu in; in^3)
Imperial pints (Imp pt)	x 0.568	= Litres (l)	x 1.76	= Imperial pints (Imp pt)
Imperial quarts (Imp qt)	x 1.137	= Litres (l)	x 0.88	= Imperial quarts (Imp qt)
Imperial quarts (Imp qt)	x 1.201	= US quarts (US qt)	x 0.833	= Imperial quarts (Imp qt)
US quarts (US qt)	x 0.946	= Litres (l)	x 1.057	= US quarts (US qt)
Imperial gallons (Imp gal)	x 4.546	= Litres (l)	x 0.22	= Imperial gallons (Imp gal)
Imperial gallons (Imp gal)	x 1.201	= US gallons (US gal)	x 0.833	= Imperial gallons (Imp gal)
US gallons (US gal)	x 3.785	= Litres (l)	x 0.264	= US gallons (US gal)

Mass (weight)

Ounces (oz)	x 28.35	= Grams (g)	x 0.035	= Ounces (oz)
Pounds (lb)	x 0.454	= Kilograms (kg)	x 2.205	= Pounds (lb)

Force

Ounces-force (ozf; oz)	x 0.278	= Newtons (N)	x 3.6	= Ounces-force (ozf; oz)
Pounds-force (lbf; lb)	x 4.448	= Newtons (N)	x 0.225	= Pounds-force (lbf; lb)
Newtons (N)	x 0.1	= Kilograms-force (kgf; kg)	x 9.81	= Newtons (N)

Pressure

Pounds-force per square inch (psi; lbf/in^2; lb/in^2)	x 0.070	= Kilograms-force per square centimetre (kgf/cm^2; kg/cm^2)	x 14.223	= Pounds-force per square inch (psi; lbf/in^2; lb/in^2)
Pounds-force per square inch (psi; lbf/in^2; lb/in^2)	x 0.068	= Atmospheres (atm)	x 14.696	= Pounds-force per square inch (psi; lbf/in^2; lb/in^2)
Pounds-force per square inch (psi; lbf/in^2; lb/in^2)	x 0.069	= Bars	x 14.5	= Pounds-force per square inch (psi; lbf/in^2; lb/in^2)
Pounds-force per square inch (psi; lbf/in^2; lb/in^2)	x 6.895	= Kilopascals (kPa)	x 0.145	= Pounds-force per square inch (psi; lbf/in^2; lb/in^2)
Kilopascals (kPa)	x 0.01	= Kilograms-force per square centimetre (kgf/cm^2; kg/cm^2)	x 98.1	= Kilopascals (kPa)
Millibar (mbar)	x 100	= Pascals (Pa)	x 0.01	= Millibar (mbar)
Millibar (mbar)	x 0.0145	= Pounds-force per square inch (psi; lbf/in^2; lb/in^2)	x 68.947	= Millibar (mbar)
Millibar (mbar)	x 0.75	= Millimetres of mercury (mmHg)	x 1.333	= Millibar (mbar)
Millibar (mbar)	x 0.401	= Inches of water (inH$_2$O)	x 2.491	= Millibar (mbar)
Millimetres of mercury (mmHg)	x 0.535	= Inches of water (inH$_2$O)	x 1.868	= Millimetres of mercury (mmHg)
Inches of water (inH$_2$O)	x 0.036	= Pounds-force per square inch (psi; lbf/in^2; lb/in^2)	x 27.68	= Inches of water (inH$_2$O)

Torque (moment of force)

Pounds-force inches (lbf in; lb in)	x 1.152	= Kilograms-force centimetre (kgf cm; kg cm)	x 0.868	= Pounds-force inches (lbf in; lb in)
Pounds-force inches (lbf in; lb in)	x 0.113	= Newton metres (Nm)	x 8.85	= Pounds-force inches (lbf in; lb in)
Pounds-force inches (lbf in; lb in)	x 0.083	= Pounds-force feet (lbf ft; lb ft)	x 12	= Pounds-force inches (lbf in; lb in)
Pounds-force feet (lbf ft; lb ft)	x 0.138	= Kilograms-force metres (kgf m; kg m)	x 7.233	= Pounds-force feet (lbf ft; lb ft)
Pounds-force feet (lbf ft; lb ft)	x 1.356	= Newton metres (Nm)	x 0.738	= Pounds-force feet (lbf ft; lb ft)
Newton metres (Nm)	x 0.102	= Kilograms-force metres (kgf m; kg m)	x 9.804	= Newton metres (Nm)

Power

Horsepower (hp)	x 745.7	= Watts (W)	x 0.0013	= Horsepower (hp)

Velocity (speed)

Miles per hour (miles/hr; mph)	x 1.609	= Kilometres per hour (km/hr; kph)	x 0.621	= Miles per hour (miles/hr; mph)

Fuel consumption*

Miles per gallon (mpg)	x 0.354	= Kilometres per litre (km/l)	x 2.825	= Miles per gallon (mpg)

Temperature

Degrees Fahrenheit = (°C x 1.8) + 32   Degrees Celsius (Degrees Centigrade; °C) = (°F - 32) x 0.56

It is common practice to convert from miles per gallon (mpg) to litres/100 kilometres (l/100km), where mpg x l/100 km = 282

Spare parts are available from many sources, including vehicle manufacturer's appointed garages, accessory shops, and motor factors. To be sure of obtaining the correct parts, it will sometimes be necessary to quote the vehicle identification number. If possible, it can also be useful to take the old parts along for positive identification. Items such as starter motors and alternators may be available under a service exchange scheme - any parts returned should always be clean.

Our advice regarding spare part sources is as follows.

Officially-appointed garages

This is the best source of parts which are peculiar to your vehicle and which are not otherwise generally available (eg: badges, interior trim, certain body panels, etc). It is also the only place at which you should buy parts if the vehicle is still under warranty.

Accessory shops

These are very good places to buy materials and components needed for the maintenance of your vehicle (oil, air and fuel filters, spark plugs, light bulbs, drivebelts, oils and greases, brake pads, touch-up paint, etc). Components of this nature sold by a reputable shop are of the same standard as those used by the vehicle manufacturer.

Besides components, these shops also sell tools and general accessories, usually have convenient opening hours, charge lower prices, and can often be found not far from home. Some accessory shops have parts counters where the components needed for almost any repair job can be purchased or ordered.

Motor factors

Good factors will stock all the more important components which wear out comparatively quickly, and can sometimes supply individual components needed for the overhaul of a larger assembly (eg: brake seals and hydraulic parts, bearing shells, pistons, valves, alternator brushes). They may also handle work such as cylinder block reboring, crankshaft regrinding and balancing, etc.

Tyre and exhaust specialists

These outlets may be independent, or members of a local or national chain. They frequently offer competitive prices when compared with a main dealer or local garage, but it will pay to obtain several quotes before making a decision. When researching prices, also ask what "extras" may be added - for instance, fitting a new valve and balancing the wheel are both commonly charged on top of the price of a new tyre.

Other sources

Beware of parts or materials obtained from market stalls, car boot sales or similar outlets. Such items are not always sub-standard, but there is little chance of compensation if they do prove unsatisfactory. In the case of safety-critical components such as brake pads, there is the risk not only of financial loss but also of an accident causing injury or death.

Second-hand components or assemblies obtained from a car breaker can be a good buy in some circumstances but this sort of purchase is best made by the experienced DIY mechanic.

Vehicle identification

Modifications are a continuing and unpublicised process in vehicle manufacture, quite apart from major model changes. Spare parts manuals and lists are compiled upon a numerical basis, the individual vehicle identification numbers being essential to correct identification of the component concerned.

When ordering spare parts, always give as much information as possible. Quote the vehicle model, year of manufacture, body and engine numbers as appropriate.

The *vehicle identification plate* is situated at the bottom of the passenger door pillar **(see illustration)**. It gives the VIN (vehicle identification number), vehicle weight information and paint and trim colour codes.

The *vehicle identification number* is repeated in the form of stamped numbers on the centre of the engine compartment bulkhead **(see illustration)**.

The *body number* is stamped into a plate fixed to the left-hand side of the spare wheel well, in the luggage compartment.

The *engine number* is stamped into a raised pad on the front left-hand end of the cylinder block/crankcase, next to the gearbox **(see illustration)**.

Other identification numbers or codes are stamped on major items such as the gearbox, final drive housing, distributor, etc. These numbers are unlikely to be needed by the home mechanic.

Vehicle identification plate on passenger door pillar

Vehicle identification number on engine compartment bulkhead

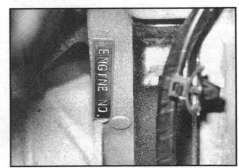

Engine number on front of cylinder block/crankcase

Whenever servicing, repair or overhaul work is carried out on the car or its components, observe the following procedures and instructions. This will assist in carrying out the operation efficiently and to a professional standard of workmanship.

Joint mating faces and gaskets

When separating components at their mating faces, never insert screwdrivers or similar implements into the joint between the faces in order to prise them apart. This can cause severe damage which results in oil leaks, coolant leaks, etc upon reassembly. Separation is usually achieved by tapping along the joint with a soft-faced hammer in order to break the seal. However, note that this method may not be suitable where dowels are used for component location.

Where a gasket is used between the mating faces of two components, a new one must be fitted on reassembly; fit it dry unless otherwise stated in the repair procedure. Make sure that the mating faces are clean and dry, with all traces of old gasket removed. When cleaning a joint face, use a tool which is unlikely to score or damage the face, and remove any burrs or nicks with an oilstone or fine file.

Make sure that tapped holes are cleaned with a pipe cleaner, and keep them free of jointing compound, if this is being used, unless specifically instructed otherwise.

Ensure that all orifices, channels or pipes are clear, and blow through them, preferably using compressed air.

Oil seals

Oil seals can be removed by levering them out with a wide flat-bladed screwdriver or similar implement. Alternatively, a number of self-tapping screws may be screwed into the seal, and these used as a purchase for pliers or some similar device in order to pull the seal free.

Whenever an oil seal is removed from its working location, either individually or as part of an assembly, it should be renewed.

The very fine sealing lip of the seal is easily damaged, and will not seal if the surface it contacts is not completely clean and free from scratches, nicks or grooves. If the original sealing surface of the component cannot be restored, and the manufacturer has not made provision for slight relocation of the seal relative to the sealing surface, the component should be renewed.

Protect the lips of the seal from any surface which may damage them in the course of fitting. Use tape or a conical sleeve where possible. Lubricate the seal lips with oil before fitting and, on dual-lipped seals, fill the space between the lips with grease.

Unless otherwise stated, oil seals must be fitted with their sealing lips toward the lubricant to be sealed.

Use a tubular drift or block of wood of the appropriate size to install the seal and, if the seal housing is shouldered, drive the seal down to the shoulder. If the seal housing is unshouldered, the seal should be fitted with its face flush with the housing top face (unless otherwise instructed).

Screw threads and fastenings

Seized nuts, bolts and screws are quite a common occurrence where corrosion has set in, and the use of penetrating oil or releasing fluid will often overcome this problem if the offending item is soaked for a while before attempting to release it. The use of an impact driver may also provide a means of releasing such stubborn fastening devices, when used in conjunction with the appropriate screwdriver bit or socket. If none of these methods works, it may be necessary to resort to the careful application of heat, or the use of a hacksaw or nut splitter device.

Studs are usually removed by locking two nuts together on the threaded part, and then using a spanner on the lower nut to unscrew the stud. Studs or bolts which have broken off below the surface of the component in which they are mounted can sometimes be removed using a stud extractor. Always ensure that a blind tapped hole is completely free from oil, grease, water or other fluid before installing the bolt or stud. Failure to do this could cause the housing to crack due to the hydraulic action of the bolt or stud as it is screwed in.

When tightening a castellated nut to accept a split pin, tighten the nut to the specified torque, where applicable, and then tighten further to the next split pin hole. Never slacken the nut to align the split pin hole, unless stated in the repair procedure.

When checking or retightening a nut or bolt to a specified torque setting, slacken the nut or bolt by a quarter of a turn, and then retighten to the specified setting. However, this should not be attempted where angular tightening has been used.

For some screw fastenings, notably cylinder head bolts or nuts, torque wrench settings are no longer specified for the latter stages of tightening, "angle-tightening" being called up instead. Typically, a fairly low torque wrench setting will be applied to the bolts/nuts in the correct sequence, followed by one or more stages of tightening through specified angles.

Locknuts, locktabs and washers

Any fastening which will rotate against a component or housing during tightening should always have a washer between it and the relevant component or housing.

Spring or split washers should always be renewed when they are used to lock a critical component such as a big-end bearing retaining bolt or nut. Locktabs which are folded over to retain a nut or bolt should always be renewed.

Self-locking nuts can be re-used in non-critical areas, providing resistance can be felt when the locking portion passes over the bolt or stud thread. However, it should be noted that self-locking stiffnuts tend to lose their effectiveness after long periods of use, and should then be renewed as a matter of course.

Split pins must always be replaced with new ones of the correct size for the hole.

When thread-locking compound is found on the threads of a fastener which is to be re-used, it should be cleaned off with a wire brush and solvent, and fresh compound applied on reassembly.

Special tools

Some repair procedures in this manual entail the use of special tools such as a press, two or three-legged pullers, spring compressors, etc. Wherever possible, suitable readily-available alternatives to the manufacturer's special tools are described, and are shown in use. In some instances, where no alternative is possible, it has been necessary to resort to the use of a manufacturer's tool, and this has been done for reasons of safety as well as the efficient completion of the repair operation. Unless you are highly-skilled and have a thorough understanding of the procedures described, never attempt to bypass the use of any special tool when the procedure described specifies its use. Not only is there a very great risk of personal injury, but expensive damage could be caused to the components involved.

Environmental considerations

When disposing of used engine oil, brake fluid, antifreeze, etc, give due consideration to any detrimental environmental effects. Do not, for instance, pour any of the above liquids down drains into the general sewage system, or onto the ground to soak away. Many local council refuse tips provide a facility for waste oil disposal, as do some garages. If none of these facilities are available, consult your local Environmental Health Department, or the National Rivers Authority, for further advice.

With the universal tightening-up of legislation regarding the emission of environmentally-harmful substances from motor vehicles, most vehicles have tamperproof devices fitted to the main adjustment points of the fuel system. These devices are primarily designed to prevent unqualified persons from adjusting the fuel/air mixture, with the chance of a consequent increase in toxic emissions. If such devices are found during servicing or overhaul, they should, wherever possible, be renewed or refitted in accordance with the manufacturer's requirements or current legislation.

OIL CARE
FOLLOW THE CODE

OIL BANK LINE
0800 66 33 66

Note: It is antisocial and illegal to dump oil down the drain. To find the location of your local oil recycling bank, call this number free.

The jack supplied with the vehicle tool kit should only be used for changing the roadwheels - see *"Wheel changing"* at the front of this Manual.

When using the jack supplied with the vehicle, position it on firm ground and locate its head in the relevant vehicle jacking point **(see illustration)**.

With jack base on firm ground, locate jack head with jacking point

On models fitted with side skirt/sill extension trim panels, the access panel must first be removed from the trim panel to gain access to jacking points 2, 3, 4 and 5 **(see illustrations)**.

When carrying out any other kind of work, raise the vehicle using a hydraulic (or trolley) jack, and always supplement this jack with

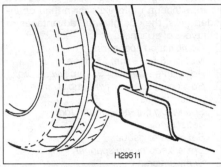

Removing side skirt/sill extension access panel to gain access to jacking point

axle stands positioned under the indicated points. Always use the recommended jacking and support points, and refer to the following Instructions:

If the front of the vehicle is to be raised, firmly apply the handbrake and place the jack head under point 1. Jack the vehicle up and position the axle stands either on the sills at points 2 and 3, or the underbody longitudinal supports at points 8.

To raise the rear of the vehicle, chock the front wheels and place the jack head under point 6, the reinforced location pad immediately in front of the rear towing eye. The axle stands should be placed either on the sills at points 4 and 5 or the underbody longitudinal supports at points 9.

To raise the side of the vehicle, place the jack head under the sill at point 2 or 3 (as applicable) at the front, then jack up the vehicle and position an axle stand under the longitudinal support at point 8. Remove the jack and position it under point 4 or 5 (as applicable) then jack up the rear of the vehicle and position an axle stand under the longitudinal support at point 9.

Never work under, around or near a raised vehicle unless it is adequately supported in at least two places.

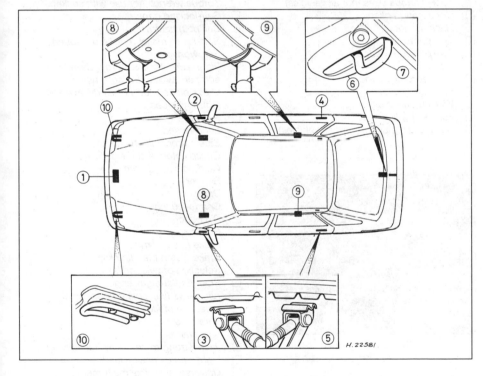

Jacking towing and support points
1 *Front central jack location pad*
2 *Right-hand sill front jacking/support point*
3 *Left-hand sill front jacking/support point*
4 *Right-hand sill rear jacking/support point*
5 *Left-hand sill rear jacking/support point*
6 *Rear reinforced jack location pad*
7 *Rear towing eye*
8 *Front underbody longitudinal support points*
9 *Rear underbody longitudinal support points*
10 *Front towing eyes*

Radio/cassette Anti-theft system - precaution

The radio/cassette unit fitted as standard equipment by Rover is equipped with a built-in security code to deter thieves. If the power source to the unit is cut, the anti-theft system will activate. Even if the power source is immediately reconnected, the radio/cassette unit will not function until the correct security code has been entered. Therefore, if you do not know the correct security code for the unit, do not disconnect the battery negative lead, or remove the radio/cassette unit from the vehicle.

The procedure for reprogramming a unit that has been disconnected from its power supply varies from model to model. Consult the handbook supplied with the unit for specific details or refer to your Rover dealer.

Introduction

A selection of good tools is a fundamental requirement for anyone contemplating the maintenance and repair of a motor vehicle. For the owner who does not possess any, their purchase will prove a considerable expense, offsetting some of the savings made by doing-it-yourself. However, provided that the tools purchased meet the relevant national safety standards and are of good quality, they will last for many years and prove an extremely worthwhile investment.

To help the average owner to decide which tools are needed to carry out the various tasks detailed in this manual, we have compiled three lists of tools under the following headings: *Maintenance and minor repair, Repair and overhaul*, and *Special*. Newcomers to practical mechanics should start off with the *Maintenance and minor repair* tool kit, and confine themselves to the simpler jobs around the vehicle. Then, as confidence and experience grow, more difficult tasks can be undertaken, with extra tools being purchased as, and when, they are needed. In this way, a *Maintenance and minor repair* tool kit can be built up into a *Repair and overhaul* tool kit over a considerable period of time, without any major cash outlays. The experienced do-it-yourselfer will have a tool kit good enough for most repair and overhaul procedures, and will add tools from the *Special* category when it is felt that the expense is justified by the amount of use to which these tools will be put.

Maintenance and minor repair tool kit

The tools given in this list should be considered as a minimum requirement if routine maintenance, servicing and minor repair operations are to be undertaken. We recommend the purchase of combination spanners (ring one end, open-ended the other); although more expensive than open-ended ones, they do give the advantages of both types of spanner.

☐ *Combination spanners:*
Metric - 8 to 19 mm inclusive
☐ *Adjustable spanner - 35 mm jaw (approx.)*
☐ *Spark plug spanner (with rubber insert) - petrol models*
☐ *Spark plug gap adjustment tool - petrol models*
☐ *Set of feeler gauges*
☐ *Brake bleed nipple spanner*
☐ *Screwdrivers:*
Flat blade - 100 mm long x 6 mm dia
Cross blade - 100 mm long x 6 mm dia
Torx - various sizes (not all vehicles)
☐ *Combination pliers*
☐ *Hacksaw (junior)*
☐ *Tyre pump*
☐ *Tyre pressure gauge*
☐ *Oil can*
☐ *Oil filter removal tool*
☐ *Fine emery cloth*
☐ *Wire brush (small)*
☐ *Funnel (medium size)*
☐ *Sump drain plug key (not all vehicles)*

Repair and overhaul tool kit

These tools are virtually essential for anyone undertaking any major repairs to a motor vehicle, and are additional to those given in the *Maintenance and minor repair* list. Included in this list is a comprehensive set of sockets. Although these are expensive, they will be found invaluable as they are so versatile - particularly if various drives are included in the set. We recommend the half-inch square-drive type, as this can be used with most proprietary torque wrenches.

The tools in this list will sometimes need to be supplemented by tools from the *Special* list:

☐ *Sockets (or box spanners) to cover range in previous list (including Torx sockets)*
☐ *Reversible ratchet drive (for use with sockets)*
☐ *Extension piece, 250 mm (for use with sockets)*
☐ *Universal joint (for use with sockets)*
☐ *Flexible handle or sliding T "breaker bar" (for use with sockets)*
☐ *Torque wrench (for use with sockets)*
☐ *Self-locking grips*
☐ *Ball pein hammer*
☐ *Soft-faced mallet (plastic or rubber)*
☐ *Screwdrivers:*
Flat blade - long & sturdy, short (chubby), and narrow (electrician's) types
Cross blade – long & sturdy, and short (chubby) types
☐ *Pliers:*
Long-nosed
Side cutters (electrician's)
Circlip (internal and external)
☐ *Cold chisel - 25 mm*
☐ *Scriber*
☐ *Scraper*
☐ *Centre-punch*
☐ *Pin punch*
☐ *Hacksaw*
☐ *Brake hose clamp*
☐ *Brake/clutch bleeding kit*
☐ *Selection of twist drills*
☐ *Steel rule/straight-edge*
☐ *Allen keys (inc. splined/Torx type)*
☐ *Selection of files*
☐ *Wire brush*
☐ *Axle stands*
☐ *Jack (strong trolley or hydraulic type)*
☐ *Light with extension lead*
☐ *Universal electrical multi-meter*

Sockets and reversible ratchet drive

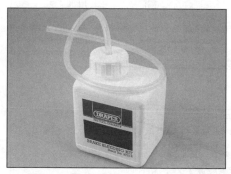

Brake bleeding kit

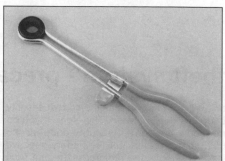

Torx key, socket and bit

Hose clamp

Angular-tightening gauge

Special tools

The tools in this list are those which are not used regularly, are expensive to buy, or which need to be used in accordance with their manufacturers' instructions. Unless relatively difficult mechanical jobs are undertaken frequently, it will not be economic to buy many of these tools. Where this is the case, you could consider clubbing together with friends (or joining a motorists' club) to make a joint purchase, or borrowing the tools against a deposit from a local garage or tool hire specialist. It is worth noting that many of the larger DIY superstores now carry a large range of special tools for hire at modest rates.

The following list contains only those tools and instruments freely available to the public, and not those special tools produced by the vehicle manufacturer specifically for its dealer network. You will find occasional references to these manufacturers' special tools in the text of this manual. Generally, an alternative method of doing the job without the vehicle manufacturers' special tool is given. However, sometimes there is no alternative to using them. Where this is the case and the relevant tool cannot be bought or borrowed, you will have to entrust the work to a dealer.

- ☐ Angular-tightening gauge
- ☐ Valve spring compressor
- ☐ Valve grinding tool
- ☐ Piston ring compressor
- ☐ Piston ring removal/installation tool
- ☐ Cylinder bore hone
- ☐ Balljoint separator
- ☐ Coil spring compressors (where applicable)
- ☐ Two/three-legged hub and bearing puller
- ☐ Impact screwdriver
- ☐ Micrometer and/or vernier calipers
- ☐ Dial gauge
- ☐ Stroboscopic timing light
- ☐ Dwell angle meter/tachometer
- ☐ Fault code reader
- ☐ Cylinder compression gauge
- ☐ Hand-operated vacuum pump and gauge
- ☐ Clutch plate alignment set
- ☐ Brake shoe steady spring cup removal tool
- ☐ Bush and bearing removal/installation set
- ☐ Stud extractors
- ☐ Tap and die set
- ☐ Lifting tackle
- ☐ Trolley jack

Buying tools

Reputable motor accessory shops and superstores often offer excellent quality tools at discount prices, so it pays to shop around.

Remember, you don't have to buy the most expensive items on the shelf, but it is always advisable to steer clear of the very cheap tools. Beware of 'bargains' offered on market stalls or at car boot sales. There are plenty of good tools around at reasonable prices, but always aim to purchase items which meet the relevant national safety standards. If in doubt, ask the proprietor or manager of the shop for advice before making a purchase.

Care and maintenance of tools

Having purchased a reasonable tool kit, it is necessary to keep the tools in a clean and serviceable condition. After use, always wipe off any dirt, grease and metal particles using a clean, dry cloth, before putting the tools away. Never leave them lying around after they have been used. A simple tool rack on the garage or workshop wall for items such as screwdrivers and pliers is a good idea. Store all normal spanners and sockets in a metal box. Any measuring instruments, gauges, meters, etc, must be carefully stored where they cannot be damaged or become rusty.

Take a little care when tools are used. Hammer heads inevitably become marked, and screwdrivers lose the keen edge on their blades from time to time. A little timely attention with emery cloth or a file will soon restore items like this to a good finish.

Working facilities

Not to be forgotten when discussing tools is the workshop itself. If anything more than routine maintenance is to be carried out, a suitable working area becomes essential.

It is appreciated that many an owner-mechanic is forced by circumstances to remove an engine or similar item without the benefit of a garage or workshop. Having done this, any repairs should always be done under the cover of a roof.

Wherever possible, any dismantling should be done on a clean, flat workbench or table at a suitable working height.

Any workbench needs a vice; one with a jaw opening of 100 mm is suitable for most jobs. As mentioned previously, some clean dry storage space is also required for tools, as well as for any lubricants, cleaning fluids, touch-up paints etc, which become necessary.

Another item which may be required, and which has a much more general usage, is an electric drill with a chuck capacity of at least 8 mm. This, together with a good range of twist drills, is virtually essential for fitting accessories.

Last, but not least, always keep a supply of old newspapers and clean, lint-free rags available, and try to keep any working area as clean as possible.

Micrometers

Dial test indicator ("dial gauge")

Strap wrench

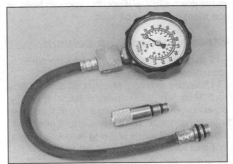
Compression tester

Fault code reader

This is a guide to getting your vehicle through the MOT test. Obviously it will not be possible to examine the vehicle to the same standard as the professional MOT tester. However, working through the following checks will enable you to identify any problem areas before submitting the vehicle for the test.

Where a testable component is in borderline condition, the tester has discretion in deciding whether to pass or fail it. The basis of such discretion is whether the tester would be happy for a close relative or friend to use the vehicle with the component in that condition. If the vehicle presented is clean and evidently well cared for, the tester may be more inclined to pass a borderline component than if the vehicle is scruffy and apparently neglected.

It has only been possible to summarise the test requirements here, based on the regulations in force at the time of printing. Test standards are becoming increasingly stringent, although there are some exemptions for older vehicles. For full details obtain a copy of the Haynes publication Pass the MOT! (available from stockists of Haynes manuals).

An assistant will be needed to help carry out some of these checks.

The checks have been sub-divided into four categories, as follows:

1 Checks carried out **FROM THE DRIVER'S SEAT**

2 Checks carried out **WITH THE VEHICLE ON THE GROUND**

3 Checks carried out **WITH THE VEHICLE RAISED AND THE WHEELS FREE TO TURN**

4 Checks carried out on **YOUR VEHICLE'S EXHAUST EMISSION SYSTEM**

1 Checks carried out **FROM THE DRIVER'S SEAT**

Handbrake

☐ Test the operation of the handbrake. Excessive travel (too many clicks) indicates incorrect brake or cable adjustment.
☐ Check that the handbrake cannot be released by tapping the lever sideways. Check the security of the lever mountings.

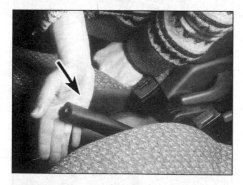

Footbrake

☐ Depress the brake pedal and check that it does not creep down to the floor, indicating a master cylinder fault. Release the pedal, wait a few seconds, then depress it again. If the pedal travels nearly to the floor before firm resistance is felt, brake adjustment or repair is necessary. If the pedal feels spongy, there is air in the hydraulic system which must be removed by bleeding.

☐ Check that the brake pedal is secure and in good condition. Check also for signs of fluid leaks on the pedal, floor or carpets, which would indicate failed seals in the brake master cylinder.
☐ Check the servo unit (when applicable) by operating the brake pedal several times, then keeping the pedal depressed and starting the engine. As the engine starts, the pedal will move down slightly. If not, the vacuum hose or the servo itself may be faulty.

Steering wheel and column

☐ Examine the steering wheel for fractures or looseness of the hub, spokes or rim.
☐ Move the steering wheel from side to side and then up and down. Check that the steering wheel is not loose on the column, indicating wear or a loose retaining nut. Continue moving the steering wheel as before, but also turn it slightly from left to right.
☐ Check that the steering wheel is not loose on the column, and that there is no abnormal

movement of the steering wheel, indicating wear in the column support bearings or couplings.

Windscreen and mirrors

☐ The windscreen must be free of cracks or other significant damage within the driver's field of view. (Small stone chips are acceptable.) Rear view mirrors must be secure, intact, and capable of being adjusted.

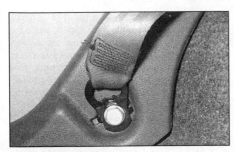

Seat belts and seats

Note: *The following checks are applicable to all seat belts, front and rear.*

☐ Examine the webbing of all the belts (including rear belts if fitted) for cuts, serious fraying or deterioration. Fasten and unfasten each belt to check the buckles. If applicable, check the retracting mechanism. Check the security of all seat belt mountings accessible from inside the vehicle.

☐ The front seats themselves must be securely attached and the backrests must lock in the upright position.

Doors

☐ Both front doors must be able to be opened and closed from outside and inside, and must latch securely when closed.

2 Checks carried out WITH THE VEHICLE ON THE GROUND

Vehicle identification

☐ Number plates must be in good condition, secure and legible, with letters and numbers correctly spaced – spacing at (A) should be twice that at (B).

☐ The VIN plate and/or homologation plate must be legible.

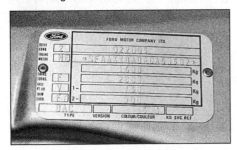

Electrical equipment

☐ Switch on the ignition and check the operation of the horn.

☐ Check the windscreen washers and wipers, examining the wiper blades; renew damaged or perished blades. Also check the operation of the stop-lights.

☐ Check the operation of the sidelights and number plate lights. The lenses and reflectors must be secure, clean and undamaged.

☐ Check the operation and alignment of the headlights. The headlight reflectors must not be tarnished and the lenses must be undamaged.

☐ Switch on the ignition and check the operation of the direction indicators (including the instrument panel tell-tale) and the hazard warning lights. Operation of the sidelights and stop-lights must not affect the indicators - if it does, the cause is usually a bad earth at the rear light cluster.

☐ Check the operation of the rear foglight(s), including the warning light on the instrument panel or in the switch.

Footbrake

☐ Examine the master cylinder, brake pipes and servo unit for leaks, loose mountings, corrosion or other damage.

☐ The fluid reservoir must be secure and the fluid level must be between the upper (**A**) and lower (**B**) markings.

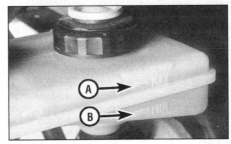

☐ Inspect both front brake flexible hoses for cracks or deterioration of the rubber. Turn the steering from lock to lock, and ensure that the hoses do not contact the wheel, tyre, or any part of the steering or suspension mechanism. With the brake pedal firmly depressed, check the hoses for bulges or leaks under pressure.

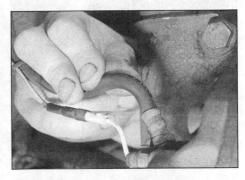

Steering and suspension

☐ Have your assistant turn the steering wheel from side to side slightly, up to the point where the steering gear just begins to transmit this movement to the roadwheels. Check for excessive free play between the steering wheel and the steering gear, indicating wear or insecurity of the steering column joints, the column-to-steering gear coupling, or the steering gear itself.

☐ Have your assistant turn the steering wheel more vigorously in each direction, so that the roadwheels just begin to turn. As this is done, examine all the steering joints, linkages, fittings and attachments. Renew any component that shows signs of wear or damage. On vehicles with power steering, check the security and condition of the steering pump, drivebelt and hoses.

☐ Check that the vehicle is standing level, and at approximately the correct ride height.

Shock absorbers

☐ Depress each corner of the vehicle in turn, then release it. The vehicle should rise and then settle in its normal position. If the vehicle continues to rise and fall, the shock absorber is defective. A shock absorber which has seized will also cause the vehicle to fail.

Exhaust system

☐ Start the engine. With your assistant holding a rag over the tailpipe, check the entire system for leaks. Repair or renew leaking sections.

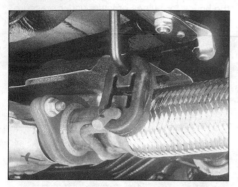

3 Checks carried out **WITH THE VEHICLE RAISED AND THE WHEELS FREE TO TURN**

Jack up the front and rear of the vehicle, and securely support it on axle stands. Position the stands clear of the suspension assemblies. Ensure that the wheels are clear of the ground and that the steering can be turned from lock to lock.

Steering mechanism

☐ Have your assistant turn the steering from lock to lock. Check that the steering turns smoothly, and that no part of the steering mechanism, including a wheel or tyre, fouls any brake hose or pipe or any part of the body structure.
☐ Examine the steering rack rubber gaiters for damage or insecurity of the retaining clips. If power steering is fitted, check for signs of damage or leakage of the fluid hoses, pipes or connections. Also check for excessive stiffness or binding of the steering, a missing split pin or locking device, or severe corrosion of the body structure within 30 cm of any steering component attachment point.

Front and rear suspension and wheel bearings

☐ Starting at the front right-hand side, grasp the roadwheel at the 3 o'clock and 9 o'clock positions and shake it vigorously. Check for free play or insecurity at the wheel bearings, suspension balljoints, or suspension mountings, pivots and attachments.
☐ Now grasp the wheel at the 12 o'clock and 6 o'clock positions and repeat the previous inspection. Spin the wheel, and check for roughness or tightness of the front wheel bearing.

☐ If excess free play is suspected at a component pivot point, this can be confirmed by using a large screwdriver or similar tool and levering between the mounting and the component attachment. This will confirm whether the wear is in the pivot bush, its retaining bolt, or in the mounting itself (the bolt holes can often become elongated).

☐ Carry out all the above checks at the other front wheel, and then at both rear wheels.

Springs and shock absorbers

☐ Examine the suspension struts (when applicable) for serious fluid leakage, corrosion, or damage to the casing. Also check the security of the mounting points.
☐ If coil springs are fitted, check that the spring ends locate in their seats, and that the spring is not corroded, cracked or broken.
☐ If leaf springs are fitted, check that all leaves are intact, that the axle is securely attached to each spring, and that there is no deterioration of the spring eye mountings, bushes, and shackles.

☐ The same general checks apply to vehicles fitted with other suspension types, such as torsion bars, hydraulic displacer units, etc. Ensure that all mountings and attachments are secure, that there are no signs of excessive wear, corrosion or damage, and (on hydraulic types) that there are no fluid leaks or damaged pipes.
☐ Inspect the shock absorbers for signs of serious fluid leakage. Check for wear of the mounting bushes or attachments, or damage to the body of the unit.

Driveshafts (fwd vehicles only)

☐ Rotate each front wheel in turn and inspect the constant velocity joint gaiters for splits or damage. Also check that each driveshaft is straight and undamaged.

Braking system

☐ If possible without dismantling, check brake pad wear and disc condition. Ensure that the friction lining material has not worn excessively, (A) and that the discs are not fractured, pitted, scored or badly worn (B).

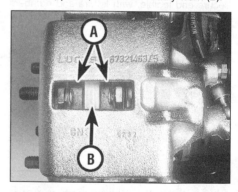

☐ Examine all the rigid brake pipes underneath the vehicle, and the flexible hose(s) at the rear. Look for corrosion, chafing or insecurity of the pipes, and for signs of bulging under pressure, chafing, splits or deterioration of the flexible hoses.
☐ Look for signs of fluid leaks at the brake calipers or on the brake backplates. Repair or renew leaking components.
☐ Slowly spin each wheel, while your assistant depresses and releases the footbrake. Ensure that each brake is operating and does not bind when the pedal is released.

□ Examine the handbrake mechanism, checking for frayed or broken cables, excessive corrosion, or wear or insecurity of the linkage. Check that the mechanism works on each relevant wheel, and releases fully, without binding.

□ It is not possible to test brake efficiency without special equipment, but a road test can be carried out later to check that the vehicle pulls up in a straight line.

Fuel and exhaust systems

□ Inspect the fuel tank (including the filler cap), fuel pipes, hoses and unions. All components must be secure and free from leaks.

□ Examine the exhaust system over its entire length, checking for any damaged, broken or missing mountings, security of the retaining clamps and rust or corrosion.

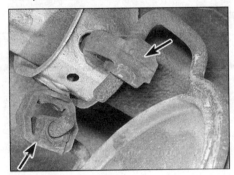

Wheels and tyres

□ Examine the sidewalls and tread area of each tyre in turn. Check for cuts, tears, lumps, bulges, separation of the tread, and exposure of the ply or cord due to wear or damage. Check that the tyre bead is correctly seated on the wheel rim, that the valve is sound and

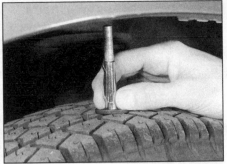

properly seated, and that the wheel is not distorted or damaged.

□ Check that the tyres are of the correct size for the vehicle, that they are of the same size and type on each axle, and that the pressures are correct.

□ Check the tyre tread depth. The legal minimum at the time of writing is 1.6 mm over at least three-quarters of the tread width. Abnormal tread wear may indicate incorrect front wheel alignment.

Body corrosion

□ Check the condition of the entire vehicle structure for signs of corrosion in load-bearing areas. (These include chassis box sections, side sills, cross-members, pillars, and all suspension, steering, braking system and seat belt mountings and anchorages.) Any corrosion which has seriously reduced the thickness of a load-bearing area is likely to cause the vehicle to fail. In this case professional repairs are likely to be needed.

□ Damage or corrosion which causes sharp or otherwise dangerous edges to be exposed will also cause the vehicle to fail.

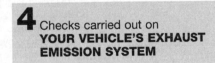

4 Checks carried out on
YOUR VEHICLE'S EXHAUST EMISSION SYSTEM

Petrol models

□ Have the engine at normal operating temperature, and make sure that it is in good tune (ignition system in good order, air filter element clean, etc).

□ Before any measurements are carried out, raise the engine speed to around 2500 rpm, and hold it at this speed for 20 seconds. Allow

the engine speed to return to idle, and watch for smoke emissions from the exhaust tailpipe. If the idle speed is obviously much too high, or if dense blue or clearly-visible black smoke comes from the tailpipe for more than 5 seconds, the vehicle will fail. As a rule of thumb, blue smoke signifies oil being burnt (engine wear) while black smoke signifies unburnt fuel (dirty air cleaner element, or other carburettor or fuel system fault).

□ An exhaust gas analyser capable of measuring carbon monoxide (CO) and hydrocarbons (HC) is now needed. If such an instrument cannot be hired or borrowed, a local garage may agree to perform the check for a small fee.

CO emissions (mixture)

□ At the time of writing, the maximum CO level at idle is 3.5% for vehicles first used after August 1986 and 4.5% for older vehicles. From January 1996 a much tighter limit (around 0.5%) applies to catalyst-equipped vehicles first used from August 1992. If the CO level cannot be reduced far enough to pass the test (and the fuel and ignition systems are otherwise in good condition) then the carburettor is badly worn, or there is some problem in the fuel injection system or catalytic converter (as applicable).

HC emissions

□ With the CO emissions within limits, HC emissions must be no more than 1200 ppm (parts per million). If the vehicle fails this test at idle, it can be re-tested at around 2000 rpm; if the HC level is then 1200 ppm or less, this counts as a pass.

□ Excessive HC emissions can be caused by oil being burnt, but they are more likely to be due to unburnt fuel.

Diesel models

□ The only emission test applicable to Diesel engines is the measuring of exhaust smoke density. The test involves accelerating the engine several times to its maximum unloaded speed.

Note: *It is of the utmost importance that the engine timing belt is in good condition before the test is carried out.*

□ Excessive smoke can be caused by a dirty air cleaner element. Otherwise, professional advice may be needed to find the cause.

Engine

- ☐ Engine fails to rotate when attempting to start
- ☐ Engine rotates but will not start
- ☐ Engine difficult to start when cold
- ☐ Engine difficult to start when hot
- ☐ Starter motor noisy or excessively rough in engagement
- ☐ Engine starts but stops immediately
- ☐ Engine idles erratically
- ☐ Engine misfires at idle speed
- ☐ Engine misfires throughout the driving speed range
- ☐ Engine hesitates on acceleration
- ☐ Engine stalls
- ☐ Engine lacks power
- ☐ Engine backfires
- ☐ Oil pressure warning light illuminated with engine running
- ☐ Engine runs-on after switching off
- ☐ Engine noises

Cooling system

- ☐ Overheating
- ☐ Overcooling
- ☐ External coolant leakage
- ☐ Internal coolant leakage
- ☐ Corrosion

Fuel and exhaust system

- ☐ Excessive fuel consumption
- ☐ Fuel leakage and/or fuel odour
- ☐ Excessive noise or fumes from exhaust system

Clutch

- ☐ Pedal travels to floor - no pressure or very little resistance
- ☐ Clutch fails to disengage (unable to select gears)
- ☐ Clutch slips (engine speed increases with no increase in vehicle speed)
- ☐ Judder as clutch is engaged
- ☐ Noise when depressing or releasing clutch pedal

Gearbox

- ☐ Noisy in neutral with engine running
- ☐ Noisy in one particular gear
- ☐ Difficulty engaging gears
- ☐ Jumps out of gear
- ☐ Vibration
- ☐ Lubricant leaks

Driveshafts

- ☐ Clicking or knocking noise on turns (at slow speed on full lock)
- ☐ Vibration when accelerating or decelerating

Braking system

- ☐ Vehicle pulls to one side under braking
- ☐ Noise (grinding or high-pitched squeal) when brakes applied
- ☐ Excessive brake pedal travel
- ☐ Brake pedal feels spongy when depressed
- ☐ Excessive brake pedal effort required to stop vehicle
- ☐ Judder felt through brake pedal or steering wheel when braking
- ☐ Brakes binding
- ☐ Rear wheels locking under normal braking

Suspension and steering

- ☐ Vehicle pulls to one side
- ☐ Wheel wobble and vibration
- ☐ Excessive pitching and/or rolling around corners or during braking
- ☐ Wandering or general instability
- ☐ Excessively stiff steering
- ☐ Excessive play in steering
- ☐ Tyre wear excessive

Electrical system

- ☐ Battery will not hold a charge for more than a few days
- ☐ Ignition warning light remains illuminated with engine running
- ☐ Ignition warning light fails to come on
- ☐ Lights inoperative
- ☐ Instrument readings inaccurate or erratic
- ☐ Horn inoperative or unsatisfactory in operation
- ☐ Windscreen/tailgate wipers inoperative or unsatisfactory in operation
- ☐ Windscreen/tailgate washers inoperative or unsatisfactory in operation
- ☐ Electric windows inoperative or unsatisfactory in operation
- ☐ Central locking system inoperative or unsatisfactory in operation

Introduction

The vehicle owner who does his or her own maintenance according to the recommended service schedules should not have to use this section of the manual very often. Modern component reliability is such that, provided those items subject to wear or deterioration are inspected or renewed at the specified intervals, sudden failure is comparatively rare. Faults do not usually just happen as a result of sudden failure, but develop over a period of time. Major mechanical failures in particular are usually preceded by characteristic symptoms over hundreds or even thousands of miles. Those components which do occasionally fail without warning are often small and easily carried in the vehicle.

With any fault finding, the first step is to decide where to begin investigations. Sometimes this is obvious, but on other occasions a little detective work will be necessary. The owner who makes half a dozen haphazard adjustments or replacements may be successful in curing a fault (or its symptoms), but will be none the wiser if the fault recurs and ultimately may have spent more time and money than was necessary. A calm and logical approach will be found to be more satisfactory in the long run. Always take into account any warning signs or abnormalities that may have been noticed in the period preceding the fault - power loss, high or low gauge readings, unusual smells, etc - and remember that failure of components such as fuses or spark plugs may only be pointers to some underlying fault.

The pages which follow provide an easy reference guide to the more common problems which may occur during the operation of the vehicle. These problems and their possible causes are grouped under headings denoting various components or systems, such as Engine, Cooling system, etc. The Chapter and/or Section which deals with the problem is also shown in brackets. Whatever the fault, certain basic principles apply. These are as follows:

Verify the fault. This is simply a matter of being sure that you know what the symptoms are before starting work. This is particularly important if you are investigating a fault for someone else who may not have described it very accurately.

Don't overlook the obvious. For example, if the vehicle won't start, is there petrol in the tank? (Don't take anyone else's word on this particular point, and don't trust the fuel gauge either!) If an electrical fault is indicated, look for loose or broken wires before digging out the test gear.

Cure the disease, not the symptom. Substituting a flat battery with a fully charged one will get you off the hard shoulder, but if the underlying cause is not attended to, the new battery will go the same way. Similarly, changing oil-fouled spark plugs for a new set will get you moving again, but remember that the reason for the fouling (if it wasn't simply an incorrect grade of plug) will have to be established and corrected.

Don't take anything for granted. Particularly, don't forget that a 'new' component may itself be defective (especially if it's been rattling around in the boot for months), and don't leave components out of a fault diagnosis sequence just because they are new or recently fitted. When you do finally diagnose a difficult fault, you'll probably realise that all the evidence was there from the start.

Engine

Engine fails to rotate when attempting to start

- [ ] Battery terminal connections loose or corroded ("Weekly checks").
- [ ] Battery discharged or faulty (Chapter 5).
- [ ] Broken, loose or disconnected wiring in the starting circuit (Chapter 5).
- [ ] Defective starter solenoid or switch (Chapter 5).
- [ ] Defective starter motor (Chapter 5).
- [ ] Starter pinion or flywheel ring gear teeth loose or broken (Chapters 2 and 5).
- [ ] Engine earth strap broken or disconnected (Chapter 5).

Engine rotates but will not start

- [ ] Fuel tank empty.
- [ ] Battery discharged (engine rotates slowly) (Chapter 5).
- [ ] Battery terminal connections loose or corroded ("Weekly Checks").
- [ ] Ignition components damp or damaged (Chapters 1 and 5).
- [ ] Broken, loose or disconnected wiring in the ignition circuit (Chapters 1 and 5).
- [ ] Worn, faulty or incorrectly gapped spark plugs (Chapter 1).
- [ ] Choke mechanism sticking, incorrectly adjusted, or faulty (Chapter 4).
- [ ] Major mechanical failure (eg camshaft drive) (Chapter 2).

Engine difficult to start when cold

- [ ] Battery discharged (Chapter 5).
- [ ] Battery terminal connections loose or corroded ("Weekly Checks").
- [ ] Worn, faulty or incorrectly gapped spark plugs (Chapter 1).
- [ ] Choke mechanism sticking, incorrectly adjusted, or faulty (Chapter 4).
- [ ] Other ignition system fault (Chapters 1 and 5).
- [ ] Low cylinder compressions (Chapter 2).

Engine difficult to start when hot

- [ ] Air filter element dirty or clogged (Chapter 1).
- [ ] Choke mechanism sticking, incorrectly adjusted, or faulty (Chapter 4).
- [ ] Carburettor float chamber flooding (Chapter 4).
- [ ] Low cylinder compressions (Chapter 2).

Starter motor noisy or excessively rough in engagement

- [ ] Starter pinion or flywheel ring gear teeth loose or broken (Chapters 2 and 5).
- [ ] Starter motor mounting bolts loose or missing (Chapter 5).
- [ ] Starter motor internal components worn or damaged (Chapter 5).

Engine starts but stops immediately

- [ ] Insufficient fuel reaching carburettor (Chapter 4).
- [ ] Loose or faulty electrical connections in the ignition circuit (Chapters 1 and 5).
- [ ] Vacuum leak at the carburettor or inlet manifold (Chapter 4).
- [ ] Blocked carburettor jet(s) or internal passages (Chapter 4).

Engine idles erratically

- [ ] Incorrectly adjusted idle speed and/or mixture settings (Chapter 1).
- [ ] Air filter element clogged (Chapter 1).
- [ ] Vacuum leak at the carburettor, inlet manifold or associated hoses (Chapter 4).
- [ ] Worn, faulty or incorrectly gapped spark plugs (Chapter 1).
- [ ] Uneven or low cylinder compressions (Chapter 2).
- [ ] Camshaft lobes worn (Chapter 2).
- [ ] Timing belt incorrectly tensioned (Chapter 2).

Engine misfires at idle speed

- [ ] Worn, faulty or incorrectly gapped spark plugs (Chapter 1).
- [ ] Faulty spark plug HT leads (Chapter 1).
- [ ] Incorrectly adjusted idle mixture settings (Chapter 1).
- [ ] Incorrect ignition timing (Chapter 1).
- [ ] Vacuum leak at the carburettor, inlet manifold or associated hoses (Chapter 4).
- [ ] Distributor cap cracked or tracking internally (Chapter 1).
- [ ] Uneven or low cylinder compressions (Chapter 2).
- [ ] Disconnected, leaking or perished crankcase ventilation hoses (Chapter 1).

Engine misfires throughout the driving speed range

- [ ] Blocked carburettor jet(s) or internal passages (Chapter 4).
- [ ] Carburettor worn or incorrectly adjusted (Chapters 1 and 4).
- [ ] Fuel filter choked (Chapter 1).
- [ ] Fuel pump faulty or delivery pressure low (Chapter 4).
- [ ] Fuel tank vent blocked or fuel pipes restricted (Chapter 4).
- [ ] Vacuum leak at the carburettor, inlet manifold or associated hoses (Chapter 4).
- [ ] Worn, faulty or incorrectly gapped spark plugs (Chapter 1).
- [ ] Faulty spark plug HT leads (Chapter 1).
- [ ] Distributor cap cracked or tracking internally (Chapter 1).
- [ ] Faulty ignition coil (Chapter 5).
- [ ] Uneven or low cylinder compressions (Chapter 2).

Engine hesitates on acceleration

- [ ] Worn, faulty or incorrectly gapped spark plugs (Chapter 1).
- [ ] Carburettor accelerator pump faulty (Chapter 4).
- [ ] Blocked carburettor jets or internal passages (Chapter 4).
- [ ] Vacuum leak at the carburettor, inlet manifold or associated hoses (Chapter 4).
- [ ] Carburettor worn or incorrectly adjusted (Chapters 1 and 4).

Engine stalls

- [ ] Incorrectly adjusted idle speed and/or mixture settings (Chapter 1).
- [ ] Blocked carburettor jet(s) or internal passages (Chapter 4).
- [ ] Vacuum leak at the carburettor, inlet manifold or associated hoses (Chapter 4).
- [ ] Fuel filter choked (Chapter 1).
- [ ] Fuel pump faulty or delivery pressure low (Chapter 4).
- [ ] Fuel tank vent blocked or fuel pipes restricted (Chapter 4).

Engine (continued)

Engine lacks power

- ☐ Incorrect ignition timing (Chapter 1).
- ☐ Carburettor worn or incorrectly adjusted (Chapter 1).
- ☐ Timing belt incorrectly fitted or tensioned (Chapter 2).
- ☐ Fuel filter choked (Chapter 1).
- ☐ Fuel pump faulty or delivery pressure low (Chapter 4).
- ☐ Uneven or low cylinder compressions (Chapter 2).
- ☐ Worn, faulty or incorrectly gapped spark plugs (Chapter 1).
- ☐ Vacuum leak at the carburettor, inlet manifold or associated hoses (Chapter 4).
- ☐ Brakes binding (Chapters 1 and 9).
- ☐ Clutch slipping (Chapter 6).

Engine backfires

- ☐ Ignition timing incorrect (Chapter 1).
- ☐ Timing belt incorrectly fitted or tensioned (Chapter 2).
- ☐ Carburettor worn or incorrectly adjusted (Chapter 1).
- ☐ Vacuum leak at the carburettor, inlet manifold or associated hoses (Chapter 4).

Oil pressure warning light illuminated with engine running

- ☐ Low oil level or incorrect grade (Chapter 1).
- ☐ Faulty oil pressure switch (Chapter 2).
- ☐ Worn engine bearings and/or oil pump (Chapter 2).
- ☐ High engine operating temperature (Chapter 3).
- ☐ Oil pressure relief valve defective (Chapter 2).
- ☐ Oil pick-up strainer clogged (Chapter 2).

Engine runs-on after switching off

- ☐ Idle speed excessively high (Chapter 1).
- ☐ Faulty anti-run-on solenoid (Chapter 4).
- ☐ Excessive carbon build-up in engine (Chapter 2).
- ☐ High engine operating temperature (Chapter 3).

Engine noises

Pre-ignition (pinking) or knocking during acceleration or under load

- ☐ Ignition timing incorrect (Chapter 1).
- ☐ Incorrect grade of fuel (Chapter 4).
- ☐ Vacuum leak at the carburettor, inlet manifold or associated hoses (Chapter 4).
- ☐ Excessive carbon build-up in engine (Chapter 2).
- ☐ Worn or damaged distributor or other ignition system component (Chapter 5).
- ☐ Carburettor worn or incorrectly adjusted (Chapter 1).

Whistling or wheezing noises

- ☐ Leaking inlet manifold or carburettor gasket (Chapter 4).
- ☐ Leaking exhaust manifold gasket or pipe to manifold joint (Chapter 1).
- ☐ Leaking vacuum hose (Chapters 4, 5 and 9).
- ☐ Blowing cylinder head gasket (Chapter 2).

Tapping or rattling noises

- ☐ Faulty hydraulic tappets (Chapter 1 or 2).
- ☐ Worn valve gear or camshaft (Chapter 2).
- ☐ Worn timing belt or tensioner (Chapter 2).
- ☐ Ancillary component fault (coolant pump, alternator etc) (Chapters 3 and 5).

Knocking or thumping noises

- ☐ Worn big-end bearings (regular heavy knocking, perhaps less under load) (Chapter 2).
- ☐ Worn main bearings (rumbling and knocking, perhaps worsening under load) (Chapter 2).
- ☐ Piston slap (most noticeable when cold) (Chapter 2).
- ☐ Ancillary component fault (alternator, coolant pump etc) (Chapters 3 and 5).

Cooling system

Overheating

- ☐ Insufficient coolant in system (Chapter 3).
- ☐ Thermostat faulty (Chapter 3).
- ☐ Radiator core blocked or grille restricted (Chapter 3).
- ☐ Electric cooling fan or thermostatic switch faulty (Chapter 3).
- ☐ Pressure cap faulty (Chapter 3).
- ☐ Timing belt worn, or incorrectly tensioned (Chapter 2).
- ☐ Ignition timing incorrect (Chapter 1).
- ☐ Inaccurate temperature gauge sender unit (Chapter 3).
- ☐ Air lock in cooling system (Chapter 1).

Overcooling

- ☐ Thermostat faulty (Chapter 3).
- ☐ Inaccurate temperature gauge sender unit (Chapter 3).

External coolant leakage

- ☐ Deteriorated or damaged hoses or hose clips (Chapter 1).
- ☐ Radiator core or heater matrix leaking (Chapter 3).
- ☐ Pressure cap faulty (Chapter 3).
- ☐ Coolant pump seal leaking (Chapter 3).
- ☐ Boiling due to overheating (Chapter 3).
- ☐ Core plug leaking (Chapter 2).

Internal coolant leakage

- ☐ Leaking cylinder head gasket (Chapter 2).
- ☐ Cracked cylinder head or cylinder bore (Chapter 2).

Corrosion

- ☐ Infrequent draining and flushing (Chapter 1).
- ☐ Incorrect antifreeze mixture or inappropriate type (Chapter 1).

Fuel and exhaust system

Excessive fuel consumption

☐ Air filter element dirty or clogged (Chapter 1).
☐ Carburettor worn or incorrectly adjusted (Chapter 4).
☐ Choke cable incorrectly adjusted or choke sticking (Chapter 4).
☐ Ignition timing incorrect (Chapter 1).
☐ Tyres underinflated ("Weekly Checks").

Fuel leakage and/or fuel odour

☐ Damaged or corroded fuel tank, pipes or connections (Chapter 1).
☐ Carburettor float chamber flooding (Chapter 4).

Excessive noise or fumes from exhaust system

☐ Leaking exhaust system or manifold joints (Chapter 1).
☐ Leaking, corroded or damaged silencers or pipe (Chapter 1).
☐ Broken mountings causing body or suspension contact (Chapter 1).

Clutch

Pedal travels to floor - no pressure or very little resistance

☐ Broken clutch cable (Chapter 6).
☐ Faulty clutch pedal self-adjust mechanism (Chapter 6).
☐ Broken clutch release bearing or fork (Chapter 6).
☐ Broken diaphragm spring in clutch pressure plate (Chapter 6).

Clutch fails to disengage (unable to select gears)

☐ Faulty clutch pedal self-adjust mechanism (Chapter 6).
☐ Clutch friction plate sticking on gearbox input shaft splines (Chapter 6).
☐ Clutch friction plate sticking to flywheel or pressure plate (Chapter 6).
☐ Faulty pressure plate assembly (Chapter 6).
☐ Gearbox input shaft seized in crankshaft spigot bearing (Chapter 2).
☐ Clutch release mechanism worn or incorrectly assembled (Chapter 6).

Noise when depressing or releasing clutch pedal

☐ Worn clutch release bearing (Chapter 6).
☐ Worn or dry clutch pedal bushes (Chapter 6).
☐ Faulty pressure plate assembly (Chapter 6).
☐ Pressure plate diaphragm spring broken (Chapter 6).
☐ Broken clutch friction plate cushioning springs (Chapter 6).

Clutch slips (engine speed increases with no increase in vehicle speed)

☐ Faulty clutch pedal self-adjust mechanism (Chapter 6).
☐ Clutch friction plate friction material excessively worn (Chapter 6).
☐ Clutch friction plate friction material contaminated with oil or grease (Chapter 6).
☐ Faulty pressure plate or weak diaphragm spring (Chapter 6).

Judder as clutch is engaged

☐ Clutch friction plate friction material contaminated with oil or grease (Chapter 6).
☐ Clutch friction plate friction material excessively worn (Chapter 6).
☐ Clutch cable sticking or frayed (Chapter 6).
☐ Faulty or distorted pressure plate or diaphragm spring (Chapter 6).
☐ Worn or loose engine or gearbox mountings (Chapter 2).
☐ Clutch friction plate hub or gearbox input shaft splines worn (Chapter 6).

Gearbox

Noisy in neutral with engine running

☐ Input shaft bearings worn (noise apparent with clutch pedal released but not when depressed) (Chapter 7).*
☐ Clutch release bearing worn (noise apparent with clutch pedal depressed, possibly less when released) (Chapter 6).

Noisy in one particular gear

☐ Worn, damaged or chipped gear teeth (Chapter 7).*

Difficulty engaging gears

☐ Clutch fault (Chapter 6).
☐ Worn or damaged gear linkage (Chapter 7).
☐ Incorrectly adjusted gear linkage (Chapter 7).
☐ Worn synchroniser units (Chapter 7).*

Jumps out of gear

☐ Worn or damaged gear linkage (Chapter 7).
☐ Incorrectly adjusted gear linkage (Chapter 7).
☐ Worn synchroniser units (Chapter 7).*
☐ Worn selector forks (Chapter 7).*

Vibration

☐ Lack of oil (Chapter 1).
☐ Worn bearings (Chapter 7).*

Lubricant leaks

☐ Leaking driveshaft oil seal (Chapter 7).
☐ Leaking housing joint (Chapter 7).*
☐ Leaking input shaft oil seal (Chapter 7).*

*Although the corrective action necessary to remedy the symptoms described is beyond the scope of the home mechanic, the above information should be helpful in isolating the cause of the condition so that the owner can communicate clearly with a professional mechanic

Driveshafts

Clicking or knocking noise on turns (at slow speed on full lock)
☐ Lack of constant velocity joint lubricant (Chapter 8).
☐ Worn outer constant velocity joint (Chapter 8).

Vibration when accelerating or decelerating
☐ Worn inner constant velocity joint (Chapter 8).
☐ Bent or distorted driveshaft (Chapter 8).

Braking system

Note: *Before assuming that a brake problem exists, make sure that the tyres are in good condition and correctly inflated, the front wheel alignment is correct and the vehicle is not loaded with weight in an unequal manner*

Vehicle pulls to one side under braking
☐ Worn, defective, damaged or contaminated front or rear brake pads/shoes on one side (Chapter 1).
☐ Seized or partially seized front or rear brake caliper/wheel cylinder piston (Chapter 9).
☐ A mixture of brake pad/shoe lining materials fitted between sides (Chapter 1).
☐ Brake caliper mounting bolts loose (Chapter 9).
☐ Rear brake backplate mounting bolts loose (Chapter 9).
☐ Worn or damaged steering or suspension components (Chapter 10).

Noise (grinding or high-pitched squeal) when brakes applied
☐ Brake pad or shoe friction lining material worn down to metal backing (Chapter 1).
☐ Excessive corrosion of brake disc or drum, especially if the vehicle has been standing for some time (Chapter 1).
☐ Foreign object (stone chipping etc) trapped between brake disc and splash shield (Chapter 1).

Brake pedal feels spongy when depressed
☐ Air in hydraulic system (Chapter 9).
☐ Deteriorated flexible rubber brake hoses (Chapter 1 or 9).
☐ Master cylinder mounting nuts loose (Chapter 9).
☐ Faulty master cylinder (Chapter 9).

Excessive brake pedal travel
☐ Faulty master cylinder (Chapter 9).
☐ Air in hydraulic system (Chapter 9).

Excessive brake pedal effort required to stop vehicle
☐ Faulty vacuum servo unit (Chapter 9).
☐ Disconnected, damaged or insecure brake servo vacuum hose (Chapter 9).
☐ Primary or secondary hydraulic circuit failure (Chapter 9).
☐ Seized brake caliper or wheel cylinder piston(s) (Chapter 9).
☐ Brake pads or brake shoes incorrectly fitted (Chapter 1).
☐ Incorrect grade of brake pads or brake shoes fitted (Chapter 1).
☐ Brake pads or brake shoe linings contaminated (Chapter 1).

Judder felt through brake pedal or steering wheel when braking
☐ Excessive run-out or distortion of front discs or rear drums (Chapter 9).
☐ Brake pad or brake shoe linings worn (Chapter 1).
☐ Brake caliper or rear brake backplate mounting bolts loose (Chapter 9).
☐ Wear in suspension, steering components or mountings (Chapter 9).

Brakes binding
☐ Seized brake caliper or wheel cylinder piston(s) (Chapter 9).
☐ Incorrectly adjusted handbrake mechanism or linkage (Chapter 1).
☐ Faulty master cylinder (Chapter 9).

Rear wheels locking under normal braking
☐ Rear brake shoe linings contaminated (Chapter 1).
☐ Faulty brake pressure regulator (Chapter 9).

Suspension and steering

Note: *Before diagnosing suspension or steering faults, be sure that the trouble is not due to incorrect tyre pressures, mixtures of tyre types or binding brakes*

Vehicle pulls to one side
☐ Defective tyre (*"Weekly Checks"*).
☐ Excessive wear in suspension or steering components (Chapter 10).
☐ Incorrect front wheel alignment (Chapter 10).
☐ Accident damage to steering or suspension components (Chapter 10).

Wheel wobble and vibration
☐ Front roadwheels out of balance (vibration felt mainly through the steering wheel) (Chapter 10).
☐ Rear roadwheels out of balance (vibration felt throughout the vehicle) (Chapter 10).
☐ Roadwheels damaged or distorted (Chapter 10).

☐ Faulty or damaged tyre (Chapter 10).
☐ Worn steering or suspension joints, bushes or components (Chapter 10).
☐ Wheel nuts loose (Chapter 1).

Excessive pitching and/or rolling around corners or during braking
☐ Broken or weak suspension components (Chapter 10).
☐ Worn or damaged anti-roll bar or mountings (Chapter 10).

Wandering or general instability
☐ Incorrect front wheel alignment (Chapter 10).
☐ Worn steering or suspension joints, bushes or components (Chapter 10).
☐ Roadwheels out of balance (Chapter 10).
☐ Faulty or damaged tyre (Chapter 10).
☐ Wheel nuts loose (Chapter 1).

Suspension and steering (continued)

Excessively stiff steering

- ☐ Lack of steering gear lubricant (Chapter 10).
- ☐ Seized track rod balljoint or suspension balljoint (Chapter 10).
- ☐ Incorrect front wheel alignment (Chapter 10).
- ☐ Steering rack or column bent or damaged (Chapter 10).

Excessive play in steering

- ☐ Worn steering column universal joint(s) or intermediate coupling (Chapter 10).
- ☐ Worn steering track rod balljoints (Chapter 10).
- ☐ Worn steering gear (Chapter 10).
- ☐ Worn steering or suspension joints, bushes or components (Chapter 10).

Tyre wear excessive

Tyres worn on inside or outside edges

- ☐ Tyres underinflated (wear on both edges) ("Weekly Checks").
- ☐ Incorrect camber or castor angles (wear on one edge only) (Chapter 10).

- ☐ Worn steering or suspension joints, bushes or components (Chapter 10).
- ☐ Excessively hard cornering.
- ☐ Accident damage.

Tyre treads exhibit feathered edges

- ☐ Incorrect toe setting (Chapter 10).

Tyres worn in centre of tread

- ☐ Tyres overinflated ("Weekly Checks").

Tyres worn on inside and outside edges

- ☐ Tyres underinflated ("Weekly Checks").

Tyres worn unevenly

- ☐ Tyres out of balance ("Weekly Checks").
- ☐ Excessive wheel or tyre run-out ("Weekly Checks").
- ☐ Worn suspension units and/or dampers (Chapter 10).
- ☐ Faulty tyre ("Weekly Checks").

Electrical system

Note: For problems associated with the starting system, refer to the faults listed under "Engine" earlier in this Section

Battery will not hold a charge for more than a few days

- ☐ Battery defective internally (Chapter 5).
- ☐ Battery electrolyte level low (Chapter 1).
- ☐ Battery terminal connections loose or corroded (Chapter 5).
- ☐ Alternator drivebelt worn or incorrectly adjusted (Chapter 1).
- ☐ Alternator not charging at correct output (Chapter 5).
- ☐ Alternator or voltage regulator faulty (Chapter 5).
- ☐ Short-circuit causing continual battery drain (Chapter 12).

Ignition warning light remains illuminated with engine running

- ☐ Alternator drivebelt broken, worn, or incorrectly adjusted (Chapter 1).
- ☐ Alternator brushes worn, sticking, or dirty (Chapter 5).
- ☐ Alternator brush springs weak or broken (Chapter 5).
- ☐ Internal fault in alternator or voltage regulator (Chapter 5).
- ☐ Broken, disconnected, or loose wiring in charging circuit (Chapter 5).

Ignition warning light fails to come on

- ☐ Warning light bulb blown (Chapter 12).
- ☐ Broken, disconnected, or loose wiring in warning light circuit (Chapter 12).
- ☐ Alternator faulty (Chapter 5).

Lights inoperative

- ☐ Bulb blown (Chapter 12).
- ☐ Corrosion of bulb or bulbholder contacts (Chapter 12).
- ☐ Blown fuse (Chapter 12).
- ☐ Faulty relay (Chapter 12).
- ☐ Broken, loose, or disconnected wiring (Chapter 12).
- ☐ Faulty switch (Chapter 12).

Instrument readings inaccurate or erratic

Instrument readings increase with engine speed

- ☐ Faulty voltage regulator (Chapter 12).

Fuel or temperature gauge give no reading

- ☐ Faulty gauge sender unit (Chapters 3 or 4).
- ☐ Wiring open circuit (Chapter 12).
- ☐ Faulty gauge (Chapter 12).

Fuel or temperature gauges give continuous maximum reading

- ☐ Faulty gauge sender unit (Chapters 3 or 4).
- ☐ Wiring short-circuit (Chapter 12).
- ☐ Faulty gauge (Chapter 12).

Horn inoperative or unsatisfactory in operation

Horn operates all the time

- ☐ Horn push either earthed or stuck down (Chapter 12).
- ☐ Horn cable to horn push earthed (Chapter 12).

Horn fails to operate

- ☐ Blown fuse (Chapter 12).
- ☐ Cable or cable connections loose, broken or disconnected (Chapter 12).
- ☐ Faulty horn (Chapter 12).

Horn emits intermittent or unsatisfactory sound

- ☐ Cable connections loose (Chapter 12).
- ☐ Horn mountings loose (Chapter 12).
- ☐ Faulty horn (Chapter 12).

Windscreen/tailgate wipers inoperative or unsatisfactory in operation

Wipers fail to operate or operate very slowly

- ☐ Wiper blades stuck to screen, or linkage seized or binding (Chapter 12).
- ☐ Blown fuse (Chapter 12).
- ☐ Cable or cable connections loose, broken or disconnected (Chapter 12).
- ☐ Faulty relay (Chapter 12).
- ☐ Faulty wiper motor (Chapter 12).

Electrical system (continued)

Wiper blades sweep over too large or too small an area of the glass

☐ Wiper arms incorrectly positioned on spindles (Chapter 12).
☐ Excessive wear of wiper linkage (Chapter 12).
☐ Wiper motor or linkage mountings loose or insecure (Chapter 12).

Wiper blades fail to clean the glass effectively

☐ Wiper blade rubbers worn or perished *("Weekly Checks")*.
☐ Wiper arm tension springs broken or arm pivots seized (Chapter 12).
☐ Insufficient windscreen washer additive to adequately remove road dirt film *("Weekly Checks")*.

Windscreen/tailgate washers inoperative or unsatisfactory in operation

One or more washer jets inoperative

☐ Blocked washer jet (Chapter 12).
☐ Disconnected, kinked or restricted fluid hose (Chapter 12).
☐ Insufficient fluid in washer reservoir *("Weekly Checks")*.

Washer pump fails to operate

☐ Broken or disconnected wiring or connections (Chapter 12).
☐ Blown fuse (Chapter 12).
☐ Faulty washer switch (Chapter 12).
☐ Faulty washer pump (Chapter 12).

Washer pump runs for some time before fluid is emitted from jets

☐ Faulty one-way valve in fluid supply hose (Chapter 12).

Electric windows inoperative or unsatisfactory in operation

Window glass will only move in one direction

☐ Faulty switch (Chapter 12).

Window glass slow to move

☐ Incorrectly adjusted door glass guide channels (Chapter 11).
☐ Regulator seized or damaged, or in need of lubrication (Chapter 11).
☐ Door internal components or trim fouling regulator (Chapter 11).
☐ Faulty motor (Chapter 12).

Window glass fails to move

☐ Incorrectly adjusted door glass guide channels (Chapter 11).
☐ Blown fuse (Chapter 12).
☐ Faulty relay (Chapter 12).
☐ Broken or disconnected wiring or connections (Chapter 12).
☐ Faulty motor (Chapter 12).

Central locking system inoperative or unsatisfactory in operation

Complete system failure

☐ Blown fuse (Chapter 12).
☐ Faulty relay (Chapter 12).
☐ Broken or disconnected wiring or connections (Chapter 12).

Latch locks but will not unlock, or unlocks but will not lock

☐ Faulty master switch (Chapter 12).
☐ Broken or disconnected latch operating rods or levers (Chapter 11).
☐ Faulty relay (Chapter 12).

One motor fails to operate

☐ Broken or disconnected wiring or connections (Chapter 12).
☐ Faulty motor (Chapter 12).
☐ Broken, binding or disconnected latch operating rods or levers (Chapter 11).
☐ Fault in door latch (Chapter 11).

A

ABS (Anti-lock brake system) A system, usually electronically controlled, that senses incipient wheel lockup during braking and relieves hydraulic pressure at wheels that are about to skid.

Air bag An inflatable bag hidden in the steering wheel (driver's side) or the dash or glovebox (passenger side). In a head-on collision, the bags inflate, preventing the driver and front passenger from being thrown forward into the steering wheel or windscreen.

Air cleaner A metal or plastic housing, containing a filter element, which removes dust and dirt from the air being drawn into the engine.

Air filter element The actual filter in an air cleaner system, usually manufactured from pleated paper and requiring renewal at regular intervals.

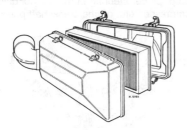

Air filter

Allen key A hexagonal wrench which fits into a recessed hexagonal hole.

Alligator clip A long-nosed spring-loaded metal clip with meshing teeth. Used to make temporary electrical connections.

Alternator A component in the electrical system which converts mechanical energy from a drivebelt into electrical energy to charge the battery and to operate the starting system, ignition system and electrical accessories.

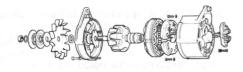

Alternator (exploded view)

Ampere (amp) A unit of measurement for the flow of electric current. One amp is the amount of current produced by one volt acting through a resistance of one ohm.

Anaerobic sealer A substance used to prevent bolts and screws from loosening. Anaerobic means that it does not require oxygen for activation. The Loctite brand is widely used.

Antifreeze A substance (usually ethylene glycol) mixed with water, and added to a vehicle's cooling system, to prevent freezing of the coolant in winter. Antifreeze also contains chemicals to inhibit corrosion and the formation of rust and other deposits that

would tend to clog the radiator and coolant passages and reduce cooling efficiency.

Anti-seize compound A coating that reduces the risk of seizing on fasteners that are subjected to high temperatures, such as exhaust manifold bolts and nuts.

Anti-seize compound

Asbestos A natural fibrous mineral with great heat resistance, commonly used in the composition of brake friction materials. Asbestos is a health hazard and the dust created by brake systems should never be inhaled or ingested.

Axle A shaft on which a wheel revolves, or which revolves with a wheel. Also, a solid beam that connects the two wheels at one end of the vehicle. An axle which also transmits power to the wheels is known as a live axle.

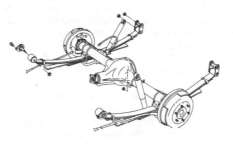

Axle assembly

Axleshaft A single rotating shaft, on either side of the differential, which delivers power from the final drive assembly to the drive wheels. Also called a driveshaft or a halfshaft.

B

Ball bearing An anti-friction bearing consisting of a hardened inner and outer race with hardened steel balls between two races.

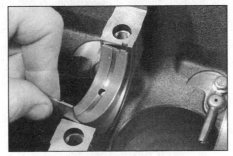

Bearing

Bearing The curved surface on a shaft or in a bore, or the part assembled into either, that permits relative motion between them with minimum wear and friction.

Big-end bearing The bearing in the end of the connecting rod that's attached to the crankshaft.

Bleed nipple A valve on a brake wheel cylinder, caliper or other hydraulic component that is opened to purge the hydraulic system of air. Also called a bleed screw.

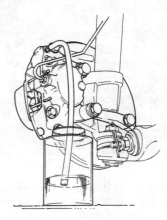

Brake bleeding

Brake bleeding Procedure for removing air from lines of a hydraulic brake system.

Brake disc The component of a disc brake that rotates with the wheels.

Brake drum The component of a drum brake that rotates with the wheels.

Brake linings The friction material which contacts the brake disc or drum to retard the vehicle's speed. The linings are bonded or riveted to the brake pads or shoes.

Brake pads The replaceable friction pads that pinch the brake disc when the brakes are applied. Brake pads consist of a friction material bonded or riveted to a rigid backing plate.

Brake shoe The crescent-shaped carrier to which the brake linings are mounted and which forces the lining against the rotating drum during braking.

Braking systems For more information on braking systems, consult the *Haynes Automotive Brake Manual*.

Breaker bar A long socket wrench handle providing greater leverage.

Bulkhead The insulated partition between the engine and the passenger compartment.

C

Caliper The non-rotating part of a disc-brake assembly that straddles the disc and carries the brake pads. The caliper also contains the hydraulic components that cause the pads to pinch the disc when the brakes are applied. A caliper is also a measuring tool that can be set to measure inside or outside dimensions of an object.

Camshaft A rotating shaft on which a series of cam lobes operate the valve mechanisms. The camshaft may be driven by gears, by sprockets and chain or by sprockets and a belt.

Canister A container in an evaporative emission control system; contains activated charcoal granules to trap vapours from the fuel system.

Canister

Carburettor A device which mixes fuel with air in the proper proportions to provide a desired power output from a spark ignition internal combustion engine.

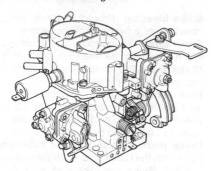

Carburettor

Castellated Resembling the parapets along the top of a castle wall. For example, a castellated balljoint stud nut.

Castellated nut

Castor In wheel alignment, the backward or forward tilt of the steering axis. Castor is positive when the steering axis is inclined rearward at the top.

Catalytic converter A silencer-like device in the exhaust system which converts certain pollutants in the exhaust gases into less harmful substances.

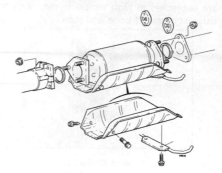

Catalytic converter

Circlip A ring-shaped clip used to prevent endwise movement of cylindrical parts and shafts. An internal circlip is installed in a groove in a housing; an external circlip fits into a groove on the outside of a cylindrical piece such as a shaft.

Clearance The amount of space between two parts. For example, between a piston and a cylinder, between a bearing and a journal, etc.

Coil spring A spiral of elastic steel found in various sizes throughout a vehicle, for example as a springing medium in the suspension and in the valve train.

Compression Reduction in volume, and increase in pressure and temperature, of a gas, caused by squeezing it into a smaller space.

Compression ratio The relationship between cylinder volume when the piston is at top dead centre and cylinder volume when the piston is at bottom dead centre.

Constant velocity (CV) joint A type of universal joint that cancels out vibrations caused by driving power being transmitted through an angle.

Core plug A disc or cup-shaped metal device inserted in a hole in a casting through which core was removed when the casting was formed. Also known as a freeze plug or expansion plug.

Crankcase The lower part of the engine block in which the crankshaft rotates.

Crankshaft The main rotating member, or shaft, running the length of the crankcase, with offset "throws" to which the connecting rods are attached.

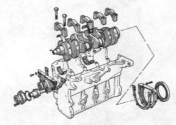

Crankshaft assembly

Crocodile clip See Alligator clip

D

Diagnostic code Code numbers obtained by accessing the diagnostic mode of an engine management computer. This code can be used to determine the area in the system where a malfunction may be located.

Disc brake A brake design incorporating a rotating disc onto which brake pads are squeezed. The resulting friction converts the energy of a moving vehicle into heat.

Double-overhead cam (DOHC) An engine that uses two overhead camshafts, usually one for the intake valves and one for the exhaust valves.

Drivebelt(s) The belt(s) used to drive accessories such as the alternator, water pump, power steering pump, air conditioning compressor, etc. off the crankshaft pulley.

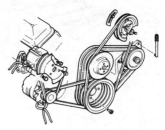

Accessory drivebelts

Driveshaft Any shaft used to transmit motion. Commonly used when referring to the axleshafts on a front wheel drive vehicle.

Driveshaft

Drum brake A type of brake using a drum-shaped metal cylinder attached to the inner surface of the wheel. When the brake pedal is pressed, curved brake shoes with friction linings press against the inside of the drum to slow or stop the vehicle.

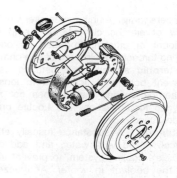

Drum brake assembly

E

EGR valve A valve used to introduce exhaust gases into the intake air stream.

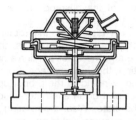

EGR valve

Electronic control unit (ECU) A computer which controls (for instance) ignition and fuel injection systems, or an anti-lock braking system. For more information refer to the *Haynes Automotive Electrical and Electronic Systems Manual*.

Electronic Fuel Injection (EFI) A computer controlled fuel system that distributes fuel through an injector located in each intake port of the engine.

Emergency brake A braking system, independent of the main hydraulic system, that can be used to slow or stop the vehicle if the primary brakes fail, or to hold the vehicle stationary even though the brake pedal isn't depressed. It usually consists of a hand lever that actuates either front or rear brakes mechanically through a series of cables and linkages. Also known as a handbrake or parking brake.

Endfloat The amount of lengthwise movement between two parts. As applied to a crankshaft, the distance that the crankshaft can move forward and back in the cylinder block.

Engine management system (EMS) A computer controlled system which manages the fuel injection and the ignition systems in an integrated fashion.

Exhaust manifold A part with several passages through which exhaust gases leave the engine combustion chambers and enter the exhaust pipe.

Exhaust manifold

F

Fan clutch A viscous (fluid) drive coupling device which permits variable engine fan speeds in relation to engine speeds.

Feeler blade A thin strip or blade of hardened steel, ground to an exact thickness, used to check or measure clearances between parts.

Feeler blade

Firing order The order in which the engine cylinders fire, or deliver their power strokes, beginning with the number one cylinder.

Flywheel A heavy spinning wheel in which energy is absorbed and stored by means of momentum. On cars, the flywheel is attached to the crankshaft to smooth out firing impulses.

Free play The amount of travel before any action takes place. The "looseness" in a linkage, or an assembly of parts, between the initial application of force and actual movement. For example, the distance the brake pedal moves before the pistons in the master cylinder are actuated.

Fuse An electrical device which protects a circuit against accidental overload. The typical fuse contains a soft piece of metal which is calibrated to melt at a predetermined current flow (expressed as amps) and break the circuit.

Fusible link A circuit protection device consisting of a conductor surrounded by heat-resistant insulation. The conductor is smaller than the wire it protects, so it acts as the weakest link in the circuit. Unlike a blown fuse, a failed fusible link must frequently be cut from the wire for replacement.

G

Gap The distance the spark must travel in jumping from the centre electrode to the side

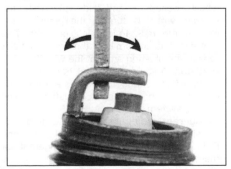

Adjusting spark plug gap

electrode in a spark plug. Also refers to the spacing between the points in a contact breaker assembly in a conventional points-type ignition, or to the distance between the reluctor or rotor and the pickup coil in an electronic ignition.

Gasket Any thin, soft material - usually cork, cardboard, asbestos or soft metal - installed between two metal surfaces to ensure a good seal. For instance, the cylinder head gasket seals the joint between the block and the cylinder head.

Gasket

Gauge An instrument panel display used to monitor engine conditions. A gauge with a movable pointer on a dial or a fixed scale is an analogue gauge. A gauge with a numerical readout is called a digital gauge.

H

Halfshaft A rotating shaft that transmits power from the final drive unit to a drive wheel, usually when referring to a live rear axle.

Harmonic balancer A device designed to reduce torsion or twisting vibration in the crankshaft. May be incorporated in the crankshaft pulley. Also known as a vibration damper.

Hone An abrasive tool for correcting small irregularities or differences in diameter in an engine cylinder, brake cylinder, etc.

Hydraulic tappet A tappet that utilises hydraulic pressure from the engine's lubrication system to maintain zero clearance (constant contact with both camshaft and valve stem). Automatically adjusts to variation in valve stem length. Hydraulic tappets also reduce valve noise.

I

Ignition timing The moment at which the spark plug fires, usually expressed in the number of crankshaft degrees before the piston reaches the top of its stroke.

Inlet manifold A tube or housing with passages through which flows the air-fuel mixture (carburettor vehicles and vehicles with throttle body injection) or air only (port fuel-injected vehicles) to the port openings in the cylinder head.

J

Jump start Starting the engine of a vehicle with a discharged or weak battery by attaching jump leads from the weak battery to a charged or helper battery.

L

Load Sensing Proportioning Valve (LSPV) A brake hydraulic system control valve that works like a proportioning valve, but also takes into consideration the amount of weight carried by the rear axle.

Locknut A nut used to lock an adjustment nut, or other threaded component, in place. For example, a locknut is employed to keep the adjusting nut on the rocker arm in position.

Lockwasher A form of washer designed to prevent an attaching nut from working loose.

M

MacPherson strut A type of front suspension system devised by Earle MacPherson at Ford of England. In its original form, a simple lateral link with the anti-roll bar creates the lower control arm. A long strut - an integral coil spring and shock absorber - is mounted between the body and the steering knuckle. Many modern so-called MacPherson strut systems use a conventional lower A-arm and don't rely on the anti-roll bar for location.

Multimeter An electrical test instrument with the capability to measure voltage, current and resistance.

N

NOx Oxides of Nitrogen. A common toxic pollutant emitted by petrol and diesel engines at higher temperatures.

O

Ohm The unit of electrical resistance. One volt applied to a resistance of one ohm will produce a current of one amp.

Ohmmeter An instrument for measuring electrical resistance.

O-ring A type of sealing ring made of a special rubber-like material; in use, the O-ring is compressed into a groove to provide the sealing action.

O-ring

Overhead cam (ohc) engine An engine with the camshaft(s) located on top of the cylinder head(s).

Overhead valve (ohv) engine An engine with the valves located in the cylinder head, but with the camshaft located in the engine block.

Oxygen sensor A device installed in the engine exhaust manifold, which senses the oxygen content in the exhaust and converts this information into an electric current. Also called a Lambda sensor.

P

Phillips screw A type of screw head having a cross instead of a slot for a corresponding type of screwdriver.

Plastigage A thin strip of plastic thread, available in different sizes, used for measuring clearances. For example, a strip of Plastigage is laid across a bearing journal. The parts are assembled and dismantled; the width of the crushed strip indicates the clearance between journal and bearing.

Plastigage

Propeller shaft The long hollow tube with universal joints at both ends that carries power from the transmission to the differential on front-engined rear wheel drive vehicles.

Proportioning valve A hydraulic control valve which limits the amount of pressure to the rear brakes during panic stops to prevent wheel lock-up.

R

Rack-and-pinion steering A steering system with a pinion gear on the end of the steering shaft that mates with a rack (think of a geared wheel opened up and laid flat). When the steering wheel is turned, the pinion turns, moving the rack to the left or right. This movement is transmitted through the track rods to the steering arms at the wheels.

Radiator A liquid-to-air heat transfer device designed to reduce the temperature of the coolant in an internal combustion engine cooling system.

Refrigerant Any substance used as a heat transfer agent in an air-conditioning system. R-12 has been the principle refrigerant for many years; recently, however, manufacturers have begun using R-134a, a non-CFC substance that is considered less harmful to

the ozone in the upper atmosphere.

Rocker arm A lever arm that rocks on a shaft or pivots on a stud. In an overhead valve engine, the rocker arm converts the upward movement of the pushrod into a downward movement to open a valve.

Rotor In a distributor, the rotating device inside the cap that connects the centre electrode and the outer terminals as it turns, distributing the high voltage from the coil secondary winding to the proper spark plug. Also, that part of an alternator which rotates inside the stator. Also, the rotating assembly of a turbocharger, including the compressor wheel, shaft and turbine wheel.

Runout The amount of wobble (in-and-out movement) of a gear or wheel as it's rotated. The amount a shaft rotates "out-of-true." The out-of-round condition of a rotating part.

S

Sealant A liquid or paste used to prevent leakage at a joint. Sometimes used in conjunction with a gasket.

Sealed beam lamp An older headlight design which integrates the reflector, lens and filaments into a hermetically-sealed one-piece unit. When a filament burns out or the lens cracks, the entire unit is simply replaced.

Serpentine drivebelt A single, long, wide accessory drivebelt that's used on some newer vehicles to drive all the accessories, instead of a series of smaller, shorter belts. Serpentine drivebelts are usually tensioned by an automatic tensioner.

Serpentine drivebelt

Shim Thin spacer, commonly used to adjust the clearance or relative positions between two parts. For example, shims inserted into or under bucket tappets control valve clearances. Clearance is adjusted by changing the thickness of the shim.

Slide hammer A special puller that screws into or hooks onto a component such as a shaft or bearing; a heavy sliding handle on the shaft bottoms against the end of the shaft to knock the component free.

Sprocket A tooth or projection on the periphery of a wheel, shaped to engage with a chain or drivebelt. Commonly used to refer to the sprocket wheel itself.

Starter inhibitor switch On vehicles with an

automatic transmission, a switch that prevents starting if the vehicle is not in Neutral or Park.

Strut See MacPherson strut.

T

Tappet A cylindrical component which transmits motion from the cam to the valve stem, either directly or via a pushrod and rocker arm. Also called a cam follower.

Thermostat A heat-controlled valve that regulates the flow of coolant between the cylinder block and the radiator, so maintaining optimum engine operating temperature. A thermostat is also used in some air cleaners in which the temperature is regulated.

Thrust bearing The bearing in the clutch assembly that is moved in to the release levers by clutch pedal action to disengage the clutch. Also referred to as a release bearing.

Timing belt A toothed belt which drives the camshaft. Serious engine damage may result if it breaks in service.

Timing chain A chain which drives the camshaft.

Toe-in The amount the front wheels are closer together at the front than at the rear. On rear wheel drive vehicles, a slight amount of toe-in is usually specified to keep the front wheels running parallel on the road by offsetting other forces that tend to spread the wheels apart.

Toe-out The amount the front wheels are closer together at the rear than at the front. On front wheel drive vehicles, a slight amount of toe-out is usually specified.

Tools For full information on choosing and using tools, refer to the *Haynes Automotive Tools Manual.*

Tracer A stripe of a second colour applied to a wire insulator to distinguish that wire from another one with the same colour insulator.

Tune-up A process of accurate and careful adjustments and parts replacement to obtain the best possible engine performance.

Turbocharger A centrifugal device, driven by exhaust gases, that pressurises the intake air. Normally used to increase the power output from a given engine displacement, but can also be used primarily to reduce exhaust emissions (as on VW's "Umwelt" Diesel engine).

U

Universal joint or U-joint A double-pivoted connection for transmitting power from a driving to a driven shaft through an angle. A U-joint consists of two Y-shaped yokes and a cross-shaped member called the spider.

V

Valve A device through which the flow of liquid, gas, vacuum, or loose material in bulk may be started, stopped, or regulated by a movable part that opens, shuts, or partially obstructs one or more ports or passageways. A valve is also the movable part of such a device.

Valve clearance The clearance between the valve tip (the end of the valve stem) and the rocker arm or tappet. The valve clearance is measured when the valve is closed.

Vernier caliper A precision measuring instrument that measures inside and outside dimensions. Not quite as accurate as a micrometer, but more convenient.

Viscosity The thickness of a liquid or its resistance to flow.

Volt A unit for expressing electrical "pressure" in a circuit. One volt that will produce a current of one ampere through a resistance of one ohm.

W

Welding Various processes used to join metal items by heating the areas to be joined to a molten state and fusing them together. For more information refer to the *Haynes Automotive Welding Manual.*

Wiring diagram A drawing portraying the components and wires in a vehicle's electrical system, using standardised symbols. For more information refer to the *Haynes Automotive Electrical and Electronic Systems Manual.*

Note: *References throughout this index relate to Chapter•page number*

Notes

Haynes Manuals – The Complete List

Title	Book No.
ALFA ROMEO	
Alfa Romeo Alfasud/Sprint (74 - 88)	0292
Alfa Romeo Alfetta (73 - 87)	0531
AUDI	
Audi 80 (72 - Feb 79)	0207
Audi 80, 90 (79 - Oct 86) & Coupe (81 - Nov 88)	0605
Audi 80, 90 (Oct 86 - 90) & Coupe (Nov 88 - 90)	1491
Audi 100 (Oct 82 - 90) & 200 (Feb 84 - Oct 89)	0907
Audi 100/A6 (May 91 - May 97)	3504
AUSTIN	
Austin/MG Maestro 1.3 & 1.6 (83 - 95)	0922
Austin/MG Metro (80 - May 90)	0718
Austin Montego 1.3 & 1.6 (84 - 94)	1066
Austin/MG Montego 2.0 (84 - 95)	1067
Mini (59 - 69)	0527
Mini (69 - Oct 96)	0646
Austin/Rover 2.0 litre Diesel Engine (86 - 93)	1857
BEDFORD	
Bedford CF (69 - 87)	0163
Bedford Rascal (86 - 93)	3015
BMW	
BMW 316, 320 & 320i (4-cyl) (75 - Feb 83)	0276
BMW 320, 320i, 323i & 325i (6-cyl) (Oct 77 - Sept 87)	0815
BMW 3-Series (Apr 91 - 96)	3210
BMW 3-Series (sohc) (83 - 91)	1948
BMW 520i & 525e (Oct 81 - June 88)	1560
BMW 525, 528 & 528i (73 - Sept 81)	0632
BMW 5-Series (sohc) (81 - 91)	1948
BMW 1500, 1502, 1600, 1602, 2000 & 2002 (59 - 77)	0240
CITROËN	
Citroën 2CV, Ami & Dyane (67 - 90)	0196
Citroën AX Petrol & Diesel (87 - 94)	3014
Citroën BX (83 - 94)	0908
Citroën C15 Van Petrol & Diesel (89 - 98)	3509
Citroën CX (75 - 88)	0528
Citroën Saxo Petrol & Diesel (96 - 98)	3506
Citroën Visa (79 - 88)	0620
Citroën Xantia Petrol & Diesel (93 - 98)	3082
Citroën XM Petrol & Diesel (89 - 98)	3451
Citroën ZX Diesel (91 - 93)	1922
Citroën ZX Petrol (91 - 94)	1881
Citroën 1.7 & 1.9 litre Diesel Engine (84 - 96)	1379
COLT	
Colt 1200, 1250 & 1400 (79 - May 84)	0600
DAIMLER	
Daimler Sovereign (68 - Oct 86)	0242
Daimler Double Six (72 - 88)	0478
FIAT	
Fiat 126 (73 - 87)	0305
Fiat 127 (71 - 83)	0193
Fiat 500 (57 - 73)	0090
Fiat Cinquecento (June 93 - 98)	3501
Fiat Panda (81 - 95)	0793
Fiat Punto (94 - 96)	3251
Fiat Regata (84 - 88)	1167
Fiat Strada (79 - 88)	0479

Title	Book No.
Fiat Tipo (88 - 91)	1625
Fiat Uno (83 - 95)	0923
Fiat X1/9 (74 - 89)	0273
FORD	
Ford Capri II (& III) 1.6 & 2.0 (74 - 87)	0283
Ford Capri II (& III) 2.8 & 3.0 (74 - 87)	1309
Ford Cortina Mk IV (& V) 1.6 & 2.0 (76 - 83)	0343
Ford Escort (75 - Aug 80)	0280
Ford Escort (Sept 80 - Sept 90)	0686
Ford Escort (Sept 90 - 97)	1737
Ford Escort Mk II Mexico, RS 1600 & RS 2000 (75 - 80)	0735
Ford Fiesta (inc. XR2) (76 - Aug 83)	0334
Ford Fiesta (inc. XR2) (Aug 83 - Feb 89)	1030
Ford Fiesta (Feb 89 - Oct 95)	1595
Ford Fiesta Petrol & Diesel (Oct 95 - 97)	3397
Ford Granada (Sept 77 - Feb 85)	0481
Ford Granada (Mar 85 - 94)	1245
Ford Mondeo (93 - 99)	1923
Ford Mondeo Diesel (93 - 96)	3465
Ford Orion (83 - Sept 90)	1009
Ford Orion (Sept 90 - 93)	1737
Ford Sierra 1.3, 1.6, 1.8 & 2.0 (82 - 93)	0903
Ford Sierra 2.3, 2.8 & 2.9 (82 - 91)	0904
Ford Scorpio (Mar 85 - 94)	1245
Ford Transit Petrol (Mk 2) (78 - Jan 86)	0719
Ford Transit Petrol (Mk 3) (Feb 86 - 89)	1468
Ford Transit Diesel (Feb 86 - 95)	3019
Ford 1.6 & 1.8 litre Diesel Engine (84 - 96)	1172
Ford 2.1, 2.3 & 2.5 litre Diesel Engine (77 - 90)	1606
FREIGHT ROVER	
Freight Rover Sherpa (74 - 87)	0463
HILLMAN	
Hillman Avenger (70 - 82)	0037
HONDA	
Honda Accord (76 - Feb 84)	0351
Honda Accord (Feb 84 - Oct 85)	1177
Honda Civic (Feb 84 - Oct 87)	1226
Honda Civic (Nov 91 - 96)	3199
HYUNDAI	
Hyundai Pony (85 - 94)	3398
JAGUAR	
Jaguar E Type (61 - 72)	0140
Jaguar MkI & II, 240 & 340 (55 - 69)	0098
Jaguar XJ6, XJ & Sovereign (68 - Oct 86)	0242
Jaguar XJ6 & Sovereign (Oct 86 - Sept 94)	3261
Jaguar XJ12, XJS & Sovereign (72 - 88)	0478
JEEP	
Jeep Cherokee Petrol (93 - 96)	1943
LADA	
Lada 1200, 1300, 1500 & 1600 (74 - 91)	0413
Lada Samara (87 - 91)	1610
LAND ROVER	
Land Rover 90, 110 & Defender Diesel (83 - 95)	3017
Land Rover Discovery Diesel (89 - 95)	3016
Land Rover Series IIA & III Diesel (58 - 85)	0529
Land Rover Series II, IIA & III Petrol (58 - 85)	0314

Title	Book No.
MAZDA	
Mazda 323 fwd (Mar 81 - Oct 89)	1608
Mazda 323 (Oct 89 - 98)	3455
Mazda 626 fwd (May 83 - Sept 87)	0929
Mazda B-1600, B-1800 & B-2000 Pick-up (72 - 88)	0267
MERCEDES-BENZ	
Mercedes-Benz 190, 190E & 190D Petrol & Diesel (83 - 93)	3450
Mercedes-Benz 200, 240, 300 Diesel (Oct 76 - 85)	1114
Mercedes-Benz 250 & 280 (68 - 72)	0346
Mercedes-Benz 250 & 280 (123 Series) (Oct 76 - 84)	0677
Mercedes-Benz 124 Series (85 - Aug 93)	3253
MG	
MGB (62 - 80)	0111
MG Maestro 1.3 & 1.6 (83 - 95)	0922
MG Metro (80 - May 90)	0718
MG Midget & AH Sprite (58 - 80)	0265
MG Montego 2.0 (84 - 95)	1067
MITSUBISHI	
Mitsubishi 1200, 1250 & 1400 (79 - May 84)	0600
Mitsubishi Shogun & L200 Pick-Ups (83 - 94)	1944
MORRIS	
Morris Ital 1.3 (80 - 84)	0705
Morris Minor 1000 (56 - 71)	0024
NISSAN	
Nissan Bluebird fwd (May 84 - Mar 86)	1223
Nissan Bluebird (T12 & T72) (Mar 86 - 90)	1473
Nissan Cherry (N12) (Sept 82 - 86)	1031
Nissan Micra (K10) (83 - Jan 93)	0931
Nissan Micra (93 - 96)	3254
Nissan Primera (90 - Oct 96)	1851
Nissan Stanza (82 - 86)	0824
Nissan Sunny (B11) (May 82 - Oct 86)	0895
Nissan Sunny (Oct 86 - Mar 91)	1378
Nissan Sunny (Apr 91 - 95)	3219
OPEL	
Opel Ascona & Manta (B Series) (Sept 75 - 88)	0316
Opel Ascona (81 - 88) (Not available in UK see Vauxhall Cavalier 0812)	3215
Opel Astra (Oct 91 - 96) (Not available in UK see Vauxhall Astra 1832)	3156
Opel Calibra (90 - 98) (See Vauxhall/Opel Calibra Book No. 3502)	
Opel Corsa (83 - Mar 93) (Not available in UK see Vauxhall Nova 0909)	3160
Opel Corsa (Mar 93 - 97) (Not available in UK see Vauxhall Corsa 1985)	3159
Opel Frontera Petrol & Diesel (91 - 98) (See Vauxhall/Opel Frontera Book No. 1985)	
Opel Kadett (Nov 79 - Oct 84)	0634
Opel Kadett (Oct 84 - Oct 91) (Not available in UK see Vauxhall Astra & Belmont 1136)	3196
Opel Omega & Senator (86 - 94) (Not available in UK see Vauxhall Carlton & Senator 1469)	3157
Opel Omega Petrol & Diesel (94 - 98) (See Vauxhall/Opel Omega Book No. 3510)	

Title	Book No.
Opel Rekord (Feb 78 - Oct 86)	0543
Opel Vectra (88 - Oct 95) (Not available in UK see Vauxhall Cavalier 1570)	3158
Opel Vectra Petrol & Diesel (95 - 98) (Not available in UK see Vauxhall Vectra 3396)	3523
PEUGEOT	
Peugeot 106 Petrol & Diesel (91 - June 96)	1882
Peugeot 205 (83 - 95)	0932
Peugeot 305 (78 - 89)	0538
Peugeot 306 Petrol & Diesel (93 - 98)	3073
Peugeot 309 (86 - 93)	1266
Peugeot 405 Petrol (88 - 96)	1559
Peugeot 405 Diesel (88 - 96)	3198
Peugeot 406 Petrol & Diesel (96 - 97)	3394
Peugeot 505 (79 - 89)	0762
Peugeot 1.7/1.8 & 1.9 litre Diesel Engines (82 - 96)	0950
Peugeot 2.0, 2.1, 2.3 & 2.5 litre Diesel Engines (74 - 90)	1607
PORSCHE	
Porsche 911 (65 - 85)	0264
Porsche 924 & 924 Turbo (76 - 85)	0397
PROTON	
Proton (89 - 97)	3255
RANGE ROVER	
Range Rover V8 (70 - Oct 92)	0606
RELIANT	
Reliant Robin & Kitten (73 - 83)	0436
RENAULT	
Renault 5 (72 - Feb 85)	0141
Renault 5 (Feb 85 - 96)	1219
Renault 9 & 11 (82 - 89)	0822
Renault 18 (79 - 86)	0598
Renault 19 Petrol (89 - 94)	1646
Renault 19 Diesel (89 - 95)	1946
Renault 21 (86 - 94)	1397
Renault 25 (84 - 92)	1228
Renault Clio Petrol (91 - 93)	1853
Renault Clio Diesel (91 - June 96)	3031
Renault Espace (85 - 96)	3197
Renault Laguna (94 - 96)	3252
Renault Mégane & Scénic Petrol & Diesel (96 - 98)	3395
ROVER	
Rover 111 & 114 (95 - 96)	1711
Rover 213 & 216 (84 - 89)	1116
Rover 214 & 414 (89 - 96)	1689
Rover 216 & 416 (89 - 96)	1830
Rover 200 Series Petrol & Diesel (95 - 98)	3399
Rover 400 Series Petrol & Diesel (95 - 98)	3453
Rover 618, 620 & 623 (93 - 97)	3257
Rover 820, 825 & 827 (86 - 95)	1380
Rover 3500 (SD1) (76 - 87)	0365
Rover Metro (May 90 - 94)	1711
SAAB	
Saab 90, 99 & 900 (79 - Oct 93)	0765
Saab 900 (Oct 93 - 98)	3512

Title	Book No.
Saab 9000 (4-cyl) (85 - 95)	1686
SEAT	
Seat Ibiza & Malaga (85 - 92)	1609
SKODA	
Skoda Estelle 105, 120, 130 & 136 (77 - 89)	0604
Skoda Favorit (89 - 92)	1801
Skoda Felicia Petrol & Diesel (95 - 98)	3505
SUBARU	
Subaru 1600 & 1800 (Nov 79 - 90)	0995
SUZUKI	
Suzuki SJ Series, Samurai & Vitara (82 - 97)	1942
Suzuki Supercarry (86 - Oct 94)	3015
TALBOT	
Talbot Alpine, Solara, Minx & Rapier (75 - 86)	0337
Talbot Horizon (78 - 86)	0473
Talbot Samba (82 - 86)	0823
TOYOTA	
Toyota Carina E (May 92 - 97)	3256
Toyota Corolla (fwd) (Sept 83 - Sept 87)	1024
Toyota Corolla (rwd) (80 - 85)	0683
Toyota Corolla (Sept 87 - 92)	1683
Toyota Corolla (Aug 92 - 97)	3259
Toyota Hi-Ace & Hi-Lux (69 - Oct 83)	0304
TRIUMPH	
Triumph Acclaim (81 - 84)	0792
Triumph GT6 & Vitesse (62 - 74)	0112
Triumph Spitfire (62 - 81)	0113
Triumph Stag (70 - 78)	0441
Triumph TR7 (75 - 82)	0322
VAUXHALL	
Vauxhall Astra (80 - Oct 84)	0635
Vauxhall Astra & Belmont (Oct 84 - Oct 91)	1136
Vauxhall Astra (Oct 91 - 96)	1832
Vauxhall/Opel Calibra (90 - 98)	3502
Vauxhall Carlton (Oct 78 - Oct 86)	0480
Vauxhall Carlton (Nov 86 - 94)	1469
Vauxhall Cavalier 1600, 1900 & 2000 (75 - July 81)	0315
Vauxhall Cavalier (81 - Oct 88)	0812
Vauxhall Cavalier (Oct 88 - Oct 95)	1570
Vauxhall Chevette (75 - 84)	0285
Vauxhall Corsa (93 - 97)	1985
Vauxhall/Opel Frontera Petrol & Diesel (91 - 98)	3454
Vauxhall Nova (83 - 93)	0909
Vauxhall/Opel Omega Petrol & Diesel (94 - 98)	3510
Vauxhall Rascal (86 - 93)	3015
Vauxhall Senator (Sept 87 - 94)	1469
Vauxhall Vectra Petrol & Diesel (95 - 98)	3396
Vauxhall/Opel 1.5, 1.6 & 1.7 litre Diesel Engines (82 - 96)	1222
VOLKSWAGEN	
VW Beetle 1200 (54 - 77)	0036
VW Beetle 1300 & 1500 (65 - 75)	0039
VW Beetle 1302 & 1302S (70 - 72)	0110
VW Beetle 1303, 1303S & GT (72 - 75)	0159
VW Golf Mk 1 1.1 & 1.3 (74 - Feb 84)	0716
VW Golf Mk 1 1.5, 1.6 & 1.8 (74 - 85)	0726

Title	Book No.
VW Golf Mk 1 Diesel (78 - Feb 84)	0451
VW Golf Mk 2 (Mar 84 - Feb 92)	1081
VW Golf Mk 3 Petrol & Diesel (Feb 92 - 96)	3097
VW Jetta Mk 1 1.1 & 1.3 (80 - June 84)	0716
VW Jetta Mk 1 1.5, 1.6 & 1.8 (80 - June 84)	0726
VW Jetta Mk 1 Diesel (81 - June 84)	0451
VW Jetta Mk 2 (July 84 - 92)	1081
VW LT vans & light trucks (76 - 87)	0637
VW Passat (Sept 81 - May 88)	0814
VW Passat (May 88 - 96)	3498
VW Polo & Derby (76 - Jan 82)	0335
VW Polo (82 - Oct 90)	0813
VW Polo (Nov 90 - Aug 94)	3245
VW Polo Hatchback (95 - 98)	3500
VW Santana (Sept 82 - 85)	0814
VW Scirocco Mk 1 1.5, 1.6 & 1.8 (74 - 82)	0726
VW Scirocco (82 - 90)	1224
VW Transporter 1600 (68 - 79)	0082
VW Transporter 1700, 1800 & 2000 (72 - 79)	0226
VW Transporter with air-cooled engine (79 - 82)	0638
VW Transporter water-cooled (82 - 90)	3452
VW Vento Petrol & Diesel (Feb 92 - 96)	3097
VOLVO	
Volvo 142, 144 & 145 (66 - 74)	0129
Volvo 240 Series (74 - 93)	0270
Volvo 262, 264 & 260/265 (75 - 85)	0400
Volvo 340, 343, 345 & 360 (76 - 91)	0715
Volvo 440, 460 & 480 (87 - 92)	1691
Volvo 740 & 760 (82 - 91)	1258
Volvo 850 (92 - 96)	3260
Volvo 940 (90 - 96)	3249
YUGO/ZASTAVA	
Yugo/Zastava (81 - 90)	1453
TECH BOOKS	
Automotive Brake Manual	3050
Automotive Carburettor Manual	3288
Automotive Diagnostic Fault Codes Manual	3472
Automotive Diesel Engine Service Guide	3286
Automotive Disc Brake Manual	3542
Automotive Electrical and Electronic Systems Manual	3049
Automotive Engine Management and Fuel Injection Systems Manual	3344
Automotive Gearbox Overhaul Manual	3473
Automotive Service Summaries Manual	3475
Automotive Timing Belt Manual - Ford	3474
Automotive Welding Manual	3053
In-Car Entertainment Manual (3rd Edition)	3363
CAR BOOKS	
Automotive Fuel Injection Systems	9755
Car Bodywork Repair Manual	9864
Caravan Manual (2nd Edition)	9894
Motorcaravan Manual, The	L7322
Small Engine Repair Manual	1755
SU Carburettors	0299
Weber Carburettors (to 79)	0393

CL07.01/99

Preserving Our Motoring Heritage

< The Model J Duesenberg Derham Tourster. Only eight of these magnificent cars were ever built – this is the only example to be found outside the United States of America

Almost every car you've ever loved, loathed or desired is gathered under one roof at the Haynes Motor Museum. Over 300 immaculately presented cars and motorbikes represent every aspect of our motoring heritage, from elegant reminders of bygone days, such as the superb Model J Duesenberg to curiosities like the bug-eyed BMW Isetta. There are also many old friends and flames. Perhaps you remember the 1959 Ford Popular that you did your courting in? The magnificent 'Red Collection' is a spectacle of classic sports cars including AC, Alfa Romeo, Austin Healey, Ferrari, Lamborghini, Maserati, MG, Riley, Porsche and Triumph.

A Perfect Day Out

Each and every vehicle at the Haynes Motor Museum has played its part in the history and culture of Motoring. Today, they make a wonderful spectacle and a great day out for all the family. Bring the kids, bring Mum and Dad, but above all bring your camera to capture those golden memories for ever. You will also find an impressive array of motoring memorabilia, a comfortable 70 seat video cinema and one of the most extensive transport book shops in Britain. The Pit Stop Cafe serves everything from a cup of tea to wholesome, home-made meals or, if you prefer, you can enjoy the large picnic area nestled in the beautiful rural surroundings of Somerset.

John Haynes O.B.E., Founder and Chairman of the museum at the wheel of a Haynes Light 12.

< Graham Hill's Lola Cosworth Formula 1 car next to a 1934 Riley Sports.

The Museum is situated on the A359 Yeovil to Frome road at Sparkford, just off the A303 in Somerset. It is about 40 miles south of Bristol, and 25 minutes drive from the M5 intersection at Taunton.
Open 9.30am - 5.30pm (10.00am - 4.00pm Winter) 7 days a week, *except Christmas Day, Boxing Day and New Years Day*
Special rates available for schools, coach parties and outings Charitable Trust No. 292048